W9-AJP-319

RAND McNALLY
WORLD ATLAS

RAND McNALLY

CONTENTS

Copyright © 1994 by Rand McNally & Company
1995 Second Revised Printing

All rights reserved. No part of this publication may be
reproduced, stored in a retrieval system, or transmitted,
in any form or by any means – electronic, mechanical,
photocopied, recorded, or other – without the prior written
permission of Rand McNally.

Library of Congress Cataloging-in-Publication Data

Rand McNally and Company.
     World Atlas.
          p.   cm.
     Includes index.
     1. Atlases.   I. Title.
G1021.R21   1991 <G&M>   91-16938
912—dc20   CIP
                                                       MAP

USING
THE ATLAS

Maps and Atlases

Satellite images of the world (figure 1) constantly give us views of the shape and size of the earth. It is hard, therefore, to imagine how difficult it once was to ascertain the look of our planet. Yet from early history we have evidence of humans trying to work out what the world actually looked like.

Twenty-five hundred years ago, on a tiny clay tablet the size of a hand, the Babylonians inscribed the earth as a flat disk (figure 2) with Babylon at the center. The section of the Cantino map of 1502 (figure 3) is an example of a *portolan* chart used to chart the newly discovered Americas. The maps in this atlas show the detail and accuracy that cartographers are now able to achieve.

In 1589 Gerardus Mercator used the word "atlas" to describe a collection of maps. Atlases now bring together not only a variety of maps, but an assortment of tables and other reference material as well. They have become a unique and indispensable reference for graphically defining the world and answering the question, "Where?" With them, routes between places can be traced, trips planned, distances measured, places imagined, and our earth visualized.

FIGURE 2

FIGURE 3

FIGURE 1

Sequence of the Maps

The world is made up of seven major landmasses: the continents of Europe, Asia, Africa, Antarctica, Australia, South America, and North America. The maps in this atlas follow this continental sequence. To allow for the inclusion of detail, each continent is broken down into a series of maps, and this grouping is arranged so that as consecutive pages are turned, a successive part of the continent is shown. Larger-scale maps are used for regions of greater detail or for areas of global significance.

Getting the Information

To realize the potential of an atlas the user must be able to:
1. Find places on the maps
2. Measure distances
3. Determine directions
4. Understand map symbols

Finding Places

One of the most common and important tasks facilitated by an atlas is finding the location of a place in the world. A river's name in a book, a city mentioned in the news, or a vacation spot may prompt your need to know where the place is located. The illustrations and text below explain how to find Yangon (Rangoon), Myanmar (Burma).

FIGURE 4

1. Look up the place-name in the index at the back of the atlas. Yangon, Myanmar can be found on the map on page 32, and it can be located on the map by the letter-number key *B2* (figure 4). If you know the general area in which a place is found, you may turn directly to the appropriate map and use the special marginal index.

2. Turn to the map of Southeastern Asia found on page 32. Note that the letters *A* through *H* and the numbers *1* through *11* appear in the margins of the map.

3. To find Yangon on the map, place your left index finger on *B* and your right index finger on *2*. Move your left finger across the map and your right finger down the map. Your fingers will meet in the area in which Yangon is located (figure 5).

FIGURE 5

Measuring Distances

When planning trips, determining the distance between two places is essential, and an atlas can help in travel preparation. For instance, to determine the approximate distance between Paris and Rouen, France, follow these three steps:

1. Lay a slip of paper on the map on page 10 so that its edge touches the two cities. Adjust the paper so one corner touches Rouen. Mark the paper directly at the spot where Paris is located (figure 6).

FIGURE 6

2. Place the paper along the scale of miles beneath the map. Position the corner at 0 and line up the edge of the paper along the scale. The pencil mark on the paper indicates Rouen is between 50 and 100 miles from Paris (figure 7).

FIGURE 7

3. To find the exact distance, move the paper to the left so that the pencil mark is at 100 on the scale. The corner of the paper stands on the fourth 5-mile unit on the scale. This means that the two towns are 50 plus 20, or 70 miles apart (figure 8).

FIGURE 8

Determining Directions

Most of the maps in the atlas are drawn so that when oriented for normal reading, north is at the top of the map, south is at the bottom, west is at the left, and east is at the right. Most maps have a series of lines drawn across them—the lines of *latitude* and *longitude*. Lines of latitude, or *parallels* of latitude, are drawn east and west. Lines of longitude, or *meridians* of longitude, are drawn north and south (figure 9).

Parallels and meridians appear as either curved or straight lines. For example, in the section of the map of Europe (figure 10) the parallels of latitude appear as curved lines. The meridians of longitude are straight lines that come together toward the top of the map. Latitude and longitude lines help locate places on maps. Parallels of latitude are numbered in degrees north and south of the *Equator*. Meridians of longitude are numbered in degrees east and west of a line called the *Prime Meridian*, running through Greenwich, England, near London. Any place on earth can be located by the latitude and longitude lines running through it.

To determine directions or locations on the map, you must use the parallels and meridians. For example, suppose you want to know which is farther north, Bergen, Norway, or Norrköping, Sweden. The map (figure 10) shows that Norrköping is south of the 60° parallel of latitude and Bergen is north of it. Bergen is farther north than Norrköping. By looking at the meridians of longitude, you can determine which city is farther east. Bergen is approximately 5° east of the 0° meridian (Prime Meridian), and Norrköping is more than 15° east of it. Norrköping is farther east than Bergen.

FIGURE 10

Understanding Map Symbols

In a very real sense, the whole map is a symbol, representing the world or a part of it. It is a reduced representation of the earth; each of the world's features—cities, rivers, etc.—is represented on the map by a symbol. Map symbols may take the form of points, such as dots or squares (often used for cities, capital cities, or points of interest), or lines (roads, railroads, rivers). Symbols may also occupy an area, showing extent of coverage (terrain, forests, deserts). They seldom look like the feature they represent and therefore must be identified and interpreted. For instance, the maps in this atlas define political units by a colored line depicting their boundaries. Neither the colors nor the boundary lines are actually found on the surface of the earth, but because countries and states are such important political components of the world, strong symbols are used to represent them. The Map Symbols page in this atlas identifies the symbols used on the maps.

FIGURE 9

WORLD PATTERNS

The five world maps in this section portray the distribution of major natural and human elements that describe the world's fundamental geographic character. The lines and colors show basic patterns caused by the movement and interaction of land, air, water, and human activity.

The world terrain map on pages I·6 and I·7 portrays the surface of the uppermost layer of the earth's crust. The crust, broken into six gigantic and several smaller plates, floats on denser rock. Constant movement of the plates in the geologic past helped create the terrain features we see today. Motion of the plates along with the erosive force of water, wind, and human development continues to reshape the earth's terrain.

The earth's oceans are in constant motion. Water near the surface and in the deeps flows in well established currents that are like rivers within the ocean. The earth's atmosphere is an ocean of gases with currents that span the globe. The sun drives these moving currents of water and air. The average of the widely varying weather phenomena caused by these movements establishes the patterns of global climate shown on pages I·8 and I·9.

Climate is the single most important factor determining where plants can grow. And vegetation is the major factor determining where animals–including humans– can live. The map on pages I·10 and I·11 shows the distribution of vegetation types that might exist if humans did not intervene. Notice how similar the patterns of vegetation and climate are. Tundra vegetation is associated with polar climates. The rain forests of South America, Africa, and Asia grow in hot, wet climates near the Equator. The steppes of Central Asia and the short-grass prairies of North America grow in cool climates with dry summers. The evergreen forests of northern Eurasia and North America coincide with moist climates with cold winters and cool summers.

The population density map on pages I·12 and I·13 indicates that almost all areas of the earth are inhabited by humankind, from the Poles to the Equator. Humanity's densest settlement has been in the most fertile regions of the earth. These areas combine adequate rainfall and growing season with terrain that is neither too rough nor mountainous. A comparison of the terrain and climate maps with the population map shows this relationship. Abundant mineral deposits as well as people's ability to develop natural resources also explain settlement preferences. Densely settled areas in Southwest Asia, Southeast Asia, and China are rural-agricultural populations. In western Europe, the northeastern United States, and parts of Japan, high-density regions are urban-industrial in character.

The environment map on pages I·14 and I·15 indicates how human habitation has impacted our planet. Compare this map with the vegetation map that shows what the world might be like if humankind had played a less dominant role. Millions of square miles of land that were once forests or grasslands are now plowed fields and pastures. Much of North America, Europe, and Southeast Asia has been almost completely remade by farmers. Though the urban areas occupy a small percentage of the land area in the world, their impact on the environment is extensive.

Terrain

Population

Climate

Environments

Vegetation

The distribution, relationship, and interaction of the major elements shown on the maps establish fundamental world patterns that distinguish one area from another. Upon the differences and similarities indicated by these patterns the world builds its intriguing variety of cultures and histories.

Terrain

Land Elevations in Profile

Ocean Depths in Profile

Arctic Ocean

30° 60° 90° 120° 150°

RUSSIA
NORWAY SWEDEN FINLAND Ob'
Moscow Volga
Berlin POLAND BELARUS
EUROPE GERMANY
Paris UKRAINE ASIA
...CE ALPS ROMANIA KAZAKHSTAN
ITALY Black Sea MONGOLIA
Rome TURKEY TURKMENISTAN GOBI
Mediterranean Sea Caspian Sea Beijing JAPAN
ISRAEL SYRIA Tehran CHINA Tokyo
Cairo IRAQ IRAN Shanghai Pacific
LIBYA EGYPT PAKISTAN HIMALAYAS
...ERIA SAUDI Ganges Tropic of Cancer Ocean
...HARA ARABIA INDIA Calcutta RANGE
NIGER CHAD SUDAN Red Sea Nile Bombay THAILAND VIETNAM PHILIPPINES
NIGERIA CENTRAL ETHIOPIA CAMB.
AFRICA AFRICAN REPUBLIC SOMALIA MALAYSIA
GABON Congo Equator Jakarta INDONESIA Equator
CONGO ZAIRE Lake Victoria PAPUA NEW GUINEA
RIFT VALLEY TANZANIA
ANGOLA Indian
ZAMBIA MADAGASCAR GREAT SANDY DESERT
NAMIBIA ZIMBABWE Tropic of Capricorn Ocean AUSTRALIA
KALAHARI DESERT BOTSWANA MOZAMBIQUE GREAT VICTORIA DESERT
SOUTH AFRICA Ocean Sydney
Cape Town NEW ZEALAND

Arctic Circle

Antarctic Circle

...ARCTICA

A-510000-792-1ᴱ-1ᴱ-1ᴱ-2

©1990 Rand McNally & Co.

30° 60° 90° 120° 150°

		1000		2000 Mi.
0		1000	2000 Km.	

Scale

EUROPE   ASIA   OCEANIA

| | | | | | | | | | | | | | 9145 | 30000 |
ALPS CAUCASUS ELBURZ K2 Everest Kanchenjunga Gongga Shan SUMATRA BORNEO NEW GUINEA 7620 25000
...340 PYRENEES Mt. Blanc KJÖLEN Gora El'brus Qullen-ye 28,250 29,028 28,208 24,790 Full-San PHILIPPINES AUSTRALIA 6095 20000
Pico de Aneto 15,771 Glittertinden Etna (Vol.) Dj. esh-Sheikh Damavand PAMIRS JAVA Klyuchevskaya Kinabalu Mt. Apo Puncak Jaya 4570 15000
MADAGASCAR 11,168 8110 10,902 (Hermon) 18,386 PLATEAU OF TIBET (Vol.) 15,584 12,455 9692 12,503 3050 10000
Maromokotro 9436 Hekla (Vol.) Narodnaya 9232 Semeru 12,060 Mt. Kosciusko 1525 5000
4,892 6,217 IRAN SRI LANKA GOBI DESERT G. Kerinci 12,467 7,316
Meters Feet

...AN MEDITERRANEAN SEA INDIAN OCEAN ARCTIC OCEAN PACIFIC OCEAN
FRANCE GIBRALTAR MALTA ISRAEL Sea Level SOEMBA NORTH POLE 65°N 65°S LITTLE AMERICA SOUTH POLE
1525 5000
3050 10000
4570 15000
10,420 6095 20000
7620 25000
A Section along 10°S. Lat. 9145 30000
10,670 35000
Meters Feet

given in feet   I·7

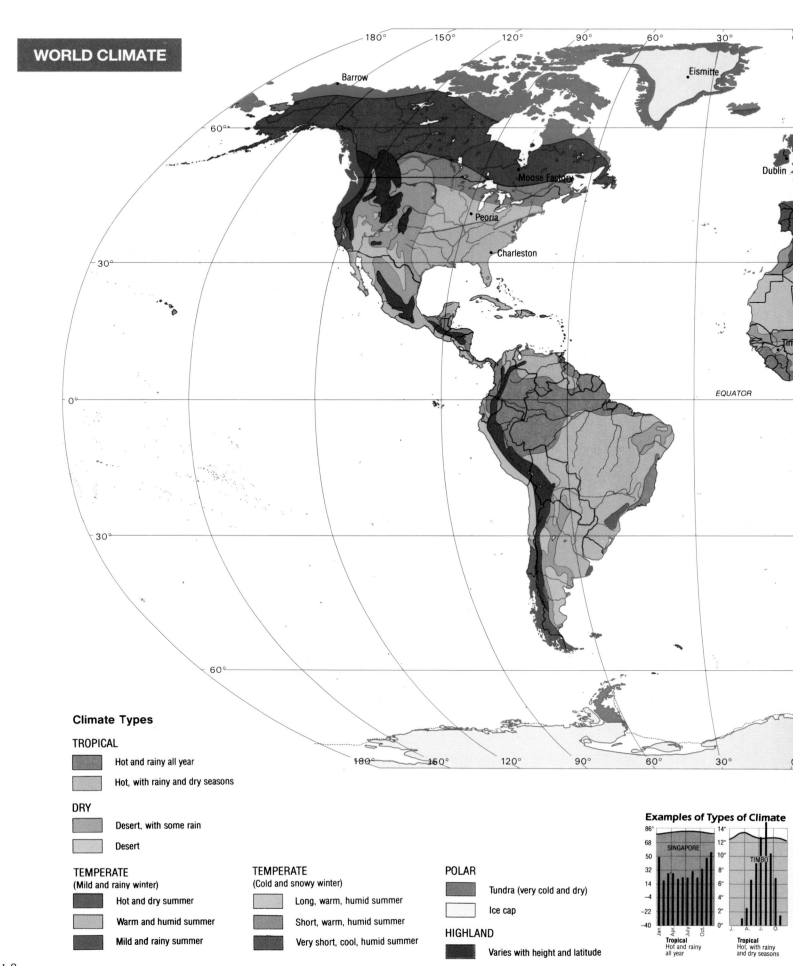

WORLD CLIMATE

Climate Types

TROPICAL

Hot and rainy all year

Hot, with rainy and dry seasons

DRY

Desert, with some rain

Desert

TEMPERATE
(Mild and rainy winter)

Hot and dry summer

Warm and humid summer

Mild and rainy summer

TEMPERATE
(Cold and snowy winter)

Long, warm, humid summer

Short, warm, humid summer

Very short, cool, humid summer

POLAR

Tundra (very cold and dry)

Ice cap

HIGHLAND

Varies with height and latitude

Examples of Types of Climate

SINGAPORE

Tropical
Hot and rainy
all year

TIMBO

Tropical
Hot, with rainy
and dry seasons

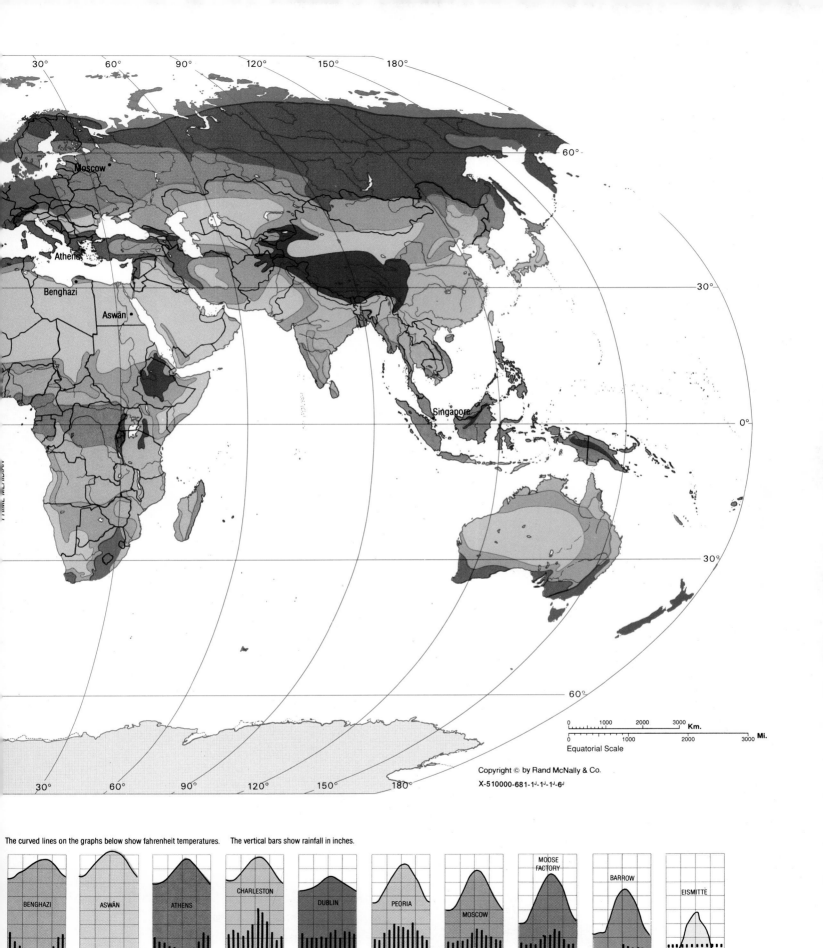

The curved lines on the graphs below show fahrenheit temperatures.   The vertical bars show rainfall in inches.

BENGHAZI
Dry
Desert, with some rain

ASWĀN
Dry
Desert

ATHENS
Temperate
Hot and dry summer; mild and rainy winter

CHARLESTON
Temperate
Warm and humid summer; mild and rainy winter

DUBLIN
Temperate
Mild and rainy all year

PEORIA
Temperate
Long, warm, humid summer; cold and snowy winter

MOSCOW
Temperate
Short, warm, humid summer; cold and snowy winter

MOOSE FACTORY
Temperate
Very short, cool, humid summer; very cold and snowy winter

BARROW
Polar
Tundra (very cold and dry)

EISMITTE
Polar
Ice cap

Copyright © by Rand McNally & Co.

X-510000-681-1ᴶ-1ᴶ-1ᴶ-6ᴶ

I·9

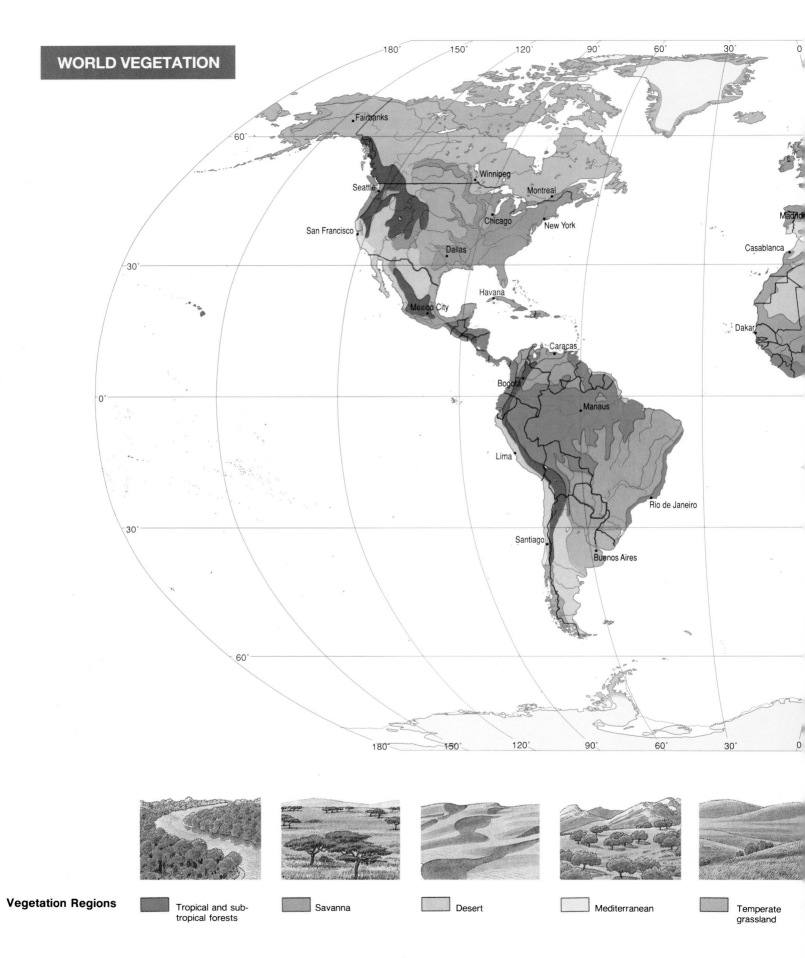

WORLD VEGETATION

180° 150° 120° 90° 60° 30° 0°

Fairbanks

60°

Winnipeg

Seattle

Montreal

San Francisco

Chicago

New York

Madrid

Casablanca

30°

Dallas

Havana

Mexico City

Dakar

Caracas

Bogotá

0°

Manaus

Lima

Rio de Janeiro

30°

Santiago

Buenos Aires

60°

180° 150° 120° 90° 60° 30° 0°

Vegetation Regions

| | Tropical and sub-tropical forests | | Savanna | | Desert | | Mediterranean | | Temperate grassland |

Stockholm
Berlin
Moscow
Novosibirsk
Volgograd
Rome
Tashkent
Damascus
Tehrán
Beijing
Cairo
New Delhi
Chongqing
Shanghai
Tōkyō
Calcutta
Hong Kong
Bombay
Khartoum
Bangkok
agos
Nairobi
Kinshasa
Jakarta
Darwin
Johannesburg
Perth
Sydney
Cape Town

60°
30°
0°
30°
60°

30° 60° 90° 120° 150° 180°

| 0 | 1000 | 2000 | 3000 | Km. |

| 0 | 1000 | 2000 | 3000 | Mi. |

Equatorial Scale

Copyright © 1991 by Rand McNally & Co.

Temperate forest

Taiga (northern forests)

Tundra (lichen and moss)

Mountain

Polar and high mountain

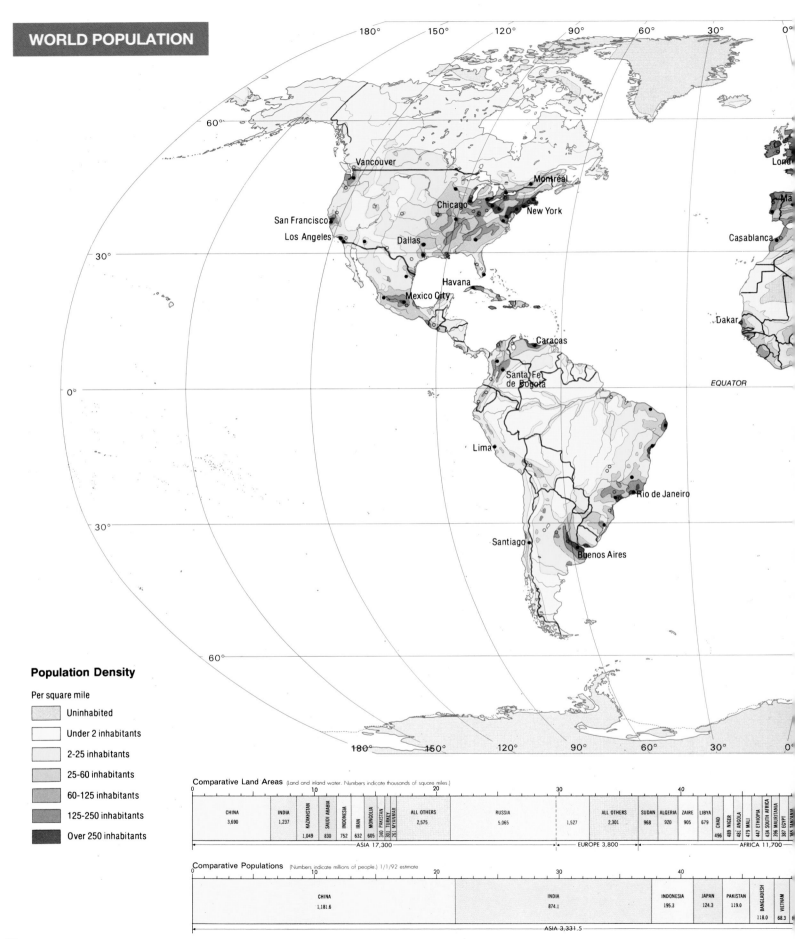

180° 150° 120° 90° 60° 30° 0°

60°

Vancouver
Montréal
Chicago
New York
San Francisco
Los Angeles
Dallas
30°
Havana
Mexico City

Caracas
0°
Santa Fe
de Bogotá
EQUATOR

Lima

Rio de Janeiro
30°

Santiago
Buenos Aires

London
Ma
Casablanca

Dakar

60°

180° 150° 120° 90° 60° 30° 0°

Population Density

Per square mile

	Uninhabited
	Under 2 inhabitants
	2-25 inhabitants
	25-60 inhabitants
	60-125 inhabitants
	125-250 inhabitants
	Over 250 inhabitants

Comparative Land Areas (Land and inland water. Numbers indicate thousands of square miles.)

0	10	20	30	40	

| CHINA 3,690 | INDIA 1,237 | KAZAKHSTAN 1,049 | SAUDI ARABIA 830 | INDONESIA 752 | IRAN 632 | MONGOLIA 605 | PAKISTAN 340 | TURKEY 301 | MYANMAR 261 | ALL OTHERS 2,575 | RUSSIA 5,065 | 1,527 | ALL OTHERS 2,301 | SUDAN 968 | ALGERIA 920 | ZAIRE 905 | LIBYA 679 | CHAD 496 | NIGER 489 | ANGOLA 481 | MALI 479 | ETHIOPIA 447 | SOUTH AFRICA 434 | MAURITANIA 396 | EGYPT 387 | TANZANIA 365 |

ASIA 17,300 — EUROPE 3,800 — AFRICA 11,700

Comparative Populations (Numbers indicate millions of people.) 1/1/92 estimate

0	10	20	30	40	

| CHINA 1,181.6 | INDIA 874.1 | INDONESIA 195.3 | JAPAN 124.3 | PAKISTAN 119.0 | BANGLADESH 118.0 | VIETNAM 68.3 |

ASIA 3,331.5

WORLD ENVIRONMENTS

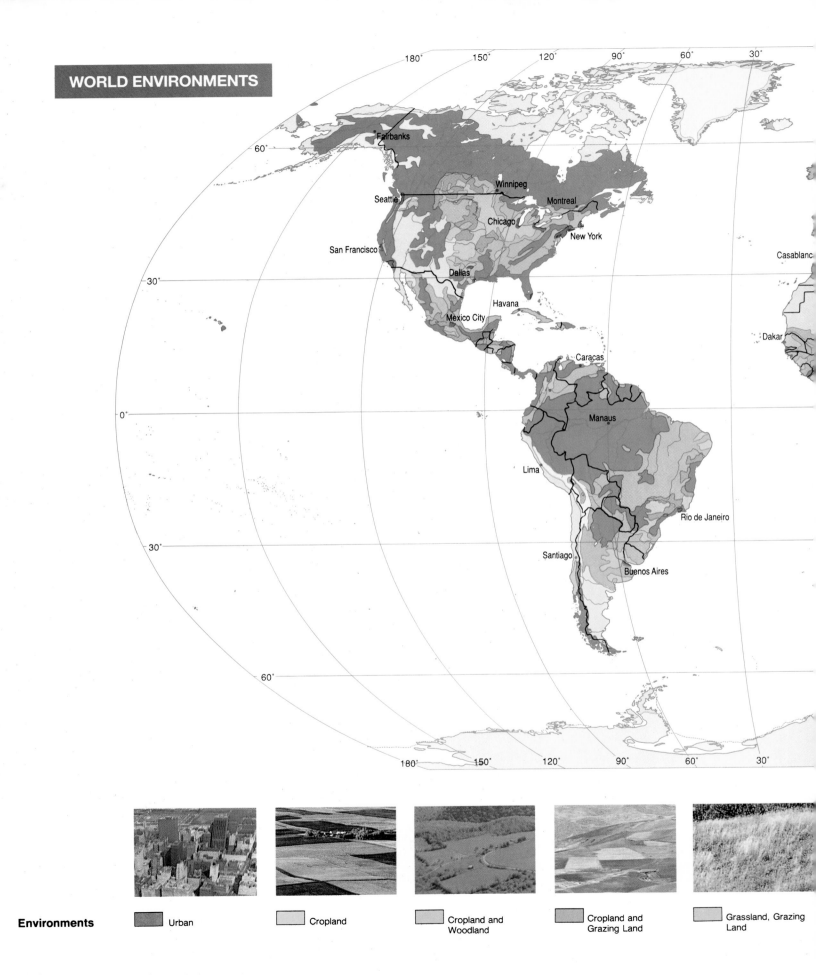

180° 150° 120° 90° 60° 30°

Fairbanks

Winnipeg
Seattle
Montreal
Chicago
New York
San Francisco
Casablanc
Dallas
Havana
Dakar
Mexico City
Caracas
Manaus
Lima
Rio de Janeiro
Santiago
Buenos Aires

60° 30° 0° 30° 60°

180° 150° 120° 90° 60° 30°

Environments

  Urban   Cropland   Cropland and Woodland   Cropland and Grazing Land   Grassland, Grazing Land

30° 60° 90° 120° 150° 180°

60°

Stockholm

Moscow
Novosibirsk

Berlin
Volgograd
Rome
Tashkent
Damascus
Tehrān
Beijing
Cairo
New Delhi
Chongqing
Tōkyō
Shanghai
30°
Calcutta
Hong Kong
Khartoum
Bombay
Lagos
Bangkok
Nairobi
Kinshasa
Jakarta
0°
Darwin
Johannesburg
Cape Town
Perth
30°
Sydney

60°

30° 60° 90° 120° 150° 180°

| 0 | 1000 | 2000 | 3000 | Km. |

| 0 | 1000 | 2000 | 3000 | Mi. |

Equatorial Scale

Copyright © 1991 by Rand McNally & Co.
X-510000-387-1-1-1-1

Forest, Woodland   Swamp, Marshland   Tundra   Shrub, Sparse Grass and Waste-land (desert)   Barren Land (polar and high mountain)

I·15

WORLD TIME ZONES

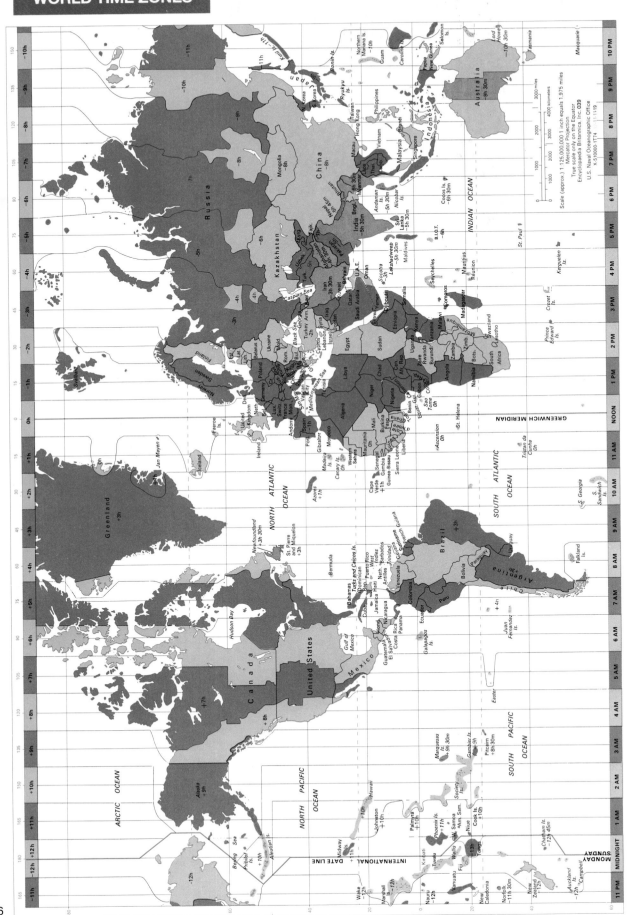

The standard time zone system, fixed by international agreement and by law in each country, is based on a theoretical division of the globe into 24 zones of 15° longitude each. The mid-meridian of each zone fixes the hour for the entire zone. The zero time zone extends 7½° east and 7½° west of the Greenwich meridian, 0° longitude. Since the earth rotates toward the east, time zones to the west of Greenwich are earlier, to the east, later.

Plus and minus hours at the top of the map are added to or subtracted from local time to find Greenwich time. Local standard time can be determined for any area in the world by adding one hour for each time zone counted in an easterly direction from one's own, or by subtracting one hour for each zone counted in a westerly direction. To separate one day from the next, the 180th meridian has been designated as the international date line. On both sides of the line the time of day is the same, but west of the line it is one day later than it is to the east. Countries that adhere to the international zone system, adopt the zone applicable to their location. Some countries, however, establish time zones based on political boundaries, or adopt the time zone of a neighboring unit. For all or part of the year some countries also advance their time by one hour, thereby utilizing more daylight hours each day.

h m | hours, minutes

Time Zones

- Standard time zone of even-numbered hours from Greenwich time
- Standard time zone of odd-numbered hours from Greenwich time
- Time varies from the standard time zone by half an hour
- Time varies from the standard time zone by other than half an hour

Map Scale

	1:4,000,000-1:6,000,000
	1:8,000,000 1:9,000,000
	1:16,000,000-1:20,500,000
62	Page Reference

World, Page 2
Asia, Page 20
Africa, Page 41
Antarctica, Page 47
Pacific Ocean, Page 48
South America, Page 53
Atlantic Ocean, Page 60
North America, Page 61
Canadian Provinces, Pages 68-75
U.S. States, Pages 78-127
North Polar Regions, Page 128

Copyright © by Rand McNally & Co.
B-519500-9Z84

World Maps Symbols

Inhabited Localities

The size of type indicates the relative economic and political importance of the locality

| Écommoy | Lisieux | **Rouen** |
| Trouville | **Orléans** | **PARIS** |

Bi'r Safâjah ° Oasis

Alternate Names

MOSKVA
MOSCOW — English or second official language names are shown in reduced size lettering

Basel
Bâle

Volgograd
(Stalingrad) — Historical or other alternates in the local language are shown in parentheses

Urban Area (Area of continuous industrial, commercial, and residential development)

Capitals of Political Units

BUDAPEST Independent Nation

Cayenne Dependency (Colony, protectorate, etc.)

Recife State, Province, County, Oblast, etc.

Political Boundaries

International (First-order political unit)

Demarcated and Undemarcated

Disputed de jure

Indefinite or Undefined

Demarcation Line

Internal

State, Province, etc. (Second-order political unit)

MURCIA Historical Region (No boundaries indicated)

GALAPAGOS (Ecuador) Administering Country

Transportation

Primary Road

Secondary Road

Minor Road, Trail

Railway

Canal du Midi Navigable Canal

Bridge

Tunnel

TO MALMÖ Ferry

Hydrographic Features

Shoreline

Undefined or Fluctuating Shoreline

Amur River, Stream

Intermittent Stream

Rapids, Falls

Irrigation or Drainage Canal

Reef

The Everglades Swamp

RIMO GLACIER Glacier

L. Victoria Lake, Reservoir

Tuz Gölü Salt Lake

Intermittent Lake, Reservoir

Dry Lake Bed

(395) Lake Surface Elevation

Topographic Features

Matterhorn △ 4478 Elevation Above Sea Level

76 ▽ Elevation Below Sea Level

Mount Cook ▲ 3764 Highest Elevation in Country

133 ▼ Lowest Elevation in Country

Khyber Pass ⋈ 1067 Mountain Pass

Elevations are given in meters.
The highest and lowest elevations in a continent are underlined

Sand Area

Lava

Salt Flat

State, Province Maps Symbols

✪	Capital
⊙	County Seat
▲	Military Installation
△	Point of Interest
+	Mountain Peak

	International Boundary
	State, Province Boundary
	County Boundary
	Railroad
	Road
	Urban Area

World

Europe

★ Population of metropolitan
area, including suburbs.

4

Miller Oblated Stereographic Projection

Scandinavia

★ Population of metropolitan area, including suburbs.
▲ Population of entire district, including rural area.

Kilometers 0 100 200 300 Km.
Miles 0 100 200 300 Mi.

1 : 8 000 000

Lambert Conformal Conic Projection

6

British Isles

Ireland
1986 CENSUS
Cork, 133,271
(173,694★) . . . . . . J 4
Dublin (Baile Átha Cliath), 502,749
(1,140,000★) . . . . H 6
Galway, 47,104 . . . . H 3
Limerick, 56,279
(76,557★) . . . . I 4
Waterford, 39,529
(41,054★) . . . . I 5

Isle of Man
1986 CENSUS
Douglas, 20,368
(28,500★) . . . . G 8

United Kingdom
England
1981 CENSUS
Birmingham, 1,013,995
(2,675,000★) I11
Blackpool, 146,297
(280,000★) . . . . . . H 9
Bournemouth, 142,829
(315,000★) K11
Bradford, 293,336 . . . H11
Brighton, 134,581
(420,000★) K12
Bristol, 413,861
(630,000★) J10
Coventry, 318,718
(645,000★) I11
Derby, 218,026
(275,000★) I11
Kingston upon Hull,
322,144 (350,000★) H12
Leeds, 445,242
(1,540,000★) H11
Leicester, 324,394
(495,000★) I11
Liverpool, 538,809
(1,525,000★) H10
London, 6,574,009
(11,100,000★) J12
Manchester, 437,612
(2,775,000★) H10
Newcastle upon Tyne,
199,064
(1,300,000★) G11
Nottingham, 273,300
(655,000★) I11
Oxford, 113,847
(230,000★) J11
Plymouth, 238,583
(290,000★) . . . . . . K 8
Portsmouth, 174,218
(485,000★) K11
Preston, 166,675
(250,000★) H10
Reading, 194,727
(200,000★) J12
Sheffield, 470,685
(710,000★) H11
Southampton, 211,321
(415,000★) K11
Southend-on-Sea,
155,720 . . . . J13
Stoke-on-Trent, 272,446
(440,000★) H10
Sunderland, 195,064 G11
Teesside, 158,516
(580,000★) G11
Wolverhampton,
263,501 . . . . I10

Northern Ireland
1987 ESTIMATE
Bangor, 70,700 . . . . G 7
Belfast, 303,800
(685,000★) . . . . . . G 7
Londonderry, 97,500
(97,200★) . . . . G 5
Newtownabbey,
72,300 . . . . G 7

Scotland
1989 ESTIMATE
Aberdeen, 210,700 . . D10
Dundee, 172,540 . . . E 9
Edinburgh, 433,200
(630,000★) . . . . . . F 9
Glasgow, 695,630
(1,800,000★) . . . . . F 8
Greenock, 58,436
(101,000★)('81) . . . F 8
Inverness, 38,204('81) D 8
Paisley, 84,330('81) . F 8

Wales
1981 CENSUS
Cardiff, 262,313
(625,000★) . . . . . . J 9
Newport, 115,896
(310,000★) . . . . . . J 9
Swansea, 172,433
(270,000★) . . . . . . J 9

★ Population of metropolitan
area, including suburbs.

7

Central Europe

★ Population of metropolitan
area, including suburbs.

8

France and the Alps

France

Kilometers 0 50 100 150 Km.

Miles 0 50 100 150 Mi.

1:4 000 000

★ Population of metropolitan area, including suburbs.
▲ Population of entire district, including rural area.

11

Copyright © by Rand McNally & Co.
B-559495-264

Lambert Conformal Conic Projection

Spain and Portugal

Andorra
1986 CENSUS

Gibraltar
1988 ESTIMATE

Portugal
1981 CENSUS

Spain
1988 ESTIMATE

★ Population of metropolitan area, including suburbs.
▲ Population of entire district, including rural area.

Copyright © by Rand McNally & Co.
B-559900-264

Conic Projection, Two Standard Parallels

Spanish North Africa

1988 ESTIMATE

13

Italy

Kilometers

Miles

1 : 4 000 000

Copyright © by Rand McNally & Co.
B-569295-264

Conic Projection, Two Standard Parallels

15

Southeastern Europe

★ Population of metropolitan area, including suburbs. ▲ Population of entire district, including rural area.

Kilometers

Miles

1 : 4 000 000

Conic Projection, Two Standard Parallels

Copyright © by Rand McNally & Co.
B-559690-264

Novi Sad, 176,000
(266,772★) .... D 3
Pančevo, 62,700 .... E 4
Podgorica, 82,500
(145,163★) .... G 3
Priština, 125,400
(244,830★) .... G 5
Subotica, 100,500
(153,306★) .... C 3
Zrenjanin, 65,400
(140,009★) .... D 4

Bucureşti (Bucharest),
1,989,823
(2,275,000★) E10
Buzău, 136,080 .... D10
Cluj-Napoca, 310,017 .. C 7
Constanţa, 327,676 .... E12
Craiova, 281,044 ...... E 7
Galaţi, 295,372 .... D12
Iaşi, 313,060 .... B11
Oradea, 213,846 .... B 5
Ploieşti, 234,886 ..... E10

Satu Mare, 130,082 .... B 6
Sibiu, 177,511 .... D 8
Târgu Mureş, 158,998 .. C 8
Timişoara, 325,272 .... D 5

Turkey
1990 CENSUS

Bursa, 838,323 .... I13
Denizli, 203,130 ...... L13
İstanbul, 6,748,435
(7,000,000★) H12

İzmir, 2,553,209
(1,620,000★) K11
Manisa, 158,283 .... K11
Ödemiş, 511,110 .... K11

Yugoslavia
1987 ESTIMATE

Beograd (Belgrade),
1,130,000
(1,400,000★) .... E 4
Niš, 168,400 (240,219★) F 5

17

Baltic and Moscow Regions

Asia

Copyright © by Rand McNally & Co.

A-519695-286

Miles 0   200   400   600   800   1000 Mi.
Kilometers 0   400   800   1200   1600 Km.

1:40 000 000

Kyōto,
1,479,218 ('85).........F16
KYRGYZSTAN............E10
Kyzyl, 80,000 ('87)......D12
Lahore, 2,707,215 ('81)
(3,025,000★) F10
Lanzhou, 1,297,000 ('88)
(1,420,000▲) F13
LAOS......................H13
LEBANON..................F 6
Lhasa, 84,400 ('86)
(107,700▲) G12
MACAU....................G14
Madras, 3,276,622 ('81)
(4,475,000★) H11
Makkah,
550,000 ('80)..........G 6
MALAYSIA..................I13
MALDIVES..................I10
Mandalay, 532,949
('83).......................G12
Manila, 1,587,000 ('90)
(6,800,000★) H15
Mashhad, 1,463,508
('86).......................F 8
Masqaṭ, 50,000 ('81)...G 8
Mawlamyine, 219,961
('83).......................H12
MONGOLIA.................E13
MYANMAR.................G12
Nāgpur, 1,219,461 ('81)
(1,302,066★) G10
Nanjing, 2,390,000
('88).......................F14
NEPAL......................G11
New Delhi, 273,036
('81).......................G10
Novosibirsk, 1,436,000
('89) (1,600,000★) ..D11
Ochotsk, 9,000...........D17
Omsk, 1,148,000 ('89)
(1,175,000★) D10
Ōsaka, 2,636,249 ('85)
(1,645,000★) F16
PAKISTAN..................G 9
Patna, 776,371 ('81)
(1,025,000★) G11
Peking see Beijing F14
Peshāwar, 506,896 ('81)
(566,248★) F10
Petropavlovsk-Kamčatskij,
269,000 ('89)...........D18
PHILIPPINES...............H15
Phnum Penh, 700,000
('86).......................H13
Pyŏngyang, 1,283,000
('81) (1,600,000★) ...F15
QATAR......................G 8
Qingdao (Tsingtao),
1,300,000 ('88)........F15
Quetta, 244,842 ('81)
(285,719★) ....F 9
Quezon City, 1,632,000
('90).......................H15
Rangoon see
Yangon H12
Rāwalpindi, 457,091 ('81)
(1,040,000★) F10
RUSSIA......................D10
Saigon see Thanh Pho Ho
Chi Minh H13
Samarkand, 366,000
('89).......................F 9
Ṣanʿāʾ, 427,150 ('86)...H 7
SAUDI ARABIA..........G 7
Semipalatinsk, 334,000
('89).......................D11
Sendai, 700,254 ('85)
(1,175,000★) F17

Shanghai,
7,220,000 ('88)
(9,300,000★) F15
Shenyang (Mukden),
3,910,000 ('88)
(4,370,000▲) E15
Shīrāz, 848,289 ('86)...G 8
SINGAPORE..................I13
Sŏul, 10,522,000 ('89)
(15,850,000★) F15
SRI LANKA..................I11
Srīnagar, 594,775 ('81)
(606,002★) F10
SYRIA.......................F 6
Tabrīz, 971,482 ('86)... F 7
T'aipei, 2,637,100 ('88)
(6,130,000★) G15
TAIWAN....................G15
Taiyuan, 1,700,000 ('88)
(1,980,000▲) F14
TAJIKISTAN.................F10
Taškent, 2,073,000 ('89)
(2,325,000★) ....E 9
Tbilisi, 1,260,000 ('89)
(1,460,000★) ....E 7
Tehrān, 6,042,584 ('86)
(7,500,000★) ....F 8
THAILAND..................H13
Thanh Pho Ho Chi Minh
(Saigon), 3,169,000 ('89)
(3,100,000★) H13
Tianjin (Tientsin),
4,950,000 ('88)
(5,540,000▲) F14
Tobol'sk,
82,000 ('87)............ D 9
Tōkyō, 8,354,615 ('85)
(27,700,000★) F16
Tomsk, 502,000 ('89)...D11
TURKEY.....................F 6
TURKMENISTAN........F 9
Ulaanbaatar, 548,400
('89).......................E13
**UNITED ARAB
EMIRATES**.............G 8
Ürümqi, 1,060,000
('88).......................E11
UZBEKISTAN..............E 9
Vārānasi, 708,647 ('81)
(925,000★) G11
Verchojansk, 1,400.....C16
Viangchan, 377,409
('85).......................H13
VIETNAM....................H13
Vladivostok, 648,000
('89).......................E16
Wuhan, 3,570,000
('88).......................F14
Xiamen, 343,700 ('86)
(546,400▲) G14
Xi'an, 2,210,000 ('88)
(2,580,000▲) F13
Yangon (Rangoon),
2,705,039 ('83)
(2,800,000★) H12
YEMEN.......................H 7
Yerevan see Jerevan ..E 7
Yerushalayim (Jerusalem),
493,500 ('89)
(530,000★) ....F 6
Yokohama, 2,992,926
('85).......................F16
Zhangjiakou,
500,000 ('88)
(640,000▲) E14

★ Population of metropolitan area, including suburbs
▲ Population of entire district, including rural area.

21

Northwest Asia

Armenia
1989 CENSUS
Jerevan, 1,199,000
(1,315,000★) . . . . . . I 6

Azerbaijan
1989 CENSUS
Baki (Baku), 1,150,000
(2,020,000★) . . . . . . I 7
Gäncä, 278,000 . . . . . I 7
Sumqayıt, 231,000 . . . I 7

Belarus
1989 CENSUS
Brest, 258,000 . . . . G 2
Gomel', 500,000 . . . . G 4
Grodno, 270,000 . . . . G 2
Minsk, 1,589,000
(1,650,000★) . . . . G 3
Mogil'ov, 356,000 . . . . G 4
Vitebsk, 350,000 . . . . F 4

Estonia
1989 CENSUS
Tallinn, 482,000 . . . . F 2

Georgia
1989 CENSUS
Kutaisi, 235,000 . . . . I 6
Tbilisi, 1,260,000
(1,460,000★) . . . . . . I 6

Kazakhstan
1989 CENSUS
Akmola, 277,000 . . . . G12
Akt'ubinsk, 253,000 G 9
Alma-Ata, 1,128,000
(1,190,000★) I13
Čimkent, 393,000 . . . I11
Džambul, 307,000 . . . I12
Karaganda, 614,000 H12
Pavlodar, 331,000 . . G13
Petropavlovsk,
241,000 . . . . G11
Semipalatinsk,
334,000 . . . . G14
Temirtau, 212,000 . . G12
Ural'sk, 200,000 . . . G 8
Ust'-Kamenogorsk,
324,000 . . . . H14

Kyrgyzstan
1989 CENSUS
Biškek, 616,000 . . . . I12
Oš, 213,000 . . . . I12

Latvia
1989 CENSUS
Rīga, 915,000
(1,005,000★) . . . . F 2

Lithuania
1989 CENSUS
Kaunas, 423,000 . . . G 2
Klaipėda, 204,000 . . . F 2
Vilnius, 582,000 . . . . F 3

Moldova
1989 CENSUS
Bălți, 131,000('81) . . H 3
Chișinău, 665,000 . . . H 3
Tiraspol, 182,000 . . H 3

Russia
1989 CENSUS
Archangel'sk, 416,000 E 6
Astrachan', 509,000 . H 7
Belgorod, 300,000 . . G 5
Br'ansk, 452,000 . . . . G 4
Čeboksary, 420,000 . . F 7
Čel'abinsk, 1,143,000
(1,325,000★) F10
Čerepovec, 310,000 . F 5
Gor'kij see Nižnij
Novgorod . . . . F 6
Groznyj, 401,000 . . . . I 7
Ivanovo, 481,000 . . . . F 6
Iževsk, 635,000 . . . . F 8
Jaroslavl', 633,000 . . F 5
Jekaterinburg
(Sverdlovsk), 1,367,000
(1,620,000★) F10
Kaliningrad, 401,000 . G 2
Kaluga, 312,000 . . . G 5
Kazan', 1,094,000
(1,140,000★) . . . . F 7
Kirov, 441,000 . . . . . F 7
Krasnodar, 620,000 . . H 5
Kurgan, 356,000 . . . F11
Kursk, 424,000 . . . . G 5
Leningrad see
Sankt-Peterburg . . F 4
Lipeck, 450,000 . . . . G 5
Machačkala, 315,000 . I 7

★ Population of metropolitan
area, including suburbs.

22

Lambert Conformal Conic Projection

Magnitogorsk, 440,000 . . . . G 9
Moskva (Moscow), 8,769,000 (13,100,000★) . . . . F 5
Murmansk, 468,000 . . D 4
Naberežnyje Čelny, 501,000 . . . . F 8
Nižnij Novgorod (Gor'kij), 1,438,000 (2,025,000★) . . . . . F 6
Nižnij Tagil, 440,000 . . F 9
Orel, 337,000 . . . . . . G 5
Orenburg, 547,000 . . G 9
Orsk, 271,000 . . . . . . G 9
Penza, 543,000 . . . . G 7
Perm', 1,091,000 (1,160,000★) . . . . . F 9
Petrozavodsk, 270,000 . . . . E 4
R'azan', 515,000 . . . . G 5
Rostov-na-Donu, 1,020,000 (1,165,000★) . . . . . H 5
Samara, 1,257,000 (1,505,000★) . . . . . G 8
Sankt-Peterburg (St. Petersburg), 4,456,000 (5,825,000★) . . . . F 4
Saransk, 312,000 . . . G 7
Saratov, 905,000 (1,155,000★) . . . . . G 7
Smolensk, 341,000 . . G 4
Soči, 337,000 . . . . . . I 5
Stalingrad see Volgograd . . . . H 6
Stavropol', 318,000 . . H 6
Sverdlovsk see Jekaterinburg F10
Syktyvkar, 233,000 . . E 8
Taganrog, 291,000 . . H 5
Tambov, 305,000 . . . G 6
Toljatti, 630,000 . . . . G 7
Tula, 540,000 (640,000★) . . . . . . G 5
Tver' (Kalinin), 451,000 . . . . F 5
Ufa, 1,083,000 (1,100,000★) . . . . . G 9
Uljanovsk, 625,000 . . G 7
Vladikavkaz, 300,000 . I 6
Vladimir, 350,000 . . . . F 6
Volgograd (Stalingrad), 999,000 (1,360,000★) . . . . . H 6
Vologda, 283,000 . . . F 5
Volžskij, 269,000 . . . . H 6
Voronež, 887,000 . . . G 5

Tajikistan
1989 CENSUS

Dušanbe, 595,000 . . J11

Turkmenistan
1989 CENSUS

Aščhabad, 398,000 . . J 9

Ukraine
1989 CENSUS

Cherkasy, 290,000 . . H 4
Chernihiv, 296,000 . . G 4
Dniprodzerzhynsk, 282,000 . . . . H 4
Dnipropetrovsk, 1,179,000 (1,600,000★) . . . . H 4
Donets'k, 1,110,000 (2,200,000★) . . . . H 5
Horlivka, 337,000 (710,000★) . . . . . H 5
Kharkiv, 1,611,000 (1,940,000★) . . . . G 5
Kherson, 355,000 . . . H 4
Kryvyy Rih, 713,000 . H 4
Kyiv (Kiev), 2,587,000 (2,900,000★) . . . . G 4
Luhansk, 497,000 . . . H 5
L'viv, 790,000 . . . . . H 2
Mariupol' (Ždanov), 517,000 . . . . H 5
Mykolayiv, 503,000 . . H 4
Odesa, 1,115,000 (1,185,000★) . . . . H 4
Poltava, 315,000 . . . H 4
Sevastopol', 356,000 . I 4
Simferopol', 344,000 . I 4
Sumy, 291,000 . . . . G 4
Vinnytsya, 374,000 . . H 3
Yalta, 89,000('87) . . . . I 4
Zaporizhzhya, 884,000 . . . . H 5
Zhytomyr, 292,000 . . G 3

Uzbekistan
1989 CENSUS

Andižan, 293,000 . . . . I12
Buchara, 224,000 . . . J10
Fergana, 200,000 . . . I12
Namangan, 308,000 . . I12
Samarkand, 366,000 . J11
Taškent, 2,073,000 (2,325,000★) I11

23

Northeast Asia

Russia

25

China, Japan, and Korea

Bhutan

1982 ESTIMATE
Thimphu, 12,000 .... F 4

China

1988 ESTIMATE
Andong, 579,800('86) C11
Anshan, 1,330,000 .. C11
Bangbu, 403,900
　(612,600)('86) E10
Baoding, 423,200
　(535,100)('86) D10
Baotou, 1,130,000 .. C 8
Beijing (Peking), 6,710,000
　(6,450,000★) D10
Benxi, 860,000 ...... C11
Canton see
　Guangzhou ...... G 9
Changchun, 1,822,000
　(2,000,000) C12
Changsha, 1,230,000 F 9
Changzhou,
　522,700('86) E10
Chengdu, 1,884,000
　(2,960,000▲) .... E 7
Chongqing, 2,502,000
　(2,890,000▲) .... F 8
Dalian, 2,280,000 .. D11
Datong, 810,000
　(1,040,000) ...... C 9
Fushun, 1,290,000 .. C11
Fuzhou, 910,000
　(1,240,000▲) F10
Guangzhou (Canton),
　3,100,000
　(3,420,000▲) ...... G 9
Guiyang, 1,030,000
　(1,430,000▲) ...... F 8
Handan, 870,000
　(1,030,000▲) ...... D 9
Hanzhou, 1,290,000 E 11
Harbin, 2,710,000 .. B12
Hefei, 740,000
　(930,000) E10
Hegang, 588,300('86) B13
Hengyang, 419,200
　(601,300)('86) .... F 9
Hohhot, 670,000
　(830,000) ...... C 9
Huainan, 700,000
　(1,110,000▲) E10
Huangshi,
　451,900('86) E10
Jilin, 1,200,000 ...... C12
Jinan (Tsinan), 1,546,000
　(2,140,000▲) D10
Jinzhou, 710,000
　(810,000▲) C11
Jixi, 700,000
　(820,000▲) B13
Kaifeng, 458,800
　(629,100)('86) .... E 9
Kunming, 1,310,000
　(1,550,000▲) ...... F 7
Lanzhou, 1,297,000
　(1,420,000▲) ...... D 7
Lasa (Lhasa), 84,400
　(107,700)('86) .... F 5
Liuzhou, 680,000 .... G 8
Luoyang, 760,000
　(1,090,000▲) ...... E 9
Mudanjiang, 650,000 C12
Nanchang, 1,090,000
　(1,260,000▲) F10
Nanjing, 2,390,000 .. E10
Nanning, 720,000
　(1,000,000▲) ...... G 8
Ningbo, 570,000
　(1,050,000▲) F11
Peking see Beijing .. D10
Qingdao (Tsingtao),
　1,300,000 ...... D11
Shanghai, 7,220,000
　(9,300,000★) E11
Shantou (Swatow),
　560,000 (790,000) G10
Shenyang (Mukden),
　3,910,000
　(4,370,000▲) C11
Shijiazhuang,
　1,220,000 ...... D 9
Suzhou, 740,000 .... E11
Taiyuan, 1,700,000
　(1,980,000▲) .... D 9
Tangshan, 1,080,000
　(1,440,000▲) D10
Tianjin (Tientsin),
　4,950,000
　(5,540,000▲) D10
Ürümqi, 1,060,000 .. C 4
Wenzhou, 372,200
　(530,600▲)('86) .. F11
Wuhan, 3,570,000 .. E 9
Wuhu, 396,000
　(502,200▲) E10
Wuxi, 880,000 ...... E11
Xi'an (Sian), 2,210,000
　(2,580,000▲) ...... E 8
Xining, 620,000 ...... D 7
Xuzhou, 860,000 .... E10
Zhangjiakou (Kalgan),
　500,000 (640,000▲) C 9

26

Zhengzhou, 1,150,000
  (1,580,000▲) . . . . . E 9
Zibo, 840,000
  (2,370,000▲) . . . D10

Hong Kong
1986 CENSUS

Kowloon (Jiulong),
  774,781 . . . . G 9
Victoria (Xianggang),
  1,175,860
  (4,770,000★) . . . . . . G 9

Japan
1985 CENSUS

Asahikawa, 363,631 . . C15
Chiba, 788,930 . . . . D15
Fukuoka, 1,160,440
  (1,750,000★) E13
Hakodate, 319,194 . . C15
Hamamatsu, 514,118 E14
Himeji, 452,917
  (660,000★) E13
Hiroshima, 1,044,118
  (1,575,000★) E13
Kagoshima, 530,502 . E13
Kanazawa, 430,481 . D14
Kitakyūshū, 1,056,402
  (1,525,000★) E13
Kōbe, 1,410,834 . . . E14
Kumamoto, 555,719 . E13
Kurashiki, 413,632 . . E13
Kyōto, 1,479,218 . . . D14
Matsuyama, 426,658 E13
Nagasaki, 449,382 . . E12
Nagoya, 2,116,381
  (4,800,000★) D14
Niigata, 475,630 . . . D14
Okayama, 572,479 . . E13
Ōsaka, 2,636,249
  (16,450,000★) E14
Sapporo, 1,542,979
  (1,900,000★) C15
Sendai, 700,254
  (1,175,000★) D15
Shizuoka, 468,362
  (975,000★) E14
Tōkyō, 8,354,615
  (27,700,000★) D14
Utsunomiya, 405,375 D14
Yokohama, 2,992,926 D14

Korea, North
1981 ESTIMATE

Ch'ŏngjin, 490,000 . . C12
Kaesŏng, 259,000 . . D12
Namp'o, 241,000 . . . D12
P'yŏngyang, 1,283,000
  (1,600,000★) D12
Sinūiju, 305,000 . . . C11
Wŏnsan, 398,000 . . . D12

Korea, South
1989 ESTIMATE

Chŏnju, 426,473('85) D12
Inch'ŏn, 1,628,000 . . D12
Kwangju, 1,165,000 . D12
Masan, 448,746
  (625,000★)('85) D12
Pusan, 3,773,000
  (3,800,000★) D12
Soŭl (Seoul), 10,522,000
  (15,850,000★) D12
Taegu, 2,207,000 . . . . D12
Taejŏn, 1,041,000 . . D12

Macau
1987 ESTIMATE

Macau (Aomen),
  429,000 . . . . G 9

Mongolia
1989 ESTIMATE

Ulaanbaatar (Ulan Bator),
  548,400 . . . . B 8

Nepal
1981 CENSUS

Kāthmāndaū
  (Kathmandu), 235,160
  (320,000★) . . . . F 4

Taiwan
1988 ESTIMATE

Kaohsiung, 1,342,797
  (1,845,000★) G11
T'aichung, 715,107 . . G11
T'ainan, 656,927 . . . . G11
T'aipei, 2,637,100
  (6,130,000★) F11

★ Population of metropolitan area, including suburbs.
▲ Population of entire district, including rural area.

27

Eastern and Southeastern China

Scale 1:4 000 000

28

Copyright © by Rand McNally & Co.
B-567500.264

Lambert Conformal Conic Projection

29

Japan

★ Population of metropolitan area, including suburbs. ◆ Population of entire district, including rural area.

Kilometers | 0 50 100 150 Km.
Miles | 0 50 100 150 Mi.

1 : 4 000 000

SEA OF JAPAN
NIHON-KAI (S. Korea)

KYŪSHŪ

PACIFIC OCEAN

IZU-SHOTŌ

NANSEI-SHOTŌ RYUKYU ISLANDS

AMAMI-SHOTŌ

SATSUNAN-SHOTŌ

Naze

OKINAWA-JIMA
Kōza Ghowan
Naha

Copyright ⓒ by Rand McNally & Co.
B-561900-264   8-1-42
Lambert Conformal Conic Projection

31

Southeastern Asia

Brunei
1981 CENSUS
Bandar Seri Begawan,
22,777 (64,000★) .. E 5

Cambodia
1986 ESTIMATE
Phnum Pénh, 700,000 C 3

Indonesia
1980 CENSUS
Ambon, 111,914
(207,702▲) . . . . F 8
Balikpapan, 208,040
(279,852▲) . . . . F 6
Bandung, 1,633,000
(1,800,000★)('85) . . m13
Banjarmasin,
424,000('83) . . . . . F 5
Banjuwangi, 90,378 . . n17
Blitar, 78,503
(100,000★) n16
Bogor, 246,946
(560,000★) m13
Cilacap, 127,017 . . . . m14
Cirebon, 223,504
(275,000★) m14
Denpasar, 159,233 . G 6
Dili, 6,890 (67,039▲) . G 8
Garut, 145,624 . . . . . m13
Jakarta, 9,200,000
(10,000,000★)('89) m13
Jambi, 155,761
(230,046▲) . . . . F 3
Jember, 171,284 . . . . n16
Kediri, 176,261
(221,830▲) m16
Kudus, 154,478 . . . . m15
Kupang, 84,587 . . . . H 7
Madiun, 150,562
(180,000★) m15
Magelang, 123,358
(160,000★) m15
Malang, 547,000('83) m16
Manado, 217,091 . . . E 7
Medan, 2,110,000('85) E 2
Padang, 405,600
(657,000▲)('83) . . . F 3
Pakanbaru, 186,199 . . E 3
Palembang,
874,000('83) . . . . . F 3
Pangkalpinang, 90,078 F 4
Pasuruan, 95,864
(125,000★) m16
Pekalongan, 132,413
(260,000★) m14
Pemalang, 72,663 . . . m14
Pematangsiantar, 150,296
(175,000★) . . . . E 2
Pontianak,
343,000('83) . . . . . F 4
Probolinggo, 100,296 m16
Purwokerto, 143,787 m14
Salatiga, 85,740 . . . . m15
Samarinda, 182,473
(264,012▲) . . . . . . F 6
Semarang,
1,206,000('83) . . . m15
Sukabumi, 109,898
(225,000★) m13
Surabaya,
2,345,000('85) . . . m16
Surakarta, 491,000
(575,000★)('83) m15
Tanjungkarang-
Telukbetung, 284,167
(375,000★) k12
Tasikmalaya, 192,267 m14
Tegal, 131,440
(340,000★) m14
Tual, 7,833 . . . . G 9
Tulungagung, 91,585 . n15
Ujungpandang,
841,000('83) . . . . . G 6
Yogyakarta, 421,000
(510,000★)('83) m15

Laos
1975 ESTIMATE
Louangphrabang,
46,000 . . . . B 3
Paksé, 47,000 . . . . . . B 4
Savannakhet, 53,000 . B 3
Viangchan,
377,409('85) . . . . . B 3

Malaysia
1980 CENSUS
Alor Setar, 69,435 . . D 3
George Town (Pinang),
248,241 (495,000★) D 3
Ipoh, 293,849 . . . . . . E 3
Johor Baharu,
246,395 . . . . E 3
Kelang, 192,080 . . . . E 3
Kota Baharu, 167,872 D 3
Kuala Lumpur, 919,610
(1,475,000★) . . . . . E 3
Kuala Terengganu,
180,296 . . . . D 3
Kuantan, 131,547 . . . E 3

32

Kilometers 0 200 400 600 Km.
Miles 0 200 400 600 Mi.
1 : 16 000 000

★ Population of metropolitan area, including suburbs.
▲ Population of entire district, including rural area.

33

Myanmar, Thailand, and Indochina

★ Population of metropolitan area, including suburbs. ▲ Population of entire district, including rural area.

Lambert Conformal Conic Projection

34

Copyright © by Rand McNally & Co.
B-561100-264

1:8 000 000

Kilometers 0 100 200 300 Km.
Miles 0 100 200 300 Mi.

India and Pakistan

The boundary between India and Pakistan through the disputed state of Jammu and Kashmir follows the "line of control" agreed upon by both countries in 1972.

Copyright © by Rand McNally & Co.
B-569400-264   -12-13-24

Lambert Conformal Conic Projection

1:16 000 000

Kilometers
Km.
Miles
Mi.

India

1981 CENSUS

Akola, 225,412 . . . . . . B 4
Amrāvati, 261,404 . . B 4
Aurangābād, 284,607
(316,421★). . . . . . . C 3
Bangalore, 2,476,355
(2,950,000★) . . . . . F 4
Baroda, 734,473
(744,881★) . . . . . . A 2
Belgaum, 274,430
(300,372★). . . . . . . E 3
Bhāvnagar, 307,121
(308,642★) . . . . . . B 2
Bhilai, 290,090
(490,214★) . . . . . . B 6
Bhubaneswar,
219,211 . . . . B 8
Bombay, 8,243,405
(9,950,000★) . . . . . C 2
Calicut, 394,447
(546,058★) . . . . . . G 3
Cochin, 513,249
(685,836★). . . . . . H 4
Coimbatore, 704,514
(965,000★) . . . . . . G 4
Cuttack, 269,950
(327,412★) . . . . . . B 8
Dhule, 210,759 . . . . . B 3
Gulbarga, 221,325 . . D 4
Guntūr, 367,699 . . . . D 6
Hubli, 527,108 . . . . . E 3
Hyderābād, 2,187,262
(2,750,000★) . . . . . D 5
Indore, 829,327
(850,000★) . . . . . . A 3
Kolhāpur, 340,625
(351,392★). . . . . . . D 3
Madras, 3,276,622
(4,475,000★) . . . . . F 6
Madurai, 820,891
(960,000★) . . . . . . H 5
Mālegaon, 245,883 . . B 3
Mysore, 441,754
(479,081★) . . . . . . F 4
Nāgpur, 1,219,461
(1,302,066★) . . . . . B 5
Nāsik, 262,428
(429,034★) . . . . . . C 2
Nellore, 237,065 . . . . E 5
Pondicherry, 162,636
(251,420★) . . . . . . G 6
Pune (Poona), 1,203,351
(1,775,000★) . . . . . C 3
Raipur, 338,245 . . . . B 6
Salem, 361,394
(518,615★) . . . . . . G 5
Sholāpur, 511,103
(514,860★) . . . . . . D 3
Surat, 776,583
(913,806★) . . . . . . B 2
Thāna, 309,897 . . . . C 2
Tiruchchirāppalli, 362,045
(609,548★) . . . . . . G 5
Trivandrum, 483,086
(520,125★) . . . . . . H 4
Ulhāsnagar, 273,668 . C 2
Vijayawāda, 454,577
(543,008★) . . . . . . D 6
Vishākhapatnam, 565,321
(603,630★) . . . . . . D 7
Warangal, 335,150 . . C 5

Sri Lanka

1986 ESTIMATE

Colombo, 683,000
(2,050,000★) . . . . . I 5
Dehiwala-Mount Lavinia,
191,000 . . . . I 5
Kandy, 130,000 . . . . . I 6
Kotte, 104,000 . . . . . I 5

★ Population of metropolitan
area, including suburbs.

Northern India and Pakistan

Afghanistan
1981 ESTIMATE
Baghlān, 41,000('82) . . . . . B 3
Ghaznī, 31,196 . . . . D 3
Jalālābād, 58,000('82) . . C 4
Kābol, 1,424,400('88) . . C 3
Khānābād, 27,482 . . . . B 3
Kholm, 28,788 . . . . . . B 2
Mazār-e Sharīf,
  130,600('88) . . . . . B 2
Meymaneh, 39,218 . . . . C 1
Qandahār,
  225,500('88) . . . . . E 1
Sheberghān, 19,475 . . B 1

Bangladesh
1981 CENSUS
Barisāl, 172,905 . . . . . I14
Brāhmanbāria, 87,570 . I14
Chittagong, 980,000
  (1,391,877★) I14
Comilla, 184,132 . . . . . I14
Dhaka, 2,365,695
  (3,430,312★) I14
Jessore, 148,927 . . . . . I13
Khulna, 648,359 . . . . . I14
Mymensingh, 190,991 H14
Nārāyanganj, 405,562 . I14
Pābna, 109,065 . . . . . H13
Rājshāhi, 253,740 . . . . H13
Rangpur, 153,174 . . . . H13
Saidpur, 126,608 . . . . H13
Sirājganj, 106,774 . . . H13
Sylhet, 168,371 . . . . . H14

Bhutan
1982 ESTIMATE
Thimphu, 12,000 . . . . G13

India
1981 CENSUS
Āgra, 694,191
  (747,318★) . . . . . . G 8
Ahmadābād, 2,059,725
  (2,400,000★) . . . . . I 5
Ajmer, 375,593 . . . . . G 6
Alīgarh, 320,861 . . . . G 8
Allāhābād, 616,051
  (650,070★) . . . . . . H 9
Alwar, 145,795 . . . . . G 7
Amritsar, 594,844 . . . E 6
Asansol, 183,375
  (1,050,000★) I12
Bareilly, 386,734
  (449,425★) . . . . . . F 8
Baroda, 734,473
  (744,881★) . . . . . . I 5
Bhāgalpur, 225,062 . . H12
Bhātpāra, 260,761 . . . I13
Bhāvnagar, 307,121
  (308,642★) . . . . . . J 5
Bhilai, 290,090
  (490,214★) . . . . . . J 9
Bhopāl, 671,018 . . . . . I 7
Bhubaneswar, 219,211 J11
Bīkaner, 253,174
  (287,712★) . . . . . . F 5
Calcutta, 3,305,006
  (11,100,000★) I13
Chandīgarh, 373,789
  (422,841★) . . . . . . E 7
Cuttack, 269,950
  (327,412★) J11
Dehra Dūn, 211,416
  (293,010★) . . . . . . E 8
Delhi, 4,884,234
  (7,200,000★) . . . . . F 7
Durgāpur, 311,798 . . . I12
Gaya, 247,075 . . . . . . H11
Ghāziābād, 271,730
  (287,170★) . . . . . . F 7
Gorakhpur, 290,814
  (307,501★) G10
Gwalior, 539,015
  (555,862★) . . . . . . G 8
Howrah, 744,429 . . . . I13
Indore, 829,327
  (850,000★) . . . . . . I 6
Jabalpur, 614,162
  (757,303★) . . . . . . I 8
Jaipur, 977,165
  (1,025,000★) . . . . . G 6
Jammu, 206,135
  (223,361★) . . . . . . D 6
Jāmnagar, 277,615
  (317,362★) . . . . . . I 4
Jamshedpur, 438,385
  (669,580★) I12
Jhānsi, 246,172
  (284,141★) . . . . . . H 8
Jodhpur, 506,345 . . . . G 5
Jullundur, 408,186
  (441,552★) . . . . . . E 6
Kānpur, 1,481,789
  (1,875,000★) . . . . . G 9
Kota, 358,241 . . . . . . H 6
Lucknow, 895,721
  (1,060,000★) . . . . . G 9
Ludhiāna, 607,052 . . . E 6
Mathura, 147,493
  (160,995★) . . . . . . G 7

★ Population of metropolitan
  area, including suburbs.

38

Meerut, 417,395
(536,615★) . . . . F 7
Morādābād, 330,051
(345,350★) . . . . F 8
Muzaffarnagar,
171,816 . . . . F 7
Muzaffarpur, 190,416 G11
Nāgpur, 1,219,461
(1,302,066★) . . . . . . J 8
New Delhi, 273,036 . . F 7
Patna, 776,371
(1,025,000★) H11
Raipur, 338,245 . . . . . J 9
Rājkot, 445,076 . . . . . I 4
Rānchī, 489,626
(502,771★) I11
Raurkela, 206,821
(322,610★) I11
Sāgar, 160,392
(207,479★) . . . . I 8
Sahāranpur, 295,355 F 7
Srīnagar, 594,775
(606,002★) . . . . C 6
Surat, 776,583
(913,806★) . . . . J 5
Ujjain, 278,454
(282,203★) . . . . I 6
Vārānasi (Benares),
708,647 (925,000★) H10

Nepal
1981 CENSUS
Bhaktapur, 48,472 . . G11
Birātnagar, 93,544 . . G12
Kathmāndaū, 235,160
(320,000★) G11

Pakistan
1981 CENSUS
Bahāwalpur, 152,009
(180,263★) . . . . F 4
Chiniot, 105,559 . . . E 5
Dera Ghāzi Khān,
102,007 . . . . E 4
Dera Ismāīl Khān, 64,358
(68,145★) . . . . E 4
Faisalabad, 1,104,209 E 5

Gujrānwāla, 600,993
(658,753★) . . . . D 6
Gujrāt, 155,058 . . . . . D 6
Hyderābād, 702,539
(800,000★) . . . . . . H 3
Islāmābād, 204,364 . . D 5
Jhang Maghiāna,
195,558 . . . . E 5
Karāchi, 4,901,627
(5,300,000★) . . . . . . H 2
Kasūr, 155,523 . . . . . E 6
Lahore, 2,707,215
(3,025,000★) . . . . . . E 6
Lārkāna, 123,890 . . . G 3
Mardān, 141,842
(147,977★) . . . . C 5
Mīrpur Khās, 124,371 H 3
Multān, 696,316
(732,070★) . . . . E 4
Nawābshāh, 102,139 G 3
Okāra, 127,455
(153,483★) . . . . E 5
Peshāwar, 506,896
(566,248★) . . . . C 4
Quetta, 244,842
(285,719★) . . . . E 2
Rahīmyār Khān, 119,036
(132,635★) . . . . F 4
Rāwalpindi, 457,091
(1,040,000★) . . . . . . D 5
Sāhiwāl (Montgomery),
150,954 . . . . E 5
Sargodha, 231,895
(291,362★) . . . . D 5
Shekhūpura, 141,168 E 5
Siālkot, 258,147
(302,009★) . . . . D 6
Sukkur, 190,551 . . . . G 3
Wah, 122,335 . . . . . . D 5

Eastern Mediterranean Lands

Cyprus
1982 CENSUS

Lemesós (Limassol),
74,782 (107,161★) . . B 3
Nicosia, 48,221
(185,000★) . . . . . B 3

Cyprus, North
1985 ESTIMATE

Nicosia, 37,400 . . . . B 3

Egypt
1986 CENSUS

Al-Iskandarīyah
(Alexandria),
2,917,327
(3,350,000★) . . . . D 1
Al-Ismāʿīlīyah (Ismailia),
212,567
(235,000★) . . . . . D 3
Al-Jīzah (Giza),
1,870,508 . . . . . D 2
Al-Qāhirah (Cairo),
6,052,836
(9,300,000★) . . . . D 2
As-Suways (Suez),
326,820 . . . . . . E 3
Asyūṭ, 273,191 . . . . F 2
Būr Saʿīd (Port Said),
399,793 . . . . . . D 3
Cairo see Al-Qāhirah D 2
Ṭanṭā, 334,505 . . . . D 2

Israel
1989 ESTIMATE

Beʾer Shevaʿ, 113,200 D 4
Ḥefa (Haifa), 222,600
(435,000★) . . . . . C 4
Jerusalem see
Yerushalayim . . . . D 4
Nābulus, 64,000 . . . C 4
Tel Aviv-Yafo, 317,800
(1,735,000★) . . . . C 4
Yerushalayim (Jerusalem),
493,500 (530,000★) D 4

Jordan
1989 ESTIMATE

ʿAmmān, 936,300
(1,450,000★) . . . . D 4
Az-Zarqāʾ, 318,055 . . C 5
Irbid, 167,785 . . . . . C 4

Lebanon
1982 ESTIMATE

Bayrūt (Beirut), 509,000
(1,675,000★) . . . . C 4
Ṭarābulus (Tripoli),
198,000 . . . . . . B 4

Saudi Arabia
1980 ESTIMATE

Al-Madīnah (Medina),
290,000 . . . . . . G 6

Syria
1988 ESTIMATE

Al-Lādhiqīyah (Latakia),
249,000 . . . . . . B 4
Al-Qāmishlī, 126,236 . A 7
Dayr az-Zawr,
112,000 . . . . . . B 7
Dimashq (Damascus),
1,326,000
(1,950,000★) . . . . C 5
Halab (Aleppo), 1,261,000
(1,275,000★) . . . . A 5
Ḥamāh, 222,000 . . . B 5
Ḥimṣ (Homs), 447,000 B 5

★ Population of metropolitan area, including suburbs.

40

Africa

Abidjan, 1,950,000 ('83)..........E 3
Accra, 859,640 ('84) (1,250,000★)..........E 3
Adis Abeba (Addis Ababa), 1,686,300 ('88) (1,500,000★)..........E 7
Alger (Algiers), 1,507,241 ('87) (2,547,983★)..B 4
ALGERIA..........C 4
Al-Iskandariyah (Alexandria), 2,917,327 ('86) (3,350,000★)..........B 6
Al-Khartūm (Khartoum), 476,218 ('83) (1,450,000★)..........D 7
Al-Qāhirah (Cairo), 6,052,836 ('86) (9,300,000★)..........B 7
ANGOLA..........G 5
BENIN..........E 4
BOTSWANA..........H 6
Brazzaville, 585,812 ('84)..........F 5
BURKINA FASO..........D 3
BURUNDI..........F 6
CAMEROON..........E 5
Cape Town, 776,617 ('85) (1,790,000★)..........I 5
Casablanca, 2,139,204 ('82) (2,475,000★)..B 3
CENTRAL AFRICAN REPUBLIC..........E 5
CHAD..........D 5
COMOROS..........G 8
CONGO..........F 5
COTE D'IVOIRE..........E 3
Dakar, 1,447,642 ('88)..D 2
Dar es Salaam, 1,300,000 ('84)..........F 7
DJIBOUTI..........D 8
EGYPT..........C 6
EQUATORIAL GUINEA..........E 4
ERITREA..........D 7

ETHIOPIA..........E 7
GABON..........F 5
GAMBIA..........D 2
GHANA..........E 3
GUINEA..........D 2
GUINEA-BISSAU..........D 2
Johannesburg, 632,369 ('85) (3,650,000★)..........H 6
Kampala, 1,008,707 ('90)..........E 7
KENYA..........E 7
Kinshasa (Léopoldville), 3,000,000 ('86)..........F 5
Lagos, 1,213,000 ('87)· (3,800,000★)..........E 4
LESOTHO..........H 6
LIBERIA..........E 3
LIBYA..........C 5
MADAGASCAR..........G 8
MALAWI..........G 7
MALI..........D 3
Maputo (Lourenço Marques), 1,069,727 ('89)..........H 7
MAURITANIA..........D 2
MOROCCO..........B 3
MOZAMBIQUE..........G 7
Nairobi, 1,505,000 ('90)..........E 7
NAMIBIA..........H 5
NIGER..........D 4
NIGERIA..........E 4
RWANDA..........F 6
SAO TOME AND PRINCIPE..........E 4
SENEGAL..........D 2
SIERRA LEONE..........E 2
SOMALIA..........E 8
SOUTH AFRICA..........I 6
SUDAN..........D 6
SWAZILAND..........H 7
TANZANIA..........F 7
Tarābulus (Tripoli), 990,697 ('84)..........B 5
TOGO..........E 4
Tunis, 596,654 ('84) (1,225,000★)..........B 5
TUNISIA..........B 4
UGANDA..........E 7
WESTERN SAHARA..........C 2
ZAIRE..........F 6
ZAMBIA..........G 6
ZIMBABWE..........G 6

★ Population of metropolitan area, including suburbs.

41

Northern Africa

Algeria
1987 CENSUS
Alger (Algiers), 1,507,241
  (2,547,983★) . . . . . . A 6
Annaba (Bône),
  305,526 . . . . A 7
Batna, 181,601 . . . . . . A 7
Blida, 170,935 . . . . . A 6
Constantine (Qacentina),
  440,842 . . . . A 7
Oran (Wahran),
  628,558 . . . . A 5
Sidi bel Abbès,
  152,778 . . . . . . A 5
Skikda, 128,747 . . . . A 7

Benin
1984 ESTIMATE
Cotonou, 478,000 . . G 6
Porto-Novo, 164,000 G 6

Burkina Faso
1985 ESTIMATE
Bobo Dioulasso,
  228,668 . . . . F 5
Ouagadougou,
  441,514 . . . . F 5

Cameroon
1986 ESTIMATE
Douala, 1,029,731 . . H 7
Yaoundé, 653,670 . . H 8

Central African Republic
1984 ESTIMATE
Bangui, 473,817 . . . . H 9

Chad
1979 ESTIMATE
N'Djamena (Fort-Lamy),
  303,000 . . . . F 9

Cote d'Ivoire
1983 ESTIMATE
Abidjan, 1,950,000 . . G 5
Bouaké, 275,000 . . . . G 4
Yamoussoukro,
  80,000 . . . . G 4

Egypt
1986 CENSUS
Al-Fayyūm, 212,523 . . C12
Al-Iskandarīyah
  (Alexandria), 2,917,327
  (3,350,000★) B11
Al-Mansūrah, 316,870
  (375,000★) B12
Al-Qāhirah (Cairo),
  6,052,836
  (9,300,000★) B12
Al-Uqsur (Luxor),
  125,404 . . . . C12
As-Suways (Suez),
  326,820 . . . . C12
Aswān, 191,461 . . . . D12
Asyūt, 273,191 . . . . C12
Banī Suwayf, 151,813 C12
Būr Sa'īd (Port Said),
  399,793 . . . . B12
Cairo see Al-Qāhirah B12
Qinā, 119,794 . . . . . C12
Tantā, 334,505 . . . . . B12

Equatorial Guinea
1983 CENSUS
Malabo, 31,630 . . . . . . H 7

Gambia
1983 CENSUS
Banjul, 44,536
  (95,000★) . . . . F 2

Ghana
1984 CENSUS
Accra, 859,640
  (1,250,000★) . . . . . G 5
Cape Coast, 86,620 . . G 5
Kumasi, 348,880
  (600,000★) . . . . . . G 5
Sekondi-Takoradi,
  93,882 . . . . H 5
Tamale, 136,828
  (168,091★) . . . . . . G 5

Guinea
1986 ESTIMATE
Conakry, 800,000 . . . . G 3
Kankan, 100,000 . . . . F 4

Guinea-Bissau
1988 ESTIMATE
Bissau, 125,000 . . . . F 2

★ Population of metropolitan area, including suburbs.

42

Copyright © by Rand McNally & Co.
B-589100-275

Kilometers
Miles

1 : 16 000 000

Southern Africa

★ Population of metropolitan area, including suburbs.
▲ Population of entire district, including rural area.

44

Miller Oblated Stereographic Projection

Somalia
1984 ESTIMATE
Kismayu, 70,000 . . . . B 8

South Africa
1985 CENSUS
Bloemfontein, 104,381
 (235,000★) . . . . . . G 5
Cape Town (Kaapstad),
 776,617
 (1,790,000★) . . . . H 3
Durban, 634,301
 (1,550,000★) . . . . G 6
East London (Oos-
 Londen), 85,699
 (320,000★) . . . . . H 5
Germiston, 116,718 . . G 5
Johannesburg, 632,369
 (3,650,000★) . . . . G 5
Kimberley, 74,061
 (145,000★) . . . . . G 4
King William's Town,
 16,123 (48,300★) . . H 5
Klerksdorp, 48,947
 (205,000★) . . . . . G 5
Ladysmith, 25,102
 (31,670★) . . . . . . G 5
Pietermaritzburg, 133,809
 (230,000★) . . . . . G 6
Port Elizabeth, 272,844
 (690,000★) . . . . . H 5
Potchefstroom, 43,766
 (78,865★) . . . . . G 5
Pretoria, 443,059
 (960,000★) . . . . . G 5
Springs, 68,235 . . . . G 5
Uitenhage, 54,987 . . . H 5
Vereeniging, 60,584
 (525,000★) . . . . . G 5
Welkom, 54,488
 (215,000★) . . . . . G 5

Swaziland
1986 CENSUS
Mbabane, 38,290 . . . G 6

Tanzania
1984 ESTIMATE
Arusha, 69,000 . . . . B 7
Dar es Salaam,
 1,300,000 . . . . . . C 7
Dodoma, 54,000('84) C 7
Tanga, 121,000 . . . . C 7
Zanzibar, 133,000('85)C 7

Uganda
1990 ESTIMATE
Kampala, 1,008,707 . . A 6

Zaire
1984 CENSUS
Boma, 88,556 . . . . . . C 2
Bukavu, 171,064 . . . . B 5
Kalemie (Albertville),
 70,694 . . . . C 5
Kananga (Luluabourg),
 290,898 . . . . C 4
Kikwit, 146,784 . . . . C 3
Kinshasa (Léopoldville),
 3,000,000('86) . . . B 3
Kisangani (Stanleyville),
 282,650 . . . . A 5
Kolwezi, 201,382 . . . . D 5
Likasi (Jadotville),
 194,465 . . . . D 5
Lubumbashi
 (Élisabethville),
 543,268 . . . . D 5
Matadi, 144,742 . . . . C 2
Mbandaka (Coquilhatville),
 125,263 . . . . A 3
Mbuji-Mayi (Bakwanga),
 423,363 . . . . C 4

Zambia
1980 CENSUS
Chingola, 130,872 . . D 5
Kabwe (Broken Hill),
 127,420 . . . . D 5
Kitwe, 207,500
 (283,962★) . . . . . . D 5
Livingstone, 61,296 . . E 5
Luanshya, 61,600
 (113,422★) . . . . . . D 5
Lusaka, 535,830 . . . E 5
Mufulira, 77,100
 (138,824★) . . . . . . D 5
Ndola, 250,490 . . . . D 5

Zimbabwe
1983 ESTIMATE
Bulawayo, 429,000 . . F 5
Harare, 681,000
 (890,000★) . . . . . . E 6

45

Eastern Africa and Middle East

Bahrain
1981 CENSUS
Al-Manāmah, 115,054
(224,643★) . . . . . . C 5

Djibouti
1976 ESTIMATE
Djibouti, 120,000 . . F 3

Eritrea
1988 ESTIMATE
Asmara, 319,353 . . E 2

Ethiopia
1988 ESTIMATE
Adis Abeba, 1,686,300
(1,500,000★) . . . . . G 2
Asmera, 319,353 . . . E 2

Iran
1986 CENSUS
Esfahān, 986,753
(1,175,000★) . . . . . B 5
Shīrāz, 848,289 . . . . C 5

Iraq
1985 ESTIMATE
Al-Basrah, 616,700 . . B 4
Baghdād,
3,841,268('87) . . . B 3

Kuwait
1985 CENSUS
Al-Kuwayt, 44,335
(1,375,000★) . . . . . C 4

Oman
1981 ESTIMATE
Masqat (Muscat),
50,000 . . . . D 6

Qatar
1986 CENSUS
Ad-Dawhah (Doha),
217,294 (310,000★) C 5

Saudi Arabia
1980 ESTIMATE
Al-Madīnah (Medina),
290,000 . . . . D 2
Ar-Riyāḍ (Riyadh),
1,250,000 . . . . . . D 4
Jiddah, 1,300,000 . . D 2
Makkah (Mecca),
550,000 . . . . D 2

Somalia
1984 ESTIMATE
Muqdisho, 600,000 . . H 4

United Arab
Emirates
1980 CENSUS
Abū Ẓaby, 242,975 . . D 5
Dubayy (Dubai),
265,702 . . . . C 6

Yemen
1984 ESTIMATE
Adan (Aden), 176,100
(318,000★) . . . . . . F 4
San'ā', 427,150('86) E 3

★ Population of metropolitan
area, including suburbs.

46

Copyright © by Rand McNally & Co.
B-589391-264

Miller Oblated Stereographic Projection

Kilometers
Km.
Miles
Mi.
1:16 000 000

Pacific Ocean

PHYSICAL FEATURES AND RELIEF

Depths	Feet	Meters
	0	0
	500	150
	5 000	1 525
	10 000	3 050
	15 000	4 575
	20 000	6 100

Scale: 1 inch = 1060 miles
1 cm = 671.5 km

A-514200-9F86   -1-1ᴱ-2ᴱ

Anchorage

GULF OF
ALASKA

Mackenzie

HUDSON
BAY

GREENLAND

KAP
FARVEL

REYKJANES
RIDGE

LABRADOR
BASIN

VANCOUVER
I.

Seattle

Columbia

NORTH

St. Lawrence

Montréal

NEWFOUNDLAND

GRAND
BANK

NEWFOUNDLAND
RIDGE

MENDOCINO ESCARPMENT

CAPE
MENDOCINO

San Francisco

AMERICA

Missouri

Chicago

New York

Ohio

Washington

ATLANTIC

OCEAN

Mississippi

CAPE
HATTERAS

NORTH
AMERICAN
BASIN

O C E A N

Los Angeles

MURRAY FRACTURE ZONE

Colorado

Golfo de California

Rio Grande

New
Orleans

GULF OF

MEXICAN
BASIN

Tropic of Cancer

MEXICO

Miami

BAHAMAS

MILWAUKEE DEPTH
—28 232 Ft.
—8 605 M.

Honolulu

La Habana

C U B A

WEST INDIES

PUERTO RICO TRENCH

CLARION FRACTURE ZONE

Ciudad de
México

CAYMAN TRENCH

CARIBBEAN
SEA

AVES RIDGE

MEXICAN TRENCH
(MIDDLE AMERICA TRENCH)

COLOMBIAN VENEZUELAN
ABYSSAL BASIN
PLAIN

CLIPPERTON FRACTURE ZONE

ISTMO
DE
PANAMA

Caracas

COCOS RIDGE

Orinoco

Equator

Santa Fe de Bogotá

THWEST CHRISTMAS ISLAND
RIDGE

ARCHIPIÉLAGO DE COLON
(GALÁPAGOS IS.)

CARNEGIE
RIDGE

SOUTH

Amazon

TUAMOTU
RIDGE

SOCIETY
RIDGE

TUAMOTU

TUAMOTU
ARCHIPELAGO

RIDGE

AMERICA

Lima

AUSTRAL SEAMOUNT CHAIN

Tropic of Capricorn

—26 457 Ft.
—8 064 M.

PERU CHILE TRENCH

Paraná

P A C I F I C

PACIFIC - ANTARCTIC RIDGE

O C E A N

Santiago

Buenos
Aires

Montevideo

CHILE RISE

ATLANTIC
OCEAN

SOUTHWESTERN

PACIFIC

BASIN

ARGENTINE
BASIN

© RAND MC NALLY & CO

Australia

Copyright © by Rand McNally & Co.
B-590200-264

1:16 000 000

Melbourne, 55,300
  (3,039,100★) . . . . . G 8
Mildura, 20,512('86) . . F 8
Mitchell, 1,212('86) . . E 9
Moora, 1,469('86) . . . . F 3
Moree, 10,215('86) . . E 9
Morwell, 16,880 . . . . G 9
Mount Gambier, 22,194
  (27,228★) . . . . G 8
Mount Isa, 24,023 . . D 7
Mount Magnet,
  1,000('86) . . . . E 3
Mullewa, 758('86) . . . E 3
Murwillumbah,
  7,678('86) E10
Nambour, 9,579('86) E10
Naracoorte,
  4,636('86) . . . . G 8
Newcastle, 130,940
  (425,610★) F10
New Norfolk,
  6,152('86) . . . . H 9
Normanton,
  1,109('86) . . . . C 8
Norseman,
  1,775('86) . . . . F 4
Northam, 6,377('86) . . F 3
Nyngan, 2,502('86) . . F 9
Onslow, 750('86) . . . D 3
Oodnadatta, 200('76) E 7
Orange, 32,980 . . . . F 9
Pemberton, 802('86) . . F 3
Perth, 82,413
  (1,158,387★) . . . . . . F 3
Peterborough,
  2,239('86) . . . . F 7
Port Augusta,
  15,752 . . . . F 7
Port Hedland,
  13,069('86) . . . . . . D 3
Port Lincoln, 12,941 . . F 7
Port Macquarie,
  22,884('86) F10
Port Pirie, 15,210 . . . F 7
Quilpie, 780('86) . . . . E 8
Ravensthorpe,
  299('86) . . . . F 3
Richmond, 704('86) . . D 8
Rockhampton, 58,890
  (61,694★) D10
Roebourne,
  1,269('86) . . . . D 3
Roma, 6,069('86) . . . E 9
Saint George,
  2,323('86) . . . . E 9
Sale, 13,800 . . . . . . G 9
Shepparton, 26,420
  (39,700★) . . . . G 9
Smithton, 3,414('86) . . H 9
Southern Cross,
  898('86) . . . . F 3
Swan Hill,
  8,831('86) . . . . G 8
Sydney, 9,800
  (3,623,550★) F10
Tamworth, 34,430 . . F10
Taree, 38,760 . . . . . F10
Tennant Creek,
  3,503('86) . . . . C 6
Tenterfield,
  3,370('86) . . . . E 9
Theodore, 576('86) . . D10
Toowoomba,
  81,071 . . . . E10
Townsville, 83,339
  (111,972★) . . . . . . C 9
Wagga Wagga,
  52,180 . . . . G 9
Walgett, 2,151('86) . . E 9
Wangaratta, 16,320 . . G 9
Warrnambool,
  24,480 . . . . G 8
Weipa, 2,406('86) . . . B 8
Whyalla, 26,706 . . . . F 7
Wilcannia, 1,048('86) . . F 8
Wiluna, 279('86) . . . . E 4
Winton, 1,281('86) . . D 8
Wollongong, 174,770
  (236,690★) F10
Woomera,
  1,805('86) . . . . F 7
Wyndham,
  1,329('86) . . . . C 5

Indonesia
1980 CENSUS
Jayapura, 60,641 . . . . k15
Kupang, 84,587 . . . . B 4
Sorong, 52,041 . . . . . k13

Papua New Guinea
1987 ESTIMATE
Lae, 79,600 . . . . m16
Madang, 24,700 . . . . m16
Port Moresby,
  152,100 . . . . m16
Rabaul, 14,954('80) . . k17
Wewak, 23,200 . . . . . . k15

51

New Zealand

New Zealand
1986 CENSUS

Alexandra, 4,842 . . . . F 2
Ashburton, 14,030 . . E 3
Auckland, 149,046
  (850,000★) . . . . . . B 5
Blenheim, 18,308
  (22,681★) . . . . . . D 4
Bluff, 2,537 . . . . G 2
Cambridge, 10,145 . . B 5
Christchurch, 168,200
  (320,000★) . . . . . E 4
Dannevirke, 5,873 . . D 6
Dargaville, 4,859 . . . . A 4
Devonport, 10,543 . . B 5
Dunedin, 76,964
  (109,000★) . . . . . . F 3
Gisborne, 30,020
  (32,238★) . . . . C 7
Gore, 8,594 (11,249★)G 2
Greymouth, 7,624
  (11,261★) . . . . . . E 3
Hamilton, 94,511
  (101,814★) . . . . . . B 5
Hastings, 37,658 . . . . C 6
Hawera, 4,151
  (11,375★) . . . . . C 5
Hokitika, 3,427 . . . . E 3
Huntly, 6,750 . . . . . . B 5
Invercargill, 48,197
  (52,807★) . . . . . . G 2
Kaiapoi, 5,234 . . . . . E 4
Kaikoura, 2,209 . . . . E 4
Levin, 15,368
  (18,962★) . . . . . . D 5
Lower Hutt, 63,862 . . D 5
Masterton, 18,511
  (20,145★) . . . . . . D 5
Milton, 2,154 . . . . . . F 3
Morrinsville, 5,281 . . B 5
Motueka, 5,052 . . . . D 4
Murapara, 2,566 . . . . C 6
Napier, 49,428
  (107,060★) . . . . . . C 6
Nelson, 34,274
  (44,593★) . . . . . . D 4
New Plymouth, 36,865
  (47,384★) . . . . . C 5
Oamaru, 12,652
  (14,247★) . . . . . . F 3
Opotiki, 3,719 . . . . . . C 6
Otaki, 4,407 . . . . . . D 5
Palmerston North, 60,503
  (67,405★) . . . . . . D 5
Picton, 4,129 . . . . . D 5
Port Chalmers, 2,871 F 3
Pukekohe, 9,398
  (13,823★) . . . . . . B 5
Queenstown, 3,659 . . F 2
Richmond, 7,204 . . . . D 4
Rotorua, 40,597
  (52,001★) . . . . . . C 6
Stratford, 5,528 . . . . C 5
Taihape, 2,472 . . . . C 5
Takapuna, 69,419 . . B 5
Taumarunui, 6,387 . . C 5
Taupo, 15,873 . . . . . C 6
Tauranga, 41,611
  (59,435★) . . . . . . B 6
Te Awamutu, 8,096 . . C 5
Te Kuiti, 4,787 . . . . C 5
Thames, 6,461 . . . . B 5
Timaru, 27,757
  (28,621★) . . . . F 3
Tokoroa, 17,628
  (18,193★) . . . . . . C 5
Waihi, 3,679 . . . . . . B 5
Waimate, 3,250 . . . . F 3
Waipukurau, 3,862 . . D 6
Wairoa, 5,094 . . . . C 5
Waitara, 6,482 . . . . C 5
Waiuku, 4,357 . . . . . B 5
Wanaka, 1,710 . . . . F 2
Wanganui, 38,084
  (40,758★) . . . . . . C 5
Wellington, 137,495
  (350,000★) . . . . . D 5
Wellsford, 1,627 . . . . B 5
Westport, 4,660 . . . . D 3
Whakatane, 12,800
  (15,954★) . . . . . . B 6
Whangarei, 40,179
  (44,043★) . . . . . . A 5
Winton, 2,082 . . . . . . G 2

★ Population of metropolitan area, including suburbs.

52

1 : 6 000 000

Conic Projection

Copyright © by Rand McNally & Co.
A-591600-286

South America

★ Population of metropolitan area, including suburbs.
▲ Population of entire district, including rural area.

Miles
Kilometers

1:40 000 000

Northern South America

ATLANTIC OCEAN

Ibagué, 292,965 . . . . C 3
Manizales, 299,352
 (330,000★) . . . . B 3
Medellín, 1,468,089
 (2,095,000★) . . . . . B 3
Montería, 157,466 . . B 3
Neiva, 194,556 . . . . C 3
Palmira, 175,186 . . . C 3
Pasto, 197,407 . . . . C 3
Pereira, 233,271
 (390,000★) . . . . C 3
Popayán, 141,964 . . . C 3
Santa Fe de Bogotá,
 3,982,941
 (4,260,000★) . . . . . . C 4
Santa Marta, 177,922 A 4
Tuluá, 99,721 . . . . . . C 3
Valledupar, 142,771 . . A 4
Villavicencio, 178,685 C 4

Ecuador
1987 ESTIMATE
Ambato, 126,067 . . . . D 3
Cuenca, 201,490 . . . . D 3
Guayaquil, 1,572,615
 (1,580,000★) . . . . . . D 3
Machala, 144,396 . . . . D 3
Manta, 135,990 . . . . . D 2
Portoviejo, 141,568 . . D 2
Quito, 1,137,705
 (1,300,000★) . . . . . . D 3

French Guiana
1982 CENSUS
Cayenne, 38,091 . . . . C 8

Guyana
1983 ESTIMATE
Georgetown, 78,500
 (188,000★) . . . . B 7

Peru
1981 CENSUS
Arequipa, 108,023
 (446,942★) . . . . G 4
Ayacucho, 57,432
 (69,533★) . . . . F 4
Cajamarca, 62,259 . . E 3
Callao, 264,133 . . . . . F 3
Cerro de Pasco, 55,597
 (66,373★) . . . . F 3

Chiclayo, 213,095
 (279,527★) . . . . E 3
Chimbote, 223,341 . . E 3
Cuzco, 89,563
 (184,550★) . . . . F 4
Huancayo, 84,845
 (164,954★) . . . . F 3
Huánuco, 61,812 . . . . E 3
Ica, 114,786 . . . . F 3
Iquitos, 178,738 . . . . D 4
Lima, 371,122
 (4,608,010★) . . . . . . F 3
Piura, 144,609
 (207,934★) . . . . E 2
Sullana, 89,037 . . . . . D 2
Tacna, 97,173 . . . . . . G 4
Trujillo, 202,469
 (354,301★) . . . . E 3
Tumbes, 47,936 . . . . D 2
Vitarte, 145,504 . . . . F 3

Suriname
1988 ESTIMATE
Paramaribo, 241,000
 (296,000★) . . . . B 7

Venezuela
1981 CENSUS
Acarigua, 91,662 . . . . B 5
Barinas, 110,462 . . . . B 4
Barquisimeto, 497,635 A 5
Cabimas, 140,435 . . . A 4
Calabozo, 61,995 . . . . B 5
Caracas, 1,816,901
 (3,600,000★) . . . . . . A 5
Ciudad Bolívar,
 182,941 . . . . B 6
Ciudad Guayana,
 314,497 . . . . B 6
Ciudad Ojeda, 83,565 A 4
Cumaná, 179,814 . . . . A 6
El Tigre, 73,595 . . . . . B 6
Maracaibo, 890,643 . . A 4
Maracay, 322,560 . . . A 5
Maturín, 154,976 . . . . B 6
Mérida, 143,209 . . . . B 4
Puerto Cabello,
 71,759 . . . . A 5
Punto Fijo, 71,114 . . . A 4
San Cristóbal,
 198,793 . . . . B 4
Valencia, 616,224 . . . A 5
Valera, 102,068 . . . . B 4

★ Population of metropolitan area, including suburbs.
▲ Population of entire district, including rural area.

Oblique Conic Conformal Projection

55

Southern South America

Argentina
1980 CENSUS
Avellaneda, 334,145 . . C 5
Bahía Blanca, 223,818 D 4
Buenos Aires, 2,922,829
  (10,750,000★) . . . . . . C 5
Catamarca, 78,799
  (90,000★) . . . . . . B 3
Comodoro Rivadavia,
  96,817 . . . . F 3
Concordia, 94,222 . . C 5
Córdoba, 993,055
  (1,070,000★) . . . . . C 4
Corrientes, 180,612 . . B 5
La Plata, 477,175 . . . C 5
Mar del Plata,
  414,696 . . . . D 5
Mendoza, 119,088
  (650,000★) . . . . . . C 3
Paraná, 161,638 . . . . C 4
Posadas, 143,889 . . . B 5
Río Cuarto, 110,254 . . C 4
Rosario, 938,120
  (1,045,000★) . . . . . C 4
Salta, 260,744 . . . . . A 3
San Isidro, 289,170 . . C 5
San Juan, 118,046
  (300,000★) . . . . . . C 3
San Miguel de Tucumán,
  392,888 (525,000★) B 3
Santa Fe, 292,165 . . C 4
Santiago del Estero,
  148,758 (200,000★) B 4

Brazil
1985 ESTIMATE
Bauru, 220,105 . . . . . A 7
Blumenau, 192,074 . . B 7
Campinas, 841,016
  (1,125,000★) . . . . . A 7
Caxias do Sul,
  266,809 . . . . B 6
Curitiba, 1,279,205
  (1,700,000★) . . . . . B 7
Florianópolis, 178,400
  (365,000★) . . . . . . B 7
Joinvile, 302,877 . . . B 7
Jundiaí, 268,900
  (313,652▲) . . . . . . A 7
Londrina, 296,400
  (346,676▲) . . . . . . A 6
Maringá, 196,871 . . . A 6
Pelotas, 210,300
  (277,730▲) . . . . . . C 6
Piracicaba, 211,000
  (252,079▲) . . . . . . A 7
Ponta Grossa,
  223,154 . . . . B 6
Porto Alegre, 1,272,121
  (2,600,000★) . . . . . C 6
Presidente Prudente,
  155,883 . . . . A 6
Ribeirão Prêto,
  383,125 . . . . A 7
Rio Grande, 164,221 C 6
Santa Maria, 163,900
  (196,827▲) . . . . . . B 6
Santos, 460,100
  (1,065,000★) . . . . . A 7
São Carlos, 140,383 A 7
São Paulo, 10,063,110
  (15,175,000★) . . . . A 7
Sorocaba, 327,468 . . A 7

Chile
1982 CENSUS
Antofagasta, 185,486 A 2
Chillán, 118,163 . . . . D 2
Concepción, 267,891
  (675,000★) . . . . . . D 2
Osorno, 95,286 . . . . . E 2
Punta Arenas, 95,332 G 2
Rancagua, 139,925 . . C 2
Santiago, 232,667
  (4,100,000★) . . . . . C 2
Talca, 128,544 . . . . . D 2
Talcahuano, 202,368 D 2
Temuco, 157,297 . . . D 2
Valdivia, 100,046 . . . D 2
Valparaíso, 265,355
  (675,000★) . . . . . . C 2
Viña del Mar, 244,899 C 2

Falkland Islands
1986 ESTIMATE
Stanley, 1,200 . . . . . . G 5

Paraguay
1985 ESTIMATE
Asunción, 477,100
  (700,000★) . . . . . . B 5

Uruguay
1985 CENSUS
Montevideo, 1,251,647
  (1,550,000★) . . . . . C 5
Paysandú, 76,191 . . . C 5
Salto, 80,823 . . . . . . C 5

★ Population of metropolitan area, including suburbs.
▲ Population of entire district, including rural area.

56

Copyright © by Rand McNally & Co.
B-549200-264

Oblique Conic Conformal Projection

Kilometers
0   200   400   600   Km.
Miles
0   200   400   600   Mi.

1 : 16 000 000

Copyright © by Rand McNally & Co.
B-560 36-594

Brazil

1985 ESTIMATE

Americana, 156,030	G 5	
Anápolis, 225,840	D 4	
Aracatuba, 129,304	F 4	
Araraquara, 87,500	F 4	
Assis, 63,100 (74,238▲)	G 3	
Barbacena, 80,200	F 7	

Barra Mansa, 149,200 G 6
Bauru, 220,105 F 4
Belo Horizonte, 2,114,429 E 7
  (2,950,000★)
Brasília, 1,567,709 C 5
Cachoeiro de Itapemirim,
  95,000 (138,156▲) F 8
Campinas, 841,016 G 5
  (1,125,000★)
Campo Grande, 384,398 F 1
  (366,716▲) F 7

Conselheiro Lafaiete,
  77,958 F 7
Divinópolis, 139,940 F 6
Duque de Caxias,
  353,200 G 7
Feira de Santana, 278,600
  (355,201▲) B 9
Franca, 182,820 F 5
Goiânia, 923,333 D 4
  (990,000★)
Governador Valadares,
  192,300 (216,957▲) E 8

Guarulhos, 571,700 G 5
Itabuna, 142,200 B 9
  (167,543▲)
Itajubá, 61,500 G 6
  (69,675▲)
Itapetininga, 76,700 G 5
  (105,512▲)
Itaquari, 163,900 F 8
  (214,472▲)
Juiz de Fora, 349,720 F 7
  (143,529▲)
Jundiaí, 268,900 G 5
  (313,652▲)
Limeira, 186,986 G 5

Londrina, 296,400 G 3
Maringá, 196,871 G 3
  (346,676▲)
Mogi das Cruzes,
  144,800 G 5
Montes Claros, 183,500 D 7
Niterói, 441,684 G 7
Nova Friburgo, 103,500 F 7
Nova Iguaçu, 592,800 G 7
Petrópolis, 170,300 G 7

Piracicaba, 211,000 G 5
Poços de Caldas,
  100,004 F 5
Presidente Prudente,
  155,883 G 3
Ribeirão Prêto, 383,125 F 5
Rio Claro, 129,859 G 5
Rio de Janeiro, 5,603,388 G 7
  (10,150,000★)
Salvador, 1,804,438 B 9
  (2,050,000★)

São Vicente, 239,778 G 5
Sete Lagoas, 121,418 E 6
Sorocaba, 327,468 G 5
Taubaté, 205,120 G 5
Uberaba, 244,875 E 5
Uberlândia, 312,024 E 4
Vitória, 201,500 F 8
  (735,000★)
Vitória da Conquista,
  145,800 (198,150▲) C 8
Volta Redonda, 219,267 G 6
  (375,000★)

Santo André, 635,129 G 5
Santos, 460,100 G 5
  (1,065,000★)
São Caetano do Sul,
  171,005 G 5
São Carlos, 140,383 G 5
São José do Rio Prêto,
  229,221 F 4
São José dos Campos,
  372,578 G 6
São Paulo, 10,063,110 G 5
  (15,175,000★)

★ Population of metropolitan area, including suburbs. ▲ Population of entire district, including rural area.

Kilometers

Miles

1:8 000 000

Colombia, Ecuador, Venezuela, and Guyana

Aruba
1987 ESTIMATE
Oranjestad, 19,800 . . A 7

Colombia
1985 CENSUS
Armenia, 187,130 . . . . . E 5
Barrancabermeja,
137,406 . . . . D 6
Barranquilla, 899,781
(1,140,000★) . . . . . . B 5
Bello, 212,861 . . . . . . D 5
Bogotá see Santa Fe de
Bogotá . . . . E 5
Bucaramanga, 352,326
(550,000★) . . . . D 6
Buenaventura,
160,342 . . . . F 4
Buga, 82,992 . . . . F 4
Cali, 1,350,565
(1,400,000★) . . . . . . F 4
Cartagena, 531,426 . . B 5
Cartago, 97,791 . . . . . E 5
Ciénaga, 56,860 . . . . B 5
Cúcuta, 379,478
(445,000★) . . . . D 6
Duitama, 56,390 . . . . E 6
Envigado, 91,391 . . . . D 5
Espinal, 37,563 . . . . . E 5
Facatativá, 44,331 . . . E 5
Florencia, 66,430 . . . . F 5
Florida, 30,040 . . . . . . F 4
Floridablanca,
143,824 . . . . D 6
Girardot, 70,078 . . . . E 5
Ibagué, 292,965 . . . . E 5
Ipiales, 45,419 . . . . . . G 4
Itagüí, 137,623 . . . . . D 5
La Dorada, 48,572 . . . E 5
Magangué, 49,160 . . . C 5
Manizales, 299,352
(330,000★) . . . . E 5
Medellín, 1,468,089
(2,095,000★) . . . . . . D 5
Montería, 157,466 . . . C 5
Neiva, 194,556 . . . . . F 5
Ocaña, 51,443 . . . . . . C 6
Palmira, 175,186 . . . . F 4
Pamplona, 34,213 . . . D 6
Pasto, 197,407 . . . . . G 4
Pereira, 233,271
(390,000★) . . . . E 5
Planeta Rica, 24,238 . C 5
Popayán, 141,964 . . . F 4
Puerto Berrio, 21,414 . D 5
Quibdó, 47,950 . . . . . E 4
Ríohacha, 46,667 . . . . B 6
Santa Fe de Bogotá,
3,982,941
(4,260,000★) . . . . . . E 5
Santa Marta,
177,922 . . . . B 5
Santa Rosa de Cabal,
37,112 . . . . E 5
Sincelejo, 120,537 . . . C 5
Sogamoso, 64,437 . . . E 6
Soledad, 165,791 . . . . B 5
Tuluá, 99,721 . . . . . . E 4
Tumaco, 45,456 . . . . G 3
Tunja, 93,792 . . . . . . E 5
Valledupar, 142,771 . . B 6
Villavicencio, 178,685 . E 5
Zipaquirá, 45,676 . . . . E 5

Ecuador
1987 ESTIMATE
Alfaro, 51,023('82) . . . . I 3
Ambato, 126,067 . . . . H 3
Babahoyo,
42,266('82) . . . . . . H 3
Chone, 33,839('82) . . H 2
Cuenca, 201,490 . . . . I 3
Esmeraldas, 120,387 . G 3
Guayaquil, 1,572,615
(1,580,000★) . . . . . . I 3
Ibarra, 53,428('82) . . . G 3
Jipijapa, 27,146('82) . . H 2
Latacunga,
28,764('82) . . . . . . H 3
Loja, 71,652('82) . . . . J 3
Machala, 144,396 . . . I 3
Manta, 135,990 . . . . H 2
Milagro, 102,884 . . . . I 3
Portoviejo, 141,568 . . H 2
Quevedo,
67,023('82) . . . . . . H 3
Quito, 1,137,705
(1,300,000★) . . . . . . H 3
Riobamba,
75,455('82) . . . . . . H 3
Santo Domingo de los
Colorados, 104,059 . H 3
Tulcán, 30,985('82) . . G 4

Guyana
1983 ESTIMATE
Georgetown, 78,500
(188,000★) . . . . D 13
New Amsterdam,
20,000('82) . . . . . . D 14

★ Population of metropolitan
area, including suburbs.

Copyright © by Rand McNally & Co.
B-549700-264

Kilometers
Miles
1:8 000 000

Atlantic Ocean

Pacific Ocean
Seattle
Hudson Bay
Missouri
NORTH
Chicago
St. Lawrence
Montréal
NEWFOUNDLAND
New York
Washington
Ohio
AMERICA
Mississippi
CAPE HATTERAS
New Orleans
Gulf of MEXICO BASIN
Mexico
Miami
BAHAMAS
La Habana
CUBA
WEST INDIES
MILWAUKEE DEPTH
-28 232 ft.
-8 605 M.
Caribbean
BEATA RIDGE
COLOMBIAN ABYSSAL PLAIN
ISTMO DE PANAMA
VENEZUELAN BASIN
AVES RIDGE
PUERTO RICO TRENCH
Caracas
Sea
COCOS RIDGE
ARCH. DE COLON
CARNEGIE RIDGE
Santa Fe de Bogotá
GUIANA BASIN
Equator
Amazon
SOUTH
Lima
AMERICA
PERU-CHILE TRENCH
-26 457 ft.
-8 064 M.
PACIFIC
OCEAN
Parana
Buenos Aires
Santiago
Rio de Janeiro
São Paulo
Tropic of Capricorn

Arctic
Circle
BAFFIN ISLAND
BAFFIN BASIN
GREENLAND
KAP FARVEL
LABRADOR BASIN
REYKJANES RIDGE
GRAND BANK
NEWFOUNDLAND BASIN
ATLANTIC
OCEAN
MID-ATLANTIC RIDGE
NORTH AMERICAN BASIN
Tropic of Cancer
CAPE VERDE BASIN
ARQ. DE CABO VERDE

SVALBARD
HOPEN RISE
GREENLAND BASIN
MOHNS RIDGE
NORWEGIAN BASIN
ICELAND
FAEROE PLATEAU
North Sea
London
WEST EUROPEAN BASIN
IBERIAN ABYSSAL PLAIN
AZORES PLATEAU
AÇORES
AZORES-GIBRALTAR RIDGE
IS. CANARIAS
CANARY BASIN
CAPE VERDE TERRACE
Dakar
SIERRA LEONE RISE
SIERRA LEONE BASIN

MURMANSK RISE
BARENTS TROUGH
Baltic Sea
Sankt-Peterburg
Moskva
Stockholm
Berlin
EUROPE
Paris
Roma
Madrid
Mediterranean Sea
El Djazair
Casablanca
SAHARA
AFRICA
Niger
Lagos
Gulf of Guinea
GUINEA BASIN
GUINEA RIDGE
Kinshasa
Congo

Black Sea
Danube
Istanbul
Volga

C. DE SÃO ROQUE
Recife
BRAZIL BASIN
ANGOLA BASIN
MID-ATLANTIC RIDGE
ATLANTIC
OCEAN
WALVIS RIDGE
CAPE BASIN
CAPE OF GOOD HOPE
Cape Town
CAPE RISE
Orange
AGULHAS BASIN
ATLANTIC-INDIAN RIDGE

BROMLEY PLATEAU
ARGENTINE BASIN
FALKLAND PLATEAU
FALKLAND IS.
BURDWOOD BANK
CABO DE HORNOS
Drake Passage
SOUTHEAST PACIFIC BASIN
S. SCOTIA RIDGE
SCOTIA RIDGE
W. SCOTIA BASIN
NORTHEASTERN GEORGIA RIDGE
S. SANDWICH TRENCH
-27 313 ft.
-8 325 M.
WEST ATLANTIC-INDIAN BASIN
ANTARCTIC PENINSULA
Weddell Sea
Antarctic Circle
ANTARCTICA

PHYSICAL FEATURES AND RELIEF

Depths	Feet	Meters
	0	0
	500	150
	5 000	1 525
	10 000	3 050
	15 000	4 575
	20 000	6 100

Scale:
1 inch = 1 200 miles
1 cm = 760 km

A-513700-9F86

© RAND M¢NALLY & CO.

North America

Miles 0 200 400 600 800 1000 Mi.
Kilometers 0 400 800 1200 1600 Km.

1:40 000 000

Copyright © by Rand McNally & Co.
A-520000-286

Lambert Azimuthal Equal Area Projection

61

Mexico

Mexico

62

63

Central America and the Caribbean

Antigua and Barbuda
1977 ESTIMATE
Saint Johns, 24,359 . . F17

Bahamas
1982 ESTIMATE
Nassau, 135,000 . . . B 9

Barbados
1980 CENSUS
Bridgetown, 7,466
  (115,000★) H18

Belize
1985 ESTIMATE
Belize City, 47,000 . . F 3
Belmopan, 4,500 . . . F 3

Cayman Islands
1988 ESTIMATE
Georgetown, 13,700 E 7

Costa Rica
1988 ESTIMATE
Limón, 40,400
  (62,600▲) . . . . I 6
San José, 278,600
  (670,000★) . . . . . . J 5

Cuba
1987 ESTIMATE
Camagüey, 265,588 . D 9
Guantánamo, 179,091 D10
Havana see La
  Habana . . . . C 6
Holguín, 199,861 . . D 9
La Habana (Havana),
  2,036,800
  (2,125,000★) . . . . C 6
Santa Clara, 182,349 C 8
Santiago de Cuba,
  364,554 . . . . D10

Dominican Republic
1981 CENSUS
Santiago, 278,638 . . E 12
Santo Domingo,
  1,313,172 . . . . . . E 13

El Salvador
1985 ESTIMATE
San Salvador, 462,652
  (920,000★) . . . . . . H 3
Santa Ana, 137,879 . . H 3

Guadeloupe
1982 CENSUS
Basse-Terre, 13,656
  (26,600★) F17

Guatemala
1989 ESTIMATE
Guatemala, 1,057,210
  (1,400,000★) . . . . G 2

★ Population of metropolitan
  area, including suburbs.

64

Haiti
1987 ESTIMATE

Port-au-Prince, 797,000
(880,000★) E11

Honduras
1988 CENSUS

San Pedro Sula,
279,356 . . . . G 4
Tegucigalpa, 551,606 G 4

Jamaica
1987 ESTIMATE

Kingston, 646,400
(770,000★) . . . . . . E 9
Montego Bay,
70,265('82) . . . . . . E 9

Martinique
1982 CENSUS

Fort-de-France, 99,844
(116,017★) G17

Netherlands Antilles
1981 CENSUS

Willemstad, 31,883
(130,000★) . . . . . H 13

Nicaragua
1985 ESTIMATE

León, 101,000 . . . . . . H 4
Managua, 682,000 . . H 4

Panama
1990 CENSUS

Colón, 54,469
(96,000★) . . . . J 8
Panamá, 411,549
(770,000★) . . . . . . J 8

Puerto Rico
1980 CENSUS

Ponce, 161,739
(232,551★) E14
San Juan, 424,600
(1,775,260★) E14

Saint Lucia
1987 ESTIMATE

Castries, 53,933 . . . . G17

Saint Vincent and the Grenadines
1987 ESTIMATE

Kingstown, 19,028
(28,936★) H17

Trinidad and Tobago
1988 ESTIMATE

Port of Spain, 59,200
(370,000★) I17

Canada

★ Population of metropolitan
  area, including suburbs.

66

1 : 16 000 000

Copyright © by Rand McNally & Co.
B-520200-264

Lambert Conformal Conic Projection

67

Alberta

Alberta
1986 CENSUS

Airdrie, 10,390 . . . . . . D 3
Athabasca, 1,970 . . . . B 4
Banff . . . . D 3
Barrhead, 3,991 . . . . B 3
Beaumont, 3,944 . . . . C 4
Beaverlodge, 1,808 . . . B 1
Blackfalds, 1,688 . . . . C 4
Bonnyville, 5,470 . . . . B 5
Bow Island, 1,650 . . . E 5
Brooks, 9,464 . . . . . . D 5
Calgary, 636,104
  (671,326★) . . . . D 3
Camrose, 12,968 . . . . C 4
Canmore, 4,182 . . . . D 3
Cardston, 3,497 . . . . E 4
Carstairs, 1,629 . . . . D 3
Claresholm, 3,382 . . . E 4
Coaldale, 4,796 . . . . E 4
Cochrane, 4,190 . . . . D 3
Cold Lake, 3,195 . . . . B 5
Coronation, 1,310 . . . C 5
Crowsnest Pass,
  6,912 . . . . E 3
Devon, 3,691 . . . . . . C 4
Didsbury, 3,184 . . . . D 3
Drayton Valley, 5,290 C 3
Drumheller, 6,366 . . . D 4
Edmonton, 573,982
  (785,465★) . . . . . . C 4
Edson, 7,323 . . . . . . C 2
Fairview, 2,998 . . . . A 1
Fort Chipewyan, 922 . f 8
Fort Macleod, 3,123 . E 4
Fort McMurray, 34,949
  (48,497★) . . . . A 5
Fort Saskatchewan,
  11,983 . . . . C 4
Fox Creek, 2,068 . . . . B 2
Gibbons, 2,335 . . . . C 4
Grand Centre, 3,655 . B 5
Grande Cache, 3,646 C 1
Grande Prairie,
  26,471 . . . . B 1
Grimshaw, 2,579 . . . . A 1
Hanna, 3,017 . . . . . . D 5
High Level, 3,004 . . . F 7
High Prairie, 2,817 . . B 2
High River, 5,096 . . . D 4
Hinton, 8,629 . . . . . . C 2
Innisfail, 5,535 . . . . . C 4
Jasper . . . . C 1
Lac La Biche, 2,553 . B 5
Lacombe, 6,080 . . . . C 4
La Crete, 689 . . . . . . f 7
Lake Louise, 688 . . . D 3
Lamont, 1,576 . . . . . C 4
Leduc, 13,126 . . . . . C 4
Lethbridge, 58,841 . . E 4
Lloydminster, 17,354 C 5
Magrath, 1,637 . . . . . E 4
Medicine Hat, 41,804
  (50,734★) . . . . . . D 5
Morinville, 5,364 . . . . C 4
Nordegg, 53 . . . . . . C 2
Okotoks, 5,214 . . . . . D 4
Olds, 4,871 . . . . D 3
Peace River, 6,288 . . A 2
Penhold, 1,580 . . . . . C 4
Picture Butte, 1,576 . E 4
Pincher Creek, 3,800 E 4
Ponoka, 5,473 . . . . . C 4
Provost, 1,725 . . . . . C 5
Raymond, 2,957 . . . . E 4
Redcliff, 3,834 . . . . . D 5
Red Deer, 54,425 . . . C 4
Redwater, 1,982 . . . . C 4
Rimbey, 1,786 . . . . . C 3
Rocky Mountain House,
  5,182 . . . . C 3
Saint Albert, 36,710 . C 4
Saint Paul, 5,030 . . . B 5
Sherwood Park . . . . C 4
Slave Lake, 5,429 . . . B 3
Smith, 251 . . . . B 4
Spruce Grove, 11,918 C 4
Stettler, 5,147 . . . . . C 4
Stony Plain, 5,802 . . C 3
Strathmore, 3,544 . . D 4
Sundre, 1,712 . . . . . D 3
Swan Hills, 2,403 . . . B 3
Sylvan Lake, 3,937 . . C 3
Taber, 6,382 . . . . . . E 4
Three Hills, 2,528 . . . D 4
Valleyview, 1,987 . . . B 2
Vegreville, 5,276 . . . C 4
Vermilion, 3,879 . . . . C 4
Vulcan, 1,420 . . . . . D 4
Wainwright, 4,665 . . . C 5
Westlock, 4,532 . . . . C 4
Wetaskiwin, 10,071 . . C 4
Whitecourt, 5,737 . . . B 3

★ Population of metropolitan
  area, including suburbs.

68

British Columbia

1986 CENSUS

Armstrong, 2,706	D 8	Clearwater, 1,375	D 7	Kimberley, 6,732	E 9	Port Alberni, 18,241
Ashcroft, 1,914	D 7	Colwood, 11,546	h12	Kitimat, 11,196	B 3	(26,134★)
Black Creek, 1,972	E 5	Comox, 6,873	E 5	Ladysmith, 3,729	m18	Port Coquitlam, 29,115
Burnaby, 145,161	E 6	Courtenay, 9,631	E 5	Lake Cowichan, 2,170	g11	Powell River, 12,440
Castlegar, 6,385	E 9	(37,553★)		Langley, 16,557	f13	Prince George, 67,621
Chetwynd, 2,774	B 7	Cranbrook, 15,893	E10	MacKenzie, 5,542	B 6	Prince Rupert, 15,755
Chilliwack, 41,337	E 7	Creston, 4,098	E 9	Matsqui, 51,449		One Hundred Mile House,
(50,288★)		Dawson Creek, 10,544	B 7	(88,420★)		1,692
		Duncan, 4,039	D 7	Merritt, 6,180	D 7	Parksville, 5,828
		Elkford, 3,187	D10	Nanaimo, 49,029		Penticton, 23,588
		Esquimalt, 15,972	E 6	(60,420★)		(38,966★)
		Fernie, 5,188	E10	Nelson, 8,113	E 9	Revelstoke, 8,279
		Fort Nelson, 3,729	m18	New Westminster,		Richmond, 108,492
		Fort Saint John, 13,355	A 7	39,972		Rossland, 3,472
		Gibsons, 2,675	E 6	North Vancouver,		Sidney, 8,982
		Golden, 3,584	D 9	35,698		Smithers, 4,713
		Grand Forks, 3,282	E 8	Oak Bay, 17,065	f13	Sparwood, 4,540
		Hope, 3,046	D 7	(88,420★)		Summerland, 7,755
		Kamloops, 61,773	D 7	1,692		Terrace, 10,532
		Kelowna, 61,213	D 8			(17,390★)
		(89,730★)				Trail, 7,948

★ Population of metropolitan area, including suburbs.

Port Alberni, 18,241			
(26,134★)	D 8	Revelstoke, 8,279	D 8
Port Coquitlam, 29,115	E 6	Richmond, 108,492	E 6
Powell River, 12,440	E 5	Rossland, 3,472	E 9
Prince George, 67,621	C 6	Sidney, 8,982	B 4
Prince Rupert, 15,755		Smithers, 4,713	E 5
One Hundred Mile House,		Sparwood, 4,540	E10
1,692	D 7	Summerland, 7,755	E 8
Parksville, 5,828	B 3	Terrace, 10,532	
Penticton, 23,588		(17,390★)	B 3
(38,966★)	E 8	Trail, 7,948 (20,257★)	E 9
		Tumbler Ridge, 4,540	B 7
		Vancouver, 431,147	
		(1,380,729★)	E 6
		Vanderhoof, 3,505	C 5
		Vernon, 20,241	
		(42,802★)	D 8
		Victoria, 66,303	
		(255,547★)	E 6
		West Vancouver, 36,266	f12
		White Rock, 14,387	E 6
		Williams Lake, 10,280	
		(33,556★)	C 6

Statute Miles 10 0 10 20 30 40 50 60 70 80 90 100

Kilometers 10 0 10 20 40 60 80 100 120 140

Oblique Cylindrical Projection

Manitoba

B-500212-02 7-3-9ME
COSMO SERIES MARITIME PROV.
Copyright by
RAND McNALLY & COMPANY
Made in U.S.A.

★ Population of metropolitan area, including suburbs.

Prince Edward Island

1986 CENSUS

Charlottetown, 15,776	C 9
(53,868★)	D 7
Parkdale, 2,065	C 6
Saint Eleanor's, 3,743	C 6
Sherwood, 5,769	C 6
Summerside, 8,020	C 6
(15,614★)	C 6

New Brunswick

1986 CENSUS

Bathurst, 14,683	
(34,895★)	B 4
Blacks Harbour, 1,224	D 3
Bouctouche, 2,420	C 5
Campbellton, 9,077	
(22,614★)	A 3
Caraquet, 4,493	B 5
Chatham, 6,218	B 4

Dalhousie, 5,363	A 3
Dieppe, 9,084	C 5
Edmundston, 11,497	
(22,614★)	B 1
Fairvale, 4,660	D 4
Fredericton, 44,352	
(65,768★)	D 3
Grand Bay, 3,319	D 3
Grand Falls (Grand-Sault),	
6,209	B 2
Hampton, 3,405	D 4

Minto, 3,197	C 3
Moncton, 55,468	
(102,084★)	C 5
Newcastle, 5,804	B 4
Oromocto, 9,656	D 3
Sackville, 5,470	C 5
Saint Basile, 3,306	B 1
Saint Jacques, 2,310	B 1
Saint John, 76,381	
(121,265★)	D 3
Saint Quentin, 2,264	B 2

Nova Scotia

1986 CENSUS

Amherst, 9,671	D 5
Antigonish, 5,291	D 8

Bedford, 8,010	E 6
Berwick, 2,058	D 5
Bridgewater, 6,617	E 5
Canso, 1,285	D 8
Chéticamp, 984	C 8
Dartmouth, 65,243	E 6
Digby, 2,525	E 4
Dominion, 2,754	C 9
Enfield, 1,775	E 6
Glace Bay, 20,467	C10

Halifax, 113,577	
(295,990★)	E 6
Kentville, 5,208	D 5
Liverpool, 3,295	E 5
Lunenburg, 2,972	E 5
New Glasgow, 10,022	D 7
New Waterford, 8,326	C 9
North Sydney, 7,472	C 9
Pictou, 4,413	D 7
Port Hawkesbury, 3,869	D 8

Springhill, 4,712	D 5
Stellarton, 5,259	D 7
Sydney, 27,754	
(119,470★)	C 9
Sydney Mines, 8,063	C 9
Trenton, 3,083	D 7
Truro, 12,124 (41,516★)	D 6
Westville, 4,271	D 7
Windsor, 3,665	E 5
Wolfville, 3,277	D 5
Yarmouth, 7,617	F 3

Saint Stephen, 5,032

Saint Stephen, 5,032	D 2
Shediac, 4,370	C 5
Shippegan, 2,801	B 5
Sussex, 4,114	D 4
Tracadie, 2,444	B 5
Woodstock, 4,549	C 2

Longitude West of Greenwich

Statute Miles 5 0 5 10 20 30 40 50
Kilometers 5 0 5 15 25 45 75

Oblique Cylindrical Projection

Newfoundland

Newfoundland and Labrador

1986 CENSUS

72

Oblique Cylindrical Projection

Quebec
1986 CENSUS

Alma, 25,923 (29,977★)	A 6		
Ancienne-Lorette, 13,747	C 6		
Anjou, 36,916★	p19		
Aylmer East, 28,976	p13		
Baie-Comeau, 26,244	A 6		
(33,047★)			
Beaconsfield, 19,301★	q19		

Beauport, 62,869	n17	
Boucherville, 31,116	D 4	
Brossard, 57,441	q20	
Cap-de-la-Madeleine, 32,800		
Charlesbourg, 68,996	n17	
Châteauguay, 37,865	D 4	
Chicoutimi, 61,083		
(158,468★)	A 6	
Drummondville, 36,020	D 5	
(56,283★)		

Gaspé, 17,350		
Gatineau, 81,244	D 2	
Granby, 38,508		
(51,176★)	D 5	
Grand-Mère, 14,582	D 5	
Hull, 58,722	D 2	
Joliette, 16,845	D 4	
(34,897★)		
Jonquière, 58,467	A 6	
Lachine, 34,906	D 4	
Lachute, 11,586	D 3	

LaSalle, 75,621	q19	
La Tuque, 10,723	B 5	
Laval, 284,164	D 4	
Lévis, 18,310	C 6	
Longueuil, 125,441	D 4	
Magog, 13,530	D 5	
(18,738★)		
Mascouche, 21,285	D 4	
Matane, 13,243	A 9	
(15,361★)		

Montréal, 1,015,420	D 4	
(2,921,357★)		
Montréal-Nord, 90,303	p19	
Outremont, 23,080	p19	
Pierrefonds, 39,605	q19	
Pointe-Claire, 26,026	q19	
Québec, 164,580	C 6	
(603,267★)		
Repentigny, 40,778	D 4	
Rimouski, 29,672	A 9	
(46,210★)		

Rivière-du-Loup, 13,321	B 8	
(22,471★)		
Rouyn, 17,319	k11	
(36,495★)		
Saint-Eustache, 32,226	D 4	
Saint-Foy, 69,615	q20	
Saint-Hubert, 66,218	h13	
Saint-Hyacinthe, 38,603	D 5	
(48,303★)		
Saint-Jean-sur-Richelieu, 34,745 (59,958★)	D 4	

Saint-Jérôme, 23,316	D 3	
(44,048★)		
Saint-Laurent, 67,002	p19	
Salaberry-de-Valleyfield, 27,942 (38,797★)	D 3	
Sept-Îles (Seven Islands), 25,637 (28,050★)	h13	
Shawinigan, 21,412	C 5	
(61,965★)		

Sorel, 19,522 (46,096★)	C 4	
Terrebonne, 31,310	D 4	
Thetford Mines, 18,561	C 6	
Trois-Rivières, 50,122	C 5	
(128,888★)		
Verdun, 60,246	q19	
Victoriaville, 21,587	C 5	
Ville Saint-Georges, 11,723	C 6	
(21,022★)	C 7	

★ Population of metropolitan area, including suburbs.

Statute Miles
Kilometers

Oblique Cylindrical Projection

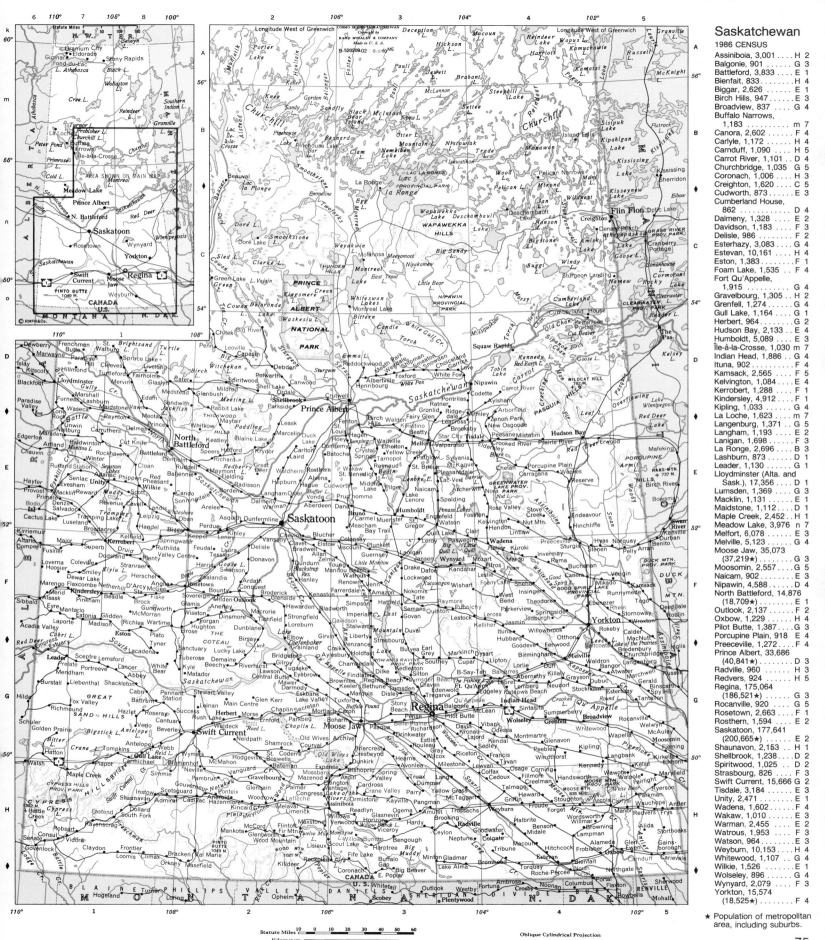

1986 CENSUS

Assiniboia, 3,001 . . . . H 2
Balgonie, 901 . . . . G 3
Battleford, 3,833 . . . . . . E 1
Bienfait, 833 . . . . H 4
Biggar, 2,626 . . . . E 1
Birch Hills, 947 . . . . . . E 3
Broadview, 837 . . . . . . G 4
Buffalo Narrows,
  1,183 . . . . m 7
Canora, 2,602 . . . . . . F 4
Carlyle, 1,172 . . . . . . H 4
Carnduff, 1,090 . . . . . H 5
Carrot River, 1,101 . . D 4
Churchbridge, 1,035 . G 5
Coronach, 1,006 . . . H 3
Creighton, 1,620 . . . C 5
Cudworth, 873 . . . . . E 3
Cumberland House,
  862 . . . . D 4
Dalmeny, 1,328 . . . . . E 2
Davidson, 1,183 . . . . F 3
Delisle, 986 . . . . F 2
Esterhazy, 3,083 . . . . G 4
Estevan, 10,161 . . . . H 4
Eston, 1,383 . . . . . . F 1
Foam Lake, 1,535 . . F 4
Fort Qu'Appelle,
  1,915 . . . . G 4
Gravelbourg, 1,305 . . H 2
Grenfell, 1,274 . . . . . G 4
Gull Lake, 1,164 . . . . G 1
Herbert, 964 . . . . G 2
Hudson Bay, 2,133 . . E 4
Humboldt, 5,089 . . . E 3
Île-à-la-Crosse, 1,030 m 7
Indian Head, 1,886 . . G 4
Ituna, 902 . . . . F 4
Kamsack, 2,565 . . . . F 5
Kelvington, 1,084 . . . E 4
Kerrobert, 1,288 . . . F 1
Kindersley, 4,912 . . . F 1
Kipling, 1,033 . . . . . G 4
La Loche, 1,623 . . . . m 7
Langenburg, 1,371 . . G 5
Langham, 1,193 . . . . E 2
Lanigan, 1,698 . . . . . F 3
La Ronge, 2,696 . . . . B 3
Lashburn, 873 . . . . . D 1
Leader, 1,130 . . . . . G 1
Lloydminster (Alta. and
  Sask.), 17,356 . . . D 1
Lumsden, 1,369 . . . . G 3
Macklin, 1,131 . . . . E 1
Maidstone, 1,112 . . . D 1
Maple Creek, 2,452 . . H 1
Meadow Lake, 3,976 . n 3
Melfort, 6,078 . . . . . E 3
Melville, 5,123 . . . . . G 4
Moose Jaw, 35,073
  (37,219★) . . . . G 3
Moosomin, 2,557 . . . G 5
Naicam, 902 . . . . . . E 3
Nipawin, 4,588 . . . . D 4
North Battleford, 14,876
  (18,709★) . . . . . . E 1
Outlook, 2,137 . . . . F 2
Oxbow, 1,229 . . . . . H 4
Pilot Butte, 1,387 . . G 3
Porcupine Plain, 918 . E 4
Preeceville, 1,272 . . F 4
Prince Albert, 33,686
  (40,841★) . . . . . . D 3
Radville, 960 . . . . . H 3
Redvers, 924 . . . . . H 5
Regina, 175,064
  (186,521★) . . . . . G 3
Rocanville, 920 . . . . G 5
Rosetown, 2,663 . . . F 1
Rosthern, 1,594 . . . E 2
Saskatoon, 177,641
  (200,665★) . . . . . E 2
Shaunavon, 2,153 . . H 1
Shellbrook, 1,238 . . D 2
Spiritwood, 1,025 . . D 2
Strasbourg, 826 . . . F 3
Swift Current, 15,666 G 2
Tisdale, 3,184 . . . . . E 3
Unity, 2,471 . . . . . . E 1
Wadena, 1,602 . . . . F 4
Wakaw, 1,010 . . . . E 3
Warman, 2,455 . . . . E 2
Watrous, 1,953 . . . . F 3
Watson, 964 . . . . . . E 3
Weyburn, 10,153 . . . H 4
Whitewood, 1,107 . . G 4
Wilkie, 1,526 . . . . . E 1
Wolseley, 896 . . . . . G 4
Wynyard, 2,079 . . . . F 3
Yorkton, 15,574
  (18,525★) . . . . . . F 4

★ Population of metropolitan
  area, including suburbs.

United States of America

Copyright © by Rand McNally & Co.
B-520591-264

Copyright © by Rand McNally & Co.

Kilometers
Miles

1:16 000 000

76

Alabama

Alaska

1990 CENSUS

Akiachak, 400('83)	C 7	Galena, 833	C10	Kenai, 6,327	C 8	Kwigillingok, 354('80)	D 7	Old Harbor, 284	D 9	Togiak, 613	D 7
Akiak, 285('80)	C 7	Gambell, 598	C 6	Ketchikan, 8,263	D13	Manokotak, 385	C 8	Palmer, 2,866	C10	Tok, 589('80)	C11
Akutan, 589('80)	E 7	Glennallen, 511('80)	B10	Kiana, 385	B 7	McGrath, 528	C 8	Petersburg, 3,207	D13	Tununak, 316	C 6
Alakanuk, 544	C 7	Haines, 1,238	C10	King Cove, 451	E 7	Metlakatla, 1,056('80)	D13	Pilot Station, 463	C 7	Unalakleet, 714	B 8
Anchorage, 226,338	C10	Healy, 334('80)	B10	King Salmon, 545('80)	D 8	Mountain Village, 674	C 7	Point Hope, 639	A 8	Unalaska, 3,089	E 6
Anderson, 628	B10	Homer, 3,660	C 9	Kipnuk, 371('80)	D 7	Nenana, 393	B10	Prudhoe Bay, 50('80)	A10	Valdez, 4,068	C10
Angoon, 638	D13	Hoonah, 795	D12	Klawock, 722	D13	Nikishka, 1,109('80)	C 9	Quinhagak, 501	D 7	Wainwright, 492	A 8
Aniak, 540	C 8	Hooper Bay, 845	C 6	Kodiak, 6,365	D 9	Nikolai, 341('80)	C 9	Saint Marys, 441	C 7	Wasilla, 4,028	C10
Barrow, 3,469	A 8	Hydaburg, 384	D13	Kotlik, 461	C 7	Ninilchik, 341('80)	C 9	Saint Paul, 763	D 5	Whittier, 243	g16
Bethel, 4,674	C 7	Juneau, 30,843	C10	Kotzebue, 26,751	B 7	Nome, 3,500	B 7	Sand Point, 878	D 7	Wrangell, 2,479	C10
Big Delta, 285('80)	B11	Kake, 700	D13	Kwethluk, 558	C 7	Noorvik, 531	B 7	Savoonga, 519	C 5	Yakutat, 534	C12
Chevak, 598	C 6					Nulato, 359	C 7	Selawik, 596	B 7		
Cold Bay, 148	E 7							Seldovia, 316	D 9		
College, 800('83)	B10							Seward, 2,699	C10		
Cordova, 2,110	C10							Shishmaref, 456	B 6		
Craig, 1,260	D13							Shungnak, 223	B 8		
Delta Junction, 652	C10							Sitka, 8,588	D12		
Dillingham, 2,017	D 8							Skagway, 692	C11		
Emmonak, 642	C 7							Soldotna, 3,482	g16		
Fairbanks, 30,843	C10							Stebbins, 400	C 6		
Fort Yukon, 580	B10							Sterling, 919('80)	g16		

Arizona

Little Rock

Statute Miles
Kilometers

Lambert Conformal Conic Projection

Arkansas

1990 CENSUS

Arkadelphia, 10,014	C 2	Dardanelle, 3,722	A 2	Forrest City, 13,364	B 5	Jacksonville, 29,101	C 3	Monticello, 8,116	D 4	Paris, 3,674	A 1	Springdale, 29,941	A 1
Ashdown, 5,150	D 1	De Queen, 4,633	B 6	Fort Smith, 72,798	C 1	Jonesboro, 46,535	B 5	Morrilton, 6,551	C 3	Stuttgart, 10,420	C 4
Bald Knob, 2,653	B 4	Dermott, 4,715	D 4	Greenwood, 3,984	C 1	Lake Village, 2,791	D 4	Mountain Home, 9,027	A 3	Texarkana, 22,631	D 1
Barling, 4,078	C 1	De Witt, 3,553	C 4	Harrison, 9,922	A 2	Little Rock, 175,795	C 3	Mountain View, 2,439	B 3	Trumann, 6,304	B 5
Batesville, 9,187	B 4	Dumas, 5,520	C 4	Harrison, 4,022	A 2	Lonoke, 4,022	C 3	Nashville, 4,639	D 2	Tuckerman, 2,020	B 4
Beebe, 4,455	B 4	Earle, 3,393	B 5	Heber Springs, 5,628	B 3	Magnolia, 11,151	D 2	Newport, 7,459	B 4	Van Buren, 14,979	A 1
Benton, 18,177	C 3	El Dorado, 23,146	D 3	Helena, 7,491	C 5	Malvern, 9,256	C 3	North Little Rock,		Walnut Ridge, 4,388	A 4
Bentonville, 11,257	A 1	Eudora, 3,155	D 4	Hope, 9,643	D 2	Marianna, 5,910	C 5	61,741	C 3	Warren, 6,455	D 3
Berryville, 3,212	A 2	Eureka Springs, 1,900	A 2	Hot Springs National Park,		Marked Tree, 3,100	B 5	Osceola, 8,930	B 6	West Helena, 9,695	C 5
Blytheville, 22,906	A 6	Fayetteville, 42,099	A 1	32,462	C 2	McGehee, 4,997	D 4	Ozark, 3,330	A 1	West Memphis, 28,259	B 5
Booneville, 3,804	B 2	Fordyce, 4,729	D 3	Hoxie, 2,676	A 5	Mena, 5,475	C 1	Paragould, 18,540	A 5	Wynne, 8,187	B 5
Brinkley, 4,234	C 4										
Bryant, 5,269	C 3										
Cabot, 8,319	C 3										
Camden, 14,380	D 3										
Clarksville, 5,833	B 2										
Conway, 26,481	C 3										
Corning, 3,323	A 5										
Crossett, 6,282	D 4										

California

Statute Miles

Kilometers

Lambert Conformal Conic Projection

Connecticut

Statute Miles

Kilometers

Lambert Conformal Conic Projection

84

Delaware

1990 CENSUS

Bear, 1,200('88) .... B 3
Bethany Beach, 326 .. F 5
Blades, 834 .... F 3
Bridgeville, 1,210 .... F 3
Broadkill Beach,
  390('88) .... E 5
Brookside, 7,450('88) B 3
Camden, 1,899 .... D 3
Canterbury, 500('88) D 3
Castle Hills, 1,475('88) i 7
Chalfonte, 1,740('88) h 7
Cheswold, 321 ...... D 3
Christiana, 500('88) .. B 3
Clarksville, 500('88) .. F 5
Claymont, 15,100('88)A 4
Clayton, 1,163 ...... C 3
Collins Park,
  2,100('88) ...... B 3
Dagsboro, 398 ...... F 5
Darley Woods,
  1,220('88) .... h 8
Delaware City, 1,682 B 3
Delmar, 962 .... G 3
Del Park Manor,
  1,550('88) .... i 7
Devonshire, 2,120('88)h 7
Dewey Beach, 204 .. F 5
Dover, 27,630 ...... D 3
Dunleith, 2,600('88) .. i 7
Dupont Manor,
  1,059('80) .... D 3
Edgemoor, 5,400('88) A 3
Ellendale, 313 ...... E 4
Elsmere, 5,935 ...... B 3
Fairfax, 2,075('88) .. A 3
Faulkland Heights,
  1,300('88) .... i 7
Felton, 683 .... D 3
Frankford, 591 ...... F 5
Frederica, 761 ...... D 4
Georgetown, 3,732 .. F 4
Graylyn Crest,
  4,380('88) .... A 3
Green Acres,
  1,140('88) .... h 8
Greenville, 800('88) .. a 3
Greenwood, 578 .... E 3
Gumboro, 200('88) .. g 4
Gwinhurst, 1,340('88) h 8
Harbeson, 500('88) .. f 5
Harrington, 2,311 .... E 3
Hockessin, 2,430('88) A 3
Houston, 487 ...... E 3
Jefferson Farms,
  3,130('88) .... i 7
Kenton, 232 .... D 3
Kirkwood, 350('88) .. b 3
Laurel, 3,226 ...... F 3
Lebanon, 130('88) .. d 4
Leipsic, 236 .... D 3
Lewes, 2,295 ...... E 5
Lincoln, 500('88) .... e 4
Little Creek, 167 .... D 4
Marshallton,
  1,765('88) .... B 3
Middletown, 3,834 .. C 3
Midway, 500('88) .... f 5
Milford, 6,040 ...... E 4
Millsboro, 1,643 .... F 4
Milton, 1,417 ...... E 4
Minquadale, 790('88)..i 7
Monroe Park,
  1,000('88) .... h 7
Montchanin, 500('88) h 7
Newark, 25,098 .... B 3
New Castle, 4,837 .. B 3
Newport, 1,240 .... B 3
North Star, 1,030('88) A 3
Oak Orchard, 350('88) f 5
Ocean View, 606 .... F 5
Odessa, 303 ...... C 3
Port Penn, 300('88) .. b 3
Rehoboth Beach,
  1,234 .... F 5
Rising Sun, 540('88) D 3
Rodney Village,
  1,100('88) .... D 3
Saint Georges,
  500('88) .... B 3
Seabreeze, 350('88) .. F 5
Seaford, 5,689 ...... F 3
Selbyville, 1,335 .... G 5
Sharpley, 1,250('88)..h 7
Sherwood Park,
  2,000('88) .... i 7
Silview, 1,500('88) .. B 3
Smyrna, 5,231 ...... C 3
Talleyville, 6,880('80) A 3
Townsend, 322 .... C 3
Tuxedo Park,
  1,300('88) .... i 7
Willow Run, 1,600('88) i 7
Wilmington, 71,529 .. B 3
Wilmington Manor,
  1,235('88) .... i 7
Wyoming, 977 ...... D 3
Yorklyn, 600('88) .... A 3

Florida

Hawaii

Lambert Conformal Conic Projection

Illinois

Statute Miles 5 0 5 10 20 30 40
Kilometers 5 0 5 15 25 35 45 55

Lambert Conformal Conic Projection

Anderson, 59,459 . . D 6
Auburn, 9,379 . . . . . B 7
Bedford, 13,817 . . G 5
Beech Grove, 13,383 . E 5
Bloomington, 60,633 . F 4
Bluffton, 9,020 . . . . C 7
Boonville, 6,724 . . H 3
Brazil, 7,640 . . . . . . E 3
Brownsburg, 7,628 . . E 5
Carmel, 25,380 . . . E 5
Cedar Lake, 8,885 . . B 3
Chesterton, 9,124 . . A 3
Clarksville, 19,833 . . H 6
Columbus, 31,802 . . F 6
Connersville, 15,550 . E 7
Corydon, 2,661 . . . H 5
Crawfordsville, 13,584 D 4
Crown Point, 17,728 . B 3
Decatur, 8,644 . . . . C 8
Dyer, 10,923 . . . . . A 2
East Chicago, 33,892 . A 3
Elkhart, 43,627 . . . . A 6
Elwood, 9,494 . . . . D 6
Evansville, 126,272 . I 2
Fort Wayne, 173,072 . B 7
Frankfort, 14,754 . . . D 4
Franklin, 12,907 . . . F 5
French Lick, 2,087 . . G 4
Gary, 116,646 . . . . . A 3
Gas City, 6,296 . . . . D 6
Goshen, 23,797 . . . A 6
Greencastle, 8,984 . . E 4
Greenfield, 11,657 . . E 6
Greensburg, 9,286 . . F 7
Greenwood, 26,265 . . E 5
Griffith, 17,916 . . . A 3
Hammond, 84,236 . . A 2
Hartford City, 6,960 . D 7
Highland, 23,696 . . A 3
Hobart, 21,822 . . . . A 3
Huntington, 16,389 . . C 7
Indianapolis, 731,327 E 5
Jasper, 10,030 . . . . H 4
Jeffersonville, 21,841 H 6
Kendallville, 7,773 . . B 7
Kokomo, 44,962 . . . D 5
Lafayette, 43,764 . . D 4
Lake Station, 13,899 . A 3
La Porte, 21,507 . . . A 4
Lawrence, 26,763 . . E 5
Lebanon, 12,059 . . . D 5
Linton, 5,814 . . . . F 3
Logansport, 16,812 . . C 5
Madison, 12,006 . . . G 7
Marion, 32,618 . . . . C 6
Martinsville, 11,677 . . F 5
Merrillville, 27,257 . . A 3
Michigan City, 33,822 A 4
Mishawaka, 42,608 . . A 5
Mount Vernon, 7,217 . I 2
Muncie, 71,035 . . . D 7
Munster, 19,949 . . . A 2
New Albany, 36,322 . H 6
New Castle, 17,753 . . E 7
New Haven, 9,320 . . B 7
Noblesville, 17,655 . . D 6
Peru, 12,843 . . . . C 5
Plainfield, 10,433 . . E 5
Plymouth, 8,303 . . . B 5
Portage, 29,060 . . . A 3
Portland, 6,483 . . . D 8
Princeton, 8,127 . . . H 2
Richmond, 38,705 . . E 7
Rockville, 2,706 . . . . E 3
Rushville, 5,533 . . . E 7
Schererville, 19,926 . B 3
Seymour, 15,576 . . . G 6
Shelbyville, 15,336 . . F 6
South Bend, 105,511 A 5
South Haven,
  6,679 ('80) . . . . . . A 3
Speedway, 13,092 . . E 5
Tell City, 8,088 . . . I 4
Terre Haute, 57,483 . . F 3
Valparaiso, 24,414 . . B 3
Vincennes, 19,859 . . G 2
Wabash, 12,127 . . . C 6
Warsaw, 10,968 . . . B 6
Washington, 10,838 . G 3
West Lafayette,
  25,907 . . . . D 4

Iowa

Statute Miles

Kilometers

Lambert Conformal Conic Projection

Statute Miles 5 0 5 15 25 35 45
Kilometers 5 0 5 15 25 35 45 55 65

Lambert Conformal Conic Projection

Kansas

1990 CENSUS

Abilene, 6,242	D 6
Andover, 4,047	g12
Arkansas City, 12,762	E 6
Atchison, 10,656	C 8
Augusta, 7,876	E 7
Baldwin City, 2,961	D 8
Baxter Springs, 4,351	E 9
Beloit, 4,066	C 5

Bonner Springs, 6,413	C 9
Burlington, 2,735	D 8
Chanute, 9,488	E 8
Clay Center, 4,613	C 6
Coffeyville, 12,917	E 8
Colby, 5,396	C 2
Columbus, 3,268	E 9
Concordia, 6,167	C 6
Derby, 14,699	E 6
Dodge City, 21,129	E 3
Edwardsville, 3,979	k16

El Dorado, 11,504	D 8
Emporia, 25,512	D 7
Eudora, 3,006	E 8
Eureka, 2,974	E 7
Fairway, 4,173	k16
Fort Scott, 8,362	E 9
Fredonia, 2,599	E 8
Galena, 3,308	E 9
Garden City, 24,097	D 3
Garnett, 3,210	E 8
Goodland, 4,983	C 2

Great Bend, 15,427	D 5
Hays, 17,767	D 4
Haysville, 8,364	g12
Herington, 2,685	D 7
Hiawatha, 3,603	C 8
Hoisington, 3,182	D 5
Holton, 3,196	C 8
Hugoton, 3,179	E 2
Hutchinson, 39,308	D 6
Independence, 9,942	E 8
Iola, 6,351	D 8

Junction City, 20,604	C 7
Kansas City, 149,767	C 9
Kingman, 3,196	E 5
Lansing, 7,120	C 9
Larned, 4,490	D 4
Lawrence, 65,608	C 8
Leavenworth, 38,495	C 8
Leawood, 19,693	m16
Lenexa, 34,034	m16
Liberal, 16,573	E 3
Lindsborg, 3,076	D 6

Lyons, 3,688	D 5
Manhattan, 37,712	C 7
Marysville, 3,359	C 7
McPherson, 12,422	D 6
Merriam, 11,821	k16
Mission, 9,504	k16
Mulvane, 4,674	E 6
Neodesha, 2,837	E 8
Newton, 16,700	D 6
Norton, 3,017	C 4
Olathe, 63,352	D 9

Osawatomie, 4,590	D 9
Ottawa, 10,667	D 8
Overland Park, 111,790	m16
Paola, 4,698	D 9
Park City, 5,050	g12
Parsons, 11,924	E 8
Phillipsburg, 2,828	C 4
Pittsburg, 17,775	E 9
Prairie Village, 23,186	m16
Pratt, 6,687	E 5
Roeland Park, 7,706	k16

Russell, 4,781	D 5
Salina, 42,303	D 6
Scott City, 3,785	D 3
Shawnee, 37,993	k16
Topeka, 119,883	C 8
Ulysses, 5,474	E 2
Valley Center, 3,624	E 6
Wamego, 3,706	C 7
Wellington, 8,411	E 6
Wichita, 304,011	E 6
Winfield, 11,931	E 7

Kentucky

Statute Miles 5 0 5 10 20 30 40

Kilometers 5 0 5 10 20 30 40 60

Lambert Conformal Conic Projection

B-520519-01 · 8 · 1 · ME
COMBO SERIES LOUISIANA
Copyright by
RAND McNALLY COMPANY
Made in U.S.A.

Statute Miles

Kilometers

Lambert Conformal Conic Projection

Louisiana
1990 CENSUS

Abbeville, 11,187	E 3	Jefferson, 15,550('80)	k11
Alexandria, 49,188	C 3	Jena, 2,626	C 3
Arabi, 10,248('80)	k11	Jennings, 11,305	D 3
Baker, 13,233	D 4	Jonesboro, 11,305	B 3
Bastrop, 13,916	B 4	Kaplan, 4,535	E 3
Baton Rouge, 219,531	D 4	Kenner, 72,033	E 5
Berwick, 4,375	E 4	Lafayette, 94,440	D 3
Bogalusa, 14,280	D 6	Lake Charles, 70,580	D 2

Bossier City, 52,721	B 2	Lake Providence, 5,380	B 4
Breaux Bridge, 6,515	D 4	La Place, 16,112('80)	h11
Bunkie, 5,044	D 3	Leesville, 7,638	C 2
Chalmette, 31,860	E 6	Lutcher, 3,907	D 5
Church Point, 4,677	D 3	Mandeville, 7,083	D 5
Covington, 7,691	D 5	Mansfield, 5,389	B 2
Crowley, 13,983	D 3	Marksville, 5,526	C 3
Cut Off, 5,049('80)	E 5	Marrero, 36,671	E 5
Denham Springs, 8,381	D 5	Metairie, 149,428	E 5
De Ridder, 9,868	C 2	Minden, 13,661	B 2
Donaldsonville, 7,949	D 4	Monroe, 54,909	B 3

Eunice, 11,162	D 3	Morgan City, 14,531	E 4
Ferriday, 4,111	C 4	Moss Bluff, 7,004('80)	h11
Franklin, 9,004	E 4	Natchitoches, 16,609	C 2
Gonzales, 7,003	D 4	New Iberia, 31,828	D 4
Grambling, 5,484	B 3	New Orleans, 496,938	E 5
Gretna, 17,208	E 5	Oakdale, 6,832	D 3
Hammond, 15,871	D 5	Opelousas, 18,151	D 3
Harahan, 9,927	k11	Patterson, 4,736	E 4
Harvey, 15,000	E 5	Pineville, 12,251	C 3
Houma, 96,982	E 5	Plaquemine, 6,200	D 4
Jeanerette, 6,205	E 4	Ponchatoula, 5,425	D 5

		Port Allen, 6,277	D 4
		Raceland, 6,302('80)	h11
		Rayne, 8,502	D 3
		Rayville, 4,411	B 4
		Reserve, 7,288('80)	h10
		River Ridge, 17,146('80)	k11
		Ruston, 20,027	B 3
		Saint Martinville, 7,137	D 4
		Scotlandville,
15,113('80)	B 2
		Shreveport, 198,525	B 2
		Slidell, 24,124	D 6

		Tallulah, 8,526	B 4
		Thibodaux, 14,035	E 5
		Vidalia, 4,953	C 4
		Ville Platte, 9,037	D 3
		Violet, 6,000	k12
		Westlake, 5,007	D 2
		West Monroe, 14,096	B 3
		Westwego, 11,218	k11
		Winnfield, 6,138	C 3
		Winnsboro, 5,755	B 4
		Zachary, 9,036	D 4
		Springhill, 5,668	A 2
		Sulphur, 20,125	D 2

95

Maine

▲ Population of entire town (township), including rural area.

Longitude West of Greenwich

B-520520-01 —5-6-7-gME
COSMO SERIES MAINE
Copyright by
RAND McNALLY & COMPANY
Made in U.S.A.

Statute Miles
Kilometers

Lambert Conformal Conic Projection

1990 CENSUS

Aberdeen, 13,087	A 5	
Annapolis, 33,187	C 4	
Baltimore, 736,014	B 4	
Bel Air, 8,860	A 5	
Beltsville, 7,670('88)	B 4	
Bethesda, 62,936	C 3	
Bladensburg, 8,064	f 9	
Bowie, 37,589	C 4	
Brunswick, 5,117	B 2	
Calverton, 7,649('80)	B 4	
Cambridge, 11,514	C 5	
Catonsville, 35,000	g 10	
Chevy Chase, 8,559	C 3	
Chillum, 12,500('88)	f 9	
Clinton, 7,570('88)	C 4	
College Park, 21,927	B 4	
Columbia, 75,883	B 4	
Crofton, 12,009('80)	B 4	
Cumberland, 23,706	k 13	

Dundalk, 65,800	B 4	
Easton, 9,372	C 5	
Edgemere, 7,410('88)	B 5	
Edgewood, 19,455('88)	B 5	
Elkton, 9,073	A 6	
Essex, 40,872	B 5	
Fallston, 5,572('80)	A 5	
Frederick, 40,148	B 3	
Frostburg, 8,075	k 13	
Gaithersburg, 39,542	B 3	
Germantown, 760('88)	B 4	
Glen Burnie, 32,700	B 4	
Greenbelt, 21,096	C 4	
Hagerstown, 35,445	A 2	
Halethorpe, 20,163	A 2	
Halfway, 9,073('80)	A 4	
Havre de Grace, 8,952	A 5	
Hyattsville, 13,864	C 4	
Langley Park, 9,150('88)	f 9	
Lanham, 5,000('88)	C 4	

La Vale, 5,000('88)	k 13	
Lutherville-Timonium, 16,871('80)	B 4	
Lynne River, 5,910('88)	B 4	
Middle River, 24,616	B 5	
Mount Rainier, 7,954	f 9	
Oakland, 1,741	D 6	
Ocean City, 5,146	D 7	
Odenton, 6,590('88)	B 4	
Olney, 9,500('88)	B 3	
Overlea, 3,320('88)	B 4	
Owings Mills, 9,526('80)	B 4	
Oxon Hill, 3,730('88)	f 9	
Parkville, 31,617	B 5	
Perry Hall, 10,285('88)	B 4	
Pikesville, 16,280	B 4	
Pocomoke City, 3,922	D 6	
Potomac, 25,370	B 3	
Randallstown, 18,680('88)	B 4	
Reisterstown, 19,385('80)	B 4	

Rockville, 44,835	B 3	
Rosedale, 11,390('88)	f 9	
Salisbury, 20,592	D 6	
Seat Pleasant, 5,359	B 5	
Severn, 20,147('80)	B 4	
Severna Park, 21,253('80)	B 4	
Sharpsburg, 659	B 2	
Silver Spring, 76,200	C 3	
Snow Hill, 2,217	D 7	
Suitland, 35,400	C 4	
Takoma Park, 16,700	f 8	
Towson, 49,445	B 4	
Westminster, 13,068	B 3	
Wheaton, 58,300	B 4	
Woodmoor, 8,630('88)	B 4	

District of Columbia

1990 CENSUS

Washington, 606,900 . . C 3

97

Massachusetts

Massachusetts
1990 CENSUS

Amherst, 17,773				
(35,228▲)		B 2		
Arlington, 44,630		A 5		
Attleboro, 38,383		C 5		
Belmont, 24,720		g11		
Beverly, 38,195		A 6		
Boston, 574,283		B 5		
Braintree, 33,836		B 5		
Brockton, 92,788		B 5		
Brookline, 54,718		B 5		
Burlington, 23,302		f11		
Cambridge, 95,802		A 5		
Chelmsford, 32,383		A 5		
Chelsea, 28,710		B 5		
Chicopee, 56,632		B 2		
Concord, 4,680				
(17,076▲)				
Danvers, 24,174		A 6		
Dedham, 23,782		B 5		
Everett, 35,701		A 5		
Fall River, 92,703		B 5		
Fitchburg, 41,194		A 4		
Framingham, 64,989		B 5		
Gardner, 20,125		A 4		
Gloucester, 28,716		A 6		
Greenfield, 14,198		B 2		
(18,666▲)				
Haverhill, 51,418		A 5		
Holyoke, 43,704		B 2		
Hyannis, 9,900		C 7		
Lawrence, 70,207		A 5		
Leominster, 38,145		A 4		
Lexington, 29,974		B 5		
Lowell, 103,439		A 5		
Lynn, 81,245		A 6		
Malden, 53,884		B 5		
Marlborough, 20,126('80)		B 4		
New Bedford, 99,922		B 6		
Newburyport, 16,317		A 6		
Newton, 82,585		B 5		
North Adams, 16,797		A 1		
Northampton, 29,289		B 2		
North Andover,				
20,129('87)		A 5		
North Attleboro, 24,200		C 5		
Norwood, 28,700		A 6		
Peabody, 47,039		A 6		
Pittsfield, 48,622		B 1		
Plymouth, 7,232				
(45,608▲)		C 6		
Quincy, 84,985		B 5		
Randolph, 30,093		B 5		
Reading, 22,539		A 5		
Revere, 42,786		B 5		
Salem, 38,091		A 6		
Saugus, 25,549		B 5		
Shrewsbury, 23,400		A 6		
Somerville, 76,210		B 5		
Springfield, 156,983		B 2		
West Springfield, 27,537		B 2		
Stoneham, 22,203		g11		
Weymouth, 54,063		g11		
Stoughton, 27,800		B 5		
Winchester, 20,701('80)		g11		
Taunton, 49,832		C 5		
Vineyard Haven,				
1,704('80)		D 6		
Wakefield, 24,825		B 5		
Waltham, 57,878		A 6		
Watertown, 33,284		g11		
Saugus, 25,549		B 2		
Wellesley, 26,615		B 5		
Westfield, 38,372		B 2		
Woburn, 35,943		B 5		
Worcester, 169,759		B 4		
Milford, 25,200		B 4		
Milton, 25,725		B 5		
Nantucket, 3,229		D 7		
Natick, 30,100		B 5		
Needham, 27,557		g11		
Winthrop, 19,294('80)		g11		

▲Population of entire town (township), including rural area.

Statute Miles 0 5 10 15 20

Kilometers 0 5 10 15 20 25

Lambert Conformal Conic Projection

98

Minnesota

Minnesota
1990 CENSUS

Albert Lea, 18,310 . . G 5
Alexandria, 7,838 . . . . E 3
Andover, 15,216 . . . m12
Anoka, 17,192 . . . . . E 5
Apple Valley, 34,598 . n12
Austin, 21,907 . . . . G 6
Bemidji, 11,245 . . . . C 4
Blaine, 38,975 . . . . . E 5
Bloomington, 86,335 . F 5
Brainerd, 12,353 . . . D 4
Brooklyn Center,
  28,887 . . . . E 5
Brooklyn Park,
  56,381 . . . . F 5
Burnsville, 51,288 . . . F 5
Champlin, 16,849 . . m12
Chisholm, 5,290 . . . C 6
Cloquet, 10,885 . . . D 6
Columbia Heights,
  18,910 . . . . E 5
Coon Rapids, 52,978 E 5
Cottage Grove,
  22,935 . . . . n13
Crookston, 8,119 . . . . C 2
Crystal, 23,788 . . . m12
Detroit Lakes, 6,635 . D 3
Duluth, 85,493 . . . . D 6
Eagan, 47,409 . . . . n12
East Bethel, 8,050 . . E 5
East Grand Forks,
  8,658 . . . . C 2
Eden Prairie, 39,311 . n12
Edina, 46,070 . . . . F 5
Ely, 3,968 . . . . C 7
Fairmont, 11,265 . . . G 4
Faribault, 17,085 . . . F 5
Fergus Falls, 12,362 . D 2
Fridley, 28,335 . . . m12
Golden Valley, 20,971 n12
Grand Marais, 1,171 . k 9
Grand Rapids, 7,976 . C 5
Hastings, 15,445 . . . F 6
Hibbing, 18,046 . . . . C 6
Hopkins, 16,534 . . . n12
Hutchinson, 11,523 . . F 4
International Falls,
  8,325 . . . . B 5
Inver Grove Heights,
  22,477 . . . . n12
Lakeville, 24,854 . . . F 5
Litchfield, 6,041 . . . . E 4
Little Falls, 7,232 . . . E 4
Mankato, 31,477 . . . F 5
Maple Grove, 38,736 m12
Maplewood, 30,954 . n12
Marshall, 12,023 . . . F 3
Minneapolis, 368,383 . F 5
Minnetonka, 48,370 . n12
Montevideo, 5,499 . . F 3
Moorhead, 32,295 . . D 2
Morris, 5,613 . . . . . E 3
Mound, 9,634 . . . . . n11
Mounds View, 12,541 m12
New Brighton, 22,207 m12
New Hope, 21,853 . . m12
New Ulm, 13,132 . . . F 4
Northfield, 14,684 . . F 5
North Mankato,
  10,164 . . . . F 4
North St. Paul,
  12,376 . . . . m13
Owatonna, 19,386 . . F 5
Pipestone, 4,554 . . . G 2
Plymouth, 50,889 . . m12
Prior Lake, 11,482 . . F 5
Ramsey, 12,408 . . . E 5
Red Wing, 15,134 . . F 6
Redwood Falls, 4,859 F 3
Richfield, 35,710 . . . F 5
Robbinsdale, 14,396 n12
Rochester, 70,745 . . F 6
Roseville, 33,485 . . m12
Saint Cloud, 48,812 . E 4
Saint Louis Park,
  43,787 . . . . n12
Saint Paul, 272,235 . . F 5
Saint Peter, 9,421 . . F 5
Shakopee, 11,739 . . F 5
Shoreview, 24,587 . m12
South St. Paul,
  20,197 . . . . n12
Stillwater, 13,882 . . . E 6
Thief River Falls,
  8,010 . . . . B 2
Virginia, 9,410 . . . . C 6
Waseca, 8,385 . . . . F 5
West Saint Paul,
  19,248 . . . . n12
White Bear Lake,
  24,704 . . . . E 5
Willmar, 17,531 . . . . E 3
Winona, 25,399 . . . . F 7
Woodbury, 20,075 . . F 6
Worthington, 9,977 . . G 3

100

Mississippi

1990 CENSUS

Aberdeen, 6,837 . . . . B 5
Amory, 7,093 . . . . . . B 5
Baldwyn, 3,204 . . . . A 5
Batesville, 6,403 . . . . A 4
Bay Saint Louis,
  8,063 . . . . E 4
Belzoni, 2,536 . . . . . . B 3
Biloxi, 46,319 . . . . . . E 5
Booneville, 7,955 . . . . A 5
Brandon, 11,077 . . . . C 4
Brookhaven, 10,243 . . D 3
Canton, 10,062 . . . . C 4
Carthage, 3,819 . . . . C 4
Charleston, 2,328 . . . . A 3
Clarksdale, 19,717 . . A 3
Cleveland, 15,384 . . . . A 3
Clinton, 21,847 . . . . C 3
Columbia, 6,815 . . . . D 4
Columbus, 23,799 . . . . B 5
Corinth, 11,820 . . . . A 5
Crystal Springs, 5,643 D 3
D'Iberville, 6,566 . . . . E 5
Durant, 2,838 . . . . . . B 4
Ellisville, 3,634 . . . . D 4
Escatawpa, 5,367('80) E 5
Forest, 5,060 . . . . . . C 4
Fulton, 3,387 . . . . . . A 5
Gautier, 10,088 . . . . f 8
Greenville, 45,226 . . B 2
Greenwood, 18,906 . . B 3
Grenada, 10,864 . . . . B 4
Gulfport, 40,775 . . . . E 4
Hattiesburg, 41,882 . . D 4
Hazlehurst, 4,221 . . . . D 3
Hernando, 3,125 . . . . A 4
Hollandale, 3,576 . . . . B 3
Holly Springs, 7,261 . . A 4
Horn Lake, 9,069 . . . . A 4
Houston, 3,903 . . . . B 4
Indianola, 11,809 . . . . B 3
Itta Bena, 2,377 . . . . B 3
Iuka, 3,122 . . . . . . A 5
Jackson, 196,637 . . C 3
Kosciusko, 6,986 . . . . C 4
Laurel, 18,827 . . . . D 4
Leland, 6,366 . . . . . . B 3
Lexington, 2,227 . . . . B 3
Long Beach, 15,804 . . g 7
Louisville, 7,169 . . . . B 4
Magee, 3,607 . . . . . . D 4
McComb, 11,591 . . . . D 3
Meridian, 41,036 . . . . C 5
Mississippi State,
  4,600('81) . . . . B 5
Morgantown,
  3,288('80) . . . . D 2
Morton, 3,212 . . . . C 4
Moss Point, 17,837 . . E 5
Mound Bayou, 2,222 B 3
Natchez, 19,460 . . . . D 2
New Albany, 6,775 . . A 4
Newton, 3,701 . . . . . C 4
North Gulfport,
  6,660('80) . . . . E 4
Ocean Springs,
  14,658 . . . . E 5
Okolona, 3,267 . . . . B 5
Orange Grove,
  3,000('81) . . . . E 5
Oxford, 9,984 . . . . . . A 4
Palmer, 2,765('80) . . D 4
Pascagoula, 25,899 . . E 5
Pass Christian, 5,557 E 4
Pearl, 19,588 . . . . . . C 3
Petal, 7,883 . . . . . . D 4
Philadelphia, 6,758 . . C 4
Picayune, 10,633 . . . . E 4
Pontotoc, 4,570 . . . . A 4
Quitman, 2,736 . . . . C 5
Ridgeland, 11,714 . . . . C 3
Ripley, 5,371 . . . . . . A 5
Rolling Fork, 2,444 . . C 3
Rosedale, 2,595 . . . . B 2
Ruleville, 3,245 . . . . . B 3
Senatobia, 4,772 . . . . A 4
Southaven, 17,949 . . A 3
Starkville, 18,458 . . . . B 5
Tupelo, 30,685 . . . . A 5
Vicksburg, 20,908 . . C 3
Water Valley, 3,610 . . A 4
Waveland, 5,369 . . . . E 4
Waynesboro, 5,143 . . D 5
West Point, 8,489 . . . . B 5
Wiggins, 3,185 . . . . E 4
Winona, 5,705 . . . . B 4
Yazoo City, 12,427 . . C 3

Statute Miles
Kilometers

Lambert Conformal Conic Projection

Missouri

Missouri
1990 CENSUS

Arnold, 18,828 .... C 7
Aurora, 6,459 .... E 4
Ballwin, 21,816 .... f12
Belton, 18,150 .... C 7
Berkeley, 12,450 .... f13
Blue Springs, 40,153 .... B 3
Bolivar, 6,845 .... D 4
Boonville, 7,095 .... C 5

Brentwood, 8,150 .... f13
Bridgeton, 17,779 .... C 7
Brookfield, 4,888 .... B 4
Cape Girardeau, 34,438 .... D 8
Carthage, 10,747 .... D 3
Caruthersville, 7,389 .... E 8
Charleston, 5,085 .... D 7
Chillicothe, 8,804 .... B 4
Clayton, 13,874 .... f13
Clinton, 8,703 .... C 4
Columbia, 69,101 .... C 5

De Soto, 5,993 .... C 6
Des Peres, 8,395 .... C 7
Dexter, 7,559 .... B 4
Ellisville, 9,053 .... f12
Eureka, 4,683 .... f12
Excelsior Springs,
  10,354 .... B 3
Farmington, 11,598 .... D 7
Ferguson, 22,286 .... f13
Festus, 8,105 .... C 7
Florissant, 51,206 .... C 5

Fulton, 10,033 .... C 6
Gladstone, 26,243 .... h10
Grandview, 24,967 .... C 3
Hannibal, 18,004 .... B 6
Harrisonville, 7,683 .... C 3
Independence, 112,301 .... B 3
Jackson, 9,256 .... D 7
Jefferson City, 35,481 .... C 5
Jennings, 15,905 .... f13
Joplin, 40,961 .... D 3
Kansas City, 435,146 .... B 3

Kennett, 10,941 .... E 7
Kirksville, 17,152 .... A 5
Kirkwood, 27,291 .... f13
Lebanon, 9,983 .... D 5
Lees Summit, 46,418 .... C 3
Liberty, 20,459 .... B 3
Macon, 5,571 .... B 5
Malden, 5,123 .... E 8
Manchester, 6,542 .... f12
Maplewood, 9,962 .... f13
Marshall, 12,711 .... B 4

Maryland Heights,
  25,407 .... f13
Mexico, 11,290 .... B 6
Moberly, 12,839 .... B 5
Monett, 6,529 .... E 4
Neosho, 9,254 .... E 3
Nevada, 8,597 .... D 3
O'Fallon, 18,698 .... f12
Overland, 17,987 .... f13
Perryville, 6,933 .... C 7

Pine Lawn, 5,092 .... f13
Poplar Bluff, 16,996 .... E 7
Raytown, 30,601 .... h11
Richmond Heights,
  10,448 .... f13
Rolla, 14,090 .... D 6
Saint Charles, 54,555 .... C 7
Sainte Genevieve, 4,411 .... D 7
Saint Joseph, 71,852 .... B 3
Saint Louis, 396,685 .... C 7
Saint Peters, 45,779 .... C 7

Sedalia, 19,800 .... C 4
Sikeston, 17,641 .... E 8
Springfield, 140,494 .... D 4
Sullivan, 5,661 .... C 6
Trenton, 6,129 .... A 4
University City, 40,087 .... C 7
Warrensburg, 15,244 .... C 4
Washington, 10,704 .... C 6
Webb City, 7,449 .... D 3
Webster Groves, 22,987 .... f13
West Plains, 8,913 .... E 6

Statute Miles
Kilometers

Lambert Conformal Conic Projection

Statute Miles 10 0 10 20 30 40 50 60 70

Kilometers 10 0 10 30 50 70 90

Lambert Conformal Conic Projection

Montana

1990 CENSUS

Anaconda, 10,278	D 4	
Baker, 1,818	D12	
Belgrade, 3,411	E 5	
Belt, 571	C 6	
Bigfork, 1,080('80)	B 2	
Big Sandy, 740	B 6	
Big Timber, 1,557	E 7	
Billings, 81,151	E 8	

Billings Heights, 8,480('80)	E 8	
Boulder, 1,316	D 4	
Bozeman, 22,660	E 5	
Bridger, 692	E11	
Broadus, 572	E11	
Browning, 1,170	B 3	
Butte, 33,336	E 4	
Cascade, 729	C 5	
Chester, 942	B 6	
Chinook, 1,512	B 7	

Choteau, 1,741	C 4	
Circle, 805	C11	
Colstrip, 1,476('80)	E10	
Columbia Falls, 2,942	B 2	
Columbus, 1,573	E 7	
Conrad, 2,891	C 6	
Culbertson, 796	B12	
Cut Bank, 3,329	B 4	
Deer Lodge, 3,378	D 4	
Dillon, 3,991	E 4	
East Helena, 1,538	D 5	

Ennis, 773	E 5	
Eureka, 1,043	B 1	
Fairview, 869	C12	
Forsyth, 2,178	D10	
Fort Benton, 1,660	C 6	
Glasgow, 3,572	B10	
Glendive, 4,802	C12	
Great Falls, 55,097	C 5	
Hamilton, 2,737	D 2	
Hardin, 2,940	E 9	
Harlem, 882	B 8	

Harlowton, 1,049	D 7	
Havre, 10,201	B 7	
Helena, 24,569	D 4	
Kalispell, 11,917	B 2	
Laurel, 5,686	E 8	
Lewistown, 6,051	C 7	
Libby, 2,532	B 1	
Livingston, 6,701	E 6	
Lockwood, 2,300('89)	E 8	
Lolo, 2,418('80)	D 2	
Malta, 2,340	B 8	

Manhattan, 1,034	D 7	
Miles City, 8,461	D 8	
Missoula, 42,918	D 2	
Orchard Homes, 4,500('89)	D 2	
Philipsburg, 925	D 3	
Plains, 992	C 2	
Plentywood, 2,136	B12	
Polson, 3,283	C 2	
Poplar, 881	B11	
Red Lodge, 1,958	E 7	

Ronan, 1,547	C 2	
Roundup, 1,808	D 8	
Saint Ignatius, 778	C 2	
Scobey, 1,154	B11	
Shelby, 2,763	B 5	
Sidney, 5,217	C12	
Stevensville, 1,221	D 2	
Superior, 881	D 2	
Terry, 659	D11	
Thompson Falls, 1,319	C 1	
Three Forks, 1,203	E 5	

Townsend, 1,635	D 5	
Troy, 953	B 1	
Vaughn, 2,270('80)	C 5	
Walkerville, 605	D 4	
West Yellowstone, 913	F 5	
Whitefish, 4,368	B 2	
Whitehall, 1,067	E 4	
White Sulphur Springs, 963	D 6	
Wibaux, 628	D12	
Wolf Point, 2,880	B11	

Longitude West of Greenwich

Montana

B-500627-01
RAND McNALLY & COMPANY
Copyright by
RAND McNALLY & COMPANY
Made in U.S.A.

Nebraska

Statute Miles
Kilometers

Lambert Conformal Conic Projection

New Hampshire

Statute Miles

Kilometers

Lambert Conformal Conic Projection

1990 CENSUS

Asbury Park, 16,799 . . C 4
Atlantic City, 37,986 . . E 4
Bayonne, 61,444 . . . . B 4
Belleville, 34,213 . . . . B 4
Bergenfield, 24,458 . . B 4
Bloomfield, 45,061 . . . h 8
Brick [Township],
  64,800('89) . . . . . . C 4
Bridgeton, 18,942 . . E 2
Camden, 87,492 . . . . D 2
Cape May, 4,668 . . . . F 3
Carteret, 19,025 . . . . B 4
Cherry Hill, 69,319 . . D 2
Cliffside Park, 20,393 . h 9
Clifton, 71,742 . . . . . B 4
Cranford, 22,624 . . . . B 4
Dover, 15,115 . . . . . . B 3
East Brunswick,
  43,548 . . . . C 4
East Orange, 73,552 . . B 4
Edison, 88,680 . . . . . B 4
Elizabeth, 110,002 . . B 4
Englewood, 24,850 . . B 5
Ewing Township,
  34,185 . . . . C 3
Fair Lawn, 30,548 . . . h 8
Fort Lee, 31,997 . . . . B 5
Freehold, 10,742 . . . . C 4
Garfield, 26,727 . . . . h 8
Glassboro, 15,614 . . D 2
Hackensack, 37,049 . . B 4
Hackettstown, 8,120 . B 3
Hammonton, 12,208 . D 3
Hazlet, 23,013('80) . . C 4
Hillside, 21,044 . . . . . k 8
Hoboken, 33,397 . . . . k 8
Irvington, 59,774 . . . . k 8
Jersey City, 228,537 . B 4
Kearny, 34,874 . . . . . h 8
Lakewood, 26,095 . . . C 4
Linden, 36,701 . . . . . k 8
Livingston, 26,609 . . B 4
Lodi, 22,355 . . . . h 8
Long Branch, 28,658 . C 5
Lyndhurst, 20,326('80) h 8
Maple Shade,
  20,525('80) . . . . . D 2
Maplewood, 21,756 . . B 4
Middletown,
  21,300('85) . . . . . C 4
Millburn, 18,630 . . . . B 4
Millville, 25,992 . . . . E 2
Montclair, 37,729 . . . B 4
Morristown, 16,189 . . B 4
Neptune, 29,800 . . . . C 4
Newark, 275,221 . . . B 4
New Brunswick,
  41,711 . . . . C 4
North Bergen, 48,414 . h 8
North Brunswick,
  31,287 . . . . C 4
North Plainfield,
  18,820 . . . . B 4
Nutley, 27,099 . . . . . B 4
Ocean [Township],
  24,700('86) . . . . . C 4
Orange, 29,925 . . . . . B 4
Paramus, 25,067 . . . . h 8
Passaic, 58,041 . . . . . B 4
Paterson, 140,891 . . B 4
Pennsauken, 34,733 . D 2
Pennsville,
  12,467('80) . . . . . D 1
Perth Amboy, 41,967 . B 4
Phillipsburg, 15,757 . . B 2
Piscataway, 43,800 . . B 4
Plainfield, 46,567 . . . B 4
Princeton, 12,016 . . . C 3
Rahway, 25,325 . . . . B 4
Red Bank, 10,636 . . . C 4
Ridgewood, 24,152 . . B 4
Roselle, 20,314 . . . . . k 7
Sayreville, 34,986 . . . C 4
Scotch Plains,
  20,774('80) . . . . . B 4
Somerset, 21,731('80) B 3
Somerville, 11,632 . . B 4
South Plainfield,
  20,489 . . . . B 4
Summit, 19,757 . . . . B 4
Sussex, 2,201 . . . . . . A 3
Teaneck, 37,825 . . . . h 8
Trenton, 88,675 . . . . C 3
Union City, 58,012 . . h 8
Vineland, 54,780 . . . E 2
Wayne, 47,025 . . . . . B 4
Westfield, 28,870 . . . B 4
West New York,
  38,125 . . . . B 4
West Orange, 39,103 . B 4
Willingboro, 36,291 . . C 3
Woodbine, 2,678 . . . . E 3
Woodbridge [Township],
  95,100('86) . . . . . B 4

107

New Mexico

B-520532-01 __841-13ME__
COSMO SERIES NEW MEXICO
Copyright by
RAND McNALLY & COMPANY
Made in U.S.A.

Statute Miles   10 0 10 20 30 40 50 60 70 80 90
Kilometers   10 0 10 20 30 40 50 60 70 80 100 120

Lambert Conformal Conic Projection

New York

1990 CENSUS

Albany, 101,082	C 7	
Amherst, 45,600	C 2	
Amityville, 9,286	E 7	
Amsterdam, 20,714	C 6	
Auburn, 31,258	C 4	
Batavia, 16,310	C 3	
Bay Shore, 53,008	C 5	
Binghamton, 53,008	D 5	

Brentwood, 45,218	E 7	
Brighton, 34,455	B 3	
Buffalo, 328,123	C 2	
Centereach, 26,720	n15	
Central Islip, 42,600	n15	
Cheektowaga, 84,387	C 2	
Cooperstown, 2,180	C 6	
Corning, 11,938	C 4	
Cortland, 19,801	C 4	
Deer Park, 28,840	E 7	
Depew, 17,673	C 5	

Dunkirk, 13,989	E 7	
Elmira, 33,724	C 4	
Elmont, 28,612	k13	
Freeport, 39,894	n15	
Fulton, 12,929	B 4	
Gates, 30,000	B 3	
Geneva, 14,143	C 4	
Glen Cove, 24,149	h13	
Glens Falls, 15,023	B 7	
Gloversville, 16,656	B 6	
Greece, 64,600	B 3	

Harrison, 23,308	h13	
Hempstead, 49,453	n15	
Hicksville, 40,174	E 7	
Hyde Park, 2,550(80)	D 7	
Irondequoit, 52,322	.f 9	
Ithaca, 29,541	C 4	
Jamestown, 34,681	C 1	
Kenmore, 17,180	h13	
Kingston, 23,095	D 6	
Lackawanna, 20,585	C 2	
Lake Placid, 2,485	A 7	

Levittown, 53,286	E 7	
Lindenhurst, 49,453	n15	
Lockport, 24,426	B 2	
Long Beach, 33,510	E 7	
Massena, 11,719	f10	
Middletown, 24,160	D 6	
Mineola, 18,994	E 7	
Mount Vernon, 67,153	h13	
New City, 33,673	D 6	
Newburgh, 26,454	D 6	
New Rochelle, 67,265	E 7	

New York, 7,322,564	E 7	
Niagara Falls, 61,840	B 1	
North Tonawanda, 34,989	B 2	
Ogdensburg, 13,521	A 5	
Olean, 16,946	C 2	
Oneonta, 13,954	C 5	
Ossining, 22,582	D 7	
Oswego, 19,195	B 4	
Palmyra, 3,566	B 3	
Peekskill, 19,536	D 7	

Plattsburgh, 21,255	A 7	
Port Chester, 24,728	E 7	
Poughkeepsie, 28,844	D 7	
Rochester, 231,636	B 3	
Rockville Centre, 24,727	n15	
Rome, 44,350	B 5	
Rotterdam, 21,228	C 6	
Saratoga Springs, 25,001	B 7	
Schenectady, 65,566	C 7	
Spring Valley, 21,802	g12	

Syracuse, 163,860	B 4	
Ticonderoga, 2,770	B 7	
Tonawanda, 17,284	C 2	
Troy, 54,269	C 7	
Utica, 68,637	B 5	
Valley Stream, 33,946	n15	
Watertown, 29,429	B 5	
West Point, 8,105(80)	D 7	
West Seneca, 47,866	C 2	
White Plains, 48,718	E 7	
Yonkers, 188,082	E 7	

Statute Miles

Kilometers

Lambert Conformal Conic Projection

North Carolina

Statute Miles
Kilometers

Lambert Conformal Conic Projection

North Dakota

Statute Miles

Kilometers

Lambert Conformal Conic Projection

Ohio

Statute Miles

Kilometers

Lambert Conformal Conic Projection

Statute Miles

Kilometers

Lambert Conformal Conic Projection

Oregon

Pennsylvania

115

Rhode Island

Rhode Island
1990 CENSUS

Abbott Run Valley,
  1,050('87)........B 4
Adamsville, 600('87)...E 6
Albion, 1,600('87)....B 4
Allenton, 600('87)....E 4
Anthony, 2,980('87)...D 3
Arnold Mills, 600('87).B 4
Ashton, 820('87)......B 4
Barrington,
  16,174('80)........D 5
Berkeley, 830('87)....B 4
Block Island, 620('87).h 7
Branch Village,
  400('87)...........B 3
Bristol, 20,128('80)..D 5
Burdickville, 500('87).F 2
Carolina, 650('87)....F 2
Central Falls, 17,637.B 4
Charlestown, 1,500
  (6,478▲)..........F 2
Chepachet, 900('87)..B 2
Common Fence Point,
  860('87)...........D 6
Coventry, 6,980
  (31,083▲).........D 3
Cranston, 76,060.....C 4
Davisville, 500('87)...E 4
Diamond Hill, 810('87).B 4
East Greenwich,
  10,211('87)........D 4
East Matunuck,
  500('87)...........F 3
East Providence,
  50,380............C 4
Esmond, 4,320('87)...B 4
Forestdale, 530('87)..B 3
Glendale, 700('87)....B 2
Greenville, 7,576('80).C 3
Harmony, 820('87)....D 3
Harris, 1,050('87)....D 3
Hope, 270('87)......D 3
Hopkinton, 550
  (6,873▲)..........F 1
Island Park,
  1,240('87)........E 6
Jamestown,
  4,040('87)........F 5
Johnston, 26,800....C 4
Kenyon, 400('87)....F 2
Kingston, 5,479('80)..F 3
La Fayette, 640('87)..E 4
Little Compton, 500
  (3,339▲)..........E 6
Lonsdale, 3,850('87)..B 4
Manville, 3,030('87)..B 4
Mapleville, 1,300('87).B 2
Matunuck, 550('87)...G 3
Middletown, 3,350
  (19,460▲).........D 5
Mount View, 610('87).D 4
Narragansett, 3,342
  (14,985▲).........F 4
Newport, 28,227....F 5
North Kingstown, 2,750
  (23,786▲).........E 4
North Providence,
  32,090............C 4
Oakland, 600('87)....B 2
Pascoag, 3,807('80)..B 2
Pawtucket, 72,644...C 4
Peace Dale,
  3,100('87)........F 3
Plum Beach, 400('87).E 4
Portsmouth, 3,540
  (16,857▲).........E 6
Primrose, 500('87)...B 3
Providence, 160,728..C 4
Quidnessett,
  3,300('87)........E 4
Quidnick, 2,300('87)..D 3
Quonochontaug,
  1,500('87)........G 2
Saunderstown,
  400('87)..........E 4
Saylesville, 3,510('87).B 4
Shannock, 950('87)...F 2
Shores Acres,
  410('87)..........E 4
Slatersville, 2,330('87).A 3
South Hopkinton,
  900('87)..........F 1
Tiverton, 7,653
  (14,312▲).........D 6
Union Village,
  2,150('87)........B 4
Usquepaug, 400('87)..F 3
Valley Falls,
  10,892('80).......B 4
Wakefield, 3,450('87)..F 3
Warren, 10,640('87)..D 5
Warwick, 85,427....D 4
Westerly, 16,477
  (21,605▲).........F 1
West Kingston,
  1,150('87)........F 3
West Warwick,
  29,268............D 3
Woonsocket, 43,877.A 3
Yorktown Manor,
  2,520('87)........C 3

▲ Population of entire town (township), including rural area.

116

South Carolina
1990 CENSUS

South Dakota

Statute Miles 5 0 5 10 20 30 40 50 60

Kilometers 5 0 5 15 25 35 45 55 65 75

Lambert Conformal Conic Projection

Texas

Vermont

Vermont
1990 CENSUS

Arlington, 700 .... E 2
  (2,299▲)
Barre, 9,482 .... C 4
Barton, 908 .... B 4
Bellows Falls, 3,313 .. E 4
Bennington, 9,349 ...... F 2
  (16,451▲)
Bethel, 1,016 .... D 3
  (1,866▲)
Bradford, 672 .... D 4
Brandon, 1,925 .... D 2
  (4,223▲)
Brattleboro, 8,596 ..... F 3
  (12,241▲)
Bristol, 1,801 .... C 2
Burlington, 39,127 .. C 2
Castleton, 600 .... D 2
  (4,278▲)
Chester, 550 (2,832▲) E 3
Chester Depot, 500 .. E 3
Derby Line, 855 ..... A 4
Dorset, 550 (1,918▲) E 2
East Arlington, 600 .. E 2
East Barre, 700 .... C 4
East Middlebury, 500 D 2
East Montpelier, 600 .. C 4
  (2,239▲)
Enosburg Falls, 1,350 B 3
Essex, 800 (16,498▲) B 2
Essex Junction, 8,396 C 2
Fair Haven, 2,887 ..... D 2
Forest Dale, 350 ...... D 2
Gilman, 500 .... C 5
Graniteville, 500 ..... C 4
Hardwick, 1,400 ...... B 4
  (2,964▲)
Hartford, 500 .... D 4
  (9,404▲)
Hydeville, 450 ...... D 2
Jericho, 1,300 .... B 3
  (4,302▲)
Johnson, 1,470 ...... B 3
Ludlow, 1,123 ...... E 3
Lyndonville, 1,255 .. B 4
Manchester, 561 .... E 2
Middlebury, 5,591 ..... C 2
  (8,034▲)
Milton, 1,578 .... C 2
Montpelier, 8,247 .. C 3
Morrisville, 1,984 .... B 3
Newport, 4,434 ...... B 4
North Bennington,
  1,520 .... F 2
North Clarendon, 500 D 3
Northfield, 1,889 .... C 3
Northfield Falls, 600 C 3
North Springfield, 750 E 3
North Troy, 723 ..... B 4
Norwich, 1,000 ...... D 4
  (3,093▲)
Orleans, 806 .... B 4
Pittsford, 650 .... D 2
  (2,919▲)
Plainfield, 600 ...... C 4
  (1,302▲)
Poultney, 1,731 ...... D 2
Proctor, 1,979 .... D 2
Proctorsville, 480 .... E 3
Putney, 1,100 .... F 3
  (2,352▲)
Quechee, 550 .... D 4
Randolph, 2,200 ...... D 3
  (4,764▲)
Richford, 1,425 ..... B 3
Richmond, 650 ...... C 2
  (3,729▲)
Riverton, 150 .... C 3
Rochester, 500 ...... D 3
  (1,181▲)
Rutland, 18,230 ..... D 3
Saint Albans, 7,339 .. B 2
Saint Johnsbury, 7,150 C 4
  (7,608▲)
Saxtons River, 541 .. E 3
Shaftsbury, 700 ..... E 2
  (3,368▲)
South Burlington,
  12,809 .... C 2
South Royalton, 700 D 3
Springfield, 5,603 .... E 4
  (9,579▲)
Stamford, 400 (773▲) F 2
Stowe, 450 .... B 3
Swanton, 2,360 .... B 2
Vergennes, 2,578 .... C 2
Wallingford, 1,141 .. D 2
  (2,184▲)
Warren, 350 (1,172▲) C 3
Waterbury, 1,702 .... C 3
Waterbury Center,
  500 .... C 3
Websterville, 600 .... C 4
West Pawlet, 350 .... D 2
West Rutland, 2,448 D 2
Williamstown, 650 .. C 3
  (2,839▲)
Wilmington, 550 .... F 3
  (1,968▲)
Windsor, 3,714 ...... E 4
Winooski, 6,649 ..... C 2
Woodstock, 1,037 .. D 3

▲ Population of entire town (township), including rural area.

122

RAND M®NALLY & COMPANY
Copyright ©
Made in U.S.A.

Statute Miles 5 0 5 10 20
Kilometers 5 0 5 10 15 20 25

Lambert Conformal Conic Projection

Statute Miles 5 0 5 10 20 30 40
Kilometers 5 0 5 15 25 35 45 55

Lambert Conformal Conic Projection

Washington

West Virginia

Statute Miles
Kilometers

Lambert Conformal Conic Projection

Wisconsin

Wisconsin
1990 CENSUS

Statute Miles
Kilometers

Lambert Conformal Conic Projection

North Polar Regions

★ Population of metropolitan area, including suburbs.

▲ Population of entire district, including rural area.

Kilometers
Miles

1:60 000 000

Lambert Azimuthal Equal-Area Projection

Index to World Reference Maps

Introduction to the Index

This universal index includes in a single alphabetical list approximately 38,000 names of features that appear on the reference maps. Each name is followed by the name of the country or continent in which it is located, a map-reference key and a page reference.

Names The names of cities appear in the index in regular type. The names of all other features appear in *italics*, followed by descriptive terms (hill, mtn., state) to indicate their nature.

Names that appear in shortened versions on the maps due to space limitations are spelled out in full in the index. The portions of these names omitted from the maps are enclosed in brackets — for example, Acapulco [de Juárez].

Abbreviations of names on the maps have been standardized as much as possible. Names that are abbreviated on the maps are generally spelled out in full in the index.

Country names and names of features that extend beyond the boundaries of one country are followed by the name of the continent in which each is located. Country designations follow the names of all other places in the index. The locations of places in the United States, Canada, and the United Kingdom are further defined by abbreviations that indicate the state, province, or political division in which each is located.

All abbreviations used in the index are defined in the List of Abbreviations below.

Alphabetization Names are alphabetized in the order of the letters of the English alphabet. Spanish *ll* and *ch*, for example, are not treated as distinct letters. Furthermore, diacritical marks are disregarded in alphabetization — German or Scandinavian ä or ö are treated as *a* or *o*.

The names of physical features may appear inverted, since they are always alphabetized under the proper, not the generic, part of the name, thus: 'Gibraltar, Strait of'. Otherwise every entry, whether consisting of one word or more, is alphabetized as a single continuous entity. 'Lakeland', for example, appears after 'La Crosse' and before 'La Salle'. Names beginning with articles (Le Havre, Den Helder, Al Manṣūrah) are not inverted. Names beginning 'St.', 'Ste.' and 'Sainte' are alphabetized as though spelled 'Saint'.

In the case of identical names, towns are listed first, then political divisions, then physical features. Entries that are completely identical are listed alphabetically by country name.

Map-Reference Keys and Page References The map-reference keys and page references are found in the last two columns of each entry.

Each map-reference key consists of a letter and number. The letters appear along the sides of the maps. Lowercase letters indicate reference to inset maps. Numbers appear across the tops and bottoms of the maps.

Map reference keys for point features, such as cities and mountain peaks, indicate the locations of the symbols. For extensive areal features, such as countries or mountain ranges, locations are given for the approximate centers of the features. Those for linear features, such as canals and rivers, are given for the locations of the names.

Names of some important places or features that are omitted from the maps due to space limitations are included in the index. Each of these places is identified by an asterisk (*) preceding the map-reference key.

The page number generally refers to the main map for the country in which the feature is located. Page references to two-page maps always refer to the left-hand page.

List of Abbreviations

Afg.	Afghanistan	*ctry.*	country	*is.*	islands	Nic.	Nicaragua
Afr.	Africa	C.V.	Cape Verde	Isr.	Israel	Nig.	Nigeria
Ak., U.S.	Alaska, U.S.	Cyp.	Cyprus	Jam.	Jamaica	N. Ire., U.K.	Northern Ireland, U.K.
Al., U.S.	Alabama, U.S.	Czech.	Czech Republic	Jord.	Jordan	N.J., U.S.	New Jersey, U.S.
Alb.	Albania	D.C., U.S.	District of Columbia, U.S.	Kaz.	Kazakhstan	N. Kor.	North Korea
Alg.	Algeria			Kir.	Kiribati	N.M., U.S.	New Mexico, U.S.
Alta., Can.	Alberta, Can.	De., U.S.	Delaware, U.S.	Ks., U.S.	Kansas, U.S.	N. Mar. Is.	Northern Mariana Islands
Am. Sam.	American Samoa	Den.	Denmark	Kuw.	Kuwait		
anch.	anchorage	*dep.*	dependency, colony	Ky., U.S.	Kentucky, U.S.	Nmb.	Namibia
And.	Andorra	*depr.*	depression	Kyrg.	Kyrgyzstan	Nor.	Norway
Ang.	Angola	*dept.*	department, district	*l.*	lake, pond	Norf. I.	Norfolk Island
Ant.	Antarctica	*des.*	desert	La., U.S.	Louisiana, U.S.	N.S., Can.	Nova Scotia, Can.
Antig.	Antigua and Barbuda	Dji.	Djibouti	Lat.	Latvia	Nv., U.S.	Nevada, U.S.
Ar., U.S.	Arkansas, U.S.	Dom.	Dominica	Leb.	Lebanon	N.W. Ter., Can.	Northwest Territories, Can.
Arg.	Argentina	Dom. Rep.	Dominican Republic	Leso.	Lesotho		
Arm.	Armenia	Ec.	Ecuador	Lib.	Liberia	N.Y., U.S.	New York, U.S.
Aus.	Austria	El Sal.	El Salvador	Liech.	Liechtenstein	N.Z.	New Zealand
Austl.	Australia	Eng., U.K.	England, U.K.	Lith.	Lithuania	Oc.	Oceania
Az., U.S.	Arizona, U.S.	Eq. Gui.	Equatorial Guinea	Lux.	Luxembourg	Oh., U.S.	Ohio, U.S.
Azer.	Azerbaijan	Erit.	Eritrea	Ma., U.S.	Massachusetts, U.S.	Ok., U.S.	Oklahoma, U.S.
b.	bay, gulf, inlet, lagoon	*est.*	estuary	Mac.	Macedonia	Ont., Can.	Ontario, Can.
Bah.	Bahamas	Est.	Estonia	Madag.	Madagascar	Or., U.S.	Oregon, U.S.
Bahr.	Bahrain	Eth.	Ethiopia	Malay.	Malaysia	Pa., U.S.	Pennsylvania, U.S.
Barb.	Barbados	Eur.	Europe	Mald.	Maldives	Pak.	Pakistan
B.A.T.	British Antarctic Territory	Faer. Is.	Faeroe Islands	Man., Can.	Manitoba, Can.	Pan.	Panama
		Falk. Is.	Falkland Islands	Marsh. Is.	Marshall Islands	Pap. N. Gui.	Papua New Guinea
B.C., Can.	British Columbia, Can.	Fin.	Finland	Mart.	Martinique	Para.	Paraguay
Bdi.	Burundi	Fl., U.S.	Florida, U.S.	Maur.	Mauritania	P.E.I., Can.	Prince Edward Island, Can.
Bel.	Belgium	*for.*	forest, moor	May.	Mayotte		
Bela.	Belarus	Fr.	France	Md., U.S.	Maryland, U.S.	*pen.*	peninsula
Ber.	Bermuda	Fr. Gu.	French Guiana	Me., U.S.	Maine, U.S.	Phil.	Philippines
Bhu.	Bhutan	Fr. Poly.	French Polynesia	Mex.	Mexico	Pit.	Pitcairn
B.I.O.T.	British Indian Ocean Territory	F.S.A.T.	French Southern and Antarctic Territory	Mi., U.S.	Michigan, U.S.	*pl.*	plain, flat
				Micron.	Federated States of Micronesia	*plat.*	plateau, highland
Bngl.	Bangladesh	Ga., U.S.	Georgia, U.S.			Pol.	Poland
Bol.	Bolivia	Gam.	Gambia	Mid. Is.	Midway Islands	Port.	Portugal
Bos.	Bosnia and Herzegovina	Geor.	Georgia	*mil.*	military installation	P.R.	Puerto Rico
		Ger.	Germany	Mn., U.S.	Minnesota, U.S.	*prov.*	province, region
Bots.	Botswana	Gib.	Gibraltar	Mo., U.S.	Missouri, U.S.	Que., Can.	Quebec, Can.
Braz.	Brazil	Golan Hts.	Golan Heights	Mol.	Moldova	*reg.*	physical region
Bru.	Brunei	Grc.	Greece	Mon.	Monaco	*res.*	reservoir
Br. Vir. Is.	British Virgin Islands	Gren.	Grenada	Mong.	Mongolia	Reu.	Reunion
Bul.	Bulgaria	Grnld.	Greenland	Monts.	Montserrat	*rf.*	reef, shoal
Burkina	Burkina Faso	Guad.	Guadeloupe	Mor.	Morocco	R.I., U.S.	Rhode Island, U.S.
c.	cape, point	Guat.	Guatemala	Moz.	Mozambique	Rom.	Romania
Ca., U.S.	California, U.S.	Gui.	Guinea	Mrts.	Mauritius	Rw.	Rwanda
Cam.	Cameroon	Gui.-B.	Guinea-Bissau	Ms., U.S.	Mississippi, U.S.	S.A.	South America
Camb.	Cambodia	Guy.	Guyana	Mt., U.S.	Montana, U.S.	S. Afr.	South Africa
Can.	Canada	Hi., U.S.	Hawaii, U.S.	*mth.*	river mouth or channel	Sask., Can.	Saskatchewan, Can.
Cay. Is.	Cayman Islands	*hist.*	historic site, ruins	*mtn.*	mountain	Sau. Ar.	Saudi Arabia
Cen. Afr. Rep.	Central African Republic	*hist. reg.*	historic region	*mts.*	mountains	S.C., U.S.	South Carolina, U.S.
		H.K.	Hong Kong	Mwi.	Malawi	*sci.*	scientific station
Christ. I.	Christmas Island	Hond.	Honduras	Mya.	Myanmar	Scot., U.K.	Scotland, U.K.
C. Iv.	Cote d'Ivoire	Hung.	Hungary	N.A.	North America	S.D., U.S.	South Dakota, U.S.
clf.	cliff, escarpment	*i.*	island	N.B., Can.	New Brunswick, Can.	Sen.	Senegal
co.	county, parish	Ia., U.S.	Iowa, U.S.	N.C., U.S.	North Carolina, U.S.	Sey.	Seychelles
Co., U.S.	Colorado, U.S.	Ice.	Iceland	N. Cal.	New Caledonia	Sing.	Singapore
Col.	Colombia	*ice*	ice feature, glacier	N. Cyp.	North Cyprus	S. Kor.	South Korea
Com.	Comoros	Id., U.S.	Idaho, U.S.	N.D., U.S.	North Dakota, U.S.	S.L.	Sierra Leone
cont.	continent	Il., U.S.	Illinois, U.S.	Ne., U.S.	Nebraska, U.S.	Slo.	Slovenia
C.R.	Costa Rica	In., U.S.	Indiana, U.S.	Neth.	Netherlands	Slov.	Slovakia
crat.	crater	Indon.	Indonesia	Neth. Ant.	Netherlands Antilles	S. Mar.	San Marino
Cro.	Croatia	I. of Man	Isle of Man	Newf., Can.	Newfoundland, Can.	Sol. Is.	Solomon Islands
Ct., U.S.	Connecticut, U.S.	Ire.	Ireland	N.H., U.S.	New Hampshire, U.S.	Som.	Somalia

Sp. N. Afr.	Spanish North Africa
Sri L.	Sri Lanka
state	state, republic, canton
St. Hel.	St. Helena
St. K./N	St. Kitts and Nevis
St. Luc.	St. Lucia
stm.	stream (river, creek)
S. Tom./P.	Sao Tome and Principe
St. P./M.	St. Pierre and Miquelon
strt.	strait, channel, sound
St. Vin.	St. Vincent and the Grenadines
Sud.	Sudan
Sur.	Suriname
sw.	swamp, marsh
Swaz.	Swaziland
Swe.	Sweden
Switz.	Switzerland
Tai.	Taiwan
Taj.	Tajikistan
Tan.	Tanzania
T./C. Is.	Turks and Caicos Islands
ter.	territory
Thai.	Thailand
Tn., U.S.	Tennessee, U.S.
Tok.	Tokelau
Trin.	Trinidad and Tobago
Tun.	Tunisia
Tur.	Turkey
Turk.	Turkmenistan
Tx., U.S.	Texas, U.S.
U.A.E.	United Arab Emirates
Ug.	Uganda
U.K.	United Kingdom
Ukr.	Ukraine
Ur.	Uruguay
U.S.	United States
Ut., U.S.	Utah, U.S.
Uzb.	Uzbekistan
Va., U.S.	Virginia, U.S.
val.	valley, watercourse
Vat.	Vatican City
Ven.	Venezuela
Viet.	Vietnam
V.I.U.S.	Virgin Islands (U.S.)
vol.	volcano
Vt., U.S.	Vermont, U.S.
Wa., U.S.	Washington, U.S.
Wal./F.	Wallis and Futuna
W. Bank	West Bank
Wi., U.S.	Wisconsin, U.S.
W. Sah.	Western Sahara
W. Sam.	Western Samoa
wtfl.	waterfall
W.V., U.S.	West Virginia, U.S.
Wy., U.S.	Wyoming, U.S.
Yugo.	Yugoslavia
Yukon, Can.	Yukon Territory, Can.
Zam.	Zambia
Zimb.	Zimbabwe

Index

A

137

Index

Index

Index

World Political Information

This table lists the area, population, population density, form of government, political status, and capital for every country in the world.

The populations are estimates for January 1, 1995 made by Rand McNally on the basis of official data, United Nations estimates, and other available information. Area figures include inland water.

The political units listed in the table are categorized by political status, as follows:

A–independent countries; B–internally independent political entities which are under the protection of other countries in matters of defense and foreign affairs; C–colonies and other dependent political units; D–the major administrative subdivisions of Australia, Canada, China, the United Kingdom, and the United States. For comparison, the table also includes the continents and the world.

All footnotes to this table appear on page 196.

Country, Division or Region English (Conventional)	Area in sq. mi.	Area in sq. km.	Estimated Population 1/1/95	Pop. per sq. mi.	Pop. per sq. km.	Form of Government and Political Status		Capital
† Afghanistan	251,826	652,225	19,715,000	78	30	Islamic republic	A	Kābol (Kabul)
Africa	11,700,000	30,300,000	697,600,000	60	23			
Alabama	52,423	135,775	4,254,000	81	31	State (U.S.)	D	Montgomery
Alaska	656,424	1,700,139	614,000	0.9	0.4	State (U.S.)	D	Juneau
† Albania	11,100	28,748	3,394,000	306	118	Republic	A	Tiranë
Alberta	255,287	661,190	2,632,000	10	4.0	Province (Canada)	D	Edmonton
† Algeria	919,595	2,381,741	27,965,000	30	12	Provisional military government	A	Alger (Algiers)
American Samoa	77	199	56,000	727	281	Unincorporated territory (U.S.)	C	Pago Pago
† Andorra	175	453	59,000	337	130	Parliamentary co-principality (Spanish and French protection)	B	Andorra
† Angola	481,354	1,246,700	10,690,000	22	8.6	Republic	A	Luanda
Anguilla	35	91	7,100	203	78	Dependent territory (U.K. protection)	B	The Valley
Anhui	53,668	139,000	59,490,000	1,108	428	Province (China)	D	Hefei
Antarctica	5,400,000	14,000,000	(1)	—	—			
† Antigua and Barbuda	171	442	67,000	392	152	Parliamentary state	A	St. Johns
† Argentina	1,073,519	2,780,400	34,083,000	32	12	Republic	A	Buenos Aires and Viedma (4)
Arizona	114,006	295,276	4,070,000	36	14	State (U.S.)	D	Phoenix
Arkansas	53,182	137,742	2,468,000	46	18	State (U.S.)	D	Little Rock
† Armenia	11,506	29,800	3,794,000	330	127	Republic	A	Jerevan
Aruba	75	193	67,000	893	347	Self-governing territory (Netherlands protection)	B	Oranjestad
Asia	17,300,000	44,900,000	3,422,700,000	198	76			
† Australia	2,966,155	7,682,300	18,205,000	6.1	2.4	Federal parliamentary state	A	Canberra
Australian Capital Territory	927	2,400	309,000	333	129	Territory (Australia)	D	Canberra
† Austria	32,377	83,856	7,932,000	245	95	Federal republic	A	Wien (Vienna)
† Azerbaijan	33,436	86,600	7,491,000	224	87	Republic	A	Baku
† Bahamas	5,382	13,939	275,000	51	20	Parliamentary state	A	Nassau
† Bahrain	267	691	563,000	2,109	815	Monarchy	A	Al-Manāmah
† Bangladesh	55,598	143,998	119,370,000	2,147	829	Republic	A	Dhaka (Dacca)
† Barbados	166	430	261,000	1,572	607	Parliamentary state	A	Bridgetown
Beijing Shi	6,487	16,800	11,490,000	1,771	684	Autonomous city (China)	D	Beijing (Peking)
† Belarus	80,155	207,600	10,425,000	130	50	Republic	A	Minsk
† Belgium	11,783	30,518	10,075,000	855	330	Constitutional monarchy	A	Bruxelles (Brussels)
† Belize	8,866	22,963	212,000	24	9.2	Parliamentary state	A	Belmopan
† Benin	43,475	112,600	5,433,000	125	48	Republic	A	Porto-Novo and Cotonou
Bermuda	21	54	61,000	2,905	1,130	Dependent territory (U.K.)	C	Hamilton
† Bhutan	17,954	46,500	1,758,000	98	38	Monarchy (Indian protection)	B	Thimphu
† Bolivia	424,165	1,098,581	6,790,000	16	6.2	Republic	A	La Paz and Sucre
† Bosnia and Herzegovina	19,741	51,129	4,481,000	227	88	Republic	A	Sarajevo
† Botswana	224,711	582,000	1,438,000	6.4	2.5	Republic	A	Gaborone
† Brazil	3,286,500	8,511,996	159,690,000	49	19	Federal republic	A	Brasília
British Columbia	365,948	947,800	3,395,000	9.3	3.6	Province (Canada)	D	Victoria
British Indian Ocean Territory	23	60	(1)	—	—	Dependent territory (U.K.)	C	
† Brunei	2,226	5,765	289,000	130	50	Monarchy	A	Bandar Seri Begawan
† Bulgaria	42,855	110,994	8,787,000	205	79	Republic	A	Sofija (Sofia)
† Burkina Faso	105,792	274,000	10,275,000	97	38	Republic	A	Ouagadougou
Burma, see Myanmar	—	—	—	—	—			
† Burundi	10,745	27,830	6,192,000	576	222	Republic	A	Bujumbura
California	163,707	424,002	32,090,000	196	76	State (U.S.)	D	Sacramento
† Cambodia	69,898	181,035	9,713,000	139	54	Constitutional monarchy	A	Phnum Pénh (Phnom Penh)
† Cameroon	183,568	475,440	13,330,000	73	28	Republic	A	Yaoundé
† Canada	3,849,674	9,970,610	28,285,000	7.3	2.8	Federal parliamentary state	A	Ottawa
† Cape Verde	1,557	4,033	429,000	276	106	Republic	A	Praia
Cayman Islands	100	259	33,000	330	127	Dependent territory (U.K.)	C	Georgetown
† Central African Republic	240,535	622,984	3,177,000	13	5.1	Republic	A	Bangui
† Chad	495,755	1,284,000	6,396,000	13	5.0	Republic	A	N'Djamena
† Chile	292,135	756,626	14,050,000	48	19	Republic	A	Santiago
† China (excl. Taiwan)	3,689,631	9,556,100	1,196,980,000	324	125	Socialist republic	A	Beijing (Peking)
Christmas Island	52	135	1,000	19	7.4	External territory (Australia)	C	
Cocos (Keeling) Islands	5.4	14	600	111	43	Territory (Australia)	C	
† Colombia	440,831	1,141,748	34,870,000	79	31	Republic	A	Santa Fe de Bogotá
Colorado	104,100	269,620	3,649,000	35	14	State (U.S.)	D	Denver
† Comoros (excl. Mayotte)	863	2,235	540,000	626	242	Federal Islamic republic	A	Moroni
† Congo	132,047	342,000	2,474,000	19	7.2	Republic	A	Brazzaville
Connecticut	5,544	14,358	3,266,000	589	227	State (U.S.)	D	Hartford
Cook Islands	91	236	19,000	209	81	Self-governing territory (New Zealand protection)	B	Avarua
† Costa Rica	19,730	51,100	3,379,000	171	66	Republic	A	San José
† Cote d'Ivoire	124,518	322,500	14,540,000	117	45	Republic	A	Abidjan and Yamoussoukro (4)
† Croatia	21,829	56,538	4,801,000	220	85	Republic	A	Zagreb
† Cuba	42,804	110,861	11,560,000	270	104	Socialist republic	A	La Habana (Havana)
† Cyprus (excl. North Cyprus)	2,276	5,896	551,000	242	93	Republic	A	Nicosia (Levkosía)
Cyprus, North (2)	1,295	3,355	182,000	141	54	Republic	A	Nicosia (Lefkoşa)
† Czech Republic	30,450	78,864	10,430,000	343	132	Republic	A	Praha (Prague)
Delaware	2,489	6,447	709,000	285	110	State (U.S.)	D	Dover
† Denmark	16,639	43,094	5,207,000	313	121	Constitutional monarchy	A	København (Copenhagen)
District of Columbia	68	177	575,000	8,456	3,249	Federal district (U.S.)	D	Washington
† Djibouti	8,958	23,200	557,000	62	24	Republic	A	Djibouti
† Dominica	305	790	89,000	292	113	Republic	A	Roseau
† Dominican Republic	18,704	48,442	7,896,000	422	163	Republic	A	Santo Domingo
† Ecuador	105,037	272,045	11,015,000	105	40	Republic	A	Quito
† Egypt	386,662	1,001,449	58,100,000	150	58	Socialist republic	A	Al-Qāhirah (Cairo)
† El Salvador	8,124	21,041	5,280,000	650	251	Republic	A	San Salvador
England	50,352	130,410	48,730,000	968	374	Administrative division (U.K.)	D	London
† Equatorial Guinea	10,831	28,051	394,000	36	14	Republic	A	Malabo
† Eritrea	36,170	93,679	3,458,000	96	37	Republic	A	Asmera
† Estonia	17,413	45,100	1,515,000	87	34	Republic	A	Tallinn
† Ethiopia	446,953	1,157,603	55,070,000	123	48	Provisional military government	A	Adis Abeba
Europe	3,800,000	9,900,000	712,100,000	187	72			
Faeroe Islands	540	1,399	49,000	91	35	Self-governing territory (Danish protection)	B	Tórshavn
Falkland Islands (3)	4,700	12,173	2,100	0.4	0.2	Dependent territory (U.K.)	C	Stanley

193

World Political Information

Country, Division or Region English (Conventional)	Area in sq. mi.	Area in sq. km.	Estimated Population 1/1/95	Pop. per sq. mi.	Pop. per sq. km.	Form of Government and Political Status	Capital
† Fiji	7,056	18,274	775,000	110	42	Republic .... A	Suva
† Finland	130,559	338,145	5,098,000	39	15	Republic .... A	Helsinki (Helsingfors)
Florida	65,758	170,313	13,995,000	213	82	State (U.S.) .... D	Tallahassee
† France (excl. Overseas Departments)	211,208	547,026	58,000	275	106	Republic .... A	Paris
French Guiana	35,135	91,000	138,000	3.9	1.5	Overseas department (France) C	Cayenne
French Polynesia	1,359	3,521	217,000	160	62	Overseas territory (France) C	Papeete
Fujian	46,332	120,000	31,720,000	685	264	Province (China) .... D	Fuzhou
† Gabon	103,347	267,667	1,035,000	10	3.9	Republic .... A	Libreville
† Gambia	4,127	10,689	1,082,000	262	101	Provisional military government .... A	Banjul
Gansu	173,746	450,000	23,700,000	136	53	Province (China) .... D	Lanzhou
Gaza Strip	146	378	774,000	5,301	2,048	Israeli territory with limited self-government	
Georgia	59,441	153,953	7,065,000	119	46	State (U.S.) .... D	Atlanta
† Georgia	26,911	69,700	5,704,000	212	82	Republic .... A	Tbilisi
† Germany	137,822	356,955	81,710,000	593	229	Federal republic .... A	Berlin and Bonn
† Ghana	92,098	238,533	17,210,000	187	72	Republic .... A	Accra
Gibraltar	2.3	6.0	32,000	13,913	5,333	Dependent territory (U.K.) C	Gibraltar
Golan Heights	454	1,176	29,000	64	25	Occupied by Israel	
† Greece	50,949	131,957	10,475,000	206	79	Republic .... A	Athínai (Athens)
Greenland	840,004	2,175,600	57,000	0.1	—	Self-governing territory (Danish protection) ...... B	Godthåb (Nuuk)
† Grenada	133	344	92,000	692	267	Parliamentary state .... A	St. George's
Guadeloupe (incl. Dependencies)	687	1,780	432,000	629	243	Overseas department (France) C	Basse-Terre
Guam	209	541	152,000	727	281	Unincorporated territory (U.S.) C	Agana
Guangdong	68,726	178,000	66,550,000	968	374	Province (China) .... D	Guangzhou (Canton)
† Guatemala	42,042	108,889	10,420,000	248	96	Republic .... A	Guatemala
Guernsey (incl. Dependencies)	30	78	64,000	2,133	821	Crown dependency (U.K. protection) .... B	St. Peter Port
† Guinea	94,926	245,857	6,469,000	68	26	Provisional military government .... A	Conakry
† Guinea-Bissau	13,948	36,125	1,111,000	80	31	Republic .... A	Bissau
Guizhou	65,637	170,000	34,355,000	523	202	Province (China) .... D	Guiyang
† Guyana	83,000	214,969	726,000	8.7	3.4	Republic .... A	Georgetown
Hainan	13,127	34,000	6,945,000	529	204	Province (China) .... D	Haikou
† Haiti	10,714	27,750	7,069,000	660	255	Provisional military government .... A	Port-au-Prince
Hawaii	10,932	28,313	1,181,000	108	42	State (U.S.) .... D	Honolulu
Hebei	73,359	190,000	64,640,000	881	340	Province (China) .... D	Shijiazhuang
Heilongjiang	181,082	469,000	37,345,000	206	80	Province (China) .... D	Harbin
Henan	64,479	167,000	90,495,000	1,403	542	Province (China) .... D	Zhengzhou
† Honduras	43,277	112,088	5,822,000	135	52	Republic .... A	Tegucigalpa
Hong Kong	414	1,072	5,927,000	14,316	5,529	Chinese territory under British administration ... C	Victoria (Xianggang)
Hubei	72,356	187,400	57,100,000	789	305	Province (China) .... D	Wuhan
Hunan	81,081	210,000	64,280,000	793	306	Province (China) .... D	Changsha
† Hungary	35,919	93,030	10,270,000	286	110	Republic .... A	Budapest
† Iceland	39,769	103,000	265,000	6.7	2.6	Republic .... A	Reykjavík
Idaho	83,574	216,456	1,129,000	14	5.2	State (U.S.) .... D	Boise
Illinois	57,918	150,007	11,870,000	205	79	State (U.S.) .... D	Springfield
† India (incl. part of Jammu and Kashmir)	1,237,062	3,203,975	909,150,000	735	284	Federal republic .... A	New Delhi
Indiana	36,420	94,328	5,805,000	159	62	State (U.S.) .... D	Indianapolis
† Indonesia	752,410	1,948,732	193,680,000	257	99	Republic .... A	Jakarta
Inner Mongolia (Nei Mongol Zizhiqu)	456,759	1,183,000	22,745,000	50	19	Autonomous region (China) .... D	Hohhot
Iowa	56,276	145,754	2,862,000	51	20	State (U.S.) .... D	Des Moines
† Iran	632,457	1,638,057	63,810,000	101	39	Islamic republic .... A	Tehrān
† Iraq	169,235	438,317	20,250,000	120	46	Republic .... A	Baghdād
† Ireland	27,137	70,285	3,546,000	131	50	Republic .... A	Dublin (Baile Átha Cliath)
Isle of Man	221	572	72,000	326	126	Crown dependency (U.K. protection) .... B	Douglas
† Israel	8,019	20,770	5,059,000	631	244	Republic .... A	Yerushalayim (Jerusalem)
† Italy	116,324	301,277	57,330,000	493	190	Republic .... A	Roma (Rome)
† Jamaica	4,244	10,991	2,568,000	605	234	Parliamentary state .... A	Kingston
† Japan	145,870	377,801	125,360,000	859	332	Constitutional monarchy .... A	Tōkyō
Jersey	45	116	86,000	1,911	741	Crown dependency (U.K. protection) .... B	St. Helier
Jiangsu	39,614	102,600	70,980,000	1,792	692	Province (China) .... D	Nanjing
Jiangxi	64,325	166,600	39,980,000	622	240	Province (China) .... D	Nanchang
Jilin	72,201	187,000	26,095,000	361	140	Province (China) .... D	Changchun
† Jordan	35,135	91,000	4,028,000	115	44	Constitutional monarchy .... A	'Ammān
Kansas	82,282	213,110	2,575,000	31	12	State (U.S.) .... D	Topeka
† Kazakhstan	1,049,156	2,717,300	17,025,000	16	6.3	Republic .... A	Alma-Ata and Akmola (4)
Kentucky	40,411	104,665	3,835,000	95	37	State (U.S.) .... D	Frankfort
† Kenya	224,961	582,646	28,380,000	126	49	Republic .... A	Nairobi
† Kiribati	313	811	79,000	252	97	Republic .... A	Bairiki
† Korea, North	46,540	120,538	23,265,000	500	193	Socialist republic .... A	P'yŏngyang
† Korea, South	38,230	99,016	44,655,000	1,168	451	Republic .... A	Sŏul (Seoul)
† Kuwait	6,880	17,818	1,866,000	271	105	Constitutional monarchy .... A	Al-Kuwayt (Kuwait)
Kwangsi Chuang (Guangxi Zhuang Zizhiqu)	91,236	236,300	44,765,000	491	189	Autonomous region (China) .... D	Nanning
† Kyrgyzstan	76,641	198,500	4,541,000	59	23	Republic .... A	Biškek
† Laos	91,429	236,800	4,768,000	52	20	Socialist republic .... A	Viangchan (Vientiane)
† Latvia	24,595	63,700	2,532,000	103	40	Republic .... A	Rīga
† Lebanon	4,015	10,400	3,660,000	912	352	Republic .... A	Bayrūt (Beirut)
† Lesotho	11,720	30,355	1,967,000	168	65	Constitutional monarchy under military rule ...... A	Maseru
Liaoning	56,255	145,700	41,775,000	743	287	Province (China) .... D	Shenyang (Mukden)
† Liberia	38,250	99,067	2,771,000	72	28	Republic .... A	Monrovia
† Libya	679,362	1,759,540	5,148,000	7.6	2.9	Socialist republic .... A	Tarābulus (Tripoli)
† Liechtenstein	62	160	30,000	484	188	Constitutional monarchy .... A	Vaduz
† Lithuania	25,212	65,300	3,757,000	149	58	Republic .... A	Vilnius
Louisiana	51,843	134,275	4,360,000	84	32	State (U.S.) .... D	Baton Rouge
† Luxembourg	998	2,586	396,000	397	153	Constitutional monarchy .... A	Luxembourg
Macau	7.0	18	396,000	56,571	22,000	Chinese territory under Portuguese administration C	Macau
† Macedonia	9,928	25,713	2,102,000	212	82	Republic .... A	Skopje
† Madagascar	226,658	587,041	13,645,000	60	23	Republic .... A	Antananarivo
Maine	35,387	91,653	1,260,000	36	14	State (U.S.) .... D	Augusta
† Malawi	45,747	118,484	8,984,000	196	76	Republic .... A	Lilongwe
† Malaysia	127,320	329,758	19,505,000	153	59	Federal constitutional monarchy .... A	Kuala Lumpur
† Maldives	115	298	251,000	2,183	842	Republic .... A	Male
† Mali	482,077	1,248,574	9,585,000	20	7.7	Republic .... A	Bamako
† Malta	122	316	368,000	3,016	1,165	Republic .... A	Valletta
Manitoba	250,947	649,950	1,131,000	4.5	1.7	Province (Canada) .... D	Winnipeg
† Marshall Islands	70	181	55,000	786	304	Republic (U.S. protection) .... A	Majuro (island)

Country, Division or Region English (Conventional)	Area in sq. mi.	Area in sq. km.	Estimated Population 1/1/95	Pop. per sq. mi.	Pop. per sq. km.	Form of Government and Political Status		Capital
Martinique	425	1,100	384,000	904	349	Overseas department (France)	C	Fort-de-France
Maryland	12,407	32,135	5,045,000	407	157	State (U.S.)	D	Annapolis
Massachusetts	10,555	27,337	6,117,000	580	224	State (U.S.)	D	Boston
† Mauritania	395,956	1,025,520	2,228,000	5.6	2.2	Republic	A	Nouakchott
† Mauritius (incl. Dependencies)	788	2,040	1,121,000	1,423	550	Republic	A	Port Louis
Mayotte (5)	144	374	95,000	660	254	Territorial collectivity (France)	C	Dzaoudzi and Mamoudzou (4)
† Mexico	759,534	1,967,183	93,860,000	124	48	Federal republic	A	Ciudad de México (Mexico City)
Michigan	96,810	250,738	9,615,000	99	38	State (U.S.)	D	Lansing
† Micronesia, Federated States of	271	702	122,000	450	174	Republic (U.S. protection)	A	Kolonia and Paliker (4)
Midway Islands	2.0	5.2	500	250	96	Unincorporated territory (U.S.)	C	....
Minnesota	86,943	225,182	4,595,000	53	20	State (U.S.)	D	St. Paul
Mississippi	48,434	125,443	2,678,000	55	21	State (U.S.)	D	Jackson
Missouri	69,709	180,546	5,330,000	76	30	State (U.S.)	D	Jefferson City
† Moldova	13,012	33,700	4,377,000	336	130	Republic	A	Chișinău (Kishinev)
† Monaco	0.7	1.9	31,000	44,286	16,316	Constitutional monarchy	A	Monaco
† Mongolia	604,829	1,566,500	2,462,000	4.1	1.6	Republic	A	Ulaanbaatar (Ulan Bator)
Montana	147,046	380,850	840,000	5.7	2.2	State (U.S.)	D	Helena
Montserrat	39	102	13,000	333	127	Dependent territory (U.K.)	C	Plymouth
† Morocco (excl. Western Sahara)	172,414	446,550	26,890,000	156	60	Constitutional monarchy	A	Rabat
† Mozambique	308,642	799,380	17,860,000	58	22	Republic	A	Maputo
† Myanmar	261,228	676,577	44,675,000	171	66	Provisional military government	A	Yangon (Rangoon)
† Namibia	318,253	824,272	1,623,000	5.1	2.0	Republic	A	Windhoek
Nauru	8.1	21	10,000	1,235	476	Republic	A	Yaren District
Nebraska	77,358	200,358	1,628,000	21	8.1	State (U.S.)	D	Lincoln
† Nepal	56,827	147,181	21,295,000	375	145	Constitutional monarchy	A	Kātmāndau (Kathmandu)
† Netherlands	16,164	41,864	15,425,000	954	368	Constitutional monarchy	A	Amsterdam and 's-Gravenhage (The Hague)
Netherlands Antilles	309	800	187,000	605	234	Self-governing territory (Netherlands protection)	B	Willemstad
Nevada	110,567	286,368	1,444,000	13	5.0	State (U.S.)	D	Carson City
New Brunswick	28,355	73,440	764,000	27	10	Province (Canada)	D	Fredericton
New Caledonia	7,358	19,058	183,000	25	9.6	Overseas territory (France)	C	Nouméa
Newfoundland	156,649	405,720	594,000	3.8	1.5	Province (Canada)	D	St. John's
New Hampshire	9,351	24,219	1,100,000	118	45	State (U.S.)	D	Concord
New Jersey	8,722	22,590	7,985,000	916	353	State (U.S.)	D	Trenton
New Mexico	121,598	314,939	1,655,000	14	5.3	State (U.S.)	D	Santa Fe
New South Wales	309,500	801,600	6,171,000	20	7.7	State (Australia)	D	Sydney
New York	54,475	141,089	18,460,000	339	131	State (U.S.)	D	Albany
† New Zealand	104,454	270,534	3,558,000	34	13	Parliamentary state	A	Wellington
† Nicaragua	50,054	129,640	4,438,000	89	34	Republic	A	Managua
† Niger	489,191	1,267,000	9,125,000	19	7.2	Provisional military government	A	Niamey
† Nigeria	356,669	923,768	97,300,000	273	105	Provisional military government	A	Lagos and Abuja
Ningsia Hui (Ningxia Huizu Zizhiqu)	25,637	66,400	4,908,000	191	74	Autonomous region (China)	D	Yinchuan
Niue	100	259	1,900	19	7.3	Self-governing territory (New Zealand protection)	B	Alofi
Norfolk Island	14	36	2,700	193	75	External territory (Australia)	C	Kingston
North America	9,500,000	24,700,000	453,300,000	48	18	....		....
North Carolina	53,821	139,397	7,065,000	131	51	State (U.S.)	D	Raleigh
North Dakota	70,704	183,123	656,000	9.3	3.6	State (U.S.)	D	Bismarck
Northern Ireland	5,461	14,144	1,636,000	300	116	Administrative division (U.K.)	D	Belfast
Northern Mariana Islands	184	477	51,000	277	107	Commonwealth (U.S. protection)	B	Saipan (island)
Northern Territory	519,771	1,346,200	182,000	0.4	0.1	Territory (Australia)	D	Darwin
Northwest Territories	1,322,910	3,426,320	57,000	—	—	Territory (Canada)	D	Yellowknife
† Norway (incl. Svalbard and Jan Mayen)	149,412	386,975	4,339,000	29	11	Constitutional monarchy	A	Oslo
Nova Scotia	21,425	55,490	933,000	44	17	Province (Canada)	D	Halifax
Oceania (incl. Australia)	3,300,000	8,500,000	28,400,000	8.6	3.3	....		....
Ohio	44,828	116,103	11,270,000	251	97	State (U.S.)	D	Columbus
Oklahoma	69,903	181,049	3,282,000	47	18	State (U.S.)	D	Oklahoma City
† Oman	82,030	212,457	2,089,000	25	9.8	Monarchy	A	Masqaṭ (Muscat)
Ontario	412,581	1,068,580	10,435,000	25	9.8	Province (Canada)	D	Toronto
Oregon	98,386	254,819	3,098,000	31	12	State (U.S.)	D	Salem
† Pakistan (incl. part of Jammu and Kashmir)	339,732	879,902	129,630,000	382	147	Federal Islamic republic	A	Islāmābād
† Palau (Belau)	196	508	17,000	87	33	Republic	A	Koror and Melekeok (4)
† Panama	29,157	75,517	2,654,000	91	35	Republic	A	Panamá
† Papua New Guinea	178,704	462,840	4,057,000	23	8.8	Parliamentary state	A	Port Moresby
† Paraguay	157,048	406,752	4,400,000	28	11	Republic	A	Asunción
Pennsylvania	46,058	119,291	12,215,000	265	102	State (U.S.)	D	Harrisburg
† Peru	496,225	1,285,216	23,095,000	47	18	Republic	A	Lima
† Philippines	115,831	300,000	67,910,000	586	226	Republic	A	Manila
Pitcairn (incl. Dependencies)	19	49	100	5.3	2.0	Dependent territory (U.K.)	C	Adamstown
† Poland	121,196	313,895	38,730,000	320	123	Republic	A	Warszawa (Warsaw)
† Portugal	35,516	91,985	9,907,000	279	108	Republic	A	Lisboa (Lisbon)
Prince Edward Island	2,185	5,660	141,000	65	25	Province (Canada)	D	Charlottetown
Puerto Rico	3,515	9,104	3,625,000	1,031	398	Commonwealth (U.S. protection)	B	San Juan
† Qatar	4,412	11,427	519,000	118	45	Monarchy	A	Ad-Dawḥah (Doha)
Qinghai	277,994	720,000	4,670,000	17	6.5	Province (China)	D	Xining
Quebec	594,860	1,540,680	7,157,000	12	4.6	Province (Canada)	D	Québec
Queensland	666,876	1,727,200	3,259,000	4.9	1.9	State (Australia)	D	Brisbane
Reunion	969	2,510	660,000	681	263	Overseas department (France)	C	Saint-Denis
Rhode Island	1,545	4,002	1,024,000	663	256	State (U.S.)	D	Providence
† Romania	91,699	237,500	22,745,000	248	96	Republic	A	București (Bucharest)
† Russia	6,592,849	17,075,400	150,500,000	23	8.8	Federal republic	A	Moskva (Moscow)
† Rwanda	10,169	26,338	7,343,000	722	279	Republic	A	Kigali
St. Helena (incl. Dependencies)	121	314	7,000	58	22	Dependent territory (U.K.)	C	Jamestown
† St. Kitts and Nevis	104	269	42,000	404	156	Parliamentary state	A	Basseterre
† St. Lucia	238	616	138,000	580	224	Parliamentary state	A	Castries
St. Pierre and Miquelon	93	242	6,700	72	28	Territorial collectivity (France)	C	Saint-Pierre
† St. Vincent and the Grenadines	150	388	110,000	733	284	Parliamentary state	A	Kingstown
† San Marino	24	61	24,000	1,000	393	Republic	A	San Marino
† Sao Tome and Principe	372	964	127,000	341	132	Republic	A	São Tomé
Saskatchewan	251,866	652,330	1,018,000	4.0	1.6	Province (Canada)	D	Regina
† Saudi Arabia	830,000	2,149,690	18,190,000	22	8.5	Monarchy	A	Ar-Riyāḍ (Riyadh)
Scotland	30,421	78,789	5,142,000	169	65	Administrative division (U.K.)	D	Edinburgh
† Senegal	75,951	196,712	8,862,000	117	45	Republic	A	Dakar
† Serbia	34,116	88,361	10,095,000	296	114	Republic (Yugoslavia)	D	Beograd (Belgrade)
† Seychelles	175	453	75,000	429	166	Republic	A	Victoria

195

Country, Division or Region English (Conventional)	Area in sq. mi.	Area in sq. km.	Estimated Population 1/1/95	Pop. per sq. mi.	Pop. per sq. km.	Form of Government and Political Status	Capital
Shandŏng	59,074	153,000	89,400,000	1,513	584	Province (China) ...... D	Jinan
Shanghai Shi	2,394	6,200	14,125,000	5,900	2,278	Autonomous city (China) ...... D	Shanghai
Shansi (Shānxī)	60,232	156,000	30,405,000	505	195	Province (China) ...... D	Taiyuan
Shensi (Shǎnxī)	79,151	205,000	34,830,000	440	170	Province (China) ...... D	Xi'an (Sian)
Sichuan	220,078	570,000	113,470,000	516	199	Province (China) ...... D	Chengdu
† Sierra Leone	27,925	72,325	4,690,000	168	65	Transitional military government ...... A	Freetown
† Singapore	246	636	2,921,000	11,874	4,593	Republic ...... A	Singapore
Sinkiang (Xinjiang Uygur Zizhiqu)	617,764	1,600,000	16,040,000	26	10	Autonomous region (China) ...... D	Ürümqi
† Slovakia	18,933	49,035	5,353,000	283	109	Republic ...... A	Bratislava
† Slovenia	7,820	20,253	1,993,000	255	98	Republic ...... A	Ljubljana
† Solomon Islands	10,954	28,370	393,000	36	14	Parliamentary state ...... A	Honiara
† Somalia	246,201	637,657	7,187,000	29	11	None ...... A	Muqdisho (Mogadishu)
† South Africa	471,010	1,219,909	44,500,000	94	36	Republic ...... A	Pretoria, Cape Town, and Bloemfontein
South America	6,900,000	17,800,000	313,900,000	45	18		
South Australia	379,925	984,000	1,493,000	3.9	1.5	State (Australia) ...... D	Adelaide
South Carolina	32,007	82,898	3,702,000	116	45	State (U.S.) ...... D	Columbia
South Dakota	77,121	199,745	735,000	9.5	3.7	State (U.S.) ...... D	Pierre
South Georgia (incl. Dependencies)	1,450	3,755	(1)	—	—	Dependent territory (U.K.) C	
† Spain	194,885	504,750	39,260,000	201	78	Constitutional monarchy ...... A	Madrid
Spanish North Africa [6]	12	32	146,000	12,167	4,563	Five possessions (Spain) C	
† Sri Lanka	24,962	64,652	18,240,000	731	282	Socialist republic ...... A	Colombo and Kotte
† Sudan	967,500	2,505,813	25,840,000	27	10	Provisional military government ...... A	Al-Khartūm (Khartoum)
† Suriname	63,251	163,820	426,000	6.7	2.6	Republic ...... A	Paramaribo
† Swaziland	6,704	17,364	889,000	133	51	Monarchy ...... A	Mbabane and Lobamba
† Sweden	173,732	449,964	8,981,000	52	20	Constitutional monarchy ...... A	Stockholm
Switzerland	15,943	41,293	7,244,000	454	175	Federal republic ...... A	Bern (Berne)
† Syria	71,498	185,180	14,100,000	197	76	Socialist republic ...... A	Dimashq (Damascus)
Taiwan	13,900	36,002	21,150,000	1,522	587	Republic ...... A	T'aipei
† Tajikistan	55,251	143,100	6,073,000	110	42	Republic ...... A	Dušanbe
† Tanzania	341,217	883,749	28,350,000	83	32	Republic ...... A	Dar es Salaam and Dodoma
Tasmania	26,178	67,800	492,000	19	7.3	State (Australia) ...... D	Hobart
Tennessee	42,146	109,158	5,175,000	123	47	State (U.S.) ...... D	Nashville
Texas	268,601	695,676	18,330,000	68	26	State (U.S.) ...... D	Austin
† Thailand	198,115	513,115	59,870,000	302	117	Constitutional monarchy ...... A	Krung Thep (Bangkok)
Tianjin Shi	4,363	11,300	9,337,000	2,140	826	Autonomous city (China) ...... D	Tianjin (Tientsin)
Tibet (Xizang Zizhiqu)	471,045	1,220,000	2,275,000	4.8	1.9	Autonomous region (China) ...... D	Lhasa
† Togo	21,925	56,785	4,332,000	198	76	Provisional military government ...... A	Lomé
Tokelau Islands	4.6	12	1,500	326	125	Island territory (New Zealand) C	
Tonga	288	747	110,000	382	147	Constitutional monarchy ...... A	Nuku'alofa
† Trinidad and Tobago	1,980	5,128	1,281,000	647	250	Republic ...... A	Port of Spain
† Tunisia	63,170	163,610	8,806,000	139	54	Republic ...... A	Tunis
† Turkey	300,948	779,452	62,030,000	206	80	Republic ...... A	Ankara
† Turkmenistan	188,456	488,100	4,035,000	21	8.3	Republic ...... A	Aschabad
Turks and Caicos Islands	193	500	14,000	73	28	Dependent territory (U.K.) C	Grand Turk
Tuvalu	10	26	10,000	1,000	385	Parliamentary state ...... A	Funafuti
† Uganda	93,104	241,139	18,270,000	196	76	Republic ...... A	Kampala
† Ukraine	233,090	603,700	52,140,000	224	86	Republic ...... A	Kyyiv (Kiev)
† United Arab Emirates	32,278	83,660	2,855,000	88	34	Federation of monarchs ...... A	Abū Zaby (Abu Dhabi)
† United Kingdom	94,249	244,101	58,430,000	620	239	Parliamentary monarchy ...... A	London
† United States	3,787,425	9,809,431	262,530,000	69	27	Federal republic ...... A	Washington
† Uruguay	68,500	177,414	3,317,000	48	19	Republic ...... A	Montevideo
Utah	84,904	219,902	1,890,000	22	8.6	State (U.S.) ...... D	Salt Lake City
† Uzbekistan	172,742	447,400	22,860,000	132	51	Republic ...... A	Taškent
† Vanuatu	4,707	12,190	161,000	34	13	Republic ...... A	Port Vila
Vatican City	0.2	0.4	1,000	5,000	2,500	Monarchical-sacerdotal state ...... A	Città del Vaticano (Vatican City)
† Venezuela	352,145	912,050	21,395,000	61	23	Federal republic ...... A	Caracas
Vermont	9,615	24,903	578,000	60	23	State (U.S.) ...... D	Montpelier
Victoria	87,877	227,600	4,570,000	52	20	State (Australia) ...... D	Melbourne
† Vietnam	127,428	330,036	73,760,000	579	223	Socialist republic ...... A	Ha Noi
Virginia	42,769	110,771	6,595,000	154	60	State (U.S.) ...... D	Richmond
Virgin Islands (U.S.)	133	344	97,000	729	282	Unincorporated territory (U.S.) C	Charlotte Amalie
Virgin Islands, British	59	153	13,000	220	85	Dependent territory (U.K.) C	Road Town
Wake Island	3.0	7.8	300	100	38	Unincorporated territory (U.S.) C	
Wales	8,015	20,758	2,922,000	365	141	Administrative division (U.K.) ...... D	Cardiff
Wallis and Futuna	98	255	14,000	143	55	Overseas territory (France) ...... D	Mata-Utu
Washington	71,303	184,674	5,360,000	75	29	State (U.S.) ...... D	Olympia
West Bank (incl. East Jerusalem and Jericho)	2,347	6,078	1,717,000	732	282	Israeli territory with limited self-government	
Western Australia	975,101	2,525,500	1,729,000	1.8	0.7	State (Australia) ...... D	Perth
Western Sahara	102,703	266,000	215,000	2.1	0.8	Occupied by Morocco C	
† Western Samoa	1,093	2,831	172,000	157	61	Constitutional monarchy ...... A	Apia
West Virginia	24,231	62,759	1,838,000	76	29	State (U.S.) ...... D	Charleston
Wisconsin	65,503	169,653	5,120,000	78	30	State (U.S.) ...... D	Madison
Wyoming	97,818	253,349	473,000	4.8	1.9	State (U.S.) ...... D	Cheyenne
† Yemen	203,850	527,968	12,910,000	63	24	Republic ...... A	Ṣan'ā'
Yugoslavia	39,449	102,173	10,765,000	273	105	Republic ...... A	Beograd (Belgrade)
Yukon Territory	186,661	483,450	28,000	0.2	0.1	Territory (Canada) ...... D	Whitehorse
Yunnan	152,124	394,000	39,140,000	257	99	Province (China) ...... D	Kunming
† Zaire	905,355	2,344,858	43,365,000	48	18	Republic ...... A	Kinshasa
† Zambia	290,587	752,618	8,809,000	30	12	Republic ...... A	Lusaka
Zhejiang	39,305	101,800	43,930,000	1,118	432	Province (China) ...... D	Hangzhou
† Zimbabwe	150,872	390,757	11,075,000	73	28	Republic ...... A	Harare
WORLD	57,900,000	150,100,000	5,628,000,000	97	37		

† Member of the United Nations (1993).
(1) No permanent population.
(2) North Cyprus unilaterally declared its independence from Cyprus in 1983.
(3) Claimed by Argentina.
(4) Future capital.
(5) Claimed by Comoros.
(6) Comprises Ceuta, Melilla, and several small islands.

World Geographical Information

General

MOVEMENTS OF THE EARTH
The earth makes one complete revolution around the sun every 365 days, 5 hours, 48 minutes, and 46 seconds.

The earth makes one complete rotation on its axis in 23 hours, 56 minutes and 4 seconds.

The earth revolves in its orbit around the sun at a speed of 66,700 miles per hour (107,343 kilometers per hour).

The earth rotates on its axis at an equatorial speed of more than 1,000 miles per hour (1,600 kilometers per hour).

MEASUREMENTS OF THE EARTH
Estimated age of the earth, at least 4.6 billion years.

Equatorial diameter of the earth, 7,926.38 miles (12,756.27 kilometers).

Polar diameter of the earth, 7,899.80 miles (12,713.50 kilometers).

Mean diameter of the earth, 7,917.52 miles (12,742.01 kilometers).

Equatorial circumference of the earth, 24,901.46 miles (40,075.02 kilometers).

Polar circumference of the earth, 24,855.34 miles (40,000.79 kilometers).

Difference between equatorial and polar circumferences of the earth, 46.12 miles (74.23 kilometers).

Weight of the earth, 6,600,000,000,000,000,000,000 tons, or 6,600 billion billion tons (6,000 billion billion metric tons).

THE EARTH'S SURFACE
Total area of the earth, 197,000,000 square miles (510,000,000 square kilometers).

Total land area of the earth (including inland water and Antarctica), 57,900,000 square miles (150,100,000 square kilometers).

Highest point on the earth's surface, Mt. Everest, Asia, 29,028 feet (8,848 meters).

Lowest point on the earth's land surface, shores of the Dead Sea, Asia, 1,299 feet (396 meters) below sea level.

Greatest known depth of the ocean, the Mariana Trench, southwest of Guam, Pacific Ocean, 35,810 feet (10,915 meters).

THE EARTH'S INHABITANTS
Population of the earth is estimated to be 5,477,000,000 (January 1, 1993).

Estimated population density of the earth, 95 per square mile (36 per square kilometer).

EXTREMES OF TEMPERATURE AND RAINFALL OF THE EARTH
Highest temperature ever recorded, 136° F. (58° C.) at Al-'Azīzīyah, Libya, Africa, on September 13, 1922.

Lowest temperature ever recorded, -129° F. (-89° C.) at Vostok, Antarctica on July 21, 1983.

Highest mean annual temperature, 94° F. (34° C.) at Dallol, Ethiopia.

Lowest mean annual temperature, -70° F. (-50° C.) at Plateau Station, Antarctica.

The greatest local average annual rainfall is at Mt. Waialeale, Kauai, Hawaii, 460 inches (11,680 millimeters).

The greatest 24-hour rainfall, 74 inches (1,880 millimeters), is at Cilaos, Reunion Island, March 15-16, 1952.

The lowest local average annual rainfall is at Arica, Chile, .03 inches (8 millimeters).

The longest dry period, over 14 years, is at Arica, Chile, October 1903 to January 1918.

The Continents

CONTINENT	Area (sq. mi.) (sq. km.)	Estimated Population Jan. 1, 1993	Population per sq. mi. (sq. km.)	Mean Elevation (feet) (M.)	Highest Elevation (feet) (m.)	Lowest Elevation (feet) (m.)	Highest Recorded Temperature	Lowest Recorded Temperature
North America	9,500,000 (24,700,000)	438,200,000	46 (18)	2,000 (610)	Mt. McKinley, Alaska, United States 20,320 (6,194)	Death Valley, California, United States 282 (84) below sea level	Death Valley, California 134° F (57° C)	Northice, Greenland -87° F (-66° C)
South America	6,900,000 (17,800,000)	310,700,000	45 (17)	1,800 (550)	Cerro Aconcagua, Argentina 22,831 (6,959)	Salinas Chicas, Argentina 138 (42) below sea level	Rivadavia, Argentina 120° F (49° C)	Sarmiento, Argentina -27° F (-33° C)
Europe	3,800,000 (9,900,000)	694,700,000	183 (70)	980 (300)	Gora El'brus, Russia 18,510 (5,642)	Caspian Sea, Asia-Europe 92 (28) below sea level	Sevilla, Spain 122° F (50° C)	Ust' Ščugor, Russia -67° F (-55° C)
Asia	17,300,000 (44,900,000)	3,337,800,000	193 (74)	3,000 (910)	Mt. Everest, China-Nepal 29,028 (8,848)	Dead Sea, Israel-Jordan 1,299 (396) below sea level	Tirat Zevi, Israel 129° F (54° C)	Ojm'akon and Verchojansk, Russia -90° F (-68° C)
Africa	11,700,000 (30,300,000)	668,700,000	57 (22)	1,900 (580)	Kilimanjaro, Tanzania 19,340 (5,895)	Lac Assal, Djibouti 502 (153) below sea level	Al-'Azīzīyah, Libya 136° F (58° C)	Ifrane, Morocco -11° F (-24° C)
Oceania, incl. Australia	3,300,000 (8,500,000)	26,700,000	8.1 (3.1)	....	Mt. Wilhelm, Papua New Guinea 14,793 (4,509)	Lake Eyre, South Australia 52 (16) below sea level	Cloncurry, Queensland, Australia 128° F (53° C)	Charlotte Pass, New South Wales, Australia -8° F (-22° C)
Australia	2,966,155 (7,682,300)	16,965,000	5.7 (2.2)	1,000 (300)	Mt. Kosciusko, New South Wales 7,316 (2,230)	Lake Eyre, South Australia 52 (16) below sea level	Cloncurry, Queensland 128° F (53° C)	Charlotte Pass, New South Wales -8° F (-22° C)
Antarctica	5,400,000 (14,000,000)	....	....	6,000 (1830)	Vinson Massif 16,066 (4,897)	sea level	Vanda Station 59° F (15° C)	Vostok -129° F (-89° C)
World	57,900,000 (150,100,000)	5,477,000,000	95 (36)	....	Mt. Everest, China-Nepal 29,028 (8,848)	Dead Sea, Israel-Jordan 1,299 (396) below sea level	Al-'Azīzīyah, Libya 136° F (58° C)	Vostok, Antarctica -129° F (-89° C)

Historical Populations *

AREA	1650	1750	1800	1850	1900	1920	1950	1970	1980	1990
North America	5,000,000	5,000,000	13,000,000	39,000,000	106,000,000	147,000,000	219,000,000	316,600,000	365,000,000	423,600,000
South America	8,000,000	7,000,000	12,000,000	20,000,000	38,000,000	61,000,000	111,000,000	187,400,000	239,000,000	293,700,000
Europe	100,000,000	140,000,000	190,000,000	265,000,000	400,000,000	453,000,000	530,000,000	623,700,000	660,300,000	688,000,000
Asia	335,000,000	476,000,000	593,000,000	754,000,000	932,000,000	1,000,000,000	1,418,000,000	2,086,200,000	2,581,000,000	3,156,100,000
Africa	100,000,000	95,000,000	90,000,000	95,000,000	118,000,000	140,000,000	199,000,000	346,900,000	463,800,000	648,300,000
Oceania, incl. Australia	2,000,000	2,000,000	2,000,000	2,000,000	6,000,000	9,000,000	13,000,000	19,200,000	22,700,000	26,300,000
Australia	*	*	*	*	4,000,000	6,000,000	8,000,000	12,460,000	14,510,000	16,950,000
World	550,000,000	725,000,000	900,000,000	1,175,000,000	1,600,000,000	1,810,000,000	2,490,000,000	3,580,000,000	4,332,000,000	5,236,000,000

* Figures prior to 1970 are rounded to the nearest million.   Figures in italics represent very rough estimates.

Largest Countries : Population

		Population 1/1/93				Population 1/1/93
1	China	1,179,030,000	16	Turkey		58,620,000
2	India	873,850,000	17	Thailand		58,030,000
3	United States	256,420,000	18	United Kingdom		57,890,000
4	Indonesia	186,180,000	19	France		57,570,000
5	Brazil	159,630,000	20	Egypt		57,050,000
6	Russia	150,500,000	21	Italy		56,550,000
7	Japan	124,710,000	22	Ukraine		51,990,000
8	Pakistan	123,490,000	23	Ethiopia		51,715,000
9	Bangladesh	120,850,000	24	South Korea		43,660,000
10	Nigeria	91,700,000	25	Myanmar		43,070,000
11	Mexico	86,170,000	26	Zaire		39,750,000
12	Germany	80,590,000	27	Spain		39,155,000
13	Vietnam	69,650,000	28	Poland		38,330,000
14	Philippines	65,500,000	29	Colombia		34,640,000
15	Iran	60,500,000	30	South Africa		33,017,000

Largest Countries : Area

		Area (sq. mi.)	Area (sq. km.)			Area (sq. mi.)	Area (sq. km.)
1	Russia	6,592,849	17,075,400	16	Indonesia	752,410	1,948,732
2	Canada	3,849,674	9,970,610	17	Libya	679,362	1,759,540
3	United States	3,787,425	9,809,431	18	Iran	632,457	1,638,057
4	China	3,689,631	9,556,100	19	Mongolia	604,829	1,566,500
5	Brazil	3,286,500	8,511,996	20	Peru	496,225	1,285,216
6	Australia	2,966,155	7,682,300	21	Chad	495,755	1,284,000
7	India	1,237,062	3,203,975	22	Niger	489,191	1,267,000
8	Argentina	1,073,519	2,780,400	23	Mali	482,077	1,248,574
9	Kazakhstan	1,049,156	2,717,300	24	Angola	481,354	1,246,700
10	Sudan	967,500	2,505,813	25	Ethiopia	446,953	1,157,603
11	Algeria	919,595	2,381,741	26	Colombia	440,831	1,141,748
12	Zaire	905,446	2,345,095	27	South Africa	433,246	1,122,102
13	Greenland	840,000	2,175,600	28	Bolivia	424,165	1,098,581
14	Saudi Arabia	830,000	2,149,690	29	Mauritania	395,956	1,025,520
15	Mexico	759,534	1,967,183	30	Egypt	386,662	1,001,449

World Geographical Information

Principal Mountains

NORTH AMERICA

	Height (feet)	Height (meters)
McKinley, Mt., Δ Alaska (Δ United States; Δ North America)	20,320	6,194
Logan, Mt., Δ Canada (Δ Yukon; Δ St. Elias Mts.)	19,524	5,951
Orizaba, Pico de, Δ Mexico	18,406	5,610
St. Elias, Mt., Alaska-Canada	18,008	5,489
Popocatépetl, Volcán, Mexico	17,930	5,465
Foraker, Mt., Alaska	17,400	5,304
Ixtacihuatl, Mexico	17,159	5,230
Lucania, Mt., Canada	17,147	5,226
Fairweather, Mt., Alaska-Canada (Δ British Columbia)	15,300	4,663
Whitney, Mt., Δ California	14,494	4,418
Elbert, Mt., Δ Colorado (Δ Rocky Mts.)	14,433	4,399
Massive, Mt., Colorado	14,421	4,396
Harvard, Mt., Colorado	14,420	4,395
Rainier, Mt., Δ Washington (Δ Cascade Range)	14,410	4,392
Williamson, Mt., California	14,375	4,382
Blanca Pk., Colorado (Δ Sangre de Cristo Mts.)	14,345	4,372
La Plata Pk., Colorado	14,336	4,370
Uncompahgre Pk., Colorado (Δ San Juan Mts.)	14,309	4,361
Grays Pk., Colorado (Δ Front Range)	14,270	4,349
Evans, Mt., Colorado	14,264	4,348
Longs Pk., Colorado	14,255	4,345
Wrangell, Mt., Alaska	14,163	4,317
Shasta, Mt., California	14,162	4,317
Pikes Pk., Colorado	14,110	4,301
Colima, Nevado de, Mexico	13,993	4,265
Tajumulco, Volcán, Δ Guatemala (Δ Central America)	13,845	4,220
Gannett Pk., Δ Wyoming	13,804	4,207
Mauna Kea, Δ Hawaii	13,796	4,205
Grand Teton, Wyoming	13,770	4,197
Mauna Loa, Hawaii	13,679	4,169
Kings Pk., Δ Utah	13,528	4,123
Cloud Pk., Wyoming (Δ Bighorn Mts.)	13,167	4,013
Wheeler Pk., Δ New Mexico	13,161	4,011
Boundary Pk., Δ Nevada	13,143	4,006
Waddington, Mt., Canada (Δ Coast Mts.)	13,104	3,994
Robson, Mt., Canada (Δ Canadian Rockies)	12,972	3,954
Granite Pk., Δ Montana	12,799	3,901
Borah Pk., Δ Idaho	12,662	3,859
Humphreys Pk., Δ Arizona	12,633	3,851
Chirripó, Cerro, Δ Costa Rica	12,530	3,819
Columbia, Mt., Canada (Δ Alberta)	12,294	3,747
Adams, Mt., Washington	12,276	3,742
Gunnbjørn Mtn., Δ Greenland	12,139	3,700
San Gorgonio Mtn., California	11,499	3,505
Barú, Volcán, Δ Panama	11,411	3,475
Hood, Mt., Δ Oregon	11,239	3,426
Lassen Pk., California	10,457	3,187
Duarte, Pico, Δ Dominican Rep. (Δ West Indies)	10,417	3,175
Haleakala Crater, Hawaii (Δ Maui)	10,023	3,055
Paricutín, Mexico	9,213	2,808
El Pital, Cerro, Δ El Salvador-Honduras	8,957	2,730
La Selle, Pic, Δ Haiti	8,773	2,674
Guadalupe Pk., Δ Texas	8,749	2,667
Olympus, Mt., Washington (Δ Olympic Mts.)	7,965	2,428
Blue Mountain Pk., Δ Jamaica	7,402	2,256
Harney Pk., Δ South Dakota (Δ Black Hills)	7,242	2,207
Mitchell, Mt., Δ North Carolina (Δ Appalachian Mts.)	6,684	2,037
Clingmans Dome, North Carolina-Δ Tennessee (Δ Great Smoky Mts.)	6,643	2,025
Turquino, Pico, Δ Cuba	6,470	1,972
Washington, Mt., Δ New Hampshire (Δ White Mts.)	6,288	1,917
Rogers, Mt., Δ Virginia	5,729	1,746
Marcy, Mt., Δ New York (Δ Adirondack Mts.)	5,344	1,629
Katahdin, Mt., Δ Maine	5,268	1,606
Kawaikini, Hawaii (Δ Kauai)	5,243	1,598
Spruce Knob, Δ West Virginia	4,862	1,482
Pelée, Montagne, Δ Martinique	4,583	1,397
Mansfield, Mt., Δ Vermont (Δ Green Mts.)	4,393	1,339
Punta, Cerro de, Δ Puerto Rico	4,389	1,338
Black Mtn., Δ Kentucky-Virginia	4,145	1,263
Kaala, Hawaii (Δ Oahu)	4,040	1,231

SOUTH AMERICA

Aconcagua, Cerro, Δ Argentina; Δ Andes; (Δ South America)	22,831	6,959
Ojos del Salado, Nevado, Argentina-Δ Chile	22,615	6,893
Illimani, Nevado, Δ Bolivia	22,579	6,882
Bonete, Cerro, Argentina	22,546	6,872
Huascarán, Nevado, Δ Peru	22,133	6,746
Llullaillaco, Volcán, Argentina-Chile	22,057	6,723
Yerupaja, Nevado, Peru	21,765	6,634

(continued)

Tupungato, Cerro, Argentina-Chile	21,555	6,570
Sajama, Nevado, Bolivia	21,463	6,542
Illampu, Nevado, Bolivia	20,873	6,362
Chimborazo, Δ Ecuador	20,702	6,310
Antofalla, Volcán, Argentina	20,013	6,100
Cotopaxi, Ecuador	19,347	5,897
Misti, Volcán, Peru	19,101	5,822
Huila, Nevado del, Colombia (Δ Cordillera Central)	16,896	5,150
Bolívar, Pico, Δ Venezuela	16,427	5,007
Fitzroy, Monte (Cerro Chaltel), Argentina-Chile	11,073	3,375
Neblina, Pico da, Δ Brazil-Venezuela	9,888	3,014

EUROPE

El'brus, gora, Δ Russia (Δ Caucasus; Δ Europe)	18,510	5,642
Dykh-Tau, Mt., Russia	17,073	5,204
Shkhara, Mt., Δ Georgia-Russia	16,627	5,068
Blanc, Mont (Monte Bianco), Δ France-Δ Italy (Δ Alps)	15,771	4,807
Dufourspitze, Italy-Δ Switzerland	15,203	4,634
Weisshorn, Switzerland	14,783	4,506
Matterhorn, Italy-Switzerland	14,692	4,478
Finsteraarhorn, Switzerland	14,022	4,274
Jungfrau, Switzerland	13,642	4,158
Écrins, Barre des, France	13,458	4,102
Viso, Monte, Italy (Δ Alpes Cottiennes)	12,602	3,841
Grossglockner, Δ Austria	12,457	3,797
Teide, Pico de, Spain (Δ Canary Is.)	12,188	3,715
Mulhacén, Δ Spain (continental)	11,410	3,478
Aneto, Pico de, Spain (Δ Pyrenees)	11,168	3,404
Perdido, Monte, Spain	11,007	3,355
Etna, Monte, Italy (Δ Sicily)	10,902	3,323
Zugspitze, Austria-Δ Germany	9,721	2,963
Musala, Δ Bulgaria	9,596	2,925
Olympus, Mount (Óros Ólimbos), Δ Greece	9,570	2,917
Corno Grande, Italy (Δ Apennines)	9,554	2,912
Triglav, Δ Slovenia	9,393	2,863
Korabit, Maja e Δ Albania-Macedonia	9,035	2,754
Cinto, Monte, France (Δ Corsica)	8,878	2,706
Gerlachovský Štít, Δ Slovakia (Δ Carpathian Mts.)	8,711	2,655
Moldoveanu, Δ Romania	8,346	2,544
Rysy, Czechoslovakia-Δ Poland	8,199	2,499
Glittertinden, Δ Norway (Δ Scandinavia)	8,110	2,472
Parnassos, Greece	8,061	2,457
Ídhi, Óros, Greece (Δ Crete)	8,057	2,456
Pico, Ponta do, Δ Portugal (Δ Azores Is.)	7,713	2,351
Hvannadalshnúkur, Δ Iceland	6,952	2,119
Kebnekaise, Δ Sweden	6,926	2,111
Estrela, Δ Portugal (continental)	6,539	1,993
Narodnaja, gora, Russia (Δ Ural Mts.)	6,217	1,895
Sancy, Puy de, France (Δ Massif Central)	6,184	1,885
Marmora, Punta la, Italy (Δ Sardinia)	6,017	1,834
Hekla, Iceland	4,892	1,491
Nevis, Ben, Δ United Kingdom (Δ Scotland)	4,406	1,343
Haltiatunturi, Δ Finland-Norway	4,357	1,328
Vesuvio, Italy	4,190	1,277
Snowdon, United Kingdom (Δ Wales)	3,560	1,085
Carrauntoohil, Δ Ireland	3,406	1,038
Kékes, Δ Hungary	3,330	1,015
Scafell Pikes, United Kingdom (Δ England)	3,210	978

ASIA

Everest, Mount, Δ China-Δ Nepal (Δ Tibet; Δ Himalayas; Δ Asia; Δ World)	29,028	8,848
K2 (Qogir Feng), China-Δ Pakistan (Δ Kashmir; Δ Karakoram Range)	28,250	8,611
Kånchenjunga, Δ India-Nepal	28,208	8,598
Makålu, China-Nepal	27,825	8,481
Dhawlagiri, Nepal	26,810	8,172
Nånga Parbat, Pakistan	26,660	8,126
Annapurna, Nepal	26,504	8,078
Gasherbrum, China-Pakistan	26,470	8,068
Xixabangma Feng, China	26,286	8,012
Nanda Devi, India	25,645	7,817
Kamet, China-India	25,447	7,756
Namjagbarwa Feng, China	25,442	7,755
Muztag, China (Δ Kunlun Shan)	25,338	7,723
Tirich Mir, Pakistan (Δ Hindu Kush)	25,230	7,690
Gongga Shan, China	24,790	7,556
Kula Kangri, Δ Bhutan	24,784	7,554
Kommunizma, pik, Δ Tajikistan (Δ Pamir)	24,590	7,495
Nowshåk, Δ Afghanistan-Pakistan	24,557	7,485
Pobedy, pik, China-Russia	24,406	7,439
Chomo Lhari, Bhutan-China	23,997	7,314
Muztag, China	23,891	7,282
Lenin, pik, Δ Kyrgyzstan-Tajikistan	23,406	7,134
Api, Nepal	23,399	7,132
Kangrinboqê Feng, China	22,028	6,714
Hkakabo Razi, Δ Myanmar	19,296	5,881
Damåvend, Qollah-ye, Δ Iran	18,386	5,604
Ağrı Dağı, Δ Turkey	16,804	5,122

(continued)

Jaya, Puncak, Δ Indonesia (Δ New Guinea)	16,503	5,030
Fûlådî, Kûh-e, Afghanistan	16,243	4,951
Kl'učevskaja Sopka, vulkan, Russia (Δ Puluostrov Kamčatka)	15,584	4,750
Trikora, Puncak, Indonesia	15,584	4,750
Belucha, gora, Russia-Kazakhstan	14,783	4,506
Munch Chajrchan Ula, Mongolia	14,311	4,362
Kinabalu, Gunung, Δ Malaysia (Δ Borneo)	13,455	4,101
Yü Shan, Δ Taiwan	13,114	3,997
Erciyes Dağı, Turkey	12,851	3,917
Kerinci, Gunung, Indonesia (Δ Sumatra)	12,467	3,800
Fuji-san, Δ Japan (Δ Honshu)	12,388	3,776
Rinjani, Indonesia (Δ Lombok)	12,224	3,726
Semeru, Indonesia (Δ Java)	12,060	3,676
Nabī Shu'ayb, Jabal an-, Δ Yemen (Δ Arabian Peninsula)	12,008	3,660
Rantekombola, Bulu, Indonesia (Δ Celebes)	11,335	3,455
Slamet, Indonesia	11,247	3,428
Phan Si Pan, Δ Vietnam	10,312	3,143
Shåm, Jabal ash-, Δ Oman	9,957	3,035
Apo, Mount, Δ Philippines (Δ Mindanao)	9,692	2,954
Pulog, Mount, Philippines (Δ Luzon)	9,626	2,934
Bia, Phou, Δ Laos	9,249	2,819
Shaykh, Jabal ash-, Lebanon-Δ Syria	9,232	2,814
Paektu-san, Δ North Korea-China	9,003	2,744
Inthanon, Doi, Δ Thailand	8,530	2,600
Pidurutalagala, Δ Sri Lanka	8,281	2,524
Mayon Volcano, Philippines	8,077	2,462
Asahi-dake, Japan (Δ Hokkaidō)	7,513	2,290
Tahan, Gunong, Malaysia (Δ Malaya)	7,174	2,187
Ólimbos, Δ Cyprus	6,401	1,951
Halla-san, Δ South Korea	6,398	1,950
Aôral, Phnum, Δ Cambodia	5,948	1,813
Kujū-san, Japan (Δ Kyūshū)	5,863	1,787
Ramm, Jabal, Δ Jordan	5,755	1,754
Meron, Hare, Δ Israel	3,963	1,208
Carmel, Mt., Israel	1,791	546

AFRICA

Kilimanjaro, Δ Tanzania (Δ Africa)	19,340	5,895
Kirinyaga (Mount Kenya), Δ Kenya	17,058	5,199
Margherita Peak, Δ Uganda-Δ Zaire	16,763	5,109
Ras Dashen Terara, Δ Ethiopia	15,158	4,620
Meru, Mount, Tanzania	14,978	4,565
Karisimbi, Volcan, Δ Rwanda-Zaire	14,787	4,507
Elgon, Mount, Kenya-Uganda	14,178	4,321
Toubkal, Jbel, Δ Morocco (Δ Atlas Mts.)	13,665	4,165
Cameroon Mountain, Δ Cameroon	13,451	4,100
Ntlenyana, Thabana, Δ Lesotho	11,425	3,482
eNjesuthi, Δ South Africa	11,306	3,446
Koussi, Emi, Δ Chad (Δ Tibesti)	11,204	3,415
Kinyeti, Δ Sudan	10,456	3,187
Santa Isabel, Pico de, Δ Equatorial Guinea (Δ Bioko)	9,869	3,008
Tahat, Δ Algeria (Δ Ahaggar)	9,541	2,908
Maromokotro, Δ Madagascar	9,436	2,876
Kātrīnā, Jabal, Δ Egypt	8,668	2,642
Sao Tome, Pico de, Δ Sao Tome	6,640	2,024

OCEANIA

Wilhelm, Mount, Δ Papua New Guinea	14,793	4,509
Giluwe, Mount, Papua New Guinea	14,330	4,368
Bangeta, Mt., Papua New Guinea	13,520	4,121
Victoria, Mount, Papua New Guinea (Δ Owen Stanley Range)	13,238	4,035
Cook, Mount, Δ New Zealand (Δ South Island)	12,349	3,764
Ruapehu, New Zealand (Δ North Island)	9,177	2,797
Balbi, Papua New Guinea (Δ Solomon Is.)	9,000	2,743
Egmont, Mount, New Zealand	8,260	2,518
Orohena, Mont, Δ French Polynesia (Δ Tahiti)	7,352	2,241
Kosciusko, Mount, Δ Australia (Δ New South Wales)	7,316	2,230
Silisili, Mount, Δ Western Samoa	6,096	1,858
Panié, Mont, Δ New Caledonia	5,341	1,628
Bartle Frere, Australia (Δ Queensland)	5,322	1,622
Ossa, Mount, Australia (Δ Tasmania)	5,305	1,617
Woodroffe, Mount, Australia (Δ South Australia)	4,724	1,440
Sinewit, Mt., Papua New Guinea (Δ Bismarck Archipelago)	4,462	1,360
Tomanivi, Δ Fiji (Δ Viti Levu)	4,341	1,323
Meharry, Mt., Australia (Δ Western Australia)	4,104	1,251
Ayers Rock, Australia	2,844	867

ANTARCTICA

Vinson Massif, Δ Antarctica	16,066	4,897
Kirkpatrick, Mount, Antarctica	14,856	4,528
Markham, Mount, Antarctica	14,049	4,282
Jackson, Mount, Antarctica	13,747	4,190
Sidley, Mount, Antarctica	13,717	4,181
Wade, Mount, Antarctica	13,399	4,084

Δ *Highest mountain in state, country, range, or region named.*

Oceans, Seas and Gulfs

	Area (sq. mi.)	Area (sq. km.)		Area (sq. mi.)	Area (sq. km.)		Area (sq. mi.)	Area (sq. km.)
Pacific Ocean	63,800,000	165,200,000	South China Sea	1,331,000	3,447,000	Okhotsk, Sea of	619,000	1,603,000
Atlantic Ocean	31,800,000	82,400,000	Caribbean Sea	1,063,000	2,753,000	Norwegian Sea	597,000	1,546,000
Indian Ocean	28,900,000	74,900,000	Mediterranean Sea	967,000	2,505,000	Mexico, Gulf of	596,000	1,544,000
Arctic Ocean	5,400,000	14,000,000	Bering Sea	876,000	2,269,000	Hudson Bay	475,000	1,230,000
Arabian Sea	1,492,000	3,864,000	Bengal, Bay of	839,000	2,173,000	Greenland Sea	465,000	1,204,000

Principal Lakes

	Area (sq. mi.)	Area (sq. km.)		Area (sq. mi.)	Area (sq. km.)		Area (sq. mi.)	Area (sq. km.)
Caspian Sea, Asia—Europe (Salt)	143,240	370,990	Ontario, Lake, Canada—U.S.	7,540	19,529	Issyk-Kul', ozero, Kyrgyzstan (Salt)	2,425	6,280
Superior, Lake, Canada—U.S.	31,700	82,100	Balchaš, ozero, Kazakhstan	△ 7,100	18,300	Torrens, Lake, Australia (Salt)	2,300	5,900
Victoria, Lake, Kenya—Tanzania—Uganda	26,820	69,463	Ladožskoje ozero, Russia	6,833	17,700	Albert, Lake, Uganda—Zaire	2,160	5,594
Aral Sea, Asia (Salt)	24,700	64,100	Chad, Lake (Lac Tchad), Cameroon—Chad—Nigeria	6,300	16,300	Vänern, Sweden	2,156	5,584
Huron, Lake, Canada—U.S.	23,000	60,000	Onežskoje ozero, Russia	3,753	9,720	Nettilling Lake, Canada	2,140	5,542
Michigan, Lake, U.S.	22,300	57,800	Eyre, Lake, Australia (Salt)	△ 3,700	9,500	Winnipegosis, Lake, Canada	2,075	5,374
Tanganyika, Lake, Africa	12,350	31,986	Titicaca, Lago, Bolivia—Peru	3,200	8,300	Bangweulu, Lake, Zambia	1,930	4,999
Bajkal, ozero, Russia	12,200	31,500	Nicaragua, Lago de, Nicaragua	3,150	8,158	Nipigon, Lake, Canada	1,872	4,848
Great Bear Lake, Canada	12,095	31,326	Mai—Ndombe, Lac, Zaire	△ 3,100	8,000	Orūmīyeh, Daryācheh-ye, Iran (Salt)	△ 1,815	4,701
Malawi, Lake (Lake Nyasa), Malawi—Mozambique—Tanzania	11,150	28,878	Athabasca, Lake, Canada	3,064	7,935	Manitoba, Lake, Canada	1,785	4,624
Great Slave Lake, Canada	11,030	28,568	Reindeer Lake, Canada	2,568	6,650	Woods, Lake of the, Canada—U.S.	1,727	4,472
Erie, Lake, Canada—U.S.	9,910	25,667	Tônlé Sab, Cambodia	△ 2,500	6,500	Kyoga, Lake, Uganda	1,710	4,429
Winnipeg, Lake, Canada	9,416	24,387	Rudolf, Lake, Ethiopia—Kenya (Salt)	2,473	6,405	Gairdner, Lake, Australia (Salt)	△ 1,700	4,300
						Great Salt Lake, U.S. (Salt)	1,680	4,351

△ *Due to seasonal fluctuations in water level, areas of these lakes vary considerably.*

Principal Rivers

	Length (miles)	Length (km.)		Length (miles)	Length (km.)		Length (miles)	Length (km.)
Nile, Africa	4,145	6,671	Euphrates, Asia	1,510	2,430	Canadian, North America	906	1,458
Amazon-Ucayali, South America	4,000	6,400	Ural, Asia	1,509	2,428	Brazos, North America	900	1,400
Yangtze (Chang), Asia	3,900	6,300	Arkansas, North America	1,459	2,348	Salado, South America	900	1,400
Mississippi-Missouri, North America	3,740	6,019	Colorado, North America (U.S.-Mexico)	1,450	2,334	Darling, Australia	864	1,390
Huang (Yellow), Asia	3,395	5,464	Aldan, Asia	1,412	2,273	Fraser, North America	851	1,370
Ob'-Irtyš, Asia	3,362	5,410	Syrdarja, Asia	1,370	2,205	Parnaíba, South America	850	1,368
Río de la Plata-Paraná, South America	3,030	4,876	Dnieper, Europe	1,400	2,200	Colorado, North America (Texas)	840	1,352
Congo (Zaïre), Africa	2,900	4,700	Araguaia, South America	1,400	2,200	Dniester, Europe	840	1,352
Paraná, South America	2,800	4,500	Kasai (Cassai), Africa	1,338	2,153	Rhine, Europe	820	1,320
Amur-Argun', Asia	2,761	4,444	Tarim, Asia	1,328	2,137	Narmada, Asia	800	1,300
Amur (Heilong), Asia	2,744	4,416	Kolyma, Asia	1,323	2,129	St. Lawrence, North America	800	1,300
Lena, Asia	2,700	4,400	Orange, Africa	1,300	2,100	Ottawa, North America	790	1,271
Mackenzie, North America	2,635	4,241	Negro, South America	1,300	2,100	Athabasca, North America	765	1,231
Mekong, Asia	2,600	4,200	Ayeyarwady, Asia	1,300	2,100	Pecos, North America	735	1,183
Niger, Africa	2,600	4,200	Red, North America	1,270	2,044	Severskij Donec, Europe	735	1,183
Jenisej, Asia	2,543	4,092	Juruá, South America	1,250	2,012	Green, North America	730	1,175
Missouri-Red Rock, North America	2,533	4,076	Columbia, North America	1,200	2,000	White, North America (Ar.-Mo.)	720	1,159
Mississippi, North America	2,348	3,779	Xingu, South America	1,230	1,979	Cumberland, North America	720	1,159
Murray-Darling, Australia	2,330	3,750	Ucayali, South America	1,220	1,963	Elbe (Labe), Europe	720	1,159
Missouri, North America	2,315	3,726	Saskatchewan-Bow, North America	1,205	1,939	James, North America (N./S. Dakota)	710	1,143
Volga, Europe	2,194	3,531	Peace North America,	1,195	1,923	Gambia, Africa	680	1,094
Madeira, South America	2,013	3,240	Tigris, Asia	1,180	1,899	Yellowstone, North America	671	1,080
São Francisco, South America	1,988	3,199	Don, Europe	1,162	1,870	Tennessee, North America	652	1,049
Grande, Rio (Río Bravo), North America	1,885	3,034	Songhua, Asia	1,140	1,835	Gila, North America	630	1,014
Purús, South America	1,860	2,993	Pečora, Europe	1,124	1,809	Wisła (Vistula), Europe	630	1,014
Indus, Asia	1,800	2,900	Kama, Europe	1,122	1,805	Tagus (Tejo) (Tajo), Europe	625	1,006
Danube, Europe	1,776	2,858	Limpopo, Africa	1,100	1,800	Loire, Europe	625	1,006
Brahmaputra, Asia	1,770	2,849	Angara, Asia	1,105	1,779	Cimarron, North America	600	1,000
Yukon, North America	1,770	2,849	Snake, North America	1,038	1,670	North Platte, North America	618	995
Salween (Nu), Asia	1,750	2,816	Uruguay, South America	1,025	1,650	Albany, North America	610	982
Zambezi, Africa	1,700	2,700	Churchill, North America	1,000	1,600	Tisza (Tisa), Europe	607	977
Vil'uj, Asia	1,647	2,650	Marañón, South America	1,000	1,600	Back, North America	605	974
Tocantins, South America	1,640	2,639	Tobol, Asia	989	1,591	Ouachita, North America	605	974
Orinoco South America,	1,600	2,600	Ohio, North America	981	1,579	Sava, Europe	585	941
Paraguay, South America	1,610	2,591	Magdalena, South America	950	1,529	Nemunas (Neman), Europe	582	937
Amu Darya, Asia	1,578	2,540	Roosevelt, South America	950	1,529	Branco, South America	580	933
Murray, Australia	1,566	2,520	Oka, Europe	900	1,500	Meuse (Maas), Europe	575	925
Ganges, Asia	1,560	2,511	Xiang, Asia	930	1,497	Oder (Odra), Europe	565	909
Pilcomayo, South America	1,550	2,494	Godāvari, Asia	930	1,497	Rhône, Europe	500	800

Principal Islands

	Area (sq. mi.)	Area (sq. km.)		Area (sq. mi.)	Area (sq. km.)		Area (sq. mi.)	Area (sq. km.)
Grønland (Greenland), North America	840,000	2,175,600	Hispaniola, North America	29,400	76,200	New Caledonia, Oceania	6,252	16,192
New Guinea, Asia—Oceania	309,000	800,000	Banks Island, Canada	27,038	70,028	Timor, Indonesia	5,743	14,874
Borneo (Kalimantan), Asia	287,300	744,100	Tasmania, Australia	26,200	67,800	Flores, Indonesia	5,502	14,250
Madagascar, Africa	226,500	587,000	Sri Lanka, Asia	24,900	64,600	Samar, Philippines	5,100	13,080
Baffin Island, Canada	195,928	507,451	Devon Island, Canada	21,331	55,247	Negros, Philippines	4,907	12,710
Sumatera (Sumatra), Indonesia	182,860	473,606	Tierra del Fuego, Isla Grande de, South America	18,600	48,200	Palawan, Philippines	4,550	11,785
Honshū, Japan	89,176	230,966	Kyūshū, Japan	17,129	44,363	Panay, Philippines	4,446	11,515
Great Britain, United Kingdom	88,795	229,978	Melville Island, Canada	16,274	42,149	Jamaica, North America	4,200	11,000
Victoria Island, Canada	83,897	217,291	Southampton Island, Canada	15,913	41,214	Hawaii, United States	4,034	10,448
Ellesmere Island, Canada	75,767	196,236	Spitsbergen, Norway	15,260	39,523	Cape Breton Island, Canada	3,981	10,311
Sulawesi (Celebes), Indonesia	73,057	189,216	New Britain, Papua New Guinea	14,093	36,500	Mindoro, Philippines	3,759	9,735
South Island, New Zealand	57,708	149,463	T'aiwan, Asia	13,900	36,000	Kodiak Island, United States	3,670	9,505
Jawa (Java), Indonesia	51,038	132,187	Hainan Dao, China	13,100	34,000	Bougainville, Papua New Guinea	3,600	9,300
North Island, New Zealand	44,332	114,821	Prince of Wales Island, Canada	12,872	33,339	Cyprus, Asia	3,572	9,251
Cuba, North America	42,800	110,800	Vancouver Island, Canada	12,079	31,285	Puerto Rico, North America	3,500	9,100
Newfoundland, Canada	42,031	108,860	Sicilia (Sicily), Italy	9,926	25,709	New Ireland, Papua New Guinea	3,500	9,000
Luzon, Philippines	40,420	104,688	Somerset Island, Canada	9,570	24,786	Corse (Corsica), France	3,367	8,720
Ísland (Iceland), Europe	39,800	103,000	Sardegna (Sardinia), Italy	9,301	24,090	Kríti (Crete), Greece	3,189	8,259
Mindanao, Philippines	36,537	94,630	Shikoku, Japan	7,258	18,799	Vrangel'a, ostrov (Wrangel Island), Russia	2,800	7,300
Ireland, Europe	32,600	84,400	Seram (Ceram), Indonesia	7,191	18,625	Leyte, Philippines	2,785	7,214
Hokkaidō, Japan	32,245	83,515	Nordaustlandet (North East Land), Norway	6,350	16,446	Guadalcanal, Solomon Islands	2,060	5,336
Novaja Zeml'a (Novaya Zemlya), Russia	31,900	82,600				Long Island, United States	1,377	3,566
Sachalin, ostrov (Sakhalin), Russia	29,500	76,400						

World Populations

This table includes every urban center of 50,000 or more population in the world, as well as many other important or well-known cities and towns.

The population figures are all from recent censuses (designated C) or official estimates (designated E), except for a few cities for which only unofficial estimates are available (designated U). The date of the census or estimate is specified for each country. Individual exceptions are dated in parentheses.

For many cities, a second population figure is given accompanied by a star (★). The starred population refers to the city's entire metropolitan area, including suburbs. These metropolitan areas have been defined by Rand McNally, following consistent rules to facilitate comparisons among the urban centers of various countries. Where a place is part of the metropolitan area of another city, that city's name is specified in parentheses preceded by a (★). Some important places that are considered to be secondary central cities of their areas are designated by (★ ★) preceding the name of the metropolitan area's main city. A population preceded by a triangle (▲) refers to an entire municipality, commune, or other district, which includes rural areas in addition to the urban center itself. The names of capital cities appear in CAPITALS; the largest city in each country is designated by the symbol (•).

For more recent population totals for countries, see the Rand McNally population estimates in the World Political Information table.

AFGHANISTAN / Afghānestān

1988 E 15,513,000

Cities and Towns

Herāt 177,300
Jalālābād (1982 E) 58,000
• KĀBOL 1,424,400
Mazār-e Sharīf 130,600
Qandahār 225,500
Qondūz (1982 E) 57,000

ALBANIA / Shqipëri

1987 E 3,084,000

Cities and Towns

Durrës 78,700
Elbasan 78,300
Korçë 61,500
Shkodër 76,300
• TIRANE 255,700
Vlorë 67,700

ALGERIA / Algérie / Djazaïr

1987 C 23,038,942

Cities and Towns

Aïn el Beïda 61,997
Aïn Oussera 44,270
Aïn Témouchent 47,479
• ALGER (ALGIERS)
  (★ 2,547,983) 1,507,241
Annaba (Bône) 305,526
Bab Ezzouar (★ Alger) 55,211
Barika 56,488
Batna 181,601
Béchar 107,311
Bejaïa (Bougie) 114,534
Biskra 128,281
Blida 170,935
Bordj Bou Arreridj 84,264
Bordj el Kiffan (★ Alger) ... 61,035
Bou Saada 66,688
Constantine 440,842
El Asnam 129,976
El Djelfa 84,207
El Eulma 67,933
El Wad 70,073
Ghardaïa 89,415
Ghilizane 80,091
Guelma 77,821
Jijel 62,793
Khemis 55,335
Khenchla 69,743
Laghouat 67,214
Lemdiyya 85,195
Maghniyya 52,275
Mostaganem 114,037
Mouaskar 64,691
M'Sila 65,805
Oran 628,558
Saïda 80,825
Sidi bel Abbès 152,778
Skikda 128,747
Souq Ahras 83,015
Stif 170,182
Tébessa 107,559
Tihert 95,821
Tizi-Ouzou 61,163
Tlemcen 126,882
Touggourt 70,645
Wargla 81,721

AMERICAN SAMOA / Amerika Samoa

1980 C 32,279

Cities and Towns

• PAGO PAGO 3,075

ANDORRA

1986 C 46,976

Cities and Towns

• ANDORRA 18,463

ANGOLA

1989 E 9,739,100

Cities and Towns

Benguela (1983 E) 155,000
Huambo (Nova Lisboa)
  (1983 E) 203,000
Lobito (1983 E) 150,000
• LUANDA 1,459,900
Lubango (1984 E) 95,915
Namibe (1981 E) 100,000

ANGUILLA

1984 C 6,680

Cities and Towns

• THE VALLEY 1,042

ANTIGUA AND BARBUDA

1977 E 72,000

Cities and Towns

• SAINT JOHNS 24,359

ARGENTINA

1980 C 27,947,446

Cities and Towns

Almirante Brown
  (★ Buenos Aires) 331,919
Avellaneda (★ Buenos
  Aires) 334,145
Bahía Blanca 223,818
Berazategui (★ Buenos
  Aires) 201,862
Berisso (★ Buenos
  Aires) 66,152
• BUENOS AIRES
  (★ 10,750,000) 2,922,829
Campana (★ Buenos
  Aires) 54,832
Caseros (Tres de
  Febrero) (★ Buenos
  Aires) 345,424
Catamarca (★ 90,000) 78,799
Comodoro Rivadavia 96,817
Concordia 94,222
Córdoba (★ 1,070,000) 993,055
Corrientes 180,612
Esteban Echeverría
  (★ Buenos Aires) 188,923
Florencio Varela
  (★ Buenos Aires) 173,452
Formosa 93,603
General San Martín
  (★ Buenos Aires) 385,625
General Sarmiento (San
  Miguel) (★ Buenos
  Aires) 502,926
Godoy Cruz
  (★ Mendoza) 142,408
Gualeguaychú 51,400
Junín 62,458
Lanús (★ Buenos Aires) ... 466,980
La Plata (★ ★ Buenos
  Aires) 477,175
La Rioja 67,043
Las Heras (★ Mendoza) 101,579
Lomas de Zamora
  (★ Buenos Aires) 510,130
Mar del Plata 414,696
Mendoza (★ 650,000) 119,088
Mercedes 50,992
Merlo (★ Buenos Aires) ... 292,587
Moreno (★ Buenos
  Aires) 194,440
Morón (★ Buenos
  Aires) 598,420
Necochea 51,069
Neuquén 90,089
Olavarría 64,097
Paraná 161,638
Pergamino 68,612
Pilar (★ Buenos Aires) 84,429
Posadas 143,889
Presidencia Roque
  Sáenz Peña 49,341
Punta Alta 56,620
Quilmes (★ Buenos
  Aires) 446,587
Rafaela 53,273
Resistencia 220,104
Río Cuarto 110,254
Rosario (★ 1,045,000) 938,120
Salta 260,744
San Carlos de
  Bariloche 48,980
San Fernando
  (★ Buenos Aires) 133,624
San Francisco
  (★ 58,536) 51,932
San Isidro (★ Buenos
  Aires) 289,170
San Juan (★ 300,000) 118,046
San Justo (★ Buenos
  Aires) 949,566
San Lorenzo
  (★ Rosario) 96,891
San Luis 70,999
San Miguel de
  Tucumán (★ 525,000) ... 392,888
San Nicolás de los
  Arroyos 98,495
San Rafael 70,959
San Salvador de Jujuy 124,950
Santa Fe 292,165
Santiago del Estero
  (★ 200,000) 148,758
San Vincente
  (★ Buenos Aires) 55,803
Tandil 79,429
Tigre (★ Buenos Aires) ... 206,349
Trelew 52,372
Vicente López
  (★ Buenos Aires) 291,072
Villa Krause (★ San
  Juan) 66,693
Villa María 67,560
Villa Nueva
  (★ Mendoza) 164,670
Zárate 67,143

ARMENIA / Hayastan

1989 C 3,283,000

Cities and Towns

Abovjan (1987 E) 53,000
Cardzou 161,000
Ečmiadzin (★ Jerevan)
  (1987 E) 53,000
• JEREVAN
  (★ 1,315,000) 1,199,000
Kirovakan (1987 E) 169,000
Kumajri 120,000
Razdan (1987 E) 56,000

ARUBA

1987 E 64,763

Cities and Towns

• ORANJESTAD 19,800

AUSTRALIA

1989 E 16,833,100

Cities and Towns

Adelaide (★ 1,036,747) ... 12,340
Albury (★ 66,530) 40,730
Auburn (★ Sydney) 49,950
Ballarat (★ 80,090) 36,680
Bankstown (★ Sydney) 158,750
Bendigo (★ 67,920) 32,050
Berwick (★ Melbourne) 64,100
Blacktown (★ Sydney) 210,900
Blue Mountains
  (★ Sydney) 70,800
Brisbane (★ 1,273,511) ... 744,828
Broadmeadows
  (★ Melbourne) 105,500
Cairns (★ 80,875) 42,839
Camberwell
  (★ Melbourne) 87,700
Campbelltown
  (★ Sydney) 139,500
CANBERRA
  (★ 271,362) (1986 C) ... 247,194
Canning (★ Perth) 69,104
Canterbury (★ Sydney) ... 135,200
Caulfield (★ Melbourne) ... 70,100
Coburg (★ Melbourne) 54,500
Cockburn (★ Perth) 49,802
Dandenong
  (★ Melbourne) 59,400
Darwin (★ 72,937) 63,900
Doncaster
  (★ Melbourne) 107,300
Enfield (★ Adelaide) 64,058
Essendon
  (★ Melbourne) 55,300
Fairfield (★ Sydney) 176,350
Footscray
  (★ Melbourne) 48,700
Frankston
  (★ Melbourne) 90,500
Geelong (★ 148,980) 13,190
Gosford 126,600
Gosnells (★ Perth) 71,862
Heidelberg
  (★ Melbourne) 63,500
Hobart (★ 181,210) 47,280
Holroyd (★ Sydney) 82,500
Hurstville (★ Sydney) 66,350
Ipswich (★ Brisbane) 75,283
Keilor (★ Melbourne) 103,700
Knox (★ Melbourne) 121,300
Lake Macquarie
  (★ Newcastle) 161,700
Launceston (★ 92,350) 32,150
Leichhardt (★ Sydney) 58,950
Liverpool (★ Sydney) 99,750
Logan (★ Brisbane) 142,222
Mackay (★ 50,885) 22,583
Marion (★ Adelaide) 74,631
Marrickville (★ Sydney) ... 84,650
Melbourne
  (★ 3,039,100) 55,300
Melville (★ Perth) 85,590
Mitcham (★ Adelaide) 63,301
Moorabbin
  (★ Melbourne) 98,900
Newcastle (★ 425,610) ... 130,940
Noarlunga (★ Adelaide) ... 77,352
Northcote
  (★ Melbourne) 49,100
North Sydney
  (★ Sydney) 53,400
Nunawading
  (★ Melbourne) 96,400
Oakleigh (★ Melbourne) ... 57,600
Parramatta (★ Sydney) ... 134,600
Penrith (★ Sydney) 152,650
Perth (★ 1,158,387) 82,413
Preston (★ Melbourne) 82,000
Randwick (★ Sydney) 119,200
Redcliffe (★ Brisbane) ... 48,123
Rockdale (★ Sydney) 88,200
Rockhampton
  (★ 61,694) 58,890
Ryde (★ Sydney) 94,400
Salisbury (★ Adelaide) ... 106,129
Shoalhaven 64,070
Southport (★ 254,861) ... 135,408
South Sydney
  (★ Sydney) 74,100
Springvale
  (★ Melbourne) 88,700
Stirling (★ Perth) 181,556
Sunshine (★ Melbourne) ... 97,700
• Sydney (★ 3,623,550) 9,800
Tea Tree Gully
  (★ Adelaide) 82,324
Toowoomba 81,071
Townsville (★ 111,972) ... 83,339
Wagga Wagga 52,180
Wanneroo (★ Perth) 163,324
Waverley (★ Melbourne) .. 126,300
Waverley (★ Sydney) 61,850
Willoughby (★ Sydney) 53,950
Wollongong
  (★ 236,690) 174,770
Woodville (★ Adelaide) ... 82,590
Woollahra (★ Sydney) 53,850

AUSTRIA / Österreich

1981 C 7,555,338

Cities and Towns

Graz (★ 325,000) 243,166
Innsbruck (★ 185,000) 117,287
Klagenfurt (★ 115,000) 87,321
Linz (★ 335,000) 199,910
Salzburg (★ 220,000) 139,426
Sankt Pölten
  (★ 67,000) 50,419
Villach (★ 65,000) 52,692
Wels (★ 56,000) 51,060
• WIEN (VIENNA)
  (★ 1,875,000)
  (1988 E) 1,482,800

AZERBAIJAN / Azärbayjan

1989 C 7,029,000

Cities and Towns

Ali-Bajramly (1987 E) 51,000
• BAKU (★ 2,020,000) 1,150,000
Chudžand 160,000
Gjandža 278,000
Kurgan-T'ube (1987 E) 55,000
Mingečaur (1987 E) 78,000
Nachičevan' (1987 E) 51,000
Šeki (Nucha) (1987 E) 54,000
Sumgait (★ Baku) 231,000

BAHAMAS

1982 E 218,000

Cities and Towns

• NASSAU 135,000

BAHRAIN / Al-Baḥrayn

1981 C 350,798

Cities and Towns

• AL-MANĀMAH
  (★ 224,643) 115,054
Al-Muharraq
  (★ Al-Manāmah) 57,688

BANGLADESH

1981 C 87,119,965

Cities and Towns

Barisāl 172,905
Begamganj 69,623
Bhairab Bāzār 63,563
Bogra 68,749
Brāhmanbāria 87,570
Chāndpur 85,656
Chittagong
  (★ 1,391,877) 980,000
Chuādanga 76,000
Comilla 184,132
• DHAKA (DACCA)
  (★ 3,430,312) 2,365,695
Dinājpur 96,718
Farīdpur 66,579
Gulshan (★ Dhaka) 215,444
Jamālpur 91,815
Jessore 148,927
Khulna 648,359
Kishorganj 52,302
Kushtia 74,892
Mādārīpur 63,917
Mīrpur (★ Dhaka) 349,031
Mymensingh 190,991
Naogaon 52,975
Nārāyanganj
  (★ ★ Dhaka) 405,562
Narsinghdi 76,841
Nawābganj 87,724
Noākhāli 59,065
Pābna 109,065
Patuākhāli 48,121
Rājshāhi 253,740
Rangpur 153,174
Saidpur 126,608
Sātkhira 52,156
Sherpur 48,214
Sirājganj 106,774
Sītākunda
  (★ Chittagong) 237,520
Sylhet 168,371
Tangail 77,518
Tongi (★ Dhaka) 94,580

BARBADOS

1980 C 244,228

Cities and Towns

• BRIDGETOWN
  (★ 115,000) 7,466

BELARUS / Byelarus'

1989 C 10,200,000

Cities and Towns

Baranoviči 159,000
Bobrujsk 223,000
Borisov 144,000
Brest 258,000
Gomel' 500,000
Grodno 270,000
Lida (1987 E) 81,000
• MINSK (★ 1,650,000) ... 1,589,000
Mogil'ov 356,000
Molodečno (1987 E) 87,000
Mozyr' 101,000
Novopolock (1987 E) 90,000
Orša 123,000
Pinsk 119,000
Polock (1987 E) 80,000
Rečica (1987 E) 71,000
Sluck (1987 E) 55,000
Soligorsk (1987 E) 92,000
Svetlogorsk (1987 E) 68,000
Vitebsk 350,000
Zlobin (1987 E) 52,000
Zodino (1987 E) 51,000

BELGIUM / België / Belgique

1987 E 9,864,751

Cities and Towns

Aalst (Alost)
  (★ Bruxelles) 77,113
Anderlecht
  (★ Bruxelles) 88,849
Antwerpen
  (★ 1,100,000) 479,748
Brugge (Bruges)
  (★ 223,000) 117,755
• BRUXELLES (BRUSSEL)
  (★ 2,385,000) 136,920
Charleroi (★ 480,000) 209,395
Forest (★ Bruxelles) 48,266
Genk (★ ★ Hasselt) 61,391
Gent (Gand)
  (★ 465,000) 233,856
Hasselt (★ 290,000) 65,563
Ixelles (★ Bruxelles) 76,241
Kortrijk (Courtrai)
  (★ 202,000) 76,216
La Louvière
  (★ 147,000) 76,340
Leuven (Louvain)
  (★ 173,000) 84,583
Liège (Luik)
  (★ 750,000) 200,891
Mechelen (Malines)
  (★ 121,000) 75,808
Molenbeek-St.-Jean
  (★ Bruxelles) 69,764
Mons (Bergen)
  (★ 242,000) 89,697
Mouscron (★ Lille,
  France) 53,713
Namur (★ 147,000) 102,670
Oostende (Ostende)
  (★ 122,000) 68,318

C Census. E Official estimate. U Unofficial estimate.
• Largest city in country.

★ Population or designation of metropolitan area, including suburbs (see headnote).
▲ Population of an entire municipality, commune, or district, including rural area.

Roeselare (Rouers)..........51,963
Schaerbeek
  (★ Bruxelles)............104,919
Seraing (★ Liège)............61,731
Sint-Niklaas (Saint-
  Nicolas)................68,082
Tournai (Doornik)
  (★ 66,998)..............44,900
Uccle (★ Bruxelles)..........75,876
Verviers (★ 101,000)........53,498

BELIZE

1985 E................166,400

Cities and Towns

• Belize City................47,000
  BELMOPAN................4,500

BENIN / Bénin

1984 E................3,825,000

Cities and Towns

Abomey................53,000
• COTONOU................478,000
Natitingou (1975 E)........51,000
Ouidah (1979 E)............53,000
Parakou................92,000
PORTO-NOVO................164,000

BERMUDA

1985 E................56,000

Cities and Towns

• HAMILTON (★ 15,000)......1,676

BHUTAN / Druk-Yul

1982 E................1,333,000

Cities and Towns

• THIMPHU................12,000

BOLIVIA

1985 E................6,429,226

Cities and Towns

Cochabamba................317,251
• LA PAZ................992,592
Oruro................178,393
Potosí................113,380
Santa Cruz................441,717
SUCRE................86,609
Tarija................60,621

BOSNIA AND HERZEGOVINA / Bosna i Hercegovina

1987 E................4,400,464

Cities and Towns

Banja Luka (▲ 193,890)....130,900
• SARAJEVO
  (▲ 479,688)............341,200
Tuzla (▲ 129,967)............67,300
Zenica (▲ 144,869)............67,500

BOTSWANA

1987 E................1,169,000

Cities and Towns

Francistown (1986 E)........43,837
• GABORONE................107,677
Selebi Phikwe (1986 E)....41,382

BRAZIL / Brasil

1985 E................135,564,395

Cities and Towns

Alagoinhas (▲ 116,959)....87,500
Alegrete (▲ 71,898)........56,700
Alvorada................105,730
Americana................156,030
Anápolis................225,840
Apucarana (▲ 92,812)........73,700
Aracaju................360,013
Araçatuba................129,304
Araguari (▲ 96,035)........84,300
Arapiraca (▲ 147,879)........91,400
Araraquara (▲ 145,042)....87,500
Araras (▲ 71,652)............59,900
Araxá................61,418
Assis (▲ 74,238)............63,100
Bagé (▲ 106,155)............70,800
Barbacena (▲ 99,337)........80,200
Barra do Piraí
  (▲ 78,189)............55,700
Barra Mansa (★ Volta
  Redonda)..............149,200
Barretos................80,202
Bauru................220,105
Bayeux (★ João
  Pessoa)................67,182
Belém (★ 1,200,000)....1,116,578
Belford Roxo (★ Rio de
  Janeiro)................340,700
Belo Horizonte
  (★ 2,950,000)........2,114,429
Betim (★ Belo
  Horizonte)..............96,810
Blumenau................192,074
Boa Vista................66,028
Botucatu (▲ 71,139)........62,600
Bragança Paulista
  (▲ 105,099)............76,300
BRASÍLIA................1,567,709

Caçapava (▲ 64,213)........56,600
Cachoeira do Sul
  (▲ 91,492)............58,900
Cachoeirinha (★ Porto
  Alegre)................73,117
Cachoeiro de
  Itapemirim
  (▲ 138,156)............95,000
Campina Grande................279,929
Campinas
  (★ 1,125,000)........841,016
Campo Grande................384,398
Campos (▲ 366,716)........187,900
Campos Elyseos (★ Rio
  de Janeiro)............188,200
Canoas (★ Porto
  Alegre)................261,222
Carapicuiba (★ São
  Paulo)................265,856
Carazinho (▲ 62,108)........48,500
Cariacica (★ Vitória)........74,300
Caruaru (▲ 190,794)........152,100
Cascavel (▲ 200,485)........123,100
Castanhal (▲ 89,703)........71,200
Catanduva (▲ 80,309)........71,400
Caucaia (★ Fortaleza)........78,500
Cavaleiro (★ Recife)........106,600
Caxias (▲ 148,230)............66,300
Caxias do Sul................266,809
Chapecó (▲ 100,997)........64,200
Coelho da Rocha
  (★ Rio de Janeiro)....164,400
Colatina (▲ 106,260)........58,600
Colombo (★ Curitiba)........65,900
Conselheiro Lafaiete........77,958
Contagem (★ Belo
  Horizonte)............152,700
Corumbá (▲ 80,666)........65,800
Crato (▲ 86,371)............52,700
Criciúma (▲ 128,410)........85,900
Cruz Alta (▲ 71,817)........58,300
Cruzeiro................63,918
Cubatão (★ Santos)........98,322
Cuiabá (▲ 279,651)........220,400
Curitiba (★ 1,700,000)....1,279,205
Diadema (★ São Paulo)....320,187
Divinópolis................139,940
Dourados (▲ 123,757)........89,200
Duque de Caxias
  (★ Rio de Janeiro)....353,200
Embu (★ São Paulo)........119,791
Erechim (▲ 70,709)........54,300
Esteio (★ Porto Alegre)....58,964
Feira de Santana
  (▲ 355,201)............278,600
Ferraz de Vasconcelos
  (★ São Paulo)..........68,831
Florianópolis
  (★ 365,000)............178,400
Fortaleza (★ 1,825,000)..1,582,414
Foz do Iguaçu
  (▲ 182,101)............124,900
Franca................182,820
Garanhuns................73,100
Goiânia (★ 990,000)........923,333
Governador Valadares
  (▲ 216,057)............192,300
Guaratinguetá
  (▲ 93,534)............80,400
Guarujá (★ Santos)........83,500
Guarulhos (★ São
  Paulo)................571,700
Ijuí (▲ 82,064)............64,400
Ilhéus (▲ 145,810)........79,400
Imperatriz (▲ 235,453)....119,500
Ipatinga (★ 270,000)........149,100
Ipiíba (★ Rio de
  Janeiro)................116,200
Itabira (▲ 81,771)............66,300
Itabuna (▲ 167,543)........142,200
Itajaí................104,232
Itajubá (▲ 69,675)............61,500
Itapecerica da Serra
  (★ São Paulo)..........65,500
Itapetininga (▲ 105,512)....76,700
Itapevi (★ São Paulo)........66,825
Itaquaquecetuba
  (★ São Paulo)..........91,366
Itaguari (★ Vitória)........163,900
Itaúna (▲ 92,786)............77,900
Ituiutaba (▲ 85,365)........74,900
Itumbiara (▲ 78,844)........57,200
Jaboatão (★ Recife)........82,900
Jacareí................149,061
Jaú (▲ 92,547)............74,500
Jequié (▲ 127,070)........92,100
João Pessoa
  (★ 550,000)............348,500
Joinville................302,877
Juàzeiro (★ Petrolina)........78,600
Juàzeiro do Norte................159,806
Juiz de Fora................349,720
Jundiaí (▲ 313,652)........268,900
Lajes (▲ 143,246)............103,600
Lavras................52,100
Limeira................186,986
Linhares (▲ 122,453)........53,400
Londrina (▲ 346,676)........296,400
Lorena................63,230
Luziânia (▲ 98,408)........71,400
Macapá (▲ 168,839)........109,400
Maceió................482,195
Manaus................809,914
Marabá (▲ 133,559)........92,700
Marília (▲ 136,187)........116,100
Maringá................196,871
Mauá (★ São Paulo)........269,321
Mesquita (★ Rio de
  Janeiro)................161,300

Mogi das Cruzes
  (★ São Paulo)..........144,800
Mogi-Guaçu (▲ 91,994)....81,800
Mogi-Mirim (▲ 63,313)........52,300
Monjolo (★ Rio de
  Janeiro)................113,900
Montes Claros
  (▲ 214,472)............183,500
Mossoró (▲ 158,723)........128,300
Muriaé (▲ 80,466)............57,600
Muribeca dos
  Guararapes
  (★ Recife)............171,200
Natal................510,106
Neves (★ Rio de
  Janeiro)................163,600
Nilópolis (★ Rio de
  Janeiro)................112,800
Niterói (★ Rio de
  Janeiro)................441,684
Nova Friburgo
  (▲ 143,529)............103,500
Nova Iguaçu (★ Rio de
  Janeiro)................592,800
Novo Hamburgo
  (★ Porto Alegre)........167,744
Olinda (★ Recife)............316,600
Osasco (★ São Paulo)....591,568
Ourinhos (▲ 65,841)........58,100
Paranaguá (▲ 94,809)........82,300
Paranavaí (▲ 75,511)........60,900
Parnaíba (▲ 116,206)........90,200
Parque Industrial
  (★ Belo Horizonte)....228,400
Passo Fundo
  (▲ 137,843)............117,500
Passos (▲ 79,393)............65,500
Patos................74,298
Patos de Minas
  (▲ 99,027)............69,000
Paulo Afonso
  (▲ 86,182)............75,300
Pelotas (▲ 277,730)........210,300
Petrolina (▲ 225,000)........92,100
Petrópolis (★ Rio de
  Janeiro)................170,300
Pindamonhangaba
  (▲ 86,990)............64,100
Pinheirinho (★ Curitiba)....51,600
Piracicaba (▲ 252,079)....211,000
Poá (★ São Paulo)............66,006
Poços de Caldas................100,004
Ponta Grossa................223,154
Porto Alegre
  (★ 2,600,000)........1,272,121
Porto Velho
  (▲ 202,011)............152,700
Pouso Alegre
  (▲ 65,958)............58,300
Praia Grande
  (★ Santos)............67,800
Presidente Prudente........155,883
Queimados (★ Rio de
  Janeiro)................113,700
Recife (★ 2,625,000)....1,287,623
Ribeirão Prêto................383,125
Rio Branco (▲ 145,486)....109,800
Rio Claro................129,859
Rio de Janeiro
  (★ 10,150,000)........5,603,388
Rio Grande................164,221
Rio Verde (▲ 92,954)........59,400
Rondonópolis
  (▲ 101,642)............65,500
Salvador (★ 2,050,000)..1,804,438
Santa Bárbara d'Oeste....95,818
Santa Cruz do Sul
  (▲ 115,288)............60,300
Santa Maria
  (▲ 196,827)............163,900
Santana do Livramento
  (▲ 70,489)............60,100
Santarém (▲ 226,618)........120,800
Santa Rita (★ João
  Pessoa)................60,100
Santo André (★ São
  Paulo)................635,129
Santo Ângelo
  (▲ 107,559)............57,700
Santos (★ 1,065,000)........460,100
São Bernardo do
  Campo (★ São Paulo)...562,485
São Caetano do Sul
  (★ São Paulo)..........171,005
São Carlos................140,383
São Gonçalo (★ Rio de
  Janeiro)................262,400
São João da Boa Vista
  (▲ 61,653)............50,400
São João del Rei
  (▲ 74,385)............61,400
São João de Meriti
  (★ Rio de Janeiro)....241,700
São José do Rio Prêto....229,221
São José dos Campos....372,578
São José dos Pinhais
  (★ Curitiba)..........64,100
São Leopoldo (★ Porto
  Alegre)................114,065
São Lourenço da Mata
  (★ Recife)............65,936
São Luís (★ 600,000)........227,900
• São Paulo
  (★ 15,175,000)......10,063,110
São Vicente (★ Santos)....239,778
Sapucaia do Sul
  (★ Porto Alegre)........91,820
Sete Lagoas................121,418
Sete Pontes (★ Rio de
  Janeiro)................72,300

Sobral (▲ 112,275)............69,400
Sorocaba................327,468
Suzano (★ São Paulo)....128,924
Taboão da Serra
  (★ São Paulo)..........122,112
Tatuí (▲ 69,358)............56,000
Taubaté................205,120
Teófilo Otoni
  (▲ 126,265)............82,700
Teresina (★ 525,000)........425,300
Teresópolis (▲ 115,859)....92,600
Timon (★ Teresina)............68,300
Tubarão (▲ 82,082)............70,400
Uberaba................244,875
Uberlândia................312,024
Uruguaiana (▲ 105,862)....91,500
Varginha................74,630
Vicente de Carvalho
  (★ Santos)............102,700
Vila Velha (★ Vitória)........91,900
Vitória (★ 735,000)........201,500
Vitória da Conquista
  (▲ 198,150)............145,800
Vitória de Santo Antão
  (▲ 100,450)............67,800
Volta Redonda
  (★ 375,000)............219,267

BRITISH VIRGIN ISLANDS

1980 C................12,034

Cities and Towns

• ROAD TOWN................2,479

BRUNEI

1981 C................192,832

Cities and Towns

• BANDAR SERI
  BEGAWAN
  (★ 64,000)............22,777

BULGARIA / Bâlgarija

1986 E................9,913,000

Cities and Towns

Blagoevgrad................67,766
Burgas................186,369
Dimitrovgrad................54,898
Dobrič................110,471
Gabrovo................81,688
Haskovo................89,273
Jambol................92,321
Kârdžali................56,906
Kazanlâk................61,780
Kjustendil................54,773
Loveč (1985 E)................48,862
Mihajlovgrad................53,529
Pazardžik................79,198
Pernik................96,277
Pleven................132,206
Plovdiv................349,148
Razgrad................51,277
Ruse................186,428
Silistra................54,627
Sliven................104,345
• SOFIJA (SOFIA)
  (★ 1,205,000)........1,119,152
Stara Zagora................153,538
Šumen................102,886
Varna................303,071
Veliko Târnovo................70,610
Vidin................63,813
Vraca................77,934

BURKINA FASO

1985 C................7,964,705

Cities and Towns

Bobo Dioulasso................228,668
Koudougou................51,926
• OUAGADOUGOU................441,514

BURUNDI

1986 E................4,782,000

Cities and Towns

• BUJUMBURA................273,000
Gitega................95,000

CAMBODIA / Kâmpŭchéa

1986 E................7,492,000

Cities and Towns

Kâmpóng Saôm
  (1981 E)..............53,000
• PHNUM PÉNH................700,000

CAMEROON / Cameroun

1986 E................10,446,409

Cities and Towns

Bafoussam (1985 E)........89,000
Bamenda (1985 E)............72,000
• Douala................1,029,731
Foumban (1985 E)............50,000
Garoua (1985 E)............96,000
Kumba (1985 E)............67,000
Maroua................103,653
Ngaoundéré (1985 E)........61,000
Nkongsamba................123,149
YAOUNDÉ................653,670

CANADA

1986 C................25,354,064

CANADA: ALBERTA

1986 C................2,375,278

Cities and Towns

Calgary (★ 671,326)........636,104
Edmonton (★ 785,465)....573,982
Fort McMurray
  (★ 48,497)............34,949
Lethbridge................58,841
Medicine Hat
  (★ 50,734)............41,804
Red Deer................54,425

CANADA: BRITISH COLUMBIA

1986 C................2,889,207

Cities and Towns

Burnaby (★ Vancouver)....145,161
Chilliwack (★ 50,288)........41,337
Kamloops................61,773
Kelowna (★ 89,730)............61,213
Matsqui (★ 88,420)............51,449
Nanaimo (★ 60,420)........49,029
Prince George................67,621
Richmond
  (★ Vancouver)..........108,492
Vancouver
  (★ 1,380,729)........431,147
Victoria (★ 255,547)........66,303

CANADA: MANITOBA

1986 C................1,071,232

Cities and Towns

Brandon................38,708
Portage la Prairie................13,198
Winnipeg (★ 625,304)....594,551

CANADA: NEW BRUNSWICK

1986 C................710,422

Cities and Towns

Fredericton (★ 65,768)....44,352
Moncton (★ 102,084)........55,468
Saint John (★ 121,265)....76,381

CANADA: NEWFOUNDLAND

1986 C................568,349

Cities and Towns

Corner Brook
  (★ 33,730)............22,719
Gander................10,207
Saint John's
  (★ 161,901)............96,216

CANADA: NORTHWEST TERRITORIES

1986 C................52,238

Cities and Towns

Inuvik................3,389
Yellowknife................11,753

CANADA: NOVA SCOTIA

1986 C................873,199

Cities and Towns

Dartmouth (★ Halifax)....65,243
Halifax (★ 295,990)........113,577
Sydney (★ 119,470)........27,754

CANADA: ONTARIO

1986 C................9,113,515

Cities and Towns

Barrie (★ 67,703)............48,287
Brampton (★ Toronto)....188,498
Brantford (★ 90,521)........76,146
Burlington (★ Hamilton)....116,675
Cambridge (Galt)
  (★ ★ Kitchener)........79,920
East York (★ Toronto)....101,085
Etobicoke (★ Toronto)....302,973
Gloucester (★ Ottawa)....89,810
Guelph (★ 85,962)............78,235
Hamilton (★ 557,029)....306,728
Kingston (★ 122,350)........55,050
Kitchener (★ 311,195)........150,604
London (★ 342,302)........269,140
Markham (★ Toronto)....114,597
Mississauga
  (★ Toronto)............374,005
Nepean (★ Ottawa)........95,490
Niagara Falls
  (★ ★ Saint
  Catharines)............72,107
North Bay (★ 57,422)........50,623
North York (★ Toronto)....556,297
Oakville (★ Toronto)........87,107
Oshawa (★ 203,543)........123,651
OTTAWA (★ 819,263)........300,763
Peterborough
  (★ 87,083)............61,049
Saint Catharines
  (★ 343,258)............123,455
Sarnia (★ 85,700)............49,033
Sault Sainte Marie
  (★ 84,617)............80,905

C Census.   E Official estimate.   U Unofficial estimate.
• Largest city in country.

★ Population or designation of metropolitan area, including suburbs (see headnote).
▲ Population of an entire municipality, commune, or district, including rural area.

World Populations

Scarborough
(★ Toronto) 484,676
Sudbury (★ 148,877) 88,717
Thunder Bay
(★ 122,217) 112,272
• Toronto (★ 3,427,168) 612,289
Vaughan (★ Toronto) 65,058
Waterloo (★ Kitchener) 58,718
Windsor (★ 253,988) 193,111
York (★ Toronto) 135,401

CANADA: PRINCE EDWARD ISLAND

1986 C 126,646

Cities and Towns

Charlottetown
(★ 53,868) 15,776
Summerside (★ 15,614) 8,020

CANADA: QUÉBEC

1986 C 6,540,276

Cities and Towns

Beauport (★ Québec) 62,869
Brossard (★ Montréal) 57,441
Charlesbourg
(★ Québec) 68,996
Chicoutimi (★ 158,468) 61,083
Gatineau (★ Ottawa) 81,244
Hull (★ Ottawa) 58,722
Jonquière
(★ Chicoutimi) 58,467
LaSalle (★ Montréal) 75,621
Laval (★ Montréal) 284,164
Longueuil (★ Montréal) 125,441
Montréal (★ 2,921,357) ...1,015,420
Montréal-Nord
(★ Montréal) 90,303
Québec (★ 603,267) 164,580
Sainte-Foy (★ Québec) 69,615
Saint-Hubert
(★ Montréal) 66,218
Saint-Laurent
(★ Montréal) 67,002
Saint-Léonard
(★ Montréal) 75,947
Sherbrooke
(★ 129,960) 74,438
Trois-Rivières
(★ 128,888) 50,122
Verdun (★ Montréal) 60,246

CANADA: SASKATCHEWAN

1986 C 1,010,198

Cities and Towns

Moose Jaw (★ 37,219) 35,073
Prince Albert
(★ 40,841) 33,686
Regina (★ 186,521) 175,064
Saskatoon (★ 200,665) 177,641

CANADA: YUKON

1986 C 23,504

Cities and Towns

Dawson 896
Whitehorse 15,199

CAPE VERDE / Cabo Verde

1990 C 336,798

Cities and Towns

• PRAIA 61,797

CAYMAN ISLANDS

1988 E 25,900

Cities and Towns

• GEORGETOWN 13,700

CENTRAL AFRICAN REPUBLIC / République centrafricaine

1984 E 2,517,000

Cities and Towns

• BANGUI 473,817
Bouar (1982 E) 48,000

CHAD / Tchad

1979 E 4,405,000

Cities and Towns

Abéché 54,000
Moundou 66,000
• N'DJAMENA 303,000
Sarh 65,000

CHILE

1982 C 11,329,736

Cities and Towns

Antofagasta 185,486
Apoquindo (★ Santiago) 175,735
Arica 139,320
Calama 81,684
Cerrillos (★ Santiago) 67,013
Cerro Navia
(★ Santiago) 137,777
Chillán 118,163

Concepción
(★ 675,000) 267,891
Conchalí (★ Santiago) 157,884
Copiapó 69,045
Coquimbo 62,186
Coronel (★ Concepción) 65,918
Curicó 60,550
El Bosque (★ Santiago) 143,717
Huechuraba
(★ Santiago) 56,313
Independencia
(★ Santiago) 86,724
Iquique 110,153
La Cisterna
(★ Santiago) 95,863
La Florida (★ Santiago) 191,883
La Granja (★ Santiago) 109,168
La Pintana (★ Santiago) 73,932
La Reina (★ Santiago) 80,452
La Serena 83,283
Las Rejas (★ Santiago) 147,918
Lo Espejo (★ Santiago) 124,462
Lo Prado (★ Santiago) 103,575
Los Ángeles 70,529
Macul (★ Santiago) 113,100
Maipú (★ Santiago) 114,117
Ñuñoa (★ Santiago) 168,919
Osorno 95,286
Pedro Aguirre Cerda
(★ Santiago) 145,207
Peñalolén (★ Santiago) 137,298
Providencia
(★ Santiago) 115,449
Pudahuel (★ Santiago) 97,578
Puente Alto
(★ Santiago) 109,239
Puerto Montt 84,410
Punta Arenas 95,332
Quilpué (★ Valparaíso) 84,136
Quinta Normal
(★ Santiago) 128,989
Rancagua 139,925
Recoleta (★ Santiago) 164,292
Renca (★ Santiago) 93,928
San Antonio 61,486
San Bernardo
(★ Santiago) 117,132
San Joaquín
(★ Santiago) 123,904
San Miguel
(★ Santiago) 88,764
San Ramón
(★ Santiago) 99,410
• SANTIAGO
(★ 4,100,000) 232,667
Talca 128,544
Talcahuano
(★ Concepción) 202,368
Temuco 157,297
Valdivia 100,046
Valparaíso (★ 675,000) 265,355
Villa Alemana
(★ Valparaíso) 55,766
Viña del Mar
(★ Valparaíso) 244,899
Vitacura (★ Santiago) 72,038

CHINA / Zhongguo

1988 E 1,103,983,000

Cities and Towns

Abagnar Qi (▲ 100,700)
(1986 E) 71,700
Acheng (1985 E) 100,304
Aihui (▲ 135,000)
(1986 E) 76,700
Akesu (▲ 345,900)
(1986 E) 143,100
Altay (▲ 141,700)
(1986 E) 62,800
Anci (Langfang)
(▲ 522,800) (1986 E) 122,100
Anda (▲ 425,500)
(1986 E) 130,200
Andong (1986 E) 579,800
Ankang (1985 E) 89,188
Anqing (▲ 433,900)
(1986 E) 213,200
Anshan (▲ 214,700)
(1986 E) 1,330,000
Anshun (▲ 214,700)
(1986 E) 128,800
Anyang (▲ 541,900)
(1986 E) 361,200
Baicheng (▲ 282,000)
(1986 E) 198,600
Baiquan (1985 E) 50,996
Baiyin (▲ 301,900)
(1986 E) 157,100
Baoding (▲ 535,100)
(1986 E) 423,200
Baoji (▲ 359,500)
(1986 E) 286,200
Baoshan (▲ 688,400)
(1986 E) 52,300
Baotou (Paotow) 1,130,000
Baoying (1985 E) 50,479
Bei'an (▲ 440,500)
(1986 E) 199,500
Beihai (▲ 175,900)
(1986 E) 119,000
BEIJING (PEKING)
(★ 6,450,000) 6,710,000
Beipiao (▲ 603,700)
(1986 E) 180,900
Bengbu (▲ 612,600)
(1986 E) 403,900
Benxi (Penhsi) 860,000
Bijie (1985 E) 54,871

Binxian (▲ 177,900)
(1986 E) 86,700
Binxian (1982 C) 127,326
Boli (1985 E) 61,990
Bose (▲ 271,400)
(1986 E) 82,000
Boshan (1975 U) 100,000
Boxian (1985 E) 63,222
Boying (1982 C) 57,554
Boyang (1985 E) 60,688
Butha Qi (Zalantun)
(▲ 389,500) (1986 E) 111,300
Cangshan (Bianzhuang)
(1982 C) 79,334
Cangzhou (▲ 293,600)
(1986 E) 196,700
Changchun
(▲ 2,000,000) 1,822,000
Changde (▲ 220,800)
(1986 E) 178,200
Changge (1982 C) 67,002
Changji (▲ 233,400)
(1986 E) 110,500
Changsha 1,230,000
Changshou (1985 E) 51,923
Changshu (▲ 998,000)
(1986 E) 281,300
Changtu (1985 E) 49,937
Changyi (1982 C) 64,513
Changzhi (▲ 463,400)
(1986 E) 273,000
Changzhou
(Changchow)
(▲ 1,214,500) 522,700
Chaoan (▲ 1,214,500)
(1986 E) 265,400
Chaoxian (▲ 739,500)
(1986 E) 116,800
Chaoyang, Guangdong
prov. (1985 E) 85,968
Chaoyang, Liaoning
prov. (▲ 318,900)
(1986 E) 180,300
Chengde (▲ 330,400)
(1986 E) 226,600
Chengdu (Chengtu)
(▲ 2,960,000) 1,884,000
Chenghai (1985 E) 50,631
Chenxian (▲ 191,900)
(1986 E) 143,500
Chifeng (Ulanhad)
(▲ 882,900) (1986 E) 299,000
Chongqing (Chungking)
(▲ 2,890,000) 2,502,000
Chuxian (▲ 365,000)
(1986 E) 113,300
Chuxiong (▲ 379,400)
(1986 E) 67,700
Da'an (1985 E) 70,552
Dachangzhen (1975 U) 50,000
Dalian (Dairen) 2,280,000
Danyang (1985 E) 48,449
Daqing (▲ 880,000) 640,000
Dashiqiao (1985 E) 68,898
Datong (1985 E) 55,529
Datong (▲ 1,040,000) 810,000
Dawa (1985 E) 142,581
Daxian (▲ 209,400)
(1986 E) 142,000
Dehui (1985 E) 60,247
Dengfeng (1982 C) 49,746
Deqing (1982 C) 48,726
Deyang (▲ 753,400)
(1986 E) 184,800
Dezhou (▲ 276,200)
(1986 E) 161,300
Didao (1975 U) 50,000
Dinghai (1985 E) 50,161
Dongchuan (Xincun)
(▲ 275,100) (1986 E) 67,400
Dongguan
(▲ 1,208,500)
(1986 E) 254,900
Dongsheng (▲ 121,300)
(1986 E) 57,500
Dongtai (1985 E) 65,788
Dongying (▲ 514,400)
(1986 E) 178,100
Dukou (▲ 551,200)
(1986 E) 380,200
Dunhua (▲ 448,000)
(1986 E) 217,100
Duyun (▲ 386,600)
(1986 E) 123,800
Echeng (▲ 938,000)
(1986 E) 217,400
Enshi (▲ 679,000)
(1986 E) 84,300
Ergun Zuoqi (1985 E) 55,970
Feixian (1982 C) 73,246
Fengcheng (1985 E) 66,745
Foshan (▲ 312,700)
(1986 E) 243,500
Fujin (1985 E) 60,948
Fuling (▲ 973,500)
(1986 E) 166,300
Fushun (Funan) 1,290,000
Fuxian (Wafangdian)
(▲ 960,700) (1986 E) 246,200
Fuxinshi 700,000
Fuyang (▲ 195,200)
(1986 E) 143,400
Fuyu, Heilongjiang
prov. (1985 E) 48,670
Fuyu, Jilin prov.
(1986 E) 98,373
Fuzhou, Fujian prov.
(▲ 1,240,000) 910,000

Fuzhou, Jiangxi prov.
(▲ 171,800) (1986 E) 106,700
Gaixian (1985 E) 67,587
Ganhe (1985 E) 48,128
Ganzhou (▲ 346,000)
(1986 E) 191,600
Gaoqing (Tianzhen)
(1982 C) 70,411
Gaoyou (1985 E) 57,844
Gejiu (Kokiu)
(▲ 341,700) (1986 E) 193,600
Golmud (1986 E) 60,300
Gongchangling
(1982 C) 49,281
Guanghua (▲ 420,000)
(1986 E) 104,400
Guangyuan (▲ 805,500)
(1986 E) 162,200
Guangzhou (Canton)
(▲ 3,420,000) 3,100,000
Guanxian, Shandong
prov. (1982 C) 49,782
Guanxian, Sichuan
prov. (1985 E) 65,039
Guilin (Kweilin)
(▲ 457,500) (1986 E) 324,200
Guixian (1985 E) 61,970
Guiyang (Kweiyang)
(▲ 1,430,000) 1,030,000
Haicheng (▲ 984,800)
(1986 E) 210,700
Haifeng (1985 E) 50,401
Haikou (▲ 289,600)
(1986 E) 209,200
Hailaer (1986 E) 180,000
Hailin (1985 E) 58,909
Hailong (Meihekou)
(▲ 534,200) (1986 E) 117,500
Hailun (1985 E) 83,448
Haiyang (Dongcun)
(1982 C) 77,098
Hami (Kumul)
(▲ 270,300) (1986 E) 146,400
Hancheng (▲ 304,200)
(1986 E) 66,600
Handan (▲ 1,030,000) 870,000
Hangu (1975 U) 100,000
Hangzhou (Hangchow) 1,290,000
Hanzhong (▲ 415,000)
(1986 E) 151,700
Harbin 2,710,000
Hebi (▲ 321,600)
(1986 E) 158,500
Hechi (▲ 266,800)
(1986 E) 74,400
Hechuan (1985 E) 65,237
Hefei (▲ 930,000) 740,000
Hegang (1986 E) 588,300
Helong (1985 E) 62,665
Hengshui (▲ 286,500)
(1986 E) 83,100
Hengyang (▲ 601,300)
(1986 E) 419,200
Heze (Caozhou)
(▲ 1,001,500)
(1986 E) 115,400
Hohhot (▲ 830,000) 670,000
Hongjiang (▲ 67,000)
(1986 E) 54,300
Horqin Youyi Qianqi
(Ulan Hot)
(▲ 192,100) (1986 E) 129,100
Hotan (▲ 122,800)
(1986 E) 71,700
Houma (▲ 158,500)
(1986 E) 67,000
Huadian (1985 E) 75,183
Huaian (1985 E) 65,673
Huaibei (▲ 447,200)
(1986 E) 252,100
Huaide (▲ 899,400)
(1986 E) 187,600
Huaihua (▲ 427,100)
(1986 E) 102,000
Huainan (▲ 1,110,000) 700,000
Huaiyin (Wangying)
(▲ 382,500) (1986 E) 201,700
Huanan (1985 E) 66,596
Huanggang (1982 C) 65,961
Huangshi (1986 E) 451,900
Huayuan (Huarong)
(▲ 313,500) (1986 E) 81,000
Huinan (Chaoyang)
(1985 E) 52,429
Huizhou (▲ 182,100)
(1986 E) 117,000
Hulan (1985 E) 74,989
Hunjiang (Badaojiang)
(▲ 687,700) (1986 E) 442,600
Huzhou (▲ 964,400)
(1986 E) 208,500
Jiading (1985 E) 60,718
Jiamusi (Kiamusze)
(▲ 570,700) (1986 E) 429,800
Jian (▲ 184,300)
(1986 E) 132,200
Jiangling (1985 E) 77,887
Jiangmen (▲ 231,700)
(1986 E) 168,800
Jiangyin (1985 E) 66,476
Jiangyou (1985 E) 72,663
Jianou (1985 E) 55,180
Jiaohe (1985 E) 51,504
Jiaojiang (▲ 385,200)
(1986 E) 82,300
Jiaoxian (1985 E) 51,869
Jiaozuo (▲ 509,900)
(1986 E) 335,400
Jiawang (1975 U) 50,000

Jiaxing (▲ 686,500)
(1986 E) 210,200
Jiayuguan (▲ 102,100)
(1986 E) 73,800
Jiexiu (1985 E) 51,300
Jieyang (1985 E) 98,531
Jilin (Kirin) 1,200,000
Jinan (Tsinan)
(▲ 2,140,000) 1,546,000
Jinchang (Baijiazui)
(▲ 136,000) (1986 E) 90,500
Jincheng (▲ 612,700)
(1986 E) 99,900
Jingdezhen
(Kingtechen)
(▲ 569,700) (1986 E) 304,000
Jingmen (▲ 946,500)
(1986 E) 227,000
Jinhua (▲ 799,900)
(1986 E) 147,800
Jining, Nei Monggol
prov. (1982 C) 163,300
Jining, Shandong prov.
(▲ 765,700) (1986 E) 222,600
Jinshi (▲ 219,700)
(1986 E) 73,700
Jinxi (▲ 634,300)
(1986 E) 223,100
Jinxian (1985 E) 95,761
Jinzhou (Chinchou)
(▲ 810,000) 710,000
Jishou (▲ 194,500)
(1986 E) 59,500
Jishu (1985 E) 75,587
Jiujiang (▲ 382,300)
(1986 E) 248,500
Jiuquan (Suzhou)
(▲ 269,900) (1986 E) 56,300
Jiutai (1985 E) 63,021
Jixi (▲ 820,000) 700,000
Jixian (1985 E) 59,725
Juancheng (1982 C) 54,110
Junan (Shizilu) (1982 C) ...90,222
Junxian (▲ 423,400)
(1986 E) 97,000
Juxian (1982 C) 51,666
Kaifeng (▲ 629,100)
(1986 E) 458,800
Kaili (▲ 342,100)
(1986 E) 96,600
Kaiping (1985 E) 54,145
Kaiyuan (▲ 342,100)
(1986 E) 96,600
Kaiyuan (1985 E) 85,762
Karamay (1986 E) 185,300
Kashi (▲ 194,500)
(1986 E) 146,300
Keshan (1985 E) 65,088
Korla (▲ 219,000)
(1986 E) 129,400
Kunming (▲ 1,550,000) ...1,310,000
Kuqa (1985 E) 63,847
Kuytun (1986 E) 60,200
Laiwu (▲ 1,041,800)
(1986 E) 143,500
Langxiang (1985 E) 64,658
Lanxi (1985 E) 53,236
Lanxi (▲ 606,800)
(1986 E) 70,500
Lanzhou (Lanchow)
(▲ 1,420,000) 1,297,000
Lechang (1986 E) 56,913
Lengshuijiang
(▲ 277,600) (1986 E) 101,700
Lengshuitan
(▲ 362,100) (1986 E) 60,900
Leshan (▲ 972,300)
(1986 E) 307,300
Lhasa (▲ 107,700)
(1986 E) 84,400
Lianyungang (Xinpu)
(▲ 459,400) (1986 E) 288,000
Liaocheng (▲ 724,300)
(1986 E) 119,000
Liaoyang (▲ 576,900)
(1986 E) 442,600
Liaoyuan (1986 E) 370,400
Liling (▲ 856,300)
(1986 E) 107,100
Linfen (▲ 530,100)
(1986 E) 157,600
Lingling (▲ 515,300)
(1986 E) 72,700
Lingyuan (1985 E) 66,825
Linhai (1985 E) 52,653
Linhe (▲ 365,900)
(1986 E) 99,800
Linkou (1985 E) 52,936
Linqing (▲ 603,000)
(1986 E) 87,000
Linqu (1982 C) 84,196
Linxia (▲ 150,200)
(1986 E) 72,900
Linyi (▲ 1,365,000)
(1986 E) 190,000
Liuzhou 680,000
Longjiang (1985 E) 51,156
Longyan (▲ 378,500)
(1986 E) 114,500
Loudi (▲ 254,300)
(1986 E) 84,200
Lu'an (▲ 163,400)
(1986 E) 122,600
Lufeng (1985 E) 53,015
Luohe (▲ 159,100)
(1986 E) 102,300
Luoyang (Loyang)
(▲ 1,090,000) 760,000
Luzhou (▲ 360,300)
(1986 E) 237,800

C Census.   E Official estimate.   U Unofficial estimate.

• Largest city in country.

★ Population or designation of metropolitan area, including suburbs (see headnote).
▲ Population of an entire municipality, commune, or district, including rural area.

202

Maanshan (▲ 367,000)
(1986 E) 258,900
Manzhouli (1986 E) 116,600
Maoming (▲ 434,900)
(1986 E) 118,600
Meixian (▲ 740,600)
(1986 E) 169,100
Mengxian (1982 C) 55,000
Mengyin (1982 C) 70,602
Mianyang, Sichuan
prov. (▲ 848,500)
(1986 E) 233,900
Minhang (1975 U) 60,000
Mishan (1985 E) 54,919
Mixian (1982 C) 64,776
Mudanjiang 650,000
Nahe (1985 E) 49,725
N'aizishen (1985 E) 51,982
Nancha (1975 U) 50,000
Nanchang
(▲ 1,260,000) 1,090,000
Nanchong (▲ 238,100)
(1986 E) 158,000
Nanjing (Nanking) 2,390,000
Nanning (▲ 1,000,000) 720,000
Nanpiao (1982 C) 67,274
Nanping (▲ 420,800)
(1986 E) 157,100
Nantong (▲ 411,000)
(1986 E) 308,800
Nanyang (▲ 294,800)
(1986 E) 199,400
Neihuang (1982 C) 56,039
Neijiang (▲ 298,500)
(1986 E) 191,100
Ningbo (▲ 1,050,000) 570,000
Ningyang (1982 C) 55,424
Nong'an (1985 E) 55,966
Nunjiang (1985 E) 59,276
Orogen Zizhiqi (1985 E) ...48,042
Panshan (▲ 343,100)
(1986 E) 248,100
Panshi (1985 E) 59,270
Pingdingshan
(▲ 819,900) (1986 E) ...363,200
Pingliang (▲ 362,500)
(1986 E) 85,400
Pingxiang
(▲ 1,286,700)
(1986 E) 368,700
Pingyi (1982 C) 89,373
Pingyin (1982 C) 62,827
Potou (▲ 456,100)
(1986 E) 59,000
Puqi (1985 E) 65,239
Putian (▲ 265,400)
(1986 E) 64,600
Putuo (1985 E) 50,962
Puyang (▲ 1,086,100)
(1986 E) 131,000
Qian Gorlos (1985 E) 79,494
Qingdao (Tsingtao) 1,300,000
Qingjiang (▲ 246,617)
(1982 C) 150,000
Qingyuan (1985 E) 51,756
Qinhuangdao
(Chinwangtao)
(★ 436,000) (1986 E) ...307,500
Qinzhou (▲ 923,400)
(1986 E) 97,100
Qiqihar (Tsitsihar)
(▲ 1,330,000) 1,180,000
Qitaihe (▲ 309,900)
(1986 E) 166,400
Qixia (1982 C) 54,158
Qixian (1982 C) 53,041
Quanzhou (Chuanchou)
(▲ 436,000) (1986 E) ...157,000
Qujing (▲ 758,000)
(1986 E) 135,000
Quxian (▲ 704,800)
(1986 E) 124,000
Raoping (1985 E) 54,831
Rizhao (▲ 970,300)
(1986 E) 93,300
Rongcheng (1982 C) 52,878
Rugao (1985 E) 50,643
Ruian (1985 E) 57,993
Sanmenxia (Shanxian)
(▲ 150,000) (1986 E) 79,000
Sanming (▲ 214,300)
(1986 E) 144,900
• Shanghai
(★ 9,300,000) 7,220,000
Shangqiu (Zhuji)
(▲ 199,400) (1986 E) ...135,400
Shangrao (▲ 142,500)
(1986 E) 113,000
Shangshui (1982 C) 50,191
Shantou (Swatow)
(▲ 790,000) 560,000
Shanwei (1985 E) 61,234
Shaoguan (1986 E) 363,100
Shaowu (▲ 266,700)
(1986 E) 81,400
Shaoxing (▲ 250,900)
(1986 E) 167,100
Shaoyang (▲ 465,900)
(1986 E) 218,600
Shashi (1986 E) 253,700
Shenxian (1982 C) 50,208
Shenyang (Mukden)
(▲ 4,370,000) 3,910,000
Shenzhen (▲ 231,900)
(1986 E) 189,600
Shiguaigou (1975 U) 50,000
Shihezi (▲ 549,300)
(1987 E) 304,700
Shijiazhuang 1,220,000

Shiyan (▲ 332,600)
(1986 E) 227,300
Shizuishan (▲ 317,400)
(1986 E) 225,500
Shouguang (1982 C) 83,400
Shuangcheng (1985 E) 91,163
Shuangliao (1985 E) 67,324
Shuangyashan (1986 E) ...427,300
Shuicheng
(▲ 2,216,500)
(1986 E) 363,500
Shulan (1986 E) 50,582
Shunde (1985 E) 50,262
Siping (▲ 357,800)
(1986 E) 280,100
Sishui (1982 C) 82,990
Songjiang (1985 E) 71,864
Songjianghe (1985 E) 53,023
Suihua (▲ 732,100)
(1986 E) 200,400
Suileng (1985 E) 68,399
Suining (▲ 1,174,900)
(1986 E) 118,500
Suixian (▲ 1,281,600)
(1986 E) 187,700
Suqian (1985 E) 50,742
Suxian (▲ 218,600)
(1986 E) 123,300
Suzhou (Soochow) 740,000
Tai'an (▲ 1,325,400)
(1986 E) 215,900
Taiyuan (▲ 1,980,000) ..1,700,000
Taizhou (▲ 210,800)
(1987 E) 143,200
Tancheng (1982 C) 61,857
Tangshan
(▲ 1,440,000) 1,080,000
Tao'an (1985 E) 76,269
Tengxian (1985 E) 53,254
Tianjin (Tientsin)
(▲ 5,540,000) 4,950,000
Tianshui (▲ 953,200)
(1986 E) 209,500
Tiefa (▲ 146,367)
(1982 C) 60,000
Tieli (1985 E) 102,527
Tieling (▲ 454,100)
(1986 E) 326,100
Tongchuan (▲ 393,200)
(1986 E) 268,900
Tonghua (▲ 367,400)
(1986 E) 290,200
Tongliao (▲ 253,100)
(1986 E) 190,100
Tongling (▲ 216,400)
(1986 E) 182,900
Tongren (1985 E) 50,307
Tongxian (1985 E) 97,168
Tumen (▲ 99,700)
(1986 E) 77,600
Tunxi (▲ 104,500)
(1986 E) 61,800
Turpan (▲ 196,800)
(1986 E) 52,300
Ürümqi 1,060,000
Wangkui (1985 E) 52,021
Wangqing (1985 E) 61,237
Wanxian (▲ 280,800)
(1986 E) 138,700
Weifang (▲ 1,042,200)
(1986 E) 312,500
Weihai (▲ 220,800)
(1986 E) 83,000
Weinan (▲ 699,400)
(1986 E) 111,300
Weishan (Xiazhen)
(1982 C) 57,932
Weixian (Hanting)
(1982 C) 50,180
Wenzhou (▲ 530,600)
(1986 E) 372,200
Wuchang (1985 E) 64,403
Wuhai (1986 E) 266,000
Wuhan 3,570,000
Wuhu (▲ 502,200)
(1986 E) 396,000
Wulian (Hongning)
(1982 C) 51,718
Wusong (1982 C) 64,017
Wuwei (Liangzhou)
(▲ 804,000) (1986 E) ...115,500
Wuxi (Wuhsi) 880,000
Wuzhong (▲ 402,400)
(1986 E) 48,600
Wuzhou (Wuchow)
(▲ 261,500) (1986 E) ...194,800
Xiaguan (▲ 395,800)
(1986 E) 112,100
Xiamen (Amoy)
(▲ 546,400) (1986 E) ...343,700
Xi'an (Sian)
(▲ 2,580,000) 2,210,000
Xiangfan (▲ 421,200)
(1986 E) 314,900
Xiangtan (▲ 511,100)
(1986 E) 389,500
Xianning (▲ 402,200)
(1986 E) 122,200
Xianyang (▲ 641,800)
(1986 E) 285,900
Xiaogan (▲ 1,204,400)
(1986 E) 125,500
Xiaoshan (1985 E) 63,074
Xichang (▲ 161,000)
(1986 E) 105,000
Xinghua (1985 E) 75,573
Xinglongzhen (1982 C) 52,961
Xingtai (▲ 350,800)
(1986 E) 265,600
Xinhui (1985 E) 77,381

Xining (Sining) 620,000
Xinmin (1985 E) 47,900
Xintai (▲ 1,157,300)
(1986 E) 171,400
Xinwen (Suncun)
(1975 U) 50,000
Xinxian (▲ 398,600)
(1986 E) 74,200
Xinxiang (▲ 540,500)
(1986 E) 411,000
Xinyang (▲ 234,200)
(1986 E) 169,100
Xinyu (▲ 610,600)
(1986 E) 140,200
Xuancheng (1985 E) 52,387
Xuanhua (1975 U) 140,000
Xuanwei (1982 C) 70,081
Xuchang (▲ 247,200)
(1986 E) 167,800
Xuguit Qi (Yakeshi)
(1986 E) 390,000
Xuzhou (Süchow) 860,000
Yaan (▲ 277,600)
(1986 E) 89,200
Yan'an (▲ 259,800)
(1986 E) 86,700
Yancheng
(▲ 1,251,400)
(1986 E) 258,400
Yangcheng (1982 C) 57,255
Yangjiang (1986 E) 91,433
Yangquan (▲ 478,900)
(1986 E) 295,100
Yangzhou (▲ 417,300)
(1986 E) 321,500
Yanji (▲ 216,900)
(1986 E) 175,000
Yanji (Longjing)
(1985 E) 55,035
Yanling (1982 C) 52,679
Yantai (Chefoo)
(▲ 717,300) (1986 E) ...327,000
Yanzhou (1985 E) 48,972
Yaxian (Sanya)
(▲ 321,700) (1986 E) 70,500
Yi'an (1986 E) 54,253
Yibin (Ipin) (▲ 636,500)
(1986 E) 218,800
Yichang (Ichang)
(1986 E) 410,500
Yichuan (1982 C) 58,914
Yichun, Heilongjiang
prov. 840,000
Yichun, Jiangxi prov.
(▲ 770,200) (1986 E) ...132,600
Yidu (1985 E) 54,838
Yilan (1985 E) 50,436
Yima (▲ 84,800)
(1986 E) 53,700
Yinan (Jiehu) (1982 C) 67,803
Yinchuan (▲ 396,900)
(1986 E) 268,200
Yingchengzi (1985 E) 59,072
Yingkou (▲ 480,000)
(1986 E) 366,900
Yingtan (▲ 116,200)
(1986 E) 64,500
Yining (Kuldja)
(▲ 232,000) (1986 E) ...153,200
Yiyang (▲ 365,000)
(1986 E) 155,300
Yiyuan (Nanma)
(1982 C) 53,800
Yongan (▲ 269,000)
(1986 E) 105,100
Yongchuan (1985 E) 70,444
Yuci (▲ 420,700)
(1986 E) 171,000
Yueyang (▲ 411,300)
(1986 E) 239,500
Yulin, Guangxi
Zhuangzu prov.
(▲ 1,228,800)
(1986 E) 115,600
Yulin, Shaanxi prov.
(1985 E) 51,610
Yumen (Laojunmiao)
(▲ 160,100) (1986 E) 84,300
Yuncheng, Shandong
prov. (1982 C) 54,262
Yuncheng, Shanxi prov.
(▲ 434,900) (1986 E) 87,000
Yunyang (1982 C) 54,903
Yushu (1985 E) 57,222
Yuyao (▲ 772,700)
(1986 E) 169,700
Zaozhuang
(▲ 1,592,000)
(1986 E) 292,200
Zhangjiakou (Kalgan)
(▲ 640,000) 500,000
Zhangye (▲ 394,200)
(1986 E) 73,000
Zhangzhou (Longxi)
(▲ 310,400) (1986 E) ...159,400
Zhanhua (Fuguo)
(1982 C) 48,193
Zhanjiang (▲ 920,900)
(1986 E) 335,500
Zhaodong (1985 E) 99,836
Zhaoqing (Gaoyao)
(▲ 187,600) (1986 E) ...145,700
Zhaotong (▲ 546,600)
(1986 E) 77,500
Zhaoyuan (1982 C) 56,389
Zhengzhou
(Chengchow)
(▲ 1,580,000) 1,150,000
Zhenjiang (1986 E) 412,400

Zhongshan (Shiqizhen)
(▲ 1,059,700)
(1986 E) 238,700
Zhoucun (1975 U) 50,000
Zhoukouzhen
(▲ 220,400) (1986 E) ...110,500
Zhuhai (▲ 155,000)
(1986 E) 88,000
Zhumadian (▲ 149,500)
(1986 E) 99,400
Zhuoxian (1985 E) 54,523
Zhuzhou (Chuchow)
(▲ 499,600) (1986 E) ...344,800
Zibo (Zhangdian)
(▲ 2,370,000) 840,000
Zigong (Tzukung)
(▲ 909,300) (1986 E) ...361,700
Zixing (▲ 334,300)
(1986 E) 97,100
Ziyang (1985 E) 57,349
Zouping (1982 C) 49,274
Zouxian (1985 E) 61,578
Zunyi (▲ 347,600)
(1986 E) 236,600

COLOMBIA

1985 C 27,867,326

Cities and Towns

Armenia 187,130
Barrancabermeja 137,406
Barranquilla
(★ 1,140,000) 899,781
Bello (★ Medellín) 212,861
Bucaramanga
(★ 550,000) 352,326
Buenaventura 160,342
Buga 82,992
Cali (★ 1,400,000) 1,350,565
Cartagena 531,426
Cartago 97,791
Ciénaga 56,860
Cúcuta (★ 445,000) 379,478
Dos Quebradas
(★ Pereira) 101,480
Duitama 56,390
Envigado (★ Medellín) 91,391
Florencia 66,430
Floridablanca
(★ Bucaramanga) 143,824
Girardot 70,078
Ibagué 292,965
Itagüí (★ Medellín) 137,623
Magangué 49,160
Malambo
(★ Barranquilla) 52,584
Manizales (★ 330,000) ...299,352
Medellín (★ 2,095,000) .1,468,089
Montería 157,466
Neiva 194,556
Ocaña 51,443
Palmira 175,186
Pasto 197,407
Pereira (★ 390,000) 233,271
Popayán 141,964
• SANTA FE DE
BOGOTÁ
(★ 4,260,000) 3,982,941
Santa Marta 177,922
Sincelejo 120,537
Soacha (★ Santa Fe de
Bogotá) 109,051
Sogamoso 64,437
Soledad
(★ Barranquilla) 165,791
Tuluá 99,721
Tunja 93,792
Valledupar 142,771
Villa Rosario (★ Cúcuta) ..63,615
Villavicencio 178,685

COMOROS / Al-Qumur / Comores

1990 E 452,742

Cities and Towns

• MORONI 23,432

CONGO

1984 C 1,912,429

Cities and Towns

• BRAZZAVILLE 585,812
Dolisie 49,134
Pointe-Noire 294,203

COOK ISLANDS

1986 C 18,155

Cities and Towns

• AVARUA 9,678

COSTA RICA

1988 E 2,851,000

Cities and Towns

Limón (▲ 62,600) 40,400
• SAN JOSÉ
(★ 670,000) 278,600

COTE D'IVOIRE / Côte d' Ivoire

1983 E 9,300,000

Cities and Towns

• ABIDJAN 1,950,000

Bouaké 275,000
Daloa 70,000
Korhogo 125,000
Man 55,000
YAMOUSSOUKRO 80,000

CROATIA / Hrvatska

1987 E 4,673,517

Cities and Towns

Osijek (★ 162,490) 106,800
Rijeka (★ 199,282) 166,400
Split 197,074
• ZAGREB 697,925

CUBA

1987 E 10,288,000

Cities and Towns

Bayamo 108,716
Camagüey 265,588
Cárdenas (1981 C) 59,352
Cienfuegos 112,225
Guantánamo 179,091
Holguín 199,861
• LA HABANA (HAVANA)
(★ 2,125,000) 2,036,800
Manzanillo (1981 C) 87,830
Matanzas 106,954
Palma Soriano (1981 C) 55,851
Pinar del Río 108,109
Santa Clara 182,349
Santiago de Cuba 364,554
Victoria de las Tunas
(1985 E) 91,400

CYPRUS / Kıbrıs / Kípros

1982 C 512,097

Cities and Towns

Lemesós (Limassol)
(★ 107,161) 74,782
• NICOSIA (LEVKOSÍA)
(★ 185,000) 48,221

CYPRUS, NORTH / Kuzey Kıbrıs

1985 E 160,287

Cities and Towns

• NICOSIA (LEFKOŞA) 37,400

CZECH REPUBLIC / Česká Republika

1990 E 10,362,553

Cities and Towns

Brno (★ 450,000) 392,285
České Budějovice
(★ 114,000) 99,428
Chomutov (★ 80,000) 55,735
Děčín (★ 72,000) 56,034
Frýdek-Místek
(★ Ostrava) 66,791
Havířov (★ Ostrava) 92,037
Hradec Králové
(★ 113,000) 101,302
Jihlava 54,855
Karlovy Vary (Carlsbad) ...58,039
Karviná (★ ★ Ostrava) 69,521
Kladno (★ 88,500) 73,347
Liberec (★ 175,000) 104,256
Mladá Boleslav 49,195
Most (★ 135,000) 71,360
Olomouc (★ 126,000) 107,044
Opava (★ 77,500) 63,440
Ostrava (★ 760,000) 331,557
Pardubice 95,909
Plzeň (★ 210,000) 175,038
• PRAHA (PRAGUE)
(★ 1,325,000) 1,215,656
Přerov 51,996
Prostějov 52,074
Teplice (★ 94,000) 55,287
Ústí nad Labem
(★ 115,000) 106,499
Zlín (★ 124,000) 87,189

DENMARK / Danmark

1990 E 5,135,409

Cities and Towns

Ålborg (★ 155,019) 114,000
Århus (▲ 261,437) 202,300
Esbjerg (▲ 81,504) 71,900
Frederiksberg
(★ København) 85,611
Gentofte
(★ København) 65,303
Gladsakse
(★ København) 60,882
Helsingør (Elsinore)
(★ København) 56,701
• KØBENHAVN
(★ 1,685,000) 466,723
Kongens Lyngby
(★ København) 49,317
Odense (▲ 176,133) 140,100
Randers 61,020

DJIBOUTI

1976 E 226,000

Cities and Towns

• DJIBOUTI 120,000

C Census.   E Official estimate.   U Unofficial estimate.
• Largest city in country.

★ Population or designation of metropolitan area, including suburbs (see headnote).
▲ Population of an entire municipality, commune, or district, including rural area.

World Populations

DOMINICA

1984 E 77,000

Cities and Towns

• ROSEAU 9,348

DOMINICAN REPUBLIC / República Dominicana

1981 C 5,647,977

Cities and Towns

Barahona 49,334
La Romana 91,571
San Cristóbal 58,520
San Francisco de
  Macorís 64,906
San Juan [de la
  Maguana] 49,764
San Pedro de Macorís 78,562
Santiago [de los
  Caballeros] 278,638
• SANTO DOMINGO 1,313,172

ECUADOR

1987 E 9,923,000

Cities and Towns

Alfaro (★ Guayaquil)
  (1982 C) 51,023
Ambato 126,067
Cuenca 201,490
Esmeraldas 120,387
• Guayaquil
  (★ 1,580,000) 1,572,615
Ibarra (1982 C) 53,428
Loja (1982 C) 71,652
Machala 144,396
Manta 135,990
Milagro 102,884
Portoviejo 141,568
Quevedo (1982 C) 67,023
QUITO (★ 1,300,000) 1,137,705
Riobamba (1982 C) 75,455
Santo Domingo de los
  Colorados 104,059

EGYPT / Miṣr

1986 C 48,205,049

Cities and Towns

Abū Kabīr 69,500
Akhmīm 70,602
Al-'Arīsh 67,638
Al-Fayyūm 212,523
Al-Hawāmidīyah
  (★ Al-Qāhirah) 73,060
Al-Iskandarīyah
  (Alexandria)
  (★ 3,350,000) 2,917,327
Al-Ismā'īlīyah
  (★ 235,000) 212,567
Al-Jīzah (Giza)
  (★ Al-Qāhirah) 1,870,508
Al-Mahallah al-Kubrā 358,844
Al-Manṣūrah
  (★ 375,000) 316,870
Al-Manzilah 55,090
Al-Maṭarīyah 74,554
Al-Minyā 179,136
• AL-QĀHIRAH (CAIRO)
  (★ 9,300,000) 6,052,836
Al-Uqṣur (Luxor) 125,404
Armant 54,650
Ashmūn 54,450
As-Sinbillāwayn 60,285
As-Suways (Suez) 326,820
Aswān 191,461
Asyūṭ 273,191
Az-Zaqāzīq 245,496
Bahtīm (★ Al-Qāhirah) 275,807
Banhā 115,571
Banī Suwayf 151,813
Bilbays 96,540
Bilqās Qism Awwal 73,162
Būlāq ad-Dakrūr
  (★ Al-Qāhirah) 148,787
Būr Sa'īd (Port Said) 399,793
Būsh 54,482
Damanhūr 190,840
Disūq 78,119
Dumyāṭ (Damietta) 89,498
Ḥawsh 'Īsā (1980 C) 53,619
Idkū 70,729
Jirjā 70,989
Kafr ad-Dawwār
  (★ Al-Iskandarīyah) 195,102
Kafr ash-Shaykh 102,910
Kafr az-Zayyāt 58,061
Kawm Umbū 52,131
Maghāghah 50,807
Mallawī 99,062
Manfalūṭ 52,644
Minūf 69,883
Mīt Ghamr (★ 100,000) 92,253
Qalyūb 86,684
Qinā 119,794
Rashīd (Rosetta) 52,014
Rummānah 50,014
Samālūṭ 62,404
Sāqiyat Makkī 51,062
Sawhāj 132,965
Shibīn al-Kawm 132,751
Shubrā al-Khaymah
  (★ Al-Qāhirah) 710,794
Sinnūris 55,323
Tahṭā 58,516
Ṭalkhā (★ Al-Manṣūrah) 55,757

Ṭanṭā 334,505
Warrāq al-'Arab
  (★ Al-Qāhirah) 127,108
Ziftā (★★ Mīt Ghamr) 69,050

EL SALVADOR

1985 E 5,337,896

Cities and Towns

Delgado (★ San
  Salvador) 67,684
Mejicanos (★ San
  Salvador) 91,465
Nueva San Salvador
  (★ San Salvador) 53,688
San Miguel 88,520
• SAN SALVADOR
  (★ 920,000) 462,652
Santa Ana 137,879
Soyapango (★ San
  Salvador) 60,000

EQUATORIAL GUINEA / Guinea Ecuatorial

1983 C 300,000

Cities and Towns

• MALABO 31,630

ERITREA

1987 E 2,951,100

Cities and Towns

• ASMERA (1988 E) 319,353
Mitsiwa (1984 C) 15,441

ESTONIA / Eesti

1989 C 1,573,000

Cities and Towns

Kohtla-Järve (1987 E) 78,000
Narva (1987 E) 81,000
Pärnu (1987 E) 53,000
• TALLINN 482,000
Tartu 114,000

ETHIOPIA / Ityopiya

1987 E 43,004,600

Cities and Towns

• ADIS ABEBA
  (★ 1,500,000)
  (1988 E) 1,686,300
Akaki Beseka (★ Adis
  Abeba) 54,146
Bahir Dar 54,800
Debre Zeyit 51,143
Dese 68,848
Dire Dawa (1988 E) 117,042
Gonder 68,958
Harer 62,160
Jima 60,992
Mekele 61,583
Nazret 76,284

FAEROE ISLANDS / Føroyar

1990 E 47,946

Cities and Towns

• TÓRSHAVN 14,767

FALKLAND ISLANDS

1986 C 1,916

Cities and Towns

• STANLEY 1,200

FIJI

1986 C 715,375

Cities and Towns

Lautoka (★ 39,057) 28,728
• SUVA (★ 141,273) 69,665

FINLAND / Suomi

1988 E 4,938,602

Cities and Towns

Espoo (Esbo)
  (★ Helsinki) 164,569
Hämeenlinna 42,486
• HELSINKI
  (HELSINGFORS)
  (★ 1,040,000) 490,034
Joensuu 47,099
Jyväskylä (★ 93,000) 65,719
Kotka 57,745
Kouvola (★ 53,821) 31,933
Kuopio 78,916
Lahti (★ 108,000) 74,300
Lappeenranta
  (▲ 53,780) 47,400
Oulu (★ 121,000) 98,582
Pori 77,395
Tampere (★ 241,000) 170,533
Turku (Åbo)
  (★ 228,000) 160,456
Vaasa (Vasa) 53,737
Vantaa (Vanda)
  (★ Helsinki) 149,063

FRANCE

1982 C 54,334,871

Cities and Towns

Aix-en-Provence
  (★ 126,552) 121,327
Ajaccio 54,089
Albi (★ 60,181) 45,947
Alès (★ 70,180) 43,268
Amiens (★ 154,498) 131,332
Angers (★ 195,859) 136,038
Angoulême (★ 103,552) 46,197
Annecy (★ 112,632) 49,965
Antibes (★★ Cannes) 62,859
Antony (★ Paris) 54,610
Argenteuil (★ Paris) 95,347
Arras (★ 80,477) 41,736
Asnières [-sur-Seine]
  (★ Paris) 71,077
Aubervilliers (★ Paris) 67,719
Aulnay-sous-Bois
  (★ Paris) 75,996
Avignon (★ 174,264) 89,132
Bayonne (★ 127,477) 41,381
Beauvais (★ 55,817) 52,365
Belfort (★ 76,221) 51,206
Besançon (★ 120,772) 113,283
Béthune (★ 258,383) 25,508
Béziers (★ 81,347) 76,647
Bordeaux (★ 640,012) 208,159
Boulogne-Billancourt
  (★ Paris) 102,582
Boulogne-sur-Mer
  (★ 98,566) 47,653
Bourges (★ 92,202) 76,432
Brest (★ 201,145) 156,060
Brive-la-Gaillarde
  (★ 64,301) 51,511
Caen (★ 183,526) 114,068
Calais (★ 100,823) 76,527
Cannes (★ 295,525) 72,259
Châlons-sur-Marne
  (★ 63,061) 51,137
Chalon-sur-Saône
  (★ 78,064) 56,194
Chambéry (★ 96,163) 53,427
Champigny-sur-Marne
  (★ Paris) 76,176
Charleville-Mézières
  (★ 67,694) 58,667
Châteauroux
  (★ 66,851) 51,942
Cherbourg (★ 85,485) 28,442
Cholet 55,524
Clermont-Ferrand
  (★ 256,189) 147,361
Colmar (★ 82,468) 62,483
Colombes (★ Paris) 78,777
Courbevoie (★ Paris) 59,830
Créteil (★ Paris) 71,693
Dieppe (★ 41,812) 35,957
Dijon (★ 215,865) 140,942
Douai (★ 202,366) 42,576
Drancy (★ Paris) 60,183
Dunkerque (★ 195,705) 73,120
Épinay-sur-Seine
  (★ Paris) 50,314
Fontenay-sous-Bois
  (★ Paris) 52,627
Forbach (★ 99,606) 27,187
Grenoble (★ 392,021) 156,637
Hagondange
  (★ 119,669) 9,091
Ivry-sur-Seine (★ Paris) 55,699
La Rochelle
  (★ 102,143) 75,840
La Seyne [-sur-Mer]
  (★ Toulon) 57,659
Laval (★ 55,984) 50,360
Le Havre (★ 254,595) 199,388
Le Mans (★ 191,080) 147,697
Levallois-Perret
  (★ Paris) 53,500
Lille (★ 1,020,000) 168,424
Limoges (★ 171,689) 140,400
Lorient (★ 104,025) 62,554
Lyon (★ 1,275,000) 413,095
Maisons-Alfort (★ Paris) 51,065
Mantes-la-Jolie
  (★ 170,265) 43,564
Marseille (★ 1,225,000) 874,436
Maubeuge (★ 105,714) 36,061
Melun (★ 82,479) 35,005
Mérignac (★ Bordeaux) 51,306
Metz (★ 186,437) 114,232
Montbéliard
  (★ 128,194) 31,836
Montluçon (★ 67,963) 49,912
Montpellier (★ 221,307) 197,231
Montreuil-sous-Bois
  (★ Paris) 93,368
Mulhouse (Mülhausen)
  (★ 220,613) 112,157
Nancy (★ 306,982) 96,317
Nanterre (★ Paris) 88,578
Nantes (★ 464,857) 240,539
Neuilly-sur-Seine
  (★ Paris) 64,170
Nice (★ 449,496) 337,085
Nîmes (★ 132,343) 124,220
Niort (★ 61,959) 58,203
Orléans (★ 220,478) 102,710
• PARIS (★ 9,775,000)
  (1987 E) 2,078,900
Pau (★ 131,265) 83,790
Perpignan (★ 137,915) 111,669
Pessac (★ Bordeaux) 50,267
Poitiers (★ 103,204) 79,350
Quimper 56,907

Reims (★ 199,388) 194,656
Rennes (★ 234,418) 117,234
Roanne (★ 81,786) 48,705
Roubaix (★★ Lille) 101,602
Rouen (★ 379,879) 101,945
Rueil-Malmaison
  (★ Paris) 63,412
Saint-Brieuc (★ 83,900) 48,563
Saint-Chamond
  (★ 82,059) 40,267
Saint-Denis (★ Paris) 90,829
Saint-Étienne
  (★ 317,228) 204,955
Saint-Maur-des-Fossés
  (★ Paris) 80,811
Saint-Nazaire
  (★ 130,271) 68,348
Saint-Quentin
  (★ 71,887) 63,567
Sarcelles (★ Paris) 53,630
Strasbourg (★ 400,000) 248,712
Tarbes (★ 78,056) 51,422
Thionville (★ 138,034) 40,573
Toulon (★ 410,393) 179,423
Toulouse (★ 541,271) 347,995
Tourcoing (★★ Lille) 96,908
Tours (★ 262,786) 132,209
Troyes (★ 125,240) 63,581
Valence (★ 106,041) 66,356
Valenciennes
  (★ 349,505) 40,275
Vénissieux (★ Lyon) 64,804
Versailles (★ Paris) 91,494
Villejuif (★ Paris) 52,448
Villeneuve-d'Ascq
  (★ Lille) 59,527
Villeurbanne (★ Lyon) 115,960
Vitry-sur-Seine (★ Paris) ... 85,263

FRENCH GUIANA / Guyane française

1982 C 73,022

Cities and Towns

• CAYENNE 38,091

FRENCH POLYNESIA / Polynésie française

1988 C 188,814

Cities and Towns

• PAPEETE (★ 80,000) 23,555

GABON

1985 E 1,312,000

Cities and Towns

Franceville 58,800
Lambaréné 49,500
LIBREVILLE 235,700
Port Gentil 124,400

GAMBIA

1983 C 696,000

Cities and Towns

• BANJUL (★ 95,000) 44,536

GEORGIA / Sakartvelo

1989 C 5,449,000

Cities and Towns

Batumi 136,000
Gori (1987 E) 62,000
Kutaisi 235,000
Poti (1977 E) 54,000
Rustavi (★ Tbilisi) 159,000
Suchumi 121,000
• TBILISI (★ 1,460,000) 1,260,000

GERMANY / Deutschland

1989 E 78,389,735

Cities and Towns

Aachen (★ 535,000) 233,255
Aalen (★ 80,000) 62,812
Ahlen 52,836
Altenburg 53,288
Arnsberg 73,912
Aschaffenburg
  (★ 145,000) 62,048
Augsburg (★ 405,000) 247,731
Baden-Baden 50,761
Bad Homburg
  (★ Frankfurt am
  Main) 51,035
Bad Salzuflen
  (★★ Herford) 50,875
Bamberg (★ 120,000) 69,809
Bautzen 52,394
Bayreuth (★ 90,000) 70,933
Bergheim (★ Köln) 55,997
Bergisch Gladbach
  (★ Köln) 101,983
Bergkamen (★★ Essen) 48,111
BERLIN (★ 3,825,000) 3,352,848
Bielefeld (★ 515,000) 311,946
Bitterfeld (★ 105,000) 20,513
Bocholt 67,565
Bochum (★★ Essen) 389,087
BONN (★ 570,000) 282,190
Bottrop (★ Essen) 116,363
Brandenburg 94,872
Braunschweig
  (★ 330,000) 253,794

Bremen (★ 800,000) 535,058
Bremerhaven
  (★ 190,000) 126,934
Castrop-Rauxel
  (★ Essen) 77,660
Celle 71,050
Chemnitz (★ 450,000) 311,765
Cottbus 128,639
Cuxhaven 55,249
Darmstadt (★ 305,000) 136,067
Delmenhorst
  (★★ Bremen) 72,901
Dessau (★ 140,000) 103,867
Detmold 66,809
Dinslaken (★ Essen) 63,246
Dormagen (★ Köln) 55,935
Dorsten (★ Essen) 75,518
Dortmund (★★ Essen) 587,328
Dresden (★ 670,000) 518,057
Duisburg (★ Essen) 527,447
Düren (★ 110,000) 83,120
Düsseldorf
  (★ 1,190,000) 569,641
Eberswalde 54,822
Eisenhüttenstadt 53,048
Emden 49,803
Erfurt 220,016
Erlangen
  (★★ Nürnberg) 100,583
Eschweiler
  (★★ Aachen) 53,516
• Essen (★ 4,950,000) 620,594
Esslingen (★ Stuttgart) 90,537
Flensburg (★ 103,000) 85,830
Frankfurt am Main
  (★ 1,855,000) 625,258
Frankfurt an der Oder 87,863
Freiberg 51,341
Freiburg [im Breisgau]
  (★ 225,000) 183,979
Friedrichshafen 52,295
Fulda (★ 79,000) 54,320
Fürth (★★ Nürnberg) 98,832
Garbsen (★ Hannover) 59,225
Garmisch-Partenkirchen 25,908
Gelsenkirchen
  (★★ Essen) 287,255
Gera 134,834
Giessen (★ 160,000) 71,751
Gladbeck (★ Essen) 79,187
Göppingen (★ 155,000) 52,873
Görlitz 77,609
Goslar (★ 84,000) 45,614
Gotha 57,365
Göttingen 118,073
Greifswald 68,597
Grevenbroich
  (★ Düsseldorf) 59,204
Gummersbach 49,017
Gütersloh
  (★★ Bielefeld) 83,407
Hagen (★★ Essen) 210,640
Halle (★ 475,000) 236,044
Halle-Neustadt (★ Halle) 93,446
Hamburg (★ 2,225,000) 1,603,070
Hameln (★ 72,000) 57,642
Hamm 173,611
Hanau (★★ Frankfurt
  am Main) 84,300
Hannover (★ 1,000,000) 498,495
Hattingen (★ Essen) 56,242
Heidelberg
  (★★ Mannheim) 131,429
Heidenheim (★ 89,000) 48,497
Heilbronn (★ 230,000) 112,278
Herford (★ 120,000) 61,700
Herne (★ Essen) 174,664
Herten (★ Essen) 68,111
Hilden (★ Düsseldorf) 53,725
Hildesheim (★ 140,000) 103,512
Hof 50,938
Hoyerswerda 69,361
Hürth (★ Köln) 49,094
Ingolstadt (★ 138,000) 97,702
Iserlohn 93,337
Jena 108,010
Kaiserslautern
  (★ 138,000) 96,990
Karlsruhe (★ 485,000) 265,100
Kassel (★ 360,000) 189,156
Kempten (Allgäu) 60,052
Kerpen (★ Köln) 54,699
Kiel (★ 335,000) 240,675
Kleve 44,416
Koblenz (★ 180,000) 107,286
Köln (Cologne)
  (★ 1,760,000) 937,482
Konstanz 72,862
Krefeld (★★ Essen) 235,423
Landshut 57,194
Langenfeld
  (★ Düsseldorf) 50,777
Leipzig (★ 700,000) 545,307
Leverkusen (★ Köln) 157,358
Lippstadt 60,396
Lübeck (★ 260,000) 210,681
Lüdenscheid 76,118
Ludwigsburg
  (★ Stuttgart) 79,342
Ludwigshafen
  (★★ Mannheim) 158,478
Lüneburg 60,053
Lünen (★ Essen) 85,584
Magdeburg (★ 400,000) 290,579
Mainz (★★ Wiesbaden) 174,828
Mannheim
  (★ 1,400,000) 300,468
Marburg an der Lahn 70,905
Marl (★ Essen) 89,651

C Census.   E Official estimate.   U Unofficial estimate.
• Largest city in country.

★ Population or designation of metropolitan area, including suburbs (see headnote).
▲ Population of an entire municipality, commune, or district, including rural area.

Column 1 (Germany continued)

Meerbusch
(★ Düsseldorf) 50,452
Menden 54,899
Minden (★ 125,000) 75,169
Moers (★ Essen) 101,809
Mönchengladbach
(★ 410,000) 252,910
Mülheim an der Ruhr
(★ Essen) 175,454
München (Munich)
(★ 1,955,000) 1,211,617
Münster 248,919
Neubrandenburg 90,471
Neumünster 79,574
Neunkirchen
(★ 135,000) 50,784
Neuss (★ Düsseldorf) 143,976
Neustadt an der
Weinstrasse 50,453
Neuwied (★ 150,000) 60,665
Norderstedt
(★ Hamburg) 66,747
Nürnberg (★ 1,030,000) ..480,078
Oberhausen
(★ ★ Essen) 221,017
Offenbach (★ Frankfurt
am Main) 112,450
Offenburg 51,730
Oldenburg 140,785
Osnabrück (★ 270,000) ...154,594
Paderborn 114,148
Passau 49,137
Pforzheim (★ 220,000) ...108,887
Plauen 77,593
Potsdam (★ Berlin) 142,862
Ratingen (★ Düsseldorf) ..89,880
Ravensburg (★ 75,000) 44,146
Recklinghausen
(★ Essen) 121,666
Regensburg
(★ 205,000) 119,078
Remscheid
(★ Wuppertal) 120,979
Reutlingen (★ 160,000) ..100,400
Rheine 69,324
Rosenheim 54,304
Rostock 253,990
Rüsselsheim
(★ ★ Wiesbaden) 58,426
Saarbrücken
(★ 385,000) 188,467
Saarlouis (★ 115,000) 37,662
Salzgitter 111,674
Sankt Augustin
(★ Bonn) 50,230
Schwäbisch Gmünd 57,861
Schwedt 52,419
Schweinfurt
(★ 110,000) 52,818
Schwerin 130,685
Schwerte (★ Essen) 49,017
Siegburg (★ 170,000) 34,402
Siegen (★ 200,000) 106,160
Sindelfingen
(★ Stuttgart) 57,524
Solingen
(★ ★ Wuppertal) 160,824
Stendal 49,906
Stolberg (★ ★ Aachen) 56,182
Stralsund 75,498
Stuttgart (★ 1,925,000) ..562,658
Suhl 56,345
Trier (★ 125,000) 95,692
Troisdorf
(★ ★ Siegburg) 62,011
Tübingen 76,046
Ulm (★ 210,000) 106,508
Unna (★ Essen) 61,989
Velbert (★ Essen) 88,058
Viersen
(★ ★ Mönchengladbach) ...76,163
Villingen-Schwenningen ...76,258
Weimar 63,412
Wesel 57,986
Wetzlar (★ 105,000) 50,299
Wiesbaden (★ 795,000) ...254,209
Wilhelmshaven
(★ 135,000) 89,892
Wismar 58,058
Witten (★ Essen) 109,637
Wittenberg 53,358
Wolfenbüttel
(★ ★ Braunschweig) 50,960
Wolfsburg 125,831
Worms
(★ ★ Mannheim) 74,809
Wuppertal (★ 830,000) ...371,283
Würzburg (★ 210,000) 125,589
Zweibrücken
(★ 105,000) 33,377
Zwickau (★ 165,000) 121,749

GHANA

1984 C 12,205,574

Cities and Towns

• ACCRA (★ 1,250,000) 859,640
Ashiaman (★ Accra) 49,427
Cape Coast 86,620
Koforidua 54,400
Kumasi (★ 600,000) 348,880
Obuasi 60,146
Sekondi-Takoradi
(★ 175,352) 93,882
Tafo (★ Kumasi) 50,432
Tamale (★ 168,091) 136,828
Tema (★ ★ Accra) 99,608
Teshie (★ Accra) 62,954

GIBRALTAR

1988 E 30,077

Cities and Towns

• GIBRALTAR 30,077

GREECE / Ellás

1981 C 9,740,417

Cities and Towns

Aiyáleo (★ Athínai) 81,906
• ATHÍNAI (ATHENS)
(★ 3,027,331) 885,737
Áyios Dhimítrios
(★ Athínai) 51,421
Galátsion (★ Athínai) 50,096
Ilioúpolis (★ Athínai) ...69,560
Iráklion (★ 110,958) 102,398
Kalamariá
(★ Thessaloníki) 51,676
Kallithéa (★ Athínai) ...117,319
Kavála 56,375
Keratsínion (★ Athínai) ..74,179
Khalándrion (★ Athínai) ..54,320
Khaniá (★ 61,976) 47,451
Khíos (★ 29,742) 24,070
Koridhallós (★ Athínai) ..61,313
Lárisa 102,048
Néa Ionía (★ Athínai) 59,202
Néa Liósia (★ Athínai) ...72,427
Néa Smírni (★ Athínai) ...67,408
Níkaia (★ Athínai) 90,368
Palaión Fáliron
(★ Athínai) 53,273
Pátrai (★ 154,596) 142,163
Peristérion (★ Athínai) .140,858
Piraiévs (Piraeus)
(★ Athínai) 196,389
Spárti (Sparta)
(★ 14,388) 12,975
Thessaloníki (Salonika)
(★ 706,180) 406,413
Víron (★ Athínai) 57,880
Vólos (★ 107,407) 71,378
Zográfos (★ Athínai) 84,548

GREENLAND / Grønland / Kalaallit Nunaat

1990 E 55,558

Cities and Towns

• GODTHÅB (NUUK) 12,217

GRENADA

1981 C 89,088

Cities and Towns

• SAINT GEORGE'S
(★ 25,000) 4,788

GUADELOUPE

1982 C 328,400

Cities and Towns

BASSE-TERRE
(★ 26,600) 13,656
Les Abymes (★ Pointe-
à-Pitre) 56,165
• Pointe-à-Pitre
(★ 83,000) 25,310

GUAM

1980 C 105,979

Cities and Towns

• AGANA (★ 44,000) 896

GUATEMALA

1989 E 8,935,395

Cities and Towns

Escuintla 60,673
• GUATEMALA
(★ 1,400,000) 1,057,210
Quetzaltenango 88,769

GUERNSEY

1986 C 55,482

Cities and Towns

• SAINT PETER PORT
(★ 36,000) 16,085

GUINEA / Guinée

1986 E 6,225,000

Cities and Towns

• CONAKRY 800,000
Kankan 100,000
Kindia 80,000
Labé 110,000
Nzérékoré (1983 C) 55,356

GUINEA-BISSAU / Guiné-Bissau

1988 E 945,000

Cities and Towns

• BISSAU 125,000

GUYANA

1983 E 918,000

• GEORGETOWN
(★ 188,000) 78,500

HAITI / Haïti

1987 E 5,531,802

Cities and Towns

Cap-Haïtien 72,161
• PORT-AU-PRINCE
(★ 880,000) 797,000

HONDURAS

1988 C 4,376,839

Cities and Towns

Choluteca 53,799
El Progreso 55,523
La Ceiba 68,289
San Pedro Sula 279,356
• TEGUCIGALPA 551,606

HONG KONG

1986 C 5,395,997

Cities and Towns

Kowloon (Jiulong)
(★ ★ Victoria) 774,781
Kwai Chung (★ Victoria) .131,362
New Kowloon
(Xinjiulong)
(★ ★ Victoria) 1,526,910
Sha Tin (★ Victoria) 355,810
Sheung Shui 87,206
Tai Po 119,679
Tsuen Wan (Quanwan)
(★ Victoria) 514,241
Tuen Mun (★ Victoria) ...262,458
• VICTORIA
(★ 4,770,000) 1,175,860
Yuen Long 75,740

HUNGARY / Magyarország

1990 C 10,375,000

Cities and Towns

Békéscsaba (▲ 67,621) 58,800
• BUDAPEST
(★ 2,565,000) 2,016,132
Debrecen 212,247
Dunaújváros 59,049
Eger 61,908
Győr 129,356
Kaposvár 71,793
Kecskemét (▲ 102,528) 81,200
Miskolc 196,449
Nagykanizsa 54,059
Nyíregyháza
(▲ 114,166) 88,500
Pécs 170,119
Sopron 55,088
Szeged 175,338
Székesfehérvár 108,990
Szolnok 78,333
Szombathely 85,418
Tatabánya 74,271
Veszprém 63,902
Zalaegerszeg 62,221

ICELAND / Ísland

1987 E 247,357

Cities and Towns

• REYKJAVÍK
(★ 137,941) 93,425

INDIA / Bhärat

1981 C 685,184,692

Cities and Towns

Abohar 86,334
Achalpur 81,186
Ādilābād 53,482
Adītyapur
(★ Jamshedpur) 53,421
Ādoni 108,939
Agartala 132,186
Āgra (★ 747,318) 694,191
Ahmadābād
(★ 2,400,000) 2,059,725
Ahmadnagar
(★ 181,210) 143,937
Ajmer 375,593
Akola 225,412
Akot 51,936
Alandur (★ Madras) 97,449
Alīgarh 320,861
Alijal 74,493
Allahābād (★ 650,070) ..616,051
Alleppey 169,940
Alwar 145,795
Amalner 67,516
Amarnāth (★ Bombay) 96,347
Ambāla (★ 233,110) 104,565
Ambāla Sadar
(★ Ambāla) 80,741
Ambattur (★ Madras) 115,901
Āmbūr 66,042
Amrāvati 261,404
Amreli (★ 58,241) 56,598
Amritsar 594,844
Amroha 112,682
Anakāpalle 73,179
Ānand 83,936

Anantapur 119,531
Arcot (★ 94,363) 38,836
Arkonam 59,405
Arni 49,365
Arrah 125,111
Aruppukkottai 72,245
Asansol (★ 1,050,000) ...183,375
Ashoknagar-Kalyangarh
(★ Hābra) 55,176
Āttūr 50,517
Aurangābād
(★ 316,421) 284,607
Avadi (★ Madras) 124,701
Azamgarh 66,523
Badagara 64,174
Bāgalkot 67,858
Baharampur
(★ 102,311) 92,889
Bahraich 99,889
Baidyabāti (★ Calcutta) ..70,573
Bālāghāt (★ 53,183) 49,564
Bālāngīr 54,943
Balasore 65,779
Ballālpur 61,398
Ballia 61,704
Bālly (★ Calcutta) 147,735
Bālly (★ Calcutta) 54,859
Bālurghāt (★ 112,621) ...104,646
Bānda 72,379
Bangalore
(★ 2,950,000) 2,476,355
Bangaon 69,885
Bānkura 94,954
Bansberia (★ Calcutta) ...77,020
Bāpatla 55,347
Bārākpur (★ Calcutta) ...115,253
Baranagar (★ Calcutta) ..170,343
Bārāsat (★ Calcutta) 66,504
Bareilly (★ 449,425) 386,734
Barmer 55,554
Baroda (★ 744,881) 734,473
Bārsi 72,537
Bāruni 56,366
Basīrhāt 81,040
Basti 69,357
Batala (★ 101,966) 87,135
Beāwar 89,998
Begusarai (★ 68,305) 56,633
Behāla (South
Suburban)
(★ Calcutta) 378,765
Bela 49,932
Belgaum (★ 300,372) 274,430
Bellary 201,579
Berhampur 162,550
Bettiah 72,167
Bhadrakh 60,600
Bhadrāvati (★ 130,606) ...53,551
Bhadrāvati New Town
(★ ★ Bhadrāvati) 77,055
Bhadreswar
(★ Calcutta) 58,858
Bhāgalpur 225,062
Bhandāra 56,025
Bharatpur 105,274
Bhathinda 124,453
Bhātpāra (★ Calcutta) ...260,761
Bhaunagar (★ 308,642) ...307,121
Bhilai (★ 490,214) 290,090
Bhīlwāra 122,625
Bhīmavaram 101,894
Bhind 74,515
Bhiwandi (★ Bombay) 115,298
Bhiwāni 101,277
Bhopāl 671,018
Bhubaneswar 219,211
Bhuj (★ 70,211) 69,693
Bhusāwal (★ 132,142) ...123,133
Bīdar 78,856
Bihār 151,343
Bijāpur 147,313
Bijnor 56,713
Bikaner (★ 287,712) 253,174
Bilāspur (★ 187,104) 147,218
Bīr 80,287
Bodhan 50,807
Bodināyakkanūr 59,168
Bokāro Steel City
(★ 264,480) 224,099
Bombay (★ 9,950,000) ..8,243,405
Botād 50,274
Brajrājnagar 54,033
Broach (★ 120,524) 110,070
Budaun 93,004
Budge Budge
(★ Calcutta) 66,424
Bulandshahr 103,436
Bulsār (★ Bombay) 54,017
Burdwān 167,364
Burhānpur 140,896
• Calcutta
(★ 11,100,000) 3,305,006
Calicut (★ 546,058) 394,447
Cambay 68,791
Cannanore (★ 157,797) 60,904
Chākdaha 59,308
Chakradharpur
(★ 44,532) 29,272
Chālisgaon 59,342
Champdāni (★ Calcutta) ...76,138
Chandannagar
(★ Calcutta) 101,925
Chandausi 66,970
Chandīgarh (★ 422,841) ..373,789
Chandrapur 115,777
Changanācheri 51,955
Channapatna 50,725
Chāpra 111,564
Chhatarpur 51,959
Chhindwāra 75,178

Chidambaram
(★ 62,543) 55,920
Chikmagalūr 60,582
Chilakalurupet 61,645
Chīrāla 72,040
Chitradurga 74,580
Chittaranjan (★ 61,045) ..50,748
Chittoor 86,230
Churu (★ 62,070) 61,811
Cochin (★ 685,836) 513,249
Coimbatore
(★ 965,000) 704,514
Cooch Behār
(★ 80,101) 62,127
Coonoor (★ 92,242) 44,750
Cuddalore 127,625
Cuddapah 103,125
Cuttack (★ 327,412) 269,950
Dabgram 76,402
Dāhod (★ 82,256) 55,256
Dāltonganj 51,952
Damoh (★ 76,758) 75,573
Dānāpur (★ Patna) 58,684
Darbhanga 176,301
Darjiling 57,603
Datia 49,386
Dāvangere 196,621
Dehra Dūn (★ 293,010) ...211,416
Dehri 90,409
Delhi (★ 7,200,000) ...4,884,234
Delhi Cantonment
(★ Delhi) 85,166
Deoband 51,270
Deoghar (★ 59,120) 52,904
Deolāli (★ Nāsik) 77,666
Deolāli Cantonment
(★ Nāsik) 57,745
Deoria 55,720
Dewās 83,465
Dhamtari 55,797
Dhānbād (★ 825,000) 120,221
Dharmapuri 51,223
Dharmavaram 50,969
Dhorāji (★ 77,716) 76,556
Dhrāngadhra 51,280
Dhule 210,759
Dibrugarh (1971 C) 80,348
Dindigul 164,103
Dombivli (★ Bombay) 103,222
Durg (★ ★ Bhilai) 114,637
Durgāpur 311,798
English Bāzār 79,010
Erode (★ 275,999) 142,252
Etah 53,784
Etāwah 112,174
Faizābād (★ 143,167) 101,873
Farīdābād New
Township (★ Delhi) 330,864
Farrukhābād
(★ 160,796) 145,793
Fatehpur, Rājasthān
state 51,084
Fatehpur, Uttar
Pradesh state 84,831
Fīrozābād 202,338
Fīrozpur (★ 105,840) 61,162
Gadag 117,368
Gandhidham (★ 61,489) 61,415
Gandhinagar 62,443
Gangāwati 58,735
Garden Reach
(★ Calcutta) 191,101
Gārulia (★ Calcutta) 57,061
Gauhāti (★ 200,377)
(1971 C) 123,783
Gaya 247,075
Ghāziābād (★ 287,170) ...271,730
Ghāzīpur 60,725
Giridih 65,444
Godhra (★ 86,228) 85,784
Gonda 70,847
Gondal (★ 66,818) 66,096
Gondia 100,423
Gorakhpur (★ 307,501) ...290,814
Gudivāda 80,198
Gudiyāttam (★ 80,674) 75,044
Gulbarga 221,325
Guna (★ 64,659) 60,255
Guntakal 84,599
Guntur 367,699
Gurgaon (★ 100,877) 89,115
Gwalior (★ 555,862) 539,015
Hābra (★ 129,610) 74,434
Hājīpur 62,520
Haldwāni 77,300
Hālisahar (★ Calcutta) ...95,579
Hānsi 50,365
Hanumāngarh 60,071
Hāpur 102,837
Hardoi 67,259
Hardwār (★ 145,946) 114,180
Harihar 52,334
Hassan 71,534
Hāthras 92,962
Hazāribāgh 80,155
Hindupur 55,901
Hinganghāt 59,075
Hisār (★ 137,369) 131,309
Hoshiārpur 85,648
Hospet (★ 115,351) 90,572
Howrah (★ Calcutta) 744,429
Hubli-Dhārwār 527,108
Hugli-Chinsurah
(★ Calcutta) 125,193
Hyderābād
(★ 2,750,000) 2,187,262
Ichaikaranji 133,751
Imphāl 156,622
Indore (★ 850,000) 829,327

C Census.   E Official estimate.   U Unofficial estimate.
• Largest city in country.

★ Population or designation of metropolitan area, including suburbs (see headnote).
▲ Population of an entire municipality, commune, or district, including rural area.

205

World Populations

Itārsi (★ 69,619) ... 62,499
Jabalpur (★ 757,303) ... 614,162
Jabalpur Cantonment (★ Jabalpur) ... 61,026
Jādabpur (★ Calcutta) ... 251,968
Jagdalpur (★ 63,632) ... 51,286
Jagtiāl ... 53,213
Jaipur (★ 1,025,000) ... 977,165
Jālgaon ... 145,335
Jālna ... 122,276
Jalpaiguri ... 61,743
Jamālpur ... 78,356
Jammu (★ 223,361) ... 206,135
Jāmnagar (★ 317,362) ... 277,615
Jamshedpur (★ 669,580) ... 438,385
Jangoon ... 70,727
Jaridih (★ 101,946) ... 46,477
Jaunpur ... 105,140
Jetpur (★ 63,074) ... 62,806
Jeypore ... 53,981
Jhānsi (★ 284,141) ... 246,172
Jharia (★ ★ Dhānbād) ... 57,496
Jhārsuguda ... 54,859
Jīnd ... 56,748
Jodhpur ... 506,345
Jotacamund ... 78,277
Jullundur (★ 441,552) ... 408,186
Junāgadh (★ 120,416) ... 118,646
Kadaiyanallūr ... 60,306
Kadiri ... 52,774
Kaithal ... 58,385
Kākināda ... 226,409
Kālahasti ... 51,306
Kālol (★ Ahmadābād) ... 69,946
Kalyān (★ Bombay) ... 136,052
Kāmārhāti (★ Calcutta) ... 234,951
Kambam ... 50,340
Kāmthi (★ Nāgpur) ... 67,364
Kānchipuram (★ 145,254) ... 130,926
Kānchrāpāra (★ Calcutta) ... 88,798
Kānpur (★ 1,875,000) ... 1,481,789
Kānpur Cantonment (★ Kānpur) ... 90,311
Kapūrthala ... 50,300
Karād ... 54,364
Kāraikkudi (★ 100,141) ... 66,993
Karīmnagar ... 86,125
Karnāl ... 132,107
Karūr (★ 93,810) ... 72,692
Kāsganj ... 61,402
Kashīpur ... 51,773
Katihār (★ 122,005) ... 104,781
Kayankulam ... 61,327
Kerkend (★ Dhānbād) ... 75,186
Khadki Cantonment (★ Pune) ... 80,835
Khāmgaon ... 61,992
Khammam ... 98,757
Khandwa ... 114,725
Khanna ... 53,761
Kharagpur (★ 232,575) ... 150,475
Kharagpur Railway Settlement (★ Kharagpur) ... 82,100
Khargon ... 52,749
Khurja ... 67,119
Kishanganj ... 51,790
Kishangarh ... 62,032
Kolār ... 65,834
Kolār Gold Fields (★ 144,385) ... 77,679
Kolhāpur (★ 351,392) ... 340,625
Konnagar (★ Calcutta) ... 51,211
Korba ... 83,387
Kota ... 358,241
Kottagūdem ... 94,894
Kottayam ... 64,431
Kovilpatti ... 63,964
Krishnanagar ... 98,141
Kumbakonam (★ 141,794) ... 132,832
Kundla (★ 51,431) ... 49,740
Kurnool ... 206,362
Lakhīmpur ... 61,003
Lalitpur ... 55,756
Lātur ... 111,986
Lucknow (★ 1,060,000) ... 895,721
Lucknow Cantonment (★ Lucknow) ... 59,614
Ludhiāna ... 607,052
Machilīpatnam (Bandar) ... 138,530
Madanapalle ... 54,938
Madgaon (Margao) (★ 64,858) ... 53,076
Madras (★ 4,475,000) ... 3,276,622
Madurai (★ 960,000) ... 820,891
Mahbūbnagar ... 87,503
Mahuva (★ 56,072) ... 53,625
Mainpuri ... 58,928
Mālegaon ... 245,883
Māler Kotla ... 65,756
Malkajgiri (★ Hyderābād) ... 65,776
Mandasor ... 77,603
Mandya ... 100,285
Mangalore (★ 306,078) ... 172,252
Mango (★ Jamshedpur) ... 67,284
Manjeri ... 53,959
Manmād ... 51,439
Mannārgudi ... 51,738
Mathura (★ 160,995) ... 147,493
Maunath Bhanjan ... 86,326
Māyūram ... 67,675
Meerut (★ 536,615) ... 417,395
Meerut Cantonment (★ Meerut) ... 94,210
Mehsāna (★ 73,024) ... 72,872

Melappālaiyam (★ Tirunelveli) ... 57,683
Mettuppālaiyam ... 59,537
Mhow (★ 76,037) ... 70,130
Midnapore ... 86,118
Miraj (★ ★ Sāngli) ... 105,455
Mirzāpur ... 127,787
Modinagar (★ 87,665) ... 78,243
Moga ... 80,272
Mokāma ... 51,047
Monghyr ... 129,260
Morādābād (★ 345,350) ... 330,051
Morena ... 69,864
Mormugao ... 69,684
Morvi ... 73,327
Motihāri (★ 63,212) ... 57,911
Muktsar ... 50,941
Murwāra (★ 123,017) ... 77,862
Muzaffarnagar ... 171,816
Muzaffarpur ... 190,416
Mysore (★ 479,081) ... 441,754
Nabadwip (★ 129,800) ... 109,108
Nadiād ... 142,689
Nāgappattinam (★ 90,650) ... 82,828
Nāgda ... 56,602
Nāgercoil ... 171,648
Nagīna ... 50,405
Nāgpur (★ 1,302,066) ... 1,219,461
Naihāti (★ Calcutta) ... 114,607
Najībābād ... 55,109
Nalgonda ... 62,458
Nānded ... 191,269
Nandurbār ... 65,394
Nandyāl ... 88,185
Nangi (★ Calcutta) ... 54,035
Narasaraopet ... 67,032
Nāsik (★ 429,034) ... 262,428
Navsāri (★ 129,266) ... 106,793
Nawābganj (★ 62,216) ... 51,518
Neemuch (★ 68,853) ... 65,860
Nellore ... 237,065
NEW DELHI (★ ★ Delhi) ... 273,036
Neyveli (★ 98,866) ... 88,000
Nizāmābād ... 183,061
North Bārākpur (★ Calcutta) ... 81,758
North Dum Dum (★ Calcutta) ... 96,418
Nowgong (1971 C) ... 56,537
Ongole ... 85,302
Orai ... 66,397
Outer Burnpur (★ Asansol) ... 86,803
Pālanpur ... 61,262
Pālayankottai (★ ★ Tirunelveli) ... 87,302
Pālghāt (★ 117,986) ... 111,245
Pāli ... 91,568
Pallavaram (★ Madras) ... 83,901
Palni (★ 68,389) ... 64,444
Pānchur (★ Calcutta) ... 51,223
Pandharpur ... 64,380
Pānihāti (★ Calcutta) ... 205,718
Pānīpat ... 137,927
Paramagudi ... 61,149
Parbhani ... 109,364
Pātan ... 79,196
Pathānkot ... 110,039
Patiāla (★ 206,254) ... 205,141
Patna (★ 1,025,000) ... 776,371
Pattukkottai ... 49,484
Phagwāra (★ 75,961) ... 72,499
Pīlibhīt ... 88,548
Pimpri-Chinchwad (★ Pune) ... 220,966
Pollāchi (★ 114,971) ... 82,354
Pondicherry (★ 251,420) ... 162,636
Ponmalai (★ Tiruchchirāppalli) ... 55,995
Ponnūru Nidubrolu ... 50,206
Porbandar (★ 133,307) ... 115,182
Port Blair ... 49,634
Proddatūr ... 107,070
Pudukkottai ... 87,952
Pune (Poona) (★ 1,775,000) ... 1,203,351
Pune Cantonment (★ Pune) ... 85,986
Puri ... 100,942
Purnea (★ 109,875) ... 91,144
Purūlia ... 73,904
Quilon (★ 167,598) ... 137,943
Rabkavi Banhatti ... 51,693
Rāe Bareli ... 89,697
Rāichūr ... 124,762
Raiganj (★ 66,705) ... 60,343
Raigarh (★ 69,791) ... 68,060
Raipur ... 338,245
Rājahmundry (★ 268,370) ... 203,358
Rājapālaiyam ... 101,640
Rajhara-Jharandalli ... 55,307
Rājkot ... 445,076
Rāj-Nāndgaon ... 86,367
Rājpura ... 58,645
Rāmpur ... 204,610
Rānāghāt (★ 83,744) ... 58,356
Rānchī (★ 502,771) ... 489,626
Rānībennur ... 58,118
Rāniganj (★ 119,101) ... 48,702
Ratlām (★ 155,578) ... 142,319
Raurkela (★ 322,610) ... 206,821
Raurkela Civil Township (★ Raurkela) ... 96,000
Rewa ... 100,641
Rewāri ... 51,562
Rishra (★ Calcutta) ... 81,001

Robertson Pet (★ Kolār Gold Fields) ... 61,099
Rohtak ... 166,767
Roorkee (★ 79,076) ... 61,851
Sāgar (★ 207,479) ... 160,392
Sahāranpur ... 295,355
Saharsa ... 57,580
Sahijpur Bogha (★ Ahmadābād) ... 65,327
Salem (★ 518,615) ... 361,394
Sambalpur (★ 162,214) ... 110,282
Sambhal ... 108,232
Sāngli (★ 268,988) ... 152,339
Sāntipur ... 82,980
Sardarnagar (★ Ahmadābād) ... 50,128
Sardārshahr (★ 56,388) ... 55,473
Sasarām ... 73,457
Sātāra ... 83,336
Satna (★ 96,667) ... 90,476
Saunda (★ 99,990) ... 50,780
Secunderābād Cantonment (★ Hyderābād) ... 135,994
Sehore ... 52,190
Seoni ... 54,017
Serampore (★ Calcutta) ... 127,304
Shāhjahānpur (★ 205,095) ... 185,396
Shāmli ... 51,850
Shillong (★ 174,703) ... 109,244
Shimoga ... 151,783
Shivpuri ... 75,738
Sholāpur (★ 514,860) ... 511,103
Shrirampur ... 55,491
Sidhpur (★ 52,706) ... 51,953
Sikar ... 102,970
Silchar (1971 C) ... 52,596
Sīliguri ... 154,378
Simla ... 70,604
Sindri (★ ★ Dhānbād) ... 70,645
Sirsa ... 89,068
Sītāpur ... 101,210
Sivakāsi (★ 83,072) ... 59,827
Siwān ... 51,284
Sonīpat ... 109,369
South Dum Dum (★ Calcutta) ... 230,266
Sri Gangānagar ... 123,692
Srīkākulam ... 68,145
Srīnagar (★ 606,002) ... 594,775
Srīrangam (★ Tiruchchirāppalli) ... 64,241
Srīvilliputtūr ... 61,458
Sujāngarh ... 55,546
Surat (★ 913,806) ... 776,583
Surendranagar (★ 130,602) ... 89,619
Tādepallegūdem ... 62,574
Tādpatri ... 53,920
Tāmbaram (★ Madras) ... 86,923
Tānda ... 54,474
Tanuku ... 53,618
Tellicherry (★ 98,704) ... 75,561
Tenāli ... 119,257
Tenkāsi ... 49,214
Thāna (★ Bombay) ... 309,897
Thānesar ... 49,052
Thanjāvūr ... 184,015
Theni-Allinagaram ... 53,018
Tindivanam ... 56,520
Tinsukia (1971 C) ... 54,911
Tiruchchirāppalli (★ 609,548) ... 362,045
Tiruchengodu ... 53,941
Tirunelveli (★ 323,344) ... 128,850
Tirupati ... 115,292
Tiruppattūr ... 52,422
Tiruppur (★ 215,859) ... 165,223
Tiruvannāmalai ... 89,462
Tiruvottiyūr (★ Madras) ... 134,014
Titāgarh (★ Calcutta) ... 104,534
Tonk ... 77,653
Trichūr (★ 170,122) ... 77,923
Trivandrum (★ 520,125) ... 483,086
Tumkūr ... 108,670
Tuticorin (★ 250,677) ... 192,949
Udaipur ... 232,588
Udamalpet ... 54,852
Udgīr ... 50,564
Ujjain (★ 282,203) ... 278,454
Ulhāsnagar (★ Bombay) ... 273,668
Unnāo ... 75,983
Upleta ... 54,907
Uttarpara-Kotrung (★ Calcutta) ... 79,598
Valparai ... 115,452
Vāniyambādi (★ 75,042) ... 59,107
Vārānasi (Benares) (★ 925,000) ... 708,647
Vellore (★ 274,041) ... 174,247
Verāval (★ 105,307) ... 85,048
Vidisha ... 65,521
Vijayawāda (★ 543,008) ... 454,577
Vikramasingapuram ... 49,319
Villupuram ... 77,091
Virudunagar ... 68,047
Vishākhapatnam (★ 603,630) ... 565,321
Vizianagaram ... 114,806
Warangal ... 335,150
Wardha ... 88,495
Yamunānagar (★ 160,424) ... 109,304
Yavatmāl ... 89,071
Yemmiganur ... 50,701

INDONESIA

1980 C ... 147,490,298

Cities and Towns

Ambon (★ 207,702) ... 111,914
Balikpapan (▲ 279,852) ... 208,040
Banda Aceh (Kuturaja) ... 71,868
Bandung (★ 1,800,000) (1985 C) ... 1,633,000
Banjarmasin (1983 E) ... 424,000
Banyuwangi ... 90,378
Batang ... 49,328
Bekasi (★ Jakarta) ... 144,290
Binjai ... 71,444
Blitar (★ 100,000) ... 78,503
Bogor (★ 560,000) ... 246,946
Bojonegoro ... 57,483
Bukittinggi (▲ 70,691) ... 55,577
Cianjur ... 105,655
Cibinong ... 87,580
Cilacap ... 127,017
Cimahi (★ Bandung) (1971 C) ... 72,367
Ciparay ... 66,854
Cirebon (★ 275,000) ... 223,504
Denpasar ... 159,233
Depok (★ Jakarta) ... 126,693
Garut ... 145,624
Genteng ... 59,481
Gorontalo (▲ 97,610) ... 63,554
Gresik ... 86,418
• JAKARTA (★ 1,000,000) (1989 E) ... 9,200,000
Jambi (▲ 230,046) ... 155,761
Jayapura (Sukarnapura) ... 60,641
Jember ... 171,284
Jombang ... 58,800
Karawang ... 72,195
Kediri (▲ 221,830) ... 176,261
Kisaran ... 58,129
Klangenang ... 64,013
Klaten ... 117,560
Kudus ... 154,478
Kupang ... 84,587
Lumajang ... 58,495
Madiun (★ 180,000) ... 150,562
Magelang (★ 160,000) ... 123,358
Majalaya ... 87,474
Malang (1983 E) ... 547,000
Manado ... 217,091
Mataram ... 210,485
Medan (1985 E) ... 2,110,000
Mojokerto ... 68,849
Padang (▲ 657,000) (1983 E) ... 405,600
Padangsidempuan ... 56,984
Palangkaraya (▲ 60,447) ... 51,686
Palembang (1983 E) ... 874,000
Pangkalpinang ... 90,078
Parepare (▲ 86,360) ... 62,865
Pasuruan (★ 125,000) ... 95,864
Pati ... 50,159
Pekalongan (★ 260,000) ... 132,413
Pekanbaru ... 186,199
Pemalang ... 72,663
Pematangsiantar (★ 175,000) ... 150,296
Ponorogo ... 55,523
Pontianak (1983 E) ... 343,000
Pringsewu ... 56,115
Probolinggo ... 100,296
Purwakarta ... 61,995
Purwokerto ... 143,787
Salatiga ... 85,740
Samarinda (▲ 264,012) ... 182,473
Semarang (1983 E) ... 1,206,000
Serang ... 78,209
Sibolga ... 59,466
Sidoarjo ... 56,090
Singaraja ... 53,368
Singkawang ... 58,693
Situbondo ... 58,299
Sorong ... 52,041
Subang ... 52,041
Sukabumi (★ 225,000) ... 109,898
Surabaya (1985 E) ... 2,345,000
Surakarta (★ 575,000) (1983 E) ... 491,000
Taman ... 64,358
Tangerang ... 97,091
Tanjungkarang-Telukbetung (★ 375,000) ... 284,167
Tasikmalaya ... 192,267
Tebingtinggi (▲ 92,068) ... 69,569
Tegal (★ 340,000) ... 131,440
Tembilahan ... 52,140
Tulungagung ... 91,585
Ujungpandang (Makasar) (1983 E) ... 841,000
Yogyakarta (★ 510,000) (1983 E) ... 421,000

IRAN / Īrān

1986 C ... 49,445,010

Cities and Towns

Ābādān (1976 C) ... 296,081
Āghā Jārī (1982 E) ... 64,000
Ahar (1982 E) ... 52,000
Ahvāz ... 579,826
Āmol ... 118,242
Andīmeshk (1982 E) ... 53,000
Arāk ... 265,349
Ardabīl ... 281,973
Bābol ... 115,320
Bakhtarān (Kermānshāh) ... 560,514
Bandar-e 'Abbās ... 201,642
Bandar-e Anzalī (Bandar-e Pahlavī) (1982 E) ... 83,000
Bandar-e Būshehr ... 120,787
Bandar-e Māh Shahr (1982 E) ... 88,000
Behbahān (1982 E) ... 84,000
Bīrjand (1982 E) ... 68,000
Bojnūrd (1982 E) ... 82,000
Borāzjān (1982 E) ... 53,000
Borūjerd ... 183,879
Dezful ... 151,420
Do Rūd (1982 E) ... 52,000
Emāmshahr (Shāhrūd) (1982 E) ... 68,000
Eşfahān (★ 1,175,000) ... 986,753
Eslāmābād (1982 E) ... 71,000
Eslāmshahr (★ Tehrān) ... 215,129
Fasā (1982 E) ... 67,000
Gonbad-e Qābūs (1982 E) ... 75,000
Gorgān ... 139,430
Hamadān ... 272,499
Īlām (1982 E) ... 75,000
Jahrom (1982 E) ... 68,000
Karaj (★ Tehrān) ... 275,100
Kāshān ... 138,599
Kāzerūn (1982 E) ... 63,000
Kermān ... 257,284
Khomeynīshahr (★ Eşfahān) ... 104,647
Khorramābād ... 208,592
Khorramshahr (1976 C) ... 146,709
Khvoy ... 115,343
Mahābād (1982 E) ... 63,000
Malāyer ... 103,640
Marāgheh ... 100,679
Marand (1982 E) ... 59,000
Marv Dasht (1982 E) ... 72,000
Mashhad ... 1,463,508
Masjed Soleymān ... 104,787
Miāndoāb (1982 E) ... 52,000
Miāneh (1982 E) ... 57,000
Najafābād ... 129,058
Neyshābūr ... 109,258
Orūmīyeh (Rezā'īyeh) ... 300,746
Qā'emshahr ... 109,288
Qazvīn ... 248,591
Qom ... 543,139
Qomsheh (1982 E) ... 67,000
Qūchān (1982 E) ... 61,000
Rafsanjān (1982 E) ... 61,000
Rāmhormoz (1982 E) ... 53,000
Rasht ... 290,897
Sabzevār ... 129,103
Sanandaj ... 204,537
Saqqez (1982 E) ... 76,000
Sārī ... 141,020
Semnān (1982 E) ... 54,000
Shahr-e Kord (1982 E) ... 63,000
Shīrāz ... 848,289
Sīrjān (1982 E) ... 67,000
Tabrīz ... 971,482
• TEHRĀN (★ 7,500,000) ... 6,042,584
Torbat-e Heydarīyeh (1982 E) ... 62,000
Varāmīn (1982 E) ... 51,000
Yazd ... 230,483
Zābol (1982 E) ... 58,000
Zāhedān ... 281,923
Zanjān ... 215,261
Zarrīn Shahr (1982 E) ... 69,000

IRAQ / Al 'Irāq

1985 E ... 15,584,987

Cities and Towns

Ad-Dīwānīyah (1970 E) ... 62,300
Al-'Amārah ... 131,758
Al-Başrah ... 616,700
Al-Hillah ... 215,249
Al-Kūt ... 73,022
Al-Mawsil ... 570,926
An-Najaf ... 242,603
An-Nāsirīyah ... 138,842
Ar-Ramādī ... 137,388
As-Samāwah ... 75,293
As-Sulaymānīyah ... 279,424
• BAGHDĀD (1987 C) ... 3,841,268
Ba'qūbah ... 114,516
Irbīl ... 333,903
Karbalā' ... 184,574
Kirkūk (1970 E) ... 207,900

IRELAND / Éire

1986 C ... 3,540,643

Cities and Towns

Cork (173,694) ... 133,271
• DUBLIN (BAILE ÁTHA CLIATH) (★ 1,140,000) ... 502,749
Dún Laoghaire (★ Dublin) ... 54,715
Galway ... 47,104
Limerick (★ 76,557) ... 56,279
Waterford (★ 41,054) ... 39,529

ISLE OF MAN

1986 C ... 64,282

Cities and Towns

• DOUGLAS (★ 28,500) ... 20,368

C Census.   E Official estimate.   U Unofficial estimate.
• Largest city in country.

★ Population or designation of metropolitan area, including suburbs (see headnote).
▲ Population of an entire municipality, commune, or district, including rural area.

ISRAEL / Isrā'īl / Yisra'el

1989 E 4,386,000

Cities and Towns

Al-Khalīl (Hebron)
  (1971 E) 43,000
Ashdod 74,700
Ashqelon 56,300
Bat Yam (★ Tel Aviv-
  Yafo) 133,100
Bayt Laḥm (Bethlehem)
  (1971 E) 25,000
Be'er Sheva
  (Beersheba) 113,200
Bene Beraq (★ Tel
  Aviv-Yafo) 109,400
Elat 24,700
Giv'atayim (★ Tel Aviv-
  Yafo) 45,600
Ḥefa (★ 435,000) 222,600
Herzliyya (★ Tel Aviv-
  Yafo) 71,600
Holon (★ Tel Aviv-Yafo) . 146,100
Kefar Sava (★ Tel Aviv-
  Yafo) 54,800
Lod (Lydda) (★ Tel
  Aviv-Yafo) 41,300
Nābulus (1971 E) 64,000
Nazerat (Nazareth)
  (★ 77,000) 50,600
Netanya (★ Tel Aviv-
  Yafo) 117,800
Petaḥ Tiqwa (★ Tel
  Aviv-Yafo) 133,600
Ra'ananna (★ Tel Aviv-
  Yafo) 49,400
Ramat Gan (★ Tel Aviv-
  Yafo) 115,700
Reḥovot (★ Tel Aviv-
  Yafo) 72,500
Rishon leẒiyyon (★ Tel
  Aviv-Yafo) 123,800
• Tel Aviv-Yafo
  (★ 1,735,000) 317,800
YERUSHALAYIM
  (AL-QUDS)
  (JERUSALEM)
  (★ 530,000) 493,500

ITALY / Italia

1987 E 57,290,519

Cities and Towns

Afragola (★ Napoli) 59,397
Alessandria (▲ 96,014) ... 76,100
Altamura 54,784
Ancona 104,409
Andria 88,348
Arezzo (▲ 91,681) 74,200
Asti (▲ 75,459) 63,600
Avellino 56,407
Aversa (★ Napoli) 57,827
Bari (★ 475,000) 362,524
Barletta 86,954
Benevento (▲ 65,661) 54,400
Bergamo (★ 345,000) 118,959
Biella 51,788
Bitonto 51,962
Bologna (★ 525,000) 432,406
Bolzano 101,515
Brescia 199,286
Brindisi 92,280
Busto Arsizio
  (★ Milano) 78,056
Cagliari (★ 305,000) 220,574
Caltanissetta 62,352
Carpi (▲ 60,614) 49,500
Carrara (★ ★ Massa) 69,229
Caserta 65,974
Casoria (★ Napoli) 54,100
Castellammare [di
  Stabia] (★ Napoli) 68,491
Catania (★ 550,000) 372,486
Catanzaro 102,558
Cava de' Tirreni
  (★ Salerno) 52,028
Cerignola 53,463
Cesena (▲ 90,012) 72,600
Chieti 55,827
Cinisello Balsamo
  (★ Milano) 78,917
Civitavecchia 50,806
Collegno (★ Torino) 49,334
Cologno Monzese
  (★ Milano) 52,554
Como (★ 165,000) 91,738
Cosenza (★ 150,000) 106,026
Cremona 76,979
Crotone (▲ 61,005) 53,600
Ercolano (★ Napoli) 62,783
Ferrara (▲ 143,950) 113,300
Firenze (★ 640,000) 425,835
Foggia 155,051
Forlì (▲ 110,482) 91,200
Gela 79,378
Genova (Genoa)
  (★ 805,000) 727,427
Giugliano in Campania
  (★ Napoli) 51,187
Grosseto (▲ 70,592) 56,400
La Spezia (★ 185,000) 108,937
Latina (▲ 98,479) 67,800
Lecce 100,981
Livorno 174,065
Lucca 88,024
Manfredonia 57,707
Mantova (▲ 56,817) 49,000

Marsala 80,468
Massa (★ 145,000) 66,872
Matera 52,819
Messina 268,896
Mestre (★ Venezia) 189,700
• Milano (Milan)
  (★ 3,750,000) 1,495,260
Modena 176,880
Molfetta 64,519
Moncalieri (★ Torino) 62,306
Monza (★ Milano) 122,064
Napoli (Naples)
  (★ 2,875,000) 1,204,211
Nicastro (▲ 67,562) 52,100
Novara 102,742
Padova (★ 270,000) 225,769
Palermo 723,732
Parma 175,842
Pavia 82,065
Perugia (▲ 146,713) 106,700
Pesaro (▲ 90,336) 78,700
Pescara 131,027
Piacenza 105,626
Pisa 104,384
Pistoia (▲ 90,689) 76,800
Pordenone 50,825
Portici (★ Napoli) 76,302
Potenza (▲ 67,114) 57,600
Pozzuoli (★ Napoli) 65,000
Prato (★ 215,000) 164,595
Quartu Sant'Elena 52,838
Ragusa 67,748
Ravenna (▲ 136,016) 86,500
Reggio di Calabria 178,821
Reggio nell'Emilia
  (▲ 130,086) 107,300
Rho (★ Milano) 50,876
Rimini (▲ 130,698) 114,600
Rivoli (★ Torino) 50,786
ROMA (ROME)
  (★ 3,175,000) 2,815,457
Salerno (★ 250,000) 154,848
San Giorgio a Cremano
  (★ Napoli) 63,656
San Remo 60,797
San Severo 55,239
Sassari 120,152
Savona (★ 112,000) 62,300
Scandicci (★ Firenze) 54,367
Sesto San Giovanni
  (★ Milano) 91,624
Siena 59,712
Siracusa 122,857
Taranto 244,997
Terni (▲ 111,157) 94,500
Torino (★ 1,550,000) 1,035,565
Torre Annunziata
  (★ Napoli) 57,508
Torre del Greco
  (★ Napoli) 105,066
Trapani (▲ 73,083) 63,000
Trento (▲ 100,202) 81,500
Treviso 85,083
Trieste (Triest) 239,031
Udine (★ 126,000) 100,211
Varese 88,353
Venezia (Venice)
  (★ 420,000) 88,700
Vercelli 51,008
Verona 259,151
Viareggio (▲ 59,146) 50,300
Vicenza 110,449
Vigevano 62,671
Vittoria 54,795

JAMAICA

1982 C 2,190,357

Cities and Towns

• KINGSTON
  (★ 770,000) (1987 E) ... 646,400
Montego Bay 70,265
Portmore (★ Kingston) 73,426
Spanish Town
  (★ Kingston) 89,097

JAPAN / Nihon

1985 C 121,048,923

Cities and Towns

Abiko (★ Tōkyō) 111,659
Ageo (★ Tōkyō) 178,587
Aizu-wakamatsu 118,140
Akashi (★ Ōsaka) 263,363
Akishima (★ Tōkyō) 97,543
Akita 296,400
Akō 52,374
Amagasaki (★ Ōsaka) 509,115
Anjō 133,059
Aomori 294,045
Asahikawa 363,631
Asaka (★ Tōkyō) 94,431
Ashikaga 167,656
Ashiya (★ Ōsaka) 87,127
Atami 49,374
Atsugi (★ Tōkyō) 175,600
Ayase (★ Tōkyō) 71,152
Beppu 134,775
Bisai (★ Nagoya) 56,234
Chiba (★ Tōkyō) 788,930
Chichibu 61,013
Chigasaki (★ Tōkyō) 185,030
Chikushino (★ Fukuoka) ... 63,242
Chiryū (★ Nagoya) 50,506
Chita (★ Nagoya) 70,013

Chitose 73,610
Chōfu (★ Tōkyō) 191,071
Chōshi 87,883
Daitō (★ Ōsaka) 122,441
Dazaifu (★ Fukuoka) 57,737
Ebetsu (★ Sapporo) 90,328
Ebina (★ Tōkyō) 93,159
Fuchū (★ Tōkyō) 201,972
Fuji (★ 370,000) 214,448
Fujieda (★ Shizuoka) 111,985
Fujiidera (★ Ōsaka) 65,252
Fujimi (★ Tōkyō) 85,697
Fujinomiya (★ Fuji) 112,642
Fujisawa (★ Tōkyō) 328,387
Fuji-yoshida 54,796
Fukaya (▲ 89,121) 71,600
Fukuchiyama
  (▲ 65,995) 56,200
Fukui 250,261
Fukuoka (★ 1,750,000) 1,160,440
Fukushima 270,762
Fukuyama 360,261
Funabashi (★ Tōkyō) 506,966
Fussa (★ Tōkyō) 51,478
Gamagōri 85,580
Gifu 411,743
Ginowan 69,206
Gotemba 74,882
Gushikawa 51,351
Gyōda 79,359
Habikino (★ Ōsaka) 111,394
Hachinohe 241,430
Hachiōji (★ Tōkyō) 426,654
Hadano (★ Tōkyō) 141,803
Hagi 52,740
Hakodate 319,194
Hamada 51,071
Hamakita 77,228
Hamamatsu 514,118
Hanamaki (▲ 69,886) 54,500
Handa (★ Nagoya) 92,883
Hannō (★ Tōkyō) 66,550
Hashima 59,760
Hasuda (★ Tōkyō) 53,991
Hatogaya (★ Tōkyō) 55,424
Hatsukaichi
  (★ Hiroshima) 52,020
Hekinan 63,778
Higashihiroshima
  (★ Hiroshima) 84,717
Higashikurume
  (★ Tōkyō) 110,079
Higashimatsuyama 70,426
Higashimurayama
  (★ Tōkyō) 123,798
Higashiōsaka (★ Ōsaka) ... 522,805
Higashiyamato
  (★ Tōkyō) 69,881
Hikari (★ Tokuyama) 49,246
Hikone 94,204
Himeji (★ 660,000) 452,917
Himi (▲ 62,112) 52,300
Hino (★ Tōkyō) 156,031
Hirakata (★ Ōsaka) 382,257
Hiratsuka (★ Tōkyō) 229,990
Hirosaki (▲ 176,082) 134,800
Hiroshima
  (★ 1,575,000) 1,044,118
Hita (▲ 65,730) 57,900
Hitachi 206,074
Hōfu 118,067
Honjō 56,495
Hōya (★ Tōkyō) 91,568
Hyūga 59,163
Ibaraki (★ Ōsaka) 250,463
Ichihara (★ Tōkyō) 237,617
Ichikawa (★ Tōkyō) 397,822
Ichinomiya
  (★ Nagoya) 257,382
Ichinoseki (▲ 60,941) 49,200
Iida (▲ 92,401) 65,000
Iizuka (★ 110,000) 81,868
Ikeda (★ Ōsaka) 101,683
Ikoma (★ Ōsaka) 86,293
Imabari 125,115
Imari (▲ 62,044) 50,700
Inagi (★ Tōkyō) 50,766
Inazawa (★ Nagoya) 94,479
Inuyama (★ Nagoya) 68,723
Iruma (★ Tōkyō) 118,603
Isahaya 88,376
Ise (Uji-yamada) 105,455
Isesaki 112,459
Ishinomaki 122,674
Itami (★ Ōsaka) 182,731
Itō 70,197
Iwaki (Taira) 350,569
Iwakuni 111,833
Iwamizawa 81,664
Iwata 80,810
Iwatsuki (★ Tōkyō) 100,903
Izumi (★ Ōsaka) 137,641
Izumi (★ Sendai) 124,216
Izumi-ōtsu (★ Ōsaka) 67,755
Izumi-sano (★ Ōsaka) 91,563
Izumo (▲ 80,749) 68,000
Jōyō (★ Ōsaka) 81,850
Kadoma (★ Ōsaka) 140,590
Kaga 68,630
Kagoshima 530,502
Kainan (★ Wakayama) 50,779
Kaizuka (★ Ōsaka) 79,591
Kakamigahara 124,464
Kakegawa (▲ 68,724) 55,600
Kakogawa (★ Ōsaka) 227,311
Kamagaya (★ Tōkyō) 85,705
Kamaishi 60,007

Kamakura (★ Tōkyō) 175,495
Kameoka 76,207
Kamifukuoka (★ Tōkyō) 57,638
Kanazawa 430,481
Kani (★ Nagoya) 69,630
Kanoya (▲ 76,029) 60,200
Kanuma (▲ 88,078) 73,200
Karatsu (▲ 78,744) 70,100
Kariya (★ Nagoya) 112,403
Kasai 52,107
Kasaoka (▲ 60,598) 53,500
Kashihara (★ Ōsaka) 112,888
Kashiwa (★ Tōkyō) 273,128
Kashiwara (★ Ōsaka) 73,252
Kashiwazaki (▲ 86,020) ... 73,350
Kasuga (★ Fukuoka) 75,555
Kasugai (★ Nagoya) 256,990
Kasukabe (★ Tōkyō) 171,890
Katano (★ Ōsaka) 64,205
Katsuta 102,763
Kawachi-nagano
  (★ Ōsaka) 91,313
Kawagoe (★ Tōkyō) 285,437
Kawaguchi (★ Tōkyō) 403,015
Kawanishi (★ Ōsaka) 136,376
Kawasaki (★ Tōkyō) 1,088,624
Kesennuma 68,137
Kimitsu (▲ 84,310) 71,900
Kiryū 131,267
Kisarazu 120,201
Kishiwada (★ Ōsaka) 185,731
Kitaibaraki 51,035
Kitakyūshū
  (★ 1,525,000) 1,056,402
Kitami 107,281
Kitamoto (★ Tōkyō) 58,114
Kiyose (★ Tōkyō) 65,066
Kōbe (★ ★ Ōsaka) 1,410,834
Kōchi 312,241
Kodaira (★ Tōkyō) 158,673
Kōfu 202,405
Koga (★ Tōkyō) 57,541
Koganei (★ Tōkyō) 104,642
Kokubunji (★ Tōkyō) 95,467
Komae (★ Tōkyō) 73,784
Komaki (★ Nagoya) 113,284
Komatsu 106,041
Kōnan (★ Nagoya) 92,049
Kōnosu (★ Tōkyō) 60,565
Kōriyama 301,673
Koshigaya (★ Tōkyō) 253,479
Kudamatsu
  (★ Tokuyama) 54,445
Kuki (★ Tōkyō) 58,636
Kumagaya 143,496
Kumamoto 555,719
Kunitachi (★ Tōkyō) 64,881
Kurashiki 413,632
Kure (★ ★ Hiroshima) 226,488
Kurume 222,847
Kusatsu (★ Ōsaka) 87,542
Kushiro 214,541
Kuwana (★ Nagoya) 94,731
Kyōto (★ ★ Ōsaka) 1,479,218
Machida (★ Tōkyō) 321,188
Maebashi 277,319
Maizuru 98,775
Marugame 74,272
Matsubara (★ Ōsaka) 136,455
Matsudo (★ Tōkyō) 427,473
Matsue 140,005
Matsumoto 197,340
Matsusaka 116,886
Matsuyama 426,658
Mihara 85,975
Miki (★ Ōsaka) 74,527
Minō (★ Ōsaka) 114,770
Misato (★ Tōkyō) 107,964
Mishima (★ ★ Numazu) 99,600
Mitaka (★ Tōkyō) 166,252
Mito 228,985
Miura (★ Tōkyō) 50,471
Miyako 61,654
Miyakonojō (▲ 132,098) ... 107,600
Miyazaki 279,114
Mobara 76,929
Moriguchi (★ Ōsaka) 159,400
Morioka 235,469
Moriyama 53,052
Mukō (★ Ōsaka) 52,216
Munakata 60,971
Muroran (★ 195,000) 136,208
Musashimurayama
  (★ Tōkyō) 60,930
Musashino (★ Tōkyō) 138,783
Mutsu 49,292
Nabari 56,474
Nagahama 55,531
Nagano 336,973
Nagaoka 183,756
Nagaokakyō (★ Ōsaka) 75,242
Nagareyama (★ Tōkyō) 124,682
Nagasaki 449,382
Nagoya (★ 4,800,000) 2,116,381
Naha 303,674
Nakama (★ Kitakyūshū) 50,294
Nakatsu 66,260
Nakatsugawa 53,277
Nanao 50,582
Nara (★ Ōsaka) 327,702
Narashino (★ Tōkyō) 136,365
Narita 77,181
Naruto 64,329
Naze 49,765
Neyagawa (★ Ōsaka) 258,228
Niigata 475,630
Niihama 132,184

Niitsu (▲ 63,846) 55,600
Niiza (★ Tōkyō) 129,287
Nishinomiya (★ Ōsaka) 421,267
Nishio 91,930
Nobeoka 136,381
Noboribetsu
  (★ Muroran) 58,370
Noda (★ Tōkyō) 105,937
Nōgata 64,479
Noshiro (▲ 59,170) 50,400
Numazu (★ 495,000) 210,490
Obihiro 162,932
Ōbu (★ Nagoya) 66,696
Ōdate (▲ 71,794) 60,900
Odawara 185,941
Ōgaki 145,910
Ōita 390,096
Okaya 61,747
Okayama 572,479
Okazaki 284,996
Okegawa (★ Tōkyō) 61,499
Okinawa 101,210
Ōme (★ Tōkyō) 110,828
Ōmi-hachiman
  (★ Ōsaka) 63,791
Ōmiya (★ Tōkyō) 373,022
Ōmura 69,472
Ōmuta (★ 225,000) 159,424
Ōnojō (★ Fukuoka) 69,435
Onomichi 100,640
• Ōsaka (★ 16,450,000) ... 2,636,249
Ōta 133,670
Otaru (★ ★ Sapporo) 172,486
Ōtsu (★ Ōsaka) 234,551
Owariashi (★ Nagoya) 57,415
Oyama (▲ 134,242) 113,100
Sabae 61,452
Saeki 54,706
Saga 168,252
Sagamihara (★ Tōkyō) 482,778
Saijō 56,516
Sakado (★ Tōkyō) 87,586
Sakai (★ Ōsaka) 818,271
Sakaide 66,087
Sakata 101,392
Sakura (★ Tōkyō) 121,213
Sakurai 58,894
Sanjō 86,325
Sano 80,753
Sapporo (★ 1,900,000) 1,542,979
Sasebo 250,633
Satte 51,462
Sayama (★ Tōkyō) 144,366
Sayama (★ Ōsaka) 50,246
Seki 64,149
Sendai, Kagoshima
  pref. (▲ 71,444) 57,800
Sendai, Miyagi pref.
  (★ 1,175,000) 700,254
Sennan (★ Ōsaka) 60,059
Seto 124,623
Settsu (★ Ōsaka) 86,332
Shibata (▲ 77,219) 62,800
Shijōnawate (★ Ōsaka) 50,352
Shiki (★ Tōkyō) 58,935
Shimada (▲ 72,388) 63,200
Shimizu (★ ★ Shizuoka) .. 242,166
Shimodate (▲ 63,958) 52,400
Shimonoseki
  (★ ★ Kitakyūshū) 269,169
Shiogama (★ Sendai) 61,825
Shizuoka (★ 975,000) 468,362
Sōka (★ Tōkyō) 194,205
Suita (★ Ōsaka) 348,948
Suwa 52,329
Suzuka 164,936
Tachikawa (★ Tōkyō) 146,523
Tagajō (★ Sendai) 54,436
Tagawa 59,727
Tajimi (★ Nagoya) 84,829
Takada 130,659
Takaishi (★ Ōsaka) 66,974
Takamatsu 326,999
Takaoka (★ 220,000) 175,780
Takarazuka (★ Ōsaka) 194,273
Takasago (★ Ōsaka) 91,434
Takasaki 231,766
Takatsuki (★ Ōsaka) 348,784
Takayama 65,033
Takefu 69,148
Takikawa 52,004
Tama (★ Tōkyō) 122,135
Tamano 76,954
Tanabe (▲ 70,835) 59,800
Tanashi (★ Tōkyō) 71,331
Tatebayashi 75,141
Tenri 69,129
Tochigi 86,290
Toda (★ Tōkyō) 76,960
Tōkai (★ Nagoya) 95,278
Toki 65,308
Tokoname (★ Nagoya) 53,077
Tokorozawa (★ Tōkyō) 275,168
Tokushima 257,884
Tokuyama (★ 250,000) 112,638
• TŌKYŌ
  (★ 27,700,000) 8,354,615
Tomakomai 158,061
Tondabayashi
  (★ Ōsaka) 102,619
Toride (★ Tōkyō) 78,608
Tosu 55,791
Tottori 137,006
Toyama 314,111
Toyoake (★ Nagoya) 57,969
Toyohashi 322,142

C Census.   E Official estimate.   U Unofficial estimate.
• Largest city in country.

★ Population or designation of metropolitan area, including suburbs (see headnote).
▲ Population of an entire municipality, commune, or district, including rural area.

World Populations

Toyokawa....107,430
Toyonaka (★ Ōsaka)....413,213
Toyota....308,111
Tsu....150,690
Tsuchiura....120,175
Tsuruga....65,670
Tsuruoka....100,200
Tsushima (★ Nagoya)....58,735
Tsuyama....86,837
Ube (★ 230,000)....174,855
Ueda....116,178
Ueno (▲ 60,812)....51,800
Uji (★ Ōsaka)....165,411
Uozu....49,826
Urasoe....81,611
Urawa (★ Tōkyō)....377,235
Urayasu (★ Tōkyō)....93,756
Ushiku....51,926
Utsunomiya....405,375
Uwajima....71,381
Wakayama (★ 495,000)....401,352
Wakkanai....51,854
Wakō (★ Tōkyō)....55,212
Warabi (★ Tōkyō)....70,408
Yachiyo (★ Tōkyō)....142,184
Yaizu (★ Shizuoka)....108,558
Yamagata....245,158
Yamaguchi....124,213
Yamato (★ Tōkyō)....177,669
Yamato-kōriyama (★ Ōsaka)....89,624
Yamato-takada (★ Ōsaka)....65,223
Yao (★ Ōsaka)....276,394
Yashio (★ Tōkyō)....67,635
Yatsushiro (▲ 108,790)....88,700
Yawata (★ Ōsaka)....72,356
Yokkaichi....263,001
Yokohama (★ ★ Tōkyō)....2,992,926
Yokosuka (★ Tōkyō)....427,116
Yonago....131,792
Yonezawa....93,721
Yono (★ Tōkyō)....71,597
Yotsukaidō (★ Tōkyō)....67,010
Yukuhashi....65,527
Zama (★ Tōkyō)....100,000
Zushi (★ Tōkyō)....57,656

JERSEY
1986 C....80,212
Cities and Towns
• SAINT HELIER (★ 46,500)....27,083

JORDAN / Al-Urdun
1989 E....3,111,000
Cities and Towns
Al-Baq'ah (★ 'Ammān) (1989 E)....63,985
• 'AMMĀN (★ 1,450,000)....936,300
Ar-Ruşayfah (★ 'Ammān)....72,580
Az-Zarqā' (★ ★ 'Ammān)....318,055
Irbid....167,785

KAZAKHSTAN
1989 C....16,538,000
Cities and Towns
Aktau....159,000
Akt'ubinsk....253,000
• ALMA-ATA (★ 1,190,000)....1,128,000
Arkalyk (1987 E)....71,000
Aterau....149,000
Balchaš (1987 E)....84,000
Čelinograd....277,000
Čimkent....393,000
Džambul....307,000
Džezkazgan....109,000
Ekibastuz....135,000
Karaganda....614,000
Kentau (1987 E)....60,000
Kokčetav....137,000
Kustanaj....224,000
Kzyl-Orda....153,000
Leninogorsk (1987 E)....69,000
Pavlodar....331,000
Petropavlovsk....241,000
Rudnyj....124,000
Šachtinsk (1987 E)....62,000
Saptajev (1987 E)....64,000
Saran' (1987 E)....64,000
Ščučinsk (1987 E)....53,000
Semipalatinsk....334,000
Taldy-Kurgan....119,000
Temirtau....212,000
Turkestan (1987 E)....77,000
Ural'sk....200,000
Ust'-Kamenogorsk....324,000
Zanatas (1987 E)....53,000
Zyr'anovsk (1987 E)....55,000

KENYA
1990 E....24,870,000
Cities and Towns
Eldoret (1979 C)....50,503
Kisumu (1984 E)....167,100
Machakos (1983 E)....92,300
Meru (1979 C)....72,049
Mombasa....537,000
• NAIROBI....1,505,000
Nakuru (1984 E)....101,700

KIRIBATI
1988 E....68,207
Cities and Towns
BAIRIKI....2,230
• Bikenibeu....4,580

KOREA, NORTH / Chosŏn-minjujuŭi-inmin-konghwaguk
1981 E....18,317,000
Cities and Towns
Ch'ŏngjin....490,000
Haeju (1983 E)....213,000
Hamhŭng (1970 E)....150,000
Hŭngnam (1976 E)....260,000
Kaesŏng....259,000
Kanggye (1967 E)....130,000
Kimch'aek (Sŏngjin) (1967 E)....265,000
Namp'o....241,000
• P'YŎNGYANG (★ 1,600,000)....1,283,000
Sinŭiju....305,000
Songnim (1944 C)....53,035
Wŏnsan (1981 E)....398,000

KOREA, SOUTH / Taehan-min'guk
1985 C....40,448,486
Cities and Towns
Andong....114,216
Anyang (★ Sŏul)....361,577
Bucheon (★ Sŏul)....456,292
Changwŏn (★ Masan)....173,508
Chech'on....102,274
Cheju....202,911
Chinhae....121,341
Chinju....227,309
Ch'ŏnan....170,196
Ch'ŏngju....350,256
Chŏnju....79,323
Chŏnju, Chŏlla Pukdo prov.....426,473
Ch'unch'ŏn....162,988
Ch'ungju....113,331
Ch'ungmu....87,459
Inch'ŏn (★ ★ Sŏul) (1989 E)....1,628,000
Iri....192,269
Kangnŭng....132,897
Kimch'ŏn....77,254
Kimhae....77,903
Kongju....142,094
Kŭmsŏng....58,897
Kunsan....185,649
Kwangju (1989 E)....1,165,000
Kwangmyŏng (★ Sŏul)....219,611
Kyŏngju....127,544
Masan (★ 625,000)....448,746
Mokp'o....236,085
Namwŏn....61,447
P'ohang....260,691
Pusan (★ 3,800,000) (1989 E)....3,773,000
P'yŏngt'aek (▲ 180,513)....63,400
Samch'ŏnp'o....62,466
Sŏgwipo....82,311
Sŏkch'o....69,501
Sŏngnam (★ Sŏul)....447,692
Songtan....66,357
• SŎUL (★ 15,850,000) (1989 E)....10,522,000
Sunch'ŏn (▲ 116,323)....121,958
Suwŏn (★ Sŏul)....430,752
T'aebaek....113,997
Taegu (1989 C)....2,207,000
Taejŏn (1989 E)....1,041,000
Tongduch'ŏn....68,633
Tonghae....91,691
Ŭijŏngbu (★ Sŏul)....162,700
Ulsan....551,014
Wŏnju....151,165
Yŏngch'ŏn....52,811
Yŏngju....84,742
Yŏsu....171,933

KUWAIT / Al-Kuwayt
1985 C....1,697,301
Cities and Towns
Al-Ahmadī (★ 285,000)....26,899
Al-Farwānīyah (★ Al-Kuwayt)....68,701
Al-Fuhayhīl (★ Al-Ahmadī)....50,081
Al-Jahrah (★ Al-Kuwayt)....111,222
• AL-KUWAYT (★ 1,375,000)....44,335
As-Sālimīyah (★ Al-Kuwayt)....153,359
Aş-Şulaybīyah (★ Al-Kuwayt)....51,314
Hawallī (★ Al-Kuwayt)....145,126
Qalīb ash-Shuyūkh (★ Al-Kuwayt)....114,771
South Khītān (★ Al-Kuwayt)....69,256
Subahiya (★ Al-Ahmadī)....60,787

KYRGYZSTAN
1989 C....4,291,000
Cities and Towns
• BIŠKEK....616,000
Džalal-Abad (1987 E)....74,000
Kara-Balta (1987 E)....55,000
Oš....213,000
Prževal'sk (1987 E)....64,000
Tokmak (1987 E)....71,000

LAOS / Lao
1985 C....3,584,803
Cities and Towns
Savannakhet (1975 E)....53,000
Viangchan (Vientiane)....377,409

LATVIA / Latvija
1989 C....2,681,000
Cities and Towns
Daugavpils....127,000
Jelgava (1987 E)....72,000
Jūrmala (★ Rīga) (1987 E)....65,000
Liepāja....114,000
• RĪGA (★ 1,005,000)....915,000
Ventspils (1987 E)....52,000

LEBANON / Lubnān
1982 U....2,637,000
Cities and Towns
• BAYRŪT....509,000
Saydā....105,000
Ṭarābulus (Tripoli)....198,000

LESOTHO
1986 C....1,577,536
Cities and Towns
• MASERU....109,382

LIBERIA
1986 E....2,221,000
Cities and Towns
• MONROVIA....465,000

LIBYA / Lībiyā
1984 C....3,637,488
Cities and Towns
Banghāzī....435,886
Darnah....62,179
Miṣrātah....131,031
• ṬARĀBULUS (TRIPOLI)....990,697
Ṭubruq (Tobruk)....75,282
Zāwiyat al-Baydā'....67,120

LIECHTENSTEIN
1990 E....28,452
Cities and Towns
• VADUZ....4,874

LITHUANIA / Lietuva
1989 C....3,690,000
Cities and Towns
Alytus (1987 E)....71,000
Kaunas....423,000
Klaipėda (Memel)....204,000
Panevėžys....126,000
Šiauliai....145,000
• VILNIUS....582,000

LUXEMBOURG
1985 E....366,000
Cities and Towns
• LUXEMBOURG (★ 136,000)....76,130

MACAU
1987 E....429,000
Cities and Towns
• MACAU....429,000

MACEDONIA / Makedonija
1987 E....2,064,581
Cities and Towns
Bitola (▲ 143,090)....76,200
• SKOPJE (▲ 547,214)....444,900

MADAGASCAR / Madagasikara
1984 E....9,731,000
Cities and Towns
• ANTANANARIVO (1985 E)....663,000
Antsirabe (★ 95,000)....50,100
Antsiranana....100,000
Fianarantsoa....130,000
Mahajanga....85,000
Toamasina....100,000
Toliara....55,000

MALAWI / Malaŵi
1987 C....7,982,607
Cities and Towns
• Blantyre....331,588
LILONGWE....233,973

MALAYSIA
1980 C....13,136,109
Cities and Towns
Alor Setar....69,435
Batu Pahat....64,727
Butterworth (★ ★ George Town)....77,982
George Town (Pinang) (★ 495,000)....248,241
Ipoh....293,849
Johor Baharu (★ Singapore, Sing.)....246,395
Kelang....192,080
Keluang....50,315
Kota Baharu....167,872
Kota Kinabalu (Jesselton)....55,997
• KUALA LUMPUR (★ 1,475,000)....919,610
Kuala Terengganu....180,296
Kuantan....131,547
Kuching....72,555
Melaka....87,494
Miri....52,125
Muar (Bandar Maharani)....65,151
Petaling Jaya (★ Kuala Lumpur)....207,805
Sandakan....70,420
Seremban....132,911
Sibu....85,231
Taiping....146,000
Telok Anson....49,148

MALDIVES
1985 C....181,453
Cities and Towns
• MALE....46,334

MALI
1987 C....7,620,225
Cities and Towns
• BAMAKO....646,163
Gao....54,874
Mopti....73,979
Ségou....88,877
Sikasso....73,050
Tombouctou (Timbuktu)....31,925

MALTA
1989 E....349,014
Cities and Towns
• VALLETTA (★ 215,000)....9,210

MARSHALL ISLANDS
1980 C....30,873
Cities and Towns
• Jarej-Uliga-Delap....8,583

MARTINIQUE
1982 C....328,566
Cities and Towns
• FORT-DE-FRANCE (★ 116,017)....99,844

MAURITANIA / Mauritanie / Mūrītāniyā
1987 E....2,007,000
Cities and Towns
• NOUAKCHOTT....285,000

MAURITIUS
1987 E....1,008,864
Cities and Towns
Beau Bassin-Rose Hill (★ Port Louis)....93,125
Curepipe (★ Port Louis)....64,243
• PORT LOUIS (★ 420,000)....139,730
Quatre Bornes (★ Port Louis)....65,480
Vacoas-Phoenix (★ Port Louis)....55,667

MAYOTTE
1985 E....67,205
Cities and Towns
• DZAOUDZI (★ 6,979)....5,865

MEXICO / México
1980 C....67,395,826
Cities and Towns
Acapulco [de Juárez]....301,902
Aguascalientes....293,152
Atlixco....53,207
Campeche....128,434
Cancún....33,273
Celaya....141,675
Chihuahua....385,603
Chilpancingo [de los Bravo]....67,498
Ciudad Chetumal....56,709
Ciudad del Carmen....72,489
• CIUDAD DE MÉXICO (MEXICO CITY) (★ 14,100,000)....8,831,079
Ciudad de Valles....65,609
Ciudad Guzmán....60,938
Ciudad Juárez....544,496
Ciudad Madero (★ Tampico)....132,444
Ciudad Mante....70,647
Ciudad Obregón....165,572
Ciudad Victoria....140,161
Coatzacoalcos....127,170
Colima....86,044
Córdoba....99,972
Cuernavaca....192,770
Culiacán....304,826
Delicias....65,504
Durango....257,915
Ecatepec (★ Ciudad de México)....741,821
Ensenada....120,483
Fresnillo....56,066
Garza García (★ Monterrey)....81,974
Gómez Palacio (★ ★ Torreón)....116,967
Guadalajara (★ 2,325,000)....1,626,152
Guadalupe (★ Monterrey)....370,524
Guaymas....54,826
Hermosillo....297,175
Hidalgo del Parral....75,590
Iguala....66,005
Irapuato....170,138
Jalapa Enríquez....204,594
La Paz....91,453
León [de los Aldamas]....593,002
Los Mochis....122,531
Matamoros....188,745
Mazatlán....199,830
Mérida....400,142
Mexicali (★ 365,000)....341,559
Minatitlán....106,765
Monclova....115,786
Monterrey (★ 2,015,000)....1,090,009
Morelia....297,544
Naucalpan de Juárez (★ Ciudad de México)....723,723
Navojoa....62,901
Nezahualcóyotl (★ Ciudad de México)....1,341,230
Nogales....65,603
Nuevo Laredo....201,731
Oaxaca [de Juárez]....154,223
Orizaba (★ 215,000)....114,848
Pachuca [de Soto]....110,351
Piedras Negras....67,455
Poza Rica de Hidalgo....166,799
Puebla [de Zaragoza] (★ 1,055,000)....835,759
Puerto Vallarta....38,645
Querétaro....215,976
Reynosa....194,693
Río Bravo....55,236
Salamanca....96,703
Saltillo....284,937
San Luis Potosí (★ 470,000)....362,371
San Luis Río Colorado....76,684
San Nicolás de los Garza (★ Monterrey)....280,696
Santa Catarina (★ Monterrey)....87,673
Soledad Díez Gutiérrez (★ San Luis Potosí)....49,173
Tampico (★ 435,000)....267,957
Tapachula....85,766
Tehuacán....79,547
Tepic....145,741
Tijuana....429,500
Tlalnepantla (★ Ciudad de México)....778,173
Tlaquepaque (★ Guadalajara)....133,500
Toluca [de Lerdo]....199,778
Torreón (★ 575,000)....328,086
Tulancingo....53,400
Tuxpan de Rodríguez Cano....56,037
Tuxtla Gutiérrez....131,096
Uruapan [del Progreso]....122,828
Veracruz [Llave] (★ 385,000)....284,822
Villahermosa....158,216
Zacatecas....80,088
Zamora de Hidalgo....86,998
Zapopan (★ Guadalajara)....345,390

MICRONESIA, FEDERATED STATES OF

C Census.   E Official estimate.   U Unofficial estimate.
• Largest city in country.
★ Population or designation of metropolitan area, including suburbs (see headnote).
▲ Population of an entire municipality, commune, or district, including rural area.

1985 E 94,534
Cities and Towns
• KOLONIA 6,306

MOLDOVA
1989 C 4,341,000
Cities and Towns
Bălti 159,000
• CHIŞINĂU 665,000
Rîbniţa (1987 E) 58,000
Tighina 130,000
Tiraspol 182,000

MONACO
1982 C 27,063
Cities and Towns
• MONACO (★ 87,000) . . . 27,063

MONGOLIA / Mongol Ard Uls
1989 E 2,040,000
Cities and Towns
Darchan (1985 E) 69,800
• ULAANBÀATAR 548,400

MONTSERRAT
1980 C 11,606
Cities and Towns
• PLYMOUTH 1,568

MOROCCO / Al-Magreb
1982 C 20,419,555
Cities and Towns
Agadir 110,479
Beni-Mellal 95,003
Berkane 60,490
• Casablanca (Dar-el-
Beida) (★ 2,475,000) . . 2,139,204
El-Jadida (Mazagan) 81,455
Fès (★ 535,000) 448,823
Kenitra 188,194
Khemisset 58,925
Khouribga 127,181
Ksar-el-Kebir 73,541
Larache 63,893
Marrakech (★ 535,000) . . . 439,728
Meknès (★ 375,000) 319,783
Mohammedia (Fedala)
(★ Casablanca) 105,120
Nador 62,040
Oued-Zem 58,744
Oujda 260,082
RABAT (★ 980,000) 518,616
Safi 197,309
Salé (★★ Rabat) 289,391
Settat 65,203
Sidi Kacem 55,833
Sidi Slimane 50,457
Tanger (Tangier)
(★ 370,000) 266,346
Taza 77,216
Tétouan 199,615

MOZAMBIQUE / Moçambique
1989 E 15,326,476
Cities and Towns
Beira 291,604
Chimoio (1986 E) 86,928
Inhambane (1986 E) 64,274
• MAPUTO 1,069,727
Nacala-Velha 101,615
Nampula 197,379
Pemba (1986 E) 50,215
Quelimane 78,520
Tete (1986 E) 56,178
Xai-Xai (1986 E) 51,620

MYANMAR
1983 C 34,124,908
Cities and Towns
Bago (Pegu) 150,528
Chauk 51,437
Dawei (Tavoy) 69,882
Henzada 82,005
Kale 52,628
Lashio 88,590
Magway 54,881
Mandalay 532,949
Mawlamyine (Moulmein) . . 219,961
Maymyo 63,782
Meiktila 96,496
Mergui (Myeik) 88,600
Mogok 49,392
Monywa 106,843
Myingyan 77,060
Myitkyinä 56,427
Pakokku 71,860
Pathein (Bassein) 144,096
Pyè (Prome) 83,332
Pyinmana 52,962
Shwebo 52,185
Sittwe (Akyab) 107,621
Taunggyi 108,231
Thaton 61,790
Toungoo 65,861
• YANGON (RANGOON)
(★ 2,800,000) 2,705,039

Yenangyaung 62,582

NAMIBIA
1988 E 1,760,000
Cities and Towns
• WINDHOEK 114,500

NAURU / Naoero
1987 E 8,000
Cities and Towns

NEPAL / Nepāl
1981 C 15,022,839
Cities and Towns
Birātnagar 93,544
• KĀTHMĀNDAU
(★ 320,000) 235,160

NETHERLANDS / Nederland
1989 E 14,880,000
Cities and Towns
Alkmaar (★ 121,000)
(1987 E) 87,034
Almelo (1986 E) 62,421
Alphen aan den Rijn
(1986 E) 55,812
Amersfoort (★ 130,158)
(1986 E) 89,596
Amstelveen
(★ Amsterdam)
(1986 E) 68,090
• AMSTERDAM
(★ 1,860,000) 696,500
Apeldoorn 147,300
Arnhem (★ 296,362) 129,000
Breda (★ 155,613) 121,400
Delft
(★★ 's-Gravenhage)
(1986 E) 87,440
Den Helder (1986 E) 63,231
Deventer (1986 E) 64,806
Dordrecht (★ 202,126) 108,300
Eindhoven (★ 379,377) 190,700
Enschede (★ 288,000) 145,200
Gouda (1986 E) 60,927
Groningen (★ 206,781) 167,800
Haarlem (★ Amsterdam) . . . 149,200
Heerlen (★ 266,617)
(1986 E) 93,871
Helmond (1987 E) 63,909
Hengelo
(★★ Enschede)
(1986 E) 76,694
Hilversum
(★ Amsterdam)
(1986 E) 86,125
Hoorn (1987 E) 53,788
IJmuiden
(★ Amsterdam)
(1986 E) 57,157
Kerkrade (★ Heerlen)
(1986 E) 52,885
Leeuwarden (1986 E) 84,966
Leiden (★ 182,244) 109,200
Maastricht (★ 160,026) 116,400
Nieuwegein (★ Utrecht)
(1987 E) 56,719
Nijmegen (★ 240,085) 145,400
Oss (1986 E) 50,343
Purmerend
(★ Amsterdam)
(1987 E) 52,257
Roosendaal (1986 E) 57,385
Rotterdam
(★ 1,110,000) 576,300
Schiedam
(★ Rotterdam)
(1986 E) 69,078
'S-GRAVENHAGE (THE
HAGUE) (★ 770,000) . . . 443,900
's-Hertogenbosch
(★ 189,067) (1986 E) . . . 89,039
Spijkenisse
(★ Rotterdam)
(1987 E) 62,394
Tilburg (★ 224,934) 155,100
Utrecht (★ 518,779) 230,700
Venlo (★ 87,000)
(1986 E) 63,475
Vlaardingen
(★ Rotterdam)
(1986 E) 75,536
Zaandam
(★ Amsterdam) 129,600
Zeist (★ Utrecht)
(1986 E) 59,743
Zoetermeer
(★ 's-Gravenhage)
(1987 E) 85,349
Zwolle (1986 E) 88,438

NETHERLANDS ANTILLES / Nederlandse Antillen
1990 E 189,687
Cities and Towns
• WILLEMSTAD
(★ 130,000) (1981 C) . . . 31,883

NEW CALEDONIA / Nouvelle-Calédonie

1989 C 164,173
Cities and Towns
• NOUMÉA (★ 88,000) . . . 65,110

NEW ZEALAND
1986 C 3,307,084
Cities and Towns
• Auckland (★ 850,000) . . . 149,046
Christchurch
(★ 320,000) 168,200
Dunedin (★ 109,000) 76,964
Hamilton (★ 101,814) 94,511
Lower Hutt
(★ Wellington) 63,862
Manukau (★ Auckland) . . . 177,248
Napier (★ 107,060) 49,428
Palmerston North
(★ 67,405) 60,503
Takapuna (★ Auckland) . . . 69,419
Waitemata
(★ Auckland) 96,365
WELLINGTON
(★ 350,000) 137,495

NICARAGUA
1985 E 3,272,100
Cities and Towns
Chinandega 75,000
Granada (1981 E) 64,642
León 101,000
• MANAGUA 682,000
Masaya 75,000
Matagalpa 68,000

NIGER
1988 C 7,250,383
Cities and Towns
Agadez 50,164
Maradi 112,965
• NIAMEY 398,265
Tahoua 51,607
Zinder 120,892

NIGERIA
1987 E 101,907,000
Cities and Towns
Aba 239,800
Abakaliki 56,800
Abeokuta 341,300
ABUJA (1993 U) 250,000
Ado-Ekiti 287,000
Afikpo 65,790
Agege 83,810
Akure 129,600
Amaigbo 53,690
Apomu 49,570
Awka 88,800
Azare 50,020
Bauchi 68,840
Benin City 183,200
Bida 100,200
Calabar 139,800
Deba 110,600
Duku 52,880
Ede 245,200
Effon-Alaiye 122,300
Ejigbo 84,570
Emure-Ekiti 58,750
Enugu 252,500
Epe 80,560
Erin-Oshogbo 59,940
Eruwa 49,140
Fiditi 49,440
Gboko 49,390
Gbongan 53,990
Gombe 86,120
Gusau 126,200
Ibadan 1,144,000
Idah 50,550
Idanre 56,080
Ife 237,000
Ifon-Oshogbo 65,980
Igboho 85,230
Igbo-Ora 68,060
Igede-Ekiti 56,570
Ihiala 73,240
Ijebu-Igbo 78,680
Ijebu-Ode 124,900
Ijero-Ekiti 76,420
Ikare 112,500
Ikerre 195,400
Ikire 94,450
Ikirun 144,900
Ikole 71,860
Ikorodu 147,700
Ikot Ekpene 69,440
Ila 210,800
Ilawe-Ekiti 147,300
Ilesha 302,100
Ilobu 159,000
Ilorin 380,000
Inisa 95,630
Ipoti-Ekiti 53,220
Ise-Ekiti 82,580
Iseyin 173,500
Iwo 289,100
Jimeta 66,130
Jos 164,700
Kaduna 273,200
Kano 538,300
Katsina 165,000
Kaura Namoda 52,910

Keffi 57,790
Kishi 77,210
Kumo 118,200
Lafia 97,810
Lafiagi 57,580
• LAGOS (★ 3,800,000) . . 1,213,000
Lalupon 56,130
Lere 49,670
Maiduguri 255,100
Makurdi 98,350
Minna 109,300
Mubi 51,190
Mushin (★ Lagos) 266,100
Nguru 78,770
Offa 157,500
Ogbomosho 582,900
Oka 114,400
Oke-Mesi 55,040
Okwe 52,550
Olupona 65,720
Ondo 135,300
Onitsha 298,200
Opobo 64,620
Oron 62,260
Oshogbo 380,800
Owo 146,600
Oyan 50,930
Oyo 204,700
Pindiga 64,130
Port Harcourt 327,300
Potiskum 56,490
Sapele 111,200
Shagamu 93,610
Shaki 139,000
Shomolu (★ Lagos) 120,700
Sokoto 163,700
Ugep 81,910
Umuahia 52,550
Uyo 60,500
Warri 100,700
Zaria 302,800

NIUE
1986 C 2,531
Cities and Towns
• ALOFI 811

NORTHERN MARIANA ISLANDS
1980 C 16,780
Cities and Towns
• Chalan Kanoa 2,678

NORWAY / Norge
1987 E 4,190,000
Cities and Towns
Bærum (★ Oslo)
(1985 E) 83,000
Bergen (★ 239,000) 209,320
Drammen (★ 73,000)
(1985 E) 50,700
Fredrikstad (★ 52,000)
(1983 E) 27,618
Hammerfest (1983 E) 7,208
Kristiansand (1985 E) 62,200
• OSLO (★ 720,000) 452,415
Stavanger (★ 132,000)
(1985 E) 94,200
Tromsø (1985 E) 47,800
Trondheim 135,010

OMAN / 'Umān
1981 E 919,000
Cities and Towns
• MASQAT (MUSCAT) 50,000
Şūr (1980 E) 30,000

PAKISTAN / Pākistān
1981 C 84,253,644
Cities and Towns
Ahmadpur East 56,979
Bahāwalnagar 74,533
Bahāwalpur
(★ 180,263) 152,009
Chārsadda 62,530
Chīchāwatni 50,241
Chiniot 105,559
Chishtiān Mandi 61,959
Daska 55,555
Dera Ghāzi Khān 102,007
Dera Ismāīl Khān
(★ 68,145) 64,358
Drigh Road
Cantonment
(★ Karāchi) 56,742
Faisalabad (Lyallpur) . . . 1,104,209
Gojra 68,000
Gujrānwāla (★ 658,753) . . . 600,993
Gujrānwāla Cantonment
(★ Gujrānwāla) 57,760
Gujrāt 155,058
Hāfizābād 83,464
Hyderābād (★ 800,000) . . . 702,539
ISLAMABAD
(★ Rāwalpindi) 204,364
Jacobābād 79,365
Jarānwāla 69,459
Jhang Maghiāna 195,558
Jhelum (★ 106,462) 92,646
Kamālia 61,107
Kāmoke 71,097
• Karāchi (★ 5,300,000) . . 4,901,627

Karāchi Cantonment
(★ Karāchi) 181,981
Kasūr 155,523
Khairpur 61,447
Khānewāl 89,090
Khānpur 70,589
Khushāb 56,274
Kohāt (★ 77,604) 55,832
Lahore (★ 3,025,000) . . . 2,707,215
Lahore Cantonment
(★ Lahore) 245,474
Lārkāna 123,890
Leiah 51,482
Mandi Būrewāla 86,311
Mardān (★ 147,977) 141,842
Miānwāli 59,159
Mingāora 88,078
Mīrpur Khās 124,371
Multān (★ 732,070) 696,316
Muzaffargarh 53,000
Nawābshāh 102,139
Okāra (★ 153,483) 127,455
Pākpattan 69,820
Peshāwar (★ 566,248) . . . 506,896
Peshāwar Cantonment
(★ Peshāwar) 59,352
Quetta (★ 285,719) 244,842
Rahīmyār Khān
(★ 132,635) 119,036
Rāwalpindi
(★ 1,040,000) 457,091
Rāwalpindi Cantonment
(★ Rāwalpindi) 337,752
Sādiqābād 63,935
Sāhīwal 150,954
Sargodha (★ 291,362) 231,895
Sargodha Cantonment
(★ Sargodha) 59,467
Shekhūpura 141,168
Shikārpur 88,138
Siālkot (★ 302,009) 258,147
Sukkur 190,551
Tando Ādam 62,744
Turbat 52,337
Vihāri 53,799
Wāh 122,335
Wazīrābād 62,725

PALAU / Belau
1986 C 13,873
Cities and Towns
• KOROR 8,629

PANAMA / Panamá
1990 C 2,315,047
Cities and Towns
Colón (★ 96,000) 54,469
David 65,635
• PANAMÁ (★ 770,000) . . . 411,549
San Miguelito
(★ Panamá) 242,529

PAPUA NEW GUINEA
1987 E 3,479,400
Cities and Towns
Lae 79,600
• PORT MORESBY 152,100
Rabaul (1980 C) 14,954

PARAGUAY
1985 E 3,279,000
Cities and Towns
• ASUNCIÓN
(★ 700,000) 477,100
Fernando de la Mora
(★ Asunción) 80,000
Lambaré (★ Asunción) 84,000
Puerto Presidente
Stroessner 64,000
San Lorenzo
(★ Asunción)
(1982 C) 74,632

PERU / Perú
1981 C 17,031,221
Cities and Towns
Arequipa (★ 446,942) 108,023
Ayacucho (★ 69,533) 57,432
Breña (★ Lima) 112,398
Cajamarca 62,259
Callao (★★ Lima) 264,133
Cerro de Pasco
(★ 66,373) 55,597
Chiclayo (★ 279,527) 213,095
Chimbote 223,341
Chorrillos (★ Lima) 141,881
Chosica 65,139
Cuzco (★ 184,550) 89,563
Huancayo (★ 164,954) 84,845
Huánuco 61,812
Ica 114,400
Iquitos 178,738
Jesús María (★ Lima) 83,179
Juliaca 87,651
La Victoria (★ Lima) 270,778
• LIMA (★ 4,608,010) 371,122
Lince (★ Lima) 80,456
Magdalena (★ Lima) 55,535
Miraflores (★ Lima) 103,453
Pisco 55,604
Piura (★ 207,934) 144,609

C Census.   E Official estimate.   U Unofficial estimate.
• Largest city in country.

★ Population or designation of metropolitan area, including suburbs (see headnote).
▲ Population of an entire municipality, commune, or district, including rural area.

World Populations

Pucallpa 112,263
Pueblo Libre (★ Lima) 83,985
Puno 67,397
Rímac (★ Lima) 184,484
San Isidro (★ Lima) 71,203
San Martín de Porras
(★ Lima) 404,856
Santiago de Surco
(★ Lima) 146,636
Sullana 89,037
Surquillo (★ Lima) 134,158
Tacna 97,173
Talara 57,351
Trujillo (★ 354,301) 202,469
Vitarte (★ Lima) 145,504

PHILIPPINES / Pilipinas

1990 C 60,477,000

Cities and Towns

Angeles 236,000
Antipolo (▲ 68,912)
(1980 C) 54,117
Bacolod 364,000
Bacoor (★ Manila)
(1980 C) 90,364
Baguio 183,000
Baliuag (1980 C) 70,555
Biñan (★ Manila)
(1980 C) 83,684
Binangonan (1980 C) 80,980
Bocaue (1980 C) 49,693
Butuan (▲ 228,000) 99,000
Cabanatuan
(▲ 173,000) 75,700
Cagayan de Oro
(▲ 340,000) 255,000
Cainta (★ Manila)
(1980 C) 59,025
Calamba (▲ 121,175)
(1980 C) 72,359
Caloocan (★ Manila) 746,000
Carmona (★ Manila)
(1980 C) 65,014
Cavite (★ 175,000) 92,000
Cebu (★ 720,000) 610,000
Cotabato 127,000
Dagupan 122,000
Davao (★ 850,000) 569,300
Dumaguete 80,000
General Santos
(Dadiangas)
(▲ 250,000) 157,600
Guagua (1980 C) 72,609
Iloilo 311,000
Isabela (Basilan)
(▲ 49,891) (1980 C) 11,491
Jolo (1980 C) 52,429
Lapu-Lapu (Opon) 146,000
Las Piñas (★ Manila)
(1984 E) 190,364
Legaspi (▲ 121,000) 63,000
Lucena 151,000
Mabalacat (▲ 80,966)
(1980 C) 54,988
Makati (★ Manila)
(1984 E) 408,991
Malabon (★ Manila)
(1984 E) 212,930
Malolos (1980 C) 95,699
Mandaluyong
(★ Manila) (1984 E) 226,670
Mandaue (★ Cebu) 180,000
Mangaldan (1980 C) 50,434
• MANILA (★ 6,800,000) . .1,587,000
Marawi 92,000
Marikina (★ Manila)
(1984 E) 248,183
Meycauayan (★ Manila)
(1980 C) 83,579
Muntinlupa (★ Manila)
(1984 E) 172,421
Naga (★ Manila) 115,000
Navotas (★ Manila)
(1984 E) 146,899
Olongapo 192,000
Pagadian (▲ 107,000) 52,400
Parañaque (★ Manila)
(1984 E) 252,791
Pasay (★ Manila) 354,000
Pasig (★ Manila)
(1984 E) 318,853
Puerto Princesa
(▲ 92,000) 52,000
Quezon City (★ Manila) . .1,632,000
San Fernando (1980 C) . . .110,891
San Juan del Monte
(★ Manila) (1984 E) 139,126
San Pablo (▲ 161,000) 83,900
San Pedro (1980 C) 74,556
Santa Cruz (1980 C) 60,620
Santa Rosa (★ Manila)
(1980 C) 64,325
Tacloban 138,000
Tagbilaran 56,000
Tagig (★ Manila)
(1984 E) 130,719
Taytay (★ Manila)
(1980 C) 75,328
Valenzuela (★ Manila)
(1984 E) 275,725
Zamboanga
(▲ 444,000) 107,000

PITCAIRN

1988 C 59

Cities and Towns

• ADAMSTOWN 59

POLAND / Polska

1989 E 37,775,100

Cities and Towns

Będzin (★ Katowice) 77,300
Bełchatów 53,600
Biała Podlaska 50,900
Białystok 263,900
Bielsko-Biała 179,600
Bydgoszcz 377,900
Bytom (Beuthen)
(★ ★ Katowice) 228,000
Chełm 63,300
Chorzów
(★ ★ Katowice) 133,300
Częstochowa 254,600
Dąbrowa Górnicza
(★ Katowice) 133,200
Elbląg (Elbing) 124,600
Ełk .49,600
Gdańsk (Danzig)
(★ 909,000) 461,500
Gdynia (★ ★ Gdańsk) 250,200
Gliwice (Gleiwitz)
(★ Katowice) 222,500
Głogów 70,100
Gniezno 68,900
Gorzów Wielkopolski
(Landsberg an der
Warthe) 121,500
Grudziądz 99,900
Inowrocław 75,100
Jastrzębie-Zdrój 102,200
Jaworzno (★ Katowice) 97,400
Jelenia Góra
(Hirschberg) 92,700
Kalisz 105,600
• Katowice
(★ 2,778,000) 365,800
Kędzierzyn Kozle 71,600
Kielce 211,100
Konin 78,500
Koszalin (Köslin) 105,600
Kraków (★ 828,000) 743,700
Legionowo
(★ Warszawa) 50,000
Legnica (Liegnitz) 102,800
Leszno 56,700
Łódź (★ 1,061,000) 851,500
Łomża 56,300
Lubin 78,800
Lublin (★ 389,000) 339,500
Mielec 58,600
Mysłowice
(★ Katowice) 91,200
Nowy Sącz 75,100
Olsztyn (Allenstein) 158,800
Opole (Oppeln) 125,800
Ostrowiec
Świętokrzyski 76,300
Ostrów Wielkopolski 71,200
Pabianice (★ Łódź) 74,400
Piekary Śląskie
(★ Katowice) 68,200
Piła (Schneidemühl)
(1988 E) 70,000
Piotrków Trybunalski 80,100
Płock 119,300
Poznań (★ 672,000) 586,500
Pruszków
(★ Warszawa) 52,700
Przemyśl 67,300
Puławy 52,200
Racibórz (Ratibor) 61,700
Radom 223,600
Radomsko 49,700
Ruda Śląska
(★ Katowice) 167,700
Rybnik 140,000
Rzeszów 148,600
Siedlce 69,200
Siemianowice Śląskie
(★ Katowice) 79,200
Skarżysko-Kamienna 50,200
Słupsk (Stolp) 98,500
Sosnowiec
(★ ★ Katowice) 258,700
Stalowa Wola 67,600
Starachowice 55,400
Stargard Szczeciński
(Stargard in
Pommern) 68,400
Suwałki 57,900
Świdnica (Schweidnitz) 61,800
Świętochłowice
(★ Katowice) 58,700
Szczecin (Stettin)
(★ 449,000) 409,500
Tarnów 119,100
Tarnowskie Góry
(★ Katowice) 72,700
Tczew 58,400
Tomaszów Mazowiecki 69,200
Toruń 199,600
Tychy (★ Katowice) 187,600
Wałbrzych
(Waldenburg)
(★ 207,000) 141,400
WARSZAWA
(★ 2,323,000) 1,651,200
Włocławek 119,500
Wodzisław Śląski 109,800
Wrocław (Breslau) 637,400
Zabrze (Hindenburg)
(★ ★ Katowice) 201,400
Zamość 59,000

Zawiercie 55,700
Zgierz (★ Łódź) 58,500
Zielona Góra
(Grünberg) 111,800
Żory 65,300

PORTUGAL

1981 C 9,833,014

Cities and Towns

Amadora (★ Lisboa) 95,518
Barreiro (★ Lisboa) 50,863
Braga 63,033
Coimbra 74,616
• LISBOA (LISBON)
(★ 2,250,000) 807,167
Porto (★ 1,225,000) 327,368
Setúbal 77,885
Vila Nova de Gaia
(★ Porto) 62,469

PUERTO RICO

1980 C 3,196,520

Cities and Towns

Aguadilla (★ 152,793) 22,039
Arecibo (★ 160,336) 48,779
Bayamón (★ San Juan) . . .185,087
Caguas (★ San Juan) 87,214
Carolina (★ San Juan) 147,835
Guaynabo (★ San Juan) . . .65,075
Mayagüez (★ 200,464) 82,968
Ponce (★ 232,551) 161,739
• SAN JUAN
(★ 1,775,260) 424,600

QATAR / Qaţar

1986 C 369,079

Cities and Towns

• AD-DAWHAH (DOHA)
(★ 310,000) 217,294
Ar-Rayyān
(★ Ad-Dawḥah) 91,996

REUNION / Réunion

1982 C 515,814

Cities and Towns

• SAINT-DENIS
(▲ 109,072) 84,400

ROMANIA / România

1986 E 22,823,479

Cities and Towns

Alba-Iulia 66,100
Alexandria 52,802
Arad 187,744
Bacău 179,877
Baia Mare 139,704
Bârlad 70,365
Bistrița 77,267
Botoșani 108,775
Brăila 235,620
Brașov 351,493
• BUCUREȘTI
(BUCHAREST)
(★ 2,275,000) 1,989,823
Buzău 136,080
Călărași 69,350
Cluj-Napoca 310,017
Constanța 327,676
Craiova 281,044
Deva 77,976
Drobeta-Turnu Severin 99,366
Focșani 86,411
Galați 295,372
Giurgiu 68,002
Hunedoara 88,514
Iași 313,060
Lugoj 53,665
Medgidia 48,409
Mediaș 72,816
Onești 52,329
Oradea 213,846
Petroșani (★ 76,000) 49,131
Piatra-Neamț 109,393
Pitești 157,190
Ploiești (★ 310,000) 234,886
Râmnicu Vâlcea 96,051
Reșița 105,914
Roman 72,415
Satu Mare 130,082
Sfântu Gheorghe 67,587
Sibiu 177,511
Slatina 76,714
Suceava 96,317
Târgoviște 91,990
Târgu Jiu 87,693
Târgu Mureș 158,998
Timișoara 325,272
Tulcea 86,336
Turda 61,594
Vaslui 65,070
Zalău 57,283

RUSSIA / Rossija

1989 C 147,386,000

Cities and Towns

Abakan 154,000
Ačinsk (1987 E) 53,000
Ačinsk 122,000
Alapajevsk (1987 E) 53,000

Aleksandrov (1987 E) 66,000
Aleksin (1987 E) 72,000
Al'metjevsk 129,000
Amursk (1987 E) 54,000
Angarsk 266,000
Anžero-Sudžensk 108,000
Apatity (1987 E) 80,000
Archangel'sk 416,000
Armavir 161,000
Arsenjev (1987 E) 67,000
Art'om (1987 E) 73,000
Arzamas 109,000
Asbest (1987 E) 83,000
Astrachan' 509,000
Azov (1987 E) 81,000
Balakovo 198,000
Balašicha (★ Moskva) 136,000
Balašov (1987 E) 99,000
Barnaul (★ 665,000) 602,000
Batajsk (★ Rostov-na-
Donu) (1987 E) 98,000
Belebej (1987 E) 51,000
Belgorod 300,000
Belogorsk (1987 E) 71,000
Beloreck (1987 E) 75,000
Belovo (1987 E) 118,000
Berdsk (★ Novosibirsk)
(1987 E) 77,000
Berezniki 201,000
Ber'ozovskij (1987 E) 51,000
Bijsk 233,000
Birobidžan (1987 E) 82,000
Blagoveščensk 206,000
Bor (★ Nižnij Novgorod)
(1987 E) 65,000
Borisoglebsk (1987 E) 69,000
Boroviči (1987 E) 64,000
Br'ansk 452,000
Bratsk 255,000
Bud'onnovsk (1987 E) 54,000
Bugul'ma (1987 E) 88,000
Buguruslan (1987 E) 53,000
Bujnaksk (1987 E) 53,000
Buzuluk (1987 E) 82,000
Čajkovskij (1987 E) 83,000
Čapajevsk (1987 E) 87,000
Čeboksary 420,000
Čechov (1987 E) 57,000
Čel'abinsk
(★ 1,325,000) 1,143,000
Čeremchovo (1987 E) 73,000
Čerepovec 310,000
Čerkessk 113,000
Černogorsk (1987 E) 80,000
Chabarovsk 601,000
Chasav'urt (1987 E) 74,000
Chimki (★ Moskva) 133,000
Cholmsk (1987 E) 50,000
Čistopol' (1987 E) 65,000
Čita 366,000
Čusovoj (1987 E) 59,000
Derbent (1987 E) 83,000
Dimitrovgrad 124,000
Dmitrov (1987 E) 64,000
Dolgoprudnyj
(★ Moskva) (1987 E) 71,000
Domodedovo
(★ Moskva) (1987 E) 51,000
Dubna (1987 E) 64,000
Dzeržinsk (★ Nižnij
Novgorod) 285,000
Elektrostal' 153,000
Elista (1987 E) 85,000
Engel's (★ ★ Saratov) 182,000
Fr'azino (★ Moskva)
(1987 E) 52,000
Gatčina (★ Sankt-
Peterburg) (1987 E) 81,000
Georgijevsk (1987 E) 62,000
Glazov 104,000
Groznyj 401,000
Gubkin (1987 E) 75,000
Gukovo (1987 E) 72,000
Gus'-Chrustal'nyj
(1987 E) 75,000
Inta (1987 E) 58,000
Irbit (1987 E) 53,000
Irkutsk 626,000
Išim (1987 E) 65,000
Išimbaj (1987 E) 67,000
Iskitim (1987 E) 69,000
Ivanovo 481,000
Ivantejevka (★ Moskva)
(1987 E) 53,000
Iževsk 635,000
Jakutsk 187,000
Jaroslavl' 633,000
Jefremov (1987 E) 58,000
Jegorjevsk (1987 E) 73,000
Jejsk (1987 E) 77,000
Jekaterinburg
(Sverdlovsk)
(★ 1,620,000) 1,367,000
Jelec 120,000
Jermolajevo (1987 E) 62,000
Jessentuki (1987 E) 84,000
Joškar-Ola 242,000
Jurga (1987 E) 92,000
Južno-Sachalinsk 157,000
Kaliningrad
(Königsberg) 401,000
Kaliningrad (★ Moskva) . . .160,000
Kaluga 312,000
Kamensk-Šachtinskij
(1987 E) 75,000
Kamensk-Ural'skij 209,000
Kamyšin 122,000
Kanaš (1987 E) 53,000
Kansk 110,000
Kaspijsk (1987 E) 61,000

Kazan' (★ 1,140,000) . . .1,094,000
Kemerovo 520,000
Kimry (1987 E) 61,000
Kinel' (1979 C) 40,873
Kinešma 105,000
Kiriši (1987 E) 51,000
Kirov 441,000
Kirovo-Čepeck (1987 E) 89,000
Kisel'ovsk
(★ Prokopjevsk) 128,000
Kislovodsk 114,000
Kizel (1979 C) 40,157
Klimovsk (★ Moskva)
(1987 E) 57,000
Klin (1987 E) 95,000
Klincy (1987 E) 72,000
Kol'čugino (1979 C) 43,686
Kolomna 162,000
Kolpino (★ Sankt-
Peterburg) 142,000
Komsomol'sk-na-Amure . . .315,000
Kopejsk (★ Čel'abinsk)
(1987 E) 99,000
Korkino (1981 E) 63,000
Korsakov (1979 C) 43,348
Kostroma 278,000
Kotlas (1987 E) 69,000
Kovrov 160,000
Krasnodar 620,000
Krasnogorsk
(★ Moskva) (1987 E) 89,000
Krasnojarsk 912,000
Krasnokamensk
(1987 E) 70,000
Krasnokamsk (1987 E) 58,000
Krasnoturjinsk (1987 E) 66,000
Krasnoufimsk (1979 C) 40,027
Krasnoural'sk (1979 C) 38,212
Krasnyj Sulin (1979 C) 42,542
Kropotkin (1987 E) 73,000
Krymsk (1983 E) 50,000
Kstovo (★ Nižnij
Novgorod) (1987 E) 64,000
Kujbyšev (1987 E) 51,000
Kulebaki (1979 C) 48,302
Kungur (1987 E) 83,000
Kurgan 356,000
Kursk 424,000
Kuša (1979 C) 43,089
Kuzneck (1987 E) 98,000
Kyzyl (1987 E) 80,000
Labinsk (1987 E) 58,000
Leninogorsk (1987 E) 61,000
Leninsk-Kuzneckij 165,000
Lipeck 450,000
Liski (1987 E) 54,000
Livny (1987 E) 51,000
Lobn'a (★ Moskva)
(1987 E) 59,000
L'ubercy (★ Moskva) 165,000
Lys'va (1987 E) 77,000
Lytkarino (★ Moskva)
(1987 E) 51,000
Machačkala 315,000
Magadan 152,000
Magnitogorsk 440,000
Majkop 149,000
Meždurečensk 107,000
Miass 168,000
Michajlovka (1987 E) 58,000
Mičurinsk 109,000
Mineral'nyje Vody
(1987 E) 75,000
Minusinsk (1987 E) 72,000
Mončegorsk (1987 E) 65,000
Moršansk (1987 E) 51,000
• MOSKVA (MOSCOW)
(★ 13,100,000) 8,769,000
Murmansk 468,000
Murom 124,000
Mytišči (★ Moskva) 154,000
Naberežnyje Čelny 501,000
Nachodka 165,000
Nal'čik 235,000
Naro-Fominsk (1987 E) 60,000
Nazarovo (1987 E) 63,000
Neftejugansk (1987 E) 86,000
Ner'ungri (1987 E) 68,000
Nevinnomyssk 121,000
Nikolo-Berjozovka 107,000
Nižnekamsk 191,000
Nižnevartovsk 242,000
Nižnij Novgorod
(★ 2,025,000) 1,438,000
Nižnij Tagil 440,000
Noginsk 123,000
Nojabr'sk (1987 E) 77,000
Noril'sk 174,000
Novgorod 229,000
Novoaltajsk (★ Barnaul)
(1987 E) 51,000
Novočeboksarsk 115,000
Novočerkassk 187,000
Novodvinsk (1987 E) 50,000
Novokujbyševsk
(★ Kujbyšev) 113,000
Novokuzneck 600,000
Novomoskovsk
(★ 365,000) 146,000
Novorossijsk 186,000
Novošachtinsk 106,000
Novosibirsk
(★ 1,600,000) 1,436,000
Novotroick 106,000
Novyj Urengoj (1987 E) 79,000
Obninsk 100,000
Odincovo (★ Moskva) 125,000
Okt'abr'skij 105,000
Omsk (★ 1,175,000) 1,148,000

C Census.   E Official estimate.   U Unofficial estimate.
• Largest city in country.

★ Population or designation of metropolitan area, including suburbs (see headnote).
▲ Population of an entire municipality, commune, or district, including rural area.

210

Orechovo-Zujevo
(★ 205,000) 137,000
Orel 337,208
Orenburg 547,000
Orsk 271,000
Osinniki (1987 E) 63,000
Partizansk (1979 C) 45,628
P'atigorsk 129,000
Pavlovo (1987 E) 72,000
Pavlovskij Posad
(1987 E) 71,000
Pečora (1987 E) 64,000
Penza 543,000
Perm' (★ 1,160,000) ...1,091,000
Pervoural'sk 142,000
Petrodvorec (★ Sankt-
Peterburg) (1987 E) 77,000
Petropavlovsk-
Kamčatskij 269,000
Petrozavodsk 270,000
Podol'sk (★ Moskva) 210,000
Polevskoj (1987 E) 71,000
Prochladnyj (1987 E) 53,000
Prokopjevsk
(★ 410,000) 274,000
Pskov 204,000
Puškin (★ Sankt-
Peterburg) (1987 E) 97,000
Puškino (1987 E) 74,000
Ramenskoje (1987 E) 86,000
R'azan' 515,000
Reutov (★ Moskva)
(1987 E) 68,000
Revda (1987 E) 66,000
Roslavl' (1987 E) 61,000
Rossoš' (1987 E) 55,000
Rostov-na-Donu
(★ 1,165,000) 1,020,000
Rubcovsk 172,000
Ruzajevka (1987 E) 53,000
Rybinsk 252,000
Ržev (1987 E) 70,000
Šachty 224,000
Sadrinsk (1987 E) 87,000
Safonovo (1987 E) 56,000
Salavat 150,000
Sal'sk (1987 E) 62,000
Samara (★ 1,505,000) ..1,257,000
Sankt-Peterburg (Saint
Petersburg)
(★ 5,825,000) 4,456,000
Saransk 312,000
Sarapul 111,000
Saratov (★ 1,155,000) ...905,000
Ščelkovo (★ Moskva) 109,000
Sčokino (1987 E) 70,000
Sergijev Posad 115,000
Serov 104,000
Serpuchov 144,000
Severodvinsk 249,000
Severomorsk (1987 E) 55,000
Slav'ansk-Na-Kubani
(1987 E) 57,000
Smolensk 341,000
Soči 337,000
Sokol (1979 C) 45,424
Solikamsk 110,000
Solncevo (★ Moskva)
(1984 E) 62,000
Solnečnogorsk
(★ Moskva) (1987 E) 53,000
Sosnovyj Bor (1987 E) 56,000
Spassk-Dal'nij (1987 E) ...60,000
Staryj Oskol 174,000
Stavropol' 318,000
Sterlitamak 248,000
Stupino (1987 E) 73,000
Suja (1987 E) 72,000
Surgut 248,000
Svobodnyj (1987 E) 78,000
Syktyvkar 233,000
Syzran' 174,000
Taganrog 291,000
Talnach (1987 E) 54,000
Tambov 305,000
Tichoreck (1987 E) 67,000
Tichvin (1987 E) 70,000
Tobol'sk (1987 E) 82,000
Toljatti 630,000
Tomsk 502,000
Toržok (1987 E) 51,000
Troick (1987 E) 91,000
Tuapse (1987 E) 64,000
Tujmazy (1987 E) 54,000
Tula (★ 640,000) 540,000
Tulun (1987 E) 56,000
T'umen' 477,000
Tver' 451,000
Tyndinskij (1987 E) 61,000
Uchta 111,000
Ufa (★ 1,100,000) 1,083,000
Uglič (1979 C) 39,872
Ulan-Ude 353,000
Uljanovsk 625,000
Usolje-Sibirskoje 107,000
Ussurijsk 162,000
Ust'-Ilimsk 109,000
Ust'-Kut (1987 E) 58,000
Uzlovaja
(★ Novomoskovsk)
(1987 E) 56,000
V'az'ma (1987 E) 57,000
Velikije Luki 114,000
Verchn'aja Salda
(1987 E) 56,000
Vičuga (1987 E) 51,000
Vladikavkaz 300,000
Vladimir 350,000
Vladivostok 648,000
Volchov (1987 E) 51,000

Volgodonsk 176,000
Volgograd (Stalingrad)
(★ 1,360,000) 999,000
Vologda 283,000
Vol'sk (1987 E) 66,000
Volžsk (1987 E) 60,000
Volžskij (★ Volgograd) ...269,000
Vorkuta 116,000
Voronež 887,000
Voskresensk (1987 E) 80,000
Votkinsk 103,000
Vyborg (1987 E) 81,000
Vyksa (1987 E) 60,000
Vyšnij Voločok (1987 E) ...70,000
Zelenograd (★ Moskva) ...158,000
Železnodorožnyj
(★ Moskva) (1987 E) 90,000
Železnogorsk (1987 E) 81,000
Zel'onodol'sk (1987 E) 93,000
Žigulevsk (1977 E) 50,000
Zima (1987 E) 51,000
Zlatoust 208,000
Žukovskij 101,000

RWANDA

1983 E 5,762,000

Cities and Towns

Butare 30,000
• KIGALI 181,600

SAINT HELENA

1987 C 5,644

Cities and Towns

• JAMESTOWN 1,413

SAINT KITTS AND NEVIS

1980 C 44,404

Cities and Towns

• BASSETERRE 14,725
Charlestown.............1,771

SAINT LUCIA

1987 E 142,342

Cities and Towns

• CASTRIES 53,933

SAINT PIERRE AND MIQUELON / Saint-Pierre-et-Miquelon

1982 C 6,041

Cities and Towns

• SAINT-PIERRE 5,371

SAINT VINCENT AND THE GRENADINES

1987 E 112,589

Cities and Towns

• KINGSTOWN
(★ 28,936) 19,028

SAN MARINO

1988 E 22,304

Cities and Towns

• SAN MARINO 2,777

SAO TOME AND PRINCIPE / São Tomé e Príncipe

1970 C 73,631

Cities and Towns

• SÃO TOMÉ 17,380

SAUDI ARABIA / Al-'Arabīyah as-Su'ūdīyah

1980 E 9,229,000

Cities and Towns

Abhā (1974 C) 30,150
Ad-Dammām 200,000
Al-Hufūf (1974 C) 101,271
Al-Khubar (1974 C) 48,817
Al-Madīnah (Medina) 290,000
Al-Mubarraz (1974 C) 54,325
AR-RIYĀD (RIYADH) ...1,250,000
At-Tā'if 300,000
Buraydah (1974 C) 69,940
Hā'il (1974 C) 40,502
• Jiddah 1,300,000
Makkah (Mecca) 550,000
Najran (1974 C) 47,501
Tabūk (1974 C) 74,825

SENEGAL / Sénégal

1988 C 6,881,919

Cities and Towns

• DAKAR 1,447,642
Diourbel 77,548
Kaolack 152,007
Louga 52,763
Saint-Louis 160,689
Thiès 184,902
Ziguinchor 124,283

SEYCHELLES

1984 E 64,718

Cities and Towns

• VICTORIA 23,000

SIERRA LEONE

1985 C 3,515,812

Cities and Towns

Bo 59,768
• FREETOWN
(★ 525,000) 469,776
Kenema 52,473
Koidu 82,474
Makeni 49,038

SINGAPORE

1989 E 2,685,400

Cities and Towns

• SINGAPORE
(★ 3,025,000) 2,685,400

SLOVAKIA / Slovenská Republika

1990 E 5,287,000

Cities and Towns

Banská Bystrica 87,834
• BRATISLAVA 442,999
Košice 237,099
Martin 66,678
Nitra 91,297
Poprad 53,039
Prešov 90,121
Prievidza 52,624
Trenčín 57,813
Trnava 72,866
Žilina 97,508

SLOVENIA / Slovenija

1987 E 1,936,606

Cities and Towns

• LJUBLJANA
(▲ 316,607) 233,200
Maribor (▲ 187,651) 107,400

SOLOMON ISLANDS

1986 C 285,176

Cities and Towns

• HONIARA 30,413

SOMALIA / Somaliya

1984 E 5,423,000

Cities and Towns

Berbera 65,000
Hargeysa 70,000
Kismayu 70,000
Marka 60,000
• MUQDISHO 600,000

SOUTH AFRICA / Suid-Afrika

1985 C 23,385,645

Cities and Towns

Alberton
(★ Johannesburg) 66,155
Alexandra
(★ Johannesburg) 67,276
Atteridgeville
(★ Pretoria) 73,439
Bellville (★ Cape Town) ...68,915
Benoni
(★ Johannesburg) 94,926
Bloemfontein
(★ 235,000) 104,381
Boksburg
(★ Johannesburg) 110,832
Botshabelo
(★ Bloemfontein) 95,625
CAPE TOWN
(KAAPSTAD)
(★ 1,790,000) 776,617
Carletonville
(★ Johannesburg) 97,874
Daveyton
(★ Johannesburg) 99,056
Diepmeadow
(★ Johannesburg) 192,682
Durban (★ 1,550,000) 634,301
East London (Oos-
Londen) (★ 320,000) 85,699
Elsies River (★ Cape
Town) 70,067
Evaton (★ Vereeniging) ...52,559
Galeshewe
(★ Kimberley) 63,238
Germiston
(★ ★ Johannesburg) 116,718
Grassy Park (★ Cape
Town) 50,193
Guguleto (★ Cape
Town) 63,893
• Johannesburg
(★ 3,650,000) 632,369
Kagiso
(★ Johannesburg) 50,647
Katlehong
(★ Johannesburg) 137,745

Kayamnandi (★ Port
Elizabeth) 220,548
Kempton Park
(★ Johannesburg) 87,721
Kimberley (★ 145,000) ...74,061
Klerksdorp (★ 205,000) ...48,947
Kroonstad (★ 65,165) 22,886
Krugersdorp
(★ Johannesburg) 73,767
Kwa Makuta
(★ Durban) 71,378
Kwa Mashu (★ Durban) ...111,593
Kwanobuhle (★ Port
Elizabeth) 52,376
Kwa-Thema
(★ Johannesburg) 78,640
Ladysmith (★ 31,670) 25,102
Lekoa (Shapeville)
(★ Vereeniging) 218,392
Madadeni
(★ Newcastle) 65,832
Mamelodi (★ Pretoria) ...127,033
Mangaung
(★ Bloemfontein) 79,851
Newcastle (★ 155,000) ...34,931
Ntuzuma (★ Durban) 61,834
Nyanga (★ Cape Town) ...148,882
Oziswen (★ Newcastle) ...51,934
Paarl (★ ★ Cape Town) ...63,671
Parow (★ Cape Town) 60,294
Pietermaritzburg
(★ 230,000) 133,809
Pinetown (★ Durban) 55,770
Port Elizabeth
(★ 690,000) 272,844
PRETORIA (★ 960,000) ...443,059
Randburg
(★ Johannesburg) 74,347
Roodepoort-Maraisburg
(★ Johannesburg) 141,764
Sandton
(★ Johannesburg) 86,089
Soshanguve
(★ Pretoria) 68,598
Soweto
(★ Johannesburg) 521,948
Springs
(★ Johannesburg) 68,235
Tembisa
(★ Johannesburg) 149,282
Uitenhage (★ ★ Port
Elizabeth) 54,987
Umlazi (★ Durban) 194,933
Vanderbijlpark
(★ ★ Vereeniging) 59,865
Vereeniging
(★ 525,000) 60,584
Verwoerdburg
(★ Pretoria) 49,891
Vosloosrus
(★ Johannesburg) 52,061
Welkom (★ 215,000) 54,488
Witbank (★ 77,171) 41,784

SPAIN / España

1988 E 39,217,804

Cities and Towns

Albacete 125,997
Alcalá de Guadaira 50,935
Alcalá de Henares
(★ Madrid) 150,021
Alcobendas (★ Madrid) ...73,455
Alcorcón (★ Madrid) 139,796
Alcoy 66,074
Algeciras 99,528
Alicante 261,051
Almería 157,644
Avilés (★ 131,000) 87,811
Badajoz (▲ 122,407) 106,400
Badalona (★ Barcelona) ..225,229
Baracaldo (★ Bilbao) 113,502
Barcelona
(★ 4,040,000) 1,714,355
Bilbao (★ 985,000) 384,733
Burgos 160,561
Cáceres 71,598
Cádiz (★ 240,000) 156,591
Cartagena (▲ 172,710) ...70,000
Castelló de la Plana 131,869
Ciudad Real 56,300
Córdoba 302,301
Cornella (★ Barcelona) ...86,866
Coslada (★ Madrid) 68,765
Dos Hermanas
(★ Sevilla) 60,600
Elche (▲ 180,256) 158,300
Elda 56,756
El Ferrol del Caudillo
(★ 129,000) 86,503
El Puerto de Santa
María (▲ 62,285) 49,900
Fuenlabrada (★ Madrid) ..128,872
Getafe (★ Madrid) 135,367
Gijón 262,156
Granada 263,334
Granollers
(★ Barcelona) 49,045
Guadalajara 61,309
Hospitalet
(★ Barcelona) 278,449
Huelva 137,826
Irún 54,886
Jaén 106,435
Jerez de la Frontera
(▲ 183,007) 156,200
La Coruña 248,862
La Línea 60,956

Las Palmas de Gran
Canaria (▲ 366,347) ...319,000
Leganés (★ Madrid) 168,403
León (★ 159,000) 136,558
Lérida (▲ 109,795) 91,500
Linares 58,622
Logroño 119,038
Lugo (▲ 78,795) 68,700
• MADRID (★ 4,650,000) .3,102,846
Málaga 574,456
Manresa 65,607
Mataró 100,817
Mérida 52,368
Móstoles (★ Madrid) 181,648
Murcia (▲ 314,124) 149,800
Orense 106,042
Oviedo (▲ 190,073) 168,900
Palencia 76,692
Palma [de Mallorca]
(▲ 314,608) 249,000
Parla (★ Madrid) 66,253
Portugalete (★ Bilbao) ...57,813
Prat del Llobregat
(★ Barcelona) 64,193
Puertollano 52,284
Reus 83,800
Sabadell (★ Barcelona) ..189,489
Salamanca 159,342
San Baudilio de
Llobregat
(★ Barcelona) 77,502
San Fernando
(★ Cádiz) 81,975
San Sebastián
(★ 285,000) 177,622
San Sebastián de los
Reyes (★ Madrid) 51,653
Santa Coloma de
Gramanet
(★ Barcelona) 136,042
Santa Cruz de Tenerife ...215,228
Santander (▲ 190,795) ..166,800
Santiago de
Compostela
(▲ 88,110) 68,800
Santurce-Antiguo
(★ Bilbao) 52,334
Segovia 54,402
Sevilla (★ 945,000) 663,132
Talavera de la Reina 68,158
Tarragona (▲ 109,586) ...63,500
Tarrasa (★ Barcelona) ...161,410
Toledo 59,551
Torrejón de Ardoz
(★ Madrid) 83,267
Torrente (★ València) 55,751
Valencia (★ 1,270,000) ..743,933
Valladolid 331,461
Vigo (▲ 271,128) 179,500
Vitoria (Gasteiz) 204,264
Zamora 62,047
Zaragoza 582,239

SPANISH NORTH AFRICA / Plazas de Soberanía en el Norte de África

1988 E 122,905

Cities and Towns

• Ceuta 67,188
Melilla 55,717

SRI LANKA

1986 E 16,117,000

Cities and Towns

Battaramulla
(★ Colombo)
(1981 C) 56,535
• COLOMBO
(★ 2,050,000) 683,000
Dehiwala-Mount Lavinia
(★ Colombo) 191,000
Galle 109,000
Jaffna 143,000
Kandy 130,000
KOTTE (★ Colombo) 104,000
Maharagama
(★ Colombo)
(1981 C) 49,765
Matale (1985 E) 57,000
Matara (1985 E) 57,000
Moratuwa (★ Colombo) ..138,000
Negombo (1985 E) 76,000
Ratnapura (1985 E) 51,000
Trincomalee (1985 E) 51,000

SUDAN / As-Sūdān

1983 C 20,564,364

Cities and Towns

Al-Fāshir (1973 C) 51,932
• AL-KHARTŪM
(★ 1,450,000) 476,218
Al-Khartūm Bahrī
(★ Al-Khartūm) 341,146
Al-Qadārif (1973 C) 66,465
Al-Ubayyid 140,000
Atbarah 73,000
Būr Sūdān (Port Sudan) ..206,727
Jūbā (1980 E) 116,000
Kassalā 143,000
Kūstī (1973 C) 65,257
Nyala (1973 C) 59,852

C Census.   E Official estimate.   U Unofficial estimate.
• Largest city in country.

★ Population or designation of metropolitan area, including suburbs (see headnote).
▲ Population of an entire municipality, commune, or district, including rural area.

211

World Populations

Umm Durmān
(Omdurman)
(★ Al-Khartūm) 526,287
Wad Madanī 141,000
Wāw (1980 E) 116,000

SURINAME

1988 E 392,000

Cities and Towns

• PARAMARIBO
(★ 296,000) 241,000

SWAZILAND

1986 C 712,131

Cities and Towns

LOBAMBA 0
Manzini (★ 30,000) 18,084
• MBABANE 38,290

SWEDEN / Sverige

1990 E 8,527,036

Cities and Towns

Borås 101,231
Borlänge 46,424
Eskilstuna 89,460
Gävle (▲ 88,081) 67,500
Göteborg (★ 710,894) ... 431,840
Halmstad (▲ 79,362) 50,900
Helsingborg 108,359
Huddinge
(★ Stockholm) 73,107
Järfälla (★ Stockholm) ... 56,386
Jönköping 110,860
Karlstad 76,120
Linköping 120,562
Luleå 67,903
Lund (★ Malmö320) 86,412
Malmö (★ 445,000) 232,908
Mölndal (★ Göteborg) 51,767
Nacka (★ Stockholm) 63,114
Norrköping 119,921
Örebro 120,353
Södertälje
(★ Stockholm) 81,460
Sollentuna
(★ Stockholm) 50,606
Solna (★ Stockholm) 51,427
• STOCKHOLM
(★ 1,449,972) 672,187
Sundsvall (▲ 93,404) 50,600
Täby (★ Stockholm) 56,553
Trollhättan 50,602
Tumba (★ Stockholm) 68,255
Umeå (▲ 90,004) 58,700
Uppsala 164,754
Västerås 118,386
Växjö (▲ 68,849) 45,500

**SWITZERLAND / Schweiz /
Suisse / Svizzera**

1990 E 6,673,850

Cities and Towns

Arbon (★ 41,100) 12,284
Baden (★ 70,700) 14,545
Basel (Bâle)
(★ 575,000) 169,587
BERN (BERNE)
(★ 298,800) 134,393
Biel (Bienne) (★ 81,900) .. 52,023
Fribourg (Freiburg)
(★ 56,800) 33,962
Genève (Geneva)
(★ 460,000) 165,404
Lausanne (★ 259,900) 122,600
Locarno (★ 42,350) 14,149
Lugano (★ 94,800) 26,055
Luzern (★ 159,500) 59,115
Sankt Gallen
(★ 125,000) 73,191
Sankt Moritz (1987 E) 5,335
Solothurn (★ 56,800) 15,429
Thun (★ 77,200) 37,707
Winterthur (★ 107,400) ... 85,174
• Zürich (★ 860,000) 342,861

SYRIA / Sūrīyah

1988 E 11,338,000

Cities and Towns

Al-Hasakah (1981 C) 73,426
Al-Lādhiqīyah (Latakia) ... 249,000
Al-Qāmishlī 126,236
As-Suwaydā' 46,844
Dar'ā (1981 C) 49,534
Dārayyā 53,204
Dayr az-Zawr 112,000
• DIMASHQ
(DAMASCUS)
(★ 1,950,000) 1,326,000
Dūmā (★ Dimashq) 66,130
Halab (Aleppo)
(★ 1,275,000) 1,261,000
Hamāh 222,000
Himş 447,000
Idlib (1981 C) 51,682
Jaramānah (★ Dimashq) .. 96,681
Madīnat ath Thawrah 58,151
Tartūs (1981 C) 52,589

TAIWAN / T'aiwan

1988 E 19,672,612

Changhua (▲ 206,603) ... 158,400
Chiai 254,875
Chilung 348,541
Chungho (★ T'aipei) 343,389
Chungli 247,639
Chutung 104,797
Fangshan
(★ Kaohsiung) 276,259
Fengyüan (▲ 144,434) 115,300
Hsichih (★ T'aipei)
(1980 C) 70,031
Hsinchu 309,899
Hsinchuang (★ T'aipei) ... 259,001
Hsintien (★ T'aipei) 205,094
Hualien 106,658
Ilan (▲ 81,751)
(1980 C) 70,900
Kangshan (1980 C) 78,049
Kaohsiung
(★ 1,845,000) 1,342,797
Lotung (1980 C) 57,925
Lukang (1980 C) 72,019
Miaoli (1980 C) 81,500
Nant'ou (1980 C) 84,038
P'ingchen (★ T'aipei) 134,925
P'ingtung (▲ 204,990) 167,600
Sanchung (★ T'aipei) 362,171
Shulin (★ T'aipei)
(1980 C) 75,700
Tach'i (1980 C) 67,209
T'aichung 715,107
T'ainan 656,927
• T'AIPEI (★ 6,130,000) . 2,637,100
T'aipeihsien (★ T'aipei) .. 506,220
T'aitung (▲ 109,358) 79,800
Taoyüan 220,255
T'oufen (1980 C) 66,536
T'uch'eng (★ T'aipei) 70,500
Yangmei (1980 C) 84,353
Yüanlin (▲ 116,936) 51,300
Yungho (★ T'aipei) 242,252
Yungkang (▲ 114,904) 59,600

TAJIKISTAN

1989 C 5,112,000

Cities and Towns

Chudžand 160,000
• DUŠANBE 595,000
Kul'ab (1987 E) 71,000

TANZANIA

1984 E 21,062,000

Cities and Towns

Arusha 69,000
• DAR ES SALAAM 1,300,000
DODOMA 54,000
Iringa 67,000
Kigoma (1978 C) 50,044
Mbeya 93,000
Morogoro 72,000
Moshi 62,000
Mtwara (1978 C) 48,510
Mwanza (1978 C) 110,611
Tabora 87,000
Tanga 121,000
Zanzibar (1985 E) 133,000

THAILAND / Prathet Thai

1988 E 54,960,917

Cities and Towns

Chiang Mai 164,030
Hat Yai 138,046
Khon Kaen 131,340
• KRUNG THEP
(BANGKOK)
(★ 6,450,000) 5,716,779
Nakhon Ratchasima 204,982
Nakhon Sawan 105,220
Nakhon Si Thammarat 72,407
Nonthaburi (★ Krung
Thep) 218,354
Pattaya 56,402
Phitsanulok 77,675
Phra Nakhon Si
Ayutthaya 60,847
Samut Prakan (★ Krung
Thep) 73,327
Samut Sakhon 53,984
Saraburi 61,206
Songkhla 84,433
Ubon Ratchathani 100,374
Udon Thani 81,202
Yala 67,383

TOGO

1981 C 2,702,945

Cities and Towns

• LOMÉ (1984 E) 400,000
Sokodé 48,098

TOKELAU

1986 C 1,690

TONGA

1986 C 94,535

Cities and Towns

• NUKU'ALOFA 21,265

TRINIDAD AND TOBAGO

1990 C 1,234,388

Cities and Towns

• PORT OF SPAIN
(★ 370,000) 50,878
San Fernando
(★ 75,000) 30,092

TUNISIA / Tunis / Tunisie

1984 C 6,975,450

Cities and Towns

Ariana (★ Tunis) 98,655
Bardo (★ Tunis) 65,669
Béja 46,708
Ben Arous (★ Tunis) 52,105
Binzert 94,509
Gabès 92,258
Gafsa 60,970
Hammam Lif (★ Tunis) 47,009
Houmt Essouk 92,269
Kairouan 72,254
Kasserine 47,606
La Goulette (★ Tunis) 61,609
Menzel Bourguiba 51,399
Nabeul (★ 75,000) 39,531
Sfax (★ 310,000) 231,911
Sousse (★ 160,000) 83,509
• TUNIS (★ 1,225,000) ... 596,654
Zarzis 49,063

TURKEY / Türkiye

1990 C 56,969,109

Cities and Towns

Adana 931,555
Adapazarı 174,353
Adıyaman 101,306
Afyon 98,618
Ağrı 57,837
Akhisar 74,002
Aksaray 92,038
Akşehir 51,669
Amasya 55,602
ANKARA (★ 2,650,000) . 2,553,209
Antakya (Antioch) 124,443
Antalya 378,726
Aydın 106,603
Bafra 66,209
Balıkesir 171,967
Bandırma 77,211
Batman 148,121
Bolu 60,600
Burdur 56,095
Bursa 838,323
Çanakkale 53,887
Çeyhan 85,000
Çorlu 77,025
Çorum 116,260
Denizli 203,130
Diyarbakır 375,767
Dörtyol 48,030
Düzce 62,606
Edirne 102,325
Elazığ 211,720
Elbistan 55,114
Ereğli, Konya prov. 74,332
Ereğli, Zonguldak prov. ... 63,776
Erzincan 90,799
Erzurum 241,344
Eskişehir 413,305
Gaziantep 627,584
Gebze (★ İstanbul) 156,594
Gemlik 50,212
Giresun 67,536
Gölcük 65,000
İçel (Mersin) 420,750
İnegöl 71,095
İskenderun 156,198
Isparta 112,100
İstanbul (★ 7,550,000) . 6,748,435
İzmir (★ 1,900,000) ... 1,762,849
İzmit 254,768
Kadirli 55,193
Kahramanmaraş 229,066
Karabük 104,869
Karaman 76,682
Kars 79,496
Kastamonu 52,363
Kayseri 416,276
Kilis 81,469
Kırıkhan 69,323
Kırıkkale 203,666
Kırşehir 74,546
Kızıltepe 60,445
Konya 509,208
Kozan 54,934
Kütahya 131,286
Lüleburgaz 51,978
Malatya 276,666
Manisa 158,283
Mardin 52,994
Nazilli 80,209
Nevşehir 52,514
Niğde 54,822
Nizip 58,259
Nusaybin 50,605
Ödemiş 511,110
Ordu 101,306
Osmaniye 122,315
Polatlı 61,026
Rize 51,586
Salihli 71,035
Samsun 301,412
Şanlıurfa 276,528
Siirt 66,607
Silvan (Miyafarkin) 59,959

Sincan (★ Ankara) 92,262
Sivas 219,122
Siverek 63,366
Söke 50,598
Soma 50,165
Tarsus 191,333
Tatvan 52,404
Tekirdağ 80,207
Tokat 83,174
Trabzon 144,805
Turgutlu 73,734
Turhal 71,406
Uşak 104,980
Van 153,525
Viranşehir 58,394
Yalova 72,874
Yarımca (1985 C) 48,420
Yozgat 51,360
Zonguldak (★ 220,000) .. 120,300

TURKMENISTAN

1989 C 3,534,000

Cities and Towns

• AŞCHADAD 398,000
Krasnovodsk (1987 E) 59,000
Mary (1987 E) 89,000
Nebit-Dag (1987 E) 85,000
Tašauz 112,000

TURKS AND CAICOS ISLANDS

1990 C 12,350

Cities and Towns

• GRAND TURK 3,761

TUVALU

1979 C 7,349

Cities and Towns

• FUNAFUTI 2,191

UGANDA

1990 E 17,213,407

Cities and Towns

Jinja (1982 E) 55,000
• KAMPALA 1,008,707

UKRAINE / Ukrayina

1989 C 51,704,000

Cities and Towns

Alchevs'k
(★ Stakhanov) 126,000
Antratsyt (★ ★ Krasnyy
Luch) (1987 E) 70,000
Artemivs'k (1987 E) 91,000
Berdjans'k 132,000
Berdychiv (1987 E) 89,000
Bila Tserkva 197,000
Bilhorod-Dnistrovs'kyy
(1987 E) 54,000
Brovary (★ Kyyiv)
(1987 E) 73,000
Bryanka (Stakhanov)
(1987 E) 65,000
Cherkasy 290,000
Chernihiv 296,000
Chernivtsi 257,000
Chervonohrad (1987 E) ... 71,000
Dniprodzerzhyns'k
(★ Dnipropetrovs'k) 282,000
Dnipropetrovs'k
(★ 1,600,000) 1,179,000
Donets'k (★ 2,200,000) . 1,110,000
Drohobych (1987 E) 76,000
Druzhkivka
(★ Kramatorsk)
(1987 E) 70,000
Dymytrov
(★ ★ Krasnoarmiys'k)
(1987 E) 62,000
Dzhankoy (1987 E) 51,000
Fastiv (1987 E) 55,000
Feodosiya (1987 E) 83,000
Horlivka (★ 710,000) 337,000
Illichivs'k (★ Odesa)
(1987 E) 52,000
Ivano-Frankivs'k 214,000
Izmayil (1987 E) 90,000
Izyum (1987 E) 63,000
Kalush (1987 E) 67,000
Kam'yanets-Podil's'kyy .. 102,000
Kerch 174,000
Kharkiv (★ 1,940,000) . 1,611,000
Khartsyz'k (★ Donets'k)
(1987 E) 69,000
Kherson 355,000
Khmel'nyts'kyy 237,000
Kirovohrad 269,000
Kolymyya (1987 E) 63,000
Konotop (1987 E) 93,000
Korosten' (1987 E) 72,000
Kostyantynivka 108,000
Kovel' (1987 E) 66,000
Kramatorsk
(★ 465,000) 198,000
Krasnoarmiys'k
(★ 175,000) (1987 E) ... 70,000
Krasnodon (1987 E) 52,000
Krasnyy Luch
(★ 250,000) 113,000
Kremenchuk 236,000
Kryvyy Rih 713,000

KYYIV (KIEV)
(★ 2,900,000) 2,587,000
Lozova (1987 E) 68,000
Lubny (1987 E) 58,000
Luhans'k 497,000
Luts'k 198,000
L'viv 790,000
Lysychans'k
(★ 410,000) 127,000
Makiyivka
(★ ★ Donets'k) 430,000
Marhanets' (1987 E) 55,000
Mariupol' (Ždanov) 517,000
Melitopol' 174,000
Mukacheve (1987 E) 88,000
Mykolayiv 503,000
Nizhyn (1987 E) 81,000
Nikopol' 158,000
Nova Kakhovka
(1987 E) 53,000
Novohrad-Volyns'kyy
(1987 E) 52,000
Novomoskovsk
(1987 E) 76,000
Novovolynsk (1987 E) 54,000
Odesa (★ 1,185,000) ... 1,115,000
Oleksandriya 103,000
Pavlohrad 131,000
Pervomays'k (1987 E) 79,000
Poltava 315,000
Pryluky (1987 E) 73,000
Rivne 228,000
Romny (1987 E) 53,000
Roven'ky (1987 E) 68,000
Rubizhne
(★ ★ Lysychans'k)
(1987 E) 72,000
Sevastopol' 356,000
Severodonets'k
(★ ★ Lysychans'k) 131,000
Shakhtars'k
(★ ★ Torez) (1987 E) ... 73,000
Shostka (1987 E) 87,000
Simferopol' 344,000
Slov'yans'k
(★ ★ Kramatorsk) 135,000
Smila (1987 E) 76,000
Snizhne (★ Torez)
(1987 E) 68,000
Stakhanov (★ 610,000) .. 112,000
Stryy (1987 E) 63,000
Sumy 291,000
Sverdlovsk (1987 E) 84,000
Svitlovods'k (1987 E) 55,000
Ternopil 205,000
Torez (★ 290,000)
(1987 E) 88,000
Uman' (1987 E) 89,000
Uzhhorod 117,000
Vinnytsya 374,000
Yalta (1987 E) 89,000
Yenakiyeve
(★ ★ Horlivka) 121,000
Yevpatoriya 108,000
Zaporizhzhya 884,000
Zhovti Zody (1987 E) 61,000
Zhytomyr 292,000

**UNITED ARAB EMIRATES /
Al-Imārāt al-'Arabīyah
al-Muttahidah**

1980 C 980,000

Cities and Towns

ABŪ ZABY (ABU
DHABI) 242,975
Al-'Ayn 101,663
Ash-Shāriqah 125,149
• Dubayy 265,702

UNITED KINGDOM

1981 C 55,678,079

UNITED KINGDOM: ENGLAND

1981 C 46,220,955

Cities and Towns

Aldershot (★ London) 53,665
Aylesbury 51,999
Barnsley 76,783
Barrow-in-Furness 50,174
Basildon (★ London) 94,800
Basingstoke 73,027
Bath 84,283
Bebington (★ Liverpool) .. 62,618
Bedford 75,632
Beeston and Stapleford
(★ Nottingham) 64,785
Benfleet (★ London) 50,783
Birkenhead
(★ Liverpool) 99,075
Birmingham
(★ 2,675,000) 1,013,995
Blackburn (★ 221,900) ... 109,564
Blackpool (★ 280,000) ... 146,297
Bognor Regis 50,323
Bolton
(★ ★ Manchester) 143,960
Bootle 70,860
Bournemouth
(★ 315,000) 142,829
Bracknell (★ London) 52,257
Bradford (★ ★ Leeds) ... 293,336
Brentwood (★ London) 51,212
Brighton (★ 420,000) 134,581
Bristol (★ 630,000) 413,861
Burnley (★ 160,000) 76,365

C Census.   E Official estimate.   U Unofficial estimate.
• Largest city in country.

★ Population or designation of metropolitan area, including suburbs (see headnote).
▲ Population of an entire municipality, commune, or district, including rural area.

Burton [upon Trent] 59,040
Bury (★ Manchester) 61,785
Cambridge 87,111
Cannock
 (★ Birmingham) 54,503
Canterbury 34,546
Carlisle 72,206
Chatham (★ London) 65,835
Cheadle and Gatley
 (★ Manchester) 59,478
Chelmsford (★ London) 91,109
Cheltenham 87,188
Cheshunt (★ London) 49,616
Chester 80,154
Chesterfield
 (★ 127,000) 73,352
Colchester 87,476
Corby 48,704
Coventry (★ 645,000) 318,718
Crawley (★ London) 80,113
Crewe 59,097
Crosby (★ Liverpool) 54,103
Darlington 85,519
Dartford (★ London) 62,032
Derby (★ 275,000) 218,026
Dewsbury (★★ Leeds) 49,612
Doncaster 74,727
Dover 33,461
Dudley
 (★★ Birmingham) 186,513
Eastbourne 86,715
Eastleigh
 (★ Southampton) 58,585
Ellesmere Port
 (★ Liverpool) 65,829
Epsom and Ewell
 (★ London) 65,830
Exeter 88,235
Fareham / Portchester
 (★ Portsmouth) 55,563
Farnborough
 (★ London) 48,063
Gateshead
 (★ Newcastle upon
 Tyne) 91,429
Gillingham (★ London) 92,531
Gloucester (★ 115,000) 106,526
Gosport (★ Portsmouth) 69,664
Gravesend (★ London) 53,450
Greasby / Moreton
 (★ Liverpool) 56,410
Great Yarmouth 54,777
Grimsby (★ 145,000) 91,532
Guildford (★ London) 61,509
Halesowen
 (★ Birmingham) 57,533
Halifax 76,675
Harlow (★ London) 79,150
Harrogate 63,637
Hartlepool
 (★ Teesside) 91,749
Hastings 74,979
Havant (★ Portsmouth) 50,098
Hemel Hempstead
 (★ London) 80,110
Hereford 48,277
High Wycombe
 (▲ 156,800) 69,575
Hove (★ Brighton) 65,587
Huddersfield
 (▲ 377,400) 147,825
Huyton-with-Roby
 (★ Liverpool) 62,011
Ipswich 129,661
Keighley (★ Leeds) 49,188
Kidderminster 50,385
Kingston upon Hull
 (★ 350,000) 322,144
Kingswood (★ Bristol) 54,736
Kirkby (★ Liverpool) 52,825
Leeds (★ 1,540,000) 445,242
Leicester (★ 495,000) 324,394
Lincoln 79,980
Littlehampton 46,028
Liverpool (★ 1,525,000) 538,809
• LONDON
 (★ 11,100,000) 6,574,009
Lowestoft 59,430
Luton (★ 220,000) 163,209
Macclesfield 47,525
Maidenhead (★ London) 59,809
Maidstone 86,067
Manchester
 (★ 2,775,000) 437,612
Mansfield (★ 198,000) 71,325
Margate 53,137
Middleton
 (★ Manchester) 51,373
Milton Keynes 36,886
Newcastle-under-Lyme
 (★ Stoke-on-Trent) 73,208
Newcastle upon Tyne
 (★ 1,300,000) 199,064
Northampton 154,172
Norwich (★ 230,000) 169,814
Nottingham (★ 655,000) 273,300
Nuneaton
 (★ Coventry) 60,337
Oldbury / Smethwick
 (★ Birmingham) 153,268
Oldham
 (★ Manchester) 107,095
Oxford (★ 230,000) 113,847
Penzance 18,501
Peterborough 113,404
Plymouth (★ 290,000) 238,583
Poole
 (★★ Bournemouth) 122,815
Portsmouth
 (★ 485,000) 174,218

Preston (★ 250,000) 166,675
Ramsgate 36,678
Reading (★ 200,000) 194,727
Redditch
 (★ Birmingham) 61,639
Rochdale
 (★★ Manchester) 97,292
Rotherham
 (★★ Sheffield) 122,374
Royal Leamington Spa
 (★★ Coventry) 56,552
Rugby 59,039
Runcorn (★ Liverpool) 63,995
Saint Albans
 (★ London) 76,709
Saint Helens 114,397
Sale (★ Manchester) 57,872
Salford (★ Manchester) 96,525
Scunthorpe 79,043
Sheffield (★ 710,000) 470,685
Shrewsbury 57,731
Slough (★ London) 106,341
Solihull (★ Birmingham) 93,940
Southampton
 (★ 415,000) 211,321
Southend-on-Sea
 (★ London) 155,720
Southport
 (★★ Liverpool) 88,596
South Shields
 (★★ Newcastle upon
 Tyne) 86,488
Stafford 60,915
Staines (★ London) 51,949
Stevenage 74,757
Stockport
 (★★ Manchester) 135,489
Stoke-on-Trent
 (★ 440,000) 272,446
Stourbridge
 (★ Birmingham) 55,136
Stratford-upon-Avon 20,941
Stretford
 (★ Manchester) 47,522
Sunderland
 (★★ Newcastle upon
 Tyne) 195,064
Sutton Coldfield
 (★ Birmingham) 102,572
Swindon 127,348
Tanworth 63,260
Taunton 47,793
Teesside (★ 580,000) 245,215
Torquay (★ 112,400) 54,430
Tunbridge Wells 57,699
Wakefield (★★ Leeds) 74,764
Wallasey (★ Liverpool) 62,465
Walsall
 (★★ Birmingham) 177,923
Walton and Weybridge
 (★ London) 50,031
Warrington 81,366
Waterlooville
 (★ Portsmouth) 57,296
Watford (★ London) 109,503
West Bromwich
 (★ Birmingham) 153,725
Weston-super-Mare 60,821
Widnes 55,973
Wigan
 (★★ Manchester) 88,725
Winchester 34,127
Windsor (★ London) 30,832
Woking (★ London) 92,667
Wolverhampton
 (★★ Birmingham) 263,501
Worcester 75,466
Worthing
 (★ Brighton) 90,687
York (★ 145,000) 123,126

UNITED KINGDOM: NORTHERN IRELAND

1987 E 1,575,200

Cities and Towns

Antrim (1981 C) 22,342
Ballymena (1981 C) 28,166
Bangor (★ Belfast) 70,700
Belfast (★ 685,000) 303,800
Castlereagh (★ Belfast) 57,900
Londonderry (★ 97,200) 97,500
Lurgan (★ 63,000)
 (1981 C) 20,991
Newtownabbey
 (★ Belfast) 72,300

UNITED KINGDOM: SCOTLAND

1989 E 5,090,700

Cities and Towns

Aberdeen 210,700
Ayr (★ 100,000)
 (1981 C) 48,493
Clydebank (★ Glasgow)
 (1981 C) 51,832
Coatbridge (1981 C) 50,831
Cumbernauld
 (★ Glasgow) 50,300
Dundee 172,540
Dunfermline
 (★ 125,817) (1981 C) 52,105
East Kilbride
 (★ Glasgow) 69,500
Edinburgh (★ 630,000) 433,200
Glasgow (★ 1,800,000) 695,630
Greenock (★ 101,000)
 (1981 C) 58,436

Hamilton (★ Glasgow)
 (1981 C) 51,666
Irvine (★ 94,000)
 (1981 C) 55,900
Kilmarnock (★ 84,000)
 (1981 C) 51,799
Kirkcaldy (★ 148,171)
 (1981 C) 46,356
Paisley (★ Glasgow)
 (1981 C) 84,330
Stirling (★ 61,000)
 (1981 C) 36,640

UNITED KINGDOM: WALES

1981 C 2,790,462

Cities and Towns

Barry (★ Cardiff) 44,443
Cardiff (★ 625,000) 262,313
Cwmbran (★ Newport) 44,592
Llanelli 45,336
Neath (★★ Swansea) 48,687
Newport (★ 310,000) 115,896
Port Talbot (★ 130,000) 40,078
Rhondda (★★ Cardiff) 70,980
Swansea (★ 275,000) 172,433

UNITED STATES

1990 C 248,709,873

UNITED STATES: ALABAMA

1990 C 4,040,587

Cities and Towns

Birmingham 265,968
Decatur 48,761
Dothan 53,589
Florence 36,426
Gadsden 42,523
Huntsville 159,789
Mobile 196,278
Montgomery 187,106
Tuscaloosa 77,759

UNITED STATES: ALASKA

1990 C 550,043

Cities and Towns

Anchorage 226,338
Fairbanks 30,843
Juneau 26,751

UNITED STATES: ARIZONA

1990 C 3,665,228

Cities and Towns

Chandler 90,533
Flagstaff 45,857
Glendale 148,134
Mesa 288,091
Peoria 50,618
Phoenix 900,013
Scottsdale 130,069
Sun City 57,000
Tempe 141,865
Tucson 405,390
Yuma 54,923

UNITED STATES: ARKANSAS

1990 C 2,350,725

Cities and Towns

Fort Smith 72,798
Little Rock 175,795
North Little Rock 61,741
Pine Bluff 57,140

UNITED STATES: CALIFORNIA

1990 C 29,760,021

Cities and Towns

Alameda 76,459
Alhambra 82,106
Anaheim 266,406
Antioch 62,195
Bakersfield 174,820
Baldwin Park 69,330
Bellflower 61,815
Berkeley 102,724
Beverly Hills 31,971
Buena Park 68,784
Burbank 93,643
Camarillo 52,303
Carlsbad 63,126
Carson 83,995
Cerritos 53,240
Chino 59,682
Chula Vista 135,163
Citrus Heights 107,439
Clovis 50,323
Compton 90,454
Concord 111,348
Corona 76,095
Costa Mesa 96,357
Cucamonga 101,409
Daly City 92,311
Diamond Bar 53,672
Downey 91,444
East Los Angeles 126,379
El Cajon 88,693
El Monte 106,209
Encinitas 55,386
Escondido 108,635
Fairfield 77,211
Fontana 87,535

Fountain Valley 53,691
Fremont 173,339
Fresno 354,202
Fullerton 114,144
Gardena 49,847
Garden Grove 143,050
Glendale 180,038
Hacienda Heights 52,354
Hawthorne 71,349
Hayward 111,498
Hesperia 50,418
Huntington Beach 181,519
Huntington Park 56,065
Inglewood 109,602
Irvine 110,330
La Habra 51,266
Lakewood 73,557
La Mesa 52,931
Lancaster 97,291
Livermore 56,741
Lodi 51,874
Long Beach 429,433
Los Angeles 3,485,398
Lynwood 61,945
Merced 56,216
Milpitas 50,686
Mission Viejo 72,820
Modesto 164,730
Montebello 59,564
Monterey Park 60,738
Moreno Valley 118,779
Mountain View 67,460
Napa 61,842
National City 54,249
Newport Beach 66,643
Norwalk 94,279
Oakland 372,242
Oceanside 128,398
Ontario 133,179
Orange 110,658
Oxnard 142,216
Palmdale 68,842
Palm Springs 40,181
Palo Alto 55,900
Pasadena 131,591
Pico Rivera 59,177
Pleasanton 50,553
Pomona 131,723
Redding 66,462
Redlands 60,394
Redondo Beach 60,167
Redwood City 66,072
Rialto 72,388
Richmond 87,425
Riverside 226,505
Rosemead 51,638
Sacramento 369,365
Salinas 108,777
San Bernardino 164,164
San Diego 1,110,549
San Francisco 723,959
San Jose 782,248
San Leandro 68,223
San Mateo 85,486
Santa Ana 293,742
Santa Barbara 85,571
Santa Clara 93,613
Santa Clarita 110,642
Santa Cruz 49,040
Santa Maria 61,284
Santa Monica 86,905
Santa Rosa 113,313
Santee 52,902
Simi Valley 100,217
South Gate 86,284
South San Francisco 54,312
Stockton 210,943
Sunnyvale 117,229
Thousand Oaks 104,352
Torrance 133,107
Tustin 50,689
Union City 53,762
Upland 63,374
Vacaville 71,479
Vallejo 109,199
Ventura (San
 Buenaventura) 92,575
Visalia 75,636
Vista 71,872
Walnut Creek 60,569
West Covina 96,086
Westminster 78,118
Whittier 77,671
Yorba Linda 52,422

UNITED STATES: COLORADO

1990 C 3,294,394

Cities and Towns

Arvada 89,235
Aurora 222,103
Boulder 83,312
Colorado Springs 281,140
Denver 467,610
Fort Collins 87,758
Greeley 60,536
Lakewood 126,481
Longmont 51,555
Pueblo 98,640
Thornton 55,031
Westminster 74,625

UNITED STATES: CONNECTICUT

1990 C 3,287,116

Cities and Towns

Bridgeport 141,686

Bristol 60,640
Danbury 65,585
East Hartford 50,452
Fairfield 52,400
Greenwich 58,000
Hamden 53,100
Hartford 139,739
Manchester 51,000
Meriden 59,479
Milford 48,168
New Britain 75,491
New Haven 130,474
Norwalk 78,331
Stamford 108,056
Stratford 50,400
Waterbury 108,961
West Hartford 59,100
West Haven 54,021

UNITED STATES: DELAWARE

1990 C 666,168

Cities and Towns

Dover 27,630
Newark 25,098
Wilmington 71,529

UNITED STATES: DISTRICT OF COLUMBIA

1990 C 606,900

Cities and Towns

WASHINGTON 606,900

UNITED STATES: FLORIDA

1990 C 12,937,926

Cities and Towns

Boca Raton 61,492
Cape Coral 74,991
Carol City 52,800
City of Sunrise 64,407
Clearwater 98,784
Coral Springs 79,443
Daytona Beach 61,921
Delray Beach 47,181
Fort Lauderdale 149,377
Gainesville 84,770
Hialeah 188,004
Hollywood 121,697
Jacksonville 635,230
Kendall 53,100
Lakeland 70,576
Largo 65,674
Lauderhill 49,708
Melbourne 59,646
Miami 358,548
Miami Beach 92,639
North Miami 49,998
Orlando 164,693
Palm Bay 62,632
Pembroke Pines 65,452
Pensacola 58,165
Plantation 66,692
Pompano Beach 72,411
Port Saint Lucie 55,866
Saint Petersburg 238,629
Sarasota 50,961
Tallahassee 124,773
Tampa 280,015
West Palm Beach 67,643

UNITED STATES: GEORGIA

1990 C 6,478,216

Cities and Towns

Albany 78,122
Athens 45,734
Atlanta 394,017
Columbus 178,681
Macon 106,612
Savannah 137,560

UNITED STATES: HAWAII

1990 C 1,108,229

Cities and Towns

Hilo 37,808
Honolulu 365,272
Pearl City 30,993

UNITED STATES: IDAHO

1990 C 1,006,749

Cities and Towns

Boise 125,738
Idaho Falls 43,929
Pocatello 46,080

UNITED STATES: ILLINOIS

1990 C 11,430,602

Cities and Towns

Arlington Heights 75,460
Aurora 99,581
Bloomington 51,972
Champaign 63,502
Chicago 2,783,726
Cicero 67,436
Decatur 83,885
Des Plaines 53,223
Elgin 77,010
Evanston 73,233
Joliet 76,836

C Census.　E Official estimate.　U Unofficial estimate.
• Largest city in country.

★ Population or designation of metropolitan area, including suburbs (see headnote).
▲ Population of an entire municipality, commune, or district, including rural area.

Column 1	
Mount Prospect	53,170
Naperville	85,351
Oak Lawn	56,182
Oak Park	53,648
Peoria	113,504
Rockford	139,426
Schaumburg	68,586
Skokie	59,432
Springfield	105,227
Waukegan	69,392
Wheaton	51,464

UNITED STATES: INDIANA

1990 C 5,544,159

Cities and Towns

Anderson	59,459
Bloomington	60,633
Evansville	126,272
Fort Wayne	173,072
Gary	116,646
Hammond	84,236
Indianapolis	731,327
Kokomo	44,962
Lafayette	43,764
Michigan City	33,822
Muncie	71,035
South Bend	105,511
Terre Haute	57,483

UNITED STATES: IOWA

1990 C 2,776,755

Cities and Towns

Ames	47,198
Cedar Rapids	108,751
Council Bluffs	54,315
Davenport	95,333
Des Moines	193,187
Dubuque	57,546
Iowa City	59,738
Sioux City	80,505
Waterloo	66,467

UNITED STATES: KANSAS

1990 C 2,477,574

Cities and Towns

Kansas City	149,767
Lawrence	65,608
Olathe	63,352
Overland Park	111,790
Topeka	119,883
Wichita	304,011

UNITED STATES: KENTUCKY

1990 C 3,685,296

Cities and Towns

Frankfort	25,968
Lexington	225,366
Louisville	269,063
Owensboro	53,549

UNITED STATES: LOUISIANA

1990 C 4,219,973

Cities and Towns

Alexandria	49,188
Baton Rouge	219,531
Bossier City	52,721
Houma	96,982
Kenner	72,033
Lafayette	94,440
Lake Charles	70,580
Metairie	149,428
Monroe	54,909
New Orleans	496,938
Shreveport	198,525

UNITED STATES: MAINE

1990 C 1,227,928

Cities and Towns

Augusta	21,325
Bangor	33,181
Lewiston	39,757
Portland	64,358

UNITED STATES: MARYLAND

1990 C 4,781,468

Cities and Towns

Annapolis	33,187
Baltimore	736,014
Bethesda	62,936
Columbia	75,883
Dundalk	65,800
Rockville	44,835
Silver Spring	76,200
Towson	49,445
Wheaton	58,300

UNITED STATES: MASSACHUSETTS

1990 C 6,016,425

Cities and Towns

Boston	574,283
Brockton	92,788
Brookline	54,718
Cambridge	95,802
Chicopee	56,632

Fall River	92,703
Framingham	64,989
Haverhill	51,418
Holyoke	43,704
Lawrence	70,207
Lowell	103,439
Lynn	81,245
Malden	53,884
Medford	57,407
New Bedford	99,922
Newton	82,585
Peabody	47,039
Pittsfield	48,622
Quincy	84,985
Salem	38,091
Somerville	76,210
Springfield	156,983
Taunton	49,832
Waltham	57,878
Weymouth	54,063
Worcester	169,759

UNITED STATES: MICHIGAN

1990 C 9,295,297

Cities and Towns

Ann Arbor	109,592
Battle Creek	53,540
Clinton	85,866
Dearborn	89,286
Dearborn Heights	60,838
Detroit	1,027,974
East Lansing	50,677
Farmington Hills	74,652
Flint	140,761
Grand Rapids	189,126
Kalamazoo	80,277
Lansing	127,321
Livonia	100,850
Pontiac	71,166
Redford	54,387
Rochester Hills	61,766
Roseville	51,412
Royal Oak	65,410
Saginaw	69,512
Saint Clair Shores	68,107
Southfield	75,728
Sterling Heights	117,810
Taylor	70,811
Troy	72,884
Warren	144,864
Westland	84,724
Wyoming	63,891

UNITED STATES: MINNESOTA

1990 C 4,375,099

Cities and Towns

Bloomington	86,335
Brooklyn Park	56,381
Burnsville	51,288
Coon Rapids	52,978
Duluth	85,493
Minneapolis	368,383
Minnetonka	48,370
Plymouth	50,889
Rochester	70,745
Saint Cloud	48,812
Saint Paul	272,235

UNITED STATES: MISSISSIPPI

1990 C 2,573,216

Cities and Towns

Biloxi	46,319
Hattiesburg	41,882
Jackson	196,637

UNITED STATES: MISSOURI

1990 C 5,117,073

Cities and Towns

Columbia	69,101
Florissant	51,206
Independence	112,301
Jefferson City	35,481
Kansas City	435,146
Saint Charles	54,555
Saint Joseph	71,852
Saint Louis	396,685
Springfield	140,494

UNITED STATES: MONTANA

1990 C 799,065

Cities and Towns

Billings	81,151
Great Falls	55,097
Helena	24,569

UNITED STATES: NEBRASKA

1990 C 1,578,385

Cities and Towns

Grand Island	39,386
Lincoln	191,972
Omaha	335,795

UNITED STATES: NEVADA

1990 C 1,201,833

Cities and Towns

Carson City	40,443
Henderson	64,942

Las Vegas	258,295
Paradise	124,682
Reno	133,850
Sparks	53,367
Sunrise Manor	95,362

UNITED STATES: NEW HAMPSHIRE

1990 C 1,109,252

Cities and Towns

Concord	36,006
Manchester	99,567
Nashua	79,662

UNITED STATES: NEW JERSEY

1990 C 7,730,188

Cities and Towns

Atlantic City	37,986
Bayonne	61,444
Brick [Township]	64,800
Camden	87,492
Cherry Hill	69,319
Clifton	71,742
East Orange	73,552
Edison	88,680
Elizabeth	110,002
Irvington	59,774
Jersey City	228,537
Newark	275,221
Passaic	58,041
Paterson	140,891
Trenton	88,675
Union	50,024
Union City	58,012
Vineland	54,780
Woodbridge [Township] (1986 U)	95,100

UNITED STATES: NEW MEXICO

1990 C 1,515,069

Cities and Towns

Albuquerque	384,736
Las Cruces	62,126
Roswell	44,654
Santa Fe	55,859

UNITED STATES: NEW YORK

1990 C 17,990,455

Cities and Towns

Albany	101,082
Binghamton	53,008
Buffalo	328,123
Cheektowaga	84,387
Greece	64,600
Irondequoit	52,322
Levittown	53,286
Mount Vernon	67,153
New Rochelle	67,265
• New York	7,322,564
Niagara Falls	61,840
Rochester	231,636
Schenectady	65,566
Syracuse	163,860
Tonawanda	65,284
Troy	54,269
Utica	68,637
Yonkers	188,082

UNITED STATES: NORTH CAROLINA

1990 C 6,628,637

Cities and Towns

Asheville	61,607
Charlotte	395,934
Durham	136,611
Fayetteville	75,695
Gastonia	54,732
Greensboro	183,521
High Point	69,496
Raleigh	207,951
Rocky Mount	48,997
Wilmington	55,530
Winston-Salem	143,485

UNITED STATES: NORTH DAKOTA

1990 C 638,800

Cities and Towns

Bismarck	49,256
Fargo	74,111
Grand Forks	49,425

UNITED STATES: OHIO

1990 C 10,847,115

Cities and Towns

Akron	223,019
Canton	84,161
Cincinnati	364,040
Cleveland	505,616
Cleveland Heights	54,052
Columbus	632,910
Dayton	182,044
Elyria	56,746
Euclid	54,875
Hamilton	61,368
Kettering	60,569
Lakewood	59,718

Lorain	71,245
Mansfield	50,627
Parma	87,876
Springfield	70,487
Toledo	332,943
Warren	50,793
Youngstown	95,732

UNITED STATES: OKLAHOMA

1990 C 3,145,585

Cities and Towns

Broken Arrow	58,043
Edmond	52,315
Lawton	80,561
Midwest City	52,267
Norman	80,071
Oklahoma City	444,719
Tulsa	367,302

UNITED STATES: OREGON

1990 C 2,842,321

Cities and Towns

Beaverton	53,310
Eugene	112,669
Gresham	68,235
Portland	437,319
Salem	107,786

UNITED STATES: PENNSYLVANIA

1990 C 11,881,643

Cities and Towns

Abington Township	59,300
Allentown	105,090
Altoona	51,881
Bensalem	56,788
Bethlehem	71,428
Bristol	57,129
Erie	108,718
Harrisburg	52,376
Haverford Township	51,800
Lancaster	55,551
Lower Merion	58,003
Penn Hills	51,430
Philadelphia	1,585,577
Pittsburgh	369,879
Reading	78,380
Scranton	81,805
Upper Darby	86,100

UNITED STATES: RHODE ISLAND

1990 C 1,003,464

Cities and Towns

Cranston	76,060
East Providence	50,380
Pawtucket	72,644
Providence	160,728
Warwick	85,427

UNITED STATES: SOUTH CAROLINA

1990 C 3,486,703

Cities and Towns

Charleston	80,414
Columbia	98,052
Greenville	58,282
North Charleston	70,218

UNITED STATES: SOUTH DAKOTA

1990 C 696,004

Cities and Towns

Pierre	12,906
Rapid City	54,523
Sioux Falls	100,814

UNITED STATES: TENNESSEE

1990 C 4,877,185

Cities and Towns

Chattanooga	152,466
Clarksville	75,494
Jackson	48,949
Knoxville	165,121
Memphis	610,337
Nashville	487,969

UNITED STATES: TEXAS

1990 C 16,986,510

Cities and Towns

Abilene	106,654
Amarillo	157,615
Arlington	261,721
Austin	465,622
Baytown	63,850
Beaumont	114,323
Brownsville	98,962
Bryan	55,002
Carrollton	82,169
College Station	52,456
Corpus Christi	257,453
Dallas	1,006,831
Denton	66,270
El Paso	515,342
Fort Worth	447,619

Galveston	59,070
Garland	180,650
Grand Prairie	99,616
Houston	1,630,553
Irving	155,037
Killeen	63,535
Laredo	122,899
Longview	70,311
Lubbock	186,206
McAllen	84,021
Mesquite	101,484
Midland	89,443
Odessa	89,699
Pasadena	119,363
Plano	128,713
Port Arthur	58,724
Richardson	74,840
San Angelo	84,474
San Antonio	935,933
Tyler	75,450
Victoria	55,076
Waco	103,590
Wichita Falls	96,259

UNITED STATES: UTAH

1990 C 1,722,850

Cities and Towns

Ogden	63,909
Orem	67,561
Provo	86,835
Salt Lake City	159,936
Sandy	75,058
West Valley City	86,976

UNITED STATES: VERMONT

1990 C 562,758

Cities and Towns

Burlington	39,127
Montpelier	8,247
Rutland	18,230

UNITED STATES: VIRGINIA

1990 C 6,187,358

Cities and Towns

Alexandria	111,183
Arlington	170,936
Chesapeake	151,976
Danville	53,056
Hampton	133,793
Lynchburg	66,049
Newport News	170,045
Norfolk	261,229
Petersburg	38,386
Portsmouth	103,907
Richmond	203,056
Roanoke	96,397
Suffolk	52,141
Virginia Beach	393,069

UNITED STATES: WASHINGTON

1990 C 4,866,692

Cities and Towns

Bellevue	86,874
Bellingham	52,179
Everett	69,961
Lakewood Center	62,000
Olympia	33,840
Seattle	516,259
Spokane	177,196
Tacoma	176,664
Yakima	54,827

UNITED STATES: WEST VIRGINIA

1990 C 1,793,477

Cities and Towns

Charleston	57,287
Huntington	54,844
Parkersburg	33,862
Wheeling	34,882

UNITED STATES: WISCONSIN

1990 C 4,891,769

Cities and Towns

Appleton	65,695
Eau Claire	56,856
Fond du Lac	37,757
Green Bay	96,466
Janesville	52,133
Kenosha	80,352
La Crosse	51,003
Madison	191,262
Milwaukee	628,088
Oshkosh	55,006
Racine	84,298
Sheboygan	49,676
Waukesha	56,958
Wausau	37,060
Wauwatosa	49,366
West Allis	63,221

UNITED STATES: WYOMING

1990 C 453,588

Cities and Towns

Casper	46,742
Cheyenne	50,008
Laramie	26,687

C Census. E Official estimate. U Unofficial estimate.
• Largest city in country.

★ Population or designation of metropolitan area, including suburbs (see headnote).
▲ Population of an entire municipality, commune, or district, including rural area.

URUGUAY

1985 C 2,955,241

Cities and Towns

Las Piedras
(★ Montevideo) 58,288
• MONTEVIDEO
(★ 1,550,000) 1,251,647
Paysandú 76,191
Rivera 57,316
Salto 80,823

UZBEKISTAN / Ŭzbekiston

1989 C 19,906,000

Cities and Towns

Almalyk 114,000
Andižan 293,000
Angren 131,000
Bekabad (1987 E) 80,000
Buchara 224,000
Chodžejli (1987 E) 55,000
Cirčik (★ Taškent) 156,000
Denau (1987 E) 53,000
Džizak 102,000
Fergana 200,000
Gulistan (1987 E) 51,000
Jangijul' (1987 E) 71,000
Karši 156,000
Kattakurgan (1987 E) 63,000
Kokand 182,000
Margilan 125,000
Namangan 308,000
Navoi 107,000
Nukus 169,000
Samarkand 366,000
• TAŠKENT
(★ 2,325,000) 2,073,000
Termez (1987 E) 72,000
Urgenč 128,000

VANUATU

1989 C 142,419

Cities and Towns

• PORT VILA (★ 23,000) 18,905

VATICAN CITY / Città del Vaticano

1988 E 766

VENEZUELA

1981 C 14,516,735

Cities and Towns

Acarigua 91,662
Barcelona 156,461
Barinas 110,462
Barquisimeto 497,635
Baruta (★ Caracas) 200,063
Cabimas 140,435
Cagua 53,704
Calabozo 61,995
• CARACAS
(★ 3,600,000) 1,816,901
Carora 58,694
Carúpano 64,579
Catia La Mar
(★ Caracas) 87,916
Chacao (★ Caracas) 72,703
Ciudad Bolívar 182,941
Ciudad Guayana 314,497
Ciudad Ojeda
(Lagunillas) 83,565
Coro 96,339
Cumaná 179,814
El Limón 65,122
El Tigre 73,595
Guacara 72,727
Guanare 64,025
Guarenas (★ Caracas) 101,742
La Victoria 70,828
Los Dos Caminos
(★ Caracas) 63,346
Los Teques
(★ Caracas) 112,857
Maiquetía (★ Caracas) 66,056
Maracaibo 890,643
Maracay 322,560
Maturín 154,976
Mérida 143,209
Petare (★ Caracas) 395,715
Porlamar 51,079
Pozuelos 80,342
Puerto Cabello 71,759
Puerto la Cruz 53,881
Punto Fijo 71,114
San Cristóbal 198,793
San Felipe 57,526
San Fernando de Apure 57,308
San Juan de los
Morros 57,219
Turmero 111,186
Valencia 616,224
Valera 102,068
Valle de la Pascua 55,761

VIETNAM / Viet Nam

1979 C 52,741,766

Cities and Towns

Bac Giang 54,506
Bien Hoa 187,254
Buon Me Thuot 71,815
Ca Mau 67,484
Cam Pha 76,697
Cam Ranh (1973 E) 118,111
Can Tho 182,856
Da Lat 87,136
Da Nang 318,653
Hai Duong 54,579
Hai Phong
(▲ 1,279,067)
(1989 C) 456,000
HÀ NOI (★ 1,500,000)
(1989 C) 1,089,000
Hoa Binh 51,187
Hon Gai 114,573
Hue 165,710
Long Xuyen 112,485
Minh Hai 72,517
My Tho 101,493
Nam Dinh 160,179
Nha Trang 172,663
Phan Thiet 75,241
Play Cu 58,088
Qui Nhon 127,211
Rach Gia 81,075
Sa Dec 73,104
Soc Trang 74,967
Thai Binh 79,566
Thai Nguyen 138,023
Thanh Hoa 72,646
• Thanh Pho Ho Chi Minh
(Saigon)
(★ 3,100,000)
(1989 C) 3,169,000
Tra Vinh 44,020
Tuy Hoa 46,617
Viet Tri 72,108
Vinh 159,753
Vinh Long 71,505
Vung Tau 81,694

VIRGIN ISLANDS OF THE UNITED STATES

1980 C 96,569

Cities and Towns

• CHARLOTTE AMALIE
(★ 32,000) 11,842

WALLIS AND FUTUNA / Wallis et Futuna

1983 E 12,408

Cities and Towns

• MATA-UTU 815

WESTERN SAHARA

1982 E 142,000

Cities and Towns

• EL AAIÚN 93,875

WESTERN SAMOA / Samoa i Sisifo

1981 C 156,349

Cities and Towns

• APIA 33,170

YEMEN / Al-Yaman

1990 E 11,282,000

Cities and Towns

'Adan (★ 318,000)
(1984 E) 176,100
Al-Hudaydah (1986 C) 155,110
Al-Mukallā (1984 E) 58,000
• SAN'Ā' (1986 C) 427,150
Ta'izz (1986 C) 178,043

YUGOSLAVIA / Jugoslavija

1987 E 10,342,020

Cities and Towns

• BEOGRAD
(★ 1,400,000) 1,130,000
Kragujevac (▲ 171,609) 94,800
Niš (▲ 240,219) 168,400
Novi Sad (▲ 266,772) 176,000
Pančevo (★ Beograd) 62,700
Podgorica (▲ 145,163) 82,500
Priština (▲ 244,830) 125,400
Subotica (▲ 153,306) 100,500
Zrenjanin (▲ 140,009) 65,400

ZAIRE / Zaïre

1984 C 29,671,407

Cities and Towns

Bandundu 63,189
Beni 73,319
Boma 88,556
Bukavu 171,064
Butembo 78,633
Gandajika 60,263
Gemena 62,641
Goma 76,745
Ilebo (Port-Francqui) 48,831
Isiro 78,871
Kabinda 81,752
Kalemie (Albertville) 70,694
Kananga (Luluabourg) 290,898
Kikwit 146,784
Kindu 68,044
• KINSHASA
(LÉOPOLDVILLE)
(1986 E) 3,000,000
Kisangani (Stanleyville) ... 282,650
Kolwezi 201,382
Likasi (Jadotville) 194,465
Lubumbashi
(Élisabethville) 543,268
Manono 51,755
Matadi 144,742
Mbandaka
(Coquilhatville) 125,263
Mbuji-Mayi (Bakwanga) 423,363
Mwene-Ditu 72,567
Tshikapa 105,484
Yangambi 53,726

ZAMBIA

1980 C 5,661,801

Cities and Towns

Chililabombwe
(Bancroft) (★ 56,582) 25,900
Chingola 130,872
Kabwe (Broken Hill) 127,420
Kalulushi 53,383
Kitwe (★ 283,962) 207,500
Livingstone 61,296
Luanshya (★ 113,422) 61,600
• LUSAKA 535,830
Mufulira (★ 138,824) 77,100
Ndola 250,490

ZIMBABWE

1983 E 7,740,000

Cities and Towns

Bulawayo 429,000
Chitungwiza (★ Harare) ... 202,000
Gweru (1982 C) 78,940
• HARARE (★ 890,000) 681,000
Kwekwe (1982 C) 47,976
Mutare (1982 C) 75,358

C Census.   E Official estimate.   U Unofficial estimate.
• Largest city in country.

★ Population or designation of metropolitan area, including suburbs (see headnote).
▲ Population of an entire municipality, commune, or district, including rural area.

215

United States General Information

Geographical Facts

ELEVATION

The highest elevation in the United States is Mount McKinley, Alaska, 20,320 feet.

The lowest elevation in the United States is in Death Valley, California, 282 feet below sea level.

The average elevation of the United States is 2,500 feet.

EXTREMITIES

Direction	Location	Latitude	Longitude
North	Point Barrow, Ak.	71° 23'N.	156° 29'W.
South	Ka Lae (point) Hi.	18° 56'N.	155° 41'W.
East	West Quoddy Head, Me.	44° 49'N.	66° 57'W.
West	Cape Wrangell, Ak.	52° 55'N.	172° 27'E.

LENGTH OF BOUNDARIES

The total length of the Canadian boundary of the United States is 5,525 miles.

The total length of the Mexican boundary of the United States is 1,933 miles.

The total length of the Atlantic coastline of the United States is 2,069 miles.

The total length of the Pacific and Arctic coastline of the United States is 8,683 miles.

The total length of the Gulf of Mexico coastline of the United States is 1,631 miles.

The total length of all coastlines and land boundaries of the United States is 19,841 miles.

The total length of the tidal shoreline and land boundaries of the United States is 96,091 miles.

GEOGRAPHIC CENTERS

The geographic center of the United States (including Alaska and Hawaii) is in Butte County, South Dakota at 44° 58'N., 103° 46'W.

The geographic center of North America is in North Dakota, a few miles west of Devils Lake, at 48° 10'N., 100° 10'W.

EXTREMES OF TEMPERATURE

The highest temperature ever recorded in the United States was 134° F., at Greenland Ranch, Death Valley, California, on July 10, 1913.

The lowest temperature ever recorded in the United States was -80° F., at Prospect Creek, Alaska, on January 23, 1971.

Historical Facts

TERRITORIAL ACQUISITIONS

Accession	Date	Area (sq. mi.)	Cost in Dollars
Original territory of the Thirteen States	1790	888,685	
Purchase of Louisiana Territory, from France	1803	827,192	$11,250,000
By treaty with Spain: Florida	1819	58,560	5,000,000
Other areas	1819	13,443	
Annexation of Texas	1845	390,144	
Oregon Territory, by treaty with Great Britain	1846	285,580	
Mexican Cession	1848	529,017	$15,000,000
Gadsden Purchase, from Mexico	1853	29,640	$10,000,000
Purchase of Alaska, from Russia	1867	586,412	7,200,000
Annexation of Hawaiian Islands	1898	6,450	
Puerto Rico, by treaty with Spain	1899	3,435	
Guam, by treaty with Spain	1899	212	
American Samoa, by treaty with Great Britain and Germany	1900	76	
Virgin Islands, by purchase from Denmark	1917	133	$25,000,000

Note: The Philippines, ceded by Spain in 1898 for $20,000,000 were a territorial possession of the United States from 1898 to 1946. On July 4, 1946 they became the independent Republic of the Philippines.

Note: The Canal Zone, ceded by Panama in 1903 for $10,000,000 was a territory of the United States from 1903 to 1979. As a result of treaties signed in 1977, sovereignty over the Canal Zone reverted to Panama in 1979.

WESTWARD MOVEMENT OF CENTER OF POPULATION

Year	U.S.Population Total at Census	Approximate Location
1790	3,929,214	23 miles east of Baltimore, Md.
1800	5,308,483	18 miles west of Baltimore, Md.
1810	7,239,881	40 miles northwest of Washington, D.C.
1820	9,638,453	16 miles east of Moorefield, W. Va.
1830	12,866,020	19 miles southwest of Moorefield, W. Va.
1840	17,069,453	16 miles south of Clarksburg, W. Va.
1850	23,191,876	23 miles southeast of Parkersburg, W. Va.
1860	31,443,321	20 miles southeast of Chillicothe, Ohio
1870	39,818,449	48 miles northeast of Cincinnati, Ohio
1880	50,155,783	8 miles southwest of Cincinnati, Ohio
1890	62,947,714	20 miles east of Columbus, Ind.
1900	75,994,575	6 miles southeast of Columbus, Ind.
1910	91,972,266	Bloomington, Ind.
1920	105,710,620	8 miles southeast of Spencer, Ind.
1930	122,775,046	3 miles northeast of Linton, Ind.
1940	131,669,275	2 miles southeast of Carlisle, Ind.
1950	150,697,361	8 miles northwest of Olney, Ill.
1960	179,323,175	6 miles northwest of Centralia, Ill.
1970	204,816,296	5 miles southeast of Mascoutah, Ill.
1980	226,549,010	1/4 mile west of DeSoto, Mo.
1990	248,709,873	10 miles southeast of Steelville, Mo.

State Areas and Populations

STATE	Land Area* square miles	Water Area* square miles	Total Area* square miles	Area Rank land area	1990 Population	1990 Population per square mile	1980 Population	1970 Population	1960 Population	Population Rank 1990	Population Rank 1980	Population Rank 1970
Alabama	50,750	1,673	52,423	28	4,040,587	80	3,894,046	3,444,354	3,266,740	22	22	21
Alaska	570,374	86,051	656,424	1	550,043	1.0	401,851	302,583	226,167	49	50	50
Arizona	113,642	364	114,006	6	3,665,228	32	2,716,756	1,775,399	1,302,161	24	29	33
Arkansas	52,075	1,107	53,182	27	2,350,725	45	2,286,357	1,923,322	1,786,272	33	33	32
California	155,973	7,734	163,707	3	29,760,021	191	23,667,372	19,971,069	15,717,204	1	1	1
Colorado	103,730	371	104,100	8	3,294,394	32	2,889,735	2,209,596	1,753,947	26	28	30
Connecticut	4,845	698	5,544	48	3,287,116	678	3,107,576	3,032,217	2,535,234	27	25	24
Delaware	1,955	535	2,489	49	666,168	341	594,317	548,104	446,292	46	47	41
District of Columbia	61	7	68	.....	606,900	9,949	638,432	756,668	763,956	.....	.....	.....
Florida	53,997	11,761	65,758	26	12,937,926	240	9,747,015	6,791,418	4,951,560	4	7	9
Georgia	57,919	1,522	59,441	21	6,478,216	112	5,462,982	4,587,930	3,943,116	11	13	15
Hawaii	6,423	4,508	10,932	47	1,108,229	173	964,691	769,913	632,772	41	39	40
Idaho	82,751	823	83,574	11	1,006,749	12	944,127	713,015	667,191	42	41	43
Illinois	55,593	2,325	57,918	24	11,430,602	206	11,427,414	11,110,285	10,081,158	6	5	5
Indiana	35,870	550	36,420	38	5,544,159	155	5,490,212	5,195,392	4,662,498	14	12	11
Iowa	55,875	401	56,276	23	2,776,755	50	2,913,808	2,825,368	2,757,537	30	27	25
Kansas	81,823	459	82,282	13	2,477,574	30	2,364,236	2,249,071	2,178,611	32	32	28
Kentucky	39,732	679	40,411	36	3,685,296	93	3,660,324	3,220,711	3,038,156	23	23	23
Louisiana	43,566	8,277	51,843	33	4,219,917	97	4,206,098	3,644,637	3,257,022	21	19	20
Maine	30,865	4,523	35,387	39	1,227,928	40	1,125,043	993,722	969,265	38	38	38
Maryland	9,775	2,633	12,407	42	4,781,468	489	4,216,933	3,923,897	3,100,689	19	18	18
Massachusetts	7,838	2,717	10,555	45	6,016,425	768	5,737,093	5,689,170	5,148,578	13	11	10
Michigan	56,809	40,001	96,810	22	9,295,297	164	9,262,044	8,881,826	7,823,194	8	8	7
Minnesota	79,617	7,326	86,943	14	4,375,099	55	4,075,970	3,806,103	3,413,864	20	21	19
Mississippi	46,914	1,520	48,434	31	2,573,216	55	2,520,698	2,216,994	2,178,141	31	31	29
Missouri	68,898	811	69,709	18	5,117,073	74	4,916,759	4,677,623	4,319,813	15	15	13
Montana	145,556	1,490	147,046	4	799,065	5.5	786,690	694,409	674,767	44	44	44
Nebraska	76,878	481	77,358	15	1,578,385	21	1,569,825	1,485,333	1,411,330	36	35	35
Nevada	109,806	761	110,567	7	1,201,833	11	800,508	488,738	285,278	39	43	47
New Hampshire	8,969	382	9,351	44	1,109,252	124	920,610	737,681	606,921	40	42	42
New Jersey	7,419	1,303	8,722	46	7,730,188	1,042	7,365,011	7,171,112	6,066,782	9	9	8
New Mexico	121,365	234	121,598	5	1,515,069	12	1,303,542	1,017,055	951,023	37	37	37
New York	47,224	7,251	54,475	30	17,990,455	381	17,558,165	18,241,391	16,782,304	2	2	2
North Carolina	48,718	5,103	53,821	29	6,628,637	136	5,880,415	5,084,411	4,556,155	10	10	12
North Dakota	68,994	1,710	70,704	17	638,800	9.3	652,717	617,792	632,446	47	46	46
Ohio	40,953	3,875	44,828	35	10,847,115	265	10,797,603	10,657,423	9,706,397	7	6	6
Oklahoma	68,679	1,224	69,903	19	3,145,585	46	3,025,487	2,559,463	2,328,284	28	26	27
Oregon	96,003	2,383	98,386	10	2,842,321	30	2,633,156	2,091,533	1,768,687	29	30	31
Pennsylvania	44,820	1,239	46,058	32	11,881,643	265	11,864,751	11,800,766	11,319,366	5	4	3
Rhode Island	1,045	500	1,545	50	1,003,464	960	947,154	949,723	859,488	43	40	39
South Carolina	30,111	1,896	32,007	40	3,486,703	116	3,120,730	2,590,713	2,382,594	25	24	26
South Dakota	75,898	1,224	77,121	16	696,004	9.2	690,768	666,257	680,514	45	45	45
Tennessee	41,220	926	42,146	34	4,877,185	118	4,591,023	3,926,018	3,567,089	17	17	17
Texas	261,914	6,687	268,601	2	16,986,510	65	14,225,288	11,198,655	9,579,677	3	3	4
Utah	82,168	2,736	84,904	12	1,722,850	21	1,461,037	1,059,273	890,627	35	36	36
Vermont	9,249	366	9,615	43	562,758	61	511,456	444,732	389,881	48	48	48
Virginia	39,598	3,171	42,769	37	6,187,358	156	5,346,797	4,651,448	3,966,949	12	14	14
Washington	66,582	4,721	71,303	20	4,866,692	73	4,132,353	3,413,244	2,853,214	18	20	22
West Virginia	24,087	145	24,231	41	1,793,477	74	1,950,186	1,744,237	1,860,421	34	34	34
Wisconsin	54,314	11,190	65,503	25	4,891,769	90	4,705,642	4,417,821	3,951,777	16	16	16
Wyoming	97,105	714	97,818	9	453,588	4.7	469,557	332,416	330,066	50	49	49
United States	3,536,342	251,083	3,787,425	.....	248,709,873	70	226,542,360	203,302,031	179,323,175	.....	.....	.....

*Area figures for all states does not equal U.S. total due to rounding.

United States Populations and Zip Codes

The following alphabetical list shows populations for all counties and over 15,000 selected cities and towns in the United States. ZIP codes are shown for all of the cities listed in the table. The state abbreviation following each name is that used by the United States Postal Service.

ZIP codes are listed for cities and towns after the state abbreviations. For each city with more than one ZIP code, the range of numbers assigned to the city is shown: For example, the ZIP code range for Chicago is 60601–99, and this indicates that the numbers between 60601 and 60699 are valid Chicago ZIP codes. ZIP codes are not listed for counties.

Populations for cities and towns appear as *italics* after the ZIP codes, and populations for counties appear after the state abbreviations. These populations are either 1990 census figures or, where census data are not available, estimates created by Rand McNally. City populations are for central cities, not metropolitan areas. For New England, 1990 census populations are given for incorporated places. Estimates are used for unincorporated places that are not treated separately by the census. 'Town' (or 'township') populations are not included unless the town is considered to be primarily urban and contains only one commonly used placename.

Counties are identified by a square symbol (□).

Abbreviations for State Names

AK	Alaska	**IA**	Iowa	**MS**	Mississippi	**PA**	Pennsylvania
AL	Alabama	**ID**	Idaho	**MT**	Montana	**RI**	Rhode Island
AR	Arkansas	**IL**	Illinois	**NC**	North Carolina	**SC**	South Carolina
AZ	Arizona	**IN**	Indiana	**ND**	North Dakota	**SD**	South Dakota
CA	California	**KS**	Kansas	**NE**	Nebraska	**TN**	Tennessee
CO	Colorado	**KY**	Kentucky	**NH**	New Hampshire	**TX**	Texas
CT	Connecticut	**LA**	Louisiana	**NJ**	New Jersey	**UT**	Utah
DC	District of	**MA**	Massachusetts	**NM**	New Mexico	**VA**	Virginia
	Columbia	**MD**	Maryland	**NV**	Nevada	**VT**	Vermont
DE	Delaware	**ME**	Maine	**NY**	New York	**WA**	Washington
FL	Florida	**MI**	Michigan	**OH**	Ohio	**WI**	Wisconsin
GA	Georgia	**MN**	Minnesota	**OK**	Oklahoma	**WV**	West Virginia
HI	Hawaii	**MO**	Missouri	**OR**	Oregon	**WY**	Wyoming

A

Abbeville, AL 36310 • *3,173*
Abbeville, LA 70510–11 • *11,187*
Abbeville, SC 29620 • *5,778*
Abbeville □, SC • *23,862*
Abbotsford, WI 54405 • *1,916*
Aberdeen, ID 83210 • *1,406*
Aberdeen, MD 21001 • *13,087*
Aberdeen, MS 39730 • *6,837*
Aberdeen, NC 28315 • *2,700*
Aberdeen, OH 45101 • *1,329*
Aberdeen, SD 57401–02 • *24,927*
Aberdeen, WA 98520 • *16,565*
Abernathy, TX 79311 • *2,720*
Abilene, KS 67410 • *6,242*
Abilene, TX 79601–08 • *106,654*
Abingdon, IL 61410 • *3,597*
Abingdon, VA 24210 • *7,003*
Abington, MA 02351 • *13,817*
Abington [Township], PA 19001 • *59,084*
Abita Springs, LA 70420 • *1,296*
Absarokee, MT 59001 • *1,067*
Absecon, NJ 08201 • *7,298*
Academia, OH 43050 • *1,447*
Acadia □, LA • *55,882*
Accomack □, VA • *31,703*
Ackerman, MS 39735 • *1,573*
Ackley, IA 50601 • *1,696*
Acton, CA 93510 • *1,471*
Acton, MA 01720 • *2,300*
Acushnet, MA 02743 • *6,030*
Acworth, GA 30101 • *4,519*
Ada, MN 56510 • *1,708*
Ada, OH 45810 • *5,413*
Ada, OK 74820–21 • *15,820*
Ada □, ID • *205,775*
Adair □, IA • *8,409*
Adair □, KY • *15,360*
Adair □, MO • *24,577*
Adair □, OK • *18,421*
Adairsville, GA 30103 • *2,131*
Adams □, CO 80022 • *2,200*
Adams, MA 01220 • *6,356*
Adams, NY 13605 • *1,753*
Adams, WI 53910 • *1,715*
Adams □, CO • *265,038*
Adams □, ID • *3,254*
Adams □, IL • *66,090*
Adams □, IN • *31,095*
Adams □, IA • *4,866*
Adams □, MS • *35,356*
Adams □, NE • *29,625*
Adams □, ND • *3,174*
Adams □, OH • *25,371*
Adams □, PA • *78,274*
Adams □, WA • *13,603*
Adams □, WI • *15,682*
Adams Center, NY 13606 • *1,675*
Adamstown, PA 19501 • *1,108*
Adamsville, AL 35005 • *4,161*
Adamsville, RI 02801 • *600*
Adamsville, TN 38310 • *1,745*
Addis, LA 70710 • *1,222*
Addison, CT 06033 • *2,460*
Addison, IL 60101 • *32,058*
Addison, NY 14801 • *1,842*
Addison, TX 75001 • *8,783*
Addison □, VT • *32,953*
Addyston, OH 45001 • *1,198*
Adel, GA 31620 • *5,093*
Adel, IA 50003 • *3,304*
Adelanto, CA 92301 • *8,517*
Adelphi, MD 20783 • *13,524*
Adobe Acres, NM 87105 • *2,400*
Adrian, MI 49221 • *22,097*
Adrian, MN 56110 • *1,141*
Adrian, MO 64720 • *1,582*
Advance, MO 63730 • *1,139*
Affton, MO 63123 • *21,106*
Afton, DE 19810 • *1,200*
Afton, MN 55001 • *2,645*
Afton, WY 83110 • *1,394*
Agawam, MA 01001 • *10,190*
Agoura Hills, CA 91301 • *20,390*
Ahoskie, NC 27910 • *4,391*
Aiea, HI 96701 • *8,906*
Aiken, SC 29801–03 • *19,872*
Aiken □, SC • *120,940*
Ainsworth, NE 69210 • *1,870*
Air Park West, NE 68524 • *3,100*
Aitkin, MN 56431 • *1,698*
Aitkin □, MN • *12,425*
Ajo, AZ 85321 • *2,919*
Akiachak, AK 99551 • *400*
Akron, CO 80720 • *1,599*
Akron, IA 51001 • *1,450*
Akron, NY 14001 • *2,906*
Akron, OH 44301–98 • *223,019*
Akron, PA 17501 • *3,869*
Alabaster, AL 35007 • *14,732*
Alachua, FL 32615 • *4,529*
Alachua □, FL • *181,596*
Alakanuk, AK 99554 • *544*
Alamance □, NC • *108,213*
Alameda, CA 94501 • *76,459*
Alameda, NM 87114 • *5,900*
Alameda □, CA • *1,279,182*

Alamo, CA 94507 • *12,277*
Alamo, NV 89001 • *400*
Alamo, TN 38001 • *2,426*
Alamo, TX 78516 • *8,210*
Alamogordo, NM 88310–11 • *27,596*
Alamo Heights, TX 78208 • *6,502*
Alamosa, CO 81101–02 • *7,579*
Alamosa □, CO • *13,617*
Alamosa East, CO 81101 • *1,389*
Albany, CA 94706 • *16,327*
Albany, GA 31701–07 • *78,122*
Albany, IN 47320 • *2,357*
Albany, KY 42602 • *2,062*
Albany, MN 56307 • *1,548*
Albany, MO 64402 • *1,958*
Albany, NY 12201–60 • *101,082*
Albany, OR 97321 • *29,462*
Albany, TX 76430 • *1,962*
Albany, WI 53502 • *1,140*
Albany □, NY • *292,594*
Albany □, WY • *30,797*
Albemarle, NC 28001–02 • *14,939*
Albemarle □, VA • *68,040*
Albert Lea, MN 56007 • *18,310*
Albertson, NY 11507 • *5,166*
Albertville, AL 35950 • *14,507*
Albertville, MN 55301 • *1,251*
Albia, IA 52531 • *3,870*
Albion, IL 62806 • *2,116*
Albion, IN 46701 • *1,823*
Albion, MI 49224 • *10,066*
Albion, NE 68620 • *1,916*
Albion, NY 14411 • *5,863*
Albion, PA 16401 • *1,575*
Albion, RI 02802 • *1,600*
Albuquerque, NM 87101–99 • *384,736*
Alburtis, PA 18011 • *1,415*
Alcester, SD 57001 • *843*
Alcoa, TN 37701 • *6,400*
Alcona □, MI • *10,145*
Alcorn □, MS • *31,722*
Alden, NY 14004 • *2,457*
Alderson, WV 24910 • *1,152*
Alderwood Manor, WA 98011 • *16,524*
Aledo, IL 61231 • *3,681*
Alexander □, IL • *10,626*
Alexander □, NC • *27,544*
Alexander City, AL 35010 • *14,917*
Alexandria, IN 46001 • *5,709*
Alexandria, KY 41001 • *5,592*
Alexandria, LA 71301–15 • *49,188*
Alexandria, MN 56308 • *7,838*
Alexandria, VA 22301–20 • *111,183*
Alexandria Bay, NY 13607 • *1,194*
Alfalfa □, OK • *6,416*
Alfred, NY 14802 • *4,559*
Alger □, MI • *8,972*
Algoma, WI 54201 • *3,353*
Algona, IA 50511 • *6,015*
Algona, WA 98001 • *1,694*
Algonac, MI 48001 • *4,551*
Algonquin, IL 60102 • *11,663*
Algood, TN 38501 • *2,399*
Alhambra, CA 91801–99 • *82,106*
Alice, TX 78332–33 • *19,788*
Aliceville, AL 35442 • *3,009*
Aliquippa, PA 15001 • *13,374*
Allamakee □, IA • *13,855*
Allegan, MI 49010 • *4,547*
Allegan □, MI • *90,509*
Allegany, NY 14706 • *1,980*
Allegany □, MD • *74,946*
Allegany □, NY • *50,470*
Alleghany □, NC • *9,590*
Alleghany □, VA • *13,176*
Allegheny □, PA • *1,336,449*
Allen, TX 75002 • *18,309*
Allen, TX 75002 • *18,309*
Allen □, IN • *300,836*
Allen □, KS • *14,638*
Allen □, KY • *14,628*
Allen □, LA • *21,226*
Allen □, OH • *109,755*
Allendale, NJ 07401 • *5,900*
Allendale, SC 29810 • *4,410*
Allendale □, SC • *11,722*
Allen Park, MI 48101 • *31,092*
Allenton, RI 02852 • *600*
Allentown, NJ 08501 • *1,828*
Allentown, PA 18101–95 • *105,090*
Alliance, NE 69301 • *9,765*
Alliance, OH 44601 • *23,376*
Allison, IA 50602 • *1,000*
Allison Park, PA 15101 • *5,600*
Allouez, WI 54301 • *14,431*
Alloway, NJ 08001 • *1,371*
Allyn, WA 98524 • *1,100*
Alma, AR 72921 • *2,959*
Alma, GA 31510 • *3,663*
Alma, MI 48801 • *9,034*
Almont, MI 48003 • *2,354*
Aloha, OR 97006 • *34,284*
Alondra Park, CA 90249 • *12,215*
Alpena, MI 49707 • *11,354*
Alpena □, MI • *30,605*
Alpha, NJ 08865 • *2,530*
Alpharetta, GA 30201–02 • *13,002*
Alpine, CA 91901 • *9,695*
Alpine, NJ 07620 • *1,716*
Alpine, TX 79830–31 • *5,637*

Alpine, UT 84003 • *3,492*
Alpine □, CA • *1,113*
Alsip, IL 60658 • *18,227*
Alta, IA 51002 • *1,820*
Altadena, CA 91001–02 • *42,658*
Altamont, IL 62411 • *2,296*
Altamont, KS 67330 • *1,048*
Altamont, NY 12009 • *1,519*
Altamont, OR 97601 • *18,591*
Altamonte Springs, FL 32701 • *34,879*
Alta Sierra, CA 95949 • *5,709*
Altavista, VA 24517 • *3,686*
Alto, TX 75925 • *1,027*
Alton, IL 62002 • *32,905*
Alton, IA 51003 • *1,063*
Alton, NH 03809 • *975*
Alton Bay, NH 03810 • *1,000*
Altoona, FL 32702 • *1,300*
Altoona, IA 50009 • *7,191*
Altoona, PA 16601–03 • *51,881*
Altoona, WI 54720 • *5,889*
Alturas, CA 96101 • *3,231*
Altus, OK 73521–23 • *21,910*
Alva, FL 33920 • *1,200*
Alva, OK 73717 • *5,495*
Alvarado, TX 76009 • *2,918*
Alvin, TX 77511–12 • *19,220*
Amador □, CA • *30,039*
Amagansett, NY 11930 • *2,188*
Amana, IA 52203 • *540*
Amarillo, TX 79101–76 • *157,615*
Ambler, PA 19002 • *6,609*
Amboy, IL 61310 • *2,377*
Ambridge, PA 15003 • *8,133*
Amelia, LA 70340 • *2,447*
Amelia, OH 45102 • *1,837*
Amelia □, VA • *8,787*
Amenia, NY 12501 • *1,057*
American Canyon, CA 94589 • *7,706*
American Falls, ID 83211 • *3,757*
American Fork, UT 84003–04 • *15,696*
Americus, GA 31709 • *16,512*
Ames, IA 50010 • *47,198*
Amesbury, MA 01913 • *12,109*
Amherst, MA 01002–04 • *17,824*
Amherst, NH 03031 • *850*
Amherst, NY 14226 • *45,600*
Amherst, OH 44001 • *10,332*
Amherst, VA 24521 • *1,060*
Amherst □, VA • *28,578*
Amherstdale, WV 25607 • *1,200*
Amite, LA 70422 • *4,236*
Amite □, MS • *13,328*
Amity, OR 97101 • *1,175*
Amityville, NY 11701 • *9,286*
Ammon, ID 83401 • *5,002*
Amory, MS 38821 • *7,093*
Amsterdam, NY 12010 • *20,714*
Anaconda, MT 59711 • *10,278*
Anacortes, WA 98221 • *11,451*
Anadarko, OK 73005 • *6,586*
Anaheim, CA 92801–25 • *266,406*
Anahola, HI 96703 • *1,181*
Anahuac, TX 77514 • *1,993*
Anamosa, IA 52205 • *5,100*
Anandale, LA 71301 • *2,000*
Anchorage, AK 99501–40 • *226,338*
Anchorage, KY 40223 • *2,082*
Andalusia, AL 36420 • *9,269*
Anderson, AK 99744 • *628*
Anderson, CA 96007 • *8,239*
Anderson, IN 46011–18 • *59,459*
Anderson, MO 64831 • *1,432*
Anderson, SC 29625–26 • *26,184*
Anderson □, KS • *7,803*
Anderson □, KY • *14,571*
Anderson □, SC • *145,196*
Anderson □, TN • *68,250*
Anderson □, TX • *48,024*
Andover, KS 67002 • *4,047*
Andover, MA 01810 • *8,242*
Andover, MN 55216 • *15,216*
Andover, NY 14806 • *1,125*
Andover, OH 44003 • *1,237*
Andrew □, MO • *14,632*
Andrews, IN 46702 • *1,118*
Andrews, NC 28901 • *2,551*
Andrews, SC 29510 • *3,050*
Andrews, TX 79714 • *10,678*
Andrews □, TX • *14,338*
Androscoggin □, ME • *105,259*
Angelina □, TX • *69,884*
Angels Camp, CA 95222 • *2,409*
Angier, NC 27501 • *2,235*
Angleton, TX 77515–16 • *17,140*
Angola, IN 46703 • *5,824*
Angola, NY 14006 • *2,231*
Angoon, AK 99820 • *638*
Aniak, AK 99557 • *540*
Anita, IA 50020 • *1,068*
Ankeny, IA 50021 • *18,482*
Anna, IL 62906 • *4,805*
Anna, OH 45302 • *1,164*
Annalee Heights, VA 22042 • *1,750*
Anna Maria, FL 34216 • *1,744*
Annandale, MN 55302 • *2,054*
Annandale, VA 22003 • *50,975*
Annapolis, MD 21401–05 • *33,187*
Ann Arbor, MI 48103–08 • *109,592*

Anne Arundel □, MD • *427,239*
Anniston, AL 36201–06 • *26,623*
Annville, PA 17003 • *4,294*
Anoka, MN 55303–04 • *17,192*
Anoka □, MN • *243,641*
Anson, TX 79501 • *2,644*
Anson □, NC • *23,474*
Ansonia, CT 06401 • *18,403*
Ansonia, OH 45303 • *1,279*
Ansted, WV 25812 • *1,643*
Antelope □, NE • *7,965*
Anthony, FL 32617 • *1,200*
Anthony, KS 67003 • *2,516*
Anthony, NM 88021 • *5,160*
Anthony, RI 02816 • *2,980*
Anthony, TX 88021 • *3,328*
Antigo, WI 54409 • *8,276*
Antioch, CA 94509 • *62,195*
Antioch, IL 60002 • *6,105*
Antlers, OK 74523 • *2,524*
Anton, TX 79313 • *1,212*
Antrim, NH 03440 • *1,325*
Antrim □, MI • *18,185*
Antwerp, OH 45813 • *1,677*
Apache, OK 73006 • *1,591*
Apache □, AZ • *61,591*
Apache Junction, AZ 85217–20 • *18,100*
Apalachicola, FL 32320 • *2,602*
Apalachin, NY 11930 • *1,208*
Apex, NC 27502 • *4,968*
Aplington, IA 50604 • *1,034*
Apollo, PA 15613 • *1,895*
Apollo Beach, FL 33572 • *6,025*
Apopka, FL 32703–04 • *13,512*
Appalachia, VA 24216 • *1,994*
Appanoose □, IA • *13,743*
Appleton, MN 56208 • *1,552*
Appleton, WI 54911–15 • *65,695*
Appleton City, MO 64724 • *1,280*
Apple Valley, CA 92307–08 • *46,079*
Apple Valley, MN 55124 • *34,598*
Applewood, CO 80401 • *11,069*
Appleyard, WA 98801 • *1,207*
Appling □, GA • *15,744*
Appomattox, VA 24522 • *1,707*
Appomattox □, VA • *12,298*
Aptos, CA 95003 • *9,061*
Aquia Harbour, VA 22554 • *6,308*
Arab, AL 35016 • *6,321*
Arabi, LA 70032 • *8,787*
Aransas □, TX • *17,892*
Aransas Pass, TX 78336 • *7,180*
Arapahoe, NE 68922 • *1,001*
Arapahoe □, CO • *391,511*
Arbuckle, CA 95912 • *1,912*
Arcade, CA 95821 • *47,900*
Arcade, NY 14009 • *2,081*
Arcadia, CA 91006–07 • *48,290*
Arcadia, FL 33821 • *6,488*
Arcadia, IN 46030 • *1,468*
Arcadia, LA 71001 • *3,079*
Arcadia, SC 29302 • *2,088*
Arcadia, WI 54612 • *2,166*
Arcanum, OH 45304 • *1,953*
Arcata, CA 95521 • *15,197*
Archbald, PA 18403 • *6,291*
Archbold, OH 43502 • *3,440*
Archdale, NC 27263 • *6,913*
Archer, FL 32618 • *1,372*
Archer □, TX • *7,973*
Archer City, TX 76351 • *1,748*
Archuleta □, CO • *5,345*
Arco, ID 83213 • *1,016*
Arcola, IL 61910 • *2,678*
Arden, CA 95825 • *62,900*
Arden Hills, MN 55112 • *9,199*
Ardmore, PA 19003 • *12,000*
Ardmore, IN 46628 • *2,250*
Ardmore, OK 73401–03 • *23,079*
Ardsley, NY 10502 • *4,272*
Arenac □, MI • *14,931*
Argos, IN 46501 • *1,642*
Arizona Sunsites, AZ 85625 • *1,100*
Arkadelphia, AR 71923 • *10,014*
Arkansas □, AR • *21,653*
Arkansas City, KS 67005 • *12,762*
Arkoma, OK 74901 • *2,393*
Arlington, GA 31713 • *1,513*
Arlington, MA 02174 • *44,630*
Arlington, MN 55307 • *1,886*
Arlington, NE 68002 • *1,178*
Arlington, NY 12603 • *11,948*
Arlington, OH 45814 • *1,267*
Arlington, SD 57212 • *908*
Arlington, TN 38002 • *1,541*
Arlington, TX 76010–18 • *261,721*
Arlington, VT 05250 • *1,311*
Arlington, VA 22201–19 • *170,936*
Arlington, WA 98223 • *4,037*
Arlington □, VA • *170,936*
Arlington Heights, IL 60004–07 • *75,460*
Arma, KS 66712 • *1,542*
Armada, MI 48005 • *1,548*
Armijo, NM 87105 • *14,600*
Armonk, NY 10504 • *2,745*
Armour, SD 57313 • *854*
Armstrong, IA 50514 • *1,025*
Armstrong □, PA • *73,478*
Armstrong □, TX • *2,021*
Arnaudville, LA 70512 • *1,444*
Arnold, MD 21012 • *20,261*

Arnold, MN 55803 • *1,500*
Arnold, MO 63010 • *18,828*
Arnold, PA 15068 • *6,113*
Arnold Mills, RI 02864 • *600*
Aroostook □, ME • *86,936*
Arroyo Grande, CA 93420–21 • *14,378*
Artesia, CA 90701–03 • *15,464*
Artesia, NM 88210–11 • *10,610*
Arthur, IL 61911 • *2,112*
Arthur □, NE • *462*
Arundel Village, MD 21225 • *3,370*
Arvada, CO 80001–06 • *89,235*
Arvin, CA 93203 • *9,286*
Asbury Park, NJ 07712 • *16,799*
Ascension □, LA • *58,214*
Ashaway, RI 02804 • *1,584*
Ashburn, GA 31714 • *4,827*
Ashburnham, MA 01430 • *1,300*
Ashdown, AR 71822 • *5,150*
Ashe □, NC • *22,209*
Asheboro, NC 27203 • *16,362*
Asherton, TX 78827 • *1,608*
Asheville, NC 28801–16 • *61,607*
Ashford, AL 36312 • *1,926*
Ash Grove, MO 65604 • *1,128*
Ashland, AL 36251 • *2,034*
Ashland, CA 94541 • *16,590*
Ashland, IL 62612 • *1,257*
Ashland, KS 67831 • *1,032*
Ashland, KY 41101–05 • *23,622*
Ashland, MA 01721 • *9,165*
Ashland, MO 65010 • *1,252*
Ashland, NE 68003 • *2,136*
Ashland, NH 03217 • *1,915*
Ashland, OH 44805 • *20,079*
Ashland, OR 97520 • *16,234*
Ashland, PA 17921 • *3,859*
Ashland, VA 23005 • *5,864*
Ashland, WI 54806 • *8,695*
Ashland □, OH • *47,507*
Ashland □, WI • *16,307*
Ashland City, TN 37015 • *2,552*
Ashley, ND 58413 • *1,052*
Ashley, OH 43003 • *1,059*
Ashley, PA 18706 • *3,291*
Ashley □, AR • *24,319*
Ashtabula, OH 44004 • *21,633*
Ashtabula □, OH • *99,821*
Ashton, ID 83420 • *1,114*
Ashton, IL 61006 • *1,042*
Ashton, MD 20861 • *1,800*
Ashton, RI 02864 • *820*
Ashville, AL 35953 • *1,494*
Ashville, OH 43103 • *2,254*
Ashwaubenon, WI 54304 • *16,376*
Asotin, WA • *17,605*
Aspen, CO 81611–15 • *5,049*
Aspen Hill, MD 20906 • *45,494*
Aspermont, TX 79502 • *1,214*
Aspinwall, PA 15215 • *2,880*
Assinippi, MA 02339 • *1,400*
Assonet, MA 02702 • *1,200*
Assumption, IL 62510 • *1,244*
Assumption □, LA • *22,753*
Astoria, IL 61501 • *1,205*
Astoria, OR 97103 • *10,069*
Atascadero, CA 93422–23 • *23,138*
Atascosa □, TX • *30,533*
Atchison, KS 66002 • *10,656*
Atchison □, KS • *16,932*
Atchison □, MO • *7,457*
Atco, NJ 08004 • *2,020*
Athens, AL 35611 • *16,901*
Athens, GA 30601–13 • *45,734*
Athens, IL 62613 • *1,404*
Athens, NY 12015 • *1,708*
Athens, OH 45701 • *21,265*
Athens, PA 18810 • *3,468*
Athens, TN 37303 • *12,054*
Athens, TX 75751 • *10,967*
Athens □, OH • *59,549*
Atherton, CA 94027 • *7,163*
Athol, MA 01331 • *8,732*
Atkins, AR 72823 • *2,834*
Atkins, VA 24311 • *1,130*
Atkinson, NE 68713 • *1,380*
Atkinson □, GA • *613*
Atlanta, GA 30301–83 • *394,017*
Atlanta, IL 61723 • *1,616*
Atlanta, TX 75551 • *6,118*
Atlantic, IA 50022 • *7,432*
Atlantic □, NJ • *224,327*
Atlantic Beach, FL 32233 • *11,636*
Atlantic City, NJ 08401–06 • *37,986*
Atlantic Highlands, NJ 07716 • *4,629*
Atmore, AL 36502 • *8,046*
Atoka, OK 74525 • *3,298*
Atoka □, OK • *12,778*
Attalla, AL 35954 • *6,859*
Attalla □, MS • *18,481*
Attica, IN 47918 • *3,457*
Attica, NY 14011 • *2,630*
Attleboro, MA 02703 • *38,383*
Atwater, CA 95301 • *22,282*
Atwater, MN 56209 • *1,053*
Atwood, IL 61913 • *1,253*
Atwood, KS 67730 • *1,388*
Atwood, TN 38220 • *1,066*
Auberry, CA 93602 • *1,866*
Auburn, AL 36830–49 • *33,830*
Auburn, CA 95603–04 • *10,592*

217

Auburn, GA 30203 • 3,139
Auburn, IL 62615 • 3,724
Auburn, IN 46706 • 9,379
Auburn, KY 42206 • 1,273
Auburn, MA 01501 • 14,845
Auburn, ME 04210-12 • 24,309
Auburn, NE 68305 • 3,443
Auburn, NY 13021-24 • 31,258
Auburn, WA 98001-02 • 33,102
Auburndale, FL 33823 • 8,858
Auburn Heights, MI 48321 • 17,076
Audrain □, MO • 23,599
Audubon, IA 50025 • 2,524
Audubon, NJ 08106 • 9,205
Audubon, PA 19407 • 6,328
Audubon □, IA • 7,334
Auglaize □, OH • 44,585
August, CA 95201 • 6,376
Augusta, AR 72006 • 2,759
Augusta, GA 30901-19 • 44,639
Augusta, KS 67010 • 7,876
Augusta, KY 41002 • 1,336
Augusta, ME 04330-38 • 21,325
Augusta, WI 54722 • 1,510
Augusta □, VA • 54,677
Aulander, NC 27805 • 1,209
Ault, CO 80610 • 1,107
Aumsville, OR 97325 • 1,650
Aurora, CO 80010-19 • 222,103
Aurora, IL 60504-07 • 99,581
Aurora, IN 47001 • 3,825
Aurora, MN 55705 • 1,965
Aurora, MO 65605 • 6,459
Aurora, NE 68818 • 3,810
Aurora, OH 44202 • 9,192
Aurora □, SD • 3,135
Au Sable, MI 48750 • 1,542
Au Sable Forks, NY 12912 • 2,100
Austell, GA 30001 • 4,173
Austin, IN 47102 • 4,310
Austin, MN 55912 • 21,907
Austin, NV 89310 • 370
Austin, TX 78701-89 • 465,622
Austin □, TX • 19,832
Austintown, OH 44515 • 32,371
Autauga □, AL • 34,222
Ava, MO 65608 • 2,938
Avalon, CA 90704 • 2,918
Avalon, NJ 08202 • 1,809
Avalon, PA 15202 • 5,784
Avella, PA 15312 • 1,200
Avenal, CA 93204 • 9,770
Avenel, MD • 5,600
Avenel, NJ 07001 • 15,504
Aventura, FL 33180 • 14,914
Averill Park, NY 12018 • 1,656
Avery □, NC • 14,867
Avilla, IN 46710 • 1,366
Avis, PA 17721 • 1,506
Avoca, IA 51521 • 1,497
Avoca, NY 14809 • 1,033
Avoca, PA 18641 • 2,897
Avocado Heights, CA 91746 • 14,232
Avon, CT 06001 • 13,937
Avon, MA 02322 • 5,026
Avon, NY 14414 • 2,995
Avon, OH 44011 • 7,337
Avon by the Sea, NJ 07717 • 2,165
Avondale, AZ 85323 • 16,169
Avondale, LA 70094 • 5,813
Avondale, OH 45404 • 5,000
Avondale Estates, GA 30002 • 2,209
Avon Lake, OH 44012 • 15,066
Avonmore, PA 15618 • 1,089
Avon Park, FL 33825 • 8,042
Avoyelles □, LA • 39,159
Ayden, NC 28513 • 4,740
Ayer, MA 01432 • 2,889
Azalea Park, FL 32807 • 8,926
Azle, TX 76020 • 8,868
Aztec, NM 87410 • 5,479
Azusa, CA 91702 • 41,333

B

Babbitt, MN 55706 • 1,562
Babbitt, NV • 1,800
Babylon, NY 11702-04 • 12,249
Baca □, CO • 4,556
Bacliff, TX 77518 • 5,549
Bacon □, GA • 9,566
Bad Axe, MI 48413 • 3,484
Baden, PA 15005 • 5,074
Badin, NC 28009 • 1,481
Bagdad, AZ 86321 • 1,858
Bagdad, FL 32530 • 1,457
Baggs, WY 82321 • 272
Bagley, MN 56621 • 1,388
Bailey □, TX • 7,064
Baileys Crossroads, VA 22041 • 19,507
Bainbridge, GA 31717 • 10,712
Bainbridge, NY 13733 • 1,550
Baird, TX 79504 • 1,658
Bairdford, PA 15006 • 1,200
Baker, LA 70714 • 13,233
Baker, MT 59313 • 1,818
Baker, OR 97814 • 9,140
Baker □, FL • 18,486
Baker □, GA • 3,615
Baker □, OR • 15,317
Bakersfield, CA 93301-89 • 174,820
Balch Springs, TX 75180 • 17,406
Bald Knob, AR 72010 • 2,653
Baldwin, FL 32234 • 1,450
Baldwin, GA 30511 • 1,439
Baldwin, LA 70514 • 2,379
Baldwin, NY 11510 • 22,719
Baldwin, PA 15234 • 21,923
Baldwin, WI 54002 • 2,022
Baldwin □, AL • 98,280
Baldwin □, GA • 39,530
Baldwin City, KS 66006 • 2,961
Baldwin Park, CA 91706 • 69,330
Baldwinsville, NY 13027 • 6,591
Baldwinville, MA 01436 • 1,795
Baldwyn, MS 38824 • 3,204
Balfour, NC 28706 • 1,118
Ball, LA 71405 • 3,305
Ballard □, KY • 7,902
Ballardvale, MA 01810 • 1,270

Ballinger, TX 76821 • 3,975
Ballston Spa, NY 12020 • 4,937
Ballwin, MO 63011 • 21,816
Balmville, NY 12550 • 2,963
Baltic, CT 06330 • 2,000
Baltimore, MD 21201-99 • 736,014
Baltimore, OH 43105 • 2,971
Baltimore □, MD • 692,134
Baltimore Highlands, MD 21227 • 7,300
Bamberg, SC 29003 • 3,843
Bamberg □, SC • 16,902
Bandera □, TX • 10,562
Bandon, OR 97411 • 2,215
Bangor, ME 04401-02 • 33,181
Bangor, MI 49013 • 1,922
Bangor, PA 18013 • 5,383
Bangor, WI 54614 • 1,076
Bangor Township, MI 48706 • 17,494
Bangs, TX 76823 • 1,555
Banks □, GA • 10,308
Banner □, NE • 852
Banning, CA 92220 • 20,570
Bannock □, ID • 66,026
Baraboo, WI 53913 • 9,203
Baraga, MI 49908 • 1,231
Baraga □, MI • 7,954
Barataria, LA 70036 • 1,160
Barber □, KS • 5,874
Barberton, OH 44203 • 27,623
Barbour □, AL • 25,417
Barbour □, WV • 15,699
Barboursville, WV 25504 • 2,774
Bardstown, KY 40004 • 6,801
Bargersville, IN 46106 • 1,681
Bar Harbor, ME 04609 • 2,768
Barker Heights, NC 28739 • 1,137
Barling, AR 72923 • 4,078
Barnegat, NJ 08005 • 1,160
Barnes □, ND • 12,545
Barnesboro, PA 15714 • 2,530
Barnesville, GA 30204 • 4,747
Barnesville, MN 56514 • 2,066
Barnesville, OH 43713 • 4,326
Barnsdall, OK 74002 • 1,316
Barnstable, MA 02630 • 2,790
Barnstable □, MA • 186,605
Barnwell, SC 29812 • 5,255
Barnwell □, SC • 20,293
Barrackville, WV 26559 • 1,443
Barre, MA 01005 • 1,094
Barre, VT 05641 • 9,482
Barren □, KY • 34,001
Barrington, IL 60010-11 • 9,504
Barrington, NJ 08007 • 6,433
Barrington, RI 02806 • 15,849
Barron, WI 54812 • 2,986
Barron □, WI • 40,750
Barron Lake, MI 49120 • 1,600
Barrow, AK 99723 • 3,469
Barrow □, GA • 29,721
Barry, IL 62312 • 1,391
Barry □, MI • 50,057
Barry □, MO • 27,547
Barstow, CA 92310-12 • 21,472
Bartholomew □, IN • 63,657
Bartlesville, OK 74003-06 • 34,256
Bartlett, IL 60103 • 19,373
Bartlett, TN 38134 • 26,989
Bartlett, TX 76511 • 1,439
Bartley, OK 43905 • 1,039
Barton, VT 05822 • 908
Barton □, KS • 29,382
Barton □, MO • 11,312
Bartonville, IL 61607 • 5,643
Bartow, FL 33830 • 14,716
Bartow □, GA • 55,911
Barview, OR 97420 • 1,402
Basalt, CO 81621 • 1,128
Basehor, KS 66007 • 1,591
Basile, LA 70515 • 1,808
Basin, WY 82410 • 1,180
Basking Ridge, NJ 07920 • 3,060
Bassett, VA 24055 • 1,579
Bass Lake, IN 46534 • 1,500
Bastrop, LA 71220-21 • 13,916
Bastrop, TX 78602 • 4,044
Bastrop □, TX • 38,263
Batavia, IL 60510 • 17,076
Batavia, NY 14020-21 • 16,310
Batavia, OH 45103 • 1,700
Bates □, MO • 15,025
Batesburg, SC 29006 • 4,082
Batesville, AR 72501-03 • 9,187
Batesville, IN 47006 • 4,720
Batesville, MS 38606 • 6,403
Bath, ME 04530 • 9,799
Bath, NY 14810 • 5,801
Bath, PA 18014 • 2,358
Bath, SC 29816 • 2,242
Bath □, KY • 9,692
Bath □, VA • 4,799
Baton Rouge, LA 70801-98 • 219,531
Battle Creek, MI 49015-17 • 53,540
Battle Ground, WA 98604 • 3,758
Battle Mountain, NV 89820 • 3,542
Baudette, MN 56623 • 1,146
Bawcomville, LA 71291 • 2,250
Baxley, GA 31513 • 3,841
Baxter, MN 56425 • 3,695
Baxter, TN 38544 • 1,289
Baxter □, AR • 31,186
Baxter Springs, KS 66713 • 4,351
Bay, AR 72411 • 1,660
Bay □, FL • 126,994
Bay □, MI • 111,723
Bayard, NE 69334 • 1,196
Bayard, NM 88023 • 2,598
Bayberry, NY 13088 • 6,710
Bay City, MI 48706-08 • 38,936
Bay City, OR 97107 • 1,027
Bay City, TX 77414 • 18,170
Bayfield, CO 81122 • 1,090
Bayfield, WI • 14,008
Bay Head, NJ 08742 • 1,226
Baylor □, TX • 4,385
Bay Minette, AL 36507 • 7,168
Bayonet Point, FL 34667 • 21,860
Bayonne, NJ 07002 • 61,444
Bayou Cane, LA 70359 • 15,876
Bayou George, FL 32401 • 1,500
Bayou La Batre, AL 36509 • 2,456
Bay Pines, FL 33504 • 4,171

Bayport, MN 55003 • 3,200
Bayport, NY 11705 • 7,702
Bay Ridge, MD 21403 • 1,989
Bay Saint Louis, MS 39520-21 • 8,063
Bay Shore, NY 11706 • 21,279
Bayshore Gardens, FL 34207 • 17,062
Bayside, WI 53217 • 4,789
Bay Springs, MS 39422 • 1,729
Baytown, TX 77520-22 • 63,850
Bay Village, OH 44140 • 17,000
Bayville, NY 11709 • 7,193
Beach, ND 58621 • 1,205
Beach Haven, NJ 08008 • 1,475
Beachwood, NJ 08722 • 9,324
Beachwood, OH 44122 • 10,677
Beacon, NY 12508 • 13,243
Beacon Falls, CT 06403 • 5,877
Beacon Square, FL 34652 • 6,265
Beadle □, SD • 18,253
Bear, DE 19701 • 1,200
Bearden, AR 71720 • 1,021
Beardstown, IL 62618 • 5,270
Bear Lake □, ID • 6,084
Bear Town, MS 39648 • 1,277
Beatrice, NE 68310 • 12,354
Beatty, NV 89003 • 1,623
Beattyville, KY 41311 • 1,131
Beaufort, NC 28516 • 3,808
Beaufort, SC 29901-03 • 9,576
Beaufort □, NC • 42,283
Beaufort □, SC • 86,425
Beaumont, CA 92223 • 9,685
Beaumont, MS 39423 • 1,054
Beaumont, TX 77701-26 • 114,323
Beauregard □, LA • 30,083
Beaver, OK 73932 • 1,584
Beaver, PA 15009 • 5,028
Beaver, UT 84713 • 1,998
Beaver, WV 25813 • 1,244
Beaver □, OK • 6,023
Beaver □, PA • 186,093
Beaver □, UT • 4,765
Beavercreek, OH 45385 • 33,626
Beaverdale, PA 15921 • 1,000
Beaver Dam, KY 42320 • 2,904
Beaver Dam, WI 53916 • 14,196
Beaver Falls, PA 15010 • 10,687
Beaverhead □, MT • 8,424
Beaverton, MI 48612 • 1,150
Beaverton, OR 97005-07 • 53,310
Beckemeyer, IL 62219 • 1,070
Becker □, MN • 27,881
Beckham □, OK • 18,812
Beckley, WV 25801-02 • 18,296
Bedford, IN 47421 • 13,817
Bedford, IA 50833 • 1,528
Bedford, MA 01730 • 13,067
Bedford, NH 03102 • 1,400
Bedford, OH 44146 • 14,822
Bedford, PA 15522 • 3,137
Bedford, TX 76021-22 • 43,762
Bedford, VA 24523 • 6,073
Bedford □, PA • 47,919
Bedford □, TN • 30,411
Bedford □, VA • 45,656
Bedford Heights, OH 44146 • 12,131
Bedford Hills, NY 10507 • 3,140
Bee □, TX • 25,135
Beebe, AR 72012 • 4,455
Beecher, IL 60401 • 2,032
Beecher, MI 48458 • 14,465
Beech Grove, IN 46107 • 13,383
Beech Island, SC 29842 • 1,500
Bee Ridge, FL 34233 • 6,406
Beeville, TX 78102-04 • 13,547
Beggs, OK 74421 • 1,150
Bel Air, MD 21014 • 8,860
Bel Aire, KS 67220 • 3,695
Belchertown, MA 01007 • 2,339
Belcourt, ND 58316 • 2,458
Belding, MI 48809 • 5,969
Belen, NM 87002 • 6,547
Belfast, ME 04915 • 6,355
Belfast, NY 14711 • 1,100
Belfield, ND 58622 • 887
Belford, NJ 07718 • 6,300
Belgrade, MT 59714 • 3,411
Belhaven, NC 27810 • 2,269
Belington, WV 26250 • 1,850
Belknap □, NH • 49,216
Bell, CA 90201 • 34,365
Bell □, KY • 31,506
Bell □, TX • 191,088
Bellair, FL 32073 • 5,200
Bellaire, MI 49615 • 1,104
Bellaire, OH 43906 • 6,028
Bellaire, TX 77401-02 • 13,842
Bella Vista, AR 72712 • 9,083
Bellbrook, OH 45305 • 6,511
Belle, MO 65013 • 1,218
Belle, WV 25015 • 1,421
Belleair, FL 34616 • 3,968
Belle Chasse, LA 70037 • 8,512
Bellefontaine, OH 43311 • 12,142
Bellefontaine Neighbors, MO 63137 • 10,922
Bellefonte, DE 19809 • 1,243
Bellefonte, PA 16823 • 6,358
Belle Fourche, SD 57717 • 4,335
Belle Glade, FL 33430 • 16,177
Belle Isle, FL 32809 • 5,272
Belle Meade, TN 37205 • 2,839
Bellemoor, DE 19802 • 1,040
Belle Plaine, IA 52208 • 2,834
Belle Plaine, KS 67013 • 1,649
Belle Plaine, MN 56011 • 3,149
Belle Vernon, PA 15012 • 1,213
Belleview, FL 32566 • 8,000
Belleview, FL 32620 • 2,666
Belle View, VA 22307 • 4,578
Belleville, IL 62220-25 • 42,785
Belleville, KS 66935 • 2,517
Belleville, MI 48111-12 • 3,270
Belleville, NJ 07109 • 34,213
Belleville, PA 17004 • 1,589
Belleville, WI 53508 • 1,456
Bellevue, ID 83313 • 1,275
Bellevue, IA 52031 • 2,239
Bellevue, KY 41073 • 6,997
Bellevue, NE 68005 • 30,982
Bellevue, OH 44811 • 8,146

Bellevue, PA 15202 • 9,126
Bellevue, WA 98004-09 • 86,874
Bellflower, CA 90706-07 • 61,815
Bell Gardens, CA 90201 • 42,355
Bellingham, MA 02019 • 4,535
Bellingham, WA 98225-27 • 52,179
Bellmawr, NJ 08031 • 12,603
Bellmead, TX 76705 • 8,336
Bellmore, NY 11710 • 16,438
Bellows Falls, VT 05101 • 3,313
Bellport, NY 11713 • 2,572
Bells, TN 38006 • 1,643
Bellville, OH 44813 • 1,568
Bellville, TX 77418 • 3,378
Bellwood, IL 60104 • 20,241
Bellwood, PA 16617 • 1,976
Bellwood, VA 23234 • 6,178
Belmar, NJ 07719 • 5,877
Belmond, IA 50421 • 2,500
Belmont, CA 94002 • 24,127
Belmont, MA 02178 • 24,720
Belmont, MS 38827 • 1,554
Belmont, NY 14813 • 1,006
Belmont, NC 28012 • 8,434
Belmont □, OH • 71,074
Bel-Nor, MO 63133 • 2,935
Beloit, KS 67420 • 4,066
Beloit, OH 44609 • 1,037
Beloit, WI 53511-12 • 35,573
Beloit North, WI 55101 • 5,457
Belpre, OH 45714 • 6,796
Belt, MT 59412 • 571
Belton, MO 64012 • 18,150
Belton, SC 29627 • 4,646
Belton, TX 76513 • 12,476
Beltrami □, MN • 34,384
Beltsville, MD 20705 • 14,476
Belvedere, GA 30032 • 6,100
Belvedere, SC 29841 • 6,133
Belvedere Park, GA 30032 • 18,089
Belvidere, IL 61008 • 15,958
Belvidere, NJ 07823 • 2,669
Belzoni, MS 39038 • 2,536
Bement, IL 61813 • 1,668
Bemidji, MN 56601-19 • 11,245
Benavides, TX 78341 • 1,788
Benbrook, TX 76126 • 19,564
Bend, OR 97701-09 • 20,469
Benewah □, ID • 7,937
Ben Hill □, GA • 16,245
Benicia, CA 94510 • 24,437
Benkelman, NE 69021 • 1,193
Benld, IL 62009 • 1,604
Ben Lomond, CA 95005 • 7,884
Bennett, CO 80102 • 1,757
Bennett □, SD • 3,206
Bennettsville, SC 29512 • 9,345
Bennington, VT 05201 • 9,532
Bennington □, VT • 35,845
Bennion, UT 84118 • 9,575
Bensalem, PA 19020-21 • 52,368
Bensenville, IL 60106 • 17,767
Bensley, VA 23234 • 5,093
Benson, AZ 85602 • 3,824
Benson, MN 56215 • 3,235
Benson, NC 27504 • 2,810
Benson □, ND • 7,198
Bent □, CO • 5,048
Bentleyville, PA 15314 • 2,673
Benton, AR 72015 • 18,177
Benton, IL 62812 • 7,216
Benton, KY 42025 • 3,899
Benton, LA 71006 • 2,047
Benton □, AR • 97,499
Benton □, IN • 9,441
Benton □, IA • 22,429
Benton □, MN • 30,185
Benton □, MS • 8,046
Benton □, MO • 13,859
Benton □, OR • 70,811
Benton □, TN • 14,524
Benton □, WA • 112,560
Benton City, WA 99320 • 1,806
Benton Harbor, MI 49022-23 • 12,818
Benton Heights, MI 49022 • 5,465
Bentonville, AR 72712-14 • 11,257
Benwood, WV 26031 • 1,669
Benzie □, MI • 12,200
Beowawe, NV 89821 • 250
Berea, KY 40403 • 9,126
Berea, OH 44017 • 19,051
Berea, SC 29611 • 13,535
Beresford, SD 57004 • 1,849
Bergen, NY 14416 • 1,103
Bergen □, NJ • 825,380
Bergenfield, NJ 07621 • 24,458
Berkeley, CA 94701-10 • 102,724
Berkeley, IL 60163 • 5,137
Berkeley, MO 63134 • 12,450
Berkeley, RI 02864 • 830
Berkeley □, SC • 128,776
Berkeley □, WV • 59,253
Berkeley Heights, NJ 07922 • 11,980
Berkley, MI 48072 • 16,960
Berks □, PA • 336,523
Berkshire □, MA • 139,352
Berlin, CT 06037 • 1,040
Berlin, MD 21811 • 2,616
Berlin, NH 03570 • 11,824
Berlin, NJ 08009 • 5,672
Berlin, NY 12022 • 1,200
Berlin, PA 15530 • 2,064
Berlin, WI 54923 • 5,371
Bernalillo, NM 87004 • 5,960
Bernalillo □, NM • 480,577
Bernardsville, NJ 07924 • 6,597
Berne, IN 46711 • 3,559
Bernice, LA 71222 • 1,543
Bernie, MO 63822 • 1,847
Berrien □, GA • 14,153
Berrien □, MI • 161,378
Berrien Springs, MI 49103 • 1,927
Berry, AL 35546 • 1,218
Berryville, AR 72616 • 3,212
Berryville, VA 22611 • 3,097
Berthoud, CO 80513 • 2,990
Bertie □, NC • 20,388
Bertrand, MI 49120 • 5,500
Berwick, LA 52031 • 4,375
Berwick, ME 03901 • 2,378
Berwick, PA 18603 • 10,976
Berwyn, IL 60402 • 45,426
Berwyn, PA 19312 • 8,150

Bessemer, AL 35020-23 • 33,497
Bessemer, MI 49911 • 2,272
Bessemer, PA 16112 • 1,196
Bessemer City, NC 28016 • 4,698
Bethalto, IL 62010 • 9,507
Bethany, CT 06525 • 1,170
Bethany, IL 61914 • 1,369
Bethany, MO 64424 • 3,005
Bethany, OK 73008 • 20,075
Bethany, WV 26032 • 1,139
Bethany Beach, DE 19930 • 326
Bethel, AK 99559 • 4,674
Bethel, CT 06801 • 8,835
Bethel, ME 04217 • 1,225
Bethel, NC 27812 • 1,842
Bethel, OH 45106 • 2,407
Bethel, VT 05032 • 1,866
Bethel Acres, OK 74801 • 2,505
Bethel Park, PA 15102 • 33,823
Bethesda, MD 20813-17 • 62,936
Bethesda, OH 43719 • 1,161
Bethlehem, CT 06751 • 1,976
Bethlehem, PA 18015-18 • 71,428
Bethpage, NY 11714 • 15,761
Bettendorf, IA 52722 • 28,132
Beulah, ND 58523 • 3,363
Beverly, MA 01915 • 38,195
Beverly, NJ 08010 • 2,973
Beverly, OH 45715 • 1,444
Beverly Hills, CA 90209-13 • 31,971
Beverly Hills, FL 32665 • 6,163
Beverly Hills, MI 48009 • 10,610
Bexar □, TX • 1,185,394
Bexley, OH 43209 • 13,088
Bibb □, AL • 16,576
Bibb □, GA • 149,967
Bicknell, IN 47512 • 3,357
Biddeford, ME 04005 • 20,710
Bienville □, LA • 15,979
Big Bear City, CA 92314 • 3,500
Big Bend, WI 53103 • 1,299
Big Delta, AK 99737 • 400
Big Flats, NY 14814 • 2,658
Bigfork, MT 59911 • 1,080
Biggs, CA 95917 • 1,581
Big Horn □, MT • 11,337
Big Horn □, WY • 10,525
Big Lake, MN 55309 • 3,113
Big Lake, TX 76932 • 3,672
Big Pine, CA 93513 • 1,158
Big Piney, WY 83113 • 454
Big Rapids, MI 49307 • 12,603
Big Sandy, MT 59520 • 740
Big Sandy, TX 75755 • 1,185
Big Spring, TX 79720-21 • 23,093
Big Stone □, MN • 6,285
Big Stone Gap, VA 24219 • 4,748
Big Timber, MT 59011 • 1,557
Billerica, MA 01821-22 • 6,840
Billings, MT 59101-08 • 81,151
Billings □, ND • 1,108
Billings Heights, MT 59105 • 8,480
Biloxi, MS 39530-35 • 46,319
Biltmore Forest, NC 28803 • 1,327
Bingham, ME 04920 • 1,071
Bingham □, ID • 37,583
Binghamton, NY 13901-05 • 53,008
Birchwood City, MD 20745 • 4,870
Birchwood Park, DE 19711 • 2,250
Bird Island, MN 55310 • 1,326
Birdsboro, PA 19508 • 4,222
Birmingham, AL 35201-61 • 265,968
Birmingham, MI 48009-12 • 19,997
Bisbee, AZ 85603 • 6,288
Biscayne Gardens, FL 33168 • 13,000
Biscayne Park, FL 33161 • 3,068
Biscoe, NC 27209 • 1,484
Bishop, CA 93514-15 • 3,475
Bishop, TX 78343 • 3,337
Bishopville, SC 29010 • 3,560
Bismarck, MO 63624 • 1,579
Bismarck, ND 58501-07 • 49,256
Biwabik, MN 55708 • 1,097
Bixby, OK 74008 • 9,502
Black Canyon City, AZ 85324 • 1,811
Black Creek, WI 54106 • 1,152
Black Diamond, WA 98010 • 1,422
Black Earth, WI 53515 • 1,248
Blackfoot, ID 83221 • 9,646
Blackford □, IN • 14,067
Black Forest, CO 80908 • 8,143
Black Hawk, SD 57718 • 1,955
Black Hawk □, IA • 123,798
Black Jack, MO 63133 • 6,128
Black Lick, PA 15716 • 1,100
Blacklick Estates, OH 43227 • 10,080
Black Mountain, NC 28711 • 5,418
Black Point Resort Club, CT 06357 • 1,200
Black River, NY 13612 • 1,349
Black River Falls, WI 54615 • 3,490
Blacksburg, SC 29702 • 1,907
Blacksburg, VA 24060-63 • 34,590
Blackshear, GA 31516 • 3,263
Blackstone, MA 01504 • 4,460
Blackstone, VA 23824 • 3,497
Blackstock, SC 29817 • 2,688
Blackwell, OK 74631 • 7,538
Blackwood, NJ 08012 • 5,120
Bladen □, NC • 28,663
Bladenboro, NC 28320 • 1,821
Bladensburg, MD 20710 • 8,064
Blades, DE 19973 • 834
Blaine, MN 55434 • 38,975
Blaine, TN 37709 • 1,326
Blaine, WA 98230 • 2,489
Blaine □, ID • 13,552
Blaine □, MT • 6,728
Blaine □, NE • 675
Blaine □, OK • 11,470
Blair, NE 68008 • 6,860
Blair, WI 54616 • 1,126
Blair □, PA • 130,542
Blairsville, PA 15717 • 3,595
Blakely, GA 31723 • 5,595
Blakely, PA 18447 • 7,222
Blanchard, LA 71009 • 1,175
Blanchard, OK 73010 • 4,206
Blanchester, OH 45107 • 4,206
Blanco, TX 78606 • 1,238
Blanco □, TX • 5,972
Bland □, VA • 6,514
Blanding, UT 84511 • 3,162
Blasdell, NY 14219 • 2,900

Blauvelt, NY 10913 • 4,470
Blawnox, PA 15238 • 1,626
Bleckley □, GA • 10,430
Bledsoe □, TN • 9,669
Blende, CO 81006 • 1,330
Blennerhassett, WV 26101 • 2,924
Blissfield, MI 49228 • 3,172
Block Island, RI 02807 • 620
Bloomer, WI 54724 • 3,085
Bloomfield, CT 06002 • 7,120
Bloomfield, IN 47424 • 2,592
Bloomfield, IA 52537 • 2,580
Bloomfield, MO 63825 • 1,800
Bloomfield, NE 68718 • 1,181
Bloomfield, NJ 07003 • 45,061
Bloomfield, NM 87413 • 5,214
Bloomfield Hills, MI 48302-04 • 4,288
Bloomfield Township, MI 48302 • 42,137
Bloomingdale, GA 31302 • 2,271
Bloomingdale, IL 60108 • 16,614
Bloomingdale, NJ 07403 • 7,530
Bloomingdale, TN 37660 • 10,953
Blooming Prairie, MN 55917 • 2,043
Bloomington, CA 92316 • 15,116
Bloomington, IL 61701-04 • 51,972
Bloomington, IN 47401-08 • 60,633
Bloomington, MN 55420 • 86,335
Bloomington, TX 77951 • 1,888
Bloomsburg, PA 17815 • 12,439
Blossburg, PA 16912 • 1,571
Blossom, TX 75416 • 1,440
Blount □, AL • 39,248
Blount □, TN • 85,969
Blountstown, FL 32424 • 2,404
Blountsville, AL 35031 • 1,527
Blountville, TN 37617 • 2,605
Blowing Rock, NC 28605 • 1,257
Blue Ash, OH 45242 • 11,860
Blue Diamond, NV 89004 • 420
Blue Earth, MN 56013 • 3,745
Blue Earth □, MN • 54,044
Bluefield, VA 24605 • 5,363
Bluefield, WV 24701 • 12,756
Blue Grass, IA 52726 • 1,214
Blue Hills, CT 06002 • 3,206
Blue Island, IL 60406 • 21,203
Blue Lake, CA 95525 • 1,235
Blue Mound, IL 62513 • 1,161
Blue Rapids, KS 66411 • 1,131
Blue Ridge, GA 30513 • 1,336
Blue Ridge, VA 24064 • 2,840
Blue Ridge Summit, PA 17214 • 1,800
Blue Springs, MO 64014-15 • 40,153
Bluewell, WV 24701 • 2,752
Bluff City, TN 37618 • 1,390
Bluffdale, UT 84065 • 2,152
Bluff Park, AL 35226 • 8,000
Bluffton, IN 46714 • 9,020
Bluffton, OH 45817 • 3,867
Blythe, CA 92225-26 • 8,428
Blytheville, AR 72315-19 • 22,906
Boalsburg, PA 16827 • 2,206
Boardman, OH 44512 • 38,596
Boardman, OR 97818 • 1,387
Boaz, AL 35957 • 6,928
Boca Grande, FL 33921 • 1,200
Boca Raton, FL 33431-34 • 61,492
Boerne, TX 78006 • 4,274
Bogalusa, LA 70427-29 • 14,280
Bogart, GA 30622 • 1,018
Bogata, TX 75417 • 1,421
Boger City, NC 28092 • 1,373
Bogota, NJ 07603 • 7,824
Bohemia, NY 11716 • 9,556
Boiling Springs, NC 28017 • 2,445
Boiling Springs, PA 17007 • 1,978
Boise, ID 83701-15 • 125,738
Boise □, ID • 3,509
Boise City, OK 73933 • 1,509
Bolingbrook, IL 60440 • 40,843
Bolivar, MO 65613 • 6,845
Bolivar, NY 14715 • 1,261
Bolivar, TN 38008 • 5,969
Bolivar □, MS • 41,875
Bollinger □, MO • 10,619
Bolton Landing, NY 12814 • 1,600
Bon Air, VA 23235 • 16,413
Bonaventure, FL 33317 • 6,000
Bond □, IL • 14,991
Bondsville, MA 01009 • 1,992
Bonduel, WI 54107 • 1,210
Bondurant, IA 50035 • 1,584
Bonham, TX 75418 • 6,686
Bon Homme □, SD • 7,089
Bonifay, FL 32425 • 2,612
Bonita, CA 91903 • 12,542
Bonita Springs, FL 33923 • 13,600
Bonneauville, PA 17325 • 1,282
Bonner □, ID • 26,622
Bonners Ferry, ID 83805 • 2,193
Bonner Springs, KS 66012 • 6,413
Bonne Terre, MO 63628 • 3,871
Bonneville □, ID • 72,207
Bonney Lake, WA 98390 • 7,494
Bonnie Doone, NC 28303 • 3,893
Bono, AR 72416 • 1,220
Booker, TX 79005 • 1,236
Boomer, WV 25031 • 1,051
Boone, IA 50036 • 12,392
Boone, NC 28607 • 12,915
Boone □, AR • 28,297
Boone □, IL • 30,806
Boone □, IN • 38,147
Boone □, IA • 25,186
Boone □, KY • 57,589
Boone □, MO • 112,379
Boone □, NE • 6,667
Boone □, WV • 25,870
Booneville, AR 72927 • 3,804
Booneville, MS 38829 • 7,955
Boonsboro, MD 21713 • 2,445
Boonton, NJ 07005 • 8,343
Booneville, CA 95415 • 1,000
Boonville, IN 47601 • 6,724
Boonville, MO 65233 • 7,095
Boonville, NY 13309 • 2,220
Boonville, NC 27011 • 1,009
Boothbay Harbor, ME 04538 • 1,267
Borden □, TX • 799
Bordentown, NJ 08505 • 4,341
Borger, TX 79007-08 • 15,675
Boron, CA 93516 • 2,101
Borrego Springs, CA 92004 • 2,244

Boscobel, WI 53805 • 2,706
Bosque □, TX • 15,125
Bossert Estates, NJ 08505 • 1,830
Bossier □, LA • 86,088
Bossier City, LA 71111-13 • 52,721
Boston, GA 31626 • 1,395
Boston, MA 02101-99 • 574,283
Boswell, PA 15531 • 1,485
Botetourt □, VA • 24,992
Bothell, WA 98011-12 • 12,345
Botkins, OH 45306 • 1,340
Bottineau, ND 58318 • 2,598
Bottineau □, ND • 8,011
Boulder, CO 80301-08 • 83,312
Boulder, MT 59632 • 1,316
Boulder □, CO • 225,339
Boulder City, NV 89005-06 • 12,567
Boulder Creek, CA 95006 • 6,725
Boulder Hill, IL 60538 • 8,894
Boulevard Heights, MD 20743 • 1,820
Boundary □, ID • 8,332
Bound Brook, NJ 08805 • 9,487
Bountiful, UT 84010-11 • 36,659
Bourbon, IN 46504 • 1,672
Bourbon, MO 65441 • 1,188
Bourbon □, KS • 14,966
Bourbon □, KY • 19,236
Bourbonnais, IL 60914 • 13,934
Bourg, LA 70343 • 2,073
Bourne, MA 02532 • 1,284
Boutte, LA 70039 • 1,200
Bovina, TX 79009 • 1,549
Bowdon, GA 30108 • 1,981
Bowie, MD 20715-21 • 37,589
Bowie, TX 76230 • 4,990
Bowie □, TX • 81,665
Bowling Green, FL 33834 • 1,836
Bowling Green, KY 42101-04 • 40,641
Bowling Green, MO 63334 • 2,976
Bowling Green, OH 43402 • 28,176
Bowman, ND 58623 • 1,741
Bowman, SC 29018 • 1,063
Bowman □, ND • 3,596
Box Butte □, NE • 13,130
Box Elder, SD 57719 • 2,680
Box Elder □, UT • 36,485
Boxford, MA 01921 • 2,472
Boyce, LA 71409 • 1,361
Boyd □, KY • 51,150
Boyd □, NE • 2,835
Boyertown, PA 19512 • 3,759
Boyes Hot Springs, CA 95416 • 5,973
Boyle □, KY • 25,641
Boyne City, MI 49712 • 3,478
Boynton Beach, FL 33435-37 • 46,194
Bozeman, MT 59715 • 22,660
Bracken □, KY • 7,766
Brackenridge, PA 15014 • 3,784
Brackettville, TX 78832 • 1,740
Braddock, PA 15104 • 4,682
Braddock Heights, MD 21714 • 4,778
Bradenton, FL 34201-10 • 43,779
Bradenville, PA 15620 • 1,100
Bradford, OH 45308 • 2,005
Bradford, PA 16701 • 9,625
Bradford, RI 02808 • 1,604
Bradford, TN 38316 • 1,154
Bradford, VT 05033 • 672
Bradford □, FL • 22,515
Bradford □, PA • 60,967
Bradfordwoods, PA 15015 • 1,329
Bradley, IL 60915 • 10,792
Bradley, WV 25818 • 2,144
Bradley □, AR • 11,793
Bradley □, TN • 73,712
Bradley Beach, NJ 07720 • 4,475
Bradner, OH 43406 • 1,093
Brady, TX 76825 • 5,946
Braham, MN 55006 • 1,139
Braidwood, IL 60408 • 3,584
Brainerd, MN 56401 • 12,353
Braintree, MA 02184 • 33,836
Branch □, MI • 41,502
Branch Village, RI 02895 • 400
Branchville, SC 29432 • 1,107
Brandenburg, KY 40108 • 1,857
Brandon, FL 33510 • 57,985
Brandon, MS 39042-43 • 11,077
Brandon, SD 29611 • 2,170
Brandon, SD 57005 • 3,543
Brandon, VT 05733 • 1,902
Brandywine, MD 20613 • 1,406
Branford, CT 06405 • 27,603
Branford Hills, CT 06405 • 3,460
Branson, MO 65616 • 3,706
Brantley, AL 36009 • 1,015
Brantley □, GA • 11,077
Brant Rock, MA 02020 • 1,850
Brattenahl, OH 44108 • 1,356
Brattleboro, VT 05301-04 • 8,612
Brawley, CA 92227 • 18,923
Braxton □, WV • 12,998
Brazil, IN 47834 • 7,640
Brazoria, TX 77422 • 2,717
Brazoria □, TX • 191,707
Brazos □, TX • 121,862
Brea, CA 92621-22 • 32,873
Breathitt □, KY • 15,703
Breaux Bridge, LA 70517 • 6,515
Breckenridge, CO 80424 • 1,285
Breckenridge, MI 48615 • 1,301
Breckenridge, MN 56520 • 3,708
Breckenridge, TX 76024 • 5,665
Breckenridge Hills, MO 63114 • 5,404
Breckinridge □, KY • 16,312
Brecksville, OH 44141 • 11,818
Breese, IL 62230 • 3,567
Bremen, GA 30110 • 4,356
Bremen, IN 46506 • 4,725
Bremen, OH 43107 • 1,386
Bremer □, IA • 22,813
Bremerton, WA 98310-15 • 38,142
Bremond, TX 76629 • 1,110
Brenham, TX 77833-34 • 11,952
Brent, AL 35034 • 2,776
Brent, FL 32503 • 21,624
Brentwood, CA 94513 • 7,563
Brentwood, MD 20722 • 3,005
Brentwood, MO 63144 • 8,150
Brentwood, NY 11717 • 45,218
Brentwood, NY • 45,218
Brentwood, OH 45231 • 3,568

Brentwood, PA 15227 • 10,823
Brentwood, SC 29405 • 2,000
Brentwood, TN 37027 • 16,392
Brevard, NC 28712 • 5,388
Brevard □, FL • 398,978
Brewer, ME 04412 • 9,021
Brewster, MA 02631 • 1,818
Brewster, NY 10509 • 1,566
Brewster, OH 44613 • 2,307
Brewster, WA 98812 • 1,633
Brewster □, TX • 8,681
Brewton, AL 36426-27 • 5,885
Briarcliff Manor, NY 10510 • 7,070
Brick [Township], NJ 08723 • 55,473
Bridge City, LA 70094 • 8,327
Bridge City, TX 77611 • 8,034
Bridgehampton, NY 11932 • 1,997
Bridgeport, AL 35740 • 2,936
Bridgeport, CT 06601-50 • 141,686
Bridgeport, IL 62417 • 2,118
Bridgeport, MI 48722 • 8,569
Bridgeport, NE 69336 • 1,581
Bridgeport, OH 43912 • 2,318
Bridgeport, PA 19405 • 4,292
Bridgeport, TX 76026 • 3,581
Bridgeport, WA 98813 • 1,498
Bridgeport, WV 26330 • 6,739
Bridger, MT 59014 • 692
Bridgeton, MO 63044 • 17,779
Bridgeton, NJ 08302 • 18,942
Bridgeton, OH 45211 • 11,460
Bridgeview, IL 60455 • 14,402
Bridgeville, DE 19933 • 1,210
Bridgeville, PA 15017 • 5,445
Bridgewater, MA 02324 • 7,242
Bridgewater, NJ 08807 • 5,630
Bridgewater, VA 22812 • 3,918
Bridgman, MI 49106 • 2,140
Bridgton, ME 04009 • 2,195
Brielle, NJ 08730 • 4,406
Brigantine, NJ 08203 • 11,354
Brigham City, UT 84302 • 15,644
Brighton, AL 35020 • 4,518
Brighton, CO 80601 • 14,203
Brighton, IL 62012 • 2,270
Brighton, MI 48116 • 5,686
Brighton, NY 14610 • 34,455
Brilliant, OH 43913 • 1,672
Brillion, WI 54110 • 2,840
Brinkley, AR 72021 • 4,234
Briscoe □, TX • 1,971
Bristol, CT 06010-11 • 60,640
Bristol, IN 46507 • 1,133
Bristol, NH 03222 • 1,483
Bristol, RI 02809 • 21,625
Bristol, TN 37620-25 • 23,421
Bristol, VT 05443 • 1,801
Bristol, VA 24201-03 • 18,426
Bristol □, MA • 506,325
Bristol □, RI • 48,859
Bristol [Township], PA 19007 • 58,773
Bristow, OK 74010 • 4,062
Britt, IA 50423 • 2,133
Britton, SD 57430 • 1,394
Broadalbin, NY 12025 • 1,397
Broad Brook, CT 06016 • 1,280
Broadkill Beach, DE 19968 • 390
Broadus, MT 59317 • 572
Broadview, IL 60153 • 8,713
Broadview Heights, OH 44141 • 12,219
Broadview Park, FL 33314 • 6,109
Broadwater □, MT • 3,318
Broadway, VA 22815 • 1,209
Brockport, NY 14420 • 8,749
Brockton, MA 02401-05 • 92,788
Brockway, PA 15824 • 2,207
Brocton, NY 14716 • 1,387
Brodhead, KY 40409 • 1,142
Brodhead, WI 53520 • 3,165
Brodheadsville, PA 18322 • 1,500
Broken Arrow, OK 74011-14 • 58,043
Broken Bow, NE 68822 • 3,778
Broken Bow, OK 74728 • 3,961
Bronson, MI 49028 • 2,342
Bronx □, NY • 1,203,789
Bronxville, NY 10708 • 6,028
Brooke □, WV • 26,992
Brookfield, CT 06804 • 1,500
Brookfield, IL 60513 • 18,876
Brookfield, MA 01506 • 2,968
Brookfield, MO 64628 • 4,888
Brookfield, WI 53005 • 35,184
Brookfield Center, CT 06804 • 1,400
Brookhaven, MS 39601 • 10,243
Brookhaven, PA 19015 • 8,567
Brookhaven, WV 26505 • 3,836
Brookings, OR 97415 • 4,400
Brookings, SD 57006 • 16,270
Brookings □, SD • 25,207
Brooklawn, NJ 08030 • 1,805
Brookline, MA 02146 • 54,718
Brooklyn, CT 06234 • 1,400
Brooklyn, IN 46111 • 1,162
Brooklyn, IA 52211 • 1,439
Brooklyn, OH 44144 • 11,706
Brooklyn, SC 29720 • 4,855
Brooklyn Center, MN 55429 • 28,887
Brooklyn Park, MD 21225 • 10,987
Brooklyn Park, MN 55443 • 56,381
Brookneal, VA 24528 • 1,344
Brook Park, OH 44142 • 22,865
Brookport, IL 62910 • 1,070
Brooks, KY 40109 • 2,464
Brooks □, GA • 15,398
Brooks □, TX • 8,204
Brookshire, TX 77423 • 2,922
Brookside, AL 35036 • 1,365
Brookside, DE 19713 • 15,307
Brookston, IN 47923 • 1,804
Brooksville, FL 34601-14 • 7,440
Brooksville, MS 39739 • 1,098
Brookville, IN 47012 • 2,529
Brookville, NY 11545 • 3,716
Brookville, OH 45309 • 4,621
Brookville, PA 15825 • 4,184
Brookwood, NJ 08527 • 5,500
Broomall, PA 19008 • 10,930
Broome □, NY • 212,160
Broomfield, CO 80020-21 • 24,638
Broussard, LA 70518 • 3,213
Broward □, FL • 1,255,488
Browardale, FL 33311 • 6,257

Brown □, IL • 5,836
Brown □, IN • 14,080
Brown □, KS • 11,128
Brown □, MN • 26,984
Brown □, NE • 3,657
Brown □, OH • 34,966
Brown □, SD • 35,580
Brown □, TX • 34,371
Brown □, WI • 194,594
Brown City, MI 48416 • 1,244
Brown Deer, WI 53209 • 12,236
Brownfield, TX 79316 • 9,560
Brownfields, LA 70811 • 5,229
Browning, MT 59417 • 1,170
Brownsburg, IN 46112 • 7,628
Browns Mills, NJ 08015 • 11,429
Brownstown, IN 47220 • 2,872
Brownsville, FL 33142 • 15,607
Brownsville, OR 97327 • 1,281
Brownsville, PA 15417 • 3,164
Brownsville, TN 38012 • 10,019
Brownsville, TX 78520-26 • 98,962
Brownville, LA 71291 • 1,700
Brownville, NY 13615 • 1,138
Brownwood, TX 76803-04 • 18,387
Broxton, GA 31519 • 1,211
Broyhill Park, VA 22042 • 3,600
Bruce, MS 38915 • 2,127
Bruceton, TN 38317 • 1,586
Brule □, SD • 5,485
Brundidge, AL 36010 • 2,472
Brunswick, GA 31520-22 • 16,433
Brunswick, ME 04011 • 14,683
Brunswick, MD 21716 • 5,117
Brunswick, MO 65236 • 1,074
Brunswick, OH 44212 • 28,230
Brunswick □, NC • 50,985
Brunswick □, VA • 15,987
Brush, CO 80723 • 4,165
Brusly, LA 70719 • 1,824
Bryan, OH 43506 • 8,348
Bryan, TX 77801-06 • 55,002
Bryan □, GA • 15,438
Bryan □, OK • 32,089
Bryans Road, MD 20616 • 3,809
Bryant, AR 72022 • 5,269
Bryantville, MA 02327 • 1,800
Bryn Mawr, WA 98178 • 1,500
Bryson City, NC 28713 • 1,145
Buchanan, GA 30113 • 1,009
Buchanan, MI 49107 • 4,992
Buchanan, VA 24066 • 1,222
Buchanan □, IA • 20,844
Buchanan □, MO • 83,083
Buchanan □, VA • 31,333
Buckeye, AZ 85326 • 5,038
Buckeye Lake, OH 43008 • 2,986
Buckhannon, WV 26201 • 5,909
Buckingham □, VA • 11,751
Buckley, WA 98321 • 3,516
Bucknell Manor, VA 22307 • 2,300
Buckner, MO 64016 • 2,873
Bucks □, PA • 541,174
Bucksport, ME 04416 • 2,989
Bucksport, SC 29527 • 1,022
Bucyrus, OH 44820 • 13,496
Buda, TX 78610 • 1,795
Budd Lake 0L, NJ • 7,272
Buechel, KY 40218 • 7,081
Buena, NJ 08310 • 4,441
Buena Park, CA 90620-24 • 68,784
Buena Vista, CO 81211 • 1,752
Buena Vista, FL 34691 • 3,000
Buena Vista, GA 31803 • 1,472
Buena Vista, VA 24416 • 6,406
Buena Vista □, IA • 19,965
Buffalo, IA 52728 • 1,260
Buffalo, MN 55313 • 6,856
Buffalo, MO 65622 • 2,414
Buffalo, NY 14201-40 • 328,123
Buffalo, OK 73834 • 1,312
Buffalo, SC 29321 • 1,569
Buffalo, TX 75831 • 1,555
Buffalo, WY 82834 • 3,302
Buffalo □, NE • 37,447
Buffalo □, SD • 1,759
Buffalo □, WI • 13,584
Buffalo Center, IA 50424 • 1,081
Buffalo Grove, IL 60089 • 36,427
Buford, GA 30518 • 8,771
Buhl, ID 83316 • 3,516
Buhler, KS 67522 • 1,277
Buies Creek, NC 27506 • 2,085
Bullhead City, AZ 86430 • 21,951
Bullitt □, KY • 47,567
Bullock □, GA • 43,125
Bullock □, AL • 11,042
Bull Shoals, AR 72619 • 1,534
Buna, TX 77612 • 1,900
Bunche Park, FL 33054 • 4,000
Buncombe □, NC • 174,821
Bunker Hill, IL 62014 • 1,722
Bunker Hill, OR 97420 • 1,242
Bunkerville, NV 89007 • 300
Bunkie, LA 71322 • 5,044
Bunnell, FL 32110 • 1,600
Buras, LA 70041 • 1,600
Burbank, CA 91501-10 • 93,643
Burbank, IL 60459 • 27,600
Burdickville, RI 02808 • 500
Bureau □, IL • 35,688
Burgaw, NC 28425 • 1,807
Burgettstown, PA 15021 • 1,634
Burgin, KY 40310 • 1,009
Burien, WA 98062 • 25,089
Burkburnett, TX 76354 • 10,145
Burke, VA 22015 • 57,734
Burke □, GA • 20,579
Burke □, NC • 75,744
Burke □, ND • 3,002
Burkesville, KY 42717 • 1,815
Burleigh □, ND • 60,131
Burleson, TX 76028 • 16,113
Burleson □, TX • 13,625
Burley, ID 83318 • 8,702
Burlingame, CA 94010-11 • 26,801
Burlingame, KS 66413 • 1,074
Burlington, CO 80807 • 2,941
Burlington, IA 52601 • 27,208
Burlington, KS 66839 • 2,735
Burlington, KY 41005 • 6,070
Burlington, MA 01803 • 23,302

Burlington, NJ 08016 • 9,835
Burlington, NC 27215-17 • 39,498
Burlington, ND 58722 • 995
Burlington, VT 05401-04 • 39,127
Burlington, WA 98233 • 4,349
Burlington, WI 53105 • 8,855
Burlington □, NJ • 395,066
Burnet, TX 78611 • 3,423
Burnet □, TX • 22,677
Burnett □, WI • 13,084
Burney, CA 96013 • 3,423
Burnham, NY 17009 • 2,197
Burns, OR 97720 • 2,913
Burns, TN 37029 • 1,127
Burns, WY 82053 • 254
Burns Flat, OK 73624 • 1,027
Burnside, LA 70738 • 5,288
Burnsville, MN 55337 • 51,288
Burnsville, NC 28714 • 1,482
Burnt Hills, NY 12027 • 1,550
Burr Ridge, IL 60521 • 7,669
Burt □, NE • 7,868
Burton, MI 48509 • 27,617
Burton, OH 44021 • 1,349
Burton, SC 29902 • 6,917
Burtonsville, MD 20866 • 5,853
Burwell, NE 68823 • 1,278
Bushnell, FL 33513 • 1,998
Bushnell, IL 61422 • 3,288
Butler, AL 36904 • 1,872
Butler, IN 46721 • 2,601
Butler, MO 64730 • 4,099
Butler, NJ 07405 • 7,392
Butler, PA 16001-03 • 15,714
Butler, WI 53007 • 2,079
Butler □, AL • 21,892
Butler □, IA • 15,731
Butler □, KS • 50,580
Butler □, KY • 11,245
Butler □, MO • 38,765
Butler □, NE • 8,601
Butler □, OH • 291,479
Butler □, PA • 152,013
Butner, NC 27509 • 4,679
Butte, MT 59701-03 • 33,336
Butte □, CA • 182,120
Butte □, ID • 2,918
Butte □, SD • 7,914
Buttonwillow, CA 93206 • 1,301
Butts □, GA • 15,326
Buxton, NC 27920 • 1,300
Buzzards Bay, MA 02532 • 3,250
Byers, CO 80103 • 1,065
Byesville, OH 43723 • 2,435
Byfield, MA 01922 • 1,200
Bylas, AZ 85530 • 1,219
Byram, CT 06010 • 2,284
Byron, GA 31008 • 2,276
Byron, IL 61010 • 2,284
Byron, MN 55920 • 2,441
Byron, WY 82412 • 470

C

Cabarrus □, NC • 98,935
Cabell □, WV • 96,827
Cabin Creek, WV 25035 • 1,300
Cabin John, MD 20818 • 1,690
Cabool, MO 65689 • 2,006
Cabot, AR 72023 • 8,319
Cache, OK 73527 • 2,251
Cache □, UT • 70,183
Caddo □, LA • 248,253
Caddo □, OK • 29,550
Cadillac, MI 49601 • 10,104
Cadiz, KY 42211 • 2,148
Cadiz, OH 43907 • 3,439
Cadott, WI 54727 • 1,328
Cahaba Heights, AL 35243 • 4,778
Cahokia, IL 62206 • 17,550
Cairnbrooke, PA 15924 • 1,081
Cairo, GA 31728 • 9,035
Cairo, IL 62914 • 4,846
Cairo, NY 12413 • 1,273
Calais, ME 04619 • 3,963
Calaveras □, CA • 31,998
Calavo Gardens, CA 91941 • 6,100
Calcasieu □, LA • 168,134
Calcutta, OH 43920 • 1,212
Caldwell, ID 83605-06 • 18,400
Caldwell, KS 67022 • 1,351
Caldwell, NJ 07006 • 7,549
Caldwell, OH 43724 • 1,786
Caldwell, TX 77836 • 3,181
Caldwell □, KY • 13,232
Caldwell □, LA • 9,810
Caldwell □, MO • 8,380
Caldwell □, NC • 70,709
Caldwell □, TX • 26,392
Caledonia, MN 55921 • 2,846
Caledonia, NY 14423 • 2,262
Caledonia □, VT • 27,846
Calera, AL 35040 • 2,136
Calera, OK 74730 • 1,536
Calexico, CA 92231-32 • 18,633
Calhoun, GA 30701 • 7,135
Calhoun □, AL • 116,034
Calhoun □, AR • 5,826
Calhoun □, FL • 11,011
Calhoun □, GA • 5,013
Calhoun □, IL • 5,322
Calhoun □, IA • 11,508
Calhoun □, MI • 135,982
Calhoun □, MS • 14,908
Calhoun □, SC • 12,753
Calhoun □, TX • 19,053
Calhoun □, WV • 7,885
Calhoun City, MS 38916 • 1,838
Calhoun Falls, SC 29628 • 2,328
Caliente, NV 89008 • 1,111
Califon, NJ 07830 • 1,073
California, MD 20619 • 7,626
California, MO 65018 • 3,465
California, PA 15419 • 5,748
Calipatria, CA 92233 • 2,690
Calistoga, CA 94515 • 4,468
Callahan □, TX • 11,859
Callaway, FL 32401 • 12,253
Callaway □, MO • 32,809
Calloway □, KY • 30,735
Calmar, IA 52132 • 1,026
Calumet □, WI • 34,291

Calumet City, IL 60409 • 37,840	Carbondale, CO 81623 • 3,004	Cassia □, ID • 19,532	Chadbourn, NC 28431 • 2,005	Cherry Hill, NJ 08002-03 • 69,319
Calumet Park, IL 60643 • 8,418	Carbondale, IL 62901-03 • 27,033	Cassopolis, MI 49031 • 1,822	Chadds Ford, PA 19317 • 1,200	Cherry Hills Village, CO 80110 • 5,245
Calvert, TX 77837 • 1,536	Carbondale, KS 66414 • 1,526	Cassville, MO 65625 • 2,371	Chadron, NE 69337 • 5,588	Cherryland, CA 94541 • 11,088
Calvert □, MD • 51,372	Carbondale, PA 18407 • 10,664	Cassville, WI 53806 • 1,144	Chadwicks, NY 13319 • 2,000	Cherryvale, KS 67335 • 2,464
Calvert City, KY 42029 • 2,531	Carbon Hill, AL 35549 • 2,115	Castanea, PA 17726 • 1,123	Chaffee, MO 63740 • 3,059	Cherry Valley, CA 92223 • 5,945
Calverton, MD 20705 • 12,046	Cardington, OH 43315 • 1,770	Castile, NY 14427 • 1,078	Chaffee □, CO • 12,684	Cherry Valley, IL 61016 • 1,615
Calverton Park, MO 63136 • 1,404	Carencro, LA 70520 • 5,429	Castle Dale, UT 84513 • 1,704	Chaffin, MA 01520 • 3,980	Cherry Valley, MA 01611 • 1,120
Camarillo, CA 93010-11 • 52,303	Carey, OH 43316 • 3,684	Castle Hayne, NC 28429 • 4,146	Chagrin Falls, OH 44022 • 4,146	Cherryville, NC 28021 • 4,756
Camanche, IA 52730 • 4,436	Caribou, ME 04736 • 9,415	Castle Hills, DE 19720 • 1,475	Chalfonte, DE 19810 • 1,740	Chesaning, MI 48616 • 2,567
Camas, WA 98607 • 6,442	Caribou □, ID • 6,963	Castle Park, CA 92011 • 6,300	Chalmette, LA 70043-44 • 31,860	Chesapeake, OH 45619 • 1,073
Camas □, ID • 727	Carle Place, NY 11514 • 5,107	Castle Point, MO 63136 • 7,800	Chama, NM 87520 • 1,048	Chesapeake, VA 23320-28 • 151,976
Cambria, CA 93428 • 5,382	Carleton, MI 48117 • 2,770	Castle Rock, CO 80104 • 8,708	Chamberlain, SD 57325 • 2,347	Chesapeake, WV 25315 • 1,896
Cambria □, PA • 163,029	Carlin, NV 89822 • 2,220	Castle Rock, WA 98611 • 2,067	Chambers □, AL • 36,876	Chesapeake Beach, MD 20732 • 2,403
Cambrian Park, CA 95124 • 2,998	Carlinville, IL 62626 • 5,416	Castle Shannon, PA 15234 • 9,135	Chambers □, TX • 20,088	Cheshire, CT 06410 • 25,684
Cambridge, IL 61238 • 2,124	Carlisle, AR 72024 • 2,253	Castleton, VT 05735 • 600	Chambersburg, PA 17201 • 16,647	Cheshire, MA 01225 • 1,100
Cambridge, MD 21613 • 11,514	Carlisle, IA 50047 • 3,241	Castleton on Hudson, NY 12033 • 1,491	Chamblee, GA 30341 • 7,668	Cheshire □, NH • 70,121
Cambridge, MA 02138 • 95,802	Carlisle, KY 40311 • 1,639	Castlewood, VA 24224 • 2,110	Champaign, IL 61820-21 • 63,502	Chesilhurst, NJ 08089 • 1,526
Cambridge, MN 55008 • 4,999	Carlisle, OH 45005 • 4,872	Castro □, TX • 9,070	Champaign □, IL • 173,025	Chesnee, SC 29323 • 1,280
Cambridge, NE 69022 • 1,107	Carlisle, PA 17013 • 18,419	Castro Valley, CA 94546 • 48,619	Champaign □, OH • 36,019	Chester, CA 96020 • 2,082
Cambridge, NY 12816 • 1,906	Carlisle □, KY • 5,238	Castroville, TX 78009 • 2,159	Champlain, NY 12919 • 1,273	Chester, CT 06412 • 1,563
Cambridge, OH 43725 • 11,748	Carl Junction, MO 64834 • 4,123	Caswell □, NC • 20,693	Champlin, MN 55316 • 16,849	Chester, IL 62233 • 8,194
Cambridge City, IN 47327 • 2,091	Carlsbad, CA 92008-09 • 63,126	Catahoula □, LA • 11,065	Champion, OH 44481 • 5,270	Chester, MT 59522 • 942
Cambridge Springs, PA 16403 • 1,837	Carlsbad, NM 88220-21 • 24,952	Catalina Foothills, AZ 85718 • 1,470	Chandler, AZ 85224-27 • 90,533	Chester, NJ 07930 • 1,214
Camden, AL 36726 • 2,414	Carlstadt, NJ 07072 • 5,510	Catasauqua, PA 18032 • 6,662	Chandler, IN 47610 • 3,099	Chester, NY 10918 • 3,270
Camden, AR 71701 • 14,380	Carlton, OR 97111 • 1,289	Cataumet, MA 02534 • 1,500	Chandler, OK 74834 • 2,596	Chester, PA 19013-16 • 41,856
Camden, DE 19934 • 1,899	Carlton □, MN • 29,259	Catawba □, NC • 118,412	Chandler, TX 75758 • 1,630	Chester, SC 29706 • 7,158
Camden, ME 04843 • 4,022	Carlyle, IL 62231 • 3,474	Catawissa, PA 17820 • 1,683	Chandler Heights, AZ 85227 • 1,000	Chester, VT 05143 • 550
Camden, NJ 08101-10 • 87,492	Carmel, CA 93921-23 • 4,239	Cathedral City, CA 92234-35 • 30,085	Chanhassen, MN 55317 • 11,732	Chester, VA 23831 • 14,896
Camden, NY 13316 • 2,552	Carmel, IN 46032 • 25,380	Catlettsburg, KY 41129 • 2,231	Channahon, IL 60410 • 4,266	Chester, WV 26034 • 2,905
Camden, OH 45311 • 2,210	Carmel, NY 10512 • 3,395	Catlin, IL 61817 • 2,173	Channel Lake, IL 60002 • 1,660	Chester □, PA • 376,396
Camden, SC 29020 • 6,696	Carmi, IL 62821 • 5,564	Catonsville, MD 21228 • 35,233	Channelview, TX 77530 • 25,564	Chester □, SC • 32,170
Camden, TN 38320 • 3,643	Carmichael, CA 95608-09 • 48,702	Catoosa, OK 74015 • 2,954	Chantilly, VA 22021-22 • 29,337	Chester □, TN • 12,819
Camden □, GA • 30,167	Carnation, WA 98014 • 1,243	Catoosa □, GA • 42,464	Chanute, KS 66720 • 9,488	Chester Depot, VT 05144 • 500
Camden □, MO • 27,495	Carnegie, OK 73015 • 1,593	Catron □, NM • 2,563	Chapel Hill, NC 27514-16 • 38,719	Chesterfield, IN 46017 • 2,730
Camden □, NC • 5,904	Carnegie, PA 15106 • 9,278	Catskill, NY 12414 • 4,690	Chapel Square, VA 22003 • 2,400	Chesterfield, SC 29709 • 1,373
Camden □, NJ • 502,824	Carney, NJ 21234 • 25,578	Cattaraugus, NY 14719 • 1,100	Chapman, KS 67431 • 1,264	Chesterfield □, SC • 38,577
Camdenton, MO 65020 • 2,561	Carneys Point, NJ 08069 • 7,686	Cattaraugus □, NY • 84,234	Chapmanville, WV 25508 • 1,110	Chesterfield □, VA • 209,274
Camelot, WA 98002 • 4,900	Carnot, PA 15108 • 4,750	Cavalier, ND 58220 • 1,508	Chappaqua, NY 10514 • 6,380	Chesterton, IN 46304 • 9,124
Cameron, LA 70631 • 2,041	Caro, MI 48723 • 4,054	Cavalier □, ND • 6,064	Chardon, OH 44024 • 4,446	Chestertown, MD 21620 • 4,005
Cameron, MO 64429 • 4,831	Carol City, FL 33055 • 53,331	Cave City, AR 72521 • 1,503	Chariton, IA 50049 • 4,616	Chester Township, PA 19013 • 5,399
Cameron, TX 76520 • 5,580	Caroleen, NC 28019 • 1,100	Cave City, KY 42127 • 1,953	Chariton □, MO • 9,202	Chestnut Hill Estates, DE 19713 • 1,730
Cameron, WV 26033 • 1,177	Carolina Beach, NC 28428 • 3,630	Cave Creek, AZ 85331 • 2,925	Charleroi, PA 15022 • 5,014	Chestnut Ridge, NY 10952 • 7,517
Cameron, WI 54822 • 1,273	Caroline □, MD • 27,035	Cave Junction, OR 97523 • 1,126	Charles □, MD • 101,154	Cheswick, PA 15024 • 1,971
Cameron □, LA • 9,260	Caroline □, VA • 19,217	Cave Spring, VA 24018 • 24,053	Charles City, IA 50616 • 7,878	Cheswold, DE 19936 • 321
Cameron □, PA • 5,913	Carol Stream, IL 60188 • 31,716	Cavetown, MD 21720 • 1,533	Charles City □, VA • 6,282	Chetek, WI 54728 • 1,953
Cameron □, TX • 260,120	Carpentersville, IL 60110 • 23,049	Cayce, SC 29033 • 11,163	Charles Mix □, SD • 9,131	Chetopa, KS 67336 • 1,357
Cameron Park, CA 95682 • 11,897	Carpinteria, CA 93013-14 • 13,747	Cayuga, IN 47928 • 1,083	Charleston, AR 72933 • 2,128	Chevak, AK 99563 • 598
Camilla, GA 31730 • 5,008	Carrabelle, FL 32322 • 1,200	Cayuga □, NY • 82,313	Charleston, IL 61920 • 20,398	Cheverly, MD 20785 • 6,023
Camino, CA 95709 • 1,500	Carrboro, NC 27510 • 11,553	Cayuga Heights, NY 14850 • 3,457	Charleston, MS 38921 • 2,328	Cheviot, OH 45211 • 9,616
Camp □, TX • 9,904	Carrier Mills, IL 62917 • 1,991	Cazenovia, NY 13035 • 3,007	Charleston, MO 63834 • 5,085	Chevy Chase, MD 20815 • 8,559
Campbell, CA 95008-09 • 36,048	Carrington, ND 58421 • 2,267	Cecil □, MD • 71,347	Charleston, SC 29401-22 • 80,414	Chewelah, WA 99109 • 1,945
Campbell, FL 34746 • 3,884	Carrizo Springs, TX 78834 • 5,745	Cedar □, IA • 17,381	Charleston, WV 25301-75 • 57,287	Cheyenne, WY 82001-09 • 50,008
Campbell, MO 63933 • 2,165	Carrizozo, NM 88301 • 1,075	Cedar □, MO • 12,093	Charleston □, SC • 295,039	Cheyenne □, CO • 2,397
Campbell, OH 44405 • 10,038	Carroll, IA 51401 • 9,579	Cedar □, NE • 10,131	Charlestown, IN 47111 • 5,889	Cheyenne □, KS • 3,243
Campbell □, KY • 83,866	Carroll □, AR • 18,654	Cedar Bluff, AL 35959 • 1,174	Charlestown, NH 03603 • 1,173	Cheyenne □, NE • 9,494
Campbell □, SD • 1,965	Carroll □, GA • 71,422	Cedar Bluff Two, TN 37722 • 2,000	Charlestown, RI 02813 • 1,500	Cheyenne Wells, CO 80810 • 1,128
Campbell □, TN • 35,079	Carroll □, IL • 16,805	Cedarburg, WI 53012 • 9,895	Charles Town, WV 25414 • 3,122	Chicago, IL 60601-99 • 2,783,726
Campbell □, VA • 47,572	Carroll □, IN • 18,809	Cedar City, UT 84720-22 • 13,443	Charlevoix, MI 49720 • 3,116	Chicago Heights, IL 60411 • 33,072
Campbell □, WY • 29,370	Carroll □, IA • 21,423	Cedar Crest, NM 87008 • 1,200	Charlevoix □, MI • 21,468	Chicago Ridge, IL 60415 • 13,643
Campbellsport, WI 53010 • 1,732	Carroll □, KY • 9,292	Cedaredge, CO 81413 • 1,380	Charlotte, MI 48813 • 8,083	Chickamauga, GA 30707 • 2,149
Campbellsville, KY 42718-19 • 9,577	Carroll □, MD • 123,372	Cedar Falls, IA 50613 • 34,298	Charlotte, NC 28201-41 • 395,934	Chickasaw, AL 36611 • 6,649
Camp Hill, AL 36850 • 1,415	Carroll □, MS • 9,237	Cedar Grove, NJ 07009 • 12,053	Charlotte, TX 78011 • 1,475	Chickasaw □, IA • 13,295
Camp Hill, PA 17011 • 7,831	Carroll □, MO • 10,748	Cedar Grove, WV 25039 • 1,473	Charlotte □, FL • 110,975	Chickasaw □, MS • 18,085
Camp Point, IL 62320 • 1,230	Carroll □, NH • 35,410	Cedar Grove, WI 53013 • 1,521	Charlotte □, VA • 11,688	Chickasha, OK 73018 • 14,988
Camp Springs, MD 20746 • 16,392	Carroll □, OH • 26,521	Cedar Hill, MO 63016 • 1,966	Charlotte Hall, MD 20622 • 1,992	Chico, CA 95926-28 • 40,079
Camp Verde, AZ 86322 • 6,243	Carroll □, TN • 27,514	Cedar Hill, TX 75104 • 19,976	Charlotte Harbor, FL 33980 • 3,327	Chicopee, MA 01013-22 • 56,632
Canaan, CT 06018 • 1,194	Carroll □, VA • 26,594	Cedar Hills, OR 97005 • 9,294	Charlottesville, VA 22901-08 • 40,341	Chicora, PA 16025 • 1,058
Canadensis, PA 18325 • 1,200	Carrollton, AL 35447 • 1,170	Cedarhurst, NY 11516 • 5,716	Charlton □, GA • 8,496	Chiefland, FL 32626 • 1,917
Canadian, TX 79014 • 2,417	Carrollton, GA 30117 • 16,029	Cedar Lake, IN 46303 • 8,885	Charlton City, MA 01508 • 1,400	Childersburg, AL 35044 • 4,579
Canadian □, OK • 74,409	Carrollton, IL 62016 • 2,507	Cedar Rapids, IA 52401-10 • 108,751	Charter Oak, CA 91724 • 8,858	Childress, TX 79201 • 5,055
Canajoharie, NY 13317 • 2,278	Carrollton, KY 41008 • 3,715	Cedar Springs, MI 49319 • 2,600	Chase □, KS • 3,021	Childress □, TX • 5,953
Canal Fulton, OH 44614 • 4,157	Carrollton, MI 48724 • 6,521	Cedartown, GA 30125 • 7,978	Chase □, NE • 4,381	Chilhowie, VA 24319 • 1,971
Canal Winchester, OH 43110 • 2,617	Carrollton, MO 64633 • 4,406	Cedarville, IL 08311 • 1,100	Chase City, VA 23924 • 2,442	Chili Center, NY 14624 • 4,360
Canandaigua, NY 14424-25 • 10,725	Carrollton, OH 44615 • 3,042	Cedarville, OH 45314 • 3,210	Chaska, MN 55318 • 11,339	Chillicothe, IL 61523 • 5,959
Canastota, NY 13032 • 4,673	Carrollton, TX 75006-08 • 82,169	Celina, OH 45822 • 9,650	Chatfield, MN 55923 • 2,226	Chillicothe, MO 64601 • 8,804
Canby, MN 56220 • 1,826	Carrolltown, PA 15722 • 1,286	Celina, TN 38551 • 1,493	Chatham, IL 62629 • 6,074	Chillicothe, OH 45601 • 21,923
Canby, OR 97013 • 8,983	Carrollwood, FL 33618 • 11,400	Celina, TX 75009 • 1,737	Chatham, MA 02633 • 1,916	Chillum, MD 20783 • 31,309
Candler □, GA • 7,744	Carson, CA 90749 • 83,995	Celoron, NY 14720 • 1,232	Chatham, NJ 07928 • 8,007	Chilton, WI 53014 • 3,240
Candlewood Isle, CT 06812 • 1,100	Carson □, TX • 6,576	Cementon, PA 18052 • 1,050	Chatham, NY 12037 • 1,920	Chilton □, AL • 32,458
Candlewood Shores, CT 06804 • 1,620	Carson City, MI 48811 • 1,158	Center, CO 81125 • 1,963	Chatham, VA 24531 • 1,354	Chimayo, NM 87522 • 2,789
Cando, ND 58324 • 1,564	Carson City, NV 89701-21 • 40,443	Center, ND 58530 • 826	Chatham □, GA • 216,935	China Grove, NC 28023 • 2,732
Caney, KS 67333 • 2,062	Carter □, KY • 24,340	Center, TX 75935 • 4,950	Chatham □, NC • 38,759	Chincoteague, VA 23336 • 3,572
Canfield, OH 44406 • 5,409	Carter □, MO • 5,515	Centerburg, OH 43011 • 1,323	Chatom, AL 36518 • 1,094	Chinle, AZ 86503 • 5,059
Canisteo, NY 14823 • 2,421	Carter □, MT • 1,503	Centereach, NY 11720 • 26,720	Chatsworth, GA 30705 • 2,865	Chino, CA 91708-10 • 59,682
Cannelton, IN 47520 • 1,786	Carter □, OK • 42,919	Center Line, MI 48015 • 9,026	Chatsworth, NJ 60921 • 1,186	Chinook, MT 59523 • 1,512
Cannon □, TN • 10,467	Carter □, TN • 51,505	Center Moriches, NY 11934 • 5,987	Chattahoochee, FL 32324 • 4,382	Chino Valley, AZ 86323 • 4,837
Cannon Beach, OR 97110 • 1,221	Carteret, NJ 07008 • 19,025	Center Point, AL 35215 • 22,657	Chattahoochee □, GA • 16,934	Chipley, FL 32428 • 3,866
Cannondale, CT 06897 • 1,500	Carteret □, NC • 52,556	Center Point, IA 52213 • 1,693	Chattanooga, TN 37401-22 • 152,466	Chippewa □, MI • 34,604
Cannon Falls, MN 55009 • 3,232	Carter Lake, IA 51510 • 3,200	Centerville, IN 47330 • 2,398	Chattaroy, WV 25667 • 1,182	Chippewa □, MN • 13,228
Canon City, CO 81212 • 12,687	Cartersville, GA 30120 • 12,035	Centerville, IA 52544 • 5,936	Chattooga □, GA • 22,242	Chippewa □, WI • 52,360
Canonsburg, PA 15317 • 9,200	Carterville, IL 62918 • 3,630	Centerville, MA 02632 • 9,190	Chautauqua □, KS • 4,407	Chippewa Falls, WI 54729 • 12,727
Canterbury, DE 19943 • 500	Carterville, MO 64835 • 2,013	Centerville, OH 45459 • 21,082	Chautauqua □, NY • 141,895	Chisago □, MN • 30,521
Canton, CT 06019 • 1,563	Carthage, IL 62321 • 2,657	Centerville, PA 15417 • 3,842	Chauvin, LA 70344 • 3,375	Chisago City, MN 55013 • 2,009
Canton, GA 30114 • 4,817	Carthage, MS 39051 • 4,373	Centerville, SD 57014 • 887	Chaves □, NM • 57,849	Chisholm, ME 04239 • 1,653
Canton, IL 61520 • 13,922	Carthage, MO 64836 • 10,747	Centerville, TN 37033 • 3,616	Chazy, NY 12921 • 1,000	Chisholm, MN 55719 • 5,290
Canton, MA 02021 • 18,182	Carthage, NY 13619 • 4,344	Centerville, UT 84014 • 11,500	Cheatham □, TN • 27,140	Chittenango, NY 13037 • 4,734
Canton, MI 48187 • 57,047	Carthage, TN 37030 • 2,386	Central, NM 88026 • 1,835	Cheboygan, MI 49721 • 4,999	Chittenden □, VT • 131,761
Canton, MS 39046 • 10,062	Carthage, TX 75633 • 6,496	Central, SC 29630 • 2,438	Cheboygan □, MI • 21,398	Choctaw, OK 73020 • 8,545
Canton, MO 63435 • 2,623	Caruthersville, MO 63830 • 7,389	Central City, CO 80427 • 335	Checotah, OK 74426 • 3,290	Choctaw □, AL • 16,018
Canton, NY 13617 • 6,379	Carver, MA 02330 • 1,500	Central City, IL 62801 • 1,390	Cheektowaga, NY 14225 • 84,387	Choctaw □, MS • 9,071
Canton, NC 28716 • 3,790	Carver □, MN • 47,915	Central City, IA 52214 • 1,063	Chehalis, WA 98532 • 6,527	Choctaw □, OK • 15,302
Canton, OH 44701-99 • 84,161	Carver Ranch Estates, FL 33023 • 5,600	Central City, KY 42330 • 4,979	Chelan, WA 98816 • 2,969	Choteau, MT 59422 • 1,741
Canton, PA 17724 • 1,966	Carville, LA 70721 • 1,108	Central City, NE 68826 • 2,868	Chelan □, WA • 52,250	Chouteau, OK 74337 • 1,771
Canton, SD 57013 • 2,787	Cary, IL 60013 • 10,043	Central City, PA 15926 • 1,246	Chelmsford, MA 01824 • 32,388	Chouteau □, MT • 5,452
Canton, TX 75103 • 2,949	Cary, NC 27511 • 43,858	Central Falls, RI 02863 • 17,637	Chelsea, MA 02150 • 28,710	Chowan □, NC • 13,506
Cantonment, FL 32533 • 3,200	Caryville, TN 37714 • 1,751	Central Heights, AZ 85501 • 1,500	Chelsea, MI 48118 • 3,772	Chowchilla, CA 93610 • 5,930
Canutillo, TX 79835 • 4,500	Casa de Oro, CA 92077 • 9,500	Centralia, IL 62801 • 14,274	Chelsea, OK 74016 • 1,620	Chrisman, IL 61924 • 1,136
Canyon, TX 79015 • 11,365	Casa Grande, AZ 85222 • 19,082	Centralia, MO 65240 • 3,414	Chelsea Estates, DE 19720 • 1,320	Christian □, IL • 34,418
Canyon □, ID • 90,076	Casas Adobes, AZ 85704 • 12,155	Centralia, WA 98531 • 12,101	Cheltenham Township, PA 19012 • 35,509	Christian □, KY • 68,941
Canyon Lake, CA 92380 • 7,938	Cascade, CO 80809 • 1,000	Central Islip, NY 11722 • 26,028	Chemung, NY • 95,195	Christian □, MO • 32,644
Canyon Lake, TX 78130 • 9,975	Cascade, ID 83611 • 877	Central Park, WA 98520 • 2,669	Chemung □, NY • 95,195	Christiana, DE 19702 • 500
Canyonville, OR 97417 • 1,219	Cascade, IA 52033 • 1,812	Central Point, OR 97502 • 7,509	Chenango □, NY • 51,768	Christiana, PA 17509 • 1,045
Capac, MI 48014 • 1,583	Cascade, MT 59421 • 729	Central Square, NY 13036 • 1,671	Chenango Bridge, NY 13745 • 2,890	Christiansburg, VA 24073 • 15,004
Cape Canaveral, FL 32920 • 8,014	Cascade □, MT • 77,691	Central Valley, CA 96019 • 4,340	Cheney, KS 67025 • 1,560	Christmas, FL 32709 • 1,200
Cape Charles, VA 23310 • 1,398	Cascade Vista, WA 98058 • 7,800	Central Valley, NY 10917 • 1,929	Cheney, WA 99004 • 7,723	Christopher, IL 62822 • 2,774
Cape Coral, FL 33904 • 74,991	Casey, IL 62420 • 2,914	Central Village, CT 06332 • 1,600	Cheneyville, LA 71325 • 1,005	Chubbuck, ID 83202 • 7,791
Cape Elizabeth, ME 04107 • 8,854	Casey □, KY • 14,211	Centre, AL 35960 • 2,893	Chenoa, IL 61726 • 1,732	Chugwater, WY 82210 • 192
Cape Girardeau, MO 63701-02 • 34,438	Cashion, AZ 85329 • 3,014	Centre □, PA • 123,786	Chenoweth, OR 97058 • 3,246	Chula Vista, CA 91909-15 • 135,163
Cape Girardeau □, MO • 61,633	Cashmere, WA 98815 • 2,544	Centre City, NJ 08051 • 2,070	Chepachet, RI 02814 • 900	Church Hill, TN 37642 • 4,834
Cape May, NJ 08204 • 4,668	Casper, WY 82601-15 • 46,742	Centre Hall, PA 16828 • 1,203	Cheraw, SC 29520 • 5,505	Churchill, OH 44505 • 7,700
Cape May □, NJ • 95,089	Caspian, MI 49915 • 1,031	Centreville, AL 35042 • 2,508	Cherokee, AL 35616 • 1,479	Churchill □, NV • 17,938
Cape May Court House, NJ 08210 • 4,426	Cass □, IL • 13,437	Centreville, IL 62207 • 7,489	Cherokee, IA 51012 • 6,026	Church Point, LA 70525 • 4,677
Cape Saint Claire, MD 21401 • 7,878	Cass □, IN • 38,413	Centreville, MD 21617 • 2,097	Cherokee, OK 73728 • 1,787	Churchville, NY 14428 • 1,731
Capitola, CA 95010 • 10,171	Cass □, IA • 15,128	Centreville, MI 49032 • 1,516	Cherokee □, AL • 19,543	Churubusco, IN 46723 • 1,781
Capitol Heights, MD 20743 • 3,633	Cass □, MI • 49,477	Centreville, MS 39631 • 1,771	Cherokee □, GA • 90,204	Cibola □, NM • 23,794
Capitol View, SC 29209 • 10,456	Cass □, MN • 21,791	Centreville, VA 22020 • 26,585	Cherokee □, IA • 14,098	Cicero, IL 60650 • 67,436
Captain Cook, HI 96704 • 2,595	Cass □, MO • 63,808	Century, FL 32535 • 1,989	Cherokee □, KS • 21,374	Cicero, IN 46034 • 3,268
Captiva, FL 33924 • 1,200	Cass □, NE • 21,318	Century Village, FL 33409 • 8,363	Cherokee □, NC • 20,170	Cimarron, KS 67835 • 1,626
Caraway, AR 72419 • 1,178	Cass □, ND • 102,874	Ceredo, WV 25507 • 1,916	Cherokee □, OK • 34,049	Cimarron □, OK • 3,301
Carbon □, MT • 8,080	Cass □, TX • 29,982	Ceres, CA 95307 • 26,314	Cherokee □, SC • 44,506	Cimarron Hills, CO 80906 • 11,160
Carbon □, PA • 56,846	Cass City, MI 48726 • 2,276	Cerritos, CA 90703 • 53,240	Cherokee □, TX • 41,049	Cincinnati, OH 45201-75 • 364,040
Carbon □, UT • 20,228	Casselberry, FL 32707-08 • 18,911	Cerro Gordo, IL 61818 • 1,436	Cherokee Village, AR 72525 • 3,200	Cinnaminson, NJ 08077 • 14,583
Carbon □, WY • 16,659	Casselton, ND 58012 • 1,601	Cerro Gordo □, IA • 46,733	Cherry □, NE • 6,307	Circle, MT 59215 • 805

Circle Pines, MN 55014 • 4,704
Circleville, OH 43113 • 11,666
Cisco, TX 76437 • 3,813
Citra, FL 32113 • 1,500
Citronelle, AL 36522 • 3,671
Citrus, CA 91702 • 9,481
Citrus Heights, CA 95610-11 • 107,439
Citrus □, FL • 93,515
City Of Sunrise, FL 33313 • 64,407
City View, SC 29611 • 1,490
Clackamas, OR 97015 • 2,578
Clackamas □, OR • 278,850
Claiborne, LA 71291 • 8,300
Claiborne □, LA • 17,405
Claiborne □, MS • 11,370
Claiborne □, TN • 26,137
Clair-Mel City, FL 33619 • 7,000
Clairton, PA 15025 • 9,656
Clallam □, WA • 56,464
Clanton, AL 35045 • 7,669
Clara City, MN 56222 • 1,307
Clare, MI 48617 • 3,021
Clare □, MI • 24,952
Claremont, CA 91711 • 32,503
Claremont, NH 03743 • 13,902
Claremore, OK 74017-18 • 13,280
Clarence, MO 63437 • 1,026
Clarendon, AR 72029 • 2,072
Clarendon, TX 79226 • 2,067
Clarendon □, SC • 28,450
Clarendon Hills, IL 60514 • 6,994
Claridge, PA 15623 • 1,200
Clarinda, IA 51632 • 5,104
Clarion, IA 50525 • 2,703
Clarion, PA 16214 • 6,457
Clarion □, PA • 41,699
Clark, NJ 07066 • 14,629
Clark, SD 57225 • 1,292
Clark □, AR • 21,437
Clark □, ID • 762
Clark □, IL • 15,921
Clark □, IN • 87,777
Clark □, KS • 2,418
Clark □, KY • 29,496
Clark □, MO • 7,547
Clark □, NV • 741,459
Clark □, OH • 147,548
Clark □, SD • 4,403
Clark □, WA • 238,053
Clark □, WI • 31,647
Clarkdale, AZ 86324 • 2,144
Clarke □, AL • 27,240
Clarke □, GA • 87,594
Clarke □, IA • 8,287
Clarke □, MS • 17,313
Clarke □, VA • 12,101
Clarkesville, GA 30523 • 1,151
Clarksburg, WV 26301-02 • 18,059
Clarksdale, MS 38614 • 19,717
Clarks Summit, PA 18411 • 5,433
Clarkston, GA 30021 • 5,385
Clarkston, MI 48346-48 • 1,005
Clarkston, WA 99403 • 6,753
Clarksville, AR 72830 • 5,833
Clarksville, DE 19970 • 500
Clarksville, IN 47129 • 19,833
Clarksville, IA 50619 • 1,382
Clarksville, TN 37040-43 • 75,494
Clarksville, TX 75426 • 4,311
Clarksville, VA 23927 • 1,243
Clarkton, MO 63837 • 1,113
Clatskanie, OR 97016 • 1,629
Clatsop □, OR • 33,301
Claude, TX 79019 • 1,199
Clawson, MI 48017 • 13,874
Claxton, GA 30417 • 2,464
Clay, KY 42404 • 1,173
Clay □, AL • 13,252
Clay □, AR • 18,107
Clay □, FL • 105,986
Clay □, GA • 3,364
Clay □, IL • 14,460
Clay □, IN • 24,705
Clay □, IA • 17,585
Clay □, KS • 9,158
Clay □, KY • 21,746
Clay □, MN • 50,422
Clay □, MS • 21,120
Clay □, MO • 153,411
Clay □, NE • 7,123
Clay □, NC • 7,155
Clay □, SD • 13,186
Clay □, TN • 7,238
Clay □, TX • 10,024
Clay □, WV • 9,983
Clay Center, KS 67432 • 4,613
Claymont, DE 19702 • 9,800
Claypool, AZ 85532 • 1,942
Claysburg, PA 16625 • 1,399
Clayton, AL 36016 • 1,564
Clayton, DE 19938 • 1,163
Clayton, GA 30525 • 1,613
Clayton, MO 63105 • 13,874
Clayton, NJ 08312 • 6,155
Clayton, NM 88415 • 2,484
Clayton, NY 13624 • 2,160
Clayton, NC 27520 • 4,756
Clayton □, GA • 182,052
Clayton □, IA • 19,054
Clear Creek □, CO • 7,619
Clearfield, KY 40313 • 1,250
Clearfield, PA 16830 • 6,633
Clearfield, UT 84015 • 21,435
Clearfield □, PA • 78,097
Clearlake, CA 95422 • 11,804
Clear Lake, IA 50428 • 8,183
Clear Lake, SD 57226 • 1,247
Clearlake, WA 98235 • 1,100
Clear Lake Shores, TX 77565 • 1,096
Clearwater, FL 34615-30 • 98,784
Clearwater, KS 67026 • 1,875
Clearwater, SC 29822 • 4,731
Clearwater □, ID • 8,505
Clearwater □, MN • 8,309
Cleburne, TX 76031-33 • 22,205
Cleburne □, AL • 12,730
Cleburne □, AR • 19,411
Cle Elum, WA 98922 • 1,778
Cleland Heights, DE 19805 • 1,120
Clementon, NJ 08021 • 5,601
Clemmons, NC 27012 • 6,020
Clemson, SC 29631-33 • 11,096

Clendenin, WV 25045 • 1,203
Cleona, PA 17042 • 2,322
Clermont, FL 34711-12 • 6,910
Clermont □, OH • 150,187
Cleveland, GA 30528 • 1,653
Cleveland, MS 38732-33 • 15,384
Cleveland, OH 44101-99 • 505,616
Cleveland, OK 74020 • 3,156
Cleveland, TN 37311-12 • 30,354
Cleveland, TX 77327-28 • 7,124
Cleveland, WI 53015 • 1,398
Cleveland □, AR • 7,781
Cleveland □, NC • 84,714
Cleveland □, OK • 174,253
Cleveland Heights, OH 44118 • 54,052
Cleves, OH 45002 • 2,208
Clewiston, FL 33440 • 6,085
Cliffside Park, NJ 07010 • 20,393
Clifton, AZ 85533 • 2,840
Clifton, CO 81520 • 12,671
Clifton, IL 60927 • 1,347
Clifton, NJ 07011-15 • 71,742
Clifton, TX 76634 • 3,195
Clifton Forge, VA 24422 • 4,679
Clifton Heights, PA 19018 • 7,111
Clifton Knolls, NY 12065 • 5,636
Clifton Springs, NY 14432 • 2,175
Clinch □, GA • 6,160
Clint, TX 79836 • 1,035
Clinton, AR 72031 • 2,213
Clinton, CT 06413 • 3,439
Clinton, IL 61727 • 7,437
Clinton, IN 47842 • 5,040
Clinton, IA 52732-33 • 29,201
Clinton, KY 42031 • 1,547
Clinton, LA 70722 • 1,904
Clinton, ME 04927 • 1,485
Clinton, MD 20735 • 19,987
Clinton, MA 01510 • 7,943
Clinton, MI 49236 • 2,475
Clinton, MS 39056 • 21,847
Clinton, MO 64735 • 8,703
Clinton, NJ 08809 • 2,054
Clinton, NY 13323 • 2,238
Clinton, NC 28328 • 8,204
Clinton, OK 73601 • 9,298
Clinton, SC 29325 • 7,987
Clinton, TN 37716 • 8,972
Clinton, UT 84015 • 7,945
Clinton, WA 98236 • 2,000
Clinton, WI 53525 • 1,849
Clinton □, IL • 33,944
Clinton □, IN • 30,974
Clinton □, IA • 51,040
Clinton □, KY • 9,135
Clinton □, MI • 57,883
Clinton □, MO • 16,595
Clinton □, NY • 85,969
Clinton □, OH • 35,415
Clinton □, PA • 37,182
Clinton Township, MI 48043 • 85,866
Clintonville, WI 54929 • 4,351
Clintwood, VA 24228 • 1,542
Clio, AL 36017 • 1,365
Clio, MI 48420 • 2,629
Clive, IA 50322 • 7,462
Cloquet, MN 55720 • 10,885
Closter, NJ 07624 • 8,094
Cloud □, KS • 11,023
Clover, SC 29710 • 3,422
Cloverdale, CA 95425 • 4,924
Cloverdale, IN 46120 • 1,681
Cloverleaf, TX 77015 • 18,230
Cloverport, KY 40111 • 1,207
Clovis, CA 93612-13 • 50,323
Clovis, NM 88101-03 • 30,954
Clute, TX 77531 • 8,910
Clyde, NY 14433 • 2,409
Clyde, NC 28721 • 1,041
Clyde, OH 43410 • 5,776
Clyde, TX 79510 • 3,002
Clymer, PA 15728 • 1,499
Coachella, CA 92236 • 16,896
Coahoma, TX 79511 • 1,133
Coahoma □, MS • 31,665
Coal □, OK • 5,780
Coal City, IL 60416 • 3,907
Coal Fork, WV 25306 • 2,100
Coalgate, OK 74538 • 1,895
Coal Grove, OH 45638 • 2,251
Coalinga, CA 93210 • 8,212
Coalville, UT 84017 • 1,065
Coatesville, PA 19320 • 11,038
Coats, NC 27521 • 1,493
Cobb □, GA • 447,745
Cobden, IL 62920 • 1,090
Cobleskill, NY 12043 • 5,268
Cochise □, AZ • 97,624
Cochituate, MA 01778 • 6,046
Cochran, GA 31014 • 4,390
Cochran □, TX • 4,377
Cochranton, PA 16314 • 1,174
Cocke □, TN • 29,141
Cockeysville, MD 21030 • 18,668
Cockrell Hill, TX 75211 • 3,746
Cocoa, FL 32922-27 • 17,722
Cocoa Beach, FL 32931-32 • 12,123
Coconino □, AZ • 96,591
Coconut Creek, FL 33060 • 27,485
Codington □, SD • 22,698
Cody, WY 82414 • 7,897
Coeburn, VA 24230 • 2,165
Coeur d'Alene, ID 83814 • 24,563
Coffee □, AL • 40,240
Coffee □, GA • 29,592
Coffee □, TN • 40,339
Coffey □, KS • 8,404
Coffeyville, KS 67337 • 12,917
Cohasset, MA 02025 • 6,661
Cohoes, NY 12047 • 16,825
Cokato, MN 55321 • 2,180
Coke □, TX • 3,424
Cokeville, WY 83114 • 493
Colbert, OK 74733 • 1,043
Colbert □, AL • 51,666
Colby, KS 67701 • 5,396
Colby, WI 54421 • 1,532
Colchester, CT 06415 • 3,212
Colchester, IL 62326 • 1,645
Cold Bay, AK 99571 • 148
Cold Spring, KY 41076 • 2,880
Cold Spring, MN 56320 • 2,459
Cold Spring Harbor, NY 11724 • 4,789

Coldwater, MI 49036 • 9,607
Coldwater, MS 38618 • 1,502
Coldwater, OH 45828 • 4,335
Cole □, MO • 63,579
Colebrook, NH 03576 • 2,444
Cole Camp, MO 65325 • 1,054
Coleman, MI 48618 • 1,237
Coleman, TX 76834 • 5,410
Coleman □, TX • 9,710
Coleraine, MN 55722 • 1,041
Coles □, IL • 51,644
Colfax, CA 95713 • 1,306
Colfax, IA 50054 • 2,462
Colfax, LA 71417 • 1,696
Colfax, WA 99111 • 2,713
Colfax, WI 54730 • 1,110
Colfax □, NE • 9,139
Colfax □, NM • 12,925
College, AK 99701 • 11,249
Collegedale, TN 37315 • 5,048
College Park, GA 30337 • 20,457
College Park, MD 20740-41 • 21,927
College Place, WA 99324 • 6,308
College Station, AR 72053 • 3,800
College Station, TX 77840-45 • 52,456
Collegeville, PA 19426 • 4,227
Colleton □, SC • 34,377
Colleyville, TX 76034 • 12,724
Collier □, FL • 152,099
Collierville, TN 38017 • 14,427
Collin □, TX • 264,036
Collingdale, PA 19023 • 9,175
Collingswood, NJ 08108 • 15,289
Collingsworth □, TX • 3,573
Collins, MS 39428 • 2,541
Collins Park, DE 19720 • 2,100
Collinsville, AL 35961 • 1,429
Collinsville, CT 06022 • 2,591
Collinsville, IL 62234 • 22,446
Collinsville, OK 74021 • 3,612
Collinsville, VA 24078 • 7,280
Collinwood, TN 38450 • 1,014
Colmar Manor, MD 20722 • 1,249
Coloma, MI 49038 • 1,679
Colon, MI 49040 • 1,224
Colonia, NJ 07067 • 18,238
Colonial Beach, VA 22443 • 3,132
Colonial Heights, TN 37663 • 6,716
Colonial Heights, VA 23834 • 16,064
Colonial Park, PA 17109 • 13,777
Colonie, NY 12212 • 8,019
Colorado □, TX • 18,383
Colorado City, AZ 86021 • 2,426
Colorado City, CO 81019 • 1,149
Colorado City, TX 79512 • 4,749
Colorado Springs, CO 80901-99 • 281,140
Colquitt, GA 31737 • 1,991
Colquitt □, GA • 36,645
Colstrip, MT 59323 • 3,035
Colton, CA 92324 • 40,213
Columbia, CA 95310 • 1,799
Columbia, IL 62236 • 5,524
Columbia, KY 42728 • 3,845
Columbia, MD 21044-46 • 75,883
Columbia, MS 39429 • 6,815
Columbia, MO 65201-05 • 69,101
Columbia, PA 17512 • 10,701
Columbia, SC 29201-92 • 98,052
Columbia, TN 38401-02 • 28,583
Columbia □, AR • 25,691
Columbia □, FL • 42,613
Columbia □, GA • 66,031
Columbia □, NY • 62,982
Columbia □, OR • 37,557
Columbia □, PA • 63,202
Columbia □, WA • 4,024
Columbia □, WI • 45,088
Columbia City, IN 46725 • 5,706
Columbia City, OR 97018 • 1,003
Columbia Falls, MT 59912 • 2,942
Columbia Heights, MN 55421 • 18,910
Columbiana, AL 35051 • 2,968
Columbiana, OH 44408 • 4,961
Columbiana □, OH • 108,276
Columbine, CO 80123 • 3,969
Columbus, GA 31901-09 • 178,681
Columbus, IN 47201-03 • 31,802
Columbus, KS 66725 • 3,268
Columbus, MS 39701-05 • 23,799
Columbus, MT 59019 • 1,573
Columbus, NE 68601 • 19,480
Columbus, OH 43201-91 • 632,910
Columbus, TX 78934 • 3,367
Columbus, WI 53925 • 4,093
Columbus □, NC • 49,587
Columbus Grove, OH 45830 • 2,231
Columbus Junction, IA 52738 • 1,616
Colusa, CA 95932 • 4,934
Colusa □, CA • 16,275
Colver, PA 15927 • 1,024
Colville, WA 99114 • 4,360
Colwich, KS 67030 • 1,091
Comal □, TX • 51,832
Comanche, OK 73529 • 1,695
Comanche, TX 76442 • 4,087
Comanche □, KS • 2,313
Comanche □, OK • 111,486
Comanche □, TX • 13,381
Combee Settlement, FL 33801 • 5,463
Combined Locks, WI 54113 • 2,190
Comfort, TX 78013 • 1,477
Commack, NY 11725 • 36,124
Commerce, CA 90040 • 12,135
Commerce, GA 30529 • 4,108
Commerce, OK 74339 • 2,426
Commerce, TX 75428 • 6,825
Commerce City, CO 80022 • 16,466
Common Fence Point, RI 02871 • 860
Como, MS 38619 • 1,387
Compton, CA 90220-24 • 90,454
Comstock, MI 49041 • 5,600
Comstock Park, MI 49321 • 6,530
Concho □, TX • 3,044
Concord, CA 94518-24 • 111,348
Concord, MA 01742 • 4,680
Concord, NC 28025-27 • 27,347
Concord, NH 03301-03 • 36,006
Concord, TN 37901 • 3,420
Concordia, KS 66901 • 6,167
Concordia, MO 64020 • 2,160
Concordia □, LA • 20,828

Conecuh □, AL • 14,054
Conejos □, CO • 7,453
Conemaugh, PA 15909 • 1,470
Congers, NY 10920 • 8,003
Conklin, NY 13748 • 1,800
Conley, GA 30027 • 5,528
Conneaut, OH 44030 • 13,241
Connell, WA 99326 • 2,005
Connellsville, PA 15425 • 9,229
Connersville, IN 47331 • 15,550
Conover, NC 28613 • 5,465
Conrad, MT 59425 • 2,891
Conroe, TX 77301-05 • 27,610
Conshohocken, PA 19428 • 8,064
Constantia, NY 13044 • 1,140
Constantine, MI 49042 • 2,032
Continental, OH 45831 • 1,214
Contoocook, NH 03229 • 1,334
Contra Costa □, CA • 803,732
Converse, IN 46919 • 1,144
Converse, SC 29329 • 1,173
Converse, TX 78109 • 8,887
Converse □, WY • 11,128
Convoy, OH 45832 • 1,200
Conway, AR 72032 • 26,481
Conway, FL 32809 • 13,159
Conway, NH 03818 • 1,604
Conway, PA 15027 • 2,424
Conway, SC 29526-27 • 9,819
Conway □, AR • 19,151
Conway Springs, KS 67031 • 1,384
Conyers, GA 30207-08 • 7,380
Cook □, GA • 13,456
Cook □, IL • 5,105,067
Cook □, MN • 3,868
Cooke □, TX • 30,777
Cookeville, TN 38501-02 • 21,744
Coolidge, AZ 85228 • 6,927
Coon Rapids, IA 50058 • 1,266
Coon Rapids, MN 55433 • 52,978
Cooper, TX 75432 • 2,153
Cooper □, MO • 14,835
Cooper City, FL 33328 • 20,791
Cooper Road, LA 71107 • 11,050
Coopersburg, PA 18036 • 2,599
Cooperstown, NY 13326 • 2,180
Cooperstown, ND 58425 • 1,247
Coopersville, MI 49404 • 3,421
Coos □, NH • 34,828
Coos □, OR • 60,273
Coosa □, AL • 11,063
Coos Bay, OR 97420 • 15,076
Copake, NY 12516 • 1,200
Copiague, NY 11726 • 20,769
Copiah □, MS • 27,592
Coplay, PA 18037 • 3,267
Copperas Cove, TX 76522 • 24,079
Coquille, OR 97423 • 4,121
Coral Gables, FL 33134 • 40,091
Coral Hills, MD 20743 • 11,032
Coral Springs, FL 33065 • 79,443
Coral Terrace, FL 33157 • 23,255
Coralville, IA 52241 • 10,347
Coral Way Village, FL 33155 • 9,000
Coram, NY 11727 • 30,111
Coraopolis, PA 15108 • 6,747
Corbin, KY 40701-02 • 7,419
Corcoran, CA 93212 • 13,364
Corcoran, MN 55340 • 5,199
Cordaville, MA 01772 • 1,530
Cordele, GA 31015 • 10,321
Cordell, OK 73632 • 2,903
Cordova, AL 35550 • 2,623
Cordova, NC 28330 • 1,200
Cordova, AK 99574 • 2,110
Corinth, MS 38834 • 11,820
Corinth, NY 12822 • 2,760
Cornelia, GA 30531 • 3,219
Cornelius, NC 28031 • 2,581
Cornelius, OR 97113 • 6,148
Cornell, WI 54732 • 1,541
Corning, AR 72422 • 3,323
Corning, CA 96021 • 5,870
Corning, IA 50841 • 1,806
Corning, NY 14830 • 11,938
Cornville, AZ 86325 • 1,200
Cornwall, PA 17016 • 3,231
Cornwall on Hudson, NY 12520 • 3,093
Corona, CA 91718-20 • 76,095
Coronado, CA 92118 • 26,540
Coronado, CO 80229 • 6,890
Corpus Christi, TX 78401-82 • 257,453
Corrigan, TX 75939 • 1,764
Corriganville, MD 21524 • 1,020
Corry, PA 16407 • 7,216
Corsicana, TX 75110 • 22,911
Corson □, SD • 4,195
Corte Madera, CA 94925 • 8,272
Cortez, CO 81321 • 7,284
Cortez, FL 34215 • 4,509
Cortland, NY 13045 • 19,801
Cortland, OH 44410 • 5,666
Cortland □, NY • 48,963
Corunna, MI 48817 • 3,091
Corvallis, OR 97330-33 • 44,757
Corydon, IN 47112 • 2,661
Corydon, IA 50060 • 1,675
Coryell □, TX • 64,213
Coshocton, OH 43812 • 12,193
Coshocton □, OH • 35,427
Cosmopolis, WA 98537 • 1,372
Costa Mesa, CA 92626-28 • 96,357
Costilla □, CO • 3,190
Cottage Grove, MN 55016 • 22,935
Cottage Grove, OR 97424 • 7,402
Cottle □, TX • 2,247
Cottleville, MO 63338 • 2,936
Cotton □, OK • 6,441
Cotton Plant, AR 72036 • 1,150
Cotton Valley, LA 71018 • 1,130
Cottondale, AL 35453 • 1,960
Cottonwood, AL 36320 • 1,385
Cottonwood, AZ 86326 • 5,918
Cottonwood, CA 96022 • 1,747
Cottonwood, ID 83522 • 822
Cottonwood, UT 84121 • 11,554
Cottonwood □, MN • 12,694
Cottonwood Heights, UT 84121 • 28,766
Cotuit, MA 02635 • 1,750
Cotulla, TX 78014 • 3,694
Coudersport, PA 16915 • 2,854
Coulee Dam, WA 99116 • 1,087

Council, ID 83612 • 831
Council Bluffs, IA 51501-03 • 54,315
Council Grove, KS 66846 • 2,228
Country Club Hills, IL 60478 • 15,431
Country Homes, WA 99218 • 5,126
Countryside, IL 60525 • 5,716
Coupeville, WA 98239 • 1,377
Coushatta, LA 71019 • 1,845
Covedale, OH 45238 • 6,669
Covelo, CA 95428 • 1,057
Coventry, CT 06238 • 10,063
Coventry, DE 19720 • 1,165
Coventry, RI 02816 • 6,980
Covina, CA 91722-24 • 43,207
Covington, GA 30209 • 10,026
Covington, IN 47932 • 2,747
Covington, KY 41011-18 • 43,264
Covington, LA 70433-34 • 7,691
Covington, OH 45318 • 2,603
Covington, TN 38019 • 7,487
Covington, VA 24426 • 6,991
Covington □, AL • 36,478
Covington □, MS • 16,527
Cowan, TN 37318 • 1,738
Cowarts, AL 36321 • 1,400
Coweta, OK 74429 • 6,159
Coweta □, GA • 53,853
Cowley, WY 82420 • 477
Cowley □, KS • 36,915
Cowlitz □, WA • 82,119
Cowpens, SC 29330 • 2,176
Coxsackie, NY 12051 • 2,789
Cozad, NE 69130 • 3,823
Crab Orchard, WV 25827 • 2,919
Crabtree, PA 15624 • 1,000
Crafton, PA 15205 • 7,188
Craig, AK 99921 • 1,260
Craig, CO 81625-26 • 8,091
Craig □, OK • 14,104
Craig □, VA • 4,372
Craighead □, AR • 68,956
Craigsville, WV 26205 • 1,955
Cramerton, NC 28032 • 2,371
Cranbury, NJ 08512 • 1,255
Crandall, TX 75114 • 1,652
Crandon, WI 54520 • 1,958
Crane, AZ 85365 • 2,650
Crane, MO 65633 • 1,218
Crane, TX 79731 • 3,533
Crane □, TX • 4,652
Cranford, NJ 07016 • 22,624
Cranston, RI 02910 • 76,060
Craven □, NC • 81,613
Crawford, NE 69339 • 1,115
Crawford □, AR • 42,493
Crawford □, GA • 8,991
Crawford □, IL • 19,464
Crawford □, IN • 9,914
Crawford □, IA • 16,775
Crawford □, KS • 35,568
Crawford □, MI • 12,260
Crawford □, MO • 19,173
Crawford □, OH • 47,870
Crawford □, PA • 86,169
Crawford □, WI • 15,940
Crawfordsville, IN 47933 • 13,584
Crawfordville, FL 32327 • 1,110
Creedmoor, NC 27522 • 1,504
Creek □, OK • 60,915
Creighton, NE 68729 • 1,223
Creighton, PA 15030 • 1,658
Crenshaw □, AL • 13,635
Creola, AL 36525 • 1,896
Cresaptown, MD 21502 • 4,645
Crescent, OK 73028 • 1,236
Crescent City, CA 95531 • 4,380
Crescent City, FL 32112 • 1,859
Crescent Springs, KY 41016 • 2,179
Cresco, IA 52136 • 3,669
Cresskill, NJ 07626 • 7,558
Cresson, PA 16630 • 1,784
Cressona, PA 17929 • 1,694
Cresthaven, FL 33064 • 2,400
Crest Hill, IL 60435 • 10,643
Crestline, CA 92325 • 8,594
Crestline, OH 44827 • 4,934
Creston, IA 50801 • 7,911
Creston, OH 44217 • 1,848
Crestview, FL 32536 • 9,886
Crestview, HI 96797 • 1,000
Crestwood, IL 60445 • 10,823
Crestwood, KY 40014 • 1,435
Crestwood, MO 63126 • 11,234
Crestwood Village, NJ 08759 • 8,030
Creswell, OR 97426 • 2,431
Crete, IL 60417 • 6,773
Crete, NE 68333 • 4,841
Creve Coeur, IL 61611 • 5,938
Creve Coeur, MO 63141 • 12,304
Crewe, VA 23930 • 2,276
Cricket, NC 28659 • 2,015
Cridersville, OH 45806 • 1,885
Crisfield, MD 21817 • 2,880
Crisp □, GA • 20,011
Crittenden, AR • 49,939
Crittenden □, KY • 9,196
Crocker, MO 65452 • 1,077
Crockett, CA 94525 • 3,228
Crockett, TX 75835 • 7,024
Crockett □, TN • 13,378
Crockett □, TX • 4,078
Crofton, MD 21114 • 12,781
Cromwell, CT 06416 • 1,100
Crook □, OR • 14,111
Crook □, WY • 5,294
Crookston, MN 56716 • 8,119
Crooksville, OH 43731 • 2,601
Crosby, MN 56441 • 2,073
Crosby, ND 58730 • 1,312
Crosby, TX 77532 • 1,811
Crosby □, TX • 7,304
Crosbyton, TX 79322 • 2,026
Cross □, AR • 19,225
Cross City, FL 32628 • 2,041
Crossett, AR 71635 • 6,282
Crosslake, MN 56442 • 1,132
Cross Lanes, WV 25313 • 10,878
Cross Plains, TN 37049 • 1,025
Cross Plains, TX 76443 • 1,063
Cross Plains, WI 53528 • 2,098
Crossville, AL 35962 • 1,350
Crossville, TN 38555 • 6,930
Croswell, MI 48422 • 2,174

United States Populations and ZIP Codes

Crothersville, IN 47229 • 1,687
Croton-on-Hudson, NY 10520 • 7,018
Crow Agency, MT 59022 • 1,446
Crowell, TX 79227 • 1,230
Crowley, LA 70526–27 • 13,983
Crowley, TX 76036 • 6,974
Crowley □, CO • 3,946
Crown Point, IN 46307 • 17,728
Crownpoint, NM 87313 • 2,108
Crow Wing □, MN • 44,249
Crozet, VA 22932 • 2,256
Crystal, MN 55428 • 23,788
Crystal Bay, NV 89402 • 1,200
Crystal Beach, FL 34681 • 1,450
Crystal City, MO 63019 • 4,088
Crystal City, TX 78839 • 8,263
Crystal Falls, MI 49920 • 1,922
Crystal Lake, CT 06029 • 1,200
Crystal Lake, IL 33803 • 5,300
Crystal Lake, IL 60014 • 24,512
Crystal Lawns, IL 60435 • 1,660
Crystal River, FL 32629 • 4,044
Crystal Springs, MS 39059 • 5,643
Cuba, IL 61427 • 1,440
Cuba, MO 65453 • 2,537
Cuba, NY 14727 • 1,690
Cuba City, WI 53807 • 2,024
Cucamonga, CA 91730 • 101,409
Cudahy, CA 90201 • 22,817
Cudahy, WI 53110 • 18,659
Cuero, TX 77954 • 6,700
Culberson □, TX • 3,407
Culbertson, MT 59218 • 796
Cullen, LA 71021 • 1,642
Cullman, AL 35055–56 • 13,367
Cullman □, AL • 67,613
Culloden, WV 25510 • 2,907
Cullowhee, NC 28723 • 1,200
Culpeper, VA 22701 • 8,581
Culpeper □, VA • 27,791
Culver, IN 46511 • 1,404
Culver City, CA 90230–33 • 38,793
Cumberland, KY 40823 • 3,112
Cumberland, MD 21501–05 • 23,706
Cumberland, WI 54829 • 2,163
Cumberland □, IL • 10,670
Cumberland □, KY • 6,784
Cumberland □, ME • 243,135
Cumberland □, NJ • 138,053
Cumberland □, NC • 274,566
Cumberland □, PA • 195,257
Cumberland □, TN • 34,736
Cumberland □, VA • 7,825
Cumberland Center, ME 04021 • 1,890
Cumberland Foreside, ME 04110 • 1,000
Cumberland Hill, RI 02864 • 6,379
Cuming □, NE • 10,117
Cumming, GA 30130 • 2,828
Cupertino, CA 95014–16 • 40,263
Currituck □, NC • 13,736
Curry □, NM • 42,207
Curry □, OR • 19,327
Curtisville, PA 15032 • 1,285
Curwensville, PA 16833 • 2,924
Cushing, OK 74023 • 7,218
Cusseta, GA 31805 • 1,107
Custer, SD 57730 • 1,741
Custer □, CO • 1,926
Custer □, ID • 4,133
Custer □, MT • 11,697
Custer □, NE • 12,270
Custer □, OK • 26,897
Custer □, SD • 6,179
Cut Bank, MT 59427 • 3,329
Cutchogue, NY 11935 • 1,730
Cuthbert, GA 31740 • 3,730
Cutler, FL 33157 • 16,201
Cutler Ridge, FL 33157 • 21,268
Cutlerville, MI 49508 • 11,228
Cut Off, LA 70345 • 5,325
Cuyahoga □, OH • 1,412,140
Cuyahoga Falls, OH 44221–24 • 48,950
Cynthiana, KY 41031 • 6,497
Cypress, CA 90630 • 42,655
Cypress Lake, FL 33919 • 10,491
Cypress Quarters, FL 34972 • 1,343
Cyril, OK 73029 • 1,072

D

Dacono, CO 80514 • 2,228
Dacula, GA 30211 • 2,217
Dade □, FL • 1,937,094
Dade □, GA • 13,147
Dade □, MO • 7,449
Dade City, FL 33525–26 • 5,633
Dadeville, AL 36853 • 3,276
Daggett □, UT • 690
Dagsboro, DE 19939 • 398
Dahlonega, GA 30533 • 3,086
Daingerfield, TX 75638 • 2,572
Dakota □, MN • 275,227
Dakota □, NE • 16,742
Dakota City, IA 50529 • 1,024
Dakota City, NE 68731 • 1,470
Dale, IN 47523 • 1,553
Dale □, AL • 49,633
Dale City, VA 22193 • 47,170
Daleville, AL 36322 • 5,117
Daleville, IN 47334 • 1,681
Dalhart, TX 79022 • 6,246
Dallam □, TX • 5,461
Dallas, GA 30132 • 2,810
Dallas, NC 28034 • 3,012
Dallas, OR 97338 • 9,422
Dallas, PA 18612 • 2,567
Dallas, TX 75201–99 • 1,006,877
Dallas □, AL • 48,130
Dallas □, AR • 9,614
Dallas □, IA • 29,755
Dallas □, MO • 12,646
Dallas □, TX • 1,852,810
Dallas Center, IA 50063 • 1,454
Dallas City, IL 62330 • 1,037
Dallastown, PA 17313 • 3,974
Dalton, GA 30720–22 • 21,761
Dalton, MA 01226–27 • 6,797
Dalton, OH 44618 • 1,377
Dalton, PA 18414 • 1,369
Dalton Gardens, ID 83814 • 1,951
Daly City, CA 94014–17 • 92,311

Damascus, MD 20872 • 9,817
Dana Point, CA 92629 • 31,896
Danbury, CT 06810–13 • 65,585
Danbury, TX 77534 • 1,447
Dandridge, TN 37725 • 1,540
Dane □, WI • 367,085
Dania, FL 33004 • 13,024
Daniels □, MT • 2,266
Danielson, CT 06239 • 4,441
Dannemora, NY 12929 • 4,005
Dansville, NY 14437 • 5,002
Dante, VA 24237 • 1,083
Danvers, MA 01923 • 24,174
Danville, AR 72833 • 1,585
Danville, CA 94526 • 31,306
Danville, IL 61832–34 • 33,828
Danville, IN 46122 • 4,345
Danville, KY 40422–23 • 12,420
Danville, OH 43014 • 1,001
Danville, PA 17821 • 5,165
Danville, VA 24540–43 • 53,056
Daphne, AL 36526 • 11,290
Darby, PA 19023 • 11,140
Darby Township, PA 19036 • 10,955
Dardanelle, AR 72834 • 3,722
Dare □, NC • 22,746
Darien, CT 06820 • 18,130
Darien, GA 31305 • 1,783
Darien, IL 60559 • 18,341
Darien, WI 53114 • 1,158
Darke □, OH • 53,619
Darley Woods, DE 19810 • 1,220
Darlington, SC 29532 • 7,311
Darlington, WI 53530 • 2,235
Darlington □, SC • 61,851
Darrington, WA 98241 • 1,042
Dartmouth Woods, DE 19810 • 1,970
Dassel, MN 55325 • 1,082
Dauphin □, PA • 237,813
Davenport, FL 33837 • 1,529
Davenport, IA 52801–09 • 95,333
Davenport, WA 99122 • 1,502
David City, NE 68632 • 2,522
Davidson, NC 28036 • 4,046
Davidson □, NC • 126,677
Davidson □, TN • 510,784
Davidsville, PA 15928 • 1,167
Davie, FL 33328 • 47,217
Davie □, NC • 27,859
Daviess □, IN • 27,533
Daviess □, KY • 87,189
Daviess □, MO • 7,865
Davis, CA 95616–17 • 46,209
Davis, OK 73030 • 2,543
Davis □, IA • 8,312
Davis □, UT • 187,941
Davison, MI 48423 • 5,693
Davison □, SD • 17,503
Davisville, RI 02852 • 500
Dawes □, NE • 9,021
Dawson, GA 31742 • 5,295
Dawson, MN 56232 • 1,626
Dawson □, GA • 9,429
Dawson □, MT • 9,505
Dawson □, NE • 19,940
Dawson □, TX • 14,349
Dawson Springs, KY 42408 • 3,129
Day □, SD • 6,978
Dayton, KY 41074 • 6,576
Dayton, MN 55327 • 4,443
Dayton, NV 89403 • 2,217
Dayton, NJ 08810 • 1,200
Dayton, OH 45401–90 • 182,044
Dayton, OR 97114 • 1,526
Dayton, TN 37321 • 5,671
Dayton, TX 77535 • 5,151
Dayton, WA 99328 • 2,468
Dayton, WY 82836 • 565
Daytona Beach, FL 32114–25 • 61,921
Dayville, CT 06241 • 1,500
Deadwood, SD 57732 • 1,830
Deaf Smith □, TX • 19,153
Deal, NJ 07723 • 1,179
Deale, MD 20751 • 4,151
Dearborn, MI 48120–26 • 89,286
Dearborn □, IN • 38,835
Dearborn Heights, MI 48127 • 60,838
De Baca □, NM • 2,252
De Bary, FL 32713 • 7,176
Decatur, AL 35601–03 • 48,761
Decatur, GA 30030–37 • 17,336
Decatur, IL 62521–26 • 83,885
Decatur, IN 46733 • 8,644
Decatur, MI 49045 • 1,760
Decatur, MS 39327 • 1,248
Decatur, TN 37322 • 1,361
Decatur, TX 76234 • 4,252
Decatur □, GA • 25,511
Decatur □, IN • 23,645
Decatur □, IA • 8,338
Decatur □, KS • 4,021
Decatur □, TN • 10,472
Decherd, TN 37324 • 2,196
Deckerville, MI 48427 • 1,015
Decorah, IA 52101 • 8,063
Dedham, MA 02026 • 23,782
Deep River, CT 06417 • 2,520
Deerfield, IL 60015 • 17,327
Deerfield, WI 53531 • 1,617
Deerfield Beach, FL 33441–43 • 46,325
Deer Lodge, MT 59722 • 3,378
Deer Lodge □, MT • 10,278
Deer Park, NY 11729 • 28,840
Deer Park, OH 45236 • 6,181
Deer Park, TX 77536 • 27,652
Deer Park, WA 99006 • 2,278
Defiance, OH 43512 • 16,768
Defiance □, OH • 39,350
De Forest, WI 53532 • 4,882
De Funiak Springs, FL 32433 • 5,120
De Graff, OH 43318 • 1,331
De Kalb, IL 60115 • 34,925
De Kalb, MS 39328 • 1,073
De Kalb, TX 75559 • 1,976
De Kalb □, AL • 54,651
De Kalb □, GA • 545,837
De Kalb □, IL • 77,932
De Kalb □, IN • 35,324
De Kalb □, MO • 9,967
De Kalb □, TN • 14,360
Delafield, WI 53018 • 5,347
Del Aire, CA 90250 • 8,040
Delanco, NJ 08075 • 3,316

De Land, FL 32720–24 • 16,491
Delano, CA 93215–16 • 22,762
Delano, MN 55328 • 2,709
Delavan, IL 61734 • 1,642
Delavan, WI 53115 • 6,073
Delavan Lake, WI 53115 • 2,177
Delaware, OH 43015 • 20,030
Delaware □, IN • 119,659
Delaware □, IA • 18,035
Delaware □, NY • 47,225
Delaware □, OH • 66,929
Delaware □, OK • 28,070
Delaware □, PA • 547,651
Delaware City, DE 19706 • 1,682
Delcambre, LA 70528 • 1,978
Del City, OK 73115 • 23,928
De Leon, TX 76444 • 2,190
De Leon Springs, FL 32130 • 1,481
Delevan, NY 14042 • 1,214
Delhi, LA 71232 • 3,169
Delhi, NY 13753 • 3,064
Delhi Hills, OH 45238 • 27,647
Dell Rapids, SD 57022 • 2,484
Dellwood, MO 63136 • 5,245
Del Mar, CA 92014 • 4,860
Delmar, DE 19940 • 962
Delmar, MD 21875 • 1,430
Delmar, NY 12054 • 8,360
Del Norte, CO 81132 • 1,674
Del Norte □, CA • 23,460
Del Park Manor, DE 19808 • 1,550
Delphi, IN 46923 • 2,531
Delphos, OH 45833 • 7,093
Delran, NJ 08075 • 14,633
Delray Beach, FL 33444–47 • 47,181
Del Rio, FL 33617 • 8,248
Del Rio, TX 78840–42 • 30,705
Delta, CO 81416 • 3,789
Delta, OH 43515 • 2,849
Delta, UT 84624 • 2,998
Delta □, CO • 20,980
Delta □, MI • 37,780
Delta □, TX • 4,857
Delta Junction, AK 99737 • 652
Deltaville, VA 23043 • 1,082
Deltona, FL 32725 • 50,828
Demarest, NJ 07627 • 4,800
Deming, NM 88030–31 • 10,970
Demopolis, AL 36732 • 7,512
Demorest, GA 30535 • 1,088
Demotte, IN 46310 • 2,482
Denham Springs, LA 70726–27 • 8,381
Denison, IA 51442 • 6,604
Denison, TX 75020–21 • 21,505
Denmark, SC 29042 • 3,762
Denmark, WI 54208 • 1,612
Dennis, MA 02638 • 2,500
Dennis □, MA • 22,746
Dennis Port, MA 02639 • 2,775
Denny Terrace, SC 29203 • 1,885
Dent □, MO • 13,702
Denton, MD 21629 • 2,977
Denton, NC 27239 • 1,292
Denton, TX 76201–06 • 66,270
Denton □, TX • 273,525
Dentsville, SC 29204 • 11,839
Denver, CO 80201–99 • 467,610
Denver, IA 50622 • 1,600
Denver, PA 17517 • 2,861
Denver □, CO • 467,610
Denville, NJ 07834 • 14,380
De Pere, WI 54115 • 16,569
Depew, NY 14043 • 17,673
Deposit, NY 13754 • 1,936
Depue, IL 61322 • 1,729
De Queen, AR 71832 • 4,633
De Quincy, LA 70633 • 3,474
Derby, CT 06418 • 12,199
Derby, KS 67037 • 14,699
Derby, NY 14047 • 1,200
Derby Line, VT 05830 • 855
De Ridder, LA 70634 • 9,868
Dermott, AR 71638 • 4,715
Derry, NH 03038 • 20,446
Derry, PA 15627 • 2,911
Derwood, MD 20855 • 1,500
Des Allemands, LA 70030 • 2,504
Des Arc, AR 72040 • 2,001
Deschutes □, OR • 74,958
Desert Hot Springs, CA 92240 • 11,668
Desha □, AR • 16,798
Deshler, OH 43516 • 1,876
Desloge, MO 63601 • 4,150
De Smet, SD 57231 • 1,172
Des Moines, IA 50301–99 • 193,187
Des Moines, WA 98188 • 17,283
Des Moines □, IA • 42,614
De Soto, IL 62924 • 1,500
De Soto, IA 50069 • 1,033
De Soto, KS 66018 • 2,291
De Soto, MO 63020 • 5,993
De Soto, TX 75115 • 30,544
De Soto □, FL • 23,865
De Soto □, LA • 25,346
De Soto □, MS • 67,910
Despard, WV 26301 • 1,018
Des Peres, MO 63131 • 8,395
Des Plaines, IL 60016–19 • 53,223
Destin, FL 32540–41 • 8,080
Destrehan, LA 70047 • 8,031
Detroit, MI 48201–44 • 1,027,974
Detroit Lakes, MN 56501–02 • 6,635
Deuel □, NE • 2,237
Deuel □, SD • 4,522
Devils Lake, ND 58301 • 7,782
Devine, TX 78016 • 3,928
Devola, OH 45750 • 2,736
Devon, PA 19333 • 6,620
Devonshire, DE 19810 • 2,120
Dewey, OK 74029 • 3,326
Dewey □, OK • 5,551
Dewey □, SD • 5,523
Dewey Beach, DE 19971 • 204
Deweyville, TX 77614 • 1,218
De Witt, AR 72042 • 3,553
De Witt, IA 52742 • 4,514
De Witt, MI 48820 • 3,964
De Witt, NY 13214 • 8,244
De Witt □, IL • 16,516
De Witt □, TX • 18,840
Dexter, ME 04930 • 2,650
Dexter, MI 48130 • 1,497

Dexter, MO 63841 • 7,559
Dexter, NY 13634 • 1,030
Diamond Bar, CA 91765 • 53,672
Diamond Hill, RI 02864 • 810
Diamond Lake, IL 60060 • 1,500
Diamond Springs, CA 95619 • 2,872
Diamondville, WY 83116 • 864
Diaz, AR 72043 • 1,363
D'Iberville, MS 39532 • 6,566
Diboll, TX 75941 • 4,341
Dickens □, TX • 2,571
Dickenson □, VA • 17,620
Dickey □, ND • 6,107
Dickinson, ND 58601–02 • 16,097
Dickinson, TX 77539 • 9,497
Dickinson □, IA • 14,909
Dickinson □, KS • 18,958
Dickinson □, MI • 26,831
Dickson, TN 37055 • 8,791
Dickson □, TN • 35,061
Dickson City, PA 18519 • 6,276
Dierks, AR 71833 • 1,263
Dighton, KS 67839 • 1,361
Dighton, MA 02715 • 1,100
Dillard, OR 97432 • 1,000
Dilley, TX 78017 • 2,632
Dillingham, AK 99576 • 2,017
Dillon, MT 59725 • 3,991
Dillon, SC 29536 • 6,829
Dillon □, SC • 29,114
Dillsboro, IN 47018 • 1,200
Dillsburg, PA 17019 • 1,925
Dilworth, MN 56529 • 2,562
Dimmit □, TX • 10,433
Dimmitt, TX 79027 • 4,408
Dimondale, MI 48821 • 1,247
Dingmans Ferry, PA 18328 • 1,200
Dinuba, CA 93618 • 12,743
Dinwiddie □, VA • 20,960
Dishman, WA 99213 • 9,671
District Heights-Forestville, MD 20747 • 6,704
District of Columbia 0T15, DC •
Divernon, IL 62530 • 1,178
Divide □, ND • 2,899
Dixfield, ME 04224 • 1,300
Dix Hills, NY 11746 • 25,849
Dixie □, FL • 10,585
Dixon, CA 95620 • 10,401
Dixon, IL 61021 • 15,144
Dixon, MO 65459 • 1,585
Dixon □, NE • 6,143
Dixonville, PA 15734 • 1,000
Dobbs Ferry, NY 10522 • 9,940
Dobson, NC 27017 • 1,195
Docena, AL 35060 • 1,000
Dock Junction, GA 31520 • 7,094
Doddridge □, WV • 6,994
Dodge □, GA • 17,607
Dodge □, MN • 15,731
Dodge □, NE • 34,500
Dodge □, WI • 76,559
Dodge Center, MN 55927 • 1,954
Dodge City, KS 67801 • 21,129
Dodge Park, MD 20785 • 4,842
Dodgeville, WI 53533 • 3,882
Dolgeville, NY 13329 • 2,452
Dolomite, AL 35061 • 2,590
Dolores, CO 81323 • 1,504
Dolton, IL 60419 • 23,930
Dona Ana, NM 88032 • 950
Dona Ana □, NM • 135,510
Donaldsonville, LA 70346 • 7,949
Donalsonville, GA 31745 • 2,761
Doneraile, SC 29532 • 1,276
Doniphan, MO 63935 • 1,713
Doniphan □, KS • 8,134
Donley □, TX • 3,696
Donna, TX 78537 • 12,652
Donora, PA 15033 • 5,928
Dooly □, GA • 9,901
Door □, WI • 25,690
Dora, AL 35062 • 2,214
Doraville, GA 30340 • 7,626
Dorchester □, MD • 30,236
Dorchester □, SC • 83,060
Dormont, PA 15216 • 9,772
Dorothy Pond, MA 01527 • 1,670
Dorr, MI 49323 • 1,450
Dorset, VT 05251 • 550
Dorsey, MD 21227 • 1,186
Dothan, AL 36301–04 • 53,589
Dougherty □, GA • 96,311
Douglas, AZ 85607–08 • 12,822
Douglas, GA 31533 • 10,464
Douglas, MI 49406 • 1,040
Douglas, WY 82633 • 5,076
Douglas □, CO • 60,391
Douglas □, GA • 71,120
Douglas □, IL • 19,464
Douglas □, KS • 81,798
Douglas □, MN • 28,674
Douglas □, MO • 11,876
Douglas □, NE • 416,444
Douglas □, NV • 27,637
Douglas □, OR • 94,649
Douglas □, SD • 3,746
Douglas □, WA • 26,205
Douglas □, WI • 41,758
Douglass, KS 67039 • 1,722
Douglasville, GA 30133–35 • 11,635
Dousman, WI 53118 • 1,277
Dover, AR 72837 • 1,055
Dover, DE 19901–03 • 27,630
Dover, FL 33527 • 2,606
Dover, MA 02030 • 2,163
Dover, NH 03820 • 25,042
Dover, NJ 07801 • 15,115
Dover, OH 44622 • 11,329
Dover, PA 17315 • 1,884
Dover, TN 37058 • 1,341
Dover-Foxcroft, ME 04426 • 3,077
Dover Plains, NY 12522 • 1,847
Dowagiac, MI 49047 • 6,409
Downers Grove, IL 60515–17 • 46,858
Downey, CA 90239–42 • 91,444
Downingtown, PA 19335 • 7,749
Downs, KS 67437 • 1,119
Downsville, NY 13755 • 1,100
Doylestown, OH 44230 • 2,668
Doylestown, PA 18901 • 8,575
Dracut, MA 01826 • 25,594

Drain, OR 97435 • 1,011
Draper, UT 84020 • 7,257
Drayton, ND 58225 • 961
Drayton, SC 29333 • 1,443
Drayton Plains, MI 48330 • 18,000
Dreamland Villa, AZ 85205 • 3,400
Dresden, OH 43821 • 1,581
Dresden, TN 38225 • 2,488
Dresslerville, NV 89410 • 180
Drew, MS 38737 • 2,349
Drew □, AR • 17,369
Drexel, NC 28619 • 1,746
Drexel, OH 45427 • 5,143
Drexel Hill, PA 19026 • 29,744
Dripping Springs, TX 78620 • 1,033
Druid Hills, GA 30333 • 12,174
Drumright, OK 74030 • 2,799
Dryden, NY 13053 • 1,908
Dry Ridge, KY 41035 • 1,601
Duarte, CA 91010 • 20,688
Dublin, CA 94568 • 23,229
Dublin, GA 31021 • 16,312
Dublin, OH 43017 • 16,366
Dublin, PA 18917 • 1,985
Dublin, TX 76446 • 3,190
Dublin, VA 24084 • 2,012
Du Bois, PA 15801 • 8,286
Dubois, WY 82513 • 895
Dubois □, IN • 36,616
Duboistown, PA 17701 • 1,201
Dubuque, IA 52001–04 • 57,546
Dubuque □, IA • 86,403
Duchesne, UT 84021 • 1,308
Duchesne □, UT • 12,645
Dudley, MA 01570–71 • 3,700
Due West, SC 29639 • 1,220
Dukes □, MA • 11,639
Dulce, NM 87528 • 2,438
Duluth, GA 30136 • 9,029
Duluth, MN 55801–16 • 85,493
Dumas, AR 71639 • 5,520
Dumas, TX 79029 • 12,871
Dumfries, VA 22026 • 4,282
Dumont, NJ 07628 • 17,187
Dunaire, GA 30032 • 7,170
Dunbar, PA 15431 • 1,213
Dunbar, WV 25064 • 8,697
Duncan, OK 73533–34 • 21,732
Duncan, SC 29334 • 2,152
Duncan Falls, OH 43734 • 1,200
Duncannon, PA 17020 • 1,450
Duncansville, PA 16635 • 1,309
Duncanville, TX 75116 • 35,748
Dundalk, MD 21222 • 65,800
Dundee, FL 33838 • 2,335
Dundee, IL 60118 • 3,728
Dundee, MI 48131 • 2,664
Dundee, NY 14837 • 1,588
Dundee, OR 97115 • 1,663
Dundy □, NE • 2,582
Dunedin, FL 34697–98 • 34,012
Dunellen, NJ 08812 • 6,528
Dunkirk, IN 47336 • 2,739
Dunkirk, NY 14048 • 13,989
Dunklin □, MO • 33,112
Dunlap, IL 61525 • 1,251
Dunlap, IA 51529 • 1,251
Dunlap, TN 37327 • 3,731
Dunleith, DE 19801 • 2,600
Dunmore, PA 18512 • 15,403
Dunn, NC 28334–35 • 8,336
Dunn □, ND • 4,005
Dunn □, WI • 35,909
Dunnellon, FL 32630 • 1,624
Dunn Loring Woods, VA 22180 • 2,800
Dunseith, ND 58329 • 723
Dunsmuir, CA 96025 • 2,129
Dunwoody, GA 30338 • 26,302
Du Page □, IL • 781,666
Duplin □, NC • 39,995
Dupont, CO 80024 • 5,200
Dupont, PA 18641 • 2,984
Dupont Manor, DE 19901 • 1,059
Duquesne, PA 15110 • 8,525
Du Quoin, IL 62832 • 6,697
Durand, IL 61024 • 1,100
Durand, MI 48429 • 4,283
Durand, WI 54736 • 2,003
Durango, CO 81301–02 • 12,430
Durant, IA 52747 • 1,549
Durant, MS 39063 • 2,838
Durant, OK 74701–02 • 12,823
Durham, CA 95938 • 1,500
Durham, CT 06422 • 2,650
Durham, NH 03824 • 9,236
Durham, NC 27701–22 • 136,611
Durham □, NC • 181,835
Duryea, PA 18642 • 4,869
Duson, LA 70529 • 1,465
Dutchess □, NY • 259,462
Duval □, FL • 672,971
Duval □, TX • 12,918
Duxbury, MA 02331–32 • 1,637
Dwight, IL 60420 • 4,230
Dyer, IN 46311 • 10,923
Dyer, TN 38330 • 2,504
Dyer □, TN • 34,854
Dyersburg, TN 38024–25 • 16,317
Dyersville, IA 52040 • 3,703
Dysart, IA 52224 • 1,230

E

Eagan, MN 55121 • 47,409
Eagar, AZ 85925 • 4,025
Eagle, CO 81631 • 1,580
Eagle, ID 83616 • 3,327
Eagle, NE 68347 • 1,047
Eagle, WI 53119 • 1,182
Eagle □, CO • 21,928
Eagle Grove, IA 50533 • 3,671
Eagle Lake, MN 56024 • 1,703
Eagle Lake, TX 77434 • 3,551
Eagle Lake, WI 53139 • 1,000
Eagle Pass, TR 78852–53 • 20,651
Eagle Point, OR 97524 • 3,008
Eagle River, WI 54521 • 1,374
Eagleton Village, TN 37801 • 5,331
Earle, AR 72331 • 3,393
Earlham, IA 50072 • 1,157
Earlimart, CA 93219 • 5,881

Earlington, KY 42410 • *1,833*
Earlville, IL 60518 • *1,435*
Early □, GA • *11,854*
Earth, TX 79031 • *1,228*
Easley, SC 29640-42 • *15,195*
East Alton, IL 62024 • *7,063*
East Arlington, VT 05252 • *600*
East Aurora, NY 14052 • *6,647*
East Bangor, PA 18013 • *1,006*
East Barre, VT 05649 • *700*
East Baton Rouge □, LA • *380,105*
East Berlin, PA 17316 • *1,175*
East Bernard, TX 77435 • *1,544*
East Bethel, MN 55005 • *8,050*
East Billerica, MA 01821 • *3,830*
East Brady, PA 16028 • *1,047*
East Brewton, AL 36426 • *2,579*
East Bridgewater, MA 02333 • *3,270*
East Brookfield, MA 01515 • *1,396*
East Brooklyn, CT 06239 • *1,481*
East Brunswick, NJ 08816 • *43,548*
East Carbon, UT 84520 • *1,270*
East Carroll □, LA • *9,709*
Eastchester, NY 10709 • *18,537*
East Cleveland, OH 44112 • *33,096*
East Compton, CA 90221 • *7,967*
East Dennis, MA 02641 • *1,500*
East Detroit, MI 48021 • *35,283*
East Douglas, MA 01516 • *1,945*
East Dubuque, IL 61025 • *1,914*
East Falmouth, MA 02536 • *5,577*
East Farmingdale, NY 11735 • *4,510*
East Feliciana □, LA • *19,211*
East Flat Rock, NC 28726 • *3,218*
East Gaffney, SC 29340 • *3,278*
Eastgate, WA 98007 • *4,434*
East Glenville, NY 12302 • *6,518*
East Granby, CT 06026 • *1,200*
East Grand Forks, MN 56721 • *8,658*
East Grand Rapids, MI 49506 • *10,807*
East Greenville, PA 18041 • *3,117*
East Greenwich, RI 02818 • *11,865*
East Half Hollow Hills, NY 11746 • *7,010*
Eastham, MA 02642 • *1,150*
East Hampton, CT 06424 • *2,167*
Easthampton, MA 01027 • *15,580*
East Hampton, NY 11937 • *1,402*
East Hanover, NJ • *9,926*
East Hartford, CT 06128 • *50,452*
East Haven, CT 06512 • *26,144*
East Helena, MT 59635 • *1,538*
East Hemet, CA 92343 • *17,611*
East Hills, NY 11576 • *6,746*
East Islip, NY 11730 • *14,325*
East Jordan, MI 49727 • *2,240*
Eastlake, OH 44094 • *21,161*
East La Mirada, CA 90638 • *9,367*
Eastland, TX 76448 • *3,690*
Eastland □, TX • *18,488*
East Lansing, MI 48823-26 • *50,677*
East Las Vegas, NV 89112 • *11,087*
East Liverpool, OH 43920 • *13,654*
East Longmeadow, MA 01028 • *12,905*
East Los Angeles, CA 90022 • *126,379*
East Lyme, CT 06333 • *1,200*
Eastman, GA 31023 • *5,153*
East Marietta, GA 30062 • *11,900*
East Marion, NY 11939 • *1,500*
East Matunuck, RI 02879 • *500*
East Meadow, NY 11554 • *36,609*
East Middlebury, VT 05740 • *500*
East Midvale, UT 84047 • *3,800*
East Millinocket, ME 04430 • *2,075*
East Moline, IL 61244 • *20,147*
East Montpelier, VT 05651 • *600*
East Naples, FL 33962 • *22,951*
East Newark, NJ 07029 • *2,157*
East Newnan, GA 30263 • *1,173*
East Norriton, PA 19401 • *13,324*
East Northport, NY 11731 • *20,411*
Easton, MD 21601 • *9,372*
East Orange, NJ 07017-19 • *73,552*
East Orleans, MA 02643 • *1,850*
Eastover, SC 29044 • *1,044*
East Palatka, FL 32131 • *1,989*
East Palestine, OH 44413 • *5,168*
East Palo Alto, CA 94303 • *23,451*
East Patchogue, NY 11772 • *20,195*
East Pea Ridge, WV 25705 • *4,980*
East Peoria, IL 61611 • *21,378*
East Pepperell, MA 01463 • *2,296*
East Petersburg, PA 17520 • *4,197*
East Pittsburgh, PA 15112 • *2,160*
Eastpoint, FL 32328 • *1,577*
East Point, GA 30344 • *34,402*
Eastport, ME 04631 • *1,965*
Eastport, NY 11941 • *1,500*
East Porterville, CA 93257 • *5,790*
East Port Orchard, WA 98366 • *5,409*
East Prairie, MO 63845 • *3,416*
East Providence, RI 02914 • *50,380*
East Quogue, NY 11942 • *4,372*
East Richmond, CA 94805 • *5,100*
East Ridge, TN 37412 • *21,101*
East River, CT 06443 • *3,440*
East Rochester, NY 14445 • *6,932*
East Rockaway, NY 11518 • *10,152*
East Rockingham, NC 28379 • *4,158*
East Rutherford, NJ 07073 • *7,902*
East Saint Louis, IL 62201-08 • *40,944*
Eastsound, WA 98245 • *1,100*
East Spencer, NC 28039 • *2,055*
East Stroudsburg, PA 18301 • *8,781*
East Tawas, MI 48730 • *2,887*
East Templeton, MA 01438 • *1,300*
East Troy, WI 53120 • *2,664*
East Tustin, CA 92705 • *10,000*
East Vestal, NY 13902 • *6,310*
East View, WV 26301 • *1,222*
East Walpole, MA 02032 • *3,760*
East Wareham, MA 02538 • *1,500*
East Washington, PA 15301 • *2,126*
East Wenatchee, WA 98802 • *2,701*
East Windsor, NJ 08520 • *15,000*
Eastwood, NY 49001 • *6,340*
Eastwood Hills, UT 84106 • *1,200*
Eaton, CO 80615 • *1,959*
Eaton, IN 47338 • *1,614*
Eaton, OH 45320 • *7,396*
Eaton □, MI • *92,879*
Eaton Rapids, MI 48827 • *4,695*

Eatonton, GA 31024 • *4,737*
Eatontown, NJ 07724 • *13,800*
Eatonville, WA 98328 • *1,374*
Eau Claire, WI 54701-03 • *56,856*
Eau Claire □, WI • *85,183*
Ebensburg, PA 15931 • *3,872*
Eccles, WV 25836 • *1,162*
Echo Bay, NV 89040 • *120*
Echols □, GA • *2,334*
Eckhart Mines, MD 21528 • *1,333*
Eclectic, AL 36024 • *1,087*
Economy, PA 15005 • *9,519*
Ecorse, MI 48229 • *12,180*
Ector □, TX • *118,934*
Edcouch, TX 78538 • *2,878*
Eddy, NM • *48,605*
Eddy □, ND • *2,951*
Eddystone, PA 19013 • *2,446*
Eddyville, IA 52553 • *1,010*
Eddyville, KY 42038 • *1,889*
Eden, NY 14057 • *3,088*
Eden, NC 27288 • *15,238*
Eden, TX 76837 • *1,567*
Eden Prairie, MN 55344 • *39,311*
Edenton, NC 27932 • *5,268*
Edgar, WI 54426 • *1,318*
Edgar □, IL • *19,595*
Edgartown, MA 02539 • *3,062*
Edgecombe □, NC • *56,558*
Edgefield, SC 29824 • *2,563*
Edgefield □, SC • *18,375*
Edgeley, ND 58433 • *680*
Edgemere, MD 21221 • *9,226*
Edgemont, SD 57735 • *906*
Edgemoor, DE 19802 • *5,853*
Edgerton, KS 66021 • *1,244*
Edgerton, MN 56128 • *1,106*
Edgerton, OH 43517 • *1,896*
Edgerton, WI 53534 • *4,254*
Edgerton, WY 82635 • *247*
Edgewater, AL 35224 • *1,120*
Edgewater, CO 80214 • *4,613*
Edgewater, FL 32132 • *15,337*
Edgewater, MD 21037 • *1,600*
Edgewater, NJ 07020 • *5,001*
Edgewater Park, NJ 08010 • *8,388*
Edgewood, IN 46011 • *2,057*
Edgewood, KY 41017 • *8,143*
Edgewood, MD • *3,470*
Edgewood, MD 21040 • *23,903*
Edgewood, OH 44004 • *5,189*
Edgewood, PA 15218 • *3,581*
Edgewood, WA 98372 • *2,650*
Edgeworth, PA 15143 • *1,670*
Edina, MN 55410 • *46,070*
Edina, MO 63537 • *1,283*
Edinboro, PA 16412 • *7,736*
Edinburg, TX 78539-40 • *29,885*
Edinburgh, IN 46124 • *4,536*
Edison, GA 31746 • *1,182*
Edison, NJ 08817-20 • *88,680*
Edmond, OK 73034 • *52,315*
Edmonds, WA 98020 • *30,744*
Edmondson Heights, MD 21207 • *4,750*
Edmonson □, KY • *10,357*
Edmonton, KY 42129 • *1,477*
Edmore, MI 48829 • *1,126*
Edmunds □, SD • *4,356*
Edna, TX 77957 • *5,343*
Edwards, MS 39066 • *1,279*
Edwards □, IL • *7,440*
Edwards □, KS • *3,787*
Edwards □, TX • *2,266*
Edwardsburg, MI 49112 • *1,142*
Edwardsville, IL 62025 • *14,579*
Edwardsville, KS 66113 • *3,979*
Edwardsville, PA 18704 • *5,399*
Effingham, IL 62401 • *11,851*
Effingham □, GA • *25,687*
Effingham □, IL • *31,704*
Egg Harbor City, NJ 08215 • *4,583*
Egypt, MA 02066 • *1,100*
Egypt Lake, FL 33614 • *14,580*
Ehrenberg, AZ 85334 • *1,500*
Elba, AL 36323 • *4,011*
Elbert, CO • *9,646*
Elbert □, GA • *18,949*
Elberta, GA 31093 • *1,559*
Elberton, GA 30635 • *5,682*
Elbow Lake, MN 56531 • *1,186*
Elburn, IL 60119 • *1,275*
El Cajon, CA 92019-22 • *88,693*
El Campo, TX 77437 • *10,511*
El Centro, CA 92243-44 • *31,384*
El Cerrito, CA 94530 • *22,869*
Eldersburg, MD 21784 • *9,720*
Eldon, IA 52554 • *1,070*
Eldon, MO 65026 • *4,419*
Eldora, IA 50627 • *3,038*
El Dorado, AR 71730-31 • *23,146*
Eldorado, IL 62930 • *4,536*
El Dorado, KS 67042 • *11,504*
Eldorado, TX 76936 • *2,019*
El Dorado □, CA • *125,995*
El Dorado Hills, CA 95630 • *6,395*
El Dorado Springs, MO 64744 • *3,830*
Eldridge, IA 52748 • *3,378*
Eleanor, WV 25070 • *1,256*
Electra, TX 76360 • *3,113*
Eleele, HI 96705 • *1,489*
El Encanto Heights, CA 93117 • *7,700*
Elfers, FL 34680 • *12,356*
Elgin, IL 60120-23 • *77,010*
Elgin, ND 58533 • *765*
Elgin, OR 97827 • *1,586*
Elgin, TX 78621 • *4,846*
Elida, OH 45807 • *1,486*
Elizabeth, NJ 07201-08 • *110,002*
Elizabeth City, NC 27906-09 • *14,292*
Elizabethton, TN 37643-44 • *11,931*
Elizabethtown, KY 42701-02 • *18,167*
Elizabethtown, NC 28337 • *3,704*
Elizabethtown, PA 17022 • *9,952*
Elizabethville, PA 17023 • *1,467*
Elk □, KS • *3,327*
Elk □, PA • *34,878*
Elkader, IA 52043 • *1,510*
Elk City, OK 73644 • *10,428*
Elk Grove, CA 95624 • *17,483*
Elk Grove Village, IL 60009 • *33,429*
Elkhart, IN 46514-17 • *43,627*
Elkhart, KS 67950 • *2,318*
Elkhart, TX 75839 • *1,076*

Elkhart □, IN • *156,198*
Elkhart Lake, WI 53020 • *1,019*
Elkhorn, NE 68022 • *1,398*
Elkhorn, WI 53121 • *5,337*
Elkin, NC 28621 • *3,790*
Elkins, WV 26241 • *7,420*
Elkland, PA 16920 • *1,849*
Elk Mountain, WY 82324 • *174*
Elko, NV 89801-02 • *14,736*
Elko □, NV • *33,530*
Elk Point, SD 57025 • *1,423*
Elk Rapids, MI 49629 • *1,626*
Elkridge, MD 21227 • *12,953*
Elk River, MN 55330 • *11,143*
Elkton, KY 42220 • *1,789*
Elkton, MD 21921-22 • *9,073*
Elkton, VA 22827 • *1,935*
Elkview, WV 25071 • *1,047*
Ellaville, GA 31806 • *1,724*
Ellendale, DE 19941 • *313*
Ellendale, ND 58436 • *1,798*
Ellensburg, WA 98926 • *12,361*
Ellenton, FL 34222 • *2,573*
Ellenville, NY 12428 • *4,243*
Ellerbe, NC 28338 • *1,132*
Ellerslie, MD 21529 • *1,500*
Ellettsville, IN 47429 • *3,275*
Ellicott City, MD 21043 • *41,396*
Ellijay, GA 30540 • *1,178*
Ellington, CT 06029 • *1,500*
Ellinwood, KS 67526 • *2,329*
Elliott □, KY • *6,455*
Ellis, KS 67637 • *1,814*
Ellis □, KS • *26,004*
Ellis □, OK • *4,497*
Ellis □, TX • *85,167*
Ellisville, MS 39437 • *3,634*
Ellisville, MO 63011 • *7,545*
Ellport, PA 16117 • *1,243*
Ellsworth, KS 67439 • *2,294*
Ellsworth, ME 04605 • *5,975*
Ellsworth, PA 15331 • *1,048*
Ellsworth, WI 54011 • *2,706*
Ellsworth □, KS • *6,586*
Ellwood City, PA 16117 • *8,894*
Elma, WA 98541 • *3,011*
Elm City, NC 27822 • *1,624*
Elmer, NJ 08318 • *1,571*
Elm Grove, WI 53122 • *6,261*
Elmhurst, IL 60126 • *42,029*
Elmira, NY 14901-05 • *33,724*
Elmira Heights, NY 14903 • *4,359*
El Mirage, AZ 85335 • *5,001*
Elmont, NY 11003 • *28,612*
Elmora, PA 15737 • *1,500*
Elmore, OH 43416 • *1,334*
Elmore □, AL • *49,210*
Elmore □, ID • *21,205*
Elmwood, IL 61529 • *1,841*
Elmwood Park, IL 60635 • *23,206*
Elmwood Park, NJ 07407 • *17,623*
Elmwood Place, OH 45216 • *2,937*
Eloise, FL 33880 • *1,408*
Elon College, NC 27244 • *4,394*
Eloy, AZ 85231 • *7,211*
El Paso, IL 61738 • *2,499*
El Paso □, CO • *397,014*
El Paso, TX 79901-99 • *515,342*
El Paso □, TX • *591,610*
El Portal, FL 33138 • *2,457*
El Reno, OK 73036 • *15,414*
Elroy, WI 53929 • *1,533*
Elsa, TX 78543 • *5,242*
Elsberry, MO 63343 • *1,898*
El Segundo, CA 90245 • *15,223*
Elsmere, DE 19805 • *5,935*
Elsmere, KY 41018 • *6,847*
Elsmere, NY 12054 • *4,140*
El Sobrante, CA 94803 • *9,852*
Elton, LA 70532 • *1,277*
El Toro, CA 92630 • *62,685*
Elvins, MO 63601 • *1,391*
Elwood, IN 46036 • *9,494*
Elwood, KS 66024 • *1,079*
Elwood, NJ 08217 • *1,400*
Elwood, NY 11731 • *10,916*
Ely, MN 55731 • *3,968*
Ely, NV 89301 • *4,756*
Elyria, OH 44035-39 • *56,746*
Elysburg, PA 17824 • *1,890*
Emanuel □, GA • *20,546*
Emerson, GA 30137 • *1,201*
Emerson, NJ 07630 • *6,930*
Emery □, UT • *10,332*
Eminence, KY 40019 • *2,055*
Emmaus, PA 18049 • *11,157*
Emmet □, IA • *11,569*
Emmet □, MI • *25,040*
Emmetsburg, IA 50536 • *3,940*
Emmett, ID 83617 • *4,601*
Emmitsburg, MD 21727 • *1,688*
Emmonak, AK 99581 • *642*
Emmons □, ND • *4,830*
Empire, NV 89405 • *300*
Emporia, KS 66801 • *25,512*
Emporia, VA 23847 • *5,306*
Emporium, PA 15834 • *2,513*
Emsworth, PA 15202 • *2,892*
Encampment, WY 82325 • *490*
Encinitas, CA 92023-24 • *55,386*
Enderlin, ND 58027 • *997*
Endicott, NY 13760 • *13,531*
Endwell, NY 13760 • *12,602*
Enfield (Thompsonville), CT 06082-83 • *8,458*
Enfield, NH 03748 • *1,560*
Enfield, NC 27823 • *3,082*
England, AR 72046 • *3,351*
Engleside, VA 22309 • *24,058*
Englewood, CO 80110-12 • *29,387*
Englewood, FL 34223-24 • *15,025*
Englewood, NJ 07631-32 • *24,850*
Englewood, OH 45322 • *11,432*
Englewood, TN 37329 • *1,611*
Englewood Cliffs, NJ 07632 • *5,634*
Englishtown, NJ 07726 • *1,268*
Enid, OK 73701-06 • *45,309*
Enka, NC 28728 • *5,567*
Ennis, MT 59729 • *773*
Ennis, TX 75119-20 • *13,883*
Enoch, UT 84720 • *1,947*
Enola, PA 17025 • *5,961*

Enon, OH 45323 • *2,605*
Enoree, SC 29335 • *1,107*
Enosburg Falls, VT 05450 • *1,350*
Ensley, FL 32504 • *16,362*
Enterprise, AL 36330-31 • *20,123*
Enterprise, OR 97828 • *1,905*
Enterprise, WV 26568 • *1,058*
Enumclaw, WA 98022 • *7,227*
Ephraim, UT 84627 • *3,363*
Ephrata, PA 17522 • *12,133*
Ephrata, WA 98823 • *5,349*
Epping, NH 03042 • *1,384*
Epworth, IA 52045 • *1,297*
Erath, LA 70533 • *2,428*
Erath □, TX • *27,991*
Erial, NJ 08081 • *2,500*
Erick, OK 73645 • *1,083*
Erie, CO 80516 • *1,258*
Erie, IL 61250 • *1,572*
Erie, KS 66733 • *1,276*
Erie, PA 16501-65 • *108,718*
Erie □, NY • *968,532*
Erie □, OH • *76,779*
Erie □, PA • *275,572*
Erin, TN 37061 • *1,586*
Erlanger, KY 41018 • *15,979*
Erma, NJ 08204 • *2,045*
Errol Heights, OR 97266 • *10,487*
Erwin, NC 28339 • *4,061*
Erwin, TN 37650 • *5,015*
Escalon, CA 95320 • *4,437*
Escambia □, AL • *35,518*
Escambia □, FL • *262,798*
Escanaba, MI 49829 • *13,659*
Escatawpa, MS 39552 • *3,902*
Escondido, CA 92025-27 • *108,635*
Esmeralda □, NV • *1,344*
Esmond, RI 02917 • *4,320*
Espanola, NM 87532 • *8,389*
Esparto, CA 95627 • *1,487*
Esperance, NM 98043 • *11,236*
Espy, PA 17815 • *1,430*
Essex, CT 06426 • *2,500*
Essex, MD 21221 • *40,872*
Essex, MA 01929 • *1,507*
Essex, VT 05451 • *800*
Essex □, MA • *670,080*
Essex □, NJ • *778,206*
Essex □, NY • *37,152*
Essex □, VT • *6,405*
Essex □, VA • *8,689*
Essex Fells, NJ 07021 • *2,363*
Essex Junction, VT 05452-53 • *8,396*
Essexville, MI 48732 • *4,088*
Estacada, OR 97023 • *2,016*
Estell Manor, NJ 08319 • *1,404*
Estelle, LA 70072 • *14,091*
Estes Park, CO 80517 • *3,184*
Estherville, IA 51334 • *6,720*
Estill, SC 29918 • *2,387*
Estill □, KY • *14,614*
Estill Springs, TN 37330 • *1,408*
Etna, PA 15223 • *4,200*
Etowah, TN 37331 • *3,815*
Etowah □, AL • *99,840*
Ettrick, VA 23803 • *5,290*
Euclid, OH 44117 • *54,875*
Eudora, AR 71640 • *3,155*
Eudora, KS 66025 • *3,006*
Eufaula, AL 36027 • *13,220*
Eufaula, OK 74432 • *2,652*
Eugene, OR 97401-05 • *112,669*
Euless, TX 76039-40 • *38,149*
Eunice, LA 70535 • *11,162*
Eunice, NM 88231 • *2,676*
Eupora, MS 39744 • *2,145*
Eureka, CA 95501-02 • *27,025*
Eureka, IL 61530 • *4,435*
Eureka, KS 67045 • *2,974*
Eureka, MO 63025 • *4,683*
Eureka, MT 59917 • *1,043*
Eureka, NV 89316 • *650*
Eureka, SD 57437 • *1,197*
Eureka □, NV • *1,547*
Eureka Springs, AR 72632 • *1,900*
Eustis, FL 32726-27 • *12,967*
Eutaw, AL 35462 • *2,281*
Evangeline □, LA • *33,274*
Evans, CO 80620 • *5,877*
Evans, GA 30809 • *2,000*
Evans □, GA • *8,724*
Evans City, PA 16033 • *2,054*
Evansdale, IA 50707 • *4,638*
Evanston, IL 60201-04 • *73,233*
Evanston, WY 82930-31 • *10,903*
Evansville, IN 47701-37 • *126,272*
Evansville, WI 53536 • *3,174*
Evansville, WY 82636 • *1,403*
Evart, MI 49631 • *1,744*
Evarts, KY 40828 • *1,063*
Eveleth, MN 55734 • *4,064*
Everett, MA 02149 • *35,701*
Everett, PA 15537 • *1,777*
Everett, WA 98201-08 • *69,961*
Evergreen, AL 36401 • *3,911*
Evergreen, CO 80439 • *7,582*
Evergreen Park, IL 60642 • *20,874*
Everman, TX 76140 • *5,672*
Everson, WA 98247 • *1,490*
Ewa, HI 96706 • *3,780*
Ewa Beach, HI 96706-07 • *14,315*
Ewing Township, NJ 08618 • *34,185*
Excelsior Springs, MO 64024 • *10,354*
Exeter, CA 93221 • *7,276*
Exeter, NH 03833 • *9,556*
Exeter, PA 18643 • *5,691*
Exmore, VA 23350 • *1,115*
Experiment, GA 30223 • *3,762*
Eyota, MN 55934 • *1,448*

F

Fabens, TX 79838 • *5,599*
Factoryville, PA 18419 • *1,310*
Fairbank, IA 50629 • *1,018*
Fairbanks, AK 99701 • *30,843*
Fair Bluff, NC 28439 • *1,068*
Fairborn, OH 45324 • *31,300*
Fairburn, GA 30213 • *4,013*
Fairbury, IL 61739 • *3,643*

Fairbury, NE 68352 • *4,335*
Fairchance, PA 15436 • *1,918*
Fairdale, KY 40118 • *6,563*
Fairfax, CA 94930 • *6,931*
Fairfax, DE 19803 • *2,075*
Fairfax, MN 55332 • *1,276*
Fairfax, OK 74637 • *1,749*
Fairfax, SC 29827 • *2,317*
Fairfax, VA 22030-39 • *19,622*
Fairfax □, VA • *818,584*
Fairfield, AL 35064 • *12,200*
Fairfield, CA 94533 • *77,211*
Fairfield, CT 06430-32 • *53,418*
Fairfield, IL 62837 • *5,439*
Fairfield, IA 52556 • *9,768*
Fairfield, ME 04937 • *2,794*
Fairfield, NJ 07004 • *7,615*
Fairfield, OH 45014 • *39,729*
Fairfield, TX 75840 • *3,234*
Fairfield □, CT • *827,645*
Fairfield □, OH • *103,461*
Fairfield □, SC • *22,295*
Fairfield Bay, AR 72088 • *2,332*
Fair Grove, NC 27360 • *1,500*
Fairhaven, MA 02719 • *15,759*
Fair Haven, NJ 07704 • *5,270*
Fair Haven, VT 05743 • *2,432*
Fairhope, AL 36532-33 • *8,485*
Fair Lawn, NJ 07410 • *30,548*
Fairlawn, OH 44313 • *5,779*
Fairlawn, VA 24141 • *2,399*
Fairlea, WV 24902 • *1,743*
Fairless Hills, PA 19030 • *9,026*
Fairmont, IL 60441 • *2,200*
Fairmont, MN 56031 • *11,265*
Fairmont, NC 28340 • *2,489*
Fairmont, WV 26554-55 • *20,210*
Fairmount, IN 46928 • *3,130*
Fairmount, NY 13031 • *12,266*
Fairmount Heights, MD 20743 • *1,238*
Fair Oaks, CA 95628 • *26,867*
Fair Oaks, GA 30060 • *6,996*
Fairoaks, PA 15003 • *1,854*
Fair Plain, MI 49022 • *8,051*
Fairport, NY 14450 • *5,943*
Fairport Harbor, OH 44077 • *2,978*
Fairton, NJ 08320 • *1,359*
Fairview □, MT 59221 • *869*
Fairview, NJ 07022 • *10,733*
Fairview, OK 73737 • *2,936*
Fairview, OR 97024 • *2,391*
Fairview, PA 16415 • *1,988*
Fairview, TN 37062 • *4,210*
Fairview Heights, IL 62208 • *14,351*
Fairview Park, IN 47842 • *1,446*
Fairview Park, OH 44126 • *18,028*
Fairview Shores, FL 32804 • *13,192*
Fairway, KS 66205 • *4,173*
Fairwood, WA 98058 • *2,000*
Fairwood, WA 99218 • *5,807*
Falconer, NY 14733 • *2,653*
Falcon Heights, MN 55113 • *5,380*
Falfurrias, TX 78355 • *5,788*
Falkville, AL 35622 • *1,337*
Fall Branch, TN 37656 • *1,203*
Fallbrook, CA 92028 • *22,095*
Fall City, WA 98024 • *1,582*
Fall Creek, WI 54742 • *1,034*
Fallon, NV 89406 • *6,438*
Fallon □, MT • *3,103*
Fall River, MA 02720-26 • *92,703*
Fall River □, SD • *7,353*
Falls □, TX • *17,712*
Falls Church, VA 22040-46 • *9,578*
Falls City, NE 68355 • *4,769*
Falls Creek, PA 15840 • *1,087*
Fallston, MD 21047 • *5,732*
Falls Township, PA 19054 • *36,083*
Falmouth, KY 41040 • *2,378*
Falmouth, ME 04105 • *7,610*
Falmouth, MA 02540 • *4,047*
Falmouth, VA 22405 • *3,541*
Fannin □, GA • *15,992*
Fannin □, TX • *24,804*
Fargo, ND 58102-09 • *74,111*
Faribault, MN 55021 • *17,085*
Faribault □, MN • *16,937*
Farley, IA 52046 • *1,354*
Farmer City, IL 61842 • *2,114*
Farmers Branch, TX 75234 • *24,250*
Farmersburg, IN 47850 • *1,159*
Farmersville, CA 93223 • *6,235*
Farmerville, LA 71241 • *3,334*
Farmingdale, ME 04345 • *2,070*
Farmingdale, NJ 07727 • *1,462*
Farmingdale, NY 11735 • *8,022*
Farmington, AR 72730 • *1,322*
Farmington, CT 06032 • *2,500*
Farmington, IL 61531 • *2,535*
Farmington, ME 04938 • *4,197*
Farmington, MI 48335-36 • *10,132*
Farmington, MN 55024 • *5,940*
Farmington, MO 63640 • *11,598*
Farmington, NH 03835 • *3,567*
Farmington, NM 87401-02 • *33,997*
Farmington, UT 84025 • *9,028*
Farmington Hills, MI 48331-34 • *74,652*
Farmingville, NY 11738 • *14,842*
Farmland, IN 47340 • *1,412*
Farmville, NC 27828 • *4,392*
Farmville, VA 23901 • *6,046*
Farragut, TN 37922 • *12,793*
Farrell, PA 16121 • *6,841*
Farwell, TX 79325 • *1,373*
Faulk □, SD • *2,744*
Faulkland Heights, DE 19808 • *1,300*
Faulkner □, AR • *60,006*
Faulkton, SD 57438 • *809*
Fauquier □, VA • *48,741*
Fayette, AL 35555 • *4,909*
Fayette, IA 52142 • *1,317*
Fayette, MS 39069 • *1,853*
Fayette, MO 65248 • *2,888*
Fayette, OH 43521 • *1,248*
Fayette □, AL • *17,962*
Fayette □, GA • *62,415*
Fayette □, IL • *20,893*
Fayette □, IN • *26,015*
Fayette □, IA • *21,843*
Fayette □, KY • *225,366*
Fayette □, OH • *27,466*
Fayette □, PA • *145,351*

United States Populations and ZIP Codes

Fayette □, TN • 25,559
Fayette □, TX • 20,095
Fayette □, WV • 47,952
Fayetteville, AR 72701-03 • 42,099
Fayetteville, GA 30214 • 5,827
Fayetteville, NC 28301-14 • 75,695
Fayetteville, TN 37334 • 6,921
Fayetteville, WV 25840 • 2,182
Fayville, MA 01745 • 1,000
Federal Heights, CO 80221 • 9,342
Federalsburg, MD 21632 • 2,365
Federal Way, WA 98003 • 67,554
Feeding Hills, MA 01030 • 5,470
Fellowship, NJ 08057 • 4,250
Fellsmere, FL 32948 • 2,179
Felton, CA 95041 • 5,350
Felton, DE 19943 • 683
Fennimore, WI 53809 • 2,378
Fennville, MI 49408 • 1,023
Fenton, MI 48430 • 8,444
Fentress □, TN • 14,669
Ferdinand, IN 47532 • 2,318
Fergus □, MT • 12,083
Fergus Falls, MN 56537-38 • 12,362
Ferguson, MO 63135 • 22,286
Fernandina Beach, FL 32034 • 8,765
Fern Creek, KY 40291 • 16,406
Ferndale, CA 95536 • 1,331
Ferndale, MD 21061 • 16,355
Ferndale, MI 48220 • 25,084
Ferndale, PA 15905 • 2,020
Ferndale, WA 98248 • 5,398
Fernley, NV 89408 • 5,164
Fern Park, FL 32730 • 8,294
Fernway, PA 16063 • 9,072
Ferriday, LA 71334 • 4,111
Ferris, TX 75125 • 2,212
Ferron, UT 84523 • 1,606
Ferry □, WA • 6,295
Ferry Farms, VA 22405 • 1,600
Fessenden, ND 58438 • 655
Festus, MO 63028 • 8,105
Fieldale, VA 24089 • 1,018
Fig Garden, CA 93704 • 9,000
Filer, ID 83328 • 1,511
Fillmore, CA 93015-16 • 11,992
Fillmore, UT 84631 • 1,956
Fillmore □, MN • 20,777
Fillmore □, NE • 7,103
Findlay, OH 45839-40 • 35,703
Finley, TN 38030 • 1,014
Finney □, KS • 33,070
Fircrest, WA 98466 • 5,258
Firebaugh, CA 93622 • 4,429
Firestone, CO 80520 • 1,358
Fisher, IL 61843 • 1,526
Fisher □, TX • 4,842
Fishers, IN 46038 • 7,508
Fishkill, NY 12524 • 1,957
Fiskdale, MA 01518 • 2,189
Fitchburg, MA 01420 • 41,194
Fitzgerald, GA 31750 • 8,612
Five Points, NM 87105 • 4,200
Flagler □, FL • 28,701
Flagler Beach, FL 32136 • 3,820
Flagstaff, AZ 86001-16 • 45,857
Flanders, NJ 07836 • 3,040
Flandreau, SD 57028 • 2,311
Flathead □, MT • 59,218
Flatonia, TX 78941 • 1,295
Flat River, MO 63601 • 4,823
Flat Rock, MI 48134 • 7,290
Flat Rock, NC 28731 • 1,200
Flatwoods, KY 41139 • 7,799
Fleetwood, PA 19522 • 3,478
Fleming □, KY • 12,292
Flemingsburg, KY 41041 • 3,071
Flemington, NJ 08822 • 4,047
Flemington, PA 17745 • 1,321
Fletcher, NC 28732 • 2,787
Fletcher, OK 73541 • 1,002
Flint, MI 48501-32 • 140,761
Flint City, AL 35601 • 1,033
Flippin, AR 72634 • 1,006
Flomaton, AL 36441 • 1,811
Flora, IL 62839 • 5,054
Flora, IN 46929 • 2,179
Flora, MS 39071 • 1,482
Florala, AL 36442 • 2,075
Floral City, FL 32636 • 2,609
Floral Park, NY 11001-05 • 15,947
Florence, AL 35630-33 • 36,426
Florence, AZ 85232 • 7,510
Florence, CA 90001 • 43,900
Florence, CO 81226 • 2,990
Florence, KY 41042 • 18,624
Florence, MS 39073 • 1,831
Florence, NJ 08518 • 4,203
Florence, OR 97439 • 5,162
Florence, SC 29501-06 • 29,813
Florence □, SC • 114,344
Florence □, WI • 4,590
Floresville, TX 78114 • 5,247
Florham Park, NJ 07932 • 8,521
Florida, NY 10921 • 2,497
Florida City, FL 33034 • 5,806
Florida Ridge, FL 32960 • 12,218
Florin, CA 95828 • 24,330
Florissant, MO 63031-34 • 51,206
Flossmoor, IL 60422 • 8,651
Flower Hill, NY 11550 • 4,490
Flowery Branch, GA 30542 • 1,251
Flowood, MS 39208 • 2,860
Floyd □, GA • 81,251
Floyd □, IN • 64,404
Floyd □, IA • 17,058
Floyd □, KY • 43,586
Floyd □, TX • 8,497
Floyd □, VA • 12,005
Floydada, TX 79235 • 3,896
Flushing, MI 48433 • 8,542
Flushing, OH 43977 • 1,042
Fluvanna □, VA • 12,429
Foard □, TX • 1,794
Folcroft, PA 19032 • 7,506
Foley, AL 36535-36 • 4,937
Foley, MN 56329 • 1,854
Folkston, GA 31537 • 2,285
Follansbee, WV 26037 • 3,339
Folly Beach, SC 29439 • 1,398
Folsom, CA 95630 • 29,802
Folsom, NJ 08037 • 2,181

Fonda, NY 12068 • 1,007
Fond du Lac, WI 54935-36 • 37,757
Fond du Lac □, WI • 90,083
Fontana, CA 92334-36 • 87,535
Fontana, WI 53125 • 1,635
Foothill Farms, CA 95841 • 17,135
Ford □, IL • 14,275
Ford □, KS • 27,463
Ford City, CA 93268 • 3,781
Ford City, PA 16226 • 3,413
Ford Heights, IL 60411 • 4,259
Fords, NJ 08863 • 14,392
Fords Prairie, WA 98531 • 2,480
Fordyce, AR 71742 • 4,729
Foreman, AR 71836 • 1,267
Forest, MS 39074 • 5,060
Forest, OH 45843 • 1,594
Forest □, PA • 4,802
Forest □, WI • 8,776
Forest Acres, SC 29206 • 7,197
Forest City, IA 50436 • 4,430
Forest City, NC 28043 • 7,475
Forest City, PA 18421 • 1,846
Forestdale, AL 35214 • 10,395
Forestdale, RI 02824 • 530
Forest Dale, VT 05745 • 350
Forest Grove, OR 97116 • 13,559
Forest Hill, TX 76119 • 11,482
Forest Hills, PA 15221 • 7,335
Forest Knolls, CA 94933 • 2,000
Forest Lake, MN 55025 • 5,833
Forest Park, GA 30050-51 • 16,925
Forest Park, IL 60130 • 14,918
Forest Park, LA 71291 • 1,400
Forest Park, OH 45240 • 18,609
Forked River, NJ 08731 • 1,950
Forks, WA 98331 • 2,862
Forney, TX 75126 • 4,070
Forrest, IL 61741 • 1,124
Forrest □, MS • 68,314
Forrest City, AR 72335 • 13,364
Forreston, IL 61030 • 1,361
Forsyth, GA 31029 • 4,268
Forsyth, IL 62535 • 1,275
Forsyth, MO 65653 • 1,175
Forsyth, MT 59327 • 2,178
Forsyth □, GA • 44,083
Forsyth □, NC • 265,878
Fort Ashby, WV 26719 • 1,288
Fort Atkinson, WI 53538 • 10,227
Fort Bend □, TX • 225,421
Fort Benton, MT 59442 • 1,660
Fort Bragg, CA 95437 • 6,078
Fort Branch, IN 47648 • 2,447
Fort Collins, CO 80521-26 • 87,758
Fort Covington, NY 12937 • 1,200
Fort Davis, TX 79734 • 1,100
Fort Defiance, AZ 86504 • 4,489
Fort Deposit, AL 36032 • 1,240
Fort Dodge, IA 50501 • 25,894
Fort Edward, NY 12828 • 3,561
Fort Fairfield, ME 04742 • 1,729
Fort Gaines, GA 31751 • 1,248
Fort Gibson, OK 74434 • 3,359
Fort Hall, ID 83203 • 2,681
Fort Kent, ME 04743 • 2,123
Fort Laramie, WY 82212 • 243
Fort Lauderdale, FL 33301-51 • 149,377
Fort Lee, NJ 07024 • 31,997
Fort Loramie, OH 45845 • 1,042
Fort Loudon, PA 17224 • 1,200
Fort Lupton, CO 80621 • 5,159
Fort Madison, IA 52627 • 11,618
Fort McKinley, OH 45426 • 9,740
Fort Meade, FL 33841 • 4,976
Fort Mill, SC 29715 • 4,930
Fort Mitchell, KY 41017 • 7,438
Fort Morgan, CO 80701 • 9,068
Fort Myers, FL 33901-19 • 45,206
Fort Myers Beach, FL 33931-32 • 9,284
Fort Myers Shores, FL 33905 • 5,460
Fort Oglethorpe, GA 30742 • 5,880
Fort Payne, AL 35967 • 11,838
Fort Pierce, FL 34945-54 • 36,830
Fort Pierre, SD 57532 • 1,854
Fort Plain, NY 13339 • 2,416
Fort Recovery, OH 45846 • 1,313
Fort Scott, KS 66701 • 8,362
Fort Shawnee, OH 45806 • 4,128
Fort Smith, AR 72901-17 • 72,798
Fort Stockton, TX 79735 • 8,524
Fort Sumner, NM 88119 • 1,269
Fort Thomas, KY 41075 • 16,032
Fortuna, CA 95540 • 8,788
Fort Valley, GA 31030 • 8,198
Fortville, IN 46040 • 2,990
Fort Walton Beach, FL 32547-48 • 21,471
Fort Washington Forest, MD 20744 • 1,010
Fort Wayne, IN 46801-99 • 173,072
Fort Wingate, NM 87316 • 950
Fort Worth, TX 76101-85 • 447,619
Fort Wright, KY 41011 • 6,570
Forty Fort, PA 18704 • 5,049
Fort Yukon, AK 99740 • 580
Fosston, MN 56542 • 1,529
Foster □, ND • 3,983
Foster City, CA 94404 • 28,176
Foster Village, HI 96818 • 3,700
Fostoria, OH 44830 • 14,983
Fountain, CO 80817 • 9,984
Fountain □, IN • 17,808
Fountain Hill, PA 18015 • 4,637
Fountain Inn, SC 29644 • 4,388
Fountain Place, LA • 9,200
Fountain Valley, CA 92708 • 53,691
Four Corners, OR 97301 • 12,156
Four Oaks, NC 27524 • 1,308
Fowler, CA 93625 • 3,208
Fowler, CO 81039 • 1,154
Fowler, IN 47944 • 2,333
Fowlerville, MI 48836 • 2,648
Foxboro, MA 02035 • 5,706
Fox Chapel, PA 15238 • 5,319
Fox Lake, IL 60020 • 7,478
Fox Lake, WI 53933 • 1,269
Fox Point, WI 53217 • 7,238
Fox River Grove, IL 60021 • 3,551
Frackville, PA 17931 • 4,700
Framingham, MA 01701 • 64,994
Franconia, VA 22310 • 19,882
Frankenmuth, MI 48734 • 4,408
Frankford, DE 19945 • 591
Frankfort, IL 60423 • 7,180

Frankfort, IN 46041 • 14,754
Frankfort, KY 40601-22 • 25,968
Frankfort, MI 49635 • 1,546
Frankfort, NY 13340 • 2,693
Frankfort □, IL • 1,065
Franklin, IN 46131 • 12,907
Franklin, KY 42134-35 • 7,607
Franklin, LA 70538 • 9,004
Franklin, MA 02038 • 9,965
Franklin, NE 68939 • 1,112
Franklin, NJ 07416 • 4,977
Franklin, NC 28734 • 2,873
Franklin, OH 45005 • 11,026
Franklin, PA 16323 • 7,329
Franklin, TN 37064-65 • 20,098
Franklin, TX 77856 • 1,336
Franklin, VA 23851 • 7,864
Franklin, WI 53132 • 21,855
Franklin □, AL • 27,814
Franklin □, AR • 14,897
Franklin □, FL • 8,967
Franklin □, GA • 16,650
Franklin □, ID • 9,232
Franklin □, IL • 40,319
Franklin □, IN • 19,580
Franklin □, IA • 11,364
Franklin □, KS • 21,994
Franklin □, KY • 43,781
Franklin □, LA • 22,387
Franklin □, ME • 29,008
Franklin □, MA • 70,092
Franklin □, MS • 8,377
Franklin □, MO • 80,603
Franklin □, NE • 3,938
Franklin □, NY • 46,540
Franklin □, NC • 36,414
Franklin □, OH • 961,437
Franklin □, PA • 121,082
Franklin □, TN • 34,725
Franklin □, TX • 7,802
Franklin □, VT • 39,980
Franklin □, VA • 39,549
Franklin □, WA • 37,473
Franklin Lakes, NJ 07417 • 9,873
Franklin Park, IL 60131 • 18,485
Franklin Park, PA 15143 • 10,109
Franklin Square, NY 11010 • 28,205
Franklinton, LA 70438 • 4,007
Franklinton, NC 27525 • 1,615
Franklinville, NJ 08322 • 1,020
Franklinville, NY 14737 • 1,739
Frankston, TX 75763 • 1,127
Frankton, IN 46044 • 1,736
Fraser, MI 48026 • 13,899
Frazee, MN 56544 • 1,176
Frazeysburg, OH 43822 • 1,165
Frazier Park, CA 93225 • 2,201
Frederic, WI 54837 • 1,124
Frederica, DE 19946 • 761
Frederick, MD 21701-02 • 40,148
Frederick, OK 73542 • 5,221
Frederick □, MD • 150,208
Frederick □, VA • 45,723
Fredericksburg, IA 50630 • 1,011
Fredericksburg, TX 78624 • 6,934
Fredericksburg, VA 22401-08 • 19,027
Fredericktown, MO 63645 • 3,950
Fredericktown, OH 43019 • 2,443
Fredericktown, PA 15333 • 1,052
Fredonia, AZ 86022 • 1,207
Fredonia, KS 66736 • 2,599
Fredonia, NY 14063 • 10,436
Fredonia, WI 53021 • 1,558
Freeborn □, MN • 33,060
Freeburg, IL 62243 • 3,115
Freedom, CA 95019 • 8,361
Freedom, PA 15042 • 1,897
Freedom, WY 83120 • 450
Freehold, NJ 07728 • 10,742
Freeland, MI 48623 • 1,421
Freeland, PA 18224 • 3,909
Freeman, SD 57029 • 1,293
Freemansburg, PA 18017 • 1,946
Freeport, IL 61032 • 25,840
Freeport, ME 04032 • 1,829
Freeport, NY 11520 • 39,894
Freeport, PA 16229 • 1,983
Freeport, TX 77541 • 11,389
Freer, TX 78357 • 3,271
Freestone □, TX • 15,818
Fremont, CA 94536-39 • 173,339
Fremont, IN 46737 • 1,407
Fremont, MI 49412 • 3,875
Fremont, NE 68025 • 23,680
Fremont, NC 27830 • 1,711
Fremont, OH 43420 • 17,648
Fremont □, CO • 32,273
Fremont □, ID • 10,937
Fremont □, IA • 8,226
Fremont □, WY • 33,662
French Island, WI 54601 • 4,478
French Lick, IN 47432 • 2,087
Frenchtown, NJ 08825 • 1,528
Fresno, CA 93701-94 • 354,202
Fresno □, CA • 667,490
Frewsburg, NY 14738 • 1,817
Friars Point, MS 38631 • 1,334
Friday Harbor, WA 98250 • 1,492
Fridley, MN 55432 • 28,335
Friend, NE 68359 • 1,111
Friendship, NY 14739 • 1,423
Friendswood, TX 77546 • 22,814
Frio □, TX • 13,472
Friona, TX 79035 • 3,688
Frisco, CO 80443 • 1,601
Frisco City, AL 36445 • 1,581
Fritch, TX 79036 • 2,335
Frontenac, KS 66762 • 2,588
Frontier □, NE • 3,101
Front Royal, VA 22630 • 11,880
Frostburg, MD 21532 • 8,075
Frostproof, FL 33843 • 2,808
Fruita, CO 81521 • 4,045
Fruit Heights, UT 84037 • 3,900
Fruitland, ID 83619 • 2,400
Fruitland, MD 21826 • 3,511
Fruitland Park, FL 34731 • 2,754
Fruitport, MI 49415 • 1,090
Fruitvale, CO 81504 • 1,070
Fruitvale, WA 98902 • 4,125
Fruitville, FL 34232 • 9,808
Fryeburg, ME 04037 • 1,580

Fulda, MN 56131 • 1,212
Fullerton, CA 92631-35 • 114,144
Fullerton, NE 68638 • 1,452
Fulton, IL 61252 • 3,698
Fulton, KY 42041 • 3,078
Fulton, MS 38843 • 3,387
Fulton, MO 65251 • 10,033
Fulton, NY 13069 • 12,929
Fulton □, AR • 10,037
Fulton □, GA • 648,951
Fulton □, IL • 38,080
Fulton □, IN • 18,840
Fulton □, KY • 8,271
Fulton □, NY • 54,191
Fulton □, OH • 38,498
Fulton □, PA • 13,837
Fultondale, AL 35068 • 6,400
Funkstown, MD 21734 • 1,136
Fuquay-Varina, NC 27526 • 4,562
Furnas □, NE • 5,553
Fyffe, AL 35971 • 1,094

G

Gabbs, NV 89409 • 667
Gadsden, AL 35901-05 • 42,523
Gadsden □, FL • 41,105
Gaffney, SC 29340-42 • 13,145
Gage □, NE • 22,794
Gages Lake, IL 60030 • 8,349
Gahanna, OH 43230 • 27,791
Gaines □, TX • 14,123
Gainesboro, TN 38562 • 1,002
Gainesville, FL 32601-14 • 84,770
Gainesville, GA 30501-07 • 17,885
Gainesville, TX 76240 • 14,256
Gaithersburg, MD 20877-79 • 39,542
Galax, VA 24333 • 6,670
Galena, AK 99741 • 833
Galena, IL 61036 • 3,647
Galena, KS 66739 • 3,308
Galesburg, IL 61401-02 • 33,530
Galesburg, MI 49053 • 1,863
Gales Ferry, CT 06335 • 1,191
Galesville, WI 54630 • 1,278
Galeton, PA 16922 • 1,370
Galion, OH 44833 • 11,859
Gallatin, MO 64640 • 1,864
Gallatin, TN 37066 • 18,794
Gallatin □, IL • 6,909
Gallatin □, KY • 5,393
Gallatin □, MT • 50,463
Gallia □, OH • 30,954
Galliano, LA 70354 • 4,294
Gallipolis, OH 45631 • 4,831
Gallup, NM 87301-05 • 19,154
Galt, CA 95632 • 8,889
Galva, IL 61434 • 2,742
Galveston, IN 46932 • 1,609
Galveston, TX 77550-54 • 59,070
Galveston □, TX • 217,399
Gambell, AK 99742 • 525
Gambier, OH 43022 • 2,073
Gambrills, MD 21054 • 1,200
Ganado, AZ 86505 • 3,400
Ganado, TX 77962 • 1,701
Gang Mills, NY 14870 • 2,738
Gantt, SC 29605 • 13,891
Gap, PA 17527 • 1,200
Garberville, CA 95440 • 1,200
Garden □, NE • 2,460
Gardena, CA 90247-49 • 49,847
Garden City, GA 31408 • 7,410
Garden City, ID 83704 • 6,369
Garden City, KS 67846 • 24,097
Garden City, MI 48135-36 • 31,846
Garden City, MO 64747 • 1,225
Garden City, NY 11530 • 21,686
Garden City Park, NY 11040 • 7,437
Gardendale, AL 35071 • 9,251
Garden Grove, CA 92640-45 • 143,050
Garden Home, OR 97223 • 5,500
Gardiner, ME 04345 • 6,746
Gardner, IL 60424 • 1,237
Gardner, KS 66030 • 3,191
Gardner, MA 01440 • 20,125
Gardnerville, NV 89410 • 2,177
Gardnerville Ranches, NV 89410 • 7,455
Garfield, NJ 07026 • 26,727
Garfield □, CO • 29,974
Garfield □, MT • 1,589
Garfield □, NE • 2,141
Garfield □, OK • 56,735
Garfield □, UT • 3,980
Garfield □, WA • 2,248
Garfield Heights, OH 44125 • 31,739
Garfield Park, DE 19720 • 1,415
Garland, TX 75040-48 • 180,650
Garland, UT 84312 • 1,637
Garland □, AR • 73,397
Garner, IA 50438 • 2,916
Garner, NC 27529 • 14,967
Garnett, KS 66032 • 3,210
Garrard □, KY • 11,579
Garretson, SD 57030 • 924
Garrett, IN 46738 • 5,349
Garrett □, MD • 28,138
Garrettsville, OH 44231 • 2,014
Garrison, MD 21055 • 5,045
Garrison, ND 58540 • 1,530
Garvin □, OK • 26,605
Garwood, NJ 07027 • 4,227
Gary, IN 46401-11 • 116,646
Gary, WV 24836 • 1,355
Garysburg, NC 27831 • 1,057
Garyville, LA 70051 • 3,181
Garza □, TX • 5,143
Gas City, IN 46933 • 6,296
Gasconade □, MO • 14,006
Gasport, NY 14067 • 1,336
Gassville, AR 72635 • 1,167
Gaston, NC 27832 • 1,003
Gaston □, NC • 175,093
Gastonia, NC 28051-56 • 54,732
Gate City, VA 24251 • 2,214
Gates, NY 14624 • 30,000
Gates □, NC • 9,305
Gatesville, TX 76528 • 11,492
Gatlinburg, TN 37738 • 3,417

Gautier, MS 39553 • 10,088
Gaylord, MI 49735 • 3,256
Gaylord, MN 55334 • 1,935
Gearhart, OR 97138 • 1,027
Geary, OK 73040 • 1,347
Geary □, KS • 30,453
Geauga □, OH • 81,129
Geistown, PA 15904 • 2,749
Gem □, ID • 11,844
Genesee, ID 83832 • 725
Genesee, MI 48437 • 1,400
Genesee □, MI • 430,459
Genesee □, NY • 60,060
Geneseo, IL 61254 • 5,990
Geneseo, NY 14454 • 7,187
Geneva, AL 36340 • 4,681
Geneva, IL 60134 • 12,617
Geneva, IN 46740 • 1,280
Geneva, NE 68361 • 2,310
Geneva, NY 14456 • 14,143
Geneva, OH 44041 • 6,597
Geneva □, AL • 23,647
Geneva-on-the-Lake, OH 44041 • 1,626
Genoa, IL 60135 • 3,083
Genoa, NE 68640 • 1,082
Genoa, NV 89411 • 190
Genoa, OH 43430 • 2,262
Genoa City, WI 53128 • 1,277
Gentry, AR 72734 • 1,726
Gentry □, MO • 6,848
George, IA 51237 • 1,066
George □, MS • 16,673
Georgetown, CA 95634 • 2,000
Georgetown, CT 06829 • 1,694
Georgetown, DE 19947 • 3,732
Georgetown, IL 61846 • 3,678
Georgetown, IN 47122 • 2,092
Georgetown, KY 40324 • 11,414
Georgetown, MA 01833 • 2,100
Georgetown, OH 45121 • 3,627
Georgetown, SC 29440-42 • 9,517
Georgetown, TX 78626-28 • 14,842
Georgetown □, SC • 46,302
George West, TX 78022 • 2,586
Georgiana, AL 36033 • 1,933
Gering, NE 69341 • 7,946
Gerlach, NV 89412 • 200
Germantown, IL 62245 • 1,167
Germantown, MD 20874 • 41,145
Germantown, OH 45327 • 4,916
Germantown, TN 38138 • 32,893
Germantown, WI 53022 • 13,658
Gettysburg, PA 17325 • 7,025
Gettysburg, SD 57442 • 1,510
Giants Neck, CT 06357 • 1,200
Gibbon, NE 68840 • 1,525
Gibbstown, NJ 80027 • 5,404
Gibsland, LA 71028 • 1,224
Gibson □, IN • 31,913
Gibson □, TN • 46,315
Gibsonburg, OH 43431 • 2,579
Gibsonia, PA 15044 • 3,500
Gibsonton, FL 33534 • 7,706
Gibsonville, NC 27249 • 3,441
Giddings, TX 78942 • 4,093
Gideon, MO 63848 • 1,104
Gifford, FL 32960 • 6,278
Gig Harbor, WA 98335 • 3,236
Gila □, AZ • 40,216
Gila Bend, AZ 85337 • 1,747
Gilbert, AZ 85234 • 29,188
Gilbert, MN 55741 • 1,934
Gilbert, WV 97266 • 4,000
Gilbertsville, PA 19525 • 3,994
Gilbertville, MA 01031 • 1,029
Gilchrist □, FL • 9,667
Gilcrest, CO 80623 • 1,084
Giles □, TN • 25,741
Giles □, VA • 16,366
Gilford Park, NJ 08753 • 8,668
Gillespie, IL 62033 • 3,645
Gillespie □, TX • 17,204
Gillett, WI 54124 • 1,303
Gillette, WY 82716-17 • 17,635
Gilliam □, OR • 1,717
Gilman, IL 60938 • 1,816
Gilman, VT 05904 • 500
Gilmer, TX 75644 • 4,822
Gilmer □, GA • 13,368
Gilmer □, WV • 7,669
Gilpin □, CO • 3,070
Gilroy, CA 95020-21 • 31,487
Girard, IL 62640 • 2,164
Girard, KS 66743 • 2,794
Girard, OH 44420 • 11,304
Girard, PA 16417 • 2,879
Girardville, PA 17935 • 1,889
Glacier □, MT • 12,121
Glades □, FL • 7,591
Glade Spring, VA 24340 • 1,435
Gladeview, FL 33138 • 15,637
Gladewater, TX 75647 • 6,027
Gladstone, MI 49837 • 4,565
Gladstone, MO 64118 • 26,243
Gladstone, NJ 07934 • 2,111
Gladstone, OR 97027 • 10,152
Gladwin, MI 48624 • 2,682
Gladwin □, MI • 21,896
Glasco, NY 12432 • 1,538
Glascock □, GA • 2,357
Glasford, IL 61533 • 1,115
Glasgow, KY 42141-42 • 12,351
Glasgow, MO 65254 • 1,295
Glasgow, MT 59230 • 3,572
Glasgow, VA 24555 • 1,140
Glasgow Village, MO 63137 • 5,199
Glassboro, NJ 08028 • 15,614
Glasscock □, TX • 1,447
Glassport, PA 15045 • 5,582
Glastonbury, CT 06033 • 7,082
Gleason, TN 38229 • 1,462
Glen Allen, VA 23060 • 9,010
Glen Avon, CA 72613 • 12,663
Glenbrook, NV 89413 • 400
Glen Burnie, MD 21061 • 37,305
Glen Burnie Park, MD 21061 • 3,260
Glen Carbon, IL 62034 • 7,731
Glencoe, AL 35905 • 4,670
Glencoe, IL 60022 • 8,499
Glencoe, MN 55336 • 4,648
Glen Cove, NY 11542 • 24,149

Glendale, AZ 85301-12 • 148,134
Glendale, CA 91201-14 • 180,038
Glendale, CO 80222 • 2,453
Glendale, MS 39401 • 1,329
Glendale, MO 63122 • 5,945
Glendale, RI 02826 • 700
Glendale, SC 29346 • 1,049
Glen Dale, WV 26038 • 1,612
Glendale, WI 53209 • 14,088
Glendale Heights, IL 60139 • 27,973
Glendive, MT 59330 • 4,802
Glendo, WY 82213 • 195
Glendola, NJ 07719 • 2,340
Glendora, CA 91740 • 47,828
Glendora, NJ 08029 • 5,201
Glen Ellyn, IL 60137-38 • 24,944
Glen Gardner, NJ 08826 • 1,665
Glenham, NY 12527 • 2,832
Glen Head, NY 11545 • 6,870
Glen Lyon, PA 18617 • 2,082
Glenmora, LA 71433 • 1,686
Glenn □, CA • 24,798
Glennallen, AK 99588 • 451
Glenn Dale, MD 20769 • 9,689
Glenns Ferry, ID 83623 • 1,304
Glennville, GA 30427 • 3,676
Glenolden, PA 19036 • 7,260
Glenpool, OK 74033 • 6,688
Glen Raven, NC 27215 • 2,616
Glen Ridge, NJ 07028 • 7,076
Glen Rock, NJ 07452 • 10,883
Glen Rock, PA 17327 • 1,688
Glenrock, WY 82637 • 2,153
Glen Rose, TX 76043 • 1,949
Glens Falls, NY 12801 • 15,023
Glenside, PA 19038 • 8,704
Glen Ullin, ND 58631 • 927
Glenview, IL 60025 • 37,093
Glenville, WV 26351 • 1,923
Glenwood, AR 71943 • 1,354
Glenwood, IL 60425 • 9,289
Glenwood, IA 51534 • 4,571
Glenwood, MN 56334 • 2,573
Glenwood, VA 24541 • 2,276
Glenwood City, WI 54013 • 1,026
Glenwood Farms, VA 23223 • 3,200
Glenwood Hills, GA 30032 • 5,240
Glenwood Springs, CO 81601-02 • 6,561
Glidden, IA 51443 • 1,099
Globe, AZ 85501-02 • 6,062
Gloster, MS 39638 • 1,323
Gloucester, MA 01930-31 • 28,716
Gloucester, VA 23061 • 1,200
Gloucester □, NJ • 230,082
Gloucester □, VA • 30,131
Gloucester City, NJ 08030 • 12,649
Gloucester Point, VA 23062 • 8,509
Glouster, OH 45732 • 2,001
Gloversville, NY 12078 • 16,656
Gloverville, SC 29828 • 2,753
Glynn □, GA • 62,496
Gnadenhutten, OH 44629 • 1,226
Goddard, KS 67052 • 1,804
Godfrey, IL 62035 • 5,436
Goffstown, NH 03045 • 2,700
Gogebic □, MI • 18,052
Golconda, NV 89414 • 200
Gold Bar, WA 98251 • 1,078
Gold Beach, OR 97444 • 1,546
Golden, CO 80401-03 • 13,116
Goldendale, WA 98620 • 3,319
Golden Gate, FL 33999 • 14,148
Golden Glades, FL 33055 • 25,474
Golden Meadow, LA 70357 • 2,049
Golden Valley, MN 55427 • 20,971
Golden Valley □, MT • 912
Golden Valley □, ND • 2,108
Goldfield, NV 89013 • 600
Goldsboro, NC 27530-34 • 40,709
Goldthwaite, TX 76844 • 1,658
Goleta, CA 93117 • 28,600
Golf Manor, OH 45237 • 4,154
Goliad, TX 77963 • 1,946
Goliad □, TX • 5,980
Gonzales, CA 93926 • 4,660
Gonzales, LA 70737 • 7,003
Gonzales, TX 78629 • 6,527
Gonzales □, TX • 17,205
Gonzalez, FL 32560 • 7,669
Goochland □, VA • 14,163
Goodhue □, MN • 40,690
Gooding, ID 83330 • 2,820
Gooding □, ID • 11,633
Goodland, FL 33933 • 1,000
Goodland, IN 47948 • 1,033
Goodland, KS 67735 • 4,983
Goodlettsville, TN 37072 • 11,219
Goodman, MS 39079 • 1,256
Goodman, MO 64843 • 1,094
Goodsprings, NV 89019 • 150
Goodview, MN 55987 • 2,878
Goodwater, AL 35072 • 1,840
Goodwell, OK 73939 • 1,065
Goodyear, AZ 85338 • 6,258
Goose Creek, SC 29445 • 24,692
Gordo, AL 35466 • 1,918
Gordon, GA 31031 • 2,468
Gordon, NE 69343 • 1,803
Gordon □, GA • 35,072
Gordonsville, VA 22942 • 1,351
Gorham, ME 04038 • 3,618
Gorham, NH 03581 • 1,910
Gorman, TX 76454 • 1,290
Goshen, IN 46526 • 23,797
Goshen, NY 10924 • 5,255
Goshen, OH 45122 • 1,400
Goshen □, WY • 12,373
Gosnell, AR 72319 • 3,783
Gosper □, NE • 1,928
Gothenburg, NE 69138 • 3,232
Gould, AR 71643 • 1,470
Goulding, FL 32503 • 4,159
Goulds, FL 33170 • 7,284
Gouverneur, NY 14070 • 4,604
Gove □, KS • 3,231
Gowanda, NY 14070 • 2,901
Gower, MO 64454 • 1,249
Gowrie, IA 50543 • 1,028
Grace, ID 83241 • 973
Graceville, FL 32440 • 2,675
Gracewood, GA 30812 • 1,000
Grady □, GA • 20,279

Grady □, OK • 41,747
Grafton, MA 01519 • 1,520
Grafton, ND 58237 • 4,840
Grafton, OH 44044 • 3,344
Grafton, WV 26354 • 5,524
Grafton, WI 53024 • 9,340
Grafton □, NH • 74,929
Graham, CA 90002 • 10,600
Graham, NC 27253 • 10,426
Graham, TX 76046 • 8,986
Graham □, AZ • 26,554
Graham □, KS • 3,543
Graham □, NC • 7,196
Grainger □, TN • 17,095
Grain Valley, MO 64029 • 1,898
Grambling, LA 71245 • 5,484
Gramercy, LA 70052 • 2,412
Granbury, TX 76048-49 • 4,045
Granby, CT 06035 • 9,369
Granby, MA 01033 • 1,327
Granby, MO 64844 • 1,945
Grand □, CO • 7,966
Grand □, UT • 6,620
Grand Bay, AL 36541 • 3,383
Grand Blanc, MI 48439 • 7,760
Grand Caillou, LA 70360 • 1,400
Grand Canyon, AZ 86023 • 1,499
Grand Coteau, LA 70541 • 1,118
Grandfield, OK 73546 • 1,224
Grand Forks, ND 58201-06 • 49,425
Grand Forks □, ND • 70,683
Grand Haven, MI 49417 • 11,951
Grand Island, NE 68801-03 • 39,386
Grand Isle, LA 70358 • 1,455
Grand Isle □, VT • 5,318
Grand Junction, CO 81501-06 • 29,034
Grand Ledge, MI 48837 • 7,579
Grand Marais, MN 55604 • 1,171
Grand Prairie, TX 75050-54 • 99,616
Grand Rapids, MI 49501-99 • 189,126
Grand Rapids, MN 55744 • 7,976
Grand Saline, TX 75140 • 2,630
Grand Terrace, CA 92324 • 10,946
Grand Traverse □, MI • 64,273
Grandview, MO 64030 • 24,967
Grandview, WA 98930 • 7,169
Grandview Heights, OH 43212 • 7,010
Grandville, MI 49418 • 15,624
Granger, IN 46530 • 20,241
Granger, TX 76530 • 1,190
Granger, WA 98932 • 2,053
Grangeville, ID 83530 • 3,226
Granite, OK 73547 • 1,844
Granite □, MT • 2,548
Granite City, IL 62040 • 32,862
Granite Falls, MN 56241 • 3,083
Granite Falls, NC 28630 • 3,253
Granite Falls, WA 98252 • 1,060
Granite Quarry, NC 28072 • 1,646
Graniteville, MA 01886 • 1,010
Graniteville, SC 29829 • 1,158
Graniteville, VT 05654 • 500
Grant, NE 69140 • 1,239
Grant □, AR • 13,948
Grant □, IN • 74,169
Grant □, KS • 7,159
Grant □, KY • 15,737
Grant □, LA • 17,526
Grant □, MN • 6,246
Grant □, NE • 769
Grant □, NM • 27,676
Grant □, ND • 3,549
Grant □, OK • 5,689
Grant □, OR • 7,853
Grant □, SD • 8,372
Grant □, WA • 54,758
Grant □, WV • 10,428
Grant □, WI • 49,264
Grant Park, IL 60940 • 1,024
Grants, NM 87020 • 8,626
Grantsburg, WI 54840 • 1,144
Grants Pass, OR 97526-27 • 17,488
Grantsville, UT 84029 • 4,500
Grantville, GA 30220 • 1,180
Granville, IL 61326 • 1,407
Granville, NY 12832 • 2,646
Granville, OH 43023 • 4,353
Granville □, NC • 38,345
Grapeland, TX 75844 • 1,450
Grapevine, TX 76051 • 29,202
Grasonville, MD 21638 • 2,439
Grass Lake, IL 60002 • 2,191
Grass Valley, CA 95945 • 9,048
Gratiot □, MI • 38,982
Graves □, KY • 33,550
Gravette, AR 72736 • 1,412
Gray, GA 31032 • 2,189
Gray, LA 70359 • 1,500
Gray □, KS • 5,396
Gray □, TX • 23,967
Grayling, MI 49738 • 1,944
Graylyn Crest, DE 19810 • 4,380
Grays Harbor □, WA • 64,175
Grayslake, IL 60030 • 7,388
Grayson, KY 41143 • 3,510
Grayson □, KY • 21,050
Grayson □, TX • 95,021
Grayson □, VA • 16,278
Graysville, AL 35073 • 2,241
Graysville, TN 37338 • 1,301
Grayville, IL 62844 • 2,043
Great Barrington, MA 01230 • 2,810
Great Bend, KS 67530 • 15,427
Great Falls, MT 59401-06 • 55,097
Great Falls, SC 29055 • 2,307
Great Falls, VA 22066 • 6,945
Great Neck, NY 11020-27 • 8,745
Great Neck Estates, NY 11021 • 2,790
Greece, NY 14626 • 15,632
Greece, NY • 15,632
Greeley, CO 80631-34 • 60,536
Greeley □, KS • 1,774
Greeley □, NE • 3,006
Green, OR 97470 • 5,076
Green □, KY • 10,371
Green □, WI • 30,339
Greenacres, CA 93308 • 7,379
Green Acres, DE 19803 • 1,140
Greenacres, CA 90016 • 4,250
Greenacres City, FL 33463 • 18,683
Green Bay, WI 54301-24 • 96,466
Greenbelt, MD 20770 • 21,096
Greenbriar, VA 22033 • 6,200

Greenbrier, AR 72058 • 2,130
Green Brier, TN 37073 • 2,873
Greenbrier □, WV • 34,693
Green Brook, NJ 08812 • 2,380
Greencastle, IN 46135 • 8,984
Greencastle, PA 17225 • 3,600
Green Cove Springs, FL 32043 • 4,497
Greendale, IN 47025 • 3,881
Greendale, WI 53129 • 15,128
Greene, IA 50636 • 1,142
Greene, NY 13778 • 1,812
Greene □, AL • 10,153
Greene □, AR • 31,804
Greene □, GA • 11,793
Greene □, IL • 15,317
Greene □, IN • 30,410
Greene □, IA • 10,045
Greene □, MS • 10,220
Greene □, MO • 207,949
Greene □, NY • 44,739
Greene □, NC • 15,384
Greene □, OH • 136,731
Greene □, PA • 39,550
Greene □, TN • 55,853
Greene □, VA • 10,297
Greeneville, TN 37743-44 • 13,532
Greenfield, CA 93927 • 7,464
Greenfield, IL 62044 • 1,162
Greenfield, IN 46140 • 11,657
Greenfield, MA 01301-02 • 14,016
Greenfield, MO 65661 • 1,416
Greenfield, OH 45123 • 5,172
Greenfield, TN 38230 • 2,105
Greenfield, WI 53220 • 33,403
Greenfield Plaza, IL 50315 • 2,200
Green Forest, AR 72638 • 2,050
Green Harbor, MA 02041 • 1,900
Greenhills, OH 45218 • 4,393
Green Island, NY 12183 • 2,490
Green Lake, WI 54941 • 1,064
Green Lake □, WI • 18,651
Greenlawn, NY 11740 • 13,208
Greenlee □, AZ • 8,008
Greenock, PA 15047 • 2,500
Greenport, NY 11944 • 2,070
Green River, WY 82935 • 12,711
Green Rock, IL 61241 • 2,615
Greensboro, AL 36744 • 3,047
Greensboro, GA 30642 • 2,860
Greensboro, MD 21639 • 1,441
Greensboro, NC 27401-95 • 183,521
Greensburg, IN 47240 • 9,286
Greensburg, KS 67054 • 1,792
Greensburg, KY 42743 • 1,990
Greensburg, PA 15601 • 16,318
Green Springs, OH 44836 • 1,446
Greensville □, VA • 8,853
Greentown, IN 46936 • 2,172
Green Tree, PA 15220 • 4,905
Greenup, IL 62428 • 1,616
Greenup, KY 41144 • 1,158
Greenup □, KY • 36,742
Green Valley, AZ 85614 • 13,231
Green Valley, MD 21771 • 9,424
Greenview, SC 29203 • 5,515
Greenville, AL 36037 • 7,492
Greenville, CA 95947 • 1,396
Greenville, DE 19807 • 800
Greenville, GA 30222 • 1,167
Greenville, IL 62246 • 4,806
Greenville, KY 42345 • 4,689
Greenville, ME 04441 • 1,601
Greenville, MI 48838 • 8,101
Greenville, MS 38701-04 • 45,226
Greenville, NH 03048 • 1,135
Greenville, NY 10583 • 9,528
Greenville, NC 27834-36 • 44,972
Greenville, OH 45331 • 12,863
Greenville, PA 16125 • 6,734
Greenville, RI 02828 • 8,303
Greenville, SC 29601-16 • 58,282
Greenville, TX 75401-03 • 23,071
Greenville □, SC • 320,167
Greenwich, CT 06830-36 • 58,441
Greenwich, NY 12834 • 1,961
Greenwich, OH 44837 • 1,442
Greenwood, AR 72936 • 3,984
Greenwood, DE 19950 • 578
Greenwood, IN 46142 • 26,265
Greenwood, LA 71033 • 2,092
Greenwood, MS 38930 • 18,906
Greenwood, MO 64034 • 1,505
Greenwood, PA 16601 • 1,510
Greenwood, SC 29646-49 • 20,807
Greenwood □, KS • 7,847
Greenwood □, SC • 59,567
Greenwood Lake, NY 10925 • 3,208
Greenwood Village, CO 80111 • 7,589
Greer, SC 29650-52 • 10,322
Greer □, OK • 6,559
Gregg □, TX • 104,948
Gregory, SD 57533 • 1,384
Gregory □, SD • 5,359
Greilickville, MI 49684 • 1,060
Grenada, MS 38901 • 10,864
Grenada □, MS • 21,555
Gresham, OR 97030 • 68,235
Gresham Park, GA 30316 • 9,000
Gretna, FL 32332 • 1,981
Gretna, LA 70053-54 • 17,208
Gretna, NE 68028 • 2,249
Gretna, VA 24557 • 1,339
Greybull, WY 82426 • 1,789
Gridley, CA 95948 • 4,631
Gridley, IL 61744 • 1,304
Griffin, GA 30223-24 • 21,347
Griffith, IN 46319 • 17,916
Grifton, NC 28530 • 2,393
Griggs □, ND • 3,303
Griggsville, IL 62340 • 1,218
Grimes, IA 50111 • 2,653
Grimes □, TX • 18,828
Grindall Creek, VA 23234 • 1,710
Grinnell, IA 50112 • 8,902
Griswold, IA 51535 • 1,049
Groesbeck, OH 45239 • 6,684
Groesbeck, TX 76642 • 3,185
Grosse Ile, MI 48138 • 9,781
Grosse Pointe, MI 48236 • 5,681
Grosse Pointe Farms, MI 48236 • 10,092
Grosse Pointe Park, MI 48230 • 12,857
Grosse Pointe Woods, MI 48225 • 17,715

Grossmont, CA 91941 • 2,600
Groton, CT 06340 • 9,837
Groton, MA 01450 • 1,044
Groton, NY 13073 • 2,398
Groton, SD 57445 • 1,196
Grottoes, VA 24441 • 1,455
Grove, OK 74344 • 4,020
Grove City, FL 34224 • 2,374
Grove City, OH 43123 • 19,661
Grove City, PA 16127 • 8,240
Grove Hill, AL 36451 • 1,551
Groveland, FL 34736 • 2,300
Groveland, MA 01834 • 3,780
Groveport, OH 43125 • 2,948
Grover City, CA 93433 • 11,656
Groves, TX 77619 • 16,513
Groveton, NH 03582 • 1,255
Groveton, TX 75845 • 1,071
Groveton, VA 22303 • 19,997
Groveton Gardens, VA 22303 • 2,600
Grovetown, GA 30813 • 3,596
Groveville, NJ 08620 • 2,900
Gruetli-Laager, TN 37339 • 1,810
Grulla, TX 78548 • 1,335
Grundy, VA 24614 • 1,305
Grundy □, IL • 32,337
Grundy □, IA • 12,029
Grundy □, MO • 10,536
Grundy □, TN • 13,362
Grundy Center, IA 50638 • 2,491
Gruver, TX 79040 • 1,172
Guadalupe, AZ 85283 • 5,458
Guadalupe, CA 93434 • 5,479
Guadalupe □, NM • 4,156
Guadalupe □, TX • 64,873
Guernsey, WY 82214 • 1,155
Guernsey □, OH • 39,024
Gueydan, LA 70542 • 1,611
Guilford, CT 06437 • 2,588
Guilford, ME 04443 • 1,082
Guilford □, NC • 347,420
Guin, AL 35563 • 2,464
Gulf □, FL • 11,504
Gulf Breeze, FL 32561 • 5,530
Gulf Gate Estates, FL 34231 • 11,622
Gulfport, FL 33707 • 11,727
Gulfport, MS 39501-07 • 40,775
Gulf Shores, AL 36542 • 3,261
Gumboro, DE 19945 • 200
Gunnison, CO 81230 • 4,636
Gunnison, UT 84634 • 1,298
Gunnison □, CO • 10,273
Guntersville, AL 35976 • 7,038
Gurdon, AR 71743 • 2,199
Gurley, AL 35748 • 1,007
Gurnee, IL 60031 • 13,701
Gustine, CA 95322 • 3,931
Guthrie, KY 42234 • 1,504
Guthrie, OK 73044 • 10,518
Guthrie □, IA • 10,935
Guthrie Center, IA 50115 • 1,614
Guttenberg, IA 52052 • 2,257
Guttenberg, NJ 07093 • 8,268
Guymon, OK 73942 • 7,803
Gwinhurst, DE 19809 • 1,340
Gwinn, MI 49841 • 2,370
Gwinner, ND 58040 • 585
Gwinnett □, GA • 352,910
Gypsum, CO 81637 • 1,750

H

Haakon □, SD • 2,624
Habersham □, GA • 27,621
Hacienda Heights, CA 91745 • 52,354
Hackensack, NJ 07601-08 • 37,049
Hackettstown, NJ 07840 • 8,120
Hackleburg, AL 35564 • 1,161
Haddam, CT 06438 • 1,200
Haddonfield, NJ 08033 • 11,628
Haddon Heights, NJ 08035 • 7,860
Hadlock, WA 98339 • 1,752
Hagerman, NM 88232 • 961
Hagerstown, IN 47346 • 1,835
Hagerstown, MD 21740 • 35,445
Hahira, GA 31632 • 1,353
Hahnville, LA 70057 • 2,599
Hailey, ID 83333 • 3,687
Haines, AK 99827 • 1,238
Haines City, FL 33844 • 11,683
Hainesport, NJ 08036 • 1,250
Halawa Heights, HI 96701 • 7,000
Hale □, AL • 15,498
Hale □, TX • 34,671
Hale Center, TX 79041 • 2,067
Haledon, NJ 07508 • 6,951
Haleiwa, HI 96712 • 2,442
Hales Corners, WI 53130 • 7,623
Halethorpe, MD 21227 • 19,750
Haleyville, AL 35565 • 4,452
Half Hollow Hills, NY 11746 • 5,110
Half Moon, NC 28540 • 8,886
Half Moon Bay, CA 94019 • 8,886
Halfway, MD 21740 • 8,873
Halifax □, NC • 55,516
Halifax □, VA • 29,033
Haliimaile, HI 96768 • 841
Hall □, GA • 95,428
Hall □, NE • 48,925
Hall □, TX • 3,905
Hallandale, FL 33009 • 30,996
Hallettsville, TX 77964 • 2,718
Hallie, WI 54729 • 1,300
Hallock, MN 56728 • 1,304
Hallowell, ME 04347 • 2,534
Halls, TN 37918 • 6,450
Halls, TN 38040 • 2,431
Halls Crossroads, TN 37918 • 1,900
Hallstead, PA 18822 • 1,274
Hallsville, TX 75650 • 2,288
Halstead, KS 67056 • 2,015
Haltom City, TX 76117 • 32,856
Hamblen □, TN • 50,480
Hamburg, AR 71646 • 3,098
Hamburg, IA 51640 • 1,248
Hamburg, NJ 07419 • 2,566
Hamburg, NY 14075 • 10,442
Hamburg, PA 19526 • 3,987
Hamden, CT 06514 • 52,434
Hamel, MN 55340 • 3,096
Hamilton, AL 35570 • 5,787

Hamilton, IL 62341 • 3,281
Hamilton, MA 01936 • 1,000
Hamilton, MI 49419 • 1,000
Hamilton, MO 64644 • 1,737
Hamilton, MT 59840 • 2,737
Hamilton, NY 13346 • 3,790
Hamilton, OH 45011-18 • 61,368
Hamilton, TX 76531 • 2,937
Hamilton □, FL • 10,930
Hamilton □, IL • 8,499
Hamilton □, IN • 108,936
Hamilton □, IA • 16,071
Hamilton □, KS • 2,388
Hamilton □, NE • 8,862
Hamilton □, NY • 5,279
Hamilton □, OH • 866,228
Hamilton □, TN • 285,536
Hamilton □, TX • 7,733
Hamilton City, CA 95951 • 1,811
Hamilton Square, NJ 08690 • 10,970
Ham Lake, MN 55304 • 8,924
Hamlet, NC 28345 • 6,196
Hamlin, TX 79520 • 2,791
Hamlin, WV 25523 • 1,030
Hamlin □, SD • 4,974
Hammond, IN 46320-27 • 84,236
Hammond, LA 70401-04 • 15,871
Hammond, WI 54015 • 1,097
Hammonton, NJ 08037 • 12,208
Hampden, ME 04444 • 3,895
Hampden □, MA • 456,310
Hampden Highlands, ME 04444 • 1,540
Hampshire, IL 60140 • 1,843
Hampshire □, MA • 146,568
Hampshire □, WV • 16,498
Hampstead, MD 21074 • 2,608
Hampton, AR 71744 • 1,562
Hampton, GA 30228 • 2,694
Hampton, IA 50441 • 4,133
Hampton, NH 03842 • 7,989
Hampton, NJ 08827 • 1,515
Hampton, SC 29924 • 2,997
Hampton, TN 37658 • 2,236
Hampton, VA 23661-70 • 133,793
Hampton □, SC • 18,191
Hampton Bays, NY 11946 • 7,893
Hamtramck, MI 48212 • 18,372
Hana, HI 96713 • 683
Hanahan, SC 29406 • 13,176
Hanamaulu, HI 96715 • 3,611
Hanapepe, HI 96716 • 1,395
Hanceville, AL 35077 • 2,246
Hancock, MD 21750 • 1,926
Hancock, MI 49930 • 4,547
Hancock, NY 13783 • 1,330
Hancock □, GA • 8,908
Hancock □, IL • 21,373
Hancock □, IN • 45,527
Hancock □, IA • 12,638
Hancock □, KY • 7,864
Hancock □, ME • 46,948
Hancock □, MS • 31,760
Hancock □, OH • 65,536
Hancock □, TN • 6,739
Hancock □, WV • 35,233
Hand □, SD • 4,272
Hanford, CA 93230-32 • 30,897
Hankinson, ND 58041 • 1,038
Hanna, WY 82327 • 1,076
Hanna City, IL 61536 • 1,205
Hannibal, MO 63401 • 18,004
Hanover, IN 47243 • 3,610
Hanover, MA 02339 • 2,500
Hanover, NH 03755 • 6,538
Hanover, PA 17331 • 14,399
Hanover □, VA • 63,306
Hanover Center, MA 02339 • 1,000
Hanover Park, IL 60103 • 32,895
Hanover Township, NJ 07981 • 11,538
Hansen, ID 83334 • 848
Hansford □, TX • 5,848
Hanson, MA 02341 • 2,188
Hanson □, SD • 2,994
Hapeville, GA 30354 • 5,483
Happy Valley, OR 97236 • 1,519
Harahan, LA 70123 • 9,927
Haralson □, GA • 21,966
Harbeson, DE 19951 • 500
Harbor, OR 97415 • 2,143
Harbor Beach, MI 48441 • 2,089
Harborcreek, PA 16421 • 1,500
Harbor Springs, MI 49740 • 1,540
Hardee □, FL • 19,499
Hardeeville, SC 29927 • 1,583
Hardeman □, TN • 23,377
Hardeman □, TX • 5,283
Hardin, IL 62047 • 1,071
Hardin, MT 59034 • 2,940
Hardin □, IL • 5,189
Hardin □, IA • 19,094
Hardin □, KY • 89,240
Hardin □, OH • 31,111
Hardin □, TN • 22,633
Hardin □, TX • 41,320
Harding □, NM • 987
Harding □, SD • 1,669
Hardinsburg, KY 40143 • 1,906
Hardwick, GA 31034 • 8,800
Hardwick, VT 05843 • 1,400
Hardy □, WV • 10,977
Harford □, MD • 182,132
Hargill, TX 78549 • 1,038
Harker Heights, TX 76543 • 12,841
Harkers Island, NC 28531 • 1,759
Harlan, IN 46743 • 1,200
Harlan, IA 51537 • 5,148
Harlan, KY 40831 • 2,686
Harlan □, KY • 36,574
Harlan □, NE • 3,810
Harlem, FL 33440 • 2,826
Harlem, GA 30814 • 2,199
Harlem, MT 59526 • 882
Harleysville, PA 19438 • 7,405
Harlingen, TX 78550-52 • 48,735
Harlowton, MT 59036 • 1,049
Harmon □, OK • 3,793
Harmony, MN 55939 • 1,081
Harmony, PA 16037 • 1,054
Harmony, RI 02829 • 820
Harnett □, NC • 67,822
Harney □, OR • 7,060
Harper, KS 67058 • 1,735
Harper □, KS • 7,124

Harper □, OK • 4,063
Harpers Ferry, WV 25425 • 308
Harper Woods, MI 48225 • 14,903
Harrah, OK 73045 • 4,206
Harriman, TN 37748 • 7,119
Harrington, DE 19952 • 2,311
Harrington Park, NJ 07640 • 4,623
Harris □, GA • 17,788
Harris □, TX • 2,818,199
Harrisburg, AR 72432 • 1,943
Harrisburg, IL 62946 • 9,289
Harrisburg, OR 97446 • 1,939
Harrisburg, PA 17101-13 • 52,376
Harris Hill, NY 14221 • 4,577
Harrison □, MI 48625 • 1,835
Harrison, NJ 07029 • 13,425
Harrison, NY 10528 • 23,308
Harrison, OH 45030 • 7,518
Harrison, TN 37341 • 7,191
Harrison □, IN • 29,890
Harrison □, IA • 14,730
Harrison □, KY • 16,248
Harrison □, MS • 165,365
Harrison □, MO • 8,469
Harrison □, OH • 16,085
Harrison □, TX • 57,483
Harrison □, WV • 69,371
Harrisonburg, VA 22801 • 30,707
Harrison Township, MI 48045 • 24,685
Harrisonville, MO 64701 • 7,683
Harristown, IL 62537 • 1,319
Harrisville, RI 02830 • 1,654
Harrisville, UT 84404 • 3,004
Harrisville, WV 26362 • 1,839
Harrodsburg, KY 40330 • 7,335
Hart, MI 49420 • 1,942
Hart, TX 79043 • 1,221
Hart □, GA • 19,712
Hart □, KY • 14,890
Hartford, AL 36344 • 2,448
Hartford, CT 06101-99 • 139,739
Hartford, IL 62048 • 1,676
Hartford, KY 42347 • 2,532
Hartford, MI 49057 • 2,341
Hartford, SD 57033 • 1,262
Hartford, VT 05047 • 500
Hartford, WI 53027 • 8,188
Hartford □, CT • 851,783
Hartford City, IN 47348 • 6,960
Hartington, NE 68739 • 1,583
Hartland, ME 04943 • 1,038
Hartland, WI 53029 • 6,906
Hartley, IA 51346 • 1,632
Hartley □, TX • 3,634
Hartsdale, NY 10530 • 9,587
Hartselle, AL 35640 • 10,795
Hartshorne, OK 74547 • 2,120
Hartsville, SC 29550 • 8,372
Hartsville, TN 37074 • 2,188
Hartville, OH 44632 • 2,031
Hartwell, GA 30643 • 4,555
Harvard, IL 60033 • 5,975
Harvard, MA 01451 • 1,200
Harvey, IL 60426 • 29,771
Harvey, LA 70058 • 21,222
Harvey, MI 49855 • 1,377
Harvey, ND 58341 • 2,263
Harvey □, KS • 31,028
Harwich, MA 02645 • 4,399
Harwich Port, MA 02646 • 2,300
Harwinton, CT 06791 • 5,228
Harwood Heights, IL 60656 • 7,680
Hasbrouck Heights, NJ 07604 • 11,488
Haskell, AR 72015 • 1,342
Haskell □, KS • 3,886
Haskell □, OK • 10,940
Haskell □, TX • 6,820
Haslett, MI 48840 • 10,230
Hastings, MI 49058 • 6,549
Hastings, MN 55033 • 15,445
Hastings, NE 68901-02 • 22,837
Hastings, PA 16646 • 1,431
Hastings-on-Hudson, NY 10706 • 8,000
Hatboro, PA 19040 • 7,382
Hatch, NM 87937 • 1,136
Hatfield, MA 01038 • 1,234
Hatfield, PA 19440 • 2,642
Hatteras, NC 27943 • 1,000
Hattiesburg, MS 39401-07 • 41,882
Hatton, ND 58240 • 800
Haubstadt, IN 47639 • 1,455
Haughton, LA 71037 • 1,664
Hauppauge, NY 11788 • 19,750
Hauula, HI 96717 • 3,479
Havana, FL 32333 • 1,654
Havana, IL 62644 • 3,610
Havelock, NC 28532 • 20,268
Haven, KS 67543 • 1,198
Haverford [Township], PA 19083 • 52,371
Haverhill, MA 01830-35 • 51,418
Haverstraw, NY 10927 • 9,438
Havre, MT 59501 • 10,201
Havre de Grace, MD 21078 • 8,952
Havre North, MT 59501 • 1,110
Hawaii □, HI • 120,317
Hawaiian Gardens, CA 90716 • 13,639
Hawarden, IA 51023 • 2,439
Hawi, HI 96719 • 928
Hawkins □, TN • 44,565
Hawkinsville, GA 31036 • 3,527
Hawley, MN 56549 • 1,655
Hawley, PA 18428 • 1,242
Haworth, NJ 07641 • 3,384
Haw River, NC 27258 • 1,855
Hawthorne, CA 90250-51 • 71,349
Hawthorne, FL 32640 • 1,305
Hawthorne, NV 89415-16 • 4,162
Hawthorne, NY 10532 • 4,764
Hayden, CO 81639 • 1,444
Hayden, ID 83835 • 3,744
Hayes □, NE • 1,222
Hayesville, OR 97303 • 14,318
Hayfield, MN 55940 • 1,283
Hayfield, VA 22310 • 2,300
Hayfork, CA 96041 • 2,605
Haynesville, LA 71038 • 2,854
Hays, KS 67601 • 17,767
Hays □, TX • 65,614

Haysville, KS 67060 • 8,364
Hayti, MO 63851 • 3,280
Hayward, CA 94540-46 • 111,498
Hayward, WI 54843 • 1,897
Hayward Addition, SD 57106 • 1,000
Haywood □, NC • 46,942
Haywood □, TN • 19,437
Hazard, KY 41701 • 5,416
Hazardville, CT 06082 • 5,179
Hazel Crest, IL 60429 • 13,334
Hazel Dell, WA 98660 • 15,386
Hazel Green, AL 35750 • 2,208
Hazel Green, WI 53811 • 1,171
Hazel Park, MI 48030 • 20,051
Hazelwood, MO 63042-45 • 15,324
Hazelwood, NC 28738 • 1,678
Hazen, AR 72064 • 1,668
Hazen, ND 58545 • 2,818
Hazlehurst, GA 31539 • 4,202
Hazlehurst, MS 39083 • 4,221
Hazlet, NJ 07730 • 23,013
Hazleton, PA 18201 • 24,730
Headland, AL 36345 • 3,266
Healdsburg, CA 95448 • 9,469
Healdton, OK 73438 • 2,872
Healy, AK 99743 • 487
Heard □, GA • 8,628
Hearne, TX 77859 • 5,132
Heath, OH 43056 • 7,231
Heavener, OK 74937 • 2,601
Hebbronville, TX 78361 • 4,465
Heber City, UT 84032 • 4,782
Heber Springs, AR 72543 • 5,628
Hebron, IN 46341 • 3,183
Hebron, KY 41048 • 1,200
Hebron, NE 68370 • 1,765
Hebron, ND 58638 • 888
Hebron, OH 43025 • 2,076
Hector, MN 55342 • 1,145
Heeia, HI 96744 • 5,010
Heflin, AL 36264 • 2,906
Hegins, PA 17938 • 1,200
Helena, AL 35080 • 3,918
Helena, AR 72342 • 7,491
Helena, GA 31037 • 1,256
Helena, MT 59601-26 • 24,569
Helena, OK 73741 • 1,043
Hellam, PA 17406 • 1,375
Hellertown, PA 18055 • 5,662
Helmetta, NJ 08828 • 1,211
Helotes, TX 78023 • 1,535
Helper, UT 84526 • 2,148
Hemet, CA 92343-44 • 36,094
Hemlock, MI 48626 • 1,601
Hemphill, TX 75948 • 1,182
Hemphill □, TX • 3,720
Hempstead, NY 11550-54 • 49,453
Hempstead, TX 77445 • 3,551
Hempstead □, AR • 21,621
Henagar, AL 35978 • 1,934
Henderson, KY 42420 • 25,945
Henderson, LA 70517 • 1,543
Henderson, NV 89015-16 • 64,942
Henderson, NC 27536 • 15,655
Henderson, TN 38340 • 4,760
Henderson, TX 75652-53 • 11,139
Henderson □, IL • 8,096
Henderson □, KY • 43,044
Henderson □, NC • 69,285
Henderson □, TN • 21,844
Henderson □, TX • 58,543
Henderson's Point, MS 39571 • 1,114
Hendersonville, NC 28739 • 7,284
Hendersonville, TN 37075 • 32,188
Hendricks □, IN • 75,717
Hendry □, FL • 25,773
Hennepin □, MN • 1,032,431
Hennessey, OK 73742 • 1,902
Henniker, NH 03242 • 1,693
Henrico □, VA • 217,881
Henrietta, NY 14467 • 1,200
Henrietta, NC 28076 • 1,412
Henrietta, TX 76365 • 2,896
Henry, IL 61537 • 2,591
Henry □, AL • 15,374
Henry □, GA • 58,741
Henry □, IL • 51,159
Henry □, IN • 48,139
Henry □, IA • 19,226
Henry □, KY • 12,823
Henry □, MO • 20,044
Henry □, OH • 29,108
Henry □, TN • 27,888
Henry □, VA • 56,942
Henryetta, OK 74437 • 5,872
Henryville, IN 47126 • 1,132
Hephzibah, GA 30815 • 2,466
Heppner, OR 97836 • 1,412
Herculaneum, MO 63048 • 2,263
Hercules, CA 94547 • 16,829
Hereford, TX 79045 • 14,745
Herington, KS 67449 • 2,685
Heritage Village, CT 06488 • 9,700
Herkimer, NY 13350 • 7,945
Herkimer □, NY • 65,797
Hermann, MO 65041 • 2,754
Hermantown, MN 55811 • 6,761
Herminie, PA 15637 • 2,000
Hermiston, OR 97838 • 10,040
Hermitage, PA 16148 • 15,300
Hermosa Beach, CA 90254 • 18,219
Hernando, FL 32642 • 2,103
Hernando, MS 38632 • 3,125
Hernando □, FL • 101,115
Herndon, VA 22070-71 • 16,139
Herrin, IL 62948 • 10,857
Herscher, IL 60941 • 1,278
Hershey, PA 17033 • 11,860
Hertford, NC 27944 • 2,105
Hertford □, NC • 22,523
Hesperia, CA 92345 • 50,418
Hesston, KS 67062 • 3,012
Hettinger, ND 58639 • 1,574
Hettinger □, ND • 3,445
Hewitt, TX 76643 • 8,983
Hewlett, NY 11557 • 6,620
Heyburn, ID 83336 • 2,714
Heyworth, IL 61745 • 1,627
Hialeah, FL 33010-16 • 188,004
Hiawatha, IA 52233 • 4,986
Hiawatha, KS 66434 • 3,603
Hibbing, MN 55746-47 • 18,046
Hickman, KY 42050 • 2,689

Hickman, NE 68372 • 1,081
Hickman □, KY • 5,566
Hickman □, TN • 16,754
Hickory, NC 28601-03 • 28,301
Hickory □, MO • 7,335
Hickory Hills, IL 60457 • 13,021
Hicksville, NY 11801-05 • 40,174
Hicksville, OH 43526 • 3,664
Hico, TX 76457 • 1,342
Hidalgo, TX 78557 • 3,292
Hidalgo □, NM • 5,958
Hidalgo □, TX • 383,545
Higganum, CT 06441 • 1,692
Higginsville, MO 64037 • 4,693
High Bridge, NJ 08829 • 3,886
Highland, CA 92346 • 34,439
Highland, IL 62249 • 7,525
Highland, IN 46322 • 23,696
Highland, MI 48356-57 • 750
Highland, NY 12528 • 4,492
Highland □, OH • 35,728
Highland □, VA • 2,635
Highland Falls, NY 10928 • 3,937
Highland Heights, OH 44124 • 6,249
Highland Lakes, NJ 07422 • 4,550
Highland Park, IL 60035 • 30,575
Highland Park, MI 48203 • 20,121
Highland Park, NJ 08904 • 13,279
Highland Park, TX 75205 • 8,739
Highlands, NJ 07732 • 4,849
Highlands, TX 77562 • 6,632
Highlands □, FL • 68,432
Highland Springs, VA 23075 • 13,823
Highmore, SD 57345 • 835
High Point, NC 27260-65 • 69,496
High Ridge, MO 63049 • 2,380
High Spire, PA 17034 • 2,668
High Springs, FL 32643 • 3,144
Hightstown, NJ 08520 • 5,126
Highview, KY 40228 • 14,814
Highwood, IL 60040 • 5,331
Hilbert, WI 54129 • 1,211
Hildale, UT 84784 • 1,325
Hill □, MT • 17,654
Hill □, TX • 27,146
Hill City, KS 67642 • 1,835
Hillcrest, NY 10977 • 6,447
Hillcrest Center, CA 93306 • 26,900
Hillcrest Heights, MD 20748 • 17,136
Hilliard, FL 32046 • 1,751
Hilliard, OH 43026 • 11,796
Hillsboro, IL 62049 • 4,400
Hillsboro, KS 67063 • 2,704
Hillsboro, MO 63050 • 1,625
Hillsboro, NH 03244 • 1,826
Hillsboro, ND 58045 • 1,488
Hillsboro, OH 45133 • 6,235
Hillsboro, OR 97123-24 • 37,520
Hillsboro, TX 76645 • 7,072
Hillsboro, WI 54634 • 1,288
Hillsborough, CA 94010 • 10,667
Hillsborough, NC 27278 • 4,263
Hillsborough □, FL • 834,054
Hillsborough □, NH • 336,073
Hillsdale, MI 49242 • 8,170
Hillsdale, NJ 07642 • 9,750
Hillsdale □, MI • 43,431
Hillside, IL 60162 • 7,672
Hillside, NJ 07205 • 21,044
Hillside Heights, DE 19711 • 1,500
Hillsville, VA 24343 • 2,408
Hillview, KY 40229 • 6,119
Hilo, HI 96720-21 • 37,808
Hilton, NY 14468 • 5,216
Hilton Head Island, SC 29928 • 23,694
Hinckley, IL 60520 • 1,682
Hinds □, MS • 254,441
Hines, OR 97738 • 1,452
Hinesville, GA 31313 • 21,603
Hingham, MA 02043 • 5,454
Hinsdale, IL 60521-22 • 16,029
Hinsdale, NH 03451 • 1,718
Hinsdale □, CO • 467
Hinton, OK 73047 • 1,233
Hinton, WV 25951 • 3,433
Hiram, GA 30141 • 1,389
Hiram, OH 44234 • 1,330
Hitchcock, TX 77563 • 5,868
Hitchcock □, NE • 3,750
Hitchcock Lake, CT 06716 • 1,640
Hobart, IN 46342 • 21,822
Hobart, OK 73651 • 4,305
Hobbs, NM 88240-41 • 29,115
Hobe Sound, FL 33455 • 11,507
Hoboken, NJ 07030 • 33,397
Hockessin, DE 19707 • 2,430
Hocking □, OH • 25,533
Hockley □, TX • 24,199
Hodgeman □, KS • 2,177
Hodgenville, KY 42748 • 2,721
Hoffman Estates, IL 60194-95 • 46,561
Hogansville, GA 30230 • 2,976
Hohenwald, TN 38462 • 3,760
Ho-Ho-Kus, NJ 07423 • 3,935
Hoisington, KS 67544 • 3,182
Hoke □, NC • 22,856
Hokes Bluff, AL 35903 • 3,739
Holbrook, AZ 86025-29 • 4,686
Holbrook, MA 02343 • 11,041
Holbrook, NY 11741 • 25,273
Holcomb, KS 67851 • 1,400
Holden, MA 01520 • 4,040
Holden, MO 64040 • 2,389
Holden, WV 25625 • 1,246
Holden Heights, FL 32805 • 4,387
Holdenville, OK 74848 • 4,792
Holdrege, NE 68949 • 5,671
Holgate, OH 43527 • 1,290
Holiday, FL 34690 • 19,360
Holiday City at Berkeley, NJ 08757 • 5,750
Holladay, UT 84117 • 22,189
Holland, MI 49422-24 • 30,745
Holland, NY 14080 • 1,288
Holland, OH 43528 • 1,210
Holland, PA 18966 • 5,250
Holland, TX 76534 • 1,118
Hollandale, MS 38748 • 3,576
Holley, NY 14470 • 1,890
Holliday, TX 76366 • 1,475
Hollidaysburg, PA 16648 • 5,624
Hollins, VA 24019 • 13,305
Hollis, OK 73550 • 2,584
Hollister, CA 95023-24 • 19,212

Hollister, MO 65672 • 2,628
Holliston, MA 01746 • 12,622
Holly, MI 48442 • 5,595
Holly Hill, FL 32117 • 11,141
Holly Hill, SC 29059 • 1,478
Holly Springs, GA 30142 • 2,406
Holly Springs, MS 38634-35 • 7,261
Hollywood, FL 33019-29 • 121,697
Hollywood, SC 29449 • 2,094
Holmen, WI 54636 • 3,220
Holmes □, FL • 15,778
Holmes □, MS • 21,604
Holmes □, OH • 32,849
Holstein, IA 51025 • 1,449
Holt, AL 35404 • 4,125
Holt, MI 48842 • 11,744
Holt □, MO • 6,034
Holt □, NE • 12,599
Holton, KS 66436 • 3,196
Holtsville, NY 11742 • 14,972
Holtville, CA 92250 • 4,820
Holualoa, HI 96725 • 3,834
Holyoke, CO 80734 • 1,931
Holyoke, MA 01040-41 • 43,704
Homedale, ID 83628 • 1,963
Home Gardens, CA 91720 • 7,780
Homeland Park, SC 29621 • 6,569
Home Place, IN 46240 • 1,300
Homer, AK 99603 • 3,660
Homer, IL 61849 • 1,264
Homer, LA 71040 • 4,152
Homer, MI 49245 • 1,758
Homer, NY 13077 • 3,476
Homer City, PA 15748 • 1,809
Homerville, GA 31634 • 2,560
Homestead, FL 33030-35 • 26,866
Homestead, PA 15120 • 4,179
Hometown, IL 60456 • 4,769
Homewood, AL 35209 • 22,922
Homewood, IL 60430 • 19,278
Homewood, OH 45015 • 2,550
Hominy, OK 74035 • 2,342
Homosassa, FL 32646 • 2,113
Hondo, TX 78861 • 6,018
Honea Path, SC 29654 • 3,841
Honeoye Falls, NY 14472 • 2,340
Honesdale, PA 18431 • 4,972
Honey Brook, PA 19344 • 1,184
Honey Grove, TX 75446 • 1,681
Honeypot Glen, CT 06410 • 1,200
Honeyville, UT 84314 • 1,112
Honokaa, HI 96727 • 2,186
Honolulu, HI 96801-50 • 365,272
Honolulu □, HI • 836,231
Honomu, HI 96728 • 532
Hood □, TX • 28,981
Hood River, OR 97031 • 4,632
Hood River □, OR • 16,903
Hoodsport, WA 98548 • 1,100
Hooker, OK 73945 • 1,551
Hooker □, NE • 793
Hooksett, NH 03106 • 2,573
Hoonah, AK 99829 • 795
Hooper Bay, AK 99604 • 845
Hoopeston, IL 60942 • 5,871
Hoosick Falls, NY 12090 • 3,490
Hoover, AL 35216 • 39,788
Hooverson Heights, WV 26037 • 3,056
Hopatcong, NJ 07843 • 15,586
Hope, AR 71801 • 9,643
Hope, IN 47246 • 2,171
Hope, RI 02831 • 270
Hopedale, MA 01747 • 3,961
Hope Mills, NC 28348 • 8,184
Hope Valley, RI 02832 • 1,446
Hopewell, NJ 08525 • 1,968
Hopewell, VA 23860 • 23,101
Hopewell Junction, NY 12533 • 1,786
Hopkins, MN 55343-47 • 16,534
Hopkins, SC 29061 • 1,600
Hopkins □, KY • 46,126
Hopkins □, TX • 28,833
Hopkinsville, KY 42240-41 • 29,809
Hopkinton, MA 01748 • 2,305
Hopkinton, RI 02833 • 550
Hopwood, PA 15445 • 2,021
Hoquiam, WA 98550 • 8,972
Horicon, WI 53032 • 3,873
Hornell, NY 14843 • 9,877
Horn Lake, MS 38637 • 9,069
Horry □, SC • 144,053
Horse Cave, KY 42749 • 2,284
Horseheads, NY 14844-45 • 6,802
Horsham, PA 19044 • 15,051
Horton, KS 66439 • 1,885
Hortonville, WI 54944 • 2,029
Hot Spring □, AR • 26,115
Hot Springs, SD 57747 • 4,325
Hot Springs □, WY • 4,809
Hot Springs National Park, AR 71901-14 • 32,462
Hot Springs Village, AR 71901 • 6,361
Houghton, MI 49931 • 7,498
Houghton, NY 14744 • 1,740
Houghton □, MI • 35,446
Houghton Lake, MI 48629 • 3,353
Houghton Lake Heights, MI 48630 • 2,449
Houlton, ME 04730 • 5,627
Houma, LA 70360-64 • 96,982
Housatonic, MA 01236 • 1,184
Houston, DE 19954 • 487
Houston, MN 55943 • 1,013
Houston, MS 38851 • 3,903
Houston, MO 65483 • 2,118
Houston, PA 15342 • 1,445
Houston, TX 77001-99 • 1,630,553
Houston □, AL • 81,331
Houston □, GA • 89,208
Houston □, MN • 18,497
Houston □, TN • 7,018
Houston □, TX • 21,375
Houtzdale, PA 16651 • 1,204
Howard, SD 57349 • 1,156
Howard, WI 54303 • 9,874
Howard □, AR • 13,569
Howard □, IN • 80,827
Howard □, IA • 9,809
Howard □, MD • 187,328
Howard □, MO • 9,631
Howard □, NE • 6,055
Howard □, TX • 32,343
Howard City, MI 49329 • 1,351
Howard Lake, MN 55349 • 1,343

Howards Grove-Millersville, WI 53083 • 2,329
Howell, MI 48843-44 • 8,184
Howell □, MO • 31,447
Howland, ME 04448 • 1,304
Howland, OH 44484 • 6,732
Hoxie, AR 72433 • 2,676
Hoxie, KS 67740 • 1,342
Hoyt Lakes, MN 55750 • 2,348
Huachuca City, AZ 85616 • 1,782
Hubbard, OH 44425 • 8,248
Hubbard □, OR 97032 • 1,881
Hubbard, TX 76648 • 1,589
Hubbard □, MN • 14,939
Hubbell, MI 49934 • 1,174
Huber Heights, OH 45424 • 38,696
Huber Ridge, OH 43081 • 5,255
Huber South, OH 45439 • 4,800
Hudson, FL 34607 • 7,344
Hudson, IL 61748 • 1,006
Hudson, IA 50643 • 2,037
Hudson, MA 01749 • 14,267
Hudson, MI 49247 • 2,580
Hudson, NH 03051 • 7,626
Hudson, NY 12534 • 8,034
Hudson, NC 28638 • 2,819
Hudson, OH 44236 • 5,159
Hudson, WI 54016 • 6,378
Hudson, WY 82515 • 392
Hudson □, NJ • 553,099
Hudson Falls, NY 12839 • 7,651
Hudson Lake, IN 46552 • 1,347
Hudsonville, MI 49426 • 6,170
Hudspeth □, TX • 2,915
Huerfano □, CO • 6,009
Hueytown, AL 35023 • 15,280
Huffakers, NV 89501 • 150
Hughes, AR 72348 • 1,810
Hughes □, OK • 13,023
Hughes □, SD • 14,817
Hughesville, MD 20637 • 1,319
Hughesville, PA 17737 • 2,049
Hugo, MN 55038 • 4,417
Hugo, OK 74743 • 5,978
Hugoton, KS 67951 • 3,179
Hulett, WY 82720 • 429
Hull, IA 51239 • 1,724
Hull, MA 02045 • 10,466
Humansville, MO 65674 • 1,084
Humble, TX 77338-39 • 12,060
Humboldt, IA 50548 • 4,438
Humboldt, KS 66748 • 2,178
Humboldt, NE 68376 • 1,003
Humboldt, TN 38343 • 9,651
Humboldt □, CA • 119,118
Humboldt □, IA • 10,756
Humboldt □, NV • 12,844
Hummels Wharf, PA 17831 • 1,069
Humphreys □, MS • 12,134
Humphreys □, TN • 15,795
Hunt □, TX • 64,343
Hunterdon □, NJ • 107,776
Huntertown, IN 46748 • 1,330
Huntingburg, IN 47542 • 5,242
Huntingdon, PA 16652 • 6,843
Huntingdon, TN 38344 • 4,180
Huntingdon □, PA • 44,164
Huntington, IN 46750 • 16,389
Huntington, MA 01050 • 1,200
Huntington, NY 11743 • 18,243
Huntington, TX 75949 • 1,794
Huntington, UT 84528 • 1,875
Huntington, VA 22303 • 7,489
Huntington, WV 25701-79 • 54,844
Huntington □, IN • 35,427
Huntington Bay, NY 11743 • 1,521
Huntington Beach, CA 92646-49 • 181,519
Huntington Park, CA 90255 • 56,065
Huntington Station, NY 11746 • 28,247
Huntington Woods, MI 48070 • 6,419
Huntley, IL 60142 • 2,453
Huntsville, AL 35801-24 • 159,789
Huntsville, AR 72740 • 1,605
Huntsville, MO 65259 • 1,567
Huntsville, TX 77340-44 • 27,925
Hurley, NM 88043 • 1,534
Hurley, NY 12443 • 4,644
Hurley, WI 54534 • 1,782
Hurlock, MD 21643 • 1,706
Huron, OH 44839 • 7,030
Huron, SD 57350 • 12,448
Huron □, MI • 34,951
Huron □, OH • 56,240
Hurricane, UT 84737 • 3,915
Hurricane, WV 25526 • 4,461
Hurst, TX 76053-54 • 33,574
Hurt, VA 24563 • 1,294
Hutchins, TX 75141 • 2,719
Hutchinson, KS 67501-05 • 39,308
Hutchinson, MN 55350 • 11,523
Hutchinson □, SD • 8,262
Hutchinson □, TX • 25,689
Huxley, IA 50124 • 2,047
Hyannis, MA 02601 • 14,120
Hyannis Port, MA 02647 • 1,100
Hyattsville, MD 20780-89 • 13,864
Hybla Valley, VA 22306 • 15,491
Hydaburg, AK 99922 • 384
Hyde, PA 16843 • 1,643
Hyde □, NC • 5,411
Hyde □, SD • 1,696
Hyde Park, NY 12538 • 2,550
Hyde Park, UT 84318 • 2,190
Hydeville, VT 05750 • 450
Hyndman, PA 15545 • 1,019
Hyrum, UT 84319 • 4,829

I

Iberia □, LA • 68,297
Iberville □, LA • 31,049
Ida, MI 48140 • 1,000
Ida □, IA • 8,365
Idabel, OK 74745 • 6,957
Ida Grove, IA 51445 • 2,357
Idaho □, ID • 13,783
Idaho Falls, ID 83401-15 • 43,929
Idaho Springs, CO 80452 • 1,834
Idalou, TX 79329 • 2,074
Ilion, NY 13357 • 8,888

Illmo, MO 63780 • 1,368
Imlay, NV 89418 • 250
Imlay City, MI 48444 • 2,921
Immokalee, FL 33934 • 14,120
Imperial, CA 92251 • 4,113
Imperial, NE 69033 • 2,007
Imperial Heights, MI 48902 • 3,200
Imperial □, CA • 109,303
Imperial Beach, CA 91932-33 • 26,512
Incline Village, NV 89450 • 4,500
Independence, CA 93526 • 1,000
Independence, KS 67301 • 9,942
Independence, KY 41051 • 10,444
Independence, LA 70443 • 1,632
Independence, MO 64050-58 • 112,301
Independence, OH 44131 • 6,500
Independence, OR 97351 • 4,425
Independence, WI 54747 • 1,041
Independence □, AR • 31,192
Indiana, PA 15701 • 15,174
Indiana □, PA • 89,994
Indianapolis, IN 46201-90 • 731,327
Indian Harbour Beach, FL 32937 • 6,933
Indian Head, MD 20640 • 3,531
Indian Heights, IN 46902 • 3,669
Indian Hills, CO 80454 • 2,000
Indian Neck, CT 06443 • 2,430
Indianola, IA 50125 • 11,340
Indianola, MS 38751 • 11,809
Indian Ridge Estates, AZ 85715 • 1,260
Indian River □, FL • 90,208
Indian Rocks Beach, FL 34635 • 3,963
Indian Springs, NV 89018 • 1,164
Indiantown, FL 34956 • 4,794
Indian Trail, NC 28079 • 1,942
Indio, CA 92201-02 • 36,793
Ingalls Park, IL 60431 • 2,730
Ingham □, MI • 281,912
Ingleside, TX 78362 • 5,696
Inglewood, CA 90301-12 • 109,602
Inglewood, TX 98011 • 6,500
Ingram, PA 15205 • 3,901
Inkom, ID 83245 • 769
Inkster, MI 48141 • 30,772
Inman, KS 67546 • 1,035
Inman, SC 29349 • 1,742
Inniswold, LA 70809 • 1,100
Inola, OK 74036 • 1,444
Institute, WV 25112 • 1,400
Interlachen, FL 32148 • 1,160
International Falls, MN 56649 • 8,325
Inver Grove Heights, MN 55076-77
    • 22,477
Inverness, CA 94937 • 1,422
Inverness, FL 32650-52 • 5,797
Inverness, IL 60067 • 6,503
Inverness, MS 38753 • 1,174
Inwood, FL 33880 • 6,824
Inwood, NY 11696 • 7,767
Inwood, WV 25428 • 1,360
Inyo □, CA • 18,281
Iola, KS 66749 • 6,351
Iola, WI 54945 • 1,125
Iona, ID 83427 • 1,049
Ione, CA 95640 • 6,516
Ionia, MI 48846 • 5,935
Ionia □, MI • 57,024
Iosco □, MI • 30,209
Iota, LA 70543 • 1,256
Iowa, LA 70647 • 2,588
Iowa □, IA • 14,630
Iowa □, WI • 20,150
Iowa City, IA 52240-46 • 59,738
Iowa Falls, IA 50126 • 5,424
Iowa Park, TX 76367 • 6,072
Ipswich, MA 01938 • 4,132
Ipswich, SD 57451 • 965
Iraan, TX 79744 • 1,322
Iredell □, NC • 92,931
Irion □, TX • 1,629
Irmo, SC 29063 • 11,280
Iron □, MI • 13,175
Iron □, MO • 10,726
Iron □, UT • 20,789
Iron □, WI • 6,153
Irondale, AL 35210 • 9,454
Irondequoit, NY 14617 • 52,322
Ironia, NJ 07845 • 1,110
Iron Mountain, MI 49801 • 8,525
Iron River, MI 49935 • 2,095
Ironton, MO 63650 • 1,539
Ironton, OH 45638 • 12,751
Ironwood, MI 49938 • 6,849
Iroquois □, IL • 30,787
Irvine, CA 92713-20 • 110,330
Irvine, KY 40336 • 2,836
Irving, TX 75060-63 • 155,037
Irvington, KY 40146 • 1,180
Irvington, NJ 07111 • 59,774
Irvington, NY 10533 • 6,348
Irwin, PA 15642 • 4,604
Irwin □, GA • 8,649
Isabella □, MI • 54,624
Isanti, MN 55040 • 1,228
Isanti □, MN • 25,921
Iselin, NJ 08830 • 16,141
Ishpeming, MI 49849 • 7,200
Islamorada, FL 33036 • 1,220
Island □, WA • 60,195
Island Heights, NJ 08732 • 1,470
Island Park, NY 11558 • 4,860
Island Park, RI 02871 • 1,240
Island Pond, VT 05846 • 1,222
Isla Vista, CA 93117 • 20,395
Isle of Palms, SC 29451 • 3,680
Isle of Wight □, VA • 25,053
Isleta, NM 87022 • 1,703
Islington, MA 02090 • 4,920
Islip, NY 11751 • 18,924
Islip Terrace, NY 11752 • 5,530
Issaquah, WA 98027 • 7,786
Issaquena □, MS • 1,909
Italy, TX 76651 • 1,699
Itasca, IL 60143 • 6,947
Itasca, TX 76055 • 1,523
Itasca □, MN • 40,863
Itawamba □, MS • 20,017
Ithaca, MI 48847 • 3,009
Ithaca, NY 14850-52 • 29,541
Itta Bena, MS 38941 • 2,377
Iuka, MS 38852 • 3,112
Iva, SC 29655 • 1,174

Ives Estates, FL 33162 • 13,531
Ivins, UT 84738 • 1,630
Ivoryton, CT 06442 • 2,200
Izard □, AR • 11,364

J

Jacinto City, TX 77029 • 9,343
Jack □, TX • 6,981
Jackpot, NV 89825 • 570
Jacksboro, TN 37757 • 1,568
Jacksboro, TX 76056 • 3,350
Jackson, AL 36545 • 5,819
Jackson, CA 95642 • 3,545
Jackson, GA 30233 • 4,076
Jackson, KY 41339 • 2,466
Jackson, LA 70748 • 3,891
Jackson, MI 49201-04 • 37,446
Jackson, MN 56143 • 3,559
Jackson, MS 39201-98 • 196,637
Jackson, MO 63755 • 9,256
Jackson, OH 45640 • 6,144
Jackson, SC 29831 • 1,681
Jackson, TN 38301-08 • 48,949
Jackson, WI 53037 • 2,486
Jackson, WY 83001-02 • 4,472
Jackson □, AL • 47,796
Jackson □, AR • 18,944
Jackson □, CO • 1,605
Jackson □, FL • 41,375
Jackson □, GA • 30,005
Jackson □, IL • 61,067
Jackson □, IN • 37,730
Jackson □, IA • 19,950
Jackson □, KS • 11,525
Jackson □, KY • 11,955
Jackson □, LA • 15,705
Jackson □, MI • 149,756
Jackson □, MN • 11,677
Jackson □, MS • 115,243
Jackson □, MO • 633,232
Jackson □, NC • 26,846
Jackson □, OH • 30,230
Jackson □, OK • 28,764
Jackson □, OR • 146,389
Jackson □, SD • 2,811
Jackson □, TN • 9,297
Jackson □, TX • 13,039
Jackson □, WV • 25,938
Jackson □, WI • 16,588
Jackson Center, OH 45334 • 1,398
Jacksonville, AL 36265 • 10,283
Jacksonville, AR 72076 • 29,101
Jacksonville, FL 32201-98 • 635,230
Jacksonville, IL 62650-51 • 19,324
Jacksonville, NC 28540-46 • 30,013
Jacksonville, OR 97530 • 1,896
Jacksonville, TX 75766 • 12,765
Jacksonville Beach, FL 32250 • 17,839
Jaffrey, NH 03452 • 2,558
Jal, NM 88252 • 2,156
Jamesburg, NJ 08831 • 5,294
James City, NC 28560 • 4,279
James City □, VA • 34,859
James Island, SC 29412 • 24,124
Jamestown, CA 95327 • 2,178
Jamestown, KY 42629 • 1,641
Jamestown, NY 14701-02 • 34,681
Jamestown, NC 27282 • 2,600
Jamestown, ND 58401-02 • 15,571
Jamestown, OH 45335 • 1,794
Jamestown, RI 02835 • 2,156
Jamestown, TN 38556 • 1,862
James Town, WY 82935 • 280
Janesville, CA 96114 • 1,200
Janesville, MN 56048 • 1,969
Janesville, WI 53545-47 • 52,133
Jarrettsville, MD 21084 • 2,148
Jasmine Estates, FL 34668 • 17,136
Jasonville, IN 47438 • 2,200
Jasper, AL 35501-02 • 13,553
Jasper, FL 32052 • 2,099
Jasper, GA 30143 • 1,772
Jasper, IN 47546-47 • 10,030
Jasper, TN 37347 • 2,780
Jasper, TX 75951 • 6,959
Jasper □, GA • 8,453
Jasper □, IL • 10,609
Jasper □, IN • 24,960
Jasper □, IA • 34,795
Jasper □, MS • 17,114
Jasper □, MO • 90,465
Jasper □, SC • 15,487
Jasper □, TX • 31,102
Jay, OK 74346 • 2,220
Jay □, IN • 21,512
Jean, NV 89019 • 150
Jeanerette, LA 70544 • 6,205
Jeannette, PA 15644 • 11,221
Jeff Davis □, GA • 12,032
Jeff Davis □, TX • 1,946
Jefferson, GA 30549 • 2,763
Jefferson, IA 50129 • 4,292
Jefferson, LA 70121 • 14,521
Jefferson, NC 28640 • 1,300
Jefferson, OH 44047 • 3,331
Jefferson, OR 97352 • 1,805
Jefferson, PA 15025 • 9,533
Jefferson, TX 75657 • 2,199
Jefferson, WI 53549 • 6,078
Jefferson □, AL • 651,525
Jefferson □, AR • 85,487
Jefferson □, CO • 438,430
Jefferson □, FL • 11,296
Jefferson □, GA • 17,408
Jefferson □, ID • 16,543
Jefferson □, IL • 37,020
Jefferson □, IN • 29,797
Jefferson □, IA • 16,310
Jefferson □, KS • 15,905
Jefferson □, KY • 664,937
Jefferson □, LA • 448,306
Jefferson □, MS • 8,653
Jefferson □, MO • 171,380
Jefferson □, MT • 7,939
Jefferson □, NE • 8,759
Jefferson □, NY • 110,943
Jefferson □, OH • 80,298
Jefferson □, OK • 7,010
Jefferson □, OR • 13,676
Jefferson □, PA • 46,083

Jefferson □, TN • 33,016
Jefferson □, TX • 239,397
Jefferson □, WA • 20,146
Jefferson □, WV • 35,926
Jefferson □, WI • 67,783
Jefferson City, MO 65101-10 • 35,481
Jefferson City, TN 37760 • 5,494
Jefferson Davis □, LA • 30,722
Jefferson Davis □, MS • 14,051
Jefferson Farms, DE 19720 • 3,130
Jefferson Manor, VA 22303 • 2,300
Jeffersontown, KY 40299 • 23,221
Jefferson Valley, NY 10535 • 6,420
Jefferson Village, VA 22042 • 2,500
Jeffersonville, IN 47129-31 • 21,841
Jeffersonville, KY 40337 • 1,854
Jeffersonville, OH 43128 • 1,281
Jeffrey City, WY 82310 • 1,452
Jellico, TN 37762 • 2,447
Jemez Pueblo, NM 87024 • 1,301
Jemison, AL 35085 • 1,898
Jena, LA 71342 • 2,626
Jenison, MI 49428-29 • 17,882
Jenkins, KY 41537 • 2,751
Jenkins □, GA • 8,247
Jenkintown, PA 19046 • 4,574
Jenks, OK 74037 • 7,493
Jennings, LA 70546 • 11,305
Jennings, MO 63136 • 15,905
Jennings □, IN • 23,661
Jennings Lodge, OR 97222 • 11,480
Jensen Beach, FL 34957-58 • 9,884
Jerauld □, SD • 2,425
Jericho, NY 11753 • 13,141
Jericho, VT 05465 • 1,300
Jermyn, PA 18433 • 2,263
Jerome, ID 83338 • 6,529
Jerome, PA 15937 • 1,074
Jerome □, ID • 15,138
Jersey □, IL • 20,539
Jersey City, NJ 07301-11 • 228,537
Jersey Shore, PA 17740 • 4,353
Jerseyville, IL 62052 • 7,382
Jessamine □, KY • 30,508
Jessup, MD 20794 • 6,537
Jessup, PA 18434 • 4,605
Jesup, GA 31545 • 8,958
Jesup, IA 50648 • 2,121
Jewell, IA 50130 • 1,106
Jewell □, KS • 4,251
Jewett City, CT 06351 • 3,349
Jim Hogg □, TX • 5,109
Jim Thorpe, PA 18229 • 5,048
Jim Wells □, TX • 37,679
Joanna, SC 29351 • 1,735
Jo Daviess □, IL • 21,821
John Day, OR 97845 • 1,836
Johnson, KS 67855 • 1,348
Johnson, VT 05656 • 1,470
Johnson □, AR • 18,221
Johnson □, GA • 8,329
Johnson □, IL • 11,347
Johnson □, IN • 88,109
Johnson □, IA • 96,119
Johnson □, KS • 355,054
Johnson □, KY • 23,248
Johnson □, MO • 42,514
Johnson □, NE • 4,673
Johnson □, TN • 13,766
Johnson □, TX • 97,165
Johnson □, WY • 6,145
Johnsonburg, PA 15845 • 3,350
Johnson City, NY 13790 • 16,890
Johnson City, TN 37601-15 • 49,381
Johnson Creek, WI 53038 • 1,259
Johnsonville, SC 29555 • 1,415
Johnston, IA 50131 • 4,702
Johnston, RI 02919 • 26,542
Johnston, SC 29832 • 2,688
Johnston □, NC • 81,306
Johnston □, OK • 10,032
Johnston City, IL 62951 • 3,706
Johnstown, CO 80534 • 1,579
Johnstown, NY 12095 • 9,058
Johnstown, OH 43031 • 3,237
Johnstown, PA 15901-09 • 28,134
Joliet, IL 60431-36 • 76,836
Jones, OK 73049 • 2,424
Jones □, GA • 20,739
Jones □, IA • 19,444
Jones □, MS • 62,031
Jones □, NC • 9,414
Jones □, SD • 1,324
Jones □, TX • 16,490
Jonesboro, AR 72401-03 • 46,535
Jonesboro, GA 30236-37 • 3,635
Jonesboro, IL 62952 • 1,728
Jonesboro, IN 46938 • 2,073
Jonesboro, LA 71251 • 4,305
Jonesborough, TN 37659 • 3,091
Jones Creek, TX 77541 • 2,160
Jonesport, ME 04649 • 1,525
Jonestown, MS 38639 • 1,467
Jonesville, LA 71343 • 2,720
Jonesville, MI 49250 • 2,283
Jonesville, NC 28642 • 1,549
Jonesville, SC 29353 • 1,229
Joplin, MO 64801-04 • 40,961
Joppatowne, MD 21085 • 11,084
Jordan, MN 55352 • 2,909
Jordan, NY 13080 • 1,325
Joseph, OR 97846 • 1,073
Josephine □, OR • 62,649
Joshua, TX 76058 • 3,828
Joshua Tree, CA 92252 • 3,898
Jourdanton, TX 78026 • 3,220
Juab □, UT • 5,817
Juanita, WA 98033 • 10,500
Judith Basin □, MT • 2,282
Judsonia, AR 72081 • 1,915
Julesburg, CO 80737 • 1,295
Julian, CA 92036 • 1,284
Junction, TX 76849 • 2,654
Junction City, KS 66441 • 20,604
Junction City, KY 40440 • 1,983
Junction City, OR 97448 • 3,670
Juneau, AK 99801-03 • 26,751
Juneau, WI 53039 • 2,157
Juneau □, WI • 21,650
Juniata □, PA • 20,625
Jupiter, FL 33458 • 24,986
Justice, IL 60458 • 11,137

Justin, TX 76247 • 1,234

K

Kaaawa, HI 96730 • 1,138
Kadoka, SD 57543 • 736
Kahaluu, HI 96725 • 380
Kahaluu, HI 96744 • 3,068
Kahoka, MO 63445 • 2,195
Kahuku, HI 96731 • 2,063
Kahului, HI 96732-33 • 16,889
Kailua, HI 96734 • 36,818
Kailua Kona, HI 96739-40 • 9,126
Kake, AK 99830 • 700
Kalaheo, HI 96741 • 3,592
Kalama, WA 98625 • 1,210
Kalamazoo, MI 49001-09 • 80,277
Kalamazoo □, MI • 223,411
Kalawao, HI • 130
Kalispell, MT 59901 • 11,917
Kalkaska, MI 49646 • 1,952
Kalkaska □, MI • 13,497
Kalona, IA 52247 • 1,942
Kamas, UT 84036 • 1,061
Kamiah, ID 83536 • 1,157
Kamuela (Waimea), HI 96743 • 5,972
Kanab, UT 84741 • 3,289
Kanabec □, MN • 12,802
Kanawha, WV 207,619
Kandiyohi □, MN • 38,761
Kane, PA 16735 • 4,590
Kane □, IL • 317,471
Kane □, UT • 5,169
Kaneohe, HI 96744 • 35,448
Kankakee, IL 60901 • 27,575
Kankakee □, IL • 96,255
Kannapolis, NC 28081-83 • 29,696
Kansas City, KS 66101-19 • 149,767
Kansas City, MO 64101-99 • 435,146
Kapaa, HI 96746 • 8,149
Kapaau, HI 96755 • 1,083
Kaplan, LA 70548 • 4,535
Karnes □, TX • 12,455
Karnes City, TX 78118 • 2,916
Karns, TN 37921 • 1,458
Kasson, MN 55944 • 3,514
Kathleen, FL 33849 • 2,743
Katy, TX 77449-50 • 8,005
Kauai □, HI • 51,177
Kaufman, TX 75142 • 5,238
Kaufman □, TX • 52,220
Kaukauna, WI 54130 • 11,982
Kaumakani, HI 96747 • 803
Kaunakakai, HI 96748 • 2,658
Kay □, OK • 48,056
Kaycee, WY 82639 • 256
Kayenta, AZ 86033 • 4,372
Kaysville, UT 84037 • 13,961
Keaau, HI 96749 • 1,584
Kealakekua, HI 96750 • 1,453
Kealia, HI 96751 • 700
Keansburg, NJ 07734 • 11,069
Kearney, MO 64060 • 1,790
Kearney, NE 68847-48 • 24,396
Kearney □, NE • 6,629
Kearns, UT 84118 • 28,374
Kearny, AZ 85237 • 2,262
Kearny, NJ 07031-32 • 34,874
Kearny □, KS • 4,027
Keego Harbor, MI 48320 • 2,932
Keene, NH 03431 • 22,430
Keene, TX 76059 • 3,944
Keeseville, NY 12944 • 1,854
Keewatin, MN 55753 • 1,118
Keith □, NE • 8,584
Keizer, OR 97303 • 21,884
Kekaha, HI 96752 • 3,506
Keller, TX 76248 • 13,683
Kellogg, ID 83837 • 2,591
Kelseyville, CA 95451 • 2,861
Kelso, WA 98626 • 11,820
Kemmerer, WY 83101 • 3,020
Kemp, TX 75143 • 1,184
Kemper □, MS • 10,356
Kenai, AK 99611 • 6,327
Kenbridge, VA 23944 • 1,264
Ken Caryl, CO 80123 • 24,391
Kendall, FL 33156 • 87,271
Kendall □, IL • 39,413
Kendall □, TX • 14,589
Kendall Park, NJ 08824 • 7,127
Kendallville, IN 46755 • 7,773
Kenedy, TX 78119 • 3,763
Kenedy □, TX • 460
Kenilworth, IL 60043 • 2,402
Kenilworth, NJ 07033 • 7,574
Kenly, NC 27542 • 1,549
Kenmare, ND 58746 • 1,214
Kenmore, NY 14217 • 17,180
Kenmore, WA 98028 • 8,917
Kennebec □, ME • 115,904
Kennebunk, ME 04043 • 4,206
Kennebunkport, ME 04046 • 1,100
Kennedy Heights, LA 70094 • 2,000
Kennedy Township, PA 15108 • 7,152
Kenner, LA 70062-65 • 72,033
Kennesaw, GA 30144 • 8,936
Kennett, MO 63857 • 10,941
Kennett Square, PA 19348 • 5,218
Kennewick, WA 99336-37 • 42,155
Kennydale, WA 98056 • 2,000
Kenosha, WI 53140-44 • 80,352
Kenosha □, WI • 128,181
Kenova, WV 25530 • 3,748
Ken Rock, IL 61109 • 3,300
Kensett, AR 72082 • 1,741
Kensington, CA 94707 • 4,974
Kensington, CT 06037 • 8,306
Kensington, MD 20895 • 1,713
Kent, OH 44240 • 28,835
Kent, WA 98031-32 • 37,960
Kent □, DE • 110,993
Kent □, MD • 17,842
Kent □, MI • 500,631
Kent □, RI • 161,135
Kent □, TX • 1,010
Kentfield, CA 94904 • 6,030
Kentland, IN 47951 • 1,798
Kenton, DE 19955 • 232
Kenton, OH 43326 • 8,356
Kenton, TN 38233 • 1,366

Kenton □, KY • 142,031
Kentwood, LA 70444 • 2,468
Kentwood, MI 49508 • 37,826
Kenvil, NJ 07847 • 3,050
Kenwood, OH 45236 • 7,469
Kenyon, MN 55946 • 1,552
Kenyon, RI 02836 • 400
Keokea, HI 96790 • 900
Keokuk, IA 52632 • 12,451
Keokuk □, IA • 11,624
Keosauqua, IA 52565 • 1,020
Keota, IA 52248 • 1,000
Kerens, TX 75144 • 1,702
Kerhonkson, NY 12446 • 1,629
Kermit, TX 79745 • 6,875
Kern □, CA • 543,477
Kernersville, NC 27284-85 • 10,836
Kernville, CA 93238 • 1,656
Kerr □, TX • 36,304
Kerrville, TX 78028-29 • 17,384
Kershaw, SC 29067 • 1,814
Kershaw □, SC • 43,599
Ketchikan, AK 99901 • 8,263
Ketchum, ID 83340 • 2,523
Kettering, MD 20772 • 9,901
Kettering, OH 45429 • 60,569
Kettle Falls, WA 99141 • 1,272
Kewanee, IL 61443 • 12,969
Kewaskum, WI 53040 • 2,515
Kewaunee, WI 54216 • 2,750
Kewaunee □, WI • 18,878
Keweenaw □, MI • 1,701
Keya Paha □, NE • 1,029
Key Biscayne, FL 33149 • 8,854
Key Largo, FL 33037 • 11,336
Keyport, NJ 07735 • 7,586
Keyser, WV 26726 • 5,870
Keystone Heights, FL 32656 • 1,315
Key West, FL 33040-41 • 24,832
Kiana, AK 99749 • 385
Kidder □, ND • 3,332
Kiel, WI 53042 • 2,910
Kihei, HI 96753 • 11,107
Kilauea, HI 96754 • 1,685
Kilgore, TX 75662-63 • 11,066
Killdeer, ND 58640 • 722
Killeen, TX 76540-47 • 63,535
Killen, AL 35645 • 1,047
Kilmarnock, VA 22482 • 1,109
Kimball, NE 69145 • 2,574
Kimball □, NE • 4,108
Kimberly, AL 35091 • 1,096
Kimberly, ID 83341 • 2,367
Kimberly, WI 54136 • 5,406
Kimble □, TX • 4,122
Kincaid, IL 62540 • 1,353
Kinder, LA 70648 • 2,246
Kinderhook, NY 12106 • 1,293
King, NC 27021 • 4,059
King □, TX • 354
King □, WA • 1,507,319
King and Queen □, VA • 6,289
King City, CA 93930 • 7,634
King Cove, AK 99612 • 451
Kingfisher, OK 73750 • 4,095
Kingfisher □, OK • 13,212
King George □, VA • 13,527
Kingman, AZ 86401-02 • 12,722
Kingman, KS 67068 • 3,196
Kingman □, KS • 8,292
King of Prussia, PA 19406 • 18,406
Kings □, CA • 101,469
Kings □, NY • 2,300,664
King Salmon, AK 99613 • 696
Kingsburg, CA 93631 • 7,205
Kingsbury □, SD • 5,925
Kingsford, MI 49801 • 5,480
Kingsgate, WA 98011 • 14,259
Kingsland, GA 31548 • 4,699
Kingsland, TX 78639 • 2,725
Kingsley, IA 51028 • 1,129
Kings Mountain, NC 28086 • 8,763
Kings Park, NY 11754 • 17,773
Kings Park, VA 22151 • 6,000
Kings Park West, VA 22032 • 6,000
Kings Point, FL 33484 • 12,422
Kings Point, NY 11024 • 4,843
Kingsport, TN 37660-65 • 36,365
Kingston, ID 83839 • 1,000
Kingston, MA 02364 • 4,774
Kingston, NJ 08528 • 1,200
Kingston, NY 12401 • 23,095
Kingston, OH 45644 • 1,153
Kingston, OK 73439 • 1,237
Kingston, PA 18704 • 14,507
Kingston, RI 02881 • 6,504
Kingston, TN 37763 • 4,552
Kingston Springs, TN 37082 • 1,529
Kingstown, MD 21620 • 1,660
Kingstree, SC 29556 • 3,858
Kingsville, OH 21087 • 3,550
Kingsville (North Kingsville), OH 44048
    • 1,243
Kingsville, TX 78363-64 • 25,276
King William □, VA • 10,913
Kingwood, TX 77339 • 37,397
Kingwood, WV 26537 • 3,243
Kinloch, MO 63140 • 2,702
Kinnelon, NJ 07405 • 8,470
Kinney □, TX • 3,119
Kinsey, AL 36301 • 1,679
Kinsley, KS 67547 • 1,875
Kinston, NC 28501-03 • 25,295
Kiowa, KS 67070 • 1,160
Kiowa □, CO • 1,688
Kiowa □, KS • 3,660
Kiowa □, OK • 11,347
Kipnuk, AK 99614 • 470
Kirby, TX 78219 • 8,326
Kirbyville, TX 75956 • 1,871
Kirkland, IL 60146 • 1,011
Kirkland, WA 98033-34 • 40,052
Kirksville, MO 63501 • 17,152
Kirkwood, DE 19708 • 350
Kirkwood, MO 63122 • 27,291
Kirtland, NM 87417 • 3,552
Kirtland, OH 44094 • 5,881
Kissimmee, FL 34741-46 • 30,050
Kit Carson □, CO • 7,140
Kitsap □, WA • 189,731
Kittanning, PA 16201 • 5,120
Kittery, ME 03904 • 5,151

United States Populations and ZIP Codes

Kittery Point, ME 03905 • 1,093
Kittitas □, WA • 26,725
Kittson □, MN • 5,767
Kitty Hawk, NC 27949 • 1,937
Klamath □, OR • 57,702
Klamath Falls, OR 97601-03 • 17,737
Klawock, AK 99925 • 722
Kleberg □, TX • 30,274
Klein, TX 77379 • 12,000
Klickitat □, WA • 16,616
Knightdale, NC 27545 • 1,884
Knightstown, IN 46148 • 2,048
Knob Noster, MO 65336 • 2,261
Knott □, KY • 17,906
Knox, IN 46534 • 3,705
Knox, PA 16232 • 1,182
Knox □, IL • 56,393
Knox □, IN • 39,884
Knox □, KY • 29,676
Knox □, ME • 36,310
Knox □, MO • 4,482
Knox □, NE • 9,534
Knox □, OH • 47,473
Knox □, TN • 335,749
Knox □, TX • 4,837
Knox City, TX 79529 • 1,440
Knoxville, IL 61448 • 3,243
Knoxville, IA 50138 • 8,232
Knoxville, TN 37901-50 • 165,121
Kodiak, AK 99615 • 6,365
Kohler, WI 53044 • 1,817
Kokomo, IN 46901-04 • 44,962
Konawa, OK 74849 • 1,508
Koochiching □, MN • 16,299
Koontz Lake, IN 46574 • 1,615
Kootenai □, ID • 69,795
Koppel, PA 16136 • 1,024
Kosciusko, MS 39090 • 6,986
Kosciusko □, IN • 65,294
Kossuth □, IA • 18,591
Kotlik, AK 99620 • 461
Kotzebue, AK 99752 • 2,751
Kountze, TX 77625 • 2,056
Kouts, IN 46347 • 1,603
Krebs, OK 74554 • 1,955
Kremmling, CO 80459 • 1,166
Krotz Springs, LA 70750 • 1,285
Kula, HI 96790 • 1,300
Kulpmont, PA 17834 • 3,233
Kuna, ID 83634 • 1,955
Kurtistown, HI 96760 • 910
Kutztown, PA 19530 • 4,704
Kwethluk, AK 99621 • 558
Kwigillingok, AK 99622 • 278
Kyle, TX 78640 • 2,225

L

Labadieville, LA 70372 • 1,821
La Barge, WY 83123 • 493
La Belle, FL 33935 • 2,703
Labette □, KS • 23,693
La Canada Flintridge, CA 91011 • 19,378
Lac du Flambeau, WI 54538 • 1,180
La Center, KY 42056 • 1,040
Lacey, WA 98503 • 19,279
Lackawanna, NY 14218 • 20,585
Lackawanna □, PA • 219,039
Laclede □, MO • 27,158
Lacombe, LA 70445 • 6,523
Lacon, IL 61540 • 1,986
Laconia, NH 03246-47 • 15,743
Lacoochee, FL 33537 • 2,072
Lac qui Parle □, MN • 8,924
La Crescent, MN 55947 • 4,311
La Crescenta, CA 91214 • 12,500
La Crosse, KS 67548 • 1,427
La Crosse, WI 54601-03 • 51,003
La Crosse □, WI • 97,904
La Cygne, KS 66040 • 1,066
Ladd, IL 61329 • 1,283
Ladera Heights, CA 90045 • 6,316
Ladoga, IN 47954 • 1,124
Ladson, SC 29456 • 13,540
Ladue, MO 63124 • 8,847
Lady Lake, FL 32159 • 8,071
Ladysmith, WI 54848 • 3,938
Lafayette, AL 36862 • 3,151
Lafayette, CA 94549 • 23,501
Lafayette, CO 80026 • 14,548
Lafayette, GA 30728 • 6,313
Lafayette, IN 47901-06 • 43,764
Lafayette, LA 70501-09 • 94,440
Lafayette, NC 28304 • 3,200
Lafayette, OR 97127 • 1,292
La Fayette, RI 02852 • 640
Lafayette, TN 37083 • 3,641
Lafayette □, AR • 9,643
Lafayette □, FL • 5,578
Lafayette □, LA • 164,762
Lafayette □, MS • 31,826
Lafayette □, MO • 31,107
Lafayette □, WI • 16,076
Lafayette Southwest, LA • 5,500
La Feria, TX 78559 • 4,360
Lafitte, LA 70067 • 1,507
La Follette, TN 37766 • 7,192
Lafourche □, LA • 85,860
La Grande, OR 97850 • 11,766
La Grange, GA 30240-41 • 25,597
La Grange, IL 60525 • 15,362
Lagrange, IN 46761 • 2,382
La Grange, KY 40031 • 3,853
La Grange, MO 63448 • 1,102
La Grange, NC 28551 • 2,805
Lagrange, OH 44050 • 1,199
La Grange, TX 78945 • 3,951
Lagrange □, IN • 29,477
La Grange Highlands, IL 60525 • 3,660
La Grange Park, IL 60525 • 12,861
Laguna Beach, CA 92651-54 • 23,170
Laguna Hills, CA 92653 • 46,731
Laguna Niguel, CA 92677 • 44,400
La Habra, CA 90631-33 • 51,266
Lahaina, HI 96761 • 9,073
La Harpe, IL 61450 • 1,407
Laie, HI 96762 • 5,577
Laingsburg, MI 48848 • 1,148
La Junta, CO 81050 • 7,637

Lake □, CA • 50,631
Lake □, CO • 6,007
Lake □, FL • 152,104
Lake □, IL • 516,418
Lake □, IN • 475,594
Lake □, MI • 8,583
Lake □, MN • 10,415
Lake □, MT • 21,041
Lake □, OH • 215,499
Lake □, OR • 7,186
Lake □, SD • 10,550
Lake □, TN • 7,129
Lake Alfred, FL 33850 • 3,622
Lake Andes, SD 57356 • 846
Lake Arrowhead, CA 92317 • 6,539
Lake Arthur, LA 70549 • 3,194
Lake Barcroft, VA 22041 • 8,686
Lake Bluff, IL 60044 • 5,513
Lake Butler, FL 32054 • 2,116
Lake Carmel, NY 10512 • 8,489
Lake Charles, LA 70601-29 • 70,580
Lake City, AR 72437 • 1,833
Lake City, FL 32055-56 • 10,005
Lake City, IA 51449 • 1,841
Lake City, MN 55041 • 4,391
Lake City, PA 16423 • 2,519
Lake City, SC 29560 • 7,153
Lake City, TN 37769 • 2,166
Lake Crystal, MN 56055 • 2,084
Lake Delta, NY 13440 • 1,980
Lake Delton, WI 53940 • 1,470
Lake Elmo, MN 55042 • 5,903
Lake Elsinore, CA 92330-31 • 18,285
Lake Erie Beach, NY 14006 • 4,509
Lakefield, MN 56150 • 1,679
Lake Forest, FL 33023 • 5,400
Lake Forest, IL 60045 • 17,836
Lake Geneva, WI 53147 • 5,979
Lake Grove, NY 11755 • 9,612
Lake Hamilton, AR 71913 • 1,331
Lake Havasu City, AZ 86403-05 • 24,363
Lake Helen, FL 32744 • 2,344
Lakehurst, NJ 08733 • 3,078
Lake in the Hills, IL 60102 • 5,866
Lake Jackson, TX 77566 • 22,776
Lake Katrine, NY 12449 • 1,998
Lakeland, FL 33801-13 • 70,576
Lakeland, GA 31635 • 2,467
Lakeland Highlands, FL 33801 • 9,972
Lakeland Village, CA 92330 • 5,159
Lake Linden, MI 49945 • 1,203
Lake Lorraine, FL 32569 • 6,779
Lake Luzerne, NY 12846 • 1,160
Lake Magdalene, FL 33612 • 15,973
Lake Mary, FL 32746 • 5,929
Lake Mills, IA 50450 • 2,143
Lake Mills, WI 53551 • 4,143
Lakemore, OH 44250 • 2,684
Lake Odessa, MI 48849 • 2,256
Lake Of The Woods □, MN • 4,076
Lake Orion, MI 48360-62 • 3,057
Lake Oswego, OR 97034-35 • 30,576
Lake Park, FL 33403 • 6,704
Lake Placid, FL 33852 • 1,158
Lake Placid, NY 12946 • 2,485
Lakeport, CA 95453 • 4,390
Lake Preston, SD 57249 • 663
Lake Providence, LA 71254 • 5,380
Lake Ridge, VA 22192 • 23,862
Lake Ronkonkoma, NY 11779 • 18,997
Lake Shore, MD 21122 • 13,269
Lakeside, CA 92040 • 39,412
Lakeside, CT 06488 • 1,200
Lakeside, FL 32073 • 29,137
Lakeside, OR 97449 • 1,437
Lakeside, VA 23228 • 12,081
Lakeside Park, KY 41017 • 3,131
Lake Station, IN 46405 • 13,899
Lake Stevens, WA 98258 • 3,380
Lake Telemark, NJ 07866 • 1,121
Lakeview, GA 30741 • 5,237
Lake View, IA 51450 • 1,303
Lakeview, MI 48850 • 1,108
Lake View, NY 14085 • 1,460
Lakeview, NY 11552 • 5,476
Lakeview, OH 43331 • 1,056
Lakeview, OR 97630 • 2,526
Lake Villa, IL 60046 • 2,857
Lake Village, AR 71653 • 2,791
Lakeville, CT 06039 • 1,800
Lakeville, MA 02346 • 1,948
Lakeville, MN 55044 • 24,854
Lakeville, NY 14480 • 1,000
Lake Wales, FL 33853 • 9,670
Lake Wissota, WI 54729 • 2,175
Lakewood, CA 90711-16 • 73,557
Lakewood, CO 80215 • 126,481
Lakewood, IL 60014 • 1,609
Lakewood, IA 50211 • 1,950
Lakewood, NJ 08701 • 26,095
Lakewood, NY 14750 • 3,564
Lakewood, OH 44107 • 59,718
Lakewood, WA 98259 • 58,412
Lakewood Center, WA 98499 • 58,412
Lakewood Park, FL 34951 • 7,211
Lake Worth, FL 33460-67 • 28,564
Lake Zurich, IL 60047 • 14,947
Lakin, KS 67860 • 2,060
Lakota, SD 58344 • 898
La Luz, NM 88337 • 1,625
Lamar, CO 81052 • 8,343
Lamar, MO 64759 • 4,168
Lamar, PA 16848 • 1,200
Lamar, SC 29069 • 1,125
Lamar □, AL • 15,715
Lamar □, GA • 13,038
Lamar □, MS • 30,424
Lamar □, TX • 43,949
La Marque, TX 77568 • 14,120
Lamb □, TX • 15,072
Lambert, MS 38643 • 1,131
Lambertville, MI 48144 • 7,860
Lambertville, NJ 08530 • 3,927
La Mesa, CA 91941-44 • 52,931
La Mesa, NM 88044 • 900
Lamesa, TX 79331 • 10,809
La Mirada, CA 90637-38 • 40,452
Lamoille, NV 89828 • 110
Lamoille □, VT • 19,735
Lamoni, IA 50140 • 2,319
Lamont, CA 93241 • 11,517
La Moure, ND 58458 • 970

La Moure □, ND • 5,383
Lampasas, TX 76550 • 6,382
Lampasas □, TX • 13,521
Lanai City, HI 96763 • 2,400
Lanark, IL 61046 • 1,382
Lancashire, DE 19810 • 1,175
Lancaster, CA 93534-39 • 97,291
Lancaster, KY 40444 • 3,421
Lancaster, NY 14086 • 11,940
Lancaster, OH 43130 • 34,507
Lancaster, PA 17601-05 • 55,551
Lancaster, SC 29720-21 • 8,914
Lancaster, TX 75146 • 22,117
Lancaster, WI 53813 • 4,192
Lancaster □, NE • 213,641
Lancaster □, PA • 422,822
Lancaster □, SC • 54,516
Lancaster □, VA • 10,896
Lancaster Village, DE 19805 • 1,100
Landen, OH 45040 • 9,263
Lander, WY 82520 • 7,023
Lander □, NV • 6,944
Landess, IN 46944 • 1,500
Landis, NC 28088 • 2,333
Land O' Lakes, FL 34639 • 7,892
Landover, MD 20784 • 5,052
Landrum, SC 29356 • 2,347
Lane □, KS • 2,375
Lane □, OR • 282,912
Lanesboro, MA 01237 • 1,000
Lanett, AL 36863 • 8,985
Langdon, ND 58249 • 2,241
Langeloth, PA 15054 • 1,112
Langhorne, PA 19047 • 1,361
Langlade □, WI • 19,505
Langley, SC 29834 • 1,714
Langley Park, MD 20783 • 17,474
Langston, OK 73050 • 1,471
Lanham, MD 20706 • 5,000
Lanier □, GA • 5,531
Lansdale, PA 19446 • 16,362
Lansdowne, MD 21227 • 9,430
Lansdowne, PA 19050 • 11,712
L'Anse, MI 49946 • 2,151
Lansford, PA 18232 • 4,583
Lansing, IL 60438 • 28,086
Lansing, IA 52151 • 1,007
Lansing, KS 66043 • 7,120
Lansing, MI 48901-33 • 127,321
Lantana, FL 33462 • 8,392
La Palma, CA 90623 • 15,392
La Paz □, AZ • 13,844
Lapeer, MI 48446 • 7,759
Lapeer □, MI • 74,768
Lapel, IN 46051 • 1,742
La Place, LA 70068-69 • 24,194
La Plata, MD 20646 • 5,841
La Plata, MO 63549 • 1,401
La Plata □, CO • 32,284
Laporte, IN 46350 • 21,507
La Porte, TX 77571-72 • 27,910
La Porte □, IN • 107,066
La Porte City, IA 50651 • 2,128
La Pryor, TX 78872 • 1,343
La Puente, CA 91744-49 • 36,955
Lapwai, ID 83540 • 932
Laramie, WY 82063-71 • 26,687
Laramie □, WY • 73,142
Larchmont, NY 10538 • 6,181
Larchmont North, NY 10538 • 11,240
Laredo, TX 78040-44 • 122,899
Largo, FL 34640-49 • 65,674
Larimer □, CO • 186,136
Larimore, ND 58251 • 1,464
La Riviera, CA 95826 • 10,802
Larkspur, CA 94939 • 11,070
Larksville, PA 18704 • 4,700
Larned, KS 67550 • 4,490
Larose, LA 70373 • 5,772
Larue □, KY • 11,679
La Salle, CO 80645 • 1,783
La Salle, IL 61301 • 9,717
La Salle □, IL • 106,913
La Salle □, LA • 13,662
La Salle □, TX • 5,254
Las Animas, CO 81054 • 2,481
Las Animas □, CO • 13,765
Las Cruces, NM 88001-08 • 62,126
Lassen □, CA • 27,598
Las Vegas, NV 89101-99 • 258,295
Las Vegas, NM 87701 • 14,753
Latah □, ID • 30,617
Lathrop, MO 64465 • 1,794
Lathrop Wells, NV 89020 • 350
Latimer □, OK • 10,333
Laton, CA 93242 • 1,415
Latrobe, PA 15650 • 9,265
Latta, SC 29565 • 1,565
Lauderdale □, AL • 79,661
Lauderdale □, MS • 75,555
Lauderdale □, TN • 23,491
Lauderdale Lakes, FL 33313 • 27,341
Lauderhill, FL 33313 • 49,708
Laughlin, NV 89028-29 • 140
Laughlintown, PA 15655 • 1,000
Laurel, DE 19956 • 3,226
Laurel, FL 34272 • 8,245
Laurel, MD 20707-09 • 19,438
Laurel, MS 39440-42 • 18,827
Laurel, MT 59044 • 5,686
Laurel, VA 23060 • 13,011
Laurel □, KY • 43,438
Laurel Bay, SC 29902 • 4,972
Laureldale, PA 19605 • 3,726
Laurel Hill, NC 28351 • 2,314
Laurence Harbor, NJ 08879 • 6,361
Laurens, IA 50554 • 1,550
Laurens, SC 29360 • 9,694
Laurens □, GA • 39,988
Laurens □, SC • 58,092
Laurinburg, NC 28352-53 • 11,643
Laurium, MI 49913 • 2,268
Lavaca, AR 72941 • 1,253
Lavaca □, TX • 18,690
La Vale, MD 21502 • 5,000
Lavallette, NJ 08735 • 2,299
La Vergne, TN 37086 • 7,499
La Verkin, UT 84745 • 1,771
La Verne, CA 91750 • 30,897
Laverne, OK 73848 • 1,269
La Vista, GA 30329 • 4,900

La Vista, NE 68128 • 9,840
Lavonia, GA 30553 • 1,840
Lawai, HI 96765 • 1,787
Lawndale, CA 90260-61 • 27,331
Lawnside, NJ 08045 • 2,841
Lawrence, IN 46226 • 26,763
Lawrence, KS 66044-46 • 65,608
Lawrence, MA 01840-45 • 70,207
Lawrence, NY 11559 • 6,513
Lawrence □, AL • 31,513
Lawrence □, AR • 17,457
Lawrence □, IL • 15,972
Lawrence □, IN • 42,836
Lawrence □, KY • 13,998
Lawrence □, MS • 12,458
Lawrence □, MO • 30,236
Lawrence □, OH • 61,834
Lawrence □, PA • 96,246
Lawrence □, TN • 35,303
Lawrenceburg, IN 47025 • 4,375
Lawrenceburg, KY 40342 • 5,911
Lawrenceburg, TN 38464 • 10,412
Lawrence Park, PA 16511 • 4,310
Lawrenceville, GA 30243-46 • 16,848
Lawrenceville, IL 62439 • 4,897
Lawrenceville, NJ 08648 • 6,446
Lawrenceville, VA 23868 • 1,486
Lawson, MO 64062 • 1,876
Lawsonia, MD 21817 • 1,326
Lawtell, LA 70550 • 1,014
Lawton, MI 49065 • 1,685
Lawton, OK 73501-07 • 80,561
Layton, UT 84040-41 • 41,784
Laytonville, CA 95454 • 1,133
Lea □, NM • 55,765
Leachville, AR 72438 • 1,743
Lead, SD 57754 • 3,632
Leadville, CO 80461 • 2,629
Leadwood, MO 63653 • 1,247
League City, TX 77573-74 • 30,159
Leake □, MS • 18,436
Leakesville, MS 39451 • 1,129
Lealman, FL 33714 • 21,748
Leavenworth, KS 66048 • 38,495
Leavenworth, WA 98826 • 1,692
Leavenworth □, KS • 64,371
Leavittsburg, OH 44430 • 2,220
Leawood, KS 66206 • 19,693
Lebanon, DE 19901 • 130
Lebanon, IN 46052 • 12,059
Lebanon, KY 40033 • 5,695
Lebanon, MO 65536 • 9,983
Lebanon, NH 03766 • 12,183
Lebanon, NJ 08833 • 1,036
Lebanon, OH 45036 • 10,453
Lebanon, OR 97355 • 10,950
Lebanon, PA 17042 • 24,800
Lebanon, TN 37087-88 • 15,208
Lebanon □, PA • 113,744
Lebanon Junction, KY 40150 • 1,741
Le Center, MN 56057 • 2,006
Le Claire, IA 52753 • 2,734
Le Flore □, OK • 43,270
Le Grand, CA 95333 • 1,205
Lehi, UT 84043 • 8,475
Lehigh □, PA • 291,130
Lehigh Acres, FL 33936 • 13,611
Lehighton, PA 18235 • 5,914
Leicester, MA 01524 • 3,200
Leipsic, DE 19901 • 236
Leipsic, OH 45856 • 2,203
Leisure City, FL 33033 • 19,379
Leitchfield, KY 42754-55 • 4,965
Leland, MS 38756 • 6,366
Le Mars, IA 51031 • 8,454
Lemay, MO 63125 • 18,005
Lemhi □, ID • 6,899
Lemmon, SD 57638 • 1,614
Lemmon Valley, NV 89501 • 4,100
Lemon Grove, CA 91945-46 • 23,984
Lemont, IL 60439 • 7,348
Lemont, PA 16851 • 2,613
Lemoore, CA 93245 • 13,622
Lena, IL 61048 • 2,605
Lenawee □, MI • 91,476
Lenexa, KS 66215 • 34,034
Lennox, CA 90304 • 22,757
Lennox, SD 57039 • 1,767
Lenoir, NC 28645 • 14,192
Lenoir □, NC • 57,274
Lenoir City, TN 37771 • 6,147
Lenox, IA 50851 • 1,303
Lenox, MA 01240 • 1,687
Leo, IN 46765 • 1,200
Leola, SD 57456 • 457
Leon, IA 50144 • 2,047
Leon □, FL • 192,493
Leon □, TX • 12,665
Leonard, TX 75452 • 1,744
Leonardo, NJ 07737 • 3,252
Leonardtown, MD 20650 • 1,475
Leonia, NJ 07605 • 8,365

Leon Valley, TX 78238 • 9,581
Leoti, KS 67861 • 1,738
Lepanto, AR 72354 • 2,033
Le Roy, IL 61752 • 2,777
Le Roy, NY 14482 • 4,974
Leslie, SC 29730 • 1,102
Leslie □, KY • 13,642
Lester Prairie, MN 55354 • 1,180
Le Sueur, MN 56058 • 3,714
Le Sueur □, MN • 23,239
Letcher □, KY • 27,000
Levelland, TX 79336-38 • 13,986
Levittown, NY 11756 • 53,286
Levittown, PA 19058 • 55,362
Levy □, FL • 25,923
Lewes, DE 19958 • 2,295
Lewis □, ID • 3,516
Lewis □, KY • 13,029
Lewis □, MO • 10,233
Lewis □, NY • 26,796
Lewis □, TN • 9,247
Lewis □, WA • 59,358
Lewis □, WV • 17,223
Lewis and Clark □, MT • 47,495
Lewisburg, OH 45338 • 1,584
Lewisburg, PA 17837 • 5,785
Lewisburg, TN 37091 • 9,879
Lewisburg, WV 24901 • 3,598
Lewisport, KY 42351 • 1,778
Lewiston, ID 83501 • 28,082
Lewiston, ME 04240-43 • 39,757
Lewiston, MN 55952 • 1,298
Lewiston, NY 14092 • 3,048
Lewiston, UT 84320 • 1,532
Lewistown, IL 61542 • 2,572
Lewistown, MT 59457 • 6,051
Lewistown, PA 17044 • 9,341
Lewisville, AR 71845 • 1,424
Lewisville, TX 75067 • 46,521
Lexington, IL 61753 • 1,809
Lexington, KY 40501-96 • 225,366
Lexington, MA 02173 • 28,974
Lexington, MS 39095 • 2,227
Lexington, MO 64067 • 4,860
Lexington, NE 68850 • 6,601
Lexington, NC 27292-93 • 16,581
Lexington, OH 44904 • 4,124
Lexington, OK 73051 • 1,776
Lexington, SC 29071-73 • 3,289
Lexington, TN 38351 • 5,810
Lexington, VA 24450 • 6,959
Lexington □, SC • 167,611
Lexington Park, MD 20653 • 9,943
Libby, MT 59923 • 2,532
Liberal, KS 67901-05 • 16,573
Liberty, IN 47353 • 2,051
Liberty, KY 42539 • 1,937
Liberty, MO 64068 • 20,459
Liberty, NY 12754 • 4,128
Liberty, NC 27298 • 2,047
Liberty, SC 29657 • 3,228
Liberty, TX 77575 • 7,733
Liberty □, FL • 5,569
Liberty □, GA • 52,745
Liberty □, MT • 2,295
Liberty □, TX • 52,726
Liberty Acres, CA 90250 • 4,700
Liberty Center, OH 43532 • 1,084
Liberty Lake, WA 99019 • 2,015
Libertyville, IL 60048 • 19,174
Licking, MO 65542 • 1,328
Licking □, OH • 128,300
Lidgerwood, ND 58053 • 799
Lighthouse Point, FL 33064 • 10,378
Ligonier, IN 46767 • 3,443
Ligonier, PA 15658 • 1,638
Lihue, HI 96766 • 5,536
Lilbourn, MO 63862 • 1,378
Lilburn, GA 30247 • 9,301
Lillington, NC 27546 • 2,048
Lilly, PA 15938 • 1,162
Lima, NY 14485 • 2,165
Lima, OH 45801-09 • 45,549
Limestone, ME 04750-51 • 1,245
Limestone □, AL • 54,135
Limestone □, TX • 20,946
Limon, CO 80828 • 1,831
Lincoln, AL 35096 • 2,941
Lincoln, AR 72744 • 1,460
Lincoln, CA 95648 • 7,248
Lincoln, DE 19960 • 500
Lincoln, IL 62656 • 15,418
Lincoln, KS 67455 • 1,381
Lincoln, ME 04457 • 3,399
Lincoln, MA 01773 • 2,860
Lincoln, NE 68501-72 • 191,972
Lincoln □, AR • 13,690
Lincoln □, CO • 4,529
Lincoln □, GA • 7,442
Lincoln □, ID • 3,308
Lincoln □, KS • 3,653
Lincoln □, KY • 20,045
Lincoln □, LA • 41,745
Lincoln □, ME • 30,357
Lincoln □, MN • 6,890
Lincoln □, MS • 30,278
Lincoln □, MO • 28,892
Lincoln □, MT • 17,481
Lincoln □, NE • 32,508
Lincoln □, NV • 3,775
Lincoln □, NM • 12,219
Lincoln □, NC • 50,319
Lincoln □, OK • 29,216
Lincoln □, OR • 38,889
Lincoln □, SD • 15,427
Lincoln □, TN • 28,157
Lincoln □, WA • 8,864
Lincoln □, WV • 21,382
Lincoln □, WI • 26,993
Lincoln □, WY • 12,625
Lincoln Acres, CA 91947 • 1,800
Lincoln City, OR 97367 • 5,892
Lincoln Heights, OH 45215 • 4,805
Lincoln Park, CO 81212 • 3,728
Lincoln Park, GA 30286 • 1,755
Lincoln Park, MI 48146 • 41,832
Lincoln Park, NJ 07035 • 10,978
Lincolnshire, IL 60069 • 4,931
Lincolnton, GA 30817 • 1,476
Lincolnton, NC 28092 • 6,657
Lincoln Village, CA 95207 • 4,236
Lincoln Village, OH 43228 • 9,958

Lincolnwood, IL 60645 • 11,365	Loganville, GA 30249 • 3,180	Luling, TX 78648 • 4,661	Madison □, NY • 69,120	Maple Bluff, WI 53704 • 1,352
Lincroft, NJ 07738 • 4,740	Lolo, MT 59847 • 2,746	Lumber City, GA 31549 • 1,429	Madison □, NC • 16,953	Maple Grove, MN 55369 • 38,736
Linda, CA 95901 • 13,033	Loma Linda, CA 92354 • 17,400	Lumberport, WV 26386 • 1,014	Madison □, OH • 37,068	Maple Heights, OH 44137 • 27,089
Lindale, GA 30147 • 4,187	Lombard, IL 60148 • 39,408	Lumberton, MS 39455 • 2,121	Madison □, TN • 77,982	Maple Lake, MN 55358 • 1,394
Lindale, TX 75771 • 2,428	Lomira, WI 53048 • 1,542	Lumberton, NC 28358-59 • 18,601	Madison □, TX • 10,931	Maple Plain, MN 55359 • 2,005
Linden, AL 36748 • 2,548	Lomita, CA 90717 • 19,382	Lumpkin, GA 31815 • 1,250	Madison □, VA • 11,949	Maple Shade, NJ 08052 • 19,211
Linden, MI 48451 • 2,415	Lompoc, CA 93436 • 37,649	Lumpkin □, GA • 14,573	Madison Heights, MI 48071 • 32,196	Mapleton, IA 51034 • 1,294
Linden, NJ 07036 • 36,701	Lonaconing, MD 21539 • 1,122	Luna, NM • 18,110	Madison Heights, VA 24572 • 11,700	Mapleton, MN 56065 • 1,526
Linden, TN 37096 • 1,099	London, KY 40741 • 5,757	Luna Pier, MI 48157 • 1,507	Madisonville, KY 42431 • 16,200	Mapleton, UT 84663 • 3,572
Linden, TX 75563 • 2,375	London, OH 43140 • 7,807	Lund, NV 89317 • 330	Madisonville, TN 37354 • 3,033	Maple Valley, WA 98038 • 1,211
Lindenhurst, IL 60046 • 8,038	Londonderry, NH 03053 • 10,114	Lunenburg, MA 01462 • 1,694	Madisonville, TX 77864 • 3,569	Mapleville, RI 02839 • 1,300
Lindenhurst, NY 11757 • 26,879	Londontown, MD 21037 • 6,992	Lunenburg □, VA • 11,419	Madras, OR 97741 • 3,443	Maplewood, MN 55109 • 30,954
Lindenwold, NJ 08021 • 18,734	Lone Grove, OK 73443 • 4,114	Luray, VA 22835 • 4,587	Madrid, IA 50156 • 2,395	Maplewood, MO 63143 • 9,962
Lindgren Acres, FL 33177 • 22,290	Lone Pine, CA 93545 • 1,818	Lusk, WY 82225 • 1,504	Magalia, CA 95954 • 8,987	Maplewood, NJ 07040 • 21,756
Lindon, UT 84042 • 3,818	Long □, GA • 6,202	Lutcher, LA 70071 • 3,907	Magdalena, NM 87825 • 861	Maquoketa, IA 52060 • 6,111
Lindsay, CA 93247 • 8,338	Long Beach, CA 90801-88 • 429,433	Luther, OK 73054 • 1,560	Magee, MS 39111 • 3,607	Marana, AZ 85653 • 861
Lindsay, OK 73052 • 2,947	Long Beach, IN 46360 • 2,044	Lutherville-Timonium, MD 21093 • 16,442	Magna, UT 84044 • 17,829	Marathon, FL 33050 • 8,857
Lindsborg, KS 67456 • 3,076	Long Beach, MS 39560 • 15,804	Lutz, FL 33549 • 10,552	Magnolia, AR 71753 • 11,151	Marathon, NY 13803 • 1,107
Lindstrom, MN 55045 • 2,461	Long Beach, NY 11561 • 33,510	Luverne, AL 36049 • 2,555	Magnolia, MS 39652 • 2,245	Marathon, WI 54448 • 1,606
Linesville, PA 16424 • 1,166	Long Beach, WA 98631 • 1,236	Luverne, MN 56156 • 4,382	Magnolia, NJ 08049 • 4,861	Marathon □, WI • 115,400
Lineville, AL 36266 • 2,394	Longboat Key, FL 34228 • 5,937	Luxemburg, WI 54217 • 1,151	Magoffin □, KY • 13,077	Marble Falls, TX 78654 • 4,007
Lingle, WY 82223 • 473	Long Branch, NJ 07740 • 28,658	Luxora, AR 72358 • 1,338	Mahanoy City, PA 17948 • 5,209	Marblehead, MA 01945 • 19,971
Linglestown, PA 17112 • 3,700	Long Lake, IL 60041 • 2,888	Luzerne, PA 18709 • 3,206	Mahaska □, IA • 21,522	Marble Hill, MO 63764 • 1,447
Linn, MO 65051 • 1,148	Longmeadow, MA 01106 • 15,467	Luzerne □, PA • 328,149	Mahnomen, MN 56557 • 1,154	Marbleton, WY 83113 • 634
Linn □, IA • 168,767	Longmont, CO 80501-02 • 51,555	Lycoming □, PA • 118,710	Mahnomen □, MN • 5,044	Marbury, MD 20658 • 1,244
Linn □, KS • 8,254	Longport, NJ 08403 • 1,224	Lyford, TX 78569 • 1,674	Mahomet, IL 61853 • 3,103	Marceline, MO 64658 • 2,645
Linn □, MO • 13,885	Long Prairie, MN 56347 • 2,786	Lykens, PA 17048 • 1,986	Mahoning □, OH • 264,806	Marcellus, MI 49067 • 1,193
Linn □, OR • 91,227	Long Valley, NJ 07853 • 1,744	Lyman, SC 29365 • 2,271	Mahopac, NY 10541 • 7,755	Marco, FL 33937 • 9,493
Lino Lakes, MN 55014 • 8,807	Long View, NC 28601 • 3,229	Lyman, WY 82937 • 1,896	Mahwah, NJ 07430 • 7,500	Marcus, IA 51035 • 1,171
Linthicum Heights, MD • 2,950	Longview, TX 75601-15 • 70,311	Lyman □, SD • 3,638	Maiden, NC 28650 • 2,574	Marcus Hook, PA 19061 • 2,546
Linthicum Heights, MD 21090 • 7,547	Longview, WA 98632 • 31,499	Lynbrook, NY 11563 • 19,208	Maili, HI 96792 • 6,059	Marengo, IA 52301 • 2,270
Linton, IN 47441 • 5,814	Longwood, FL 32750 • 13,316	Lynch, KY 40855 • 1,166	Maine, NY 13802 • 1,110	Marengo □, AL • 23,084
Linton, ND 58552 • 1,410	Lonoke, AR 72086 • 4,022	Lynchburg, OH 45142 • 1,212	Maitland, FL 32751 • 9,110	Marfa, TX 79843 • 2,424
Linwood, NJ 08221 • 6,866	Lonoke □, AR • 39,268	Lynchburg, TN 37352 • 4,721	Maize, KS 67101 • 1,520	Margate, FL 33063 • 42,985
Lipscomb, AL 35020 • 2,892	Lonsdale, MN 55046 • 1,252	Lynchburg, VA 24501-06 • 66,049	Major □, OK • 8,055	Margate, MD 21060 • 1,900
Lipscomb □, TX • 3,143	Lonsdale, RI 02865 • 3,850	Lyncourt, NY 13208 • 4,516	Makaha, HI 96792 • 7,990	Margate City, NJ 08402 • 8,431
Lisbon, IA 52253 • 1,452	Loogootee, IN 47553 • 2,884	Lynden, WA 98264 • 5,709	Makakilo City, HI 96706 • 9,828	Marianna, AR 72360 • 5,910
Lisbon, ME 04250 • 1,240	Lookout Mountain, TN 37350 • 1,901	Lyndhurst, NJ 07071 • 18,262	Makawao, HI 96768 • 5,405	Marianna, FL 32446 • 6,292
Lisbon, NH 03585 • 1,246	Lorain, OH 44052-55 • 71,245	Lyndhurst, OH 44124 • 15,982	Makaweli, HI 96769 • 700	Maricopa, AZ 85239 • 1,600
Lisbon, ND 58054 • 2,177	Lorain □, OH • 271,126	Lyndon, KY 40222 • 8,037	Malabar, FL 32950 • 1,977	Maricopa, CA 93252 • 1,193
Lisbon, OH 44432 • 3,037	Lordsburg, NM 88045 • 2,951	Lyndonville, VT 05851 • 1,255	Malad City, ID 83252 • 1,946	Maricopa □, AZ • 2,122,101
Lisbon Falls, ME 04252 • 4,674	Lorenzo, TX 79343 • 1,208	Lyndora, PA 16045 • 3,000	Malaga, NM 08328 • 2,140	Mariemont, OH 45227 • 3,118
Lisle, IL 60532 • 19,512	Loretto, PA 15940 • 1,072	Lynn, IN 47355 • 1,183	Malakoff, TX 75148 • 2,038	Marienville, PA 16239 • 1,400
Litchfield, CT 06759 • 1,378	Loretto, TN 38469 • 1,515	Lynn, MA 01901-08 • 81,245	Malden, MA 02148 • 53,884	Maries □, MO • 7,976
Litchfield, IL 62056 • 6,883	Loris, SC 29569 • 2,067	Lynn □, TX • 6,758	Malden, MO 63863 • 5,123	Marietta, GA 30060-68 • 44,129
Litchfield, MI 49252 • 1,317	Lorton, VA 22079 • 15,385	Lynne Acres, MD 21207 • 5,910	Malheur □, OR • 26,038	Marietta, OH 45750 • 15,026
Litchfield, MN 55355 • 6,041	Los Alamitos, CA 90720-21 • 11,676	Lynnfield, MA 01940 • 11,274	Malibu, CA 90264-65 • 10,000	Marietta, OK 73448 • 2,306
Litchfield □, CT • 174,092	Los Alamos, NM 87544 • 11,455	Lynn Garden, TN 37665 • 7,213	Malone, NY 12953 • 6,777	Marin □, CA • 230,096
Litchfield Park, AZ 85340 • 3,303	Los Alamos □, NM • 18,115	Lynn Garden, TN 37665 • 3,950	Malta, MT 59538 • 2,340	Marina, CA 93933 • 26,436
Lithia Springs, GA 30057 • 11,403	Los Altos, CA 94022-24 • 26,303	Lynn Haven, FL 32444 • 9,298	Malvern, AR 72104 • 9,256	Marina del Rey, CA 90292 • 7,431
Lithonia, GA 30058 • 2,448	Los Altos Hills, CA 94022 • 7,514	Lynnwood, WA 98036-37 • 28,695	Malvern, IA 51551 • 1,210	Marine City, MI 48039 • 4,556
Lititz, PA 17543 • 8,280	Los Angeles, CA 90001-99 • 3,485,398	Lynwood, CA 90262 • 61,945	Malvern, OH 44644 • 1,112	Marinette, WI 54143 • 11,843
Little Canada, MN 55110 • 8,971	Los Angeles □, CA • 8,863,164	Lyon □, IA • 11,952	Malvern, PA 19355 • 2,944	Marinette □, WI • 40,548
Little Chute, WI 54140 • 9,207	Los Banos, CA 93635 • 14,519	Lyon □, KS • 34,732	Malverne, NY 11565 • 9,054	Maringouin, LA 70757 • 1,149
Little Compton, RI 02837 • 500	Los Fresnos, TX 78566 • 2,473	Lyon □, KY • 6,624	Mamaroneck, NY 10543 • 17,325	Marion, AL 36756 • 4,211
Little Creek, DE 19961 • 167	Los Gatos, CA 95030-32 • 27,357	Lyon □, MN • 24,789	Mammoth, AZ 85618 • 1,845	Marion, AR 72364 • 4,391
Little Falls, MN 56345 • 7,232	Los Lunas, NM 87031 • 6,013	Lyon □, NV • 20,001	Mammoth Lakes, CA 93546 • 4,785	Marion, IL 62959 • 14,545
Little Falls, NJ 07424 • 11,294	Los Molinos, CA 96055 • 1,709	Lyon Mountain, NY 12952 • 1,000	Mammoth Spring, AR 72554 • 1,097	Marion, IN 46952-53 • 32,618
Little Falls, NY 13365 • 5,829	Los Nietos, CA 90606 • 7,100	Lyons, CO 80540 • 1,227	Mamou, LA 70554 • 3,483	Marion, IA 52302 • 20,403
Little Ferry, NJ 07643 • 9,989	Los Osos, CA 93402 • 8,000	Lyons, GA 30436 • 4,502	Manahawkin, NJ 08050 • 1,594	Marion, KS 66861 • 1,906
Littlefield, TX 79339 • 6,489	Los Padillas, NM 87105 • 2,400	Lyons, IL 60534 • 9,828	Manasquan, NJ 08736 • 5,369	Marion, KY 42064 • 3,320
Little River □, AR • 13,966	Los Ranchos de Albuquerque, NM 87107 • 3,955	Lyons, KS 67554 • 3,688	Manassas, VA 22110-11 • 27,957	Marion, MA 02738 • 1,426
Little Rock, AR 72201-31 • 175,795	Los Serranos, CA 91709 • 7,099	Lyons, NE 68038 • 1,144	Manassas Park, VA 22111 • 6,734	Marion, MS 39342 • 1,359
Little Silver, NJ 07739 • 5,721	Lost Hills, CA 93249 • 1,212	Lyons, NY 14489 • 4,280	Manatee □, FL • 211,707	Marion, NY 14505 • 1,080
Littlestown, PA 17340 • 2,974	Loudon, TN 37774 • 4,026	Lytle, TX 78052 • 2,255	Manawa, WI 54949 • 1,169	Marion, NC 28752 • 4,765
Littleton, CO 80120-27 • 33,685	Loudon □, TN • 31,255		Mancelona, MI 49659 • 1,370	Marion, OH 43301-02 • 34,075
Littleton, MA 01460 • 2,867	Loudonville, NY 12211 • 10,822	**M**	Manchaug, MA 01526 • 1,000	Marion, PA 17235 • 1,000
Littleton, NH 03561 • 4,633	Loudonville, OH 44842 • 2,915		Manchester, CT 06040 • 51,618	Marion, SC 29571 • 7,658
Little Valley, NY 14755 • 1,188	Loudoun □, VA • 86,129	Mabank, TX 75147 • 1,739	Manchester, GA 31816 • 4,104	Marion, SD 57043 • 831
Live Oak, CA 95062 • 15,212	Louisa, KY 41230 • 1,990	Mableton, GA 30059 • 25,725	Manchester, IA 52057 • 5,137	Marion, VA 24354 • 6,630
Live Oak, CA 95953 • 4,320	Louisa, VA 23093 • 1,088	Mabscott, WV 25871 • 1,543	Manchester, KY 40962 • 1,634	Marion, WI 54950 • 1,242
Live Oak, FL 32060 • 6,332	Louisa □, IA • 11,592	Mabton, WA 98935 • 1,482	Manchester, MD 21102 • 2,810	Marion □, AL • 29,830
Live Oak, TX 78233 • 10,023	Louisa □, VA • 20,325	MacClenny, FL 32063 • 3,966	Manchester, MI 48158 • 1,753	Marion □, AR • 12,001
Live Oak □, TX • 9,556	Louisburg, KS 66053 • 1,964	Macedon, NY 14502 • 1,400	Manchester, NY 14504 • 1,598	Marion □, FL • 194,833
Live Oak Manor, LA 70094 • 2,150	Louisburg, NC 27549 • 3,037	Macedonia, OH 44056 • 7,509	Manchester, NH 03101-10 • 99,567	Marion □, GA • 5,590
Livermore, CA 94550 • 56,741	Louisiana, MO 63353 • 3,967	Machesney Park, IL 61111 • 19,033	Manchester, OH 45144 • 2,223	Marion □, IL • 41,561
Livermore, KY 42352 • 1,534	Louisville, CO 80027 • 12,361	Machias, ME 04654 • 1,773	Manchester, PA 17345 • 1,830	Marion □, IN • 797,159
Livermore Falls, ME 04254 • 1,935	Louisville, GA 30434 • 2,429	Mackinac □, MI • 10,674	Manchester, TN 37355 • 7,709	Marion □, IA • 30,001
Livingston, AL 35470 • 3,530	Louisville, IL 62858 • 1,098	Mackinaw, IL 61755 • 1,331	Manchester, VT 05254 • 561	Marion □, KS • 12,888
Livingston, CA 95334 • 7,317	Louisville, KY 40201-99 • 269,063	Mackinaw City, MI 49701 • 875	Manchester Center, VT 05255 • 1,574	Marion □, KY • 16,499
Livingston, MT 59047 • 6,701	Louisville, MS 39339 • 7,169	Macomb, IL 61455 • 19,952	Mandan, ND 58554 • 15,177	Marion □, MS • 25,544
Livingston, NJ 07039 • 26,609	Louisville, OH 44641 • 8,087	Macomb □, MI • 717,400	Mandeville, LA 70448 • 7,083	Marion □, MO • 27,682
Livingston, TN 38570 • 3,809	Loup □, NE • 683	Macon, GA 31201-95 • 106,612	Mangum, OK 73554 • 3,344	Marion □, OH • 64,274
Livingston, TX 77351 • 5,019	Loup City, NE 68853 • 1,104	Macon, IL 62544 • 1,282	Manhasset, NY 11030 • 7,718	Marion □, OR • 228,483
Livingston □, IL • 39,301	Love □, OK • 8,157	Macon, MS 39341 • 2,256	Manhattan, KS 66502 • 37,712	Marion □, SC • 33,899
Livingston □, KY • 9,062	Loveland, CO 80537-39 • 37,352	Macon, MO 63552 • 5,571	Manhattan, MT 59741 • 1,034	Marion □, TN • 24,860
Livingston □, LA • 70,526	Loveland, OH 45140 • 9,990	Macon □, AL • 24,928	Manhattan Beach, CA 90266 • 32,063	Marion □, TX • 9,984
Livingston □, MI • 115,645	Loveland Park, OH 45140 • 1,357	Macon □, GA • 13,114	Manheim, PA 17545 • 5,011	Marion □, WV • 57,249
Livingston □, MO • 14,592	Lovell, WY 82431 • 2,131	Macon □, IL • 117,206	Manila, AR 72442 • 2,635	Marionville, MO 65705 • 1,920
Livingston □, NY • 62,372	Lovelock, NV 89419 • 2,069	Macon □, MO • 15,345	Manistee, MI 49660 • 6,734	Mariposa, CA 95338 • 1,152
Livingston Manor, NY 12758 • 1,482	Loves Park, IL 61111 • 15,462	Macon □, NC • 23,499	Manistee □, MI • 21,265	Mariposa □, CA • 14,302
Livonia, MI 48150-54 • 100,850	Loving, NM 88256 • 1,243	Macon □, TN • 15,906	Manistique, MI 49854 • 3,456	Marissa, IL 62257 • 2,375
Livonia, NY 14487 • 1,434	Loving □, TX • 107	Macoupin □, IL • 47,679	Manito, IL 61546 • 1,711	Marked Tree, AR 72365 • 3,100
Llangollen Estates, DE 19720 • 1,070	Lovington, IL 61937 • 1,143	Macungie, PA 18062 • 2,597	Manitou Springs, CO 80829 • 4,535	Markesan, WI 53946 • 1,496
Llano, TX 78643 • 2,962	Lovington, NM 88260 • 9,322	Madawaska, ME 04756 • 3,653	Manitowoc, WI 54220-21 • 32,520	Markham, IL 60426 • 13,136
Llano □, TX • 11,631	Lowell, AR 72745 • 1,224	Madeira, OH 45243 • 9,141	Manitowoc □, WI • 80,421	Markham, TX 77456 • 1,206
Lloyd Harbor, NY 11743 • 3,343	Lowell, IN 46356 • 6,430	Madelia, MN 56062 • 2,237	Mankato, KS 66956 • 1,037	Marks, MS 38646 • 1,758
Lochearn, MD 21207 • 25,240	Lowell, MA 01850-54 • 103,439	Madera, CA 93637-39 • 29,281	Mankato, MN 56001-03 • 31,477	Marksville, LA 71351 • 5,526
Loch Lomond, VA 22110 • 3,292	Lowell, MI 49331 • 3,983	Madera □, CA • 88,090	Manlius, NY 13104 • 4,764	Marlboro, NY 12542 • 2,200
Lockhart, FL 32810 • 11,636	Lowell, NC 28098 • 2,704	Madill, OK 73446 • 3,069	Manly, IA 50456 • 1,349	Marlboro □, SC • 29,361
Lockhart, TX 78644 • 9,205	Lowellville, OH 44436 • 1,349	Madison, AL 35758 • 14,904	Mannford, OK 74044 • 1,826	Marlborough, CT 06447 • 5,535
Lock Haven, PA 17745 • 9,230	Lower Burrell, PA 15068 • 12,251	Madison, AR 72359 • 1,263	Manning, IA 51455 • 1,484	Marlborough, MA 01752 • 31,813
Lockland, OH 45215 • 4,357	Lower Merion Township, PA 19003 • 59,629	Madison, CT 06443 • 2,139	Manning, SC 29102 • 4,428	Marlborough, NH 03455 • 1,211
Lockney, TX 79241 • 2,207	Lower Paia, HI 96779 • 1,500	Madison, FL 32340 • 3,345	Mannington, WV 26582 • 2,184	Marlene Village, OR 97005 • 1,500
Lockport, IL 60441 • 9,401	Lowndes □, AL • 12,658	Madison, GA 30650 • 3,483	Manokotak, AK 99628 • 385	Marlette, MI 48453 • 1,924
Lockport, LA 70374 • 2,503	Lowndes □, GA • 75,981	Madison, IL 62060 • 4,629	Manomet, MA 02345 • 1,500	Marley, MD 21060 • 7,100
Lockport, NY 14094 • 24,426	Lowndes □, MS • 59,308	Madison, IN 47250 • 12,006	Manor, TX 78653 • 1,041	Marlin, TX 76661 • 6,386
Lockwood, MO 65682 • 1,041	Lowville, NY 13367 • 3,632	Madison, ME 04950 • 2,956	Manorhaven, NY 11050 • 5,672	Marlinton, WV 24954 • 1,148
Lockwood, MT 59101 • 3,967	Loxley, AL 36551 • 1,161	Madison, MN 56256 • 1,951	Mansfield, AR 72944 • 1,018	Marlow, OK 73055 • 4,416
Locust, NC 28097 • 1,940	Loyal, WI 54446 • 1,244	Madison, MS 39110 • 7,471	Mansfield, LA 71052 • 5,389	Marlton, NJ 08053 • 10,228
Locust Grove, GA 30248 • 1,681	Loyall, KY 40854 • 1,100	Madison, NE 68748 • 2,135	Mansfield, MA 02048 • 7,170	Marmaduke, AR 72443 • 1,164
Locust Grove, OK 74352 • 1,326	Lubbock, TX 79401-99 • 186,206	Madison, NJ 07940 • 15,850	Mansfield, MO 65704 • 1,429	Marmet, WV 25315 • 1,879
Lodi, CA 95240-42 • 51,874	Lubbock □, TX • 222,636	Madison, NC 27025 • 2,371	Mansfield, OH 44901-07 • 50,627	Maroa, IL 61756 • 1,602
Lodi, NJ 07644 • 22,355	Lucas □, IA • 9,070	Madison, OH 44057 • 2,477	Mansfield, PA 16933 • 3,538	Marquette, MI 49855 • 21,977
Lodi, OH 44254 • 3,042	Lucas □, OH • 462,361	Madison, SD 57042 • 6,257	Mansfield, TX 76063 • 15,607	Marquette □, MI • 70,887
Lodi, WI 53555 • 2,093	Lucasville, OH 45648 • 1,575	Madison, WV 25130 • 3,051	Mansfield Center, CT 06250 • 1,043	Marquette □, WI • 12,321
Logan, IA 51546 • 1,401	Luce □, MI • 5,763	Madison, WI 53701-19 • 191,262	Manson, IA 50563 • 1,844	Marquette Heights, IL 61554 • 3,077
Logan, OH 43138 • 6,725	Lucedale, MS 39452 • 2,592	Madison □, AL • 238,912	Mansura, LA 71350 • 1,651	Marrero, LA 70072-73 • 36,671
Logan, UT 84321 • 32,762	Lucerne, CA 95458 • 2,011	Madison □, AR • 11,618	Manteca, CA 95336 • 40,773	Mars, PA 16046 • 1,713
Logan, WV 25601 • 2,206	Lucernemines, PA 15754 • 1,074	Madison □, FL • 16,569	Manteno, IL 60950 • 3,488	Marseilles, IL 61341 • 4,811
Logan □, AR • 20,557	Lucerne Valley, CA 92356 • 1,300	Madison □, GA • 21,050	Manti, UT 84642 • 2,268	Marshall, AR 72650 • 1,318
Logan □, CO • 17,567	Luck, WI 54853 • 1,022	Madison □, ID • 23,674	Manton, MI 49663 • 1,161	Marshall, IL 62441 • 3,555
Logan □, IL • 30,798	Ludington, MI 49431 • 8,507	Madison □, IL • 249,238	Mantua, NJ 08051 • 1,350	Marshall, MI 49068 • 6,891
Logan □, KS • 3,081	Ludlow, KY 41016 • 4,736	Madison □, IN • 130,669	Mantua, OH 44255 • 1,178	Marshall, MN 56258 • 12,023
Logan □, KY • 24,416	Ludlow, MA 01056 • 18,150	Madison □, IA • 12,483	Manua Hills, VA 22031 • 1,600	Marshall, MO 65340 • 12,711
Logan □, NE • 878	Ludlow, VT 05149 • 1,123	Madison □, KY • 57,508	Manvel, TX 77578 • 3,733	Marshall, TX 75670-71 • 23,682
Logan □, ND • 2,847	Ludowici, GA 31316 • 1,291	Madison □, LA • 12,463	Manville, NJ 08835 • 10,567	Marshall, WI 53559 • 2,329
Logan □, OH • 42,310	Lufkin, TX 75901-03 • 30,206	Madison □, MS • 53,794	Manville, RI 02838 • 3,030	Marshall □, AL • 70,832
Logan □, OK • 29,011	Lugoff, SC 29078 • 3,211	Madison □, MO • 11,127	Many, LA 71449 • 3,112	Marshall □, IL • 12,846
Logan □, WV • 43,032	Lula, GA 30554 • 1,018	Madison □, MT • 5,989	Many Farms, AZ 86538 • 1,294	Marshall □, IN • 42,182
Logandale, NV 89021 • 500	Luling, LA 70070 • 2,803	Madison □, NE • 32,655		
Logansport, IN 46947 • 16,812				
Logansport, LA 71049 • 1,390				

Marshall □, IA • 38,276
Marshall □, KS • 11,705
Marshall □, KY • 27,205
Marshall □, MN • 10,993
Marshall □, MS • 30,361
Marshall □, OK • 10,829
Marshall □, SD • 4,844
Marshall □, TN • 21,539
Marshall □, WV • 37,356
Marshallton, DE 19808 • 1,765
Marshalltown, IA 50158 • 25,178
Marshallville, GA 31057 • 1,457
Marshfield, MA 02050 • 4,002
Marshfield, MO 65706 • 4,374
Marshfield, WI 54449 • 19,291
Marshfield Hills, MA 02051 • 2,201
Mars Hill, ME 04758 • 1,500
Mars Hill, NC 28754 • 1,611
Marshville, NC 28103 • 2,020
Marsing, ID 83639 • 798
Marstons Mills, MA 02648 • 8,017
Mart, TX 76664 • 2,004
Martha Lake, WA 98012 • 10,155
Martin, SD 57551 • 1,151
Martin, TN 38237 • 8,600
Martin □, FL • 100,900
Martin □, IN • 10,369
Martin □, KY • 12,526
Martin □, MN • 22,914
Martin □, NC • 25,078
Martin □, TX • 4,956
Martinez, CA 94553 • 31,808
Martinez, GA 30907 • 33,731
Martinsburg, PA 16662 • 2,119
Martinsburg, WV 25401 • 14,073
Martins Ferry, OH 43935 • 7,990
Martinsville, IL 62442 • 1,161
Martinsville, IN 46151 • 11,677
Martinsville, VA 24112–15 • 16,162
Marvell, AR 72366 • 1,545
Maryland City, MD 20724 • 6,813
Maryland Heights, MO 63043 • 25,407
Marysville, CA 95901 • 12,324
Marysville, KS 66508 • 3,359
Marysville, MI 48040 • 8,515
Marysville, OH 43040 • 9,656
Marysville, PA 17053 • 2,425
Marysville, WA 98270 • 10,328
Maryville, MO 64468 • 10,663
Maryville, TN 37801–04 • 19,208
Mascot, TN 37806 • 2,138
Mascoutah, IL 62258 • 5,511
Mason, MI 48854 • 6,768
Mason, NV 89447 • 400
Mason, OH 45040 • 11,452
Mason, TX 76856 • 2,041
Mason, WV 25260 • 1,053
Mason □, IL • 16,269
Mason □, KY • 16,666
Mason □, MI • 25,537
Mason □, TX • 3,423
Mason □, WA • 38,341
Mason □, WV • 25,178
Masonboro, NC 28403 • 7,010
Mason City, IL 62664 • 2,323
Mason City, IA 50401 • 29,040
Masontown, PA 15461 • 3,759
Massac □, IL • 14,752
Massapequa, NY 11758 • 22,018
Massapequa Park, NY 11762 • 18,044
Massena, NY 13662 • 11,719
Massillon, OH 44646–48 • 31,007
Mastic, NY 11950 • 13,778
Mastic Beach, NY 11951 • 10,293
Masury, OH 44438 • 1,836
Matagorda, TX • 36,928
Matamoras, PA 18336 • 1,934
Matawan, NJ 07747 • 9,270
Mather, PA 15346 • 1,300
Mathews, VA • 8,348
Mathis, TX 78368 • 5,423
Matoaca, VA 23803 • 1,967
Mattapoisett, MA 02739 • 2,949
Matteson, IL 60443 • 11,378
Mattituck, NY 11952 • 3,902
Mattoon, IL 61938 • 18,441
Mattydale, NY 13211 • 6,418
Matunuck, RI 02879 • 550
Maud, OK 74854 • 1,204
Maugansville, MD 21767 • 1,707
Maui □, HI • 100,374
Mauldin, SC 29662 • 11,587
Maumee, OH 43537 • 15,561
Maunaloa, HI 96770 • 405
Maunawili, HI 96734 • 4,847
Maury □, TN • 54,812
Mauston, WI 53948 • 3,439
Maverick □, TX • 36,378
Maxton, NC 28364 • 2,373
Maxwell Acres, WV 26041 • 1,000
Mayer, AZ 86333 • 1,800
Mayes □, OK • 33,366
Mayfield, KY 42066 • 9,935
Mayfield, PA 18433 • 1,800
Mayfield Heights, OH 44124 • 19,847
Mayflower, AR 72106 • 1,415
Mayflower Village, CA 91016 • 4,978
Maynard, MA 01754 • 10,325
Maynardville, TN 37807 • 1,298
Mayo, MD 21106 • 2,537
Mayodan, NC 27027 • 2,471
Mays Landing, NJ 08330 • 2,090
Maysville, KY 41056 • 7,169
Maysville, MO 64469 • 1,176
Maysville, OK 73057 • 1,203
Mayville, MI 48744 • 1,010
Mayville, NY 14757 • 1,636
Mayville, ND 58257 • 2,092
Mayville, WI 53050 • 4,374
Maywood, CA 90270 • 27,850
Maywood, IL 60153–54 • 27,139
Maywood, NJ 07607 • 9,473
Mazomanie, WI 53560 • 1,377
McAdoo, PA 18237 • 2,459
McAlester, OK 74501–02 • 16,370
McAllen, TX 78501–04 • 84,021
McAlmont, AR 72117 • 1,800
McAlpine, MD 21043 • 2,392
McArthur, OH 45651 • 1,541
McCall, ID 83638 • 2,005
McCamey, TX 79752 • 2,493
McCandless, PA 15237 • 28,781

McCaysville, GA 30555 • 1,065
McClain □, OK • 22,795
McCleary, WA 98557 • 1,235
McCloud, CA 96057 • 1,555
McClure, PA 17841 • 1,070
McColl, SC 29570 • 2,685
McComb, MS 39648 • 11,591
McComb, OH 45858 • 1,544
McCone □, MT • 2,276
McConnellsburg, PA 17233 • 1,106
McConnelsville, OH 43756 • 1,804
McCook, NE 69001 • 8,112
McCook □, SD • 5,688
McCormick, SC 29835 • 1,659
McCormick □, SC • 8,868
McCracken □, KY • 62,879
McCreary □, KY • 15,603
McCrory, AR 72101 • 1,971
McCulloch □, TX • 8,778
McCurtain □, OK • 33,433
McDermitt, NV 89421 • 373
McDonald □, MO • 16,938
McDonough, GA 30253 • 2,929
McDonough □, IL • 35,244
McDowell □, NC • 35,681
McDowell □, WV • 35,233
McDuffie □, GA • 20,119
McEwen, TN 37101 • 1,442
McFarland, CA 93250 • 7,005
McFarland, WI 53558 • 5,232
McGehee, AR 71654 • 4,997
McGill, NV 89318 • 1,258
McGrath, AK 99627 • 528
McGraw, NY 13101 • 1,074
McGregor, TX 76657 • 4,683
McHenry, IL 60050–51 • 16,177
McHenry □, IL • 183,241
McHenry □, ND • 6,528
McIntosh □, GA • 8,634
McIntosh □, ND • 4,021
McIntosh □, OK • 16,779
McKean □, PA • 47,131
McKee City, NJ 08232 • 1,200
McKeesport, PA 15130–35 • 26,016
McKees Rocks, PA 15136 • 7,691
McKenzie, TN 38201 • 5,168
McKenzie □, ND • 6,383
McKinley □, NM • 60,686
McKinleyville, CA 95521 • 10,749
McKinney, TX 75069–70 • 21,283
McLaughlin, SD 57642 • 780
McLean, VA 22101 • 38,168
McLean □, IL • 129,180
McLean □, KY • 9,628
McLean □, ND • 10,457
McLeansboro, IL 62859 • 2,677
McLennan □, TX • 189,123
McLeod □, MN • 32,030
McLoud, OK 74851 • 2,493
McMechen, WV 26040 • 2,130
McMinn □, TN • 42,383
McMinnville, OR 97128 • 17,894
McMinnville, TN 37110 • 11,194
McMullen □, TX • 817
McNairy □, TN • 22,422
McPherson, KS 67460 • 12,422
McPherson □, KS • 27,268
McPherson □, NE • 546
McPherson □, SD • 3,228
McQueeney, TX 78123 • 2,063
McRae, GA 31055 • 3,007
McRoberts, KY 41835 • 1,101
McSherrystown, PA 17344 • 2,769
Mead, WA 99021 • 2,150
Meade, KS 67864 • 1,526
Meade □, KS • 4,247
Meade □, KY • 24,170
Meade □, SD • 21,878
Meadowbrook, FL 32808 • 5,200
Meadowood, DE 61548 • 2,100
Meadville, PA 16335 • 14,318
Meagher □, MT • 1,819
Mebane, NC 27302 • 4,754
Mecca, CA 92254 • 1,966
Mechanic Falls, ME 04256 • 2,388
Mechanicsburg, OH 43044 • 1,803
Mechanicsburg, PA 17055 • 9,452
Mechanicsville, MD 20659 • 1,012
Mechanicsville, VA 23111 • 22,027
Mechanicville, NY 12118 • 5,249
Mecklenburg □, NC • 511,433
Mecklenburg □, VA • 29,241
Mecosta □, MI • 37,308
Medfield, MA 02052 • 5,985
Medford, MA 02155 • 57,407
Medford, NJ 08055 • 1,800
Medford, NY 11763 • 21,274
Medford, OK 73759 • 1,172
Medford, OR 97501–04 • 46,951
Medford, WI 54451 • 4,283
Medford Lakes, NJ 08055 • 4,462
Media, PA 19063–65 • 5,957
Mediapolis, IA 52637 • 1,637
Medical Lake, WA 99022 • 3,664
Medicine Bow, WY 82329 • 389
Medicine Lodge, KS 67104 • 2,453
Medina, NY 14103 • 6,686
Medina, OH 44256 • 19,231
Medina, WA 98039 • 2,981
Medina □, OH • 122,354
Medina □, TX • 27,312
Medway, MA 02053 • 3,890
Meeker, CO 81641 • 2,098
Meeker, OK 74855 • 1,003
Meeker □, MN • 20,846
Meeteetse, WY 82433 • 368
Mehlville, MO 63129 • 27,557
Meigs, GA 31765 • 1,120
Meigs □, OH • 22,987
Meigs □, TN • 8,033
Meiners Oaks, CA 93023 • 3,329
Melbourne, AR 72556 • 1,562
Melbourne, FL 32901–10 • 59,646
Melbourne Beach, FL 32951 • 3,021
Melcher, IA 50163 • 1,300
Mellette □, SD • 2,137
Melrose, FL 32666 • 1,310
Melrose, MA 02176 • 28,150
Melrose, NM 56352 • 2,321
Melrose Park, FL 33312 • 6,477
Melrose Park, IL 60160–63 • 20,859
Melville, LA 71353 • 1,562
Melville, NY 11747 • 12,586

Melvindale, MI 48122 • 11,216
Memphis, FL 34221 • 6,760
Memphis, MI 48041 • 1,221
Memphis, MO 63555 • 2,094
Memphis, TN 38101–87 • 610,337
Memphis, TX 79245 • 2,465
Mena, AR 71953 • 5,475
Menahga, MN 56464 • 1,076
Menands, NY 12204 • 4,333
Menard, TX 76859 • 1,606
Menard □, IL • 11,164
Menard □, TX • 2,252
Menasha, WI 54952 • 14,711
Mendenhall, MS 39114 • 2,463
Mendham, NJ 07945 • 4,890
Mendocino, CA 95460 • 1,008
Mendocino □, CA • 80,345
Mendota, CA 93640 • 6,821
Mendota, IL 61342 • 7,018
Mendota Heights, MN 55120 • 9,431
Menifee □, KY • 5,092
Menlo Park, CA 94025–28 • 28,040
Menno, SD 57045 • 768
Menominee, MI 49858 • 9,398
Menominee □, MI • 24,920
Menominee □, WI • 3,890
Menomonee Falls, WI 53051–52 • 26,840
Menomonie, WI 54751 • 13,547
Mentor, OH 44060–61 • 47,358
Mentor-on-the-Lake, OH 44060 • 8,271
Mequon, WI 53092 • 18,885
Meraux, LA 70075 • 8,000
Merced, CA 95339–44 • 56,216
Merced □, CA • 178,403
Mercedes, TX 78570 • 12,694
Mercer, PA 16137 • 2,444
Mercer, WI 54547 • 1,308
Mercer □, IL • 17,290
Mercer □, KY • 19,148
Mercer □, MO • 3,723
Mercer □, NJ • 325,824
Mercer □, ND • 9,808
Mercer □, OH • 39,443
Mercer □, PA • 121,003
Mercer □, WV • 64,980
Mercer Island, WA 98040 • 20,816
Mercersburg, PA 17236 • 1,640
Mercerville, NJ 08619 • 15,600
Merchantville, NJ 08109 • 4,095
Meredith, NH 03253 • 1,654
Meredosia, IL 62665 • 1,134
Meriden, CT 06450 • 59,479
Meridian, ID 83642 • 9,596
Meridian, MS 39301–09 • 41,036
Meridian, PA 16001 • 3,473
Meridian, TX 76665 • 1,390
Meridian Hills, IN 46260 • 1,728
Meridianville, AL 35759 • 2,852
Meriwether □, GA • 22,411
Merkel, TX 79536 • 2,469
Merriam, KS 66203 • 11,821
Merrick, NY 11566 • 23,042
Merrick □, NE • 8,042
Merrifield, VA 22031 • 8,399
Merrill, WI 54452 • 9,860
Merrillville, IN 46410 • 27,257
Merrimac, MA 01860 • 2,050
Merrimack, NH 03054 • 1,300
Merrimack □, NH • 120,005
Merritt Island, FL 32952–54 • 32,886
Merryville, LA 70653 • 1,235
Merton, WI 53056 • 1,199
Mesa, AZ 85201–16 • 288,091
Mesa □, CO • 93,145
Mescalero, NM 88340 • 1,159
Mesilla, NM 88046 • 1,975
Mesquite, NV 89024 • 1,871
Mesquite, TX 75149–50 • 101,484
Metairie, LA 70001–11 • 149,428
Metamora, IL 61548 • 2,520
Metcalfe, MS 38760 • 1,092
Metcalfe □, KY • 8,963
Methuen, MA 01844 • 39,990
Metlakatla, AK 99926 • 1,407
Metropolis, IL 62960 • 6,734
Metter, GA 30439 • 3,707
Metuchen, NJ 08840 • 12,804
Metzger, OR 97223 • 3,149
Mexia, TX 76667 • 6,933
Mexico, ME 04257 • 2,302
Mexico, MO 65265 • 11,290
Mexico, NY 13114 • 1,555
Meyersdale, PA 15552 • 2,518
Miami, AZ 85539 • 2,018
Miami, FL 33101–99 • 358,548
Miami, OK 74354–55 • 13,142
Miami □, IN • 36,897
Miami □, KS • 23,466
Miami □, OH • 93,182
Miami Beach, FL 33139 • 92,639
Miami Lakes, FL 33014 • 4,341
Miami Shores, FL 33138 • 10,084
Miami Springs, FL 33166 • 13,268
Micco, FL 32958 • 8,757
Michigan Center, MI 49254 • 4,863
Michigan City, IN 46360 • 33,822
Middleboro (Middleborough Center), MA 02346 • 6,837
Middleburg, FL 32068 • 6,223
Middleburg, GA 30207 • 1,500
Middleburgh, NY 12122 • 1,436
Middleburg Heights, OH 44130 • 14,702
Middlebury, CT 06762 • 4,140
Middlebury, IN 46540 • 2,004
Middlebury, VT 05753 • 6,007
Middlefield, CT 06455 • 1,200
Middlefield, OH 44062 • 1,898
Middle Island, NY 11953 • 7,848
Middleport, NY 14105 • 1,876
Middleport, OH 45760 • 2,725
Middle River, MD 21220 • 24,616
Middlesboro, KY 40965 • 11,328
Middlesex, NJ 08846 • 13,055
Middlesex □, CT • 143,196
Middlesex □, MA • 1,398,468
Middlesex □, NJ • 671,780
Middlesex □, VA • 8,653
Middleton, ID 83644 • 1,851
Middleton, MA 01949 • 4,135
Middletown, CA 95461 • 2,000
Middletown, CT 06457 • 42,762

Middletown, DE 19709 • 3,834
Middletown, IN 47356 • 2,333
Middletown, KY 40243 • 5,016
Middletown, MD 21769 • 1,834
Middletown, NJ 07718 • 62,298
Middletown, NY 10940 • 24,160
Middletown, OH 45042–44 • 46,022
Middletown, PA 17057 • 9,254
Middletown, RI 02840 • 3,350
Middletown, VA 22645 • 1,061
Middletown Township, PA 19037 • 6,866
Middleville, MI 49333 • 1,966
Midfield, AL 35228 • 5,559
Midland, MI 48640–42 • 38,053
Midland, PA 15059 • 3,321
Midland, TX 79701–12 • 89,443
Midland □, MI • 75,651
Midland □, TX • 106,611
Midland City, AL 36350 • 1,819
Midland Park, KS 66716 • 1,200
Midland Park, NJ 07432 • 7,047
Midland Park, SC 29405 • 1,300
Midlothian, IL 60445 • 14,372
Midlothian, TX 76065 • 5,141
Midvale, UT 84047 • 11,886
Midvale, DE 19971 • 500
Midway, KY 40347 • 1,290
Midway, OR 97233 • 19,000
Midway, PA 15060 • 1,043
Midway, UT 84049 • 1,554
Midwest, WY 82643 • 495
Midwest City, OK 73110 • 52,267
Mifflin □, PA • 46,197
Mifflinburg, PA 17844 • 3,480
Mifflintown, PA 18631 • 1,329
Milaca, MN 56353 • 2,182
Milam □, TX • 22,946
Milan, GA 31060 • 1,056
Milan, IL 61264 • 5,831
Milan, IN 47031 • 1,529
Milan, MI 48160 • 4,040
Milan, MO 63556 • 1,767
Milan, NM 87021 • 1,911
Milan, OH 44846 • 1,464
Milan, TN 38358 • 7,512
Milbank, SD 57252 • 3,879
Milesburg, PA 16853 • 1,144
Miles City, MT 59301 • 8,461
Milford, CT 06460 • 48,168
Milford, DE 19963 • 6,040
Milford, IL 60953 • 1,512
Milford, IN 46542 • 1,388
Milford, IA 51351 • 2,239
Milford, ME 04461 • 2,228
Milford, MA 01757 • 23,339
Milford, MI 48380–82 • 5,511
Milford, NE 68405 • 1,886
Milford, NH 03055 • 8,015
Milford, NJ 08848 • 1,273
Milford, OH 45150 • 5,660
Milford, PA 18337 • 1,064
Milford, UT 84751 • 1,107
Millard, UT • 11,333
Millbrae, CA 94030 • 20,412
Millbrook, AL 36054 • 6,050
Millbrook, NY 12545 • 1,339
Millburn, NJ 07041 • 18,630
Millbury, MA 01527 • 4,940
Millbury, OH 43447 • 1,081
Mill City, OR 97360 • 1,555
Mill Creek, WA 98012 • 32,230
Millcreek Township, PA 16505 • 46,100
Milledgeville, GA 31061 • 17,727
Milledgeville, IL 61051 • 1,076
Mille Lacs □, MN • 18,670
Millen, GA 30442 • 3,808
Miller, SD 57362 • 1,678
Miller □, AR • 38,467
Miller □, GA • 6,280
Miller □, MO • 20,700
Miller Place, NY 11764 • 9,315
Millersburg, OH 44654 • 3,051
Millersburg, PA 17061 • 2,729
Millers Falls, MA 01349 • 1,084
Millersport, OH 43046 • 1,010
Millersville, PA 17551 • 8,099
Mill Hall, PA 17751 • 1,702
Milliken, CO 80543 • 1,605
Millington, MD 21651 • 1,114
Millington, TN 38053 • 17,866
Millinocket, ME 04462 • 6,922
Millis, MA 02054 • 3,777
Millport, AL 35576 • 1,203
Mills, WY 82644 • 1,574
Mills □, IA • 13,202
Mills □, TX • 4,531
Millsboro, DE 19966 • 1,643
Millstadt, IL 62260 • 2,566
Milltown, NJ 08850 • 6,968
Millville, MA 01529 • 1,693
Millville, NJ 08332 • 25,992
Millville, UT 84326 • 1,202
Millwood, WA 99212 • 1,559
Milnor, ND 58060 • 651
Milo, ME 04463 • 2,129
Milpitas, CA 95035–36 • 50,686
Milroy, PA 17063 • 1,456
Milstead, GA 30207 • 1,500
Milton, DE 19968 • 1,417
Milton, FL 32570–71 • 7,216
Milton, MA 02186 • 25,725
Milton, NH 03851 • 1,000
Milton, NY 12547 • 1,140
Milton, PA 17847 • 6,746
Milton, VT 05468 • 1,578
Milton, WA 98354 • 4,995
Milton, WV 25541 • 2,242
Milton, WI 53563 • 4,434
Milton-Freewater, OR 97862 • 5,533
Milwaukee, WI 53201–95 • 628,088
Milwaukie, OR 97222 • 18,692
Mimosa Park, LA 70070 • 4,516
Mims, FL 32754 • 9,412
Minco, OK 73059 • 1,411
Minden, LA 71055 • 13,661
Minden, NE 68959 • 2,929
Minden, NV 89423 • 1,441
Mine Hill, NJ 07801 • 3,250

Mineola, NY 11501 • 18,994
Mineola, TX 75773 • 4,321
Miner, MO 63801 • 1,218
Miner □, SD • 3,272
Mineral, CO • 558
Mineral □, MT • 3,551
Mineral □, NV • 6,475
Mineral □, WV • 26,697
Mineral Point, WI 53565 • 2,428
Mineral Springs, AR 71851 • 1,004
Mineral Wells, TX 76067 • 14,870
Minersville, PA 17954 • 4,877
Minerva, OH 44657 • 4,318
Minetto, NY 13115 • 1,252
Mineville, NY 12956 • 1,000
Mingo □, WV • 33,739
Mingo Junction, OH 43938 • 4,297
Minidoka □, ID • 19,361
Minier, IL 61759 • 1,155
Minneapolis, KS 67467 • 1,983
Minneapolis, MN 55401–80 • 368,383
Minnehaha □, SD • 123,809
Minneola, FL 34715 • 1,417
Minnetonka, MN 55345 • 48,370
Minocqua, WI 54548 • 1,280
Minonk, IL 61760 • 1,982
Minooka, IL 60447 • 2,561
Minot, ND 58701–02 • 34,544
Minquadale, DE 19720 • 790
Minster, OH 45865 • 2,650
Mint Hill, NC 28212 • 11,567
Minturn, CO 81645 • 1,066
Mio, MI 48647 • 1,500
Mira Loma, CA 91752 • 15,786
Miramar, FL 33023 • 40,663
Misenheimer, NC 28109 • 1,000
Mishawaka, IN 46544–46 • 42,608
Mishicot, WI 54228 • 1,296
Missaukee □, MI • 12,147
Mission, KS 66205 • 9,504
Mission, TX 78572 • 28,653
Mission Hills, KS 66205 • 3,446
Mission Viejo, CA 92691 • 72,820
Mississippi □, AR • 57,525
Mississippi □, MO • 14,442
Mississippi State, MS 39762 • 12,400
Missoula, MT 59801–07 • 42,918
Missoula □, MT • 78,687
Missouri City, TX 77459 • 36,176
Missouri Valley, IA 51555 • 2,888
Mitchell, IN 47446 • 4,669
Mitchell, NE 69357 • 1,743
Mitchell, SD 57301 • 13,798
Mitchell □, GA • 20,275
Mitchell □, IA • 10,928
Mitchell □, KS • 7,203
Mitchell □, NC • 14,433
Mitchell □, TX • 8,016
Mitchellville, IA 50169 • 1,670
Mizpah, NJ 08342 • 1,100
Moab, UT 84532 • 3,971
Moberly, MO 65270 • 12,839
Mobile, AL 36601–95 • 196,278
Mobile □, AL • 378,643
Mobridge, SD 57601 • 3,768
Mocanaqua, PA 18655 • 1,100
Mocksville, NC 27028 • 3,399
Modesto, CA 95350–56 • 164,730
Modoc □, CA • 9,678
Moenkopi, AZ 86045 • 1,200
Moffat □, CO • 11,357
Mogadore, OH 44260 • 4,008
Mohall, ND 58761 • 931
Mohave □, AZ • 93,497
Mohawk, NY 13407 • 2,986
Mohnton, PA 19540 • 2,484
Mojave, CA 93501–02 • 3,763
Mokena, IL 60448 • 6,128
Molalla, OR 97038 • 3,651
Moline, IL 61265 • 43,202
Molino, FL 32577 • 1,207
Momence, IL 60954 • 2,968
Monaca, PA 15061 • 6,739
Monahans, TX 79756 • 8,101
Monarch Mills, SC 29379 • 2,613
Moncks Corner, SC 29461 • 5,607
Mondovi, WI 54755 • 2,491
Monee, IL 60449 • 1,044
Monessen, PA 15062 • 9,901
Monett, MO 65708 • 6,529
Monette, AR 72447 • 1,115
Monfort Heights, OH 45239 • 9,745
Moniteau □, MO • 12,298
Monmouth, IL 61462 • 9,489
Monmouth, OR 97361 • 6,288
Monmouth □, NJ • 553,124
Monmouth Beach, NJ 07750 • 3,303
Monmouth Junction, NJ 08852 • 1,570
Mono □, CA • 9,956
Monon, IN 47959 • 1,585
Monona, IA 52159 • 1,520
Monona, WI 53716 • 8,637
Monona □, IA • 10,034
Monongah, WV 26554 • 1,018
Monongahela, PA 15063 • 4,928
Monongalia □, WV • 75,509
Monroe, GA 30655 • 9,759
Monroe, IA 50170 • 1,739
Monroe, LA 71201–13 • 54,909
Monroe, MI 48161 • 22,902
Monroe, NY 10950 • 6,672
Monroe, NC 28110–12 • 16,127
Monroe, OH 45050 • 4,490
Monroe, UT 84754 • 1,472
Monroe, WA 98272 • 4,278
Monroe, WI 53566 • 10,241
Monroe □, AL • 23,968
Monroe □, AR • 11,333
Monroe □, FL • 78,024
Monroe □, GA • 17,113
Monroe □, IL • 22,422
Monroe □, IN • 108,978
Monroe □, IA • 8,114
Monroe □, KY • 11,401
Monroe □, MI • 133,600
Monroe □, MS • 36,582
Monroe □, MO • 9,104
Monroe □, NY • 713,968
Monroe □, OH • 15,497
Monroe □, PA • 95,709
Monroe □, TN • 30,541
Monroe □, WV • 12,406

Monroe □, WI • 36,633
Monroe Center, CT 06468 • 7,900
Monroe City, MO 63456 • 2,701
Monroe Park, DE 19807 • 1,000
Monroeville, AL 36460-61 • 6,993
Monroeville, IN 46773 • 1,232
Monroeville, OH 44847 • 1,381
Monroeville, PA 15146 • 29,169
Monrovia, CA 91016 • 35,761
Monsey, NY 10952 • 13,986
Monson, MA 01057 • 2,101
Montague, CA 96064 • 1,415
Montague, MI 49437 • 2,276
Montague □, TX • 17,274
Mont Alto, PA 17237 • 1,395
Montauk, NY 11954 • 3,001
Mont Belvieu, TX 77580 • 1,323
Montcalm □, MI • 53,059
Montchanin, DE 19710 • 500
Montclair, CA 91763 • 28,434
Montclair, NJ 07042-44 • 37,729
Monteagle, TN 37356 • 1,138
Montebello, CA 90640 • 59,564
Montecito, CA 93108 • 9,300
Montello, NV 89830 • 200
Montello, WI 53949 • 1,329
Monterey, CA 93940 • 31,954
Monterey, TN 38574 • 2,559
Monterey □, CA • 355,660
Monterey Park, CA 91754 • 60,738
Montesano, WA 98563 • 3,064
Montevallo, AL 35115 • 4,239
Montevideo, MN 56265 • 5,499
Monte Vista, CO 81144 • 4,324
Montezuma, GA 31063 • 4,506
Montezuma, IN 47862 • 1,134
Montezuma, IA 50171 • 1,651
Montezuma □, CO • 18,672
Montgomery, AL 36101-99 • 187,106
Montgomery, IL 60538 • 4,267
Montgomery, MN 56069 • 2,399
Montgomery, NY 12549 • 2,696
Montgomery, OH 45242 • 9,753
Montgomery, PA 17752 • 1,631
Montgomery, WV 25136 • 2,449
Montgomery □, AL • 209,085
Montgomery □, AR • 7,841
Montgomery □, GA • 7,163
Montgomery □, IL • 30,728
Montgomery □, IN • 34,436
Montgomery □, IA • 12,076
Montgomery □, KS • 38,816
Montgomery □, KY • 19,561
Montgomery □, MD • 757,027
Montgomery □, MS • 12,388
Montgomery □, MO • 11,355
Montgomery □, NY • 51,981
Montgomery □, NC • 23,346
Montgomery □, OH • 573,809
Montgomery □, PA • 678,111
Montgomery □, TN • 100,498
Montgomery □, TX • 182,201
Montgomery □, VA • 73,913
Montgomery City, MO 63361 • 2,281
Montgomery Village, MD 20879 • 32,315
Monticello, AR 71655 • 8,116
Monticello, FL 32344 • 2,573
Monticello, GA 31064 • 2,289
Monticello, IL 61856 • 4,549
Monticello, IN 47960 • 5,237
Monticello, IA 52310 • 3,522
Monticello, KY 42633 • 5,357
Monticello, MN 55362 • 4,941
Monticello, MS 39654 • 1,755
Monticello, NY 12701 • 6,597
Monticello, UT 84535 • 1,806
Monticello, WI 53570 • 1,140
Montmorency □, MI • 8,936
Montour □, PA • 17,735
Montour Falls, NY 14865 • 1,845
Montoursville, PA 17754 • 4,983
Montpelier, ID 83254 • 2,656
Montpelier, IN 47359 • 1,880
Montpelier, OH 43543 • 4,299
Montpelier, VT 05601-02 • 8,247
Montrose, AL 36559 • 1,400
Montrose, CO 81401-02 • 8,854
Montrose, MI 48457 • 1,811
Montrose, PA 18801 • 1,982
Montrose, VA 23231 • 6,405
Montrose □, CO • 24,423
Montvale, NJ 07645 • 6,946
Montville, CT 06353 • 16,673
Montville, NJ 07045 • 2,600
Monument, CO 80132 • 1,020
Monument Beach, MA 02553 • 1,800
Monument Heights, VA 23226 • 2,500
Moodus, CT 06469 • 1,170
Moody, TX 76557 • 1,329
Moody □, SD • 6,507
Moonachie, NJ 07074 • 2,817
Moorcroft, WY 82721 • 768
Moore, OK 73160 • 40,318
Moore □, NC • 59,013
Moore □, TN • 4,721
Moore □, TX • 17,865
Moorefield, WV 26836 • 2,148
Moore Haven, FL 33471 • 1,432
Mooreland, OK 73852 • 1,157
Moorestown, NJ 08057 • 16,500
Mooresville, IN 46158 • 5,541
Mooresville, NC 28115 • 9,317
Moorhead, MN 56560-61 • 32,295
Moorhead, MS 38761 • 2,417
Moorpark, CA 93020-21 • 25,494
Moose Lake, MN 55767 • 1,206
Moosic, PA 18507 • 5,339
Moosup, CT 06354 • 3,289
Mora, MN 55051 • 2,905
Mora, NM 87732 • 1,200
Mora □, NM • 4,264
Moraga, CA 94556 • 15,852
Moraine, OH 45439 • 5,989
Moravia, NY 13118 • 1,559
Morehead, KY 40351 • 8,357
Morehead City, NC 28557 • 6,046
Morehouse, MO 63868 • 1,068
Morehouse □, LA • 31,938
Morenci, AZ 85540 • 1,799
Morenci, MI 49256 • 2,342
Moreno Valley, CA 92387-88 • 118,779
Morgan, UT 84050 • 2,023

Morgan □, AL • 100,043
Morgan □, CO • 21,939
Morgan □, GA • 12,883
Morgan □, IL • 36,397
Morgan □, IN • 55,920
Morgan □, KY • 11,648
Morgan □, MO • 15,574
Morgan □, OH • 14,194
Morgan □, TN • 17,300
Morgan □, UT • 5,528
Morgan □, WV • 12,128
Morgan City, LA 70380-81 • 14,531
Morganfield, KY 42437 • 3,776
Morgan Hill, CA 95037-38 • 23,928
Morganton, NC 28655 • 15,085
Morgantown, KY 42261 • 2,284
Morgantown, MS 39120 • 3,288
Morgantown, WV 26502-07 • 25,879
Moriarty, NM 87035 • 1,399
Morningdale, MA 01505 • 1,130
Morocco, IN 47963 • 1,044
Moroni, UT 84646 • 1,115
Morrill □, NE • 5,423
Morrilton, AR 72110 • 6,551
Morris, AL 35116 • 1,136
Morris, IL 60450 • 10,270
Morris, MN 56267 • 5,613
Morris, OK 74445 • 1,216
Morris □, KS • 6,198
Morris □, NJ • 421,353
Morris □, TX • 13,200
Morrison, IL 61270 • 4,363
Morrison □, MN • 29,604
Morrison City, TN 37660 • 2,032
Morrisonville, IL 62546 • 1,113
Morrisonville, NY 12962 • 1,742
Morris Plains, NJ 07950 • 5,219
Morristown, NJ 07960-63 • 16,189
Morristown, TN 37813-16 • 21,385
Morrisville, NY 13408 • 2,732
Morrisville, PA 19067 • 9,765
Morrisville, VT 05661 • 1,984
Morro Bay, CA 93442-43 • 9,664
Morrow, GA 30260 • 5,168
Morrow, OH 45152 • 1,206
Morrow □, OH • 27,749
Morrow □, OR • 7,625
Morton, IL 61550 • 13,799
Morton, MS 39117 • 3,212
Morton, TX 79346 • 2,597
Morton, WA 98356 • 1,130
Morton □, KS • 3,480
Morton □, ND • 23,700
Morton Grove, IL 60053 • 22,408
Moscow, ID 83843 • 18,519
Moscow, PA 18444 • 1,527
Moses Lake, WA 98837 • 11,235
Mosheim, TN 37818 • 1,451
Mosinee, WI 54455 • 3,820
Moss Bluff, LA 70611 • 8,039
Moss Point, MS 39563 • 17,837
Motley □, TX • 1,532
Mott, ND 58646 • 1,019
Moulton, AL 35650 • 3,248
Moultrie, GA 31768 • 14,865
Moultrie □, IL • 13,930
Mound, MN 55364 • 9,634
Mound Bayou, MS 38762 • 2,222
Mound City, MO 64470 • 1,273
Moundridge, KS 67107 • 1,531
Mounds, IL 62964 • 1,407
Mounds View, MN 55432 • 12,541
Moundsville, WV 26041 • 10,753
Moundville, AL 35474 • 1,348
Mountainair, NM 87036 • 926
Mountain Brook, AL 35223 • 19,810
Mountain City, NV 89831 • 110
Mountain City, TN 37683 • 2,169
Mountain Grove, MO 65711 • 4,182
Mountain Home, AR 72653 • 9,027
Mountain Home, ID 83647 • 7,913
Mountain Iron, MN 55768 • 3,362
Mountain Lake, MN 56159 • 1,906
Mountain Lake Park, MD 21550 • 1,938
Mountain Lakes, NJ 07046 • 3,847
Mountain Park, GA 30087 • 11,025
Mountainside, NJ 07092 • 6,657
Mountain View, AR 72560 • 2,439
Mountain View, CA 94039-43 • 67,460
Mountain View, CO 80521 • 2,100
Mountain View, MO 65548 • 2,036
Mountain View, NM 87105 • 2,300
Mountain View, OK 73062 • 1,086
Mountain View, WY 82604 • 1,200
Mountain Village, AK 99632 • 674
Mount Airy, MD 21771 • 3,730
Mount Airy, NC 27030 • 7,156
Mount Angel, OR 97362 • 2,778
Mount Arlington, NJ 07856 • 3,630
Mount Ayr, IA 50854 • 1,796
Mount Carmel, IL 62863 • 8,287
Mount Carmel, PA 17851 • 7,196
Mount Carroll, IL 61053 • 1,726
Mount Clemens, MI 48043-46 • 18,405
Mount Dora, FL 32757 • 7,196
Mount Ephraim, NJ 08059 • 4,517
Mount Freedom, NJ 07970 • 1,920
Mount Gay, WV 25637 • 1,200
Mount Gilead, NC 27306 • 1,336
Mount Gilead, OH 43338 • 2,846
Mount Healthy, OH 45231 • 7,580
Mount Holly, NJ 08060 • 10,639
Mount Holly, NC 28120 • 7,710
Mount Holly Springs, PA 17065 • 1,925
Mount Hope, WV 25880 • 1,573
Mount Horeb, WI 53572 • 4,182
Mount Jackson, VA 22842 • 1,583
Mount Jewett, PA 16740 • 1,029
Mount Joy, PA 17552 • 6,398
Mount Juliet, TN 37122 • 5,389
Mount Kisco, NY 10549 • 9,108
Mountlake Terrace, WA 98043 • 19,320
Mount Lebanon, PA 15228 • 33,362
Mount Morris, IL 61054 • 2,919
Mount Morris, MI 48458 • 3,292
Mount Morris, NY 14510 • 3,137
Mount Olive, IL 62069 • 2,126
Mount Olive, NC 28365 • 4,582
Mount Olympus, UT 84117 • 7,413
Mount Orab, OH 45154 • 1,929
Mount Penn, PA 19606 • 2,883

Mount Pleasant, IA 52641 • 8,027
Mount Pleasant, MI 48858-59 • 23,285
Mount Pleasant, NC 28124 • 1,027
Mount Pleasant, PA 15666 • 4,787
Mount Pleasant, SC 29464-65 • 30,108
Mount Pleasant, TN 38474 • 4,278
Mount Pleasant, TX 75455 • 12,291
Mount Pleasant, UT 84647 • 2,092
Mount Pocono, PA 18344 • 1,795
Mount Prospect, IL 60056 • 53,170
Mount Pulaski, IL 62548 • 1,610
Mountrail □, ND • 7,021
Mount Rainier, MD 20712 • 7,954
Mount Savage, MD 21545 • 1,640
Mount Shasta, CA 96067 • 3,460
Mount Sinai, NY 11766 • 8,023
Mount Sterling, IL 62353 • 1,922
Mount Sterling, KY 40353 • 5,362
Mount Sterling, OH 43143 • 1,647
Mount Union, PA 17066 • 2,878
Mount Vernon, GA 30445 • 1,914
Mount Vernon, IL 62864 • 16,988
Mount Vernon, IN 47620 • 7,217
Mount Vernon, IA 52314 • 3,726
Mount Vernon, KY 40456 • 2,654
Mount Vernon, MO 65712 • 3,726
Mount Vernon, NY 10550-53 • 67,153
Mount Vernon, OH 43050 • 14,550
Mount Vernon, TX 75457 • 2,219
Mount Vernon, WA 98273 • 17,647
Mount View, RI 02852 • 610
Mount Washington, KY 40047 • 5,226
Mount Wolf, PA 17347 • 1,365
Mount Zion, IL 62549 • 4,522
Moville, IA 51039 • 1,306
Moweaqua, IL 62550 • 1,785
Mower □, MN • 37,385
Moyock, NC 27958 • 1,400
Muenster, TX 76252 • 1,387
Muhlenberg □, KY • 31,318
Mukilteo, WA 98275 • 7,007
Mukwonago, WI 53149 • 4,457
Mulberry, AR 72947 • 1,448
Mulberry, FL 33860 • 2,988
Mulberry, IN 46058 • 1,262
Mulberry, NC 28659 • 2,339
Muldraugh, KY 40155 • 1,376
Muldrow, OK 74948 • 2,889
Muleshoe, TX 79347 • 4,571
Mullan, ID 83846 • 821
Mullens, WV 25882 • 2,006
Mullica Hill, NJ 08062 • 1,117
Mullins, SC 29574 • 5,910
Multnomah □, OR • 583,887
Mulvane, KS 67110 • 4,674
Muncie, IN 47302-08 • 71,035
Muncy, PA 17756 • 2,702
Munday, TX 76371 • 1,600
Mundelein, IL 60060 • 21,215
Munford, TN 38058 • 2,326
Munfordville, KY 42765 • 1,556
Munhall, PA 15120 • 13,158
Munising, MI 49862 • 2,783
Munster, IN 46321 • 19,949
Murfreesboro, AR 71958 • 1,542
Murfreesboro, NC 27855 • 2,580
Murfreesboro, TN 37129-33 • 44,922
Murphy, MO 63026 • 9,342
Murphy, NC 28906 • 1,575
Murphys, CA 95247 • 1,517
Murphysboro, IL 62966 • 9,176
Murray, KY 42071 • 14,439
Murray, UT 84107 • 31,282
Murray □, GA • 26,147
Murray □, MN • 9,660
Murray □, OK • 12,042
Murrells Inlet, SC 29576 • 3,334
Murrysville, PA 15668 • 17,240
Muscatine, IA 52761 • 22,881
Muscatine □, IA • 39,907
Muscle Shoals, AL 35661 • 9,611
Muscoda, WI 53573 • 1,287
Muscogee □, GA • 179,278
Muscoy, CA 92405 • 7,541
Muse, PA 15350 • 1,250
Muskego, WI 53150 • 16,813
Muskegon, MI 49440-45 • 40,283
Muskegon □, MI • 158,983
Muskegon Heights, MI 49444 • 13,176
Muskingum □, OH • 82,068
Muskogee, OK 74401-03 • 37,708
Muskogee □, OK • 68,078
Musselshell □, MT • 4,106
Mustang, OK 73064 • 10,434
Myerstown, PA 17067 • 3,236
Myrtle Beach, SC 29577-78 • 24,848
Myrtle Grove, FL 32506 • 17,402
Myrtle Point, OR 97458 • 2,712
Mystic, CT 06355 • 2,618
Mystic Island, NJ 08087 • 7,400

N

Naalehu, HI 96772 • 1,027
Naamans Gardens, DE 19810 • 1,500
Nabnasset, MA 01886 • 3,600
Nacogdoches, TX 75961-63 • 30,872
Nacogdoches □, TX • 54,753
Nags Head, NC 27959 • 1,838
Nahant, MA 01908 • 3,828
Nahunta, GA 31553 • 1,049
Nampa, ID 83651-53 • 28,365
Nanakuli, HI 96792 • 9,575
Nance □, NE • 4,275
Nanticoke, PA 18634 • 12,267
Nantucket, MA 02554 • 3,069
Nantucket □, MA • 6,012
Nanty Glo, PA 15943 • 3,190
Nanuet, NY 10954 • 14,065
Napa, CA 94558-59 • 61,842
Napa □, CA • 110,765
Napanoch, NY 12458 • 1,068
Naperville, IL 60540 • 85,351
Naples, FL 33939-42 • 19,505
Naples, NY 14512 • 1,237
Naples, TX 75568 • 1,508
Naples, UT 84078 • 1,334
Naples Park, FL 33963 • 8,002
Napoleon, ND 58561 • 930
Napoleon, OH 43545 • 8,884
Nappanee, IN 46550 • 5,510

Naranja, FL 33032 • 5,790
Narberth, PA 19072 • 4,278
Narragansett, RI 02882 • 3,721
Narrows, VA 24124 • 2,082
Naselle, WA 98638 • 1,000
Nash, TX 75569 • 2,162
Nash □, NC • 76,677
Nashua, IA 50658 • 1,476
Nashua, NH 03060-63 • 79,662
Nashville, AR 71852 • 4,639
Nashville, GA 31639 • 4,782
Nashville, IL 62263 • 3,202
Nashville, MI 49073 • 1,654
Nashville, NC 27856 • 3,617
Nashville, TN 37201-35 • 487,969
Nashwauk, MN 55769 • 1,026
Nassau, NY 12123 • 1,254
Nassau □, FL • 43,941
Nassau □, NY • 1,287,348
Nassau Shores, NY 11758 • 5,110
Natalia, TX 78059 • 1,216
Natchez, MS 39120-22 • 19,460
Natchitoches, LA 71457-58 • 16,609
Natchitoches □, LA • 36,689
Natick, MA 01760 • 30,100
National City, CA 91950-51 • 54,249
National Park, NJ 08063 • 3,413
Natrona □, WY • 61,226
Natrona Heights, PA 15065 • 12,200
Naugatuck, CT 06770 • 30,625
Nautilus Park, CT 06340 • 6,500
Nauvoo, IL 62354 • 1,108
Navajo □, AZ • 77,658
Navarre, OH 44662 • 1,635
Navarro □, TX • 39,926
Navasota, TX 77868-69 • 6,296
Navesink, NJ 07752 • 1,420
Nazareth, PA 18064 • 5,713
Neah Bay, WA 98357 • 1,300
Nebraska City, NE 68410 • 6,547
Nederland, CO 80466 • 1,099
Nederland, TX 77627 • 16,192
Nedrow, NY 13120 • 2,980
Needham, MA 02192 • 27,557
Needles, CA 92363 • 5,191
Needville, TX 77461 • 2,199
Neenah, WI 54956-57 • 23,219
Neffs, OH 43940 • 1,213
Negaunee, MI 49866 • 4,741
Neillsville, WI 54456 • 2,680
Nekoosa, WI 54457 • 2,557
Neligh, NE 68756 • 1,742
Nelson □, KY • 29,710
Nelson □, ND • 4,410
Nelson □, VA • 12,778
Nelsonville, OH 45764 • 4,563
Nemacolin, PA 15351 • 1,097
Nemaha □, KS • 10,446
Nemaha □, NE • 7,980
Nenana, AK 99760 • 393
Neodesha, KS 66757 • 2,837
Neoga, IL 62447 • 1,678
Neosho, MO 64850 • 9,254
Neosho □, KS • 17,035
Nephi, UT 84648 • 3,515
Neptune, NJ 07753 • 28,366
Neptune Beach, FL 32233 • 6,816
Neptune City, NJ 07753 • 4,997
Nesconset, NY 11767 • 10,712
Nescopeck, PA 18635 • 1,651
Neshoba □, MS • 24,800
Nesquehoning, PA 18240 • 3,364
Ness □, KS • 4,033
Ness City, KS 67560 • 1,724
Netcong, NJ 07857 • 3,311
Nether Providence Township, PA 19013 • 13,229
Nettleton, MS 38858 • 2,462
Nevada, IA 50201 • 6,009
Nevada, MO 64772 • 8,597
Nevada □, AR • 10,101
Nevada □, CA • 78,510
Nevada City, CA 95959 • 2,855
New Albany, IN 47150-51 • 36,322
New Albany, MS 38652 • 6,775
New Albany, OH 43054 • 1,621
Newark, AR 72562 • 1,159
Newark, CA 94560 • 37,861
Newark, DE 19711-15 • 25,098
Newark, NJ 07101-75 • 275,221
Newark, NY 14513 • 9,849
Newark, OH 43055-58 • 44,389
Newark Valley, NY 13811 • 1,082
New Athens, IL 62264 • 2,010
Newaygo, MI 49337 • 1,336
Newaygo □, MI • 38,202
New Baden, IL 62265 • 2,602
New Baltimore, MI 48047 • 5,798
New Bedford, MA 02740-48 • 99,922
Newberg, OR 97132 • 13,086
New Berlin, NY 13411 • 1,220
New Berlin, WI 53151 • 33,592
New Bern, NC 28560-64 • 17,363
Newbern, TN 38059 • 2,515
Newberry, FL 32669 • 1,644
Newberry, MI 49868 • 1,873
Newberry, SC 29108 • 10,542
Newberry □, SC • 33,172
New Bethlehem, PA 16242 • 1,151
New Bloomfield, PA 17068 • 1,092
New Boston, MI 48164 • 1,200
New Boston, OH 45662 • 2,717
New Boston, TX 75570 • 5,057
New Braunfels, TX 78130-33 • 27,334
New Bremen, OH 45869 • 2,393
New Brighton, MN 55112 • 22,207
New Brighton, PA 15066 • 6,854
New Britain, CT 06050-53 • 75,491
New Brockton, AL 36351 • 1,184
New Brunswick, NJ 08901-06 • 41,711
New Buffalo, MI 49117 • 2,317
Newburg, KY 40218 • 21,647
Newburgh, IN 47629-30 • 2,880
Newburgh, NY 12550-53 • 26,454
Newburgh Heights, OH 44105 • 2,310
Newburyport, MA 01950-52 • 16,317
New Canaan, CT 06840 • 17,864
New Carlisle, IN 46552 • 1,446
New Carlisle, OH 45344 • 6,049
New Carrollton, MD 20784 • 12,002
New Castle, AL 35119 • 1,100
New Castle, DE 19720 • 4,837

New Castle, IN 47362 • 17,753
Newcastle, OK 73065 • 4,214
New Castle, PA 16101-08 • 28,334
Newcastle, WY 82701 • 3,003
New Castle □, DE • 441,946
New City, NY 10956 • 33,673
Newcomerstown, OH 43832 • 4,012
New Concord, OH 43762 • 2,086
New Cumberland, PA 17070 • 7,665
New Cumberland, WV 26047 • 1,363
New Egypt, NJ 08533 • 2,327
Newell, IA 50568 • 1,089
Newell, WV 26050 • 1,724
New Ellenton, SC 29809 • 2,515
Newellton, LA 71357 • 1,576
New England, ND 58647 • 663
Newfane, NY 14108 • 3,001
Newfield, NJ 08344 • 1,592
New Franklin, MO 65274 • 1,107
New Freedom, PA 17349 • 2,920
New Glarus, WI 53574 • 1,899
New Hampton, IA 50659 • 3,660
New Hanover □, NC • 120,284
New Hartford, CT 06057 • 1,269
New Haven, CT 06510-36 • 130,474
New Haven, IN 46774 • 9,320
New Haven, MI 48048 • 2,331
New Haven, MO 63068 • 1,757
New Haven, WV 25265 • 1,632
New Haven □, CT • 804,219
New Holland, GA 30501 • 1,200
New Holland, PA 17557 • 4,484
New Holstein, WI 53061 • 3,342
New Hope, AL 35760 • 2,248
New Hope, MN 55428 • 21,853
New Hope, NC 27604 • 5,694
New Hope, PA 18938 • 1,400
New Hyde Park, NY 11040 • 9,728
New Iberia, LA 70560-62 • 31,828
Newington, CT 06031 • 29,208
Newington, VA 22122 • 17,965
New Johnsonville, TN 37134 • 1,643
New Kensington, PA 15068 • 15,894
New Kent □, VA • 10,445
Newkirk, OK 74647 • 2,168
New Lenox, IL 60451 • 9,627
New Lexington, OH 43764 • 5,117
New Lisbon, WI 53950 • 1,491
Newllano, LA 71461 • 2,660
New London, CT 06320 • 28,540
New London, IA 52645 • 1,922
New London, NH 03257 • 3,180
New London, OH 44851 • 2,642
New London, WI 54961 • 6,658
New London □, CT • 254,957
New Madrid, MO 63869 • 3,350
New Madrid □, MO • 20,928
Newman, CA 95360 • 4,151
Newmanstown, PA 17073 • 1,410
Newmarket, NH 03857 • 4,917
New Market, TN 37820 • 1,086
New Market, VA 22844 • 1,435
New Martinsville, WV 26155 • 6,705
New Matamoras, OH 45767 • 1,002
New Miami, OH 45011 • 2,555
New Milford, CT 06776 • 5,775
New Milford, NJ 07646 • 15,990
Newnan, GA 30263-65 • 12,497
New Orleans, LA 70101-95 • 496,938
New Oxford, PA 17350 • 1,617
New Paris, IN 46553 • 1,007
New Paris, OH 45347 • 1,801
New Philadelphia, OH 44663 • 15,698
New Philadelphia, PA 17959 • 1,283
New Plymouth, ID 83655 • 1,313
Newport, AR 72112 • 7,459
Newport, DE 19804 • 1,240
Newport, KY 41071-76 • 18,871
Newport, ME 04953 • 1,843
Newport, MN 55055 • 3,720
Newport, NH 03773 • 3,772
Newport, NC 28570 • 2,516
Newport, OR 97365 • 8,437
Newport, PA 17074 • 1,568
Newport, RI 02840 • 28,227
Newport, TN 37821 • 7,123
Newport, VT 05855 • 4,434
Newport, WA 99156 • 1,691
Newport □, RI • 87,194
Newport Beach, CA 92657-63 • 66,643
Newport East, RI 02840 • 11,080
Newport Hills, WA 98002 • 14,736
Newport News, VA 23601-09 • 170,045
New Port Richey, FL 34652-56 • 14,044
New Prague, MN 56071 • 3,569
New Preston, CT 06777 • 1,217
New Providence, NJ 07974 • 11,439
New Richland, MN 56072 • 1,237
New Richmond, OH 45157 • 2,408
New Richmond, WI 54017 • 5,106
New River Station, NC 28542 • 9,732
New Roads, LA 70760 • 5,303
New Rochelle, NY 10801-05 • 67,265
New Rockford, ND 58356 • 1,604
New Salem, ND 58563 • 909
New Sarpy, LA 70078 • 2,946
New Sharon, IA 50207 • 1,136
New Smyrna Beach, FL 32168-70 • 16,543
New Tazewell, TN 37825 • 1,864
Newton, AL 36352 • 1,580
Newton, IL 62448 • 3,154
Newton, IA 50208 • 14,789
Newton, KS 67114 • 16,700
Newton, MA 02158 • 82,585
Newton, MS 39345 • 3,701
Newton, NJ 07860 • 7,521
Newton, NC 28658 • 9,304
Newton, TX 75966 • 1,885
Newton □, AR • 7,666
Newton □, GA • 41,808
Newton □, IN • 13,551
Newton □, MS • 20,291
Newton □, MO • 44,445
Newton □, TX • 13,569
Newton Falls, OH 44444 • 4,866
New Town, ND 58763 • 1,388
Newtown, CT 06470 • 1,800
Newtown, OH 45244 • 1,589
Newtown Square, PA 19073 • 11,366

New Ulm, MN 56073 • 13,132
Newville, PA 17241 • 1,349
New Washington, OH 44854 • 1,057
New Washoe City, NV 89701 • 2,875
New Waterford, OH 44445 • 1,278
New Whiteland, IN 46184 • 4,097
New Wilmington, PA 16142 • 2,706
New Windsor, NY 12553 • 8,898
New York, NY 10001-99 • 7,322,564
New York ▫, NY • 1,487,536
Nez Perce ▫, ID • 33,754
Niagara, WI 54151 • 1,999
Niagara ▫, NY • 220,756
Niagara Falls, NY 14301-05 • 61,840
Niantic, CT 06357 • 3,048
Nibley, UT 84321 • 1,167
Niceville, FL 32578 • 10,507
Nicholas ▫, KY • 6,725
Nicholas ▫, WV • 26,775
Nicholasville, KY 40356 • 13,603
Nicholls, GA 31554 • 1,003
Nichols Hills, OK 73116 • 4,020
Nickerson, KS 67561 • 1,137
Nicollet ▫, MN • 28,076
Nicoma Park, OK 73066 • 2,353
Nikishka, AK 99635 • 1,109
Niland, CA 92257 • 1,183
Niles, IL 60648 • 28,284
Niles, MI 49120 • 12,458
Niles, OH 44446 • 21,128
Ninety Six, SC 29666 • 2,099
Ninilchik, AK 99639 • 456
Niobrara ▫, WY • 2,499
Nipomo, CA 93444 • 7,109
Niskayuna, NY 12309 • 4,942
Nisswa, MN 56468 • 1,391
Nitro, WV 25143 • 6,851
Nixa, MO 65714 • 4,707
Nixon, NV 89424 • 150
Nixon, TX 78140 • 1,995
Noank, CT 06340 • 1,406
Noble ▫, IN • 37,877
Noble ▫, OH • 11,336
Noble ▫, OK • 11,045
Nobles ▫, MN • 20,098
Noblesville, IN 46060 • 17,655
Nocatee, FL 33864 • 1,300
Nocona, TX 76255 • 2,870
Nodaway ▫, MO • 21,709
Noel, MO 64854 • 1,169
Nogales, AZ 85621 • 19,489
Nokomis, FL 34274-75 • 3,448
Nokomis, IL 62075 • 2,534
Nolan ▫, TX • 16,594
Nome, AK 99762 • 3,500
Noorvik, AK 99763 • 531
Nora Springs, IA 50458 • 1,505
Norco, CA 91760 • 23,302
Norco, LA 70079 • 3,385
Norcross, GA 30071 • 5,947
Norfolk ▫, CT 06058 • 1,500
Norfolk, NE 68701 • 21,476
Norfolk, NY 13667 • 1,412
Norfolk, VA 23501-93 • 261,229
Norfolk ▫, MA • 616,087
Norland, FL 33169 • 22,109
Normal, IL 61761 • 40,023
Norman, OK 73069-72 • 80,071
Norman ▫, MN • 7,975
Normandy, MO 63121 • 4,480
Norridge, IL 60656 • 14,459
Norridgewock, ME 04957 • 1,496
Norris, TN 37828 • 1,303
Norris City, IL 62869 • 1,322
Norristown, PA 19401-09 • 30,749
North Adams, MA 01247 • 16,797
North Albany, OR 97321 • 4,325
North Amherst, MA 01059 • 6,239
North Amityville, NY 11701 • 13,849
Northampton, MA 01060-61 • 29,289
Northampton, PA 18067 • 8,717
Northampton ▫, NC • 20,798
Northampton ▫, PA • 247,105
Northampton ▫, VA • 13,061
North Andover, MA 01845 • 20,129
North Andrews Gardens, FL 33308 • 9,002
North Apollo, PA 15673 • 1,391
North Arlington, NJ 07032 • 13,790
North Atlanta, GA 30319 • 27,812
North Attleboro, MA 02760-63 • 16,178
North Auburn, CA 95603 • 10,301
North Augusta, SC 29841 • 15,351
North Aurora, IL 60542 • 5,940
North Babylon, NY 11703 • 18,081
North Baltimore, OH 45872 • 3,139
North Bay Shore, NY 11706 • 12,799
North Beach, MD 20714 • 1,173
North Bellmore, NY 11710 • 19,707
North Bellport, NY 11713 • 8,182
North Belmont, NC 28012 • 10,762
North Bend, NE 68649 • 1,249
North Bend, OR 97459 • 9,614
North Bend, WA 98045 • 2,578
North Bennington, VT 05257 • 1,520
North Bergen, NJ 07047 • 48,414
North Berwick, ME 03906 • 1,568
North Billerica, MA 01862 • 5,400
Northborough, MA 01532 • 5,761
North Braddock, PA 15104 • 7,036
North Branch, MI 48461 • 1,023
North Branch, MN 55056 • 1,867
North Branch, NJ 08876 • 2,620
North Branford, CT 06471 • 6,600
Northbridge, MA 01534 • 3,570
Northbrook, IL 60062 • 32,308
Northbrook, OH 45231 • 11,471
North Brookfield, MA 01535 • 2,635
North Brunswick, NJ 08902 • 31,287
North Brunswick Township, NJ 08902 • 31,287
North Caldwell, NJ 07006 • 7,375
North Canton, OH 44720 • 14,748
North Cape May, NJ 08204 • 3,341
North Charleston, SC 29406 • 70,218
North Chicago, IL 60064 • 34,978
North City, WA 98155 • 8,200
North Cohasset, MA 02025 • 1,045
North College Hill, OH 45239 • 11,002
North Collins, NY 14111 • 1,335
North Conway, NH 03860 • 2,032
North Corbin, KY 40701 • 1,601

North Crossett, AR 71635 • 3,358
North Dartmouth, MA 02747 • 8,080
North Decatur, GA 30033 • 13,936
North Dighton, MA 02764 • 1,174
North Druid Hills, GA 30033 • 14,170
North Eagle Butte, SD 57625 • 1,423
North East, MD 21901 • 1,913
North East, PA 16428 • 4,617
North Eastham, MA 02651 • 1,570
Northeast Henrietta, NY 14534 • 10,650
North Easton, MA 02356 • 4,420
North Fair Oaks, CA 94025 • 13,912
North Falmouth, MA 02556 • 3,150
Northfield, IL 60093 • 4,635
Northfield, MA 01360 • 1,322
Northfield, MN 55057 • 14,684
Northfield, NH 03276 • 1,375
Northfield, NJ 08225 • 7,305
Northfield, OH 44067 • 3,624
Northfield, VT 05663 • 1,889
Northfield Falls, VT 05664 • 600
North Fond du Lac, WI 54935 • 4,292
Northford, CT 06472 • 3,180
North Fort Myers, FL 33903 • 30,027
Northglenn, CO 80233 • 27,195
North Grafton, MA 01536 • 3,050
North Great River, NY 11722 • 3,964
North Grosvenordale, CT 06255 • 1,705
North Gulfport, MS 39501 • 4,966
North Haledon, NJ 07508 • 7,987
North Hampton, NH 03862 • 1,000
North Haven, CT 06473 • 22,249
North Highlands, CA 95660 • 42,105
North Hill, WA 98166 • 5,706
North Houston, TX 77086 • 2,800
North Hudson, WI 54016 • 3,101
North Industry, OH 44707 • 3,250
North Judson, IN 46366 • 1,582
North Kansas City, MO 64116 • 4,130
North Kingstown, RI 02852-54 • 2,750
North Kingsville, OH 44068 • 2,672
North La Junta, CO 81050 • 1,076
Northlake, IL 60164 • 12,505
North Las Vegas, NV 89030-31 • 47,707
North Lauderdale, FL 33068 • 26,506
North Lewisburg, OH 43060 • 1,160
North Liberty, IN 46554 • 1,366
North Liberty, IA 52317 • 2,926
North Lindenhurst, NY 11757 • 10,563
North Little Rock, AR 72114-20 • 61,741
North Logan, UT 84321 • 3,768
North Madison, OH 44057 • 8,699
North Manchester, IN 46962 • 6,383
North Mankato, MN 56001 • 10,164
North Massapequa, NY 11758 • 19,365
North Merrick, NY 11566 • 12,113
North Merrydale, LA 70812 • 4,000
North Miami, FL 33161 • 49,998
North Miami Beach, FL 33162 • 35,359
North Muskegon, MI 49445 • 3,919
North Myrtle Beach, SC 29582 • 8,636
North Naples, FL 33963 • 13,422
North New Hyde Park, NY 11040 • 14,359
North Ogden, UT 84404 • 11,668
North Olmsted, OH 44070 • 34,204
North Oxford, MA 01537 • 1,250
North Palm Beach, FL 33408 • 11,343
North Park, IL 61111 • 15,806
North Patchogue, NY 11772 • 7,374
North Pembroke, MA 02358 • 2,485
North Plainfield, NJ 07060 • 18,820
North Platte, NE 69101-03 • 22,605
Northport, AL 35476 • 17,366
North Port, FL 34287 • 11,973
Northport, NY 11768 • 7,572
North Prairie, WI 53153 • 1,322
North Providence, RI 02911 • 32,090
North Reading, MA 01864 • 11,455
North Richland Hills, TX 76118 • 45,895
Northridge, OH 44509 • 5,939
Northridge, OH 45414 • 9,448
North Ridgeville, OH 44039 • 21,564
North Riverside, IL 60546 • 6,005
North Royalton, OH 44133 • 23,197
North Salt Lake, UT 84054 • 6,474
North Sarasota, FL 34234 • 6,702
North Scituate, MA 02060 • 4,891
North Sioux City, SD 57049 • 2,019
North Springfield, OR 97477 • 5,451
North Springfield, VT 05150 • 750
North Springfield, VA 22151 • 8,996
North Star, DE 19711 • 1,030
North St. Paul, MN 55109 • 12,376
North Sudbury, MA 01776 • 2,630
North Syracuse, NY 13212 • 7,363
North Tarrytown, NY 10591 • 8,152
North Terre Haute, IN 47805 • 2,000
North Tewksbury, MA 01876 • 1,030
North Tonawanda, NY 14120 • 34,989
North Troy, VT 05859 • 723
North Tunica, MS 38676 • 1,314
Northumberland, PA 17857 • 3,860
Northumberland ▫, PA • 96,771
Northumberland ▫, VA • 10,524
North Uxbridge, MA 01538 • 1,500
Northvale, NJ 07647 • 4,563
North Valley Stream, NY 11580 • 14,574
North Vernon, IN 47265 • 5,311
North Versailles, PA 15137 • 12,302
Northview, MI 49505 • 13,712
Northview, OH 45322 • 10,337
Northville, MI 48167 • 6,226
Northville, NY 12134 • 1,180
North Wales, PA 19454 • 3,802
North Wantagh, NY 11793 • 12,276
North Warren, PA 16365 • 1,232
North Wildwood, NJ 08260 • 5,017
North Windham, ME 04062 • 4,077
Northwood, IA 50459 • 1,940
Northwood, ND 58267 • 1,166
Northwood, OH 43619 • 5,506
Northwoods, MO 63121 • 5,106
North York, PA 17404 • 1,689
Norton, KS 67654 • 3,017
Norton, MA 02766 • 1,899
Norton, OH 44203 • 11,477
Norton, VA 24273 • 4,247
Norton ▫, KS • 5,947
Norton Shores, MI 49441 • 21,755
Nortonville, KY 42442 • 1,209
Norwalk, CA 90650-52 • 94,279
Norwalk, CT 06850-56 • 78,331

Norwalk, IA 50211 • 5,726
Norwalk, OH 44857 • 14,731
Norway, ME 04268 • 3,023
Norway, MI 49870 • 2,910
Norwell, MA 02061 • 1,200
Norwich, CT 06360 • 37,391
Norwich, NY 13815 • 7,613
Norwich, VT 05055 • 1,000
Norwood, MA 02062 • 28,700
Norwood, MN 55368 • 1,351
Norwood, NJ 07648 • 4,858
Norwood, NY 13668 • 1,841
Norwood, NC 28128 • 1,617
Norwood, OH 45212 • 23,674
Norwood, PA 19074 • 6,162
Norwoodville, IA 50317 • 1,200
Nottoway ▫, VA • 14,993
Novato, CA 94947-49 • 47,585
Novi, MI 48374-77 • 32,998
Nowata, OK 74048 • 3,896
Nowata ▫, OK • 9,992
Noxubee ▫, MS • 12,604
Nuckolls ▫, NE • 5,786
Nueces ▫, TX • 291,145
Nulato, AK 99765 • 359
Nunda, NY 14517 • 1,347
Nutley, NJ 07110 • 27,099
Nutter Fort, WV 26301 • 1,819
Nutting Lake, MA 01865 • 3,180
Nyack, NY 10960 • 6,558
Nye ▫, NV • 17,781
Nyssa, OR 97913 • 2,629

O

Oak Bluffs, MA 02557 • 1,124
Oak Brook, IL 60521 • 9,178
Oak Creek, WI 53154 • 19,513
Oakdale, CA 95361 • 11,961
Oakdale, GA 30080 • 1,080
Oakdale, LA 71463 • 6,832
Oakdale, MN 55128 • 18,374
Oakdale, NY 11769 • 7,875
Oakdale, PA 15071 • 1,752
Oakes, ND 58474 • 1,775
Oakfield, NY 14125 • 1,818
Oakfield, WI 53065 • 1,003
Oak Forest, IL 60452 • 26,203
Oak Grove, KY 42262 • 2,863
Oak Grove, LA 71263 • 2,126
Oak Grove, OR 97267 • 12,576
Oak Grove, SC 29073 • 7,173
Oak Harbor, OH 43449 • 2,637
Oak Harbor, WA 98277 • 17,176
Oak Hill, MI 49660 • 1,000
Oak Hill, OH 45656 • 1,831
Oak Hill, WV 25901 • 6,812
Oakhurst, OK 74050 • 2,200
Oakland, CA 94601-62 • 372,242
Oakland, IA 51560 • 1,496
Oakland, ME 04963 • 3,510
Oakland, MD 21550 • 2,078
Oakland, NE 68045 • 1,279
Oakland, NJ 07436 • 11,997
Oakland, RI 02830 • 600
Oakland ▫, MI • 1,083,592
Oakland City, IN 47660 • 2,810
Oakland Park, FL 33334 • 26,326
Oak Lawn, IL 60453-59 • 56,182
Oaklawn, KS 67216 • 4,200
Oakley, CA 94561 • 18,374
Oakley, KS 67748 • 2,045
Oaklyn, NJ 08107 • 4,430
Oakmont, PA 15139 • 6,961
Oak Orchard, DE 19966 • 350
Oak Park, CA 91301 • 5,000
Oak Park, IL 60301-05 • 53,648
Oak Park, MI 48237 • 30,462
Oak Ridge, FL 32809 • 15,388
Oakridge, OR 97463 • 3,063
Oak Ridge, TN 37830 • 27,310
Oakton, VA 22124 • 24,610
Oak Valley, NJ 08090 • 5,400
Oakville, CT 06779 • 8,741
Oakville, MO 63129 • 31,750
Oakwood, GA 30566 • 1,464
Oakwood, IL 61858 • 1,533
Oakwood, OH 45419 • 3,392
Oberlin, KS 67749 • 2,197
Oberlin, LA 70655 • 1,808
Oberlin, OH 44074 • 8,191
Obetz, OH 43207 • 3,167
Obion, TN 38240 • 1,241
Obion ▫, TN • 31,717
Oblong, IL 62449 • 1,616
O'Brien ▫, IA • 15,444
Ocala, FL 32670-78 • 42,045
Ocean ▫, NJ • 433,203
Oceana, WV 24870 • 1,791
Oceana ▫, MI • 22,454
Ocean Bluff, MA 02065 • 2,500
Ocean City, FL 32548 • 5,422
Ocean City, MD 21842 • 5,146
Ocean City, NJ 08226 • 15,512
Ocean Gate, NJ 08740 • 2,078
Ocean Grove, MA 02777 • 4,560
Oceano, CA 93445 • 6,169
Ocean Park, WA 98640 • 1,650
Ocean Pointe, NJ 07757 • 6,146
Oceanside, CA 92054-56 • 128,398
Oceanside, NY 11572 • 32,423
Ocean Springs, MS 39564-65 • 14,658
Ocean [Township], NJ 07712 • 23,570
Ocean View, DE 19970 • 606
Oceanville, NJ 08231 • 1,000
Ochiltree ▫, TX • 9,128
Ocilla, GA 31774 • 3,182
Ocoee, FL 34761 • 12,778
Oconee ▫, GA • 17,618
Oconee ▫, SC • 57,494
Oconomowoc, WI 53066 • 10,993
Oconto, WI 54153 • 4,474
Oconto ▫, WI • 30,226
Oconto Falls, WI 54154 • 2,584
Odebolt, IA 51458 • 1,158
Odell, IL 60460 • 1,030
Odem, TX 78370 • 2,366
Odenton, MD 21113 • 12,833
Odessa, DE 19730 • 303
Odessa, MO 64076 • 3,695
Odessa, TX 79760-68 • 89,699

Odin, IL 62870 • 1,150
Odon, IN 47562 • 1,475
O'Donnell, TX 79351 • 1,102
Oelwein, IA 50662 • 6,493
O'Fallon, IL 62269 • 16,073
O'Fallon, MO 63366 • 18,698
Ogallala, NE 69153 • 5,095
Ogden, UT 84201 • 1,000
Ogden, KS 66517 • 1,494
Ogden, UT 84401-14 • 63,909
Ogdensburg, NJ 07439 • 2,722
Ogdensburg, NY 13669 • 13,521
Ogemaw ▫, MI • 18,681
Ogle ▫, IL • 45,957
Oglesby, IL 61348 • 3,619
Oglethorpe, GA 31068 • 1,302
Oglethorpe ▫, GA • 9,763
Ogunquit, ME 03907 • 1,492
Ohatchee, AL 36271 • 1,042
Ohio ▫, IN • 5,315
Ohio ▫, KY • 21,105
Ohio ▫, WV • 50,871
Ohioville, PA 15009 • 3,865
Oil City, LA 71061 • 1,282
Oil City, PA 16301 • 11,949
Oildale, CA 93308 • 26,553
Oilton, OH 74052 • 1,060
Ojai, CA 93023-24 • 7,613
Okaloosa ▫, FL • 143,776
Okanogan, WA 98840 • 2,370
Okanogan ▫, WA • 33,350
Okarche, OK 73762 • 1,160
Okauchee, WI 53069 • 2,300
Okauchee Lake, WI 53058 • 3,819
Okawville, IL 62271 • 1,274
Okeechobee, FL 34972-74 • 4,943
Okeechobee ▫, FL • 29,627
Okeene, OK 73763 • 1,343
Okemah, OK 74859 • 3,380
Okemos, MI 48864 • 20,216
Okfuskee ▫, OK • 11,551
Oklahoma ▫, OK • 599,611
Oklahoma City, OK 73101-80 • 444,719
Oklawaha, FL 32179 • 1,200
Okmulgee, OK 74447 • 13,441
Okmulgee ▫, OK • 36,490
Okolona, KY 40219 • 18,902
Okolona, MS 38860 • 3,267
Oktibbeha ▫, MS • 38,375
Ola, AR 72853 • 1,090
Olathe, CO 81425 • 1,263
Olathe, KS 66061-62 • 63,352
Olcott, NY 14126 • 1,432
Old Bethpage, NY 11804 • 5,610
Old Bridge, NJ 08857 • 22,151
Old Forge, NY 13420 • 1,061
Old Forge, PA 18518 • 8,834
Oldham ▫, KY • 33,263
Oldham ▫, TX • 2,278
Old Harbor, AK 99643 • 284
Old Orchard Beach, ME 04064 • 7,789
Old Saybrook, CT 06475 • 1,820
Oldsmar, FL 34677 • 8,361
Old Tappan, NJ 07675 • 4,254
Old Town, ME 04468 • 8,317
Olean, NY 14760 • 16,946
Olive Branch, MS 38654 • 3,567
Olive Hill, KY 41164 • 1,809
Olivehurst, CA 95961 • 9,738
Oliver, PA 15472 • 3,271
Oliver ▫, ND • 2,381
Oliver Springs, TN 37840 • 3,433
Olivet, MI 49076 • 1,604
Olivette, MO 63132 • 7,573
Olivia, MN 56277 • 2,623
Olla, LA 71465 • 1,410
Olmito, TX 78575 • 1,400
Olmos Park, TX 78212 • 2,161
Olmsted ▫, MN • 106,470
Olmsted Falls, OH 44138 • 6,741
Olney, IL 62450 • 8,664
Olney, MD 20832 • 23,019
Olney, TX 76374 • 3,519
Olton, TX 79064 • 2,116
Olympia, WA 98501-07 • 33,840
Olympia Heights, FL 33175 • 36,900
Olyphant, PA 18447 • 5,222
Omaha, NE 68101-72 • 335,795
Omak, WA 98841 • 4,117
Omro, WI 54963 • 2,836
Onalaska, WI 54650 • 11,284
Onancock, VA 23417 • 1,434
Onarga, IL 60955 • 1,281
Onawa, IA 51040 • 2,936
Onaway, MI 49765 • 1,039
Oneco, FL 34264 • 6,417
Oneida, NY 13421 • 10,850
Oneida, OH 45042 • 1,650
Oneida, TN 37841 • 3,502
Oneida ▫, ID • 3,492
Oneida ▫, NY • 250,836
Oneida ▫, WI • 31,679
O'Neill, NE 68763 • 3,852
Oneonta, AL 35121 • 4,844
Oneonta, NY 13820 • 13,954
Onida, SD 57564 • 761
Onondaga ▫, NY • 468,973
Onset, MA 02558 • 1,461
Onslow ▫, NC • 149,838
Ontario, CA 91761-62 • 133,179
Ontario, OH 44862 • 4,026
Ontario, OR 97914 • 9,392
Ontario ▫, NY • 95,101
Ontonagon, MI 49953 • 2,040
Ontonagon ▫, MI • 8,854
Oolitic, IN 47451 • 1,424
Ooltewah, TN 37363 • 1,200
Oostburg, WI 53070 • 1,931
Opal Cliffs, CA 95062 • 5,940
Opa-Locka, FL 33054-56 • 15,283
Opelika, AL 36801-03 • 22,122
Opelousas, LA 70570-71 • 18,151
Opp, AL 36467 • 6,985
Opportunity, WA 99206 • 22,326
Oquawka, IL 61469 • 1,442
Oracle, AZ 85623 • 3,043
Oradell, NJ 07649 • 8,024
Oran, MO 63771 • 1,164
Orange, CA 92664-69 • 110,658
Orange ▫ 06477 • 12,830
Orange, MA 01364 • 3,791
Orange, NJ 07050-52 • 29,925
Orange, TX 77630-31 • 19,381

Orange, VA 22960 • 2,582
Orange ▫, CA • 2,410,556
Orange ▫, FL • 677,491
Orange ▫, IN • 18,409
Orange ▫, NY • 307,647
Orange ▫, NC • 93,851
Orange ▫, TX • 80,509
Orange ▫, VT • 26,149
Orange ▫, VA • 21,421
Orange Beach, AL 36561 • 2,253
Orangeburg, SC 29115-16 • 13,739
Orangeburg ▫, SC • 84,803
Orange City, FL 32763 • 5,347
Orange City, IA 51041 • 4,940
Orange Cove, MS 39503 • 15,676
Orange Grove, TX 78372 • 1,175
Orange Lake, FL 32681 • 1,000
Orange Park, FL 32073 • 9,488
Orangevale, CA 95662 • 26,266
Orangeville, UT 84537 • 1,459
Orchard City, CO 81410 • 2,218
Orchard Homes, MT 59801 • 10,317
Orchard Mesa, CO 81501 • 5,977
Orchard Park, NY 14127 • 3,280
Orchards, WA 98662 • 8,828
Orchard Valley, WY 82007 • 3,321
Orcutt, CA 93455 • 1,500
Ord, NE 68862 • 2,481
Ordway, CO 81063 • 1,025
Oregon, IL 61061 • 3,891
Oregon, OH 43616 • 18,334
Oregon, WI 53575 • 4,519
Oregon ▫, MO • 9,470
Oregon City, OR 97045 • 14,698
Orem, UT 84057-59 • 67,561
Orfordville, WI 53576 • 1,219
Orient, NY 11957 • 1,000
Orinda, CA 94563 • 16,642
Orion, IL 61273 • 1,821
Oriskany, NY 13424 • 1,450
Orland, CA 95963 • 5,052
Orland Park, IL 60462 • 35,720
Orlando, FL 32801-72 • 164,693
Orland Park, IL 60462 • 35,720
Orleans, IN 47452 • 2,083
Orleans, IN 47452 • 2,161
Orleans, MA 02653 • 1,699
Orleans, VT 05860 • 806
Orleans ▫, LA • 496,938
Orleans ▫, NY • 41,846
Orleans ▫, VT • 24,053
Orlovista, FL 32811 • 5,990
Ormond Beach, FL 32174-76 • 29,721
Ormond By The Sea, FL 32174 • 8,157
Orofino, ID 83544 • 2,868
Orono, ME 04473 • 9,789
Orono, MN 55323 • 7,285
Orosi, CA 93647 • 5,486
Oroville, CA 95965-66 • 11,960
Oroville, WA 98844 • 1,505
Orrville, OH 44667 • 7,712
Orting, WA 98360 • 2,106
Ortonville, MI 48462 • 1,252
Ortonville, MN 56278 • 2,205
Orwell, OH 44076 • 1,258
Orwigsburg, PA 17961 • 2,780
Osage, IA 50461 • 3,439
Osage, WY 82723 • 350
Osage ▫, KS • 15,248
Osage ▫, MO • 12,018
Osage ▫, OK • 41,645
Osage Beach, MO 65065 • 2,599
Osage City, KS 66523 • 2,689
Osakis, MN 56360 • 1,256
Osawatomie, KS 66064 • 4,590
Osborne, KS 67473 • 1,778
Osborne ▫, KS • 4,867
Osburn, ID 83849 • 1,579
Osceola, AR 72370 • 8,930
Osceola, IN 46561 • 1,999
Osceola, IA 50213 • 4,164
Osceola, WI 54020 • 2,075
Osceola ▫, FL • 107,728
Osceola ▫, IA • 7,267
Osceola ▫, MI • 20,146
Osceola Mills, PA 16666 • 1,310
Oscoda, MI 48750 • 1,061
Oscoda ▫, MI • 7,842
Osgood, IN 47037 • 1,688
Oshkosh, WI 54901-04 • 55,006
Oskaloosa, IA 52577 • 10,632
Oskaloosa, KS 66066 • 1,074
Osprey, FL 34229 • 2,597
Osseo, MN 55369 • 2,704
Osseo, WI 54758 • 1,551
Ossian, IN 46777 • 2,428
Ossining, NY 10562 • 22,582
Osterville, MA 02655 • 2,911
Oswego, IL 60543 • 3,876
Oswego, KS 67356 • 1,870
Oswego, NY 13126 • 19,195
Oswego ▫, NY • 121,771
Otay, CA 92010 • 6,400
Oteen, NC 28805 • 1,400
Otego, NY 13825 • 1,068
Otero ▫, CO • 20,185
Otero ▫, NM • 51,928
Othello, WA 99327 • 4,638
Otis Orchards, WA 99027 • 3,200
Otoe ▫, NE • 14,252
Otsego, MI 49078 • 3,937
Otsego ▫, MI • 17,957
Otsego ▫, NY • 60,517
Ottawa, IL 61350 • 17,451
Ottawa, KS 66067 • 10,667
Ottawa, OH 45875 • 3,999
Ottawa ▫, KS • 5,634
Ottawa ▫, MI • 187,768
Ottawa ▫, OH • 40,029
Ottawa ▫, OK • 30,561
Ottawa Hills, OH 43606 • 4,543
Otterbein, IN 47970 • 1,291
Otter Tail ▫, MN • 50,714
Ottumwa, IA 52501 • 24,488
Ouachita ▫, AR • 30,574
Ouachita ▫, LA • 142,191
Ouray, CO 81427 • 644
Ouray ▫, CO • 2,295
Outagamie ▫, WI • 140,510
Overland, MO 63114 • 17,987
Overland Park, KS 66204 • 111,790
Overlea, MD 21206 • 12,137
Overlook, OH 45431 • 6,000
Overton, NV 89040 • 1,111

Robbins, IL 60472 • 7,498
Robbinsdale, MN 55422 • 14,396
Robert Lee, TX 76945 • 1,276
Roberts, WI 54023 • 1,043
Roberts □, SD • 9,914
Roberts □, TX • 1,025
Robertsdale, AL 36567 • 2,401
Robertson □, KY • 2,124
Robertson □, TN • 41,494
Robertson □, TX • 15,511
Robertsville, NJ 07746 • 9,841
Robeson □, NC • 105,179
Robinson, IL 62454 • 6,740
Robinson, TX 76706 • 7,111
Robstown, TX 78380 • 12,849
Rochdale, MA 01542 • 1,105
Rochelle, GA 31079 • 1,510
Rochelle, IL 61068 • 8,769
Rochelle Park, NJ 07662 • 5,587
Rochester, IL 62563 • 2,676
Rochester, IN 46975 • 5,969
Rochester, MI 48306-09 • 7,130
Rochester, MN 55901-06 • 70,745
Rochester, NH 03867-68 • 26,630
Rochester, NY 14601-92 • 231,636
Rochester, PA 15074 • 4,156
Rochester, VT 05767 • 500
Rochester, WA 98579 • 1,150
Rochester Hills, MI 48309 • 61,766
Rock □, MN • 9,806
Rock □, NE • 2,019
Rock □, WI • 139,510
Rockaway, NJ 07866 • 6,243
Rockbridge □, VA • 18,350
Rockcastle □, KY • 14,803
Rock Creek, MN 55067 • 1,040
Rock Creek 0M, OR • 8,282
Rockdale, IL 60436 • 1,709
Rockdale, MD 21207 • 5,885
Rockdale, TX 76567 • 5,235
Rockdale □, GA • 54,091
Rock Falls, IL 61071 • 9,654
Rockford, IL 61101-32 • 139,426
Rockford, MI 49341 • 3,750
Rockford, MN 55373 • 2,665
Rockford, OH 45882 • 1,119
Rock Hall, MD 21661 • 1,584
Rock Hill, MO 63124 • 5,217
Rock Hill, SC 29730-32 • 41,643
Rockingham, NC 28379 • 9,399
Rockingham □, NH • 245,845
Rockingham □, NC • 86,064
Rockingham □, VA • 57,482
Rock Island, IL 61201-04 • 40,552
Rock Island □, IL • 148,723
Rockland, ME 04841 • 7,972
Rockland, MA 02370 • 15,695
Rockland □, NY • 265,475
Rockledge, FL 32955-56 • 16,023
Rockledge, PA 19111 • 2,679
Rocklin, CA 95677 • 19,033
Rockmart, GA 30153 • 3,356
Rockport, IN 47635 • 2,315
Rockport, ME 04856 • 1,100
Rockport, MA 01966 • 4,690
Rock Port, MO 64482 • 1,438
Rockport, TX 78382 • 4,753
Rock Rapids, IA 51246 • 2,601
Rock River, WY 82083 • 190
Rocksprings, TX 78880 • 1,339
Rock Springs, WY 82901-02 • 19,050
Rockton, IL 61072 • 2,928
Rock Valley, IA 51247 • 2,540
Rockville, IN 47872 • 2,706
Rockville, MD 20847-59 • 44,835
Rockville Centre, NY 11570-71 • 24,727
Rockwall, TX 75087 • 10,486
Rockwall □, TX • 25,604
Rockwell, IA 50469 • 1,008
Rockwell, NC 28138 • 1,598
Rockwell City, IA 50579 • 1,981
Rockwell Park, NC 28213 • 2,600
Rockwood, MI 48173 • 3,141
Rockwood, OR 97233 • 11,000
Rockwood, PA 15557 • 1,014
Rockwood, TN 37854 • 5,348
Rocky Creek, FL 33615 • 7,800
Rocky Ford, CO 81067 • 4,162
Rocky Hill, CT 06067 • 14,559
Rocky Mount, NC 27801-04 • 48,997
Rocky Mount, VA 24151 • 4,098
Rocky Point, NY 11778 • 8,596
Rocky River, OH 44116 • 20,410
Rodeo, CA 94572 • 7,589
Roderfield, WV 24881 • 1,200
Rodney Village, DE 19901 • 1,745
Roebling, NJ 08554 • 2,415
Roebuck, SC 29376 • 1,966
Roeland Park, KS 66203 • 7,706
Roessleville, NY 12205 • 10,753
Roger Mills □, OK • 4,147
Rogers, AR 72756-57 • 24,692
Rogers, TX 76569 • 1,131
Rogers □, OK • 55,170
Rogers City, MI 49779 • 3,642
Rogersville, AL 35652 • 1,125
Rogersville, TN 37857 • 4,149
Rogue River, OR 97537 • 1,759
Rohnert Park, CA 94927-28 • 36,326
Roland, IA 50236 • 1,035
Roland, OK 74954 • 2,481
Rolette, ND • 12,772
Rolette □, ND • 12,772
Rolla, MO 65401 • 14,090
Rolla, ND 58367 • 1,286
Rolling Fork, MS 39159 • 2,444
Rolling Hills Estates, CA 90274 • 7,789
Rolling Meadows, IL 60008 • 22,591
Rollinsford, NH 03869 • 2,645
Roma, TX 78584 • 8,059
Rome, GA 30161-65 • 30,326
Rome, IL 61562 • 1,902
Rome, NY 13440 • 44,350
Rome City, IN 46784 • 1,138
Romeo, MI 48065 • 3,520
Romeoville, IL 60441 • 14,074
Romney, WV 26757 • 1,966
Romulus, MI 48174 • 22,897
Ronan, MT 59864 • 1,547
Ronceverte, WV 24970 • 1,754
Ronkonkoma, NY 11779 • 20,391
Roodhouse, IL 62082 • 2,139
Rooks □, KS • 6,039

Roosevelt, NY 11575 • 15,030
Roosevelt, UT 84066 • 3,915
Roosevelt □, MT • 10,999
Roosevelt □, NM • 16,702
Roosevelt Park, MI 49441 • 3,885
Rosamond, CA 93560 • 7,430
Roscoe, IL 61073 • 2,079
Roscoe, TX 79545 • 1,446
Roscommon □, MI • 19,776
Roseau, MN 56751 • 2,396
Roseau □, MN • 15,026
Roseboro, NC 28382 • 1,441
Rosebud, TX 76570 • 1,638
Rosebud □, MT • 10,505
Roseburg, OR 97470 • 17,032
Rosedale, MD 21237 • 18,703
Rosedale, MS 38769 • 2,595
Rose Hill, KS 67133 • 2,399
Rose Hill, NC 28458 • 1,287
Rose Hill, VA 22310 • 12,675
Roseland, CA 95407 • 8,779
Roseland, FL 32957 • 1,379
Roseland, LA 70456 • 1,093
Roseland, NJ 07068 • 4,847
Roseland, OH 44906 • 3,000
Roselle, IL 60172 • 20,819
Roselle, NJ 07203 • 20,314
Roselle Park, NJ 07204 • 12,805
Rosemead, CA 91770 • 51,638
Rosemont, CA 95826 • 22,851
Rosemount, MN 55068 • 8,622
Rosenberg, TX 77471 • 20,183
Rosepine, LA 70659 • 1,135
Roseto, PA 18013 • 1,555
Roseville, CA 95678 • 44,685
Roseville, IL 61473 • 1,151
Roseville, MI 48066 • 51,412
Roseville, MN 55113 • 33,485
Roseville, OH 43777 • 1,847
Rosewood Heights, IL 62024 • 4,821
Rosiclare, IL 62982 • 1,378
Roslyn Heights, NY 11577 • 6,405
Ross □, 45061 • 2,124
Ross □, OH • 69,303
Rossford, OH 43460 • 5,861
Rossmoor, CA 90720 • 9,893
Ross Township, PA 15237 • 33,482
Rossville, GA 30741-42 • 3,601
Rossville, IL 60963 • 1,334
Rossville, IN 46065 • 1,175
Rossville, KS 66533 • 1,052
Roswell, GA 30075-77 • 47,923
Roswell, NM 88201-02 • 44,654
Rotan, TX 79546 • 1,913
Rothschild, WI 54474 • 3,310
Rothsville, PA 17543 • 2,097
Rotterdam, NY 12303 • 21,228
Roulette, PA 16746 • 1,500
Round Lake, IL 60073 • 3,550
Round Lake Beach, IL 60073 • 16,434
Round Mountain, NV 89045 • 210
Round Rock, TX 78664 • 30,923
Roundup, MT 59072 • 1,808
Rouses Point, NY 12979 • 2,377
Routt □, CO • 14,088
Rouzerville, PA 17250 • 1,188
Rowan □, KY • 20,353
Rowan □, NC • 110,605
Rowland, NC 28383 • 1,139
Rowland Heights, CA 91748 • 32,700
Rowlett, TX 75088 • 23,260
Rowley, MA 01969 • 1,144
Roxboro, NC 27573 • 7,332
Roxbury, MO • 48,043
Roy, UT 84067 • 24,603
Royal Oak, MI 48067-73 • 65,410
Royal Pines, NC 28704 • 1,600
Royalton, IL 62983 • 1,191
Royersford, PA 19468 • 4,458
Royse City, TX 75089 • 2,206
Royston, GA 30662 • 2,758
Rubidoux, CA 92509 • 24,367
Rugby, ND 58368 • 2,909
Ruidoso, NM 88345 • 4,600
Ruidoso Downs, NM 88346 • 920
Ruleville, MS 38771 • 3,245
Rumford, ME 04276 • 5,419
Rumson, NJ 07760 • 6,701
Runge, TX 78151 • 1,139
Runnels □, TX • 11,294
Runnemede, NJ 08078 • 9,042
Rupert, ID 83350 • 5,455
Rupert, WV 25984 • 1,104
Rural Hall, NC 27045 • 1,652
Rush □, IN • 18,129
Rush □, KS • 3,842
Rush City, MN 55069 • 1,497
Rushford, MN 55971 • 1,485
Rushmere, VA 23430 • 1,064
Rush Springs, OK 73082 • 1,229
Rushville, IL 62681 • 3,229
Rushville, IN 46173 • 5,533
Rushville, NE 69360 • 1,127
Rusk, TX 75785 • 4,366
Rusk □, TX • 43,735
Rusk □, WI • 15,079
Ruskin, FL 33570-73 • 6,046
Russell, KS 67665 • 4,781
Russell, KY 41169 • 4,014
Russell, PA 16345 • 1,000
Russell □, AL • 46,860
Russell □, KS • 7,835
Russell □, KY • 14,716
Russell □, VA • 28,667
Russell Springs, KY 42642 • 2,363
Russellville, AL 35653 • 7,812
Russellville, AR 72801 • 21,260
Russellville, KY 42276 • 7,454
Russellville, OR 97216 • 6,500
Russellville, TN 37860 • 1,069
Ruston, LA 71270-73 • 20,027
Ruth, NV 89319 • 550
Rutherford, NJ 07070-75 • 17,790
Rutherford, TN 38369 • 1,303
Rutherford □, NC • 56,918
Rutherford □, TN • 118,570
Rutherfordton, NC 28139 • 3,617
Rutland, MA 01543 • 2,145
Rutland, VT 05701-02 • 18,230
Rutland □, VT • 62,142
Rye, NH 03870 • 835
Rye, NY 10580 • 14,936
Rye Brook, NY 10573 • 7,765

S

Sabattus, ME 04280 • 3,696
Sabetha, KS 66534 • 2,341
Sabina, OH 45169 • 2,662
Sabinal, TX 78881 • 1,446
Sabine □, LA • 22,646
Sabine □, TX • 9,586
Sac □, IA • 12,324
Sacaton, AZ 85221 • 1,452
Sac City, IA 50583 • 2,492
Sachse, TX 75040 • 5,346
Sackets Harbor, NY 13685 • 1,313
Saco, ME 04072 • 15,181
Sacramento, CA 95801-66 • 369,365
Sacramento □, CA • 1,041,219
Saddle Brook, NJ 07662 • 13,296
Saddle River, NJ 07458 • 2,950
Saegertown, PA 16433 • 1,066
Safety Harbor, FL 34695 • 15,124
Safford, AZ 85546 • 7,359
Sagadahoc □, ME • 33,535
Sagamore, MA 02561 • 2,589
Sagamore Hills, OH 44067 • 4,700
Sag Harbor, NY 11963 • 2,134
Saginaw, MI 48601-08 • 69,512
Saginaw, TX 76179 • 8,551
Saginaw □, MI • 211,946
Saguache, CO • 4,619
Saint Albans, VT 05478 • 7,339
Saint Albans, WV 25177 • 11,194
Saint Andrews, SC 29407 • 9,908
Saint Andrews, SC 29210 • 25,692
Saint Ann, MO 63074 • 14,489
Saint Anne, IL 60964 • 1,153
Saint Ansgar, IA 50472 • 1,063
Saint Anthony, ID 83445 • 3,010
Saint Augustine, FL 32084-86 • 11,692
Saint Bernard, OH 45217 • 5,344
Saint Bernard □, LA • 66,631
Saint Charles, IL 60174-75 • 22,501
Saint Charles, MD 20601 • 28,717
Saint Charles, MI 48655 • 2,144
Saint Charles, MN 55972 • 2,642
Saint Charles, MO 63301-03 • 54,555
Saint Charles □, LA • 42,437
Saint Charles □, MO • 212,907
Saint Charles Mesa, CO 81006 • 7,050
Saint Clair, MI 48079 • 5,116
Saint Clair, MO 63077 • 3,917
Saint Clair, PA 17970 • 3,524
Saint Clair □, AL • 50,009
Saint Clair □, IL • 262,852
Saint Clair □, MI • 145,607
Saint Clair □, MO • 8,457
Saint Clair Shores, MI 48080-82 • 68,107
Saint Clairsville, OH 43950 • 5,162
Saint Cloud, FL 34769-73 • 12,453
Saint Cloud, MN 56301-04 • 48,812
Saint Croix □, WI • 50,251
Saint Croix Falls, WI 54024 • 1,640
Saint David, AZ 85630 • 1,500
Saint Elmo, IL 62458 • 1,473
Saint Francis, KS 67756 • 1,495
Saint Francis, MN 55070 • 2,538
Saint Francis, SD 57572 • 815
Saint Francis, WI 53207 • 9,245
Saint Francis □, AR • 28,497
Saint Francisville, LA 70775 • 1,700
Saint Francisville, MO • 48,904
Sainte Genevieve, MO 63670 • 4,411
Sainte Genevieve □, MO • 16,037
Saint George, SC 29477 • 2,077
Saint George, UT 84770-71 • 28,502
Saint Georges, DE 19733 • 500
Saint Helena, CA 94574 • 4,990
Saint Helena □, LA • 9,874
Saint Helens, OR 97051 • 7,535
Saint Henry, OH 45883 • 1,907
Saint Ignace, MI 49781 • 2,568
Saint Ignatius, MT 59865 • 778
Saint James, MN 56081 • 4,364
Saint James, MO 65559 • 3,256
Saint James, NY 11780 • 12,703
Saint James □, LA • 20,879
Saint James City, FL 33956 • 1,094
Saint Jo, TX 76265 • 1,048
Saint John, IN 46373 • 4,921
Saint John, KS 67576 • 1,357
Saint Johns, AZ 85936 • 3,294
Saint Johns, MI 48879 • 7,284
Saint Johns, MO 63114 • 7,466
Saint Johns □, FL • 83,829
Saint Johnsbury, VT 05819 • 6,424
Saint Johnsville, NY 13452 • 1,825
Saint John the Baptist □, LA • 39,996
Saint Joseph, IL 61873 • 2,052
Saint Joseph, LA 71366 • 1,517
Saint Joseph, MI 49085 • 9,214
Saint Joseph, MN 56374 • 3,294
Saint Joseph, MO 64501-08 • 71,852
Saint Joseph □, IN • 247,052
Saint Joseph □, MI • 58,913
Saint Landry □, LA • 80,331
Saint Lawrence □, NY • 111,974
Saint Leo, FL 33574 • 1,009
Saint Louis, MO 63101-88 • 396,685
Saint Louis □, MN • 198,213
Saint Louis □, MO • 993,529
Saint Louis Park, MN 55426 • 43,787
Saint Lucie □, FL • 150,171
Saint Maries, ID 83861 • 2,442
Saint Martin □, LA • 43,978
Saint Martinville, LA 70582 • 7,137
Saint Mary □, LA • 58,086
Saint Marys, AK 99658 • 441
Saint Marys, GA 31558 • 8,187
Saint Marys, KS 66536 • 1,791
Saint Marys, OH 45885 • 8,441
Saint Marys, PA 15857 • 5,511
Saint Marys, WV 26170 • 2,148
Saint Marys □, MD • 75,974
Saint Marys City, MD 20686 • 3,200
Saint Matthews, KY 40207 • 15,800
Saint Matthews, SC 29135 • 2,345
Saint Michael, MN 55376 • 2,506
Saint Michaels, MD 21663 • 1,301

Saint Paris, OH 43072 • 1,842
Saint Paul, AK 99660 • 763
Saint Paul, IN 47272 • 1,032
Saint Paul, MN 55101-89 • 272,235
Saint Paul, MO 63366 • 1,192
Saint Paul, NE 68873 • 2,009
Saint Paul, VA 24283 • 1,007
Saint Paul Park, MN 55071 • 4,965
Saint Pauls, NC 28384 • 1,992
Saint Peter, MN 56082 • 9,421
Saint Peters, MO 63376 • 45,779
Saint Petersburg, FL 33701-84 • 238,629
Saint Petersburg Beach, FL 33706 • 9,200
Saint Rose, LA 70087 • 2,800
Saint Simons Island, GA 31522 • 12,026
Saint Stephen, SC 29479 • 1,697
Saint Stephens, NC 28601 • 8,734
Saint Tammany □, LA • 144,508
Salamanca, NY 14779 • 6,566
Sale Creek, TN 37373 • 1,050
Salem, AR 72576 • 1,474
Salem, IL 62881 • 7,470
Salem, IN 47167 • 5,619
Salem, MA 01970-71 • 38,091
Salem, MO 65560 • 4,486
Salem, NH 03079 • 12,000
Salem, NJ 08079 • 6,883
Salem, OH 44460 • 12,233
Salem, OR 97301-14 • 107,786
Salem, SD 57058 • 1,289
Salem, UT 84653 • 2,284
Salem, VA 24153 • 23,756
Salem, WV 26426 • 2,063
Salem, WI 53168 • 1,020
Salem □, NJ • 65,294
Salida, CO 81201 • 4,737
Salina, KS 67401-02 • 42,303
Salina, OK 74365 • 1,153
Salina, UT 84654 • 1,943
Salinas, CA 93901-15 • 108,777
Saline, MI 48176 • 6,660
Saline □, AR • 64,183
Saline □, IL • 26,551
Saline □, KS • 49,301
Saline □, MO • 23,523
Saline □, NE • 12,715
Salineville, OH 43945 • 1,474
Salisbury, CT 06068 • 1,600
Salisbury, MD 21801-03 • 20,592
Salisbury, MA 01952 • 3,729
Salisbury, MO 65281 • 1,881
Salisbury, NC 28144-46 • 23,087
Sallisaw, OK 74955 • 7,122
Salmon, ID 83467 • 2,941
Salmon Creek, WA 98665 • 11,989
Saltillo, MS 38866 • 1,782
Salt Lake □, UT • 725,956
Salt Lake City, UT 84101-90 • 159,936
Salt Springs, FL 32113 • 1,500
Saltville, VA 24370 • 2,300
Saltwater, WA 98188 • 2,200
Saluda, SC 29138 • 2,798
Saluda □, SC • 16,357
Salyersville, KY 41465 • 1,917
Samoset, FL 34208 • 3,119
Sampson □, NC • 47,297
Samson, AL 36477 • 2,190
Samtown, LA 71301 • 3,500
San Andreas, CA 95249 • 2,115
San Angelo, TX 76901-06 • 84,474
San Anselmo, CA 94960 • 11,743
San Antonio, TX 78201-99 • 935,933
Sanatoga, PA 19464 • 5,534
San Augustine, TX 75972 • 2,337
San Augustine □, TX • 7,999
San Benito, TX 78586 • 20,125
San Benito □, CA • 36,697
San Bernardino, CA 92401-27 • 164,164
San Bernardino □, CA • 1,418,380
Sanborn, IA 51248 • 1,345
Sanborn □, SD • 2,833
San Bruno, CA 94066 • 38,961
San Carlos, AZ 85550 • 2,918
San Carlos, CA 94070 • 26,167
San Carlos Park, FL 33912 • 11,785
San Clemente, CA 92672-74 • 41,100
Sandalfoot Cove, FL 33433 • 14,214
Sanders □, MT • 8,669
Sanderson, TX 79848 • 1,128
Sandersville, GA 31082 • 6,290
Sand Hill, MA 02066 • 1,800
Sandia, NM 87047 • 6,742
San Diego, CA 92101-99 • 1,110,549
San Diego, TX 78384 • 4,983
San Diego □, CA • 2,498,016
San Dimas, CA 91773 • 32,397
Sandoval, IL 62882 • 1,535
Sandoval □, NM • 63,319
Sand Point, AK 99661 • 878
Sandpoint, ID 83862-65 • 5,203
Sand Springs, OK 74063 • 15,346
Sandston, VA 23150 • 3,630
Sandstone, MN 55072 • 2,057
Sandusky, MI 48471 • 2,403
Sandusky, OH 44870-71 • 29,764
Sandusky □, OH • 61,963
Sandwich, IL 60548 • 5,567
Sandwich, MA 02563 • 2,998
Sandy, OR 97055 • 4,152
Sandy, UT 84070 • 75,058
Sandy Hook, CT 06482 • 1,100
Sandy Springs, GA 30328 • 67,842
Sandy Springs, SC 29677 • 1,200
San Felipe Pueblo, NM 87001 • 1,557
San Fernando, CA 91340-46 • 22,580
Sanford, FL 32771-73 • 32,387
Sanford, ME 04073 • 10,296
Sanford, NC 27330-31 • 14,475
San Francisco, CA 94101-88 • 723,959
San Francisco □, CA • 723,959
Sangamon □, IL • 178,386
Sanger, CA 93657 • 16,839
Sanger, TX 76266 • 1,800
Sanibel, FL 33957 • 5,468
Sanilac □, MI • 39,928
San Jacinto, CA 92383 • 16,210
San Jacinto □, TX • 16,372
San Joaquin □, CA • 480,628
San Jose, CA 95101-96 • 782,248
San Juan, TX 78589 • 10,815
San Juan □, CO • 745
San Juan □, NM • 91,605
San Juan □, UT • 12,621

San Juan □, WA • 10,035
San Juan Capistrano, CA 92690-93 • 26,183
San Leandro, CA 94577-79 • 68,223
San Lorenzo, CA 94580 • 19,987
San Luis, AZ 85634 • 4,212
San Luis Obispo, CA 93401-12 • 41,958
San Luis Obispo □, CA • 217,162
San Manuel, AZ 85631 • 4,009
San Marcos, CA 92069 • 38,974
San Marcos, TX 78666-67 • 28,743
San Marino, CA 91108 • 12,959
San Mateo, CA 94401-04 • 85,486
San Mateo □, CA • 649,623
San Miguel, CO • 3,653
San Miguel □, NM • 25,743
San Pablo, CA 94806 • 25,158
San Patricio □, TX • 58,749
Sanpete □, UT • 16,259
San Rafael, CA 94901-15 • 48,404
San Ramon, CA 94583 • 35,303
San Remo, NY 11754 • 7,770
San Saba, TX 76877 • 2,626
San Saba □, TX • 5,401
Sans Souci, SC 29609 • 7,612
Santa Ana, CA 92701-08 • 293,742
Santa Anna, TX 76878 • 1,249
Santa Barbara, CA 93101-90 • 85,571
Santa Barbara □, CA • 369,608
Santa Clara, CA 95050-56 • 93,613
Santa Clara, OR 97404 • 12,834
Santa Clara □, CA • 1,497,577
Santa Clara, NM 84765 • 2,322
Santa Cruz, CA 95060-67 • 49,040
Santa Cruz, NM 87567 • 975
Santa Cruz □, AZ • 29,676
Santa Cruz □, CA • 229,734
Santa Fe, NM 87501-06 • 55,859
Santa Fe, TX 77510 • 8,429
Santa Fe □, NM • 98,928
Santa Fe Springs, CA 90670-71 • 15,520
Santa Margarita, CA 93453 • 1,200
Santa Maria, CA 93454-56 • 61,284
Santa Monica, CA 90401-11 • 86,905
Santa Paula, CA 93060-61 • 25,062
Santaquin, UT 84655 • 2,386
Santa Rosa, CA 95401-09 • 113,313
Santa Rosa, NM 88435 • 2,263
Santa Rosa □, FL • 81,608
Santa Venetia, CA 94901 • 6,000
Santa Ynez, CA 93460 • 4,200
Santee, CA 92071 • 52,902
Santo Domingo Pueblo, NM 87052 • 2,866
San Ygnacio, TX 78067 • 1,000
Sappington, MO 63126 • 10,917
Sapulpa, OK 74066-67 • 18,074
Saraland, AL 36571 • 11,751
Saranac, MI 48881 • 1,461
Saranac Lake, NY 12983 • 5,377
Sarasota, FL 34230-43 • 50,961
Sarasota □, FL • 277,776
Sarasota Springs, FL 34232 • 16,088
Saratoga, CA 95070-71 • 28,061
Saratoga, TX 77585 • 1,200
Saratoga, WY 82331 • 1,969
Saratoga □, NY • 181,276
Saratoga Springs, NY 12866 • 25,001
Sarcoxie, MO 64862 • 1,330
Sardis, GA 30456 • 1,116
Sardis, MS 38666 • 2,128
Sargent □, ND • 4,549
Sarpy □, NE • 102,583
Sartell, MN 56377 • 5,393
Satanta, KS 67870 • 1,073
Satellite Beach, FL 32937 • 9,889
Satsuma, AL 36572 • 5,194
Saugerties, NY 12477 • 3,915
Saugus, MA 01906 • 25,549
Sauk □, WI • 46,975
Sauk Centre, MN 56378 • 3,581
Sauk City, WI 53583 • 3,019
Sauk Rapids, MN 56379 • 7,825
Sauk Village, IL 60411 • 9,926
Saukville, WI 53080 • 3,695
Sault Sainte Marie, MI 49783 • 14,689
Saunders □, NE • 18,285
Saunderstown, RI 02874 • 400
Sausalito, CA 94965-66 • 7,152
Savage, MD 20763 • 2,850
Savage, MN 55378 • 9,906
Savanna, IL 61074 • 3,819
Savannah, GA 31401-20 • 137,560
Savannah, MO 64485 • 4,352
Savannah, TN 38372 • 6,547
Savoonga, AK 99769 • 519
Savoy, IL 61874 • 2,674
Sawyer □, WI • 14,181
Saxonburg, PA 16056 • 1,345
Saxtons River, VT 05154 • 541
Saybrook Manor, CT 06475 • 1,073
Saydel, IA 50313 • 3,500
Saylesville, RI 02865 • 3,510
Saylorsburg, PA 18353 • 1,500
Sayre, OK 73662 • 2,881
Sayre, PA 18840 • 5,791
Sayreville, NJ 08872 • 34,986
Sayville, NY 11782 • 16,550
Scalp Level, PA 15963 • 1,158
Scappoose, OR 97056 • 3,529
Scarborough, ME 04074 • 2,586
Scarsdale, NY 10583 • 16,987
Schaumburg, IL 60192-94 • 68,586
Schenectady, NY 12301-09 • 65,566
Schenectady □, NY • 149,285
Schererville, IN 46375 • 19,926
Schertz, TX 78154 • 10,555
Schiller Park, IL 60176 • 11,189
Schleicher □, TX • 2,990
Schley □, GA • 3,588
Schofield, WI 54476 • 2,415
Schoharie, NY 12157 • 1,045
Schoharie □, NY • 31,859
Schoolcraft, MI 49087 • 1,517
Schoolcraft □, MI • 8,302
Schroon Lake, NY 12870 • 1,100
Schulenburg, TX 78956 • 2,455
Schurz, NV 89427 • 617
Schuyler, NE 68661 • 4,052
Schuyler □, IL • 7,498
Schuyler □, MO • 4,236
Schuyler □, NY • 18,662
Schuylerville, NY 12871 • 1,364
Schuylkill □, PA • 152,585

United States Populations and ZIP Codes

Schuylkill Haven, PA 17972 • 5,610
Scioto □, OH • 80,327
Scituate, MA 02066 • 5,180
Scobey, MT 59263 • 1,154
Scotch Plains, NJ 07076 • 21,160
Scotchtown, NY 10940 • 8,765
Scotia, CA 95565 • 1,200
Scotia, NY 12302 • 7,359
Scotland, SD 57059 • 968
Scotland □, MO • 4,822
Scotland □, NC • 33,754
Scotland Neck, NC 27874 • 2,575
Scotlandville, LA 70807 • 15,113
Scott, LA 70583 • 4,912
Scott □, AR • 10,205
Scott □, IL • 5,644
Scott □, IN • 20,991
Scott □, IA • 150,979
Scott □, KS • 5,289
Scott □, KY • 23,867
Scott □, MN • 57,846
Scott □, MS • 24,137
Scott □, MO • 39,376
Scott □, TN • 18,358
Scott □, VA • 23,204
Scott City, KS 67871 • 3,785
Scott City, MO 63780 • 4,292
Scottdale, GA 30079 • 8,636
Scottdale, PA 15683 • 5,184
Scott Lake, FL 33055 • 14,588
Scottsbluff, NE 69361–63 • 13,711
Scotts Bluff □, NE • 36,025
Scottsboro, AL 35768 • 13,786
Scottsburg, IN 47170 • 5,334
Scottsdale, AZ 85250–71 • 130,069
Scotts Valley, CA 95066–67 • 8,615
Scottsville, KY 42164 • 4,278
Scottsville, NY 14546 • 1,912
Scott Township, PA 15106 • 17,118
Scottville, MI 49454 • 1,287
Scranton, PA 18501–19 • 81,805
Screven □, GA • 13,842
Scurry □, TX • 18,634
Seabreeze, DE 19971 • 350
Sea Bright, NJ 07760 • 1,693
Seabrook, MD 20706 • 7,660
Seabrook, NJ 08302 • 1,457
Seabrook, TX 77586 • 6,685
Sea Cliff, NY 11579 • 5,054
Seadrift, TX 77983 • 1,277
Seaford, DE 19973 • 5,689
Seaford, NY 11783 • 15,597
Seaford, VA 23696 • 2,340
Seagate, NC 28403 • 5,444
Sea Girt, NJ 08750 • 2,099
Seagoville, TX 75159 • 8,969
Seagraves, TX 79359 • 2,398
Sea Isle City, NJ 08243 • 2,692
Seal Beach, CA 90740 • 25,098
Sealy, TX 77474 • 4,541
Seaman, OH 45679 • 1,013
Searchlight, NV 89029 • 430
Searcy, AR 72143 • 15,180
Searcy □, AR • 7,841
Searsport, ME 04974 • 1,151
Seaside, CA 93955 • 38,901
Seaside, OR 97138 • 5,359
Seaside Heights, NJ 08751 • 2,366
Seaside Park, NJ 08752 • 1,871
Seat Pleasant, MD 20743 • 5,359
Seattle, WA 98101–99 • 516,259
Sebastian, FL 32958 • 10,205
Sebastian □, AR • 99,590
Sebewaing, MI 48759 • 1,923
Sebree, KY 42455 • 1,510
Sebring, FL 33870–72 • 8,900
Sebring, OH 44672 • 4,848
Secaucus, NJ 07094 • 14,061
Security, CO 80911 • 6,660
Sedalia, MO 65301–02 • 19,800
Sedan, KS 67361 • 1,306
Sedgwick, KS 67135 • 1,438
Sedgwick □, CO • 2,690
Sedgwick □, KS • 403,662
Sedona, AZ 86336 • 7,720
Sedro Woolley, WA 98284 • 6,031
Seekonk, MA 02771 • 12,269
Seeley, CA 92273 • 1,228
Seelyville, IN 47878 • 1,090
Seguin, TX 78155–56 • 18,853
Selah, WA 98942 • 5,113
Selawik, AK 99770 • 596
Selby, SD 57472 • 707
Selbyville, DE 19975 • 1,335
Selden, NY 11784 • 20,608
Seldovia, AK 99663 • 316
Selinsgrove, PA 17870 • 5,384
Sellersburg, IN 47172 • 5,745
Sellersville, PA 18960 • 4,419
Sells, AZ 85634 • 2,750
Selma, AL 36701–02 • 23,755
Selma, CA 93662 • 14,757
Selma, NC 27576 • 4,600
Selmer, TN 38375 • 3,838
Seminole, OK 74868 • 7,071
Seminole, TX 79360 • 6,342
Seminole □, FL • 287,529
Seminole □, GA • 9,010
Seminole □, OK • 25,412
Seminole Park, FL 34647 • 8,000
Semmes, AL 36575 • 2,250
Senath, MO 63876 • 1,622
Senatobia, MS 38668 • 4,772
Seneca, IL 61360 • 1,878
Seneca, KS 66538 • 2,027
Seneca, MO 64865 • 1,885
Seneca, PA 16346 • 1,300
Seneca, SC 29678–79 • 7,726
Seneca □, NY • 33,683
Seneca □, OH • 59,733
Seneca Falls, NY 13148 • 7,370
Sequatchie □, TN • 8,863
Sequim, WA 98382 • 3,616
Sequoyah □, OK • 33,828
Sergeant Bluff, IA 51054 • 2,772
Sesser, IL 62884 • 2,087
Seven Hills, OH 44131 • 12,339
Seven Oaks, SC 29210 • 15,722
Severn, MD 21144 • 24,499
Severna Park, MD 21146 • 25,879
Sevier □, AR • 13,637
Sevier □, TN • 51,043

Sevier □, UT • 15,431
Sevierville, TN 37862 • 7,178
Seville, OH 44273 • 1,810
Sewanee, TN 37375 • 2,128
Seward, AK 99664 • 2,699
Seward, NE 68434 • 5,634
Seward □, KS • 18,743
Seward □, NE • 15,450
Sewell, NJ 08080 • 1,870
Sewickley, PA 15143 • 4,134
Seymour, CT 06483 • 14,288
Seymour, IN 47274 • 15,576
Seymour, MO 65746 • 1,636
Seymour, TN 37865 • 7,026
Seymour, TX 76380 • 3,185
Seymour, WI 54165 • 2,782
Seymourville, LA 70764 • 2,891
Shackelford □, TX • 3,316
Shady Cove, OR 97539 • 1,351
Shady Side, MD 20764 • 4,107
Shadyside, OH 43947 • 3,934
Shady Spring, WV 25918 • 1,929
Shafter, CA 93263 • 8,409
Shaftsbury, VT 05262 • 700
Shaker Heights, OH 44120 • 30,831
Shakopee, MN 55379 • 11,739
Shaler Township, PA 15116 • 30,533
Shallowater, TX 79363 • 1,708
Shamokin, PA 17872 • 9,184
Shamokin Dam, PA 17876 • 1,690
Shamrock, TX 79079 • 2,286
Shannock, RI 02875 • 950
Shannon, GA 30172 • 1,703
Shannon, MS 38868 • 1,419
Shannon □, MO • 7,613
Shannon □, SD • 9,902
Shannontown, SC 29150 • 7,900
Sharkey □, MS • 7,066
Sharon, CT 06069 • 2,815
Sharon, MA 02067 • 14,366
Sharon, PA 16146 • 17,493
Sharon, TN 38255 • 1,047
Sharon, WI 53585 • 1,250
Sharon Hill, PA 19079 • 5,771
Sharonville, OH 45241 • 13,153
Sharp □, AR • 14,109
Sharpes, FL 32922 • 3,348
Sharpley, DE 19803 • 1,243
Sharpsburg, MD 21782 • 659
Sharpsburg, PA 15215 • 3,781
Sharpsville, PA 16150 • 4,729
Shasta □, CA • 147,036
Shattuck, OK 73858 • 1,454
Shaw, MS 38773 • 2,349
Shawano, WI 54166 • 7,598
Shawano □, WI • 37,157
Shawnee, KS 66203 • 37,993
Shawnee, OK 74801–02 • 26,017
Shawnee □, KS • 160,976
Shawneetown, IL 62984 • 1,575
Sheboygan, WI 53081–83 • 49,676
Sheboygan □, WI • 103,877
Sheboygan Falls, WI 53085 • 5,823
Sheffield, AL 35660–62 • 10,380
Sheffield, IA 50475 • 1,174
Sheffield, MA 01257 • 1,100
Sheffield, PA 16347 • 1,294
Sheffield Lake, OH 44054 • 9,825
Shelbina, MO 63468 • 2,172
Shelburn, IN 47879 • 1,147
Shelburne Falls, MA 01370 • 1,996
Shelby, MI 49455 • 48,655
Shelby, MS 38774 • 2,806
Shelby, NC 28150–51 • 14,669
Shelby, OH 44875 • 9,564
Shelby □, AL • 99,358
Shelby □, IL • 22,261
Shelby □, IN • 40,307
Shelby □, IA • 13,230
Shelby □, KY • 24,824
Shelby □, MO • 6,942
Shelby □, OH • 44,915
Shelby □, TN • 826,330
Shelby □, TX • 22,034
Shelbyville, IL 62565 • 4,943
Shelbyville, IN 46176 • 15,336
Shelbyville, KY 40065 • 6,238
Shelbyville, TN 37160 • 14,049
Sheldon, IA 51201 • 4,937
Sheldon, IL 60966 • 1,109
Sheldon, TX 77028 • 1,653
Shelley, ID 83274 • 3,536
Shell Lake, WI 54871 • 1,161
Shellman, GA 31786 • 1,162
Shell Rock, IA 50670 • 1,385
Shelter Island, NY 11964 • 1,193
Shelton, CT 06484 • 35,418
Shelton, WA 98584 • 7,241
Shenandoah, IA 51601 • 5,572
Shenandoah, PA 17976 • 6,221
Shenandoah, VA 22849 • 2,213
Shenandoah □, VA • 31,636
Shepherd, MI 48883 • 1,413
Shepherd, TX 77371 • 1,823
Shepherdstown, WV 25443 • 1,287
Shepherdsville, KY 40165 • 4,805
Sherborn, MA 01770 • 1,490
Sherburn, MN 56171 • 1,105
Sherburne, NY 13460 • 1,531
Sherburne □, MN • 41,945
Sheridan, AR 72150 • 3,098
Sheridan, CO 80110 • 4,976
Sheridan, IL 60551 • 1,288
Sheridan, IN 46069 • 2,046
Sheridan, OR 97378 • 3,979
Sheridan, WY 82801 • 13,900
Sheridan □, KS • 3,043
Sheridan □, MT • 4,732
Sheridan □, NE • 6,750
Sheridan □, ND • 2,148
Sheridan □, WY • 23,562
Sheridan Beach, WA 98155 • 6,518
Sherman, TX 75090–91 • 31,601
Sherman □, KS • 6,926
Sherman □, NE • 3,718
Sherman □, OR • 1,918
Sherman □, TX • 2,858
Sherrelwood, CO 80221 • 16,636
Sherrill, NY 13461 • 2,864
Sherwood, AR 72116 • 18,893
Sherwood, OR 97140 • 3,093
Sherwood Manor, CT 06082 • 6,357

Sherwood Park, DE 19808 • 2,000
Shiawassee □, MI • 69,770
Shickshinny, PA 18655 • 1,108
Shillington, PA 19607 • 5,062
Shiloh, OH 44878 • 11,607
Shiloh, PA 17404 • 8,245
Shiner, TX 77984 • 2,074
Shinglehouse, PA 16748 • 1,243
Shinnston, WV 26431 • 2,543
Ship Bottom, NJ 08008 • 1,352
Shippensburg, PA 17257 • 5,331
Shiprock, NM 87420 • 7,687
Shirley, MA 01464 • 1,559
Shirley, NY 11967 • 22,936
Shishmaref, AK 99772 • 456
Shively, KY 40216 • 15,535
Shoemakersville, PA 19555 • 1,443
Shore Acres, MA 02066 • 1,200
Shores Acres, RI 02852 • 410
Shoreview, MN 55112 • 24,587
Shorewood, IL 60435 • 6,264
Shorewood, MN 55331 • 5,917
Shorewood, WI 53211 • 14,116
Shorewood Hills, WI 53705 • 1,680
Short Beach, CT 06405 • 2,500
Shortsville, NY 14548 • 1,485
Shoshone, ID 83352 • 1,249
Shoshone □, ID • 13,931
Shoshoni, WY 82649 • 497
Show Low, AZ 85901 • 5,019
Shreve, OH 44676 • 1,584
Shreveport, LA 71101–10 • 198,525
Shrewsbury, MA 01545 • 23,400
Shrewsbury, MO 63119 • 6,416
Shrewsbury, NJ 07702 • 3,096
Shrewsbury, PA 17361 • 2,672
Shullsburg, WI 53586 • 1,236
Shungnak, AK 99773 • 223
Sibley, IA 51249 • 2,815
Sibley □, MN • 14,366
Sicklerville, NJ 08081 • 1,750
Sidney, IL 61877 • 1,027
Sidney, IA 51652 • 1,253
Sidney, MT 59270 • 5,217
Sidney, NE 69162 • 5,959
Sidney, NY 13838 • 4,720
Sidney, OH 45365 • 18,710
Siegle, LA 71291 • 1,600
Sierra □, CA • 3,318
Sierra □, NM • 9,912
Sierra Madre, CA 91024 • 10,762
Sierra Vista, AZ 85635–36 • 32,983
Siesta Key, FL 34242 • 7,772
Signal Hill, CA 90806 • 8,371
Signal Mountain, TN 37377 • 7,034
Sigourney, IA 52591 • 2,117
Sikeston, MO 63801 • 17,641
Siler City, NC 27344 • 4,808
Siloam Springs, AR 72761 • 8,151
Silsbee, TX 77656 • 6,368
Silt, CO 81652 • 1,095
Silver Bay, MN 55614 • 1,894
Silver Bow □, MT • 33,941
Silver City, NV 89428 • 100
Silver City, NM 88061–62 • 10,683
Silver Creek, NY 14136 • 2,927
Silverdale, WA 98383 • 7,660
Silver Grove, KY 41085 • 1,102
Silver Hill, MD 20746 • 1,580
Silver Lake, KS 66539 • 1,390
Silver Lake, MA 01887 • 2,900
Silver Lake, WI 53170 • 1,801
Silverpeak, NV 89047 • 190
Silver Spring, MD 20901–12 • 76,046
Silver Springs, FL 32688 • 1,082
Silver Springs, NV 89429 • 2,223
Silver Springs Shores, FL 32672 • 6,421
Silverton, CO 81433 • 716
Silverton, OH 45236 • 5,859
Silverton, OR 97381 • 5,635
Silview, DE 19804 • 1,500
Silvis, IL 61282 • 6,926
Simi Valley, CA 93062–65 • 100,217
Simmesport, LA 71369 • 2,092
Simpson, PA 18407 • 1,670
Simpson □, KY • 15,145
Simpson □, MS • 23,953
Simpsonville, SC 29681 • 11,708
Simsbury, CT 06070 • 5,577
Sinclair, WY 82334 • 500
Sinton, TX 78387 • 5,549
Sioux □, IA • 29,903
Sioux □, NE • 1,549
Sioux □, ND • 3,761
Sioux Center, IA 51250 • 5,074
Sioux City, IA 51101–11 • 80,505
Sioux Falls, SD 57101–18 • 100,814
Siskiyou □, CA • 43,531
Sisseton, SD 57262 • 2,181
Sistersville, WV 26175 • 1,797
Sitka, AK 99835 • 8,588
Skagit □, WA • 79,555
Skagway, AK 99840 • 692
Skamania □, WA • 8,289
Skaneateles, NY 13152 • 2,724
Skiatook, OK 74070 • 4,910
Skokie, IL 60076–77 • 59,432
Skowhegan, ME 04976 • 6,990
Sky Lake, FL 32809 • 6,202
Skyland, NV 89448 • 660
Skyland, NC 28776 • 1,100
Skyway, WA 98178 • 8,500
Slackwoods, NJ 08638 • 8,100
Slater, IA 50244 • 1,268
Slater, MO 65349 • 2,186
Slater, SC 29683 • 1,000
Slatersville, RI 02876 • 2,330
Slatington, PA 18080 • 4,678
Slaton, TX 79364 • 6,078
Slayton, MN 56172 • 2,147
Sleepy Eye, MN 56085 • 3,694
Slickville, PA 15684 • 1,178
Slidell, LA 70458–61 • 24,124
Slinger, WI 53086 • 2,340
Slippery Rock, PA 16057 • 3,008
Sloan, NY 14225 • 3,830
Sloatsburg, NY 10974 • 3,035
Slocomb, AL 36375 • 1,906
Slope □, ND • 907
Smackover, AR 71762 • 2,232
Smethport, PA 16749 • 1,734
Smith □, KS • 5,078
Smith □, MS • 14,798

Smith □, TN • 14,143
Smith □, TX • 151,309
Smith Center, KS 66967 • 2,016
Smithers, WV 25186 • 1,162
Smithfield, NC 27577 • 7,540
Smithfield, PA 15478 • 1,000
Smithfield, UT 84335 • 5,566
Smithfield, VA 23430 • 4,686
Smith River, CA 95567 • 1,000
Smiths, AL 36877 • 1,700
Smithsburg, MD 21783 • 1,221
Smithton, IL 62285 • 1,587
Smithtown, NY 11787 • 25,638
Smithville, MO 64089 • 2,525
Smithville, OH 44677 • 1,354
Smithville, TN 37166 • 3,791
Smithville, TX 78957 • 3,196
Smyrna, DE 19977 • 5,231
Smyrna, GA 30080–82 • 30,981
Smyrna, TN 37167 • 13,647
Smyth □, VA • 32,370
Sneads, FL 32460 • 1,746
Sneedville, TN 37869 • 1,446
Snellville, GA 30278 • 12,084
Snohomish, WA 98290 • 6,499
Snohomish □, WA • 465,642
Snoqualmie, WA 98065 • 1,546
Snowflake, AZ 85937 • 3,679
Snow Hill, MD 21863 • 2,217
Snow Hill, NC 28580 • 1,378
Snyder, OK 73566 • 1,619
Snyder, TX 79549 • 12,195
Snyder □, PA • 36,680
Soap Lake, WA 98851 • 1,149
Socastee, SC 29577 • 10,426
Social Circle, GA 30279 • 2,755
Socorro, NM 87801 • 8,159
Socorro □, NM • 14,764
Soda Springs, ID 83276 • 3,111
Soddy-Daisy, TN 37379 • 8,240
Sodus, NY 14551 • 1,904
Sodus Point, NY 14555 • 1,190
Solana, FL 33950 • 1,128
Solana Beach, CA 92075 • 12,962
Solano □, CA • 340,421
Soldotna, AK 99669 • 3,482
Soledad, CA 93960 • 7,146
Solomons, MD 20688 • 1,500
Solon, IA 52333 • 1,050
Solon, OH 44139 • 18,548
Solvay, NY 13209 • 6,717
Somerdale, NJ 08083 • 5,440
Somers, CT 06071 • 9,108
Somerset, KY 42501–02 • 10,733
Somerset, MA 02725 • 17,655
Somerset, NJ 08873–75 • 22,070
Somerset, OH 43783 • 1,390
Somerset, PA 15501 • 6,454
Somerset, TX 78069 • 1,144
Somerset, WI 54025 • 1,065
Somerset □, ME • 49,767
Somerset □, MD • 23,440
Somerset □, NJ • 240,279
Somerset □, PA • 78,218
Somers Point, NJ 08244 • 11,216
Somersville, CT 06072 • 1,200
Somersworth, NH 03878 • 11,249
Somerton, AZ 85350 • 5,282
Somervell □, TX • 5,360
Somerville, MA 02143 • 76,210
Somerville, NJ 08876–77 • 11,632
Somerville, TN 38068 • 2,047
Somerville, TX 77879 • 1,542
Somonauk, IL 60552 • 1,263
Sonoma, CA 95476 • 8,121
Sonoma □, CA • 388,222
Sonora, CA 95370 • 4,153
Sonora, TX 76950 • 2,751
Soperton, GA 30457 • 2,797
Sophia, WV 25921 • 1,182
Soquel, CA 95073 • 9,188
Sorrento, LA 70778 • 1,119
Souderton, PA 18964 • 5,957
Sound Beach, NY 11789 • 9,102
South Acton, MA 01720 • 3,220
South Amboy, NJ 08879 • 7,863
South Amherst, MA 01002 • 5,053
South Amherst, OH 44001 • 1,765
Southampton, NY 11968–69 • 3,980
Southampton □, VA • 17,550
South Ashburnham, MA 01466 • 1,110
Southaven, MS 38671 • 17,949
South Bay, FL 33493 • 3,558
South Belmar, NJ 07719 • 1,482
South Beloit, IL 61080 • 4,072
South Bend, IN 46601–80 • 105,511
South Bend, WA 98586 • 1,551
South Berwick, ME 03908 • 5,877
Southborough, MA 01772 • 1,450
South Boston, VA 24592 • 6,997
South Bound Brook, NJ 08880 • 4,185
South Bradenton, FL 34205 • 20,398
South Broadway, WA 98902 • 2,574
Southbridge, MA 01550 • 13,631
South Burlington, VT 05403 • 12,809
Southbury, CT 06488 • 3,000
South Charleston, OH 45368 • 1,626
South Charleston, WV 25303 • 13,645
South Chicago Heights, IL 60411 • 3,597
South Congaree, SC 29169 • 2,406
South Connellsville, PA 15425 • 2,204
South Dartmouth, MA 02748 • 9,850
South Daytona, FL 32121 • 12,482
South Decatur, GA 30034 • 19,350
South Deerfield, MA 01373 • 1,906
South Dennis, MA 02660 • 2,500
South Duxbury, MA 02332 • 3,017
South Easton, MA 02375 • 1,530
South Elgin, IL 60177 • 7,474
South El Monte, CA 91733 • 20,850
Southern Pines, NC 28387–88 • 9,129
South Euclid, OH 44121 • 23,866
South Fallsburg, NY 12779 • 2,115
South Farmingdale, NY 11735 • 15,377
Southfield, MI 48034 • 75,728
South Fork, PA 15956 • 1,197
South Fulton, TN 38257 • 2,479
South Gastonia, NC 28052 • 5,487
South Gate, CA 90280 • 86,284
Southgate, FL 34239 • 7,324
Southgate, KY 41071 • 3,266
South Gate, MD 21061 • 27,564

Southgate, MI 48195 • 30,771
South Glastonbury, CT 06073 • 1,570
Southglenn, CO 80122 • 43,087
South Glens Falls, NY 12801 • 3,506
South Grafton, MA 01560 • 2,610
South Hackensack, NJ 07606 • 2,229
South Hadley, MA 01075 • 5,340
South Hadley Falls, MA 01075 • 5,100
South Hamilton, MA 01982 • 2,720
South Haven, IN 46383 • 6,112
South Haven, MI 49090 • 5,563
South Hill, NY 14850 • 5,423
South Hill, VA 23970 • 4,217
South Hingham, MA 02043 • 4,080
South Holland, IL 60473 • 22,105
South Hooksett, NH 03106 • 3,638
South Hopkinton, RI 02813 • 900
South Houston, TX 77587 • 14,207
South Huntington, NY 11746 • 9,624
South Hutchinson, KS 67505 • 2,444
Southington, CT 06489 • 38,518
South International Falls, MN 56679 • 2,806
South Jacksonville, IL 62650 • 3,187
South Jordan, UT 84065 • 12,220
South Lake Tahoe, CA 95702 • 21,586
South Lancaster, MA 01561 • 1,772
South Laramie, WY 82070 • 1,500
South Laurel, MD 20708 • 18,591
South Lebanon, OH 45065 • 2,696
South Lockport, NY 14094 • 7,112
South Lyon, MI 48178 • 5,857
South Miami, FL 33143 • 10,404
South Miami Heights, FL 33157 • 30,030
South Milwaukee, WI 53172 • 20,958
South Nyack, NY 10960 • 3,352
South Ogden, UT 84403 • 12,105
Southold, NY 11971 • 5,192
South Orange, NJ 07079 • 16,390
South Paris, ME 04281 • 2,320
South Pasadena, CA 91030 • 23,936
South Patrick Shores, FL 32937 • 10,249
South Pekin, IL 61564 • 1,184
South Pittsburg, TN 37380 • 3,295
South Plainfield, NJ 07080 • 20,489
Southport, FL 32409 • 1,992
Southport, IN 46227 • 1,969
Southport, NY 14904 • 7,753
Southport, NC 28461 • 2,369
South Portland, ME 04106 • 23,163
South River, NJ 08882 • 13,692
South Royalton, VT 05068 • 700
South Saint Paul, MN 55075–77 • 20,197
South Salt Lake, UT 84115 • 10,129
South San Francisco, CA 94080–83 • 54,312
South San Gabriel, CA 91770 • 7,700
South San Jose Hills, CA 91744 • 17,814
South Sarasota, FL 34239 • 5,298
South Setauket, NY 11733 • 5,990
Southside, AL 35901 • 5,580
Southside Place, TX 77005 • 1,392
South Sioux City, NE 68776 • 9,677
South Stony Brook, NY 11790 • 6,120
South Streator, IL 61364 • 2,334
South Sumter, SC 29150 • 4,371
South Toms River, NJ 08757 • 3,869
South Torrington, WY 82240 • 300
South Tucson, AZ 85713 • 5,093
South Valley Stream, NY 11581 • 5,328
South Venice, FL 34293 • 11,951
South Walpole, MA 02071 • 1,300
South Waverly, PA 14892 • 1,049
South Wellfleet, MA 02663 • 2,300
South Westbury, NY 11590 • 9,732
Southwest Harbor, ME 04679 • 1,952
South Whitley, IN 46787 • 1,482
South Whittier, CA 90605 • 51,100
Southwick, MA 01077 • 1,170
South Williamsport, PA 17701 • 6,496
South Windham, CT 06266 • 1,644
South Windham, ME 04082 • 1,320
South Windsor, CT 06074 • 10,800
Southwood, CO 80120 • 2,050
Southwood Acres, CT 06082 • 8,963
South Woodstock, CT 06267 • 1,112
South Yarmouth, MA 02664 • 10,358
South Yuba City, CA 95991 • 8,816
South Zanesville, OH 43701 • 1,969
Spalding □, GA • 54,457
Spanaway, WA 98387 • 15,001
Spangler, PA 15775 • 2,068
Spanish Fork, UT 84660 • 11,272
Spanish Fort, AL 36527 • 3,732
Spanish Lake, MO 63138 • 20,322
Sparks, GA 31647 • 1,205
Sparks, NV 89431–36 • 53,367
Sparr, FL 32192 • 1,100
Sparta, GA 31087 • 1,710
Sparta, IL 62286 • 4,853
Sparta, MI 49345 • 3,968
Sparta (Lake Mohawk), NJ 07871 • 8,930
Sparta, NC 28675 • 1,957
Sparta, TN 38583 • 4,681
Sparta, WI 54656 • 7,788
Spartanburg, SC 29301–18 • 43,467
Spartanburg □, SC • 226,800
Spearfish, SD 57783 • 6,966
Spearman, TX 79081 • 3,197
Speedway, IN 46224 • 13,092
Spencer, IN 47460 • 2,609
Spencer, IA 51301 • 11,066
Spencer, MA 01562 • 6,306
Spencer, NC 28159 • 3,219
Spencer, TN 38585 • 1,125
Spencer, WV 25276 • 2,279
Spencer, WI 54479 • 1,757
Spencer □, IN • 19,490
Spencer □, KY • 6,801
Spencerport, NY 14559 • 3,606
Spencerville, MD 20868 • 1,780
Spencerville, OH 45887 • 2,288
Spicer, MN 56288 • 1,020
Spindale, NC 28160 • 4,040
Spink □, SD • 7,981
Spirit Lake, ID 83869 • 790
Spirit Lake, IA 51360 • 3,871
Spiro, OK 74959 • 2,146
Spokane, WA 99201 • 177,196
Spokane □, WA • 361,364
Spooner, WI 54801 • 2,464
Spotswood, NJ 08884 • 7,983
Spotsylvania □, VA • 57,403
Sprague, WV 25926 • 2,090

Spring, TX 77373 • *33,111*
Spring Arbor, MI 49283 • *2,010*
Springboro, OH 45066 • *6,590*
Spring City, PA 19475 • *3,433*
Spring City, TN 37381 • *2,199*
Spring Creek □M, NV • *5,866*
Springdale, AR 72754–66 • *29,941*
Springdale, OH 45246 • *10,621*
Springdale, PA 15144 • *3,992*
Springdale, SC 29169 • *3,226*
Springer, NM 87747 • *1,262*
Springerville, AZ 85938 • *1,802*
Springfield, FL 32401 • *8,715*
Springfield, GA 31329 • *1,415*
Springfield, IL 62701–94 • *105,227*
Springfield, KY 40069 • *2,875*
Springfield, MA 01101–05 • *156,983*
Springfield, MI 49015 • *5,582*
Springfield, MN 56087 • *2,173*
Springfield, MO 65801–99 • *140,494*
Springfield, NE 68059 • *1,426*
Springfield, NJ 07081 • *13,240*
Springfield, OH 45501–06 • *70,487*
Springfield, OR 97477–78 • *44,683*
Springfield, PA 19064 • *24,160*
Springfield, SD 57062 • *834*
Springfield, TN 37172 • *11,227*
Springfield, VA 22150 • *23,706*
Spring Garden, PA 17403 • *11,127*
Spring Green, WI 53588 • *1,283*
Spring Grove, IL 60081 • *1,066*
Spring Grove, MN 55974 • *1,153*
Spring Grove, PA 17362 • *1,863*
Spring Hill, FL 34606 • *31,117*
Springhill, LA 71075 • *5,668*
Spring Hill, KS 66083 • *2,191*
Spring Hill, TN 37174 • *1,464*
Spring Hope, NC 27882 • *1,221*
Spring Lake, MI 49456 • *2,537*
Spring Lake, NJ 07762 • *3,499*
Spring Lake, NC 28390 • *7,524*
Spring Lake Heights, NJ 07762 • *5,341*
Spring Lake Park, MN 55432 • *6,532*
Springvale, ME 04083 • *3,542*
Spring Valley, IL 61362 • *5,246*
Spring Valley, MN 55975 • *2,461*
Spring Valley, NY 10977 • *21,802*
Spring Valley, WI 54767 • *1,051*
Springville, AL 35146 • *1,910*
Springville, NY 14141 • *4,310*
Springville, UT 84663–64 • *13,950*
Spruce Pine, NC 28777 • *2,010*
Spur, TX 79370 • *1,300*
Staatsburg, NY 12580 • *1,100*
Stafford, KS 67578 • *1,344*
Stafford □, KS • *5,365*
Stafford □, VA • *61,236*
Stafford Springs, CT 06076 • *4,100*
Stambaugh, MI 49964 • *1,281*
Stamford, CT 06901–12 • *108,056*
Stamford, NY 12167 • *1,211*
Stamford, TX 79553 • *3,817*
Stamford, VT 05352 • *400*
Stamps, AR 71860 • *2,478*
Stanaford, WV 25927 • *1,706*
Stanberry, MO 64489 • *1,310*
Standish, MI 48658 • *1,377*
Stanfield, AZ 85272 • *1,700*
Stanfield, OR 97875 • *1,568*
Stanford, CA 94305 • *18,097*
Stanford, KY 40484 • *2,686*
Stanhope, NJ 07874 • *3,393*
Stanislaus □, CA • *370,522*
Stanley, NC 28164 • *2,823*
Stanley, ND 58784 • *1,371*
Stanley, VA 22851 • *1,186*
Stanley, WI 54768 • *2,019*
Stanley □, SD • *2,453*
Stanleytown, VA 24168 • *1,563*
Stanleyville, NC 27045 • *4,779*
Stanly □, NC • *51,765*
Stanton, CA 90680 • *30,491*
Stanton, KY 40380 • *2,795*
Stanton, MI 48888 • *1,504*
Stanton, NE 68779 • *1,549*
Stanton, TX 79782 • *2,576*
Stanton □, KS • *2,333*
Stanton □, NE • *6,244*
Stanwood, WA 98292 • *1,961*
Staples, MN 56479 • *2,754*
Stapleton, AL 36578 • *1,300*
Starbuck, MN 56381 • *1,143*
Star City, AR 71667 • *2,138*
Star City, WV 26505 • *1,251*
Stargo, AZ 85540 • *1,038*
Stark □, IL • *6,534*
Stark □, ND • *22,832*
Stark □, OH • *367,585*
Starke, FL 32091 • *5,226*
Starke □, IN • *22,747*
Starkville, MS 39759 • *18,458*
Starr □, TX • *40,518*
Startex, SC 29377 • *1,162*
State Center, IA 50247 • *1,248*
State College, PA 16801–05 • *38,923*
Stateline, NV 89449 • *1,379*
State Line, PA 17263 • *1,253*
Statesboro, GA 30458 • *15,854*
Statesville, NC 28677 • *17,567*
Statham, GA 30666 • *1,360*
Staunton, IL 62088 • *4,806*
Staunton, VA 24401 • *24,461*
Stayton, OR 97383 • *5,011*
Steamboat, NV 89511 • *450*
Steamboat Springs, CO 80487 • *6,695*
Stearns, KY 42647 • *1,550*
Stearns □, MN • *118,791*
Stebbins, AK 99671 • *400*
Steele, AL 35987 • *1,046*
Steele, MO 63877 • *2,395*
Steele, ND 58482 • *762*
Steele □, MN • *30,729*
Steele □, ND • *2,420*
Steeleville, IL 62288 • *2,059*
Steelton, PA 17113 • *5,152*
Steeleville, MO 65565 • *1,465*
Steger, IL 60475 • *8,584*
Steilacoom, WA 98388 • *5,728*
Stephens, AR 71764 • *1,137*
Stephens □, GA • *23,257*

Stephens □, OK • *42,299*
Stephens □, TX • *9,010*
Stephens City, VA 22655 • *1,186*
Stephenson □, IL • *48,052*
Stephenville, TX 76401 • *13,502*
Sterling, AK 99672 • *3,802*
Sterling, CO 80751 • *10,362*
Sterling, IL 61081 • *15,132*
Sterling, KS 67579 • *2,115*
Sterling, MA 01564 • *1,250*
Sterling, VA 22170 • *20,512*
Sterling □, TX • *1,438*
Sterling City, TX 76951 • *1,096*
Sterling Heights, MI 48310–14 • *117,810*
Sterlington, LA 71280 • *1,140*
Steuben □, IN • *27,446*
Steuben □, NY • *99,088*
Steubenville, OH 43952 • *22,125*
Stevens □, KS • *5,048*
Stevens □, MN • *10,634*
Stevens □, WA • *30,948*
Stevenson, AL 35772 • *2,046*
Stevenson, WA 98648 • *1,147*
Stevens Point, WI 54481 • *23,006*
Stevensville, MI 49127 • *1,230*
Stevensville, MT 59870 • *1,221*
Stewart □, GA • *5,654*
Stewart □, TN • *9,479*
Stewartstown, PA 17363 • *1,308*
Stewartville, MN 55976 • *4,520*
Stickney, IL 60402 • *5,678*
Stigler, OK 74462 • *2,574*
Stillwater, MN 55082–83 • *13,882*
Stillwater, NY 12170 • *1,531*
Stillwater, OK 74074–76 • *36,676*
Stillwater □, MT • *6,536*
Stilwell, OK 74960 • *2,663*
Stinnett, TX 79083 • *2,166*
Stirling, NJ 07980 • *1,800*
Stockbridge, GA 30281 • *3,359*
Stockbridge, MA 01262 • *2,408*
Stockbridge, MI 49285 • *1,202*
Stockdale, TX 78160 • *1,268*
Stockholm, NJ 07460 • *1,200*
Stockton, CA 95201–19 • *210,943*
Stockton, IL 61085 • *1,871*
Stockton, KS 67669 • *1,507*
Stockton, MO 65785 • *1,579*
Stoddard □, MO • *28,895*
Stokes □, NC • *37,223*
Stokesdale, NC 27357 • *2,134*
Stollings, WV 25646 • *1,200*
Stone □, AR • *9,775*
Stone □, MS • *10,750*
Stone □, MO • *19,078*
Stoneboro, PA 16153 • *1,091*
Stoneham, MA 02180 • *22,203*
Stone Harbor, NJ 08247 • *1,025*
Stone Mountain, GA 30083 • *6,494*
Stoneville, NC 27048 • *1,109*
Stonewall, LA 71078 • *1,266*
Stonewall, MS 39363 • *1,148*
Stonewall □, TX • *2,013*
Stonewood, WV 26301 • *1,996*
Stonington, CT 06378 • *1,100*
Stonington, IL 62567 • *1,006*
Stony Brook, NY 11790 • *13,726*
Stony Point, NY 10980 • *10,587*
Stony Point, NC 28678 • *1,286*
Storey □, NV • *2,526*
Storm Lake, IA 50588 • *8,769*
Storrs, CT 06268 • *12,198*
Story, WY 82842 • *700*
Story □, IA • *74,252*
Story City, IA 50248 • *2,959*
Stottville, NY 12172 • *1,369*
Stoughton, MA 02072 • *26,777*
Stoughton, WI 53589 • *8,786*
Stow, MA 01775 • *1,200*
Stow, OH 44224 • *27,702*
Stowe, PA 19464 • *3,598*
Stowe, VT 05672 • *440*
Stowe Township, PA 15136 • *7,681*
Strabane, PA 15363 • *1,200*
Strafford, MO 65757 • *1,166*
Strafford □, NH • *104,233*
Strasburg, CO 80136 • *1,005*
Strasburg, OH 44680 • *1,995*
Strasburg, PA 17579 • *2,568*
Strasburg, VA 22657 • *3,762*
Stratford Landing, VA 22308 • *2,800*
Stratford, CT 06497 • *49,389*
Stratford, DE 19720 • *1,950*
Stratford, NJ 08084 • *7,614*
Stratford, OK 74872 • *1,404*
Stratford, TX 79084 • *1,781*
Stratford, WI 54484 • *1,515*
Strathmore, CA 93267 • *2,353*
Strathmore, NJ 07747 • *7,060*
Strawberry Point, IA 52076 • *1,357*
Streamwood, IL 60103 • *30,987*
Streator, IL 61364 • *14,121*
Stromsburg, NE 68666 • *1,241*
Strongsville, OH 44136 • *35,308*
Stroud, OK 74079 • *2,666*
Stroudsburg, PA 18360 • *5,312*
Struthers, OH 44471 • *12,284*
Stryker, OH 43557 • *1,468*
Stuart, FL 34994–97 • *11,936*
Stuart, IA 50250 • *1,522*
Stuarts Draft, VA 24477 • *5,087*
Sturbridge, MA 01566 • *2,093*
Sturgeon Bay, WI 54235 • *9,176*
Sturgis, KY 42459 • *2,184*
Sturgis, MI 49091 • *10,130*
Sturgis, SD 57785 • *5,330*
Sturtevant, WI 53177 • *3,803*
Stutsman □, ND • *22,241*
Stuttgart, AR 72160 • *10,420*
Sublette, KS 67877 • *1,378*
Sublette □, WY • *4,843*
Sublimity, OR 97385 • *1,491*
Succasunna, NJ 07876 • *7,750*
Sudbury, MA 01776 • *1,860*
Sudbury Center, MA 01776 • *2,590*
Sudley, VA 22110 • *7,321*
Suffern, NY 10901 • *11,055*
Suffolk, PA 15218 • *10,637*
Suffolk, VA 23432–38 • *52,141*
Suffolk □, MA • *663,906*
Suffolk □, NY • *1,321,864*
Sugar City, ID 83448 • *1,275*

Sugar Creek, MO 64054 • *3,982*
Sugarcreek, PA 16323 • *5,532*
Sugar Grove, VA 24375 • *1,027*
Sugar Hill, GA 30518 • *4,557*
Sugar Land, TX 77478–79 • *24,529*
Sugarland Run, VA 22170 • *9,357*
Sugar Loaf, VA 24018 • *2,000*
Sugar Notch, PA 18706 • *1,044*
Suisun City, CA 94585 • *22,686*
Suitland, MD 20746 • *35,400*
Sulligent, AL 35586 • *1,886*
Sullivan, IL 61951 • *4,354*
Sullivan, IN 47882 • *4,663*
Sullivan, MO 63080 • *5,661*
Sullivan □, IN • *18,993*
Sullivan □, MO • *6,326*
Sullivan □, NH • *38,592*
Sullivan □, NY • *69,277*
Sullivan □, PA • *6,104*
Sullivan □, TN • *143,596*
Sullivans Island, SC 29482 • *1,623*
Sully □, SD • *1,589*
Sulphur, LA 70663–64 • *20,125*
Sulphur, OK 73086 • *4,824*
Sulphur Springs, TX 75482 • *14,062*
Sultan, WA 98294 • *2,236*
Sumiton, AL 35148 • *2,604*
Summerfield, NC 27358 • *2,051*
Summers □, WV • *14,204*
Summersville, WV 26651 • *2,906*
Summerville, GA 30747 • *5,025*
Summerville, SC 29483–85 • *22,519*
Summit, IL 60501 • *9,971*
Summit, MS 39666 • *1,566*
Summit, NJ 07901 • *19,757*
Summit, TN 37363 • *8,307*
Summit □, CO • *12,881*
Summit □, OH • *514,990*
Summit □, UT • *15,518*
Summit Hill, PA 18250 • *3,332*
Sumner, IL 62466 • *1,083*
Sumner, IA 50674 • *2,078*
Sumner, WA 98390 • *6,281*
Sumner □, KS • *25,841*
Sumner □, TN • *103,281*
Sumter, SC 29150–54 • *41,943*
Sumter □, AL • *16,174*
Sumter □, FL • *31,577*
Sumter □, GA • *30,228*
Sumter □, SC • *102,637*
Sunbury, OH 43074 • *2,046*
Sunbury, PA 17801 • *11,591*
Sun City, AZ 85351 • *38,126*
Sun City, CA 92381 • *14,930*
Sun City Center, FL 33573 • *8,326*
Suncook, NH 03275 • *5,214*
Sundance, WY 82729 • *1,139*
Sundown, TX 79372 • *1,759*
Sunflower □, MS • *32,867*
Sunland Park, NM 88063 • *8,179*
Sunny Isles, FL 33160 • *11,772*
Sunnyside, CA 93727 • *5,000*
Sunnyside, WA 98944 • *11,238*
Sunnyvale, CA 94086–89 • *117,229*
Sun Prairie, WI 53590 • *15,333*
Sunray, TX 79086 • *1,729*
Sunrise Manor, NV 89110 • *95,362*
Sunset, FL 33143 • *15,810*
Sunset, LA 70584 • *2,201*
Sunset, UT 84015 • *5,128*
Sunset Beach, HI 96712 • *800*
Sun Valley, ID 83353–54 • *938*
Sun Valley, NV 89433 • *11,391*
Superior, AZ 85273 • *3,468*
Superior, NE 68978 • *2,397*
Superior, WI 54880 • *27,134*
Superior, WY 82945 • *273*
Squamish, WA 98392 • *3,105*
Surf City, NJ 08008 • *1,375*
Surfside, FL 33154 • *4,108*
Surfside Beach, SC 29575 • *3,845*
Surgoinsville, TN 37873 • *1,499*
Surprise, AZ 85374 • *7,122*
Surrey, ND 58785 • *856*
Surry □, NC • *61,704*
Surry □, VA • *6,145*
Susanville, CA 96130 • *7,279*
Susquehanna, PA 18847 • *1,760*
Susquehanna □, PA • *40,380*
Sussex, NJ 07461 • *2,201*
Sussex, WI 53089 • *5,039*
Sussex □, DE • *113,229*
Sussex □, NJ • *130,943*
Sussex □, VA • *10,248*
Sutherland, NE 69165 • *1,032*
Sutherlin, OR 97479 • *5,020*
Sutter □, CA • *64,415*
Sutter Creek, CA 95685 • *1,835*
Sutton, NE 68979 • *1,353*
Sutton □, TX • *4,135*
Suwanee, GA 30174 • *2,412*
Suwannee □, FL • *26,780*
Swain □, NC • *11,268*
Swainsboro, GA 30401 • *7,361*
Swampscott, MA 01907 • *13,650*
Swannanoa, NC 28778 • *3,538*
Swansboro, NC 28584 • *1,165*
Swansea, IL 62221 • *8,201*
Swanton, OH 43558 • *3,557*
Swanton, VT 05488 • *2,360*
Swanwyck Estates, DE 19720 • *1,320*
Swarthmore, PA 19081 • *6,157*
Swartz Creek, MI 48473 • *4,851*
Swayzee, IN 46986 • *1,059*
Swedesboro, NJ 08085 • *2,024*
Sweeny, TX 77480 • *3,297*
Sweet Grass □, MT • *3,154*
Sweet Home, OR 97386 • *6,850*
Sweet Springs, MO 65351 • *1,595*
Sweetwater, FL 33152 • *13,909*
Sweetwater, TN 37874 • *5,066*
Sweetwater, TX 79556 • *11,967*
Sweetwater □, WY • *38,823*
Sweetwater Creek, FL 33614 • *18,000*
Swift □, MN • *10,724*
Swisher □, TX • *8,133*
Swissvale, PA 15218 • *10,637*
Switzer, WV 25647 • *1,004*
Switzerland, FL 32043 • *2,400*
Switzerland □, IN • *7,738*
Swoyerville, PA • *5,630*

Sycamore, AL 35149 • *1,250*
Sycamore, IL 60178 • *9,708*
Sykesville, MD 21784 • *2,303*
Sykesville, PA 15865 • *1,387*
Sylacauga, AL 35150 • *12,520*
Sylva, NC 28779 • *1,809*
Sylvan Beach, NY 13157 • *1,119*
Sylvania, GA 30467 • *2,871*
Sylvania, OH 43560 • *17,301*
Sylvan Lake, MI 48320 • *1,884*
Sylvester, GA 31791 • *5,702*
Syosset, NY 11791 • *18,967*
Syracuse, IN 46567 • *2,729*
Syracuse, KS 67878 • *1,606*
Syracuse, NE 68446 • *1,646*
Syracuse, NY 13201–90 • *163,860*
Syracuse, UT 84075 • *4,658*

T

Tabor City, NC 28463 • *2,330*
Tacoma, WA 98401–99 • *176,664*
Taft, CA 93268 • *5,902*
Taft, TX 78390 • *3,222*
Tahlequah, OK 74464–65 • *10,398*
Tahoe City, CA 95730 • *1,300*
Tahoka, TX 79373 • *2,868*
Takoma Park, MD 20912 • *16,700*
Talbot □, GA • *6,524*
Talbot □, MD • *30,549*
Talbotton, GA 31827 • *1,046*
Talent, OR 97540 • *3,274*
Taliaferro □, GA • *1,915*
Talihina, OK 74571 • *1,297*
Talladega, AL 35160 • *18,175*
Talladega □, AL • *74,107*
Tallahassee, FL 32301–17 • *124,773*
Tallahatchie □, MS • *15,210*
Tallapoosa, GA 30176 • *2,805*
Tallapoosa □, AL • *38,826*
Tallassee, AL 36078 • *5,112*
Talleyville, DE 19803 • *6,346*
Tallmadge, OH 44278 • *14,870*
Tallulah, LA 71282–84 • *8,526*
Tama, IA 52339 • *2,697*
Tama □, IA • *17,419*
Tamalpais Valley, CA 94941 • *5,000*
Tamaqua, PA 18252 • *7,943*
Tamarac, FL 33321 • *44,822*
Tamiami, FL 33165 • *33,845*
Tampa, FL 33601–97 • *280,015*
Tanana, AK 99777 • *345*
Taney □, MO • *25,561*
Taneytown, MD 21787 • *3,695*
Tangipahoa □, LA • *85,709*
Taos, NM 87571 • *4,065*
Taos □, NM • *23,118*
Taos Pueblo, NM 87571 • *1,030*
Tappahannock, VA 22560 • *1,550*
Tappan, NY 10983 • *6,867*
Tarboro, NC 27886 • *11,037*
Tarentum, PA 15084 • *5,674*
Tariffville, CT 06081 • *1,477*
Tarkio, MO 64491 • *2,243*
Tarpey, CA 93727 • *4,000*
Tarpon Springs, FL 34688–91 • *17,906*
Tarrant, AL 35217 • *8,046*
Tarrant □, TX • *1,170,103*
Tarrytown, NY 10591 • *10,739*
Tate, GA 30177 • *1,000*
Tate □, MS • *21,432*
Tattnall □, GA • *17,722*
Taunton, MA 02780 • *49,832*
Tavares, FL 32778 • *7,383*
Tavernier, FL 33070 • *2,433*
Tawas City, MI 48763–64 • *2,009*
Taylor, AZ 85939 • *2,418*
Taylor, MI 48180 • *70,811*
Taylor, PA 18517 • *6,941*
Taylor, TX 76574 • *11,472*
Taylor □, FL • *17,111*
Taylor □, GA • *7,642*
Taylor □, IA • *7,114*
Taylor □, KY • *21,146*
Taylor □, TX • *119,655*
Taylor □, WV • *15,144*
Taylor □, WI • *18,901*
Taylor Mill, KY 41015 • *5,530*
Taylors, SC 29687 • *19,619*
Taylorsville, IN 47280 • *1,044*
Taylorsville, MS 39168 • *1,412*
Taylorsville, NC 28681 • *1,566*
Taylorville, IL 62568 • *11,133*
Tazewell, TN 37879 • *2,150*
Tazewell, VA 24651 • *4,176*
Tazewell □, IL • *123,692*
Tazewell □, VA • *45,960*
Tchula, MS 39169 • *2,186*
Teague, TX 75860 • *3,268*
Teaneck, NJ 07666 • *37,825*
Teaticket, MA 02536 • *2,600*
Tecumseh, MI 49286 • *7,462*
Tecumseh, NE 68450 • *1,702*
Tecumseh, OK 74873 • *5,750*
Tehachapi, CA 93561 • *5,791*
Tehama □, CA • *49,625*
Tekamah, NE 68061 • *1,852*
Telfair □, GA • *11,000*
Telford, PA 18969 • *4,238*
Tell City, IN 47586 • *8,088*
Teller □, CO • *12,468*
Telluride, CO 81435 • *1,309*
Temecula, CA 92390 • *27,099*
Tempe, AZ 85280–85 • *141,865*
Temperance, MI 48182 • *6,542*
Temple, GA 30179 • *1,870*
Temple, OK 73568 • *1,223*
Temple, PA 19560 • *1,491*
Temple, TX 76501–05 • *46,109*
Temple City, CA 91780 • *31,100*
Temple Terrace, FL 33617 • *16,444*
Templeton, MA 01468 • *1,000*
Tenafly, NJ 07670 • *13,326*
Tenaha, TX 75974 • *1,072*
Tenino, WA 98589 • *1,292*
Tennessee Ridge, TN 37178 • *1,271*
Tennille, GA 31089 • *1,552*
Tensas □, LA • *7,103*
Ten Sleep, WY 82442 • *311*
Terra Alta, WV 26764 • *1,713*

Terrebonne □, LA • *96,982*
Terre Haute, IN 47801–08 • *57,483*
Terre Hill, PA 17581 • *1,282*
Terrell, TX 75160 • *12,490*
Terrell □, GA • *10,653*
Terrell □, TX • *1,410*
Terrell Hills, TX 78209 • *4,592*
Terry, MT 59349 • *659*
Terry □, TX • *13,218*
Terrytown, LA 70053 • *23,787*
Terryville, CT 06786 • *5,426*
Terryville, NY 11776 • *7,380*
Tesuque, NM 87574 • *1,490*
Teton □, ID • *3,439*
Teton □, MT • *6,271*
Teton □, WY • *11,172*
Teton Village, WY 83025 • *250*
Teutopolis, IL 62467 • *1,417*
Tewksbury, MA 01876 • *10,540*
Texarkana, AR 75502 • *22,631*
Texarkana, TX 75501–05 • *31,656*
Texas □, MO • *21,476*
Texas □, OK • *16,419*
Texas City, TX 77590–92 • *40,822*
Texico, NM 88135 • *966*
Thatcher, AZ 85552 • *3,763*
Thayer, MO 65791 • *1,996*
Thayer □, NE • *6,635*
Thayne, WY 83127 • *267*
The Colony, TX 75056 • *22,113*
The Dalles, OR 97058 • *11,060*
Theodore, AL 36582 • *6,509*
The Plains, OH 45780 • *2,644*
Thermalito, CA 95965 • *5,646*
The Village, OK 73120 • *10,353*
The Village of Indian Hill, OH 45243 • *5,383*
The Woodlands, TX 77380 • *29,205*
Thibodaux, LA 70301–02 • *14,035*
Thief River Falls, MN 56701 • *8,010*
Thiensville, WI 53092 • *3,301*
Thomas, OK 73669 • *1,246*
Thomas □, GA • *38,986*
Thomas □, KS • *8,258*
Thomas □, NE • *851*
Thomasboro, IL 61878 • *1,250*
Thomaston, CT 06787 • *3,590*
Thomaston, GA 30286 • *9,127*
Thomaston, ME 04861 • *2,445*
Thomasville, AL 36784 • *4,301*
Thomasville, GA 31792 • *17,457*
Thomasville, NC 27360–61 • *15,915*
Thompson, ND 58278 • *930*
Thompson Falls, MT 59873 • *1,319*
Thomson, GA 30824 • *6,862*
Thonotosassa, FL 33592 • *1,500*
Thoreau, NM 87323 • *1,099*
Thorndale, TX 76577 • *1,092*
Thorndike, MA 01079 • *1,100*
Thornton, CO 80229 • *55,031*
Thornton □, IN 46071 • *1,506*
Thornwood, NY 10594 • *7,025*
Thorofare, NJ 08086 • *1,800*
Thorp, WI 54771 • *1,657*
Thorsby, AL 35171 • *1,465*
Thousand Oaks, CA 91359–62 • *104,352*
Three Forks, MT 59752 • *1,203*
Three Oaks, MI 49128 • *1,786*
Three Rivers, MA 01080 • *3,006*
Three Rivers, MI 49093 • *7,413*
Three Rivers, TX 78071 • *1,889*
Throckmorton, TX 76083 • *1,036*
Throckmorton □, TX • *1,880*
Throop, PA 18512 • *4,070*
Thunderbolt, GA 31404 • *2,786*
Thurmont, MD 21788 • *3,398*
Thurston □, NE • *6,936*
Thurston □, WA • *161,238*
Tiburon, CA 94920 • *7,532*
Tice, FL 33905 • *3,971*
Ticonderoga, NY 12883 • *2,770*
Tierra Amarilla, NM 87575 • *900*
Tiffin, OH 44883 • *18,604*
Tift □, GA • *34,998*
Tifton, GA 31793–94 • *14,215*
Tigard, OR 97223 • *29,344*
Tillamook, OR 97141 • *4,001*
Tillamook □, OR • *21,570*
Tillar □, IN • *10,384*
Tillmans Corner, AL 36619 • *17,988*
Tillson, NY 12486 • *1,888*
Tilton, IL 61833 • *2,729*
Tilton, NH 03276 • *1,380*
Tiltonsville, OH 43963 • *1,517*
Timberlake, VA 24502 • *10,314*
Timberville, VA 22853 • *1,596*
Timmonsville, SC 29161 • *2,182*
Timpson, TX 75975 • *1,029*
Tinley Park, IL 60477 • *37,121*
Tinton Falls, NJ 07724 • *12,361*
Tioga, LA 71477 • *1,200*
Tioga, ND 58852 • *1,278*
Tioga □, NY • *52,337*
Tioga □, PA • *41,126*
Tippah □, MS • *19,523*
Tipp City, OH 45371 • *6,027*
Tippecanoe □, IN • *130,598*
Tipton, CA 93272 • *1,383*
Tipton, IN 46072 • *4,751*
Tipton, IA 52772 • *2,998*
Tipton, MO 65081 • *2,026*
Tipton, OK 73570 • *1,043*
Tipton □, IN • *16,119*
Tipton □, TN • *37,568*
Tiptonville, TN 38079 • *2,149*
Tishomingo, OK 73460 • *3,116*
Tishomingo □, MS • *17,683*
Titus □, TX • *24,009*
Titusville, FL 32780–83 • *39,394*
Titusville, PA 16354 • *6,434*
Tiverton, RI 02878 • *7,259*
Tivoli, NY 12583 • *1,035*
Toast, NC 27049 • *2,125*
Tobyhanna, PA 18466 • *1,200*
Toccoa, GA 30577 • *8,266*
Todd □, KY • *10,940*
Todd □, MN • *23,363*
Todd □, SD • *8,352*
Todd Estates, DE 19713 • *2,000*
Togiak, AK 99678 • *613*
Tohatchi, NM 87325 • *661*
Tok, AK 99780 • *935*
Toledo, IL 62468 • *1,199*

Toledo, IA 52342 • *2,380*
Toledo, OH 43601-99 • *332,943*
Toledo, OR 97391 • *3,174*
Tolland, CT 06084 • *1,200*
Tolland □, CT • *128,699*
Tolleson, AZ 85353 • *4,434*
Tolono, IL 61880 • *2,605*
Toluca, IL 61369 • *1,315*
Tomah, WI 54660 • *7,570*
Tomahawk, WI 54487 • *3,328*
Tomball, TX 77375 • *6,370*
Tombstone, AZ 85638 • *1,220*
Tom Green □, TX • *98,458*
Tompkins □, NY • *94,097*
Tompkinsville, KY 42167 • *2,861*
Toms River, NJ 08753-57 • *7,524*
Tonawanda, NY 14150-51 • *17,284*
Tonawanda, NY 14223 • *65,284*
Tonganoxie, KS 66086 • *2,347*
Tonkawa, OK 74653 • *3,127*
Tonopah, NV 89049 • *3,616*
Tooele, UT 84074 • *13,887*
Tooele □, UT • *26,601*
Toole □, MT • *5,046*
Toombs □, GA • *24,072*
Topeka, KS 66601-99 • *119,883*
Toppenish, WA 98948 • *7,419*
Topsfield, MA 01983 • *2,711*
Topsham, ME 04086 • *6,147*
Topton, PA 19562 • *1,987*
Toronto, OH 43964 • *6,127*
Torrance, CA 90501-10 • *133,107*
Torrance □, NM • *10,285*
Torrington, CT 06790 • *33,687*
Torrington, WY 82240 • *5,651*
Totowa, NJ 07512 • *10,177*
Touisset, MA 02777 • *1,520*
Toulon, IL 61483 • *1,328*
Towaco, NJ 07082 • *1,020*
Towanda, KS 67144 • *1,289*
Towanda, PA 18848 • *3,242*
Tower City, PA 17980 • *1,518*
Town and Country, WA 99210 • *4,921*
Town Creek, AL 35672 • *1,379*
Towner, ND 58788 • *669*
Towner □, ND • *3,627*
Town 'n Country, FL 33615 • *60,946*
Towns □, GA • *6,754*
Townsend, DE 19734 • *322*
Townsend, MA 01469 • *1,164*
Townsend, MT 59644 • *1,635*
Towson, MD 21204 • *49,445*
Tracy, CA 95376-78 • *33,558*
Tracy, MN 56175 • *2,059*
Tracy City, TN 37387 • *1,556*
Tracyton, WA 98393 • *2,621*
Traer, IA 50675 • *1,552*
Trafford, PA 15085 • *3,345*
Trail Creek, IN 46360 • *2,463*
Traill □, ND • *8,752*
Transylvania □, NC • *25,520*
Travelers Rest, SC 29690 • *3,069*
Traverse □, MN • *4,463*
Traverse City, MI 49684 • *15,155*
Travis □, TX • *576,407*
Treasure □, MT • *874*
Treasure Island, FL 33706 • *7,266*
Trego □, KS • *3,694*
Tremont, IL 61568 • *2,088*
Tremont, PA 17981 • *1,814*
Tremonton, UT 84337 • *4,264*
Trempealeau, WI 54661 • *1,039*
Trempealeau □, WI • *25,263*
Trenton, FL 32693 • *1,287*
Trenton, GA 30752 • *1,994*
Trenton, IL 62293 • *2,481*
Trenton, MI 48183 • *20,586*
Trenton, MO 64683 • *6,129*
Trenton, NJ 08601-91 • *88,675*
Trenton, OH 45067 • *6,189*
Trenton, TN 38382 • *4,836*
Tresckow, PA 18254 • *1,033*
Treutlen □, GA • *5,994*
Trevorton, PA 17881 • *2,058*
Triangle, VA 22172 • *4,740*
Tri City, OR 97457 • *3,585*
Trigg □, KY • *10,361*
Tri Lakes, IN 46725 • *3,299*
Trimble □, KY • *6,090*
Trinidad, CO 81082 • *8,580*
Trinidad, TX 75163 • *1,056*
Trinity, AL 35673 • *1,380*
Trinity, NC 27370 • *5,469*
Trinity, TX 75862 • *2,648*
Trinity □, CA • *13,063*
Trinity □, TX • *11,445*
Trion, GA 30753 • *1,661*
Tripoli, IA 50676 • *1,188*
Tripp □, SD • *6,924*
Triumph, LA 70041 • *1,200*
Trona, CA 93562 • *1,400*
Trooper, PA 19401 • *5,137*
Trotwood, OH 45426 • *8,816*
Troup □, GA • *55,536*
Trousdale □, TN • *5,920*
Troutdale, OR 97060 • *7,852*
Troutman, NC 28166 • *1,493*
Troy, AL 36081 • *13,051*
Troy, ID 83871 • *699*
Troy, IL 62294 • *6,046*
Troy, KS 66087 • *1,073*
Troy, MI 48083-84 • *72,884*
Troy, MO 63379 • *3,811*
Troy, MT 59935 • *953*
Troy, NH 03465 • *2,097*
Troy, NY 12180-83 • *54,269*
Troy, NC 27371 • *3,404*
Troy, OH 45373 • *19,478*
Troy, PA 16947 • *1,262*
Troy, TN 38260 • *1,047*
Truckee, CA 95734 • *3,484*
Truman, MN 56088 • *1,292*
Trumann, AR 72472 • *6,304*
Trumansburg, NY 14886 • *1,611*
Trumbull, CT 06611 • *32,000*
Trumbull □, OH • *227,813*
Trussville, AL 35173 • *8,266*
Truth or Consequences (Hot Springs), NM 87901 • *6,221*
Tryon, NC 28782 • *1,680*
Tualatin, OR 97062 • *15,013*
Tuba City, AZ 86045 • *7,323*
Tuckahoe, NY 10707 • *6,302*

Tucker, GA 30084 • *25,781*
Tucker □, WV • *7,728*
Tuckerman, AR 72473 • *2,020*
Tuckerton, NJ 08087 • *3,048*
Tucson, AZ 85701-99 • *405,390*
Tucumcari, NM 88401 • *6,831*
Tukwila, WA 98188 • *11,874*
Tulare, CA 93274-75 • *33,249*
Tulare □, CA • *311,921*
Tularosa, NM 88352 • *2,615*
Tulelake, CA 96134 • *1,010*
Tulia, TX 79088 • *4,699*
Tullahoma, TN 37388 • *16,761*
Tulsa, OK 74101-94 • *367,302*
Tulsa □, OK • *503,341*
Tumwater, WA 98502 • *9,976*
Tunica, MS 38676 • *1,175*
Tunica □, MS • *8,164*
Tunkhannock, PA 18657 • *2,251*
Tununak, AK 99681 • *316*
Tuolumne, CA 95379 • *1,686*
Tuolumne □, CA • *48,456*
Tupelo, MS 38801-03 • *30,685*
Tupper Lake, NY 12986 • *4,087*
Turley, OK 74156 • *2,930*
Turlock, CA 95380-81 • *42,198*
Turner, OR 97392 • *1,281*
Turner □, GA • *8,703*
Turner □, SD • *8,576*
Turners Falls, MA 01376 • *4,731*
Turtle Creek, PA 15145 • *6,556*
Turtle Lake, ND 58575 • *681*
Tuscaloosa, AL 35401-06 • *77,759*
Tuscaloosa □, AL • *150,522*
Tuscarawas □, OH • *84,090*
Tuscola, IL 61953 • *4,155*
Tuscola □, MI • *55,498*
Tuscumbia, AL 35674 • *8,413*
Tuskegee, AL 36083 • *12,257*
Tustin, CA 92680-81 • *50,689*
Tuttle, OK 73089 • *2,807*
Tutwiler, MS 38963 • *1,391*
Tuxedo Park, DE 19804 • *1,300*
Twentynine Palms, CA 92277-78 • *11,821*
Twiggs □, GA • *9,806*
Twin City, GA 30471 • *1,466*
Twin Falls, ID 83301-03 • *27,591*
Twin Falls □, ID • *53,580*
Twin Knolls, AZ 85207 • *5,210*
Twin Lakes, CA 95060 • *5,379*
Twin Lakes, WI 53181 • *3,989*
Twin Rivers, NJ 08520 • *7,715*
Twinsburg, OH 44087 • *9,606*
Two Harbors, MN 55616 • *3,651*
Two Rivers, WI 54241 • *13,030*
Tybee Island, GA 31328 • *2,842*
Tyler, MN 56178 • *1,257*
Tyler, TX 75701-13 • *75,450*
Tyler □, TX • *16,646*
Tyler □, WV • *9,796*
Tyler Heights, WV 25312 • *4,070*
Tylertown, MS 39667 • *1,938*
Tyndall, SD 57066 • *1,201*
Tyrone, NM 88065 • *950*
Tyrone, PA 16686 • *5,743*
Tyrrell □, NC • *3,856*
Tysons Corner, VA 22102 • *13,124*

U

Ucon, ID 83454 • *895*
Uhrichsville, OH 44683 • *5,604*
Uinta □, WY • *18,705*
Uintah □, UT • *22,211*
Ukiah, CA 95482 • *14,599*
Uleta, FL 33162 • *10,000*
Ulster □, NY • *165,304*
Ulysses, KS 67880 • *5,474*
Umatilla, FL 32784 • *2,350*
Umatilla, OR 97882 • *3,046*
Umatilla □, OR • *59,249*
Unadilla, GA 31091 • *1,620*
Unadilla, NY 13849 • *1,246*
Unalakleet, AK 99684 • *714*
Unalaska, AK 99685 • *3,089*
Uncasville, CT 06382 • *1,597*
Underwood, AL 35630 • *1,950*
Underwood, ND 58576 • *976*
Unicoi □, TN • *16,549*
Union, KY 41091 • *1,001*
Union, MS 39365 • *1,875*
Union, MO 63084 • *5,909*
Union, NJ 07083 • *50,024*
Union, OH 45322 • *5,501*
Union, OR 97883 • *1,847*
Union, SC 29379 • *9,836*
Union, UT 84047 • *13,684*
Union □, AR • *46,719*
Union □, FL • *10,252*
Union □, GA • *11,993*
Union □, IL • *17,619*
Union □, IN • *6,976*
Union □, IA • *12,750*
Union □, KY • *16,557*
Union □, LA • *20,690*
Union □, MS • *22,085*
Union □, NJ • *493,819*
Union □, NM • *4,124*
Union □, NC • *84,211*
Union □, OH • *31,969*
Union □, OR • *23,598*
Union □, PA • *36,176*
Union □, SC • *30,337*
Union □, SD • *10,189*
Union □, TN • *13,694*
Union Beach, NJ 07735 • *6,156*
Union City, CA 94587 • *53,762*
Union City, GA 30291 • *8,375*
Union City, IN 47390 • *3,612*
Union City, MI 49094 • *1,767*
Union City, NJ 07087 • *58,012*
Union City, OH 45390 • *1,984*
Union City, OK 73090 • *1,000*
Union City, PA 16438 • *3,537*
Union City, TN 38261 • *10,513*
Uniondale, NY 11553 • *20,328*
Union Gap, WA 98903 • *3,120*
Union Grove, WI 53182 • *3,669*
Union Lake, MI 48386-87 • *8,500*
Union Park, FL 32817 • *6,890*
Union Pier, MI 49129 • *1,039*

Union Point, GA 30669 • *1,753*
Union Springs, AL 36089 • *3,975*
Union Springs, NY 13160 • *1,142*
Uniontown, AL 36786 • *1,730*
Uniontown, KY 42461 • *1,008*
Uniontown, OH 44685 • *1,500*
Uniontown, PA 15401 • *12,034*
Union Village, RI 02895 • *2,150*
Unionville, CT 06085 • *3,500*
Unionville, MO 63565 • *1,989*
Universal City, TX 78148 • *13,057*
University City, MO 63130 • *40,087*
University Gardens, NY 11020 • *4,600*
University Heights, IA 52240 • *1,042*
University Heights, OH 44118 • *14,790*
University Park, IL 60466 • *6,204*
University Park, NM 88003 • *4,520*
University Park, TX 75205 • *22,259*
University Place, WA 98465 • *27,701*
Upland, CA 91785-86 • *63,374*
Upland, IN 46989 • *3,295*
Upper Arlington, OH 43221 • *34,128*
Upper Darby, PA 19082-83 • *84,054*
Upper Dublin Township, PA 19002 • *22,348*
Upper Greenwood Lake, NJ 07421 • *2,734*
Upper Merion Township, PA 19406 • *26,138*
Upper Moreland Township, PA 19090 • *25,874*
Upper Providence Township, PA 19063 • *9,727*
Upper Saddle River, NJ 07458 • *7,198*
Upper Saint Clair, PA 15241 • *19,692*
Upper Sandusky, OH 43351 • *5,906*
Upshur □, TX • *31,370*
Upshur □, WV • *22,867*
Upson □, GA • *26,300*
Upton, MA 01568 • *1,500*
Upton, WY 82730 • *980*
Upton □, TX • *4,447*
Urbana, IL 61801 • *36,344*
Urbana, OH 43078 • *11,353*
Urbandale, IA 50322 • *23,500*
Usquepaug, RI 02892 • *400*
Utah □, UT • *263,590*
Utica, MI 48315-18 • *5,081*
Utica, MS 39175 • *1,033*
Utica, NY 13501-05 • *68,637*
Utica, OH 43080 • *1,997*
Uvalde, TX 78801-02 • *14,729*
Uvalde □, TX • *23,340*
Uxbridge, MA 01569 • *3,340*

V

Vacaville, CA 95687-88 • *71,479*
Vacherie, LA 70090 • *2,169*
Vadnais Heights, MN 55110 • *11,041*
Vail, CO 81657-58 • *3,659*
Valatie, NY 12184 • *1,487*
Valdese, NC 28690 • *3,914*
Valdez, AK 99686 • *4,068*
Valdosta, GA 31601-04 • *39,806*
Vale, OR 97918 • *1,491*
Valencia, AZ 85326 • *1,200*
Valencia □, NM • *45,235*
Valencia Heights, SC 29205 • *4,122*
Valhalla, NY 10595 • *6,200*
Valinda, CA 91744 • *18,735*
Vallejo, CA 94589-92 • *109,199*
Valle Vista, CA 92343 • *8,751*
Valley, AL 36854 • *8,173*
Valley, NE 68064 • *1,775*
Valley □, ID • *6,109*
Valley □, MT • *8,239*
Valley □, NE • *5,169*
Valley Center, KS 67147 • *3,624*
Valley City, ND 58072 • *7,163*
Valley Cottage, NY 10989 • *9,007*
Valley Falls, KS 66088 • *1,253*
Valley Falls, RI 02864 • *11,175*
Valley Forge, PA 19481-82 • *1,500*
Valley Mills, TX 76689 • *1,085*
Valley Park, MO 63088 • *4,165*
Valley Ridge, WA 98188 • *6,500*
Valley Springs, SD 57068 • *739*
Valley Station, KY 40272 • *22,840*
Valley Stream, NY 11580-82 • *33,946*
Valley View, PA 17983 • *1,749*
Valparaiso, FL 32580 • *4,672*
Valparaiso, IN 46383-84 • *24,414*
Val Verda, UT 84010 • *3,712*
Val Verde □, TX • *38,721*
Van, TX 75790 • *1,854*
Van Alstyne, TX 75095 • *2,090*
Van Buren, AR 72956 • *14,979*
Van Buren, ME 04785 • *2,759*
Van Buren □, AR • *14,008*
Van Buren □, IA • *7,676*
Van Buren □, MI • *70,060*
Van Buren □, TN • *4,846*
Vance □, NC • *38,892*
Vanceburg, KY 41179 • *1,713*
Vancleave, MS 39564 • *3,214*
Vancouver, WA 98660-68 • *46,380*
Vandalia, IL 62471 • *6,114*
Vandalia, MO 63382 • *2,683*
Vandalia, OH 45377 • *13,882*
Vandenberg Village, CA 93436 • *5,871*
Vander, NC 28301 • *1,179*
Vanderburgh □, IN • *165,058*
Vandergrift, PA 15690 • *5,904*
Van Horn, TX 79855 • *2,930*
Van Lear, KY 41265 • *1,050*
Vansant, VA 24656 • *1,187*
Van Vleck, TX 77482 • *1,534*
Van Wert, OH 45891 • *10,891*
Van Wert □, OH • *30,464*
Van Zandt □, TX • *37,944*
Varina, VA 23231 • *2,500*
Varnville, SC 29944 • *1,970*
Vassar, MI 48768 • *2,559*
Vaughn, MT 59487 • *2,270*
Veazie, ME 04401 • *1,610*
Veedersburg, IN 47987 • *2,192*
Velda Rose Estates, AZ 85205 • *2,330*
Velva, ND 58790 • *968*
Venango □, PA • *59,381*
Veneta, OR 97487 • *2,519*
Venice, FL 34292-93 • *16,922*

Venice, IL 62090 • *3,571*
Venice Gardens, FL 34293 • *7,701*
Ventnor City, NJ 08406 • *11,005*
Ventura (San Buenaventura), CA 93001-07 • *92,575*
Ventura □, CA • *669,016*
Veradale, WA 99037 • *7,836*
Verda, KY 40828 • *1,133*
Verdi, NV 89439 • *1,140*
Vergennes, VT 05491 • *2,578*
Vermilion, OH 44089 • *11,127*
Vermilion □, IL • *88,257*
Vermilion □, LA • *50,055*
Vermillion, SD 57069 • *10,034*
Vermillion □, IN • *16,773*
Vernal, UT 84078-79 • *6,644*
Vernon, AL 35592 • *2,247*
Vernon, CT 06066 • *30,200*
Vernon, TX 76384 • *12,001*
Vernon □, LA • *61,961*
Vernon □, MO • *19,041*
Vernon □, WI • *25,617*
Vernon Hills, IL 60061 • *15,319*
Vernonia, OR 97064 • *1,808*
Vero Beach, FL 32960-68 • *17,350*
Verona, MS 38879 • *2,893*
Verona, NJ 07044 • *13,597*
Verona, PA 15147 • *3,260*
Verona, WI 53593 • *5,374*
Versailles, IN 47042 • *1,791*
Versailles, KY 40383 • *7,269*
Versailles, MO 65084 • *2,365*
Versailles, OH 45380 • *2,351*
Vestal, NY 13850-51 • *5,530*
Vestavia Hills, AL 35216 • *19,749*
Vevay, IN 47043 • *1,393*
Vian, OK 74962 • *1,414*
Vicksburg, MI 49097 • *2,216*
Vicksburg, MS 39180-82 • *20,908*
Victor, NY 14564 • *2,308*
Victoria, KS 67671 • *1,157*
Victoria, TX 77901-05 • *55,076*
Victoria, VA 23974 • *1,830*
Victoria □, TX • *74,361*
Victorville, CA 92392-93 • *40,674*
Vidalia, GA 30474 • *11,078*
Vidalia, LA 71373 • *4,953*
Vidor, TX 77662 • *10,935*
Vienna, GA 31092 • *2,708*
Vienna, IL 62995 • *1,408*
Vienna, VA 22180-83 • *14,852*
Vienna, WV 26105 • *10,862*
View Park, CA 90043 • *5,900*
Vigo □, IN • *106,107*
Vilas □, WI • *17,707*
Villa Grove, IL 61956 • *2,734*
Villa Hills, KY 41016 • *7,739*
Villa Park, CA 92667 • *6,299*
Villa Park, IL 60181 • *22,253*
Villa Rica, GA 30180 • *6,542*
Villas, NJ 08251 • *8,136*
Ville Platte, LA 70586 • *9,037*
Villisca, IA 50864 • *1,332*
Vilonia, AR 72173 • *1,133*
Vincennes, IN 47591 • *19,859*
Vincent, AL 35178 • *1,767*
Vine Grove, KY 40175 • *3,586*
Vineland, NJ 08360 • *54,780*
Vineyard Haven, MA 02568 • *1,762*
Vinita, OK 74301 • *5,804*
Vinton, IA 52349 • *5,103*
Vinton, LA 70668 • *3,154*
Vinton, VA 24179 • *7,665*
Vinton □, OH • *11,098*
Viola, NY 10952 • *4,504*
Violet, LA 70092 • *8,574*
Virden, IL 62690 • *3,635*
Virginia, IL 62691 • *1,767*
Virginia, MN 55792 • *9,410*
Virginia Beach, VA 23450-67 • *393,069*
Virginia City, NV 89440 • *920*
Viroqua, WI 54665 • *3,922*
Visalia, CA 93277-79 • *75,636*
Vista, CA 92083-84 • *71,872*
Vivian, LA 71082 • *4,156*
Volcano, HI 96785 • *1,516*
Volga, SD 57071 • *1,263*
Volusia □, FL • *370,712*

W

Wabash, IN 46992 • *12,127*
Wabash □, IL • *13,111*
Wabash □, IN • *35,069*
Wabasha, MN 55981 • *2,384*
Wabasha □, MN • *19,744*
Wabasso, FL 32970 • *1,145*
Wabaunsee □, KS • *6,603*
Waco, TX 76701-16 • *103,590*
Waconia, MN 55387 • *3,498*
Wade Hampton, SC 29607 • *20,014*
Wadena, MN 56482 • *4,131*
Wadena □, MN • *13,154*
Wadesboro, NC 28170 • *3,645*
Wading River, NY 11792 • *5,317*
Wadley, GA 30477 • *2,473*
Wadsworth, IL 60083 • *1,826*
Wadsworth, NV 89442 • *640*
Wadsworth, OH 44281 • *15,718*
Wagner, SD 57380 • *1,462*
Wagoner, OK 74467 • *6,894*
Wagoner □, OK • *47,883*
Wahiawa, HI 96786 • *17,386*
Wahkiakum □, WA • *3,327*
Wahoo, NE 68066 • *3,681*
Wahpeton, ND 58074-75 • *8,751*
Waialua, HI 96791 • *3,943*
Waianae, HI 96792 • *8,758*
Waikapu, HI 96793 • *729*
Waikele, HI 96746 • *2,018*
Wailuku, HI 96793 • *10,688*
Waimanalo, HI 96795 • *3,508*
Waimea, HI 96712 • *600*
Waimea, HI 96796 • *5,972*
Wainwright, AK 99782 • *492*
Waipahu, HI 96797 • *31,435*
Waipio Acres, HI 96786 • *5,304*
Waite Park, MN 56387 • *5,020*
Wakarusa, IN 46573 • *1,667*
Wake □, NC • *423,380*
Wa Keeney, KS 67672 • *2,161*

Wakefield, MA 01880 • *24,825*
Wakefield, MI 49968 • *2,318*
Wakefield, NE 68784 • *1,082*
Wakefield, RI 02879-83 • *3,450*
Wakefield, VA 23888 • *1,070*
Wake Forest, NC 27587-88 • *5,769*
Wakulla □, FL • *14,202*
Walbridge, OH 43465 • *2,736*
Walcott, IA 52773 • *1,356*
Walden, NY 12586 • *5,836*
Waldo, AR 71770 • *1,495*
Waldo, FL 32694 • *1,017*
Waldo □, ME • *33,018*
Waldoboro, ME 04572 • *1,420*
Waldport, OR 97394 • *1,595*
Waldron, AR 72958 • *3,024*
Waldwick, NJ 07463 • *9,757*
Walhalla, ND 58282 • *1,131*
Walhalla, SC 29691 • *3,755*
Walker, LA 70785 • *3,727*
Walker, MI 49504 • *17,279*
Walker □, AL • *67,670*
Walker □, GA • *58,340*
Walker □, TX • *50,917*
Walkersville, MD 21793 • *4,145*
Walkerton, IN 46574 • *2,061*
Walkertown, NC 27051 • *1,200*
Walkerville, MT 59701 • *605*
Wall, SD 57790 • *834*
Wallace, ID 83873 • *1,010*
Wallace, NC 28466 • *2,939*
Wallace □, KS • *1,821*
Walla Walla, WA 99362 • *26,478*
Walla Walla □, WA • *48,439*
Walled Lake, MI 48390 • *6,278*
Wallen, IN 46806 • *1,000*
Waller, TX 77484 • *1,493*
Waller □, TX • *23,390*
Wallingford, CT 06492 • *17,827*
Wallingford, VT 05773 • *1,148*
Wallington, NJ 07057 • *10,828*
Wallis, TX 77485 • *1,001*
Wallkill, NY 12589 • *2,125*
Wallowa □, OR • *6,911*
Walnut, CA 91789 • *29,105*
Walnut, IL 61376 • *1,463*
Walnut Cove, NC 27052 • *1,088*
Walnut Creek, CA 94583-98 • *60,569*
Walnut Park, CA 90255 • *14,722*
Walnutport, PA 18088 • *2,055*
Walnut Ridge, AR 72476 • *4,388*
Walpole, MA 02081 • *5,495*
Walsenburg, CO 81089 • *3,300*
Walsh □, ND • *13,840*
Walterboro, SC 29488 • *5,492*
Walters, OK 73572 • *2,519*
Walthall □, MS • *14,352*
Waltham, MA 02154 • *57,878*
Walthourville, GA 31333 • *2,024*
Walton, IN 46994 • *1,053*
Walton, KY 41094 • *2,034*
Walton, NY 13856 • *3,326*
Walton □, FL • *27,760*
Walton □, GA • *38,586*
Walworth, WI 53184 • *1,614*
Walworth □, SD • *6,087*
Walworth □, WI • *75,000*
Wamac, IL 62801 • *1,501*
Wamego, KS 66547 • *3,706*
Wamesit, MA 01876 • *2,700*
Wamsutter, WY 82336 • *240*
Wanaque, NJ 07465 • *9,711*
Wanchese, NC 27981 • *1,380*
Wando Woods, SC 29405 • *5,253*
Wantagh, NY 11793 • *18,567*
Wapakoneta, OH 45895 • *9,214*
Wapato, WA 98951 • *3,795*
Wapello, IA 52653 • *2,013*
Wapello □, IA • *35,687*
Wappingers Falls, NY 12590 • *4,605*
War, WV 24892 • *1,081*
Ward, AR 72176 • *1,269*
Ward □, ND • *57,921*
Ward □, TX • *13,115*
Warden, WA 98857 • *1,639*
Ware, MA 01082 • *6,533*
Ware □, GA • *35,471*
Wareham, MA 02571 • *2,607*
Ware Shoals, SC 29692 • *2,497*
Waretown, NJ 08758 • *1,283*
Warminster, PA 18974 • *35,463*
Warner, OK 74469 • *1,479*
Warner Robins, GA 31088 • *43,726*
Warr Acres, OK 73132 • *9,288*
Warren, AR 71671 • *6,455*
Warren, IL 61087 • *1,550*
Warren, IN 46792 • *1,185*
Warren, MA 01083 • *1,516*
Warren, MI 48089-93 • *144,864*
Warren, MN 56762 • *1,813*
Warren, OH 44481-85 • *50,793*
Warren, PA 16365 • *11,122*
Warren, RI 02885 • *11,385*
Warren, VT 05674 • *350*
Warren □, GA • *6,078*
Warren □, IL • *19,181*
Warren □, IN • *8,176*
Warren □, IA • *36,033*
Warren □, KY • *76,673*
Warren □, MS • *47,880*
Warren □, MO • *19,534*
Warren □, NJ • *91,607*
Warren □, NY • *59,209*
Warren □, NC • *17,265*
Warren □, OH • *113,909*
Warren □, PA • *45,050*
Warren □, TN • *32,992*
Warren □, VA • *26,142*
Warren Park, IN 46219 • *1,763*
Warrensburg, IL 62573 • *1,274*
Warrensburg, MO 64093 • *15,244*
Warrensburg, NY 12885 • *3,204*
Warrensville Heights, OH 44122 • *15,745*
Warrenton, GA 30828 • *2,056*
Warrenton, MO 63383 • *3,564*
Warrenton, OR 97146 • *2,681*
Warrenton, VA 22186 • *4,830*
Warrenville, SC 29851 • *1,029*
Warrick □, IN • *44,920*
Warrington, FL 32507 • *16,040*
Warrington, PA 18976 • *6,980*

Warrior, AL 35180 • 3,280
Warroad, MN 56763 • 1,679
Warsaw, IN 46580-81 • 10,968
Warsaw, IL 62379 • 1,882
Warsaw, KY 41095 • 1,202
Warsaw, MO 65355 • 1,696
Warsaw, NY 14569 • 3,830
Warsaw, NC 28398 • 2,859
Warwick, NY 10990 • 5,984
Warwick, RI 02886-89 • 85,427
Wasatch ☐, UT • 10,089
Wasco, CA 93280 • 12,412
Wasco ☐, OR • 21,683
Waseca, MN 56093 • 8,385
Waseca ☐, MN • 18,079
Washakie ☐, WY • 8,388
Washburn, IL 61570 • 1,075
Washburn, IA 50706 • 1,400
Washburn, ME 04786 • 1,880
Washburn, ND 58577 • 1,506
Washburn, WI 54891 • 2,285
Washburn ☐, WI • 13,772
Washington, DC 20001-99 • 606,900
Washington, GA 30673 • 4,279
Washington, IL 61571 • 10,099
Washington, IN 47501 • 10,838
Washington, IA 52353 • 7,074
Washington, KS 66968 • 1,304
Washington, LA 70589 • 1,253
Washington, MO 63090 • 10,704
Washington, NJ 07882 • 6,474
Washington, NC 27889 • 9,075
Washington, PA 15301 • 15,864
Washington, UT 84780 • 4,198
Washington ☐, AL • 16,694
Washington ☐, AR • 113,409
Washington ☐, CO • 4,812
Washington ☐, FL • 16,919
Washington ☐, GA • 19,112
Washington ☐, ID • 8,550
Washington ☐, IL • 14,965
Washington ☐, IN • 23,717
Washington ☐, IA • 19,612
Washington ☐, KS • 7,073
Washington ☐, KY • 10,441
Washington ☐, LA • 43,185
Washington ☐, ME • 35,308
Washington ☐, MD • 121,393
Washington ☐, MN • 145,896
Washington ☐, MS • 67,935
Washington ☐, MO • 20,380
Washington ☐, NE • 16,607
Washington ☐, NY • 59,330
Washington ☐, NC • 13,997
Washington ☐, OH • 62,254
Washington ☐, OK • 48,066
Washington ☐, OR • 311,554
Washington ☐, PA • 204,584
Washington ☐, RI • 110,006
Washington ☐, TN • 92,315
Washington ☐, TX • 26,154
Washington ☐, UT • 48,560
Washington ☐, VT • 54,928
Washington ☐, VA • 45,887
Washington ☐, WI • 95,328
Washington Court House, OH 43160 • 12,983
Washington Park, FL 33314 • 6,930
Washington Park, IL 62204 • 7,431
Washington Terrace, UT 84403 • 8,189
Washington Township, NJ 07675 • 9,245
Washita ☐, OK • 11,441
Washoe ☐, NV • 254,667
Washoe City, NV 89701 • 400
Washougal, WA 98671 • 4,764
Washtenaw ☐, MI • 282,937
Wasilla, AK 99687 • 4,028
Waskom, TX 75692 • 1,812
Watauga, TX 76148 • 20,009
Watauga ☐, NC • 36,952
Watchung, NJ 07060 • 5,110
Waterbury, CT 06701-26 • 108,961
Waterbury, VT 05676 • 1,702
Waterbury Center, VT 05677 • 500
Waterford, CT 06385 • 17,930
Waterford, MI 48327-29 • 66,692
Waterford, NY 12188 • 2,370
Waterford, PA 16444 • 1,492
Waterford, WI 53185 • 2,431
Waterford Works, NJ 08089 • 1,200
Waterloo, IL 62298 • 5,072
Waterloo, IN 46793 • 2,040
Waterloo, IA 50701-07 • 66,467
Waterloo, NY 13165 • 5,116
Waterloo, WI 53594 • 2,712
Waterman, IL 60556 • 1,074
Waterproof, LA 71375 • 1,080
Watertown, CT 06795 • 20,456
Watertown, FL 32055 • 3,340
Watertown, MA 02172 • 33,284
Watertown, NY 13601-03 • 29,429
Watertown, SD 57201 • 17,592
Watertown, TN 37184 • 1,250
Watertown, WI 53094 • 19,142
Water Valley, MS 38965 • 3,610
Waterville, ME 04901-03 • 17,173
Waterville, MN 56096 • 1,771
Waterville, NY 13480 • 1,664
Waterville, OH 43566 • 4,517
Watervliet, MI 49098 • 1,867
Watervliet, NY 12189 • 11,061
Watford City, ND 58854 • 1,784
Wathena, KS 66090 • 1,160
Watkins Glen, NY 14891 • 2,207
Watkinsville, GA 30677 • 1,600
Watonga, OK 73772 • 3,408
Watonwan ☐, MN • 11,682
Watseka, IL 60970 • 5,424
Watsontown, PA 17777 • 2,310
Watsonville, CA 95076-77 • 31,099
Wattsville, GA 29360 • 1,324
Wauchula, FL 33873 • 3,253
Wauconda, IL 60084 • 6,294
Waukee, IA 50263 • 2,512
Waukegan, IL 60085-87 • 69,392
Waukesha, WI 53186-88 • 56,958
Waukesha ☐, WI • 304,715
Waukomis, OK 73773 • 1,322
Waukon, IA 52172 • 4,019
Waunakee, WI 53597 • 5,897
Waupaca, WI 54981 • 4,957
Waupaca ☐, WI • 46,104
Waupun, WI 53963 • 8,207

Wauregan, CT 06387 • 1,200
Waurika, OK 73573 • 2,088
Wausau, WI 54401-02 • 37,060
Wauseon, OH 43567 • 6,322
Waushara ☐, WI • 19,385
Wautoma, WI 54982 • 1,784
Wauwatosa, WI 53213 • 49,366
Waveland, MS 39576 • 5,369
Waverly, IL 62692 • 1,402
Waverly, IA 50677 • 8,539
Waverly, MI 48917 • 15,614
Waverly, NE 68462 • 1,869
Waverly, NY 14892 • 4,787
Waverly, OH 45690 • 4,477
Waverly, TN 37185 • 3,925
Waverly, VA 23890 • 2,223
Waxahachie, TX 75165 • 18,168
Waxhaw, NC 28173 • 1,294
Waycross, GA 31501 • 16,410
Wayland, MA 01778 • 2,550
Wayland, MI 49348 • 2,751
Wayland, NY 14572 • 1,976
Waylyn, SC 29405 • 2,400
Waymart, PA 18472 • 1,327
Wayne, MI 48184-88 • 19,899
Wayne, NE 68787 • 5,142
Wayne, NJ 07470-74 • 47,025
Wayne, WV 25570 • 1,128
Wayne ☐, GA • 22,356
Wayne ☐, IL • 17,241
Wayne ☐, IN • 71,951
Wayne ☐, IA • 7,067
Wayne ☐, KY • 17,468
Wayne ☐, MI • 2,111,687
Wayne ☐, MS • 19,517
Wayne ☐, MO • 11,543
Wayne ☐, NE • 9,364
Wayne ☐, NY • 89,123
Wayne ☐, NC • 104,666
Wayne ☐, OH • 101,461
Wayne ☐, PA • 39,944
Wayne ☐, TN • 13,935
Wayne ☐, UT • 2,177
Wayne ☐, WV • 41,636
Wayne City, IL 62895 • 1,099
Waynesboro, GA 30830 • 5,701
Waynesboro, MS 39367 • 5,143
Waynesboro, PA 17268 • 9,578
Waynesboro, TN 38485 • 1,824
Waynesboro, VA 22980 • 18,549
Waynesburg, OH 44688 • 1,068
Waynesburg, PA 15370 • 4,270
Waynesville, MO 65583 • 3,207
Waynesville, NC 28786 • 6,758
Waynesville, OH 45068 • 1,949
Waynewood, VA 22308 • 5,000
Wayzata, MN 55391 • 3,806
Weakley ☐, TN • 31,972
Weatherford, OK 73096 • 10,124
Weatherford, TX 76086-87 • 14,804
Weatherly, PA 18255 • 2,640
Weatogue, CT 06089 • 2,521
Weaver, AL 36277 • 2,715
Weaverville, CA 96093 • 3,370
Weaverville, NC 28787 • 2,107
Webb, AL 36376 • 1,039
Webb ☐, TX • 133,239
Webb City, MO 64870 • 7,449
Webberville, MI 48892 • 1,698
Weber ☐, UT • 158,330
Weber City, VA 24251 • 1,377
Webster, MA 01570 • 11,849
Webster, NY 14580 • 5,464
Webster, PA 15087 • 1,000
Webster, SD 57274 • 2,017
Webster ☐, GA • 2,263
Webster ☐, IA • 40,342
Webster ☐, KY • 13,955
Webster ☐, LA • 41,989
Webster ☐, MS • 10,222
Webster ☐, MO • 23,753
Webster ☐, NE • 4,279
Webster ☐, WV • 10,729
Webster City, IA 50595 • 7,894
Webster Groves, MO 63119 • 22,987
Websterville, VT 05678 • 600
Wedgewood, MO 63031 • 6,700
Weed, CA 96094 • 3,062
Weed Heights, NV 89447 • 230
Weedsport, NY 13166 • 1,996
Weehawken, NJ 07087 • 12,385
Weeping Water, NE 68463 • 1,098
Weigelstown, PA 17315 • 8,665
Weimar, TX 78962 • 2,052
Weippe, ID 83553 • 532
Weirsdale, FL 32195 • 1,500
Weirton, WV 26062 • 22,124
Weiser, ID 83672 • 4,571
Wekiva Springs, FL 32750 • 23,026
Welch, WV 24801 • 3,028
Welcome, SC 29611 • 6,560
Weld ☐, CO • 131,821
Weldon, NC 27890 • 1,392
Weleetka, OK 74880 • 1,112
Wellesley, MA 02181 • 26,615
Wellfleet, MA 02667 • 1,200
Wellford, SC 29385 • 2,511
Wellington, CO 80549 • 1,340
Wellington, FL 33414 • 20,670
Wellington, KS 67152 • 8,411
Wellington, NV 89444 • 280
Wellington, OH 44090 • 4,140
Wellington, TX 79095 • 2,456
Wellington, UT 84542 • 1,632
Wellman, IA 52356 • 1,085
Wells, ME 04090 • 1,200
Wells, MI 49894 • 1,150
Wells, NE 56097 • 2,465
Wells, NV 89835 • 1,256
Wells, NY 25,948
Wells ☐, ND • 5,864
Wellsboro, PA 16901 • 3,430
Wellsburg, WV 26070 • 3,385
Wellston, OH 45692 • 6,049
Wellsville, KS 66092 • 1,563
Wellsville, MO 63384 • 1,430
Wellsville, NY 14895 • 5,241
Wellsville, OH 43968 • 4,532
Wellsville, UT 84339 • 2,206
Wellton, AZ 85356 • 1,066
Welsh, LA 70591 • 3,299
Wenatchee, WA 98801-07 • 21,756
Wendell, ID 83355 • 1,963

Wendell, NC 27591 • 2,822
Wendover, UT 84083 • 1,127
Wenham, MA 01984 • 3,897
Wenonah, NJ 08090 • 2,331
Wentzville, MO 63385 • 5,088
Weslaco, TX 78596 • 21,877
Wesleyville, PA 16510 • 3,655
Wessington Springs, SD 57382 • 1,083
Wesson, MS 39191 • 1,510
West, TX 76691 • 2,515
West Acton, MA 01720 • 5,230
West Alexandria, OH 45381 • 1,460
West Allis, WI 53214 • 63,221
West Andover, MA 01810 • 1,970
West Athens, CA 90247 • 8,859
West Babylon, NY 11704 • 42,410
West Barnstable, MA 02668 • 1,000
West Baton Rouge ☐, LA • 19,419
West Bay Shore, NY 11706 • 4,907
West Bend, WI 53095 • 23,916
West Berlin, NJ 08091 • 2,970
West Billerica, MA 01862 • 1,920
West Blocton, AL 35184 • 1,468
Westborough, MA 01581 • 3,130
West Bountiful, UT 84087 • 4,477
West Bradenton, FL 34205 • 4,528
West Branch, IA 52358 • 1,908
West Branch, MI 48661 • 1,914
West Bridgewater, MA 02379 • 2,140
Westbrook, CT 06498 • 2,060
Westbrook, ME 04092 • 16,121
West Brookfield, MA 01585 • 1,419
West Burlington, IA 52655 • 3,083
Westbury, NY 11590 • 13,060
Westby, WI 54667 • 1,866
West Caldwell, NJ 07004 • 10,422
West Cape May, NJ 08204 • 1,026
West Carroll ☐, LA • 12,093
West Carrollton, OH 45449 • 14,403
West Carson, CA 90502 • 20,143
West Carthage, NY 13619 • 2,166
West Chatham, MA 02669 • 1,504
Westchester, FL 33136 • 29,883
Westchester, IL 60153 • 17,301
West Chester, PA 19380-82 • 18,041
Westchester ☐, NY • 874,866
West Chicago, IL 60185-86 • 14,796
West Columbia, SC 29169-72 • 10,588
West Columbia, TX 77486 • 4,372
West Compton, CA 90220 • 5,451
West Concord, MA 01742 • 5,761
West Concord, NC 28027 • 5,859
West Covina, CA 91790-93 • 96,086
West Crossett, AR 71635 • 2,019
West Dennis, MA 02670 • 2,307
West Des Moines, IA 50265 • 31,702
West Elmira, NY 14905 • 5,218
Westerly, RI 02891 • 16,477
Westernport, MD 21562 • 2,454
Western Springs, IL 60558 • 11,984
Westerville, OH 43081-82 • 30,269
West Fairview, PA 17025 • 1,403
West Falmouth, MA 02574 • 1,600
West Fargo, ND 58078 • 12,287
West Feliciana ☐, LA • 12,915
Westfield, IN 46074 • 3,304
Westfield, MA 01085-86 • 38,372
Westfield, NJ 07090-92 • 28,870
Westfield, NY 14787 • 3,451
Westfield, PA 16950 • 1,119
Westfield, WI 53964 • 1,125
Westford, MA 01886 • 1,200
West Fork, AR 72774 • 1,607
West Frankfort, IL 62896 • 8,526
West Freehold, NJ 07728 • 11,166
Westgate, FL 33401 • 2,100
West Gate, VA 22110 • 6,565
West Gate of Lomond, VA 22110 • 5,400
West Glens Falls, NY 12801 • 5,964
West Goshen, PA 19380 • 8,943
West Grove, PA 19390 • 2,128
Westham, VA 23229 • 3,200
West Hanover, MA 02339 • 1,700
West Hartford, CT 06127 • 60,110
West Haven, CT 06516 • 54,021
West Haven, OR 97225 • 3,400
West Haverstraw, NY 10993 • 9,183
West Hazleton, PA 18201 • 4,136
West Helena, AR 72390 • 9,695
West Hempstead, NY 11552 • 17,689
West Hollywood, CA 90069 • 36,118
Westhope, ND 58793 • 578
West Hyannisport, MA 02672 • 1,200
West Islip, NY 11795 • 28,419
West Jefferson, NC 28694 • 1,002
West Jefferson, OH 43162 • 4,504
West Jordan, UT 84084 • 42,892
West Kingston, RI 02892 • 1,150
West Lafayette, IN 47906-07 • 25,907
West Lafayette, OH 43845 • 2,129
Westlake, LA 70669 • 4,600
Westlake, OH 44145 • 27,018
Westlake Village, CA 91361 • 7,455
Westland, MI 48185 • 84,724
West Lawn, PA 19609 • 1,606
West Liberty, IA 52776 • 2,935
West Liberty, KY 41472 • 1,887
West Liberty, OH 43357 • 1,613
West Liberty, WV 26074 • 1,434
West Linn, OR 97068 • 16,367
West Long Branch, NJ 07764 • 7,690
West Marion, NC 28752 • 1,291
West Medway, MA 02053 • 1,940
West Melbourne, FL 32901 • 8,399
West Memphis, AR 72301 • 28,259
Westmere, NY 12203 • 6,750
West Miami, FL 33174 • 5,727
West Mifflin, PA 15122-23 • 23,644
West Milford, NJ 07480 • 25,430
West Milton, OH 45383 • 4,348
West Milwaukee, WI 53214 • 3,973
Westminster, CA 92683-84 • 78,118
Westminster, CO 80030-31 • 74,625
Westminster, MD 21157 • 13,068
Westminster, SC 29693 • 3,120
West Modesto, CA 95351 • 6,135
West Monroe, LA 71291-94 • 14,096
Westmont, CA 90044 • 31,100
Westmont, IL 60559 • 21,228
Westmont, NJ 08108 • 5,630
Westmont, PA 15905 • 5,789
Westmoreland, TN 37186 • 1,726

Westmoreland ☐, PA • 370,321
Westmoreland ☐, VA • 15,480
Westmorland, CA 92281 • 1,380
West Mystic, CT 06388 • 3,595
West Newton, PA 15089 • 3,152
West New York, NJ 07093 • 38,125
West Norriton, PA 19401 • 15,209
West Nyack, NY 10960 • 3,437
Weston, CT 06883 • 1,370
Weston, MA 02193 • 11,169
Weston, MO 64098 • 1,528
Weston, OH 43569 • 1,716
Weston, WV 26452 • 4,994
Weston, WI 54476 • 9,714
Weston ☐, WY • 6,518
West Orange, NJ 07052 • 39,103
Westover, WV 26505 • 4,201
West Palm Beach, FL 33401-20 • 67,643
West Pasco, WA 99301 • 7,312
West Paterson, NJ 07424 • 10,982
West Pawlet, VT 05775 • 350
West Pensacola, FL 32505 • 22,107
West Peoria, IL 61604 • 5,314
West Pittsburg, CA 94565 • 17,453
West Pittsburg, PA 16160 • 1,133
West Pittston, PA 18643 • 5,590
West Plains, MO 65775 • 8,913
West Point, CA 95255 • 1,500
West Point, GA 31833 • 3,571
West Point, IA 52656 • 1,079
West Point, KY 40177 • 1,216
West Point, MS 39773 • 8,489
West Point, NE 68788 • 3,250
West Point, NY 10996-97 • 8,024
West Point, UT 84015 • 4,258
West Point, VA 23181 • 2,938
Westport, CT 06880-83 • 24,407
Westport, IN 47283 • 1,478
Westport, WA 98595 • 1,892
West Portsmouth, OH 45662 • 3,551
West Puente Valley, CA 91744 • 20,254
West Reading, PA 19611 • 4,142
West Rutland, VT 05777 • 2,246
West Sacramento, CA 95691 • 28,898
West Saint Paul, MN 55118 • 19,248
West Salem, IL 62476 • 1,042
West Salem, OH 44287 • 1,534
West Salem, WI 54669 • 3,611
West Sayville, NY 11796 • 4,680
West Seneca, NY 14224 • 47,866
West Simsbury, CT 06092 • 2,149
West Slope, OR 97225 • 7,959
West Springfield, MA 01089-90 • 27,537
West Springfield, VA 22152 • 28,126
West Swanzey, NH 03469 • 1,055
West Terre Haute, IN 47885 • 2,495
West Union, IA 52175 • 2,490
West Union, OH 45693 • 3,096
West Unity, OH 43570 • 1,677
West University Place, TX 77005 • 12,920
West Upton, MA 01587 • 1,300
Westvale, NY 13219 • 5,552
West Valley City, UT 84120 • 86,976
Westview, FL 33168 • 9,668
West View, PA 15229 • 7,734
Westville, IL 61883 • 3,387
Westville, IN 46391 • 5,255
Westville, NJ 08093 • 4,573
Westville, OK 74965 • 1,374
West Wareham, MA 02576 • 2,059
West Warren, MA 01092 • 1,200
West Warwick, RI 02893 • 29,268
West Webster, NY 14580 • 8,690
Westwego, LA 70094-96 • 11,218
West Whittier, CA 90606 • 4,936
West Willow, MI 48198 • 4,300
Westwood, CA 96137 • 2,017
Westwood, KS 66205 • 1,772
Westwood, KY 41101 • 5,300
Westwood, MA 02090 • 6,500
Westwood, MI 49007 • 8,957
Westwood, NJ 07675 • 10,446
Westwood Lakes, FL 33165 • 11,522
West Wyoming, PA 18644 • 3,117
West Yarmouth, MA 02673 • 5,409
West Yellowstone, MT 59758 • 913
West York, PA 17404 • 4,283
Wethersfield, CT 06129 • 25,651
Wetumka, OK 74883 • 1,427
Wetumpka, AL 36092 • 4,670
Wetzel ☐, WV • 19,258
Wewahitchka, FL 32465 • 1,779
Wewoka, OK 74884 • 4,050
Wexford ☐, MI • 26,360
Weyauwega, WI 54983 • 1,665
Weymouth, MA 02188 • 54,063
Whalom, MA 01420 • 1,340
Wharton, NJ 07885 • 5,405
Wharton, TX 77488 • 9,011
Wharton ☐, TX • 39,955
Whatcom ☐, WA • 127,780
Wheatland, CA 95692 • 1,631
Wheatland, WY 82201 • 3,271
Wheatland ☐, MT • 2,246
Wheaton, IL 60187-89 • 51,464
Wheaton, MD 20902 • 58,300
Wheaton, MN 56296 • 1,615
Wheat Ridge, CO 80033-34 • 29,419
Wheeler, TX 79096 • 1,393
Wheeler ☐, GA • 4,903
Wheeler ☐, NE • 948
Wheeler ☐, OR • 1,396
Wheeler ☐, TX • 5,879
Wheelersburg, OH 45694 • 5,113
Wheeling, IL 60090 • 29,911
Wheeling, WV 26003 • 34,882
Whitacres, CT 06082 • 2,410
White ☐, AR • 54,676
White ☐, GA • 13,006
White ☐, IL • 16,522
White ☐, IN • 23,265
White ☐, TN • 20,090
White Bear Lake, MN 55110 • 24,704
White Bluff, TN 37187 • 1,988
White Castle, LA 70788 • 2,102
White Center, WA 98126 • 15,700
White City, OR 97503 • 5,891
White City, UT 84070 • 6,506
White Cloud, MI 49349 • 1,147
White Deer, TX 79097 • 1,125
Whitefield, NH 03598 • 1,041
Whitefish, MT 59937 • 4,368
Whitefish Bay, WI 53217 • 14,272

White Hall, AR 71602 • 3,849
White Hall, IL 62092 • 2,814
Whitehall, MI 49461 • 3,027
Whitehall, MT 59759 • 1,067
Whitehall, NY 12887 • 3,071
Whitehall, OH 43213 • 20,572
Whitehall, PA 15227 • 14,451
Whitehall, WI 54773 • 1,494
White Haven, PA 18661 • 1,132
White Horse, NJ 08610 • 9,397
White Horse Beach, MA 02381 • 1,200
Whitehouse, OH 43571 • 2,528
White House, TN 37188 • 2,987
White House Station, NJ 08889 • 1,400
White Island Shores, MA 02538 • 2,000
White Meadow Lake, NJ 07866 • 8,002
White Oak, MD 20901 • 18,671
White Oak, OH 45239 • 12,430
White Oak, PA 15131 • 8,761
White Pigeon, MI 49099 • 1,458
White Pine, MI 49971 • 1,142
White Pine, TN 37890 • 1,771
White Pine ☐, NV • 9,264
White Plains, MD 20695 • 3,560
White Plains, NY 10601-07 • 48,718
Whiteriver, AZ 85941 • 3,775
White River Junction, VT 05001 • 2,521
White Rock, NM 87544 • 6,192
White Salmon, WA 98672 • 1,861
Whitesboro, NY 13492 • 4,195
Whitesboro, TX 76273 • 3,209
Whitesburg, KY 41858 • 1,636
White Settlement, TX 76108 • 15,472
Whiteside ☐, IL • 60,186
White Sulphur Springs, MT 59645 • 963
White Sulphur Springs, WV 24986 • 2,779
Whiteville, NC 28472 • 5,078
Whiteville, TN 38075 • 1,050
Whitewater, WI 53190 • 12,636
Whitewood, SD 57793 • 891
Whitewright, TX 75491 • 1,713
Whitfield ☐, GA • 72,462
Whitfield Estates, FL 34243 • 3,152
Whiting, IN 46394 • 5,155
Whiting, WI 54481 • 1,838
Whitinsville, MA 01588 • 5,639
Whitley ☐, IN • 27,651
Whitley ☐, KY • 33,326
Whitley City, KY 42653 • 1,133
Whitman, MA 02382 • 13,534
Whitman, WV 25652 • 1,651
Whitman ☐, WA • 38,775
Whitman Square, NJ 08012 • 3,490
Whitmire, SC 29178 • 1,702
Whitmore Lake, MI 48189 • 3,251
Whitmore Village, HI 96786 • 3,373
Whitney, SC 29303 • 4,052
Whitney, TX 76692 • 1,626
Whitney Point, NY 13862 • 1,054
Whittier, AK 99693 • 243
Whittier, CA 90601-12 • 77,671
Whitwell, TN 37397 • 1,622
Wibaux, MT 59353 • 628
Wibaux ☐, MT • 1,191
Wichita, KS 67201-78 • 304,011
Wichita ☐, KS • 2,758
Wichita ☐, TX • 122,378
Wichita Falls, TX 76301-11 • 96,259
Wickenburg, AZ 85358 • 4,515
Wickliffe, OH 44092 • 14,558
Wickliffe, OH 44515 • 7,240
Wicomico ☐, MD • 74,339
Wiconisco, PA 17097 • 1,321
Widefield, CO 80911 • 12,112
Wiggins, MS 39577 • 3,185
Wilbarger ☐, TX • 15,121
Wilber, NE 68465 • 1,527
Wilberforce, OH 45384 • 2,639
Wilbraham, MA 01095 • 3,352
Wilburton, OK 74578 • 3,092
Wilcox, PA 15870 • 1,000
Wilcox ☐, AL • 13,568
Wilcox ☐, GA • 7,008
Wilder, ID 83676 • 1,232
Wilder, VT 05088 • 1,576
Wildorado, TX 79098 • 2,000
Wildwood, CA 34785 • 3,421
Wildwood, IL 60030 • 2,034
Wildwood, NJ 08260 • 4,484
Wildwood Crest, NJ 08260 • 3,631
Wilkes ☐, GA • 10,597
Wilkes ☐, NC • 59,393
Wilkes-Barre, PA 18701-73 • 47,523
Wilkesboro, NC 28697 • 2,573
Wilkin ☐, MN • 7,516
Wilkinsburg, PA 15221 • 21,080
Wilkinson ☐, GA • 10,228
Wilkinson ☐, MS • 9,678
Wilkins Township, PA 15145 • 7,487
Will ☐, IL • 357,313
Willacoochee, GA 31650 • 1,205
Willacy ☐, TX • 17,705
Willamina, OR 97396 • 1,717
Willard, MO 65781 • 2,177
Willard, NY 14588 • 1,339
Willard, OH 44890 • 6,210
Willard, UT 84340 • 1,298
Willcox, AZ 85643 • 3,122
Williams, AZ 86046 • 2,532
Williams, CA 95987 • 2,297
Williams ☐, ND • 21,129
Williams ☐, OH • 36,956
Williams Bay, WI 53191 • 2,108
Williamsburg, IA 52361 • 2,174
Williamsburg, KY 40769 • 5,493
Williamsburg, MA 01096 • 1,200
Williamsburg, OH 45176 • 2,322
Williamsburg, PA 16693 • 1,456
Williamsburg, VA 23185-88 • 11,530
Williamsburg ☐, SC • 36,815
Williamson, NY 14589 • 1,768
Williamson, WV 25661 • 4,154
Williamson ☐, IL • 57,733
Williamson ☐, TN • 81,021
Williamson ☐, TX • 139,551
Williamsport, IN 47993 • 1,798
Williamsport, MD 21795 • 2,103
Williamsport, PA 17701-03 • 31,933
Williamston, MI 48895 • 2,922
Williamston, NC 27892 • 5,503
Williamston, SC 29697 • 3,876
Williamstown, KY 41097 • 3,023
Williamstown, MA 01267 • 4,791

United States Populations and ZIP Codes

Williamstown, NJ 08094 • 10,891
Williamstown, PA 17098 • 1,509
Williamstown, WV 26187 • 2,774
Williamsville, IL 62693 • 1,140
Williamsville, NY 14221 • 5,583
Willimantic, CT 06226 • 14,746
Willingboro, NJ 08046 • 36,291
Willis, TX 77378 • 2,764
Williston, FL 32696 • 2,179
Williston, ND 58801-02 • 13,131
Williston, SC 29853 • 3,099
Williston Park, NY 11596 • 7,516
Willits, CA 95490 • 5,027
Willmar, MN 56201 • 17,531
Willoughby, OH 44094-95 • 20,510
Willoughby Hills, OH 44092 • 8,427
Willow Brook, CA 90222 • 32,772
Willowbrook, IL 60521 • 8,598
Willow Grove, PA 19090 • 16,325
Willowick, OH 44094 • 15,269
Willow Run, DE 19805 • 1,600
Willow Run, MI 48198 • 7,200
Willows, CA 95988 • 5,988
Willow Springs, IL 60480 • 4,509
Willow Springs, MO 65793 • 2,038
Willston, VA 22044 • 2,000
Wilmerding, PA 15148 • 2,222
Wilmette, IL 60091 • 26,690
Wilmington, DE 19801-99 • 71,529
Wilmington, IL 60481 • 4,743
Wilmington, MA 01887 • 17,654
Wilmington, NC 28401-12 • 55,530
Wilmington, OH 45177 • 11,199
Wilmington, VT 05363 • 550
Wilmington Island, GA 31410 • 11,230
Wilmington Manor, DE 19720 • 8,568
Wilmington Manor Gardens, DE 19720 • 1,500
Wilmore, KY 40390 • 4,215
Wilmot, AR 71676 • 1,047
Wilson, AR 72395 • 1,068
Wilson, NY 14172 • 1,307
Wilson, NC 27893-95 • 36,930
Wilson, OK 73463 • 1,639
Wilson, PA 18042 • 7,830
Wilson, WY 83014 • 500
Wilson □, KS • 10,289
Wilson □, NC • 66,061
Wilson □, TN • 67,675
Wilson □, TX • 22,650
Wilsonville, AL 35186 • 1,185
Wilsonville, OR 97070 • 7,106
Wilton, CT 06897 • 7,200
Wilton, IA 52778 • 2,577
Wilton, ME 04294 • 2,453
Wilton, NH 03086 • 1,165
Wilton, ND 58579 • 728
Wilton Manors, FL 33334 • 11,804
Wimauma, FL 33598 • 2,932
Winamac, IN 46996 • 2,262
Winchendon, MA 01475 • 4,316
Winchester, IL 62694 • 1,769
Winchester, IN 47394 • 5,095
Winchester, KY 40391-92 • 15,799
Winchester, MA 01890 • 20,267
Winchester, NV 89101 • 23,365
Winchester, NH 03470 • 1,735
Winchester, TN 37398 • 6,305
Winchester, VA 22601 • 21,947
Windber, PA 15963 • 4,756
Windcrest, TX 78239 • 5,331
Winder, GA 30680 • 7,373
Windgap, PA 18091 • 2,741
Windham, CT 06280 • 1,100
Windham, OH 44288 • 2,943
Windham □, CT • 102,525
Windham □, VT • 41,588
Wind Lake, WI 53185 • 3,000
Windom, MN 56101 • 4,283
Window Rock, AZ 86515 • 3,306
Wind Point, WI 53402 • 1,941
Windsor, CO 80550 • 5,062
Windsor, CT 06095 • 27,817
Windsor, IL 61957 • 1,143
Windsor, MO 65360 • 3,044

Windsor, NC 27983 • 2,056
Windsor, PA 17366 • 1,355
Windsor, VT 05089 • 3,478
Windsor, VA 23487 • 1,025
Windsor □, VT • 54,055
Windsor Heights, IA 50311 • 5,190
Windsor Hills, CA 90052 • 6,200
Windsor Locks, CT 06096 • 12,358
Windy Hill, SC 29506 • 1,622
Windy Hills, DE 19711 • 1,130
Winfield, AL 35594 • 3,689
Winfield, IA 52659 • 1,051
Winfield, KS 67156 • 11,931
Winfield, NJ 07036 • 1,785
Winfield, WV 25213 • 1,164
Wingate, NC 28174 • 2,821
Wink, TX 79789 • 1,189
Winkler □, TX • 8,626
Winlock, WA 98596 • 1,027
Winn □, LA • 16,269
Winnebago, IL 61088 • 1,840
Winnebago, MN 56098 • 1,565
Winnebago, WI 54985 • 1,433
Winnebago □, IL • 252,913
Winnebago □, IA • 12,122
Winnebago □, WI • 140,320
Winneconne, WI 54986 • 2,059
Winnemucca, NV 89445 • 6,134
Winner, SD 57580 • 3,354
Winneshiek □, IA • 20,847
Winnetka, IL 60093 • 12,174
Winnfield, LA 71483 • 6,138
Winnsboro, LA 71295 • 5,755
Winnsboro, SC 29180 • 3,475
Winnsboro, TX 75494 • 2,904
Winnsboro Mills, SC 29180 • 2,275
Winona, MN 55987 • 25,399
Winona, MS 38967 • 5,705
Winona, MO 65588 • 1,081
Winona □, MN • 47,828
Winona Lake, IN 46590 • 4,053
Winooski, VT 05404 • 6,649
Winslow, AZ 86047 • 8,190
Winslow, ME 04901 • 5,436
Winsted, CT 06098 • 8,254
Winsted, MN 55395 • 1,581
Winston, FL 33801 • 9,118
Winston, OR 97496 • 3,773
Winston □, AL • 22,053
Winston □, MS • 19,433
Winston-Salem, NC 27101-27 • 143,485
Winter Garden, FL 34787 • 9,745
Winter Haven, FL 33880-84 • 24,725
Winter Park, FL 32789-90 • 22,242
Winter Park, NC 28403 • 4,504
Winterport, ME 04496 • 1,274
Winters, CA 95694 • 4,639
Winters, TX 79567 • 2,905
Winterset, IA 50273 • 4,196
Winter Springs, FL 32708 • 22,151
Wintersville, OH 43952 • 4,102
Winterville, NC 28590 • 2,816
Winthrop, ME 04364 • 2,819
Winthrop, MA 02152 • 18,127
Winthrop, MN 55396 • 1,279
Winthrop Harbor, IL 60096 • 6,240
Winton, CA 95388 • 7,559
Wirt □, WV • 5,192
Wiscasset, ME 04578 • 1,350
Wisconsin Dells, WI 53965 • 2,393
Wisconsin Rapids, WI 54494-95 • 18,245
Wise, VA 24293 • 3,193
Wise □, TX • 34,679
Wise □, VA • 39,573
Wishek, ND 58495 • 1,171
Wisner, LA 71378 • 1,153
Wisner, NE 68791 • 1,253
Withamsville, OH 45245 • 5,000
Witherbee, NY 12998 • 1,000
Wittenberg, WI 54499 • 1,145
Wixom, MI 48393 • 8,550
Wolcott, CT 06716 • 6,070
Wolcott, NY 14590 • 1,544
Wolfe □, KY • 6,503
Wolfeboro, NH 03894 • 2,783

Wolfe City, TX 75496 • 1,505
Wolf Lake, MI 49442 • 4,110
Wolf Point, MT 59201 • 2,880
Wolf Trap, VA 22182 • 13,133
Womelsdorf, PA 19567 • 2,270
Wonder Lake, IL 60097 • 6,664
Wood □, OH • 113,269
Wood □, TX • 29,380
Wood □, WV • 86,915
Wood □, WI • 73,605
Woodbine, GA 31569 • 1,212
Woodbine, IA 51579 • 1,500
Woodbine, NJ 08270 • 2,678
Woodbourne, NY 12788 • 1,155
Woodbourne, OH 45459 • 6,000
Woodbridge, CT 06525 • 7,924
Woodbridge, NJ 07095 • 17,434
Woodbridge, VA 22191-94 • 26,401
Woodbridge [Township], NJ 07095 • 17,434
Woodburn, IN 46797 • 1,321
Woodburn, OR 97071 • 13,404
Woodbury, CT 06798 • 1,212
Woodbury, GA 30293 • 1,429
Woodbury, MN 55125 • 20,075
Woodbury, NJ 08096 • 10,904
Woodbury, NY 11797 • 8,008
Woodbury, TN 37190 • 2,287
Woodbury □, IA • 98,276
Woodcliff Lake, NJ 07675 • 5,303
Wood Dale, IL 60191 • 12,425
Woodfield, SC 29206 • 8,862
Woodford □, IL • 32,653
Woodford □, KY • 19,955
Woodhaven, MI 48183 • 11,631
Woodlake, CA 93286 • 5,678
Woodland, CA 95695 • 39,802
Woodland, ME 04694 • 1,287
Woodland, WA 98674 • 2,500
Woodland Park, CO 80863 • 4,610
Woodlawn, KY 42001 • 1,600
Woodlawn, MD 21207 • 5,329
Woodlawn, MD 20784 • 5,329
Woodlawn, OH 45215 • 2,674
Woodlawn, VA 24381 • 1,689
Woodlynne, NJ 08107 • 2,547
Woodmere, NY 11598 • 15,578
Woodmont, CT 06460 • 1,770
Woodmoor, MD 21207 • 8,630
Woodridge, IL 60517 • 26,256
Wood-Ridge, NJ 07075 • 7,506
Wood River, IL 62095 • 11,490
Wood River, NE 68883 • 1,156
Woodruff, SC 29388 • 4,365
Woodruff, WI 54568 • 1,500
Woodruff □, AR • 9,520
Woods □, OK • 9,103
Woodsboro, TX 78393 • 1,731
Woods Cross, UT 84087 • 5,384
Woodsfield, OH 43793 • 2,832
Woods Hole, MA 02543 • 1,080
Woodside, CA 94062 • 5,035
Woodson □, KS • 4,116
Woodstock, GA 30188 • 4,361
Woodstock, IL 60098 • 14,353
Woodstock, NY 12498 • 1,870
Woodstock, VT 05091 • 1,037
Woodstock, VA 22664 • 3,182
Woodstown, NJ 08098 • 3,154
Woodsville, NH 03785 • 1,122
Woodville, FL 32362 • 2,760
Woodville, MS 39669 • 1,393
Woodville, OH 43469 • 1,953
Woodville, TX 75979 • 2,636
Woodward, IA 50276 • 1,197
Woodward, OK 73801-02 • 12,340
Woodward □, OK • 18,976
Woodway, TX 76710 • 8,695
Woonsocket, RI 02895 • 43,877
Woonsocket, SD 57385 • 766
Wooster, OH 44691 • 22,191
Worcester, MA 01601-15 • 169,759
Worcester □, MD • 35,028
Worcester □, MA • 709,705
Worland, WY 82401 • 5,742

Worth, IL 60482 • 11,208
Worth □, GA • 19,745
Worth □, IA • 7,991
Worth □, MO • 2,440
Wortham, TX 76693 • 1,020
Worthington, IN 47471 • 1,473
Worthington, KY 41183 • 1,751
Worthington, MN 56187 • 9,977
Worthington, OH 43085 • 14,869
Wrangell, AK 99929 • 2,479
Wray, CO 80758 • 1,998
Wrens, GA 30833 • 2,414
Wrentham, MA 02093 • 2,110
Wright, FL 32548 • 18,945
Wright □, IA • 14,269
Wright □, MN • 68,710
Wright □, MO • 16,758
Wright City, MO 63390 • 1,250
Wrightsboro, NC 28562 • 3,843
Wrightstown, WI 54180 • 1,262
Wrightsville, AR 72183 • 1,062
Wrightsville, GA 31096 • 2,331
Wrightsville, PA 17368 • 2,396
Wrightsville Beach, NC 28480 • 2,937
Wrightwood, CA 92397 • 3,308
Wurtsboro, NY 12790 • 1,048
Wyandanch, NY 11798 • 8,950
Wyandot □, OH • 22,254
Wyandotte, MI 48192 • 30,938
Wyandotte □, KS • 161,993
Wyanet, IL 61379 • 1,017
Wyckoff, NJ 07481 • 15,372
Wymore, NE 68466 • 1,611
Wynne, AR 72396-97 • 8,187
Wynnewood, OK 73098 • 2,451
Wyoming, DE 19934 • 977
Wyoming, IL 61491 • 1,462
Wyoming, MI 49509 • 63,891
Wyoming, MN 55092 • 2,142
Wyoming, OH 45215 • 8,128
Wyoming, PA 18644 • 3,255
Wyoming □, NY • 42,507
Wyoming □, PA • 28,076
Wyoming □, WV • 28,990
Wyomissing, PA 19610 • 7,332
Wythe □, VA • 25,466
Wytheville, VA 24382 • 8,038

X

Xenia, OH 45385 • 24,664

Y

Yadkin □, NC • 30,488
Yadkinville, NC 27055 • 2,525
Yakima, WA 98901-09 • 54,827
Yakima □, WA • 188,823
Yakutat, AK 99689 • 534
Yale, MI 48097 • 1,977
Yale, OK 74085 • 1,392
Yalobusha □, MS • 12,033
Yamhill □, OR • 65,551
Yancey □, NC • 15,419
Yanceyville, NC 27379 • 1,973
Yankton, SD 57078 • 12,703
Yankton □, SD • 19,252
Yaphank, NY 11980 • 5,000
Yardley, PA 19067 • 2,288
Yardville, NJ 08620 • 6,190
Yarmouth, ME 04096 • 3,338
Yarmouth, MA 02675 • 1,200
Yarnell, AZ 85362 • 1,500
Yates □, NY • 22,810
Yates Center, KS 66783 • 1,815
Yavapai □, AZ • 107,714
Yazoo □, MS • 25,506
Yazoo City, MS 39194 • 12,427
Yeadon, PA 19050 • 11,980
Yeagertown, PA 17099 • 1,150
Yell □, AR • 17,759
Yellow Medicine □, MN • 11,684

Yellow Springs, OH 45387 • 3,973
Yellowstone □, MT • 113,419
Yellowstone National Park, WY 82190 • 400
Yellowstone National Park □, MT • 52
Yellville, AR 72687 • 1,181
Yelm, WA 98597 • 1,337
Yerington, NV 89447 • 2,367
Yermo, CA 92398 • 1,092
Yoakum, TX 77995 • 5,611
Yoakum □, TX • 8,786
Yolo □, CA • 141,092
Yonkers, NY 10701-10 • 188,082
Yorba Linda, CA 92686 • 52,422
York, AL 36925 • 3,160
York, ME 03909 • 3,130
York, NE 68467 • 7,884
York, PA 17401-07 • 42,192
York, SC 29745 • 6,709
York □, ME • 164,587
York □, NE • 14,428
York □, PA • 339,574
York □, SC • 131,497
York □, VA • 42,422
Yorketown, NJ 07726 • 6,313
York Harbor, ME 03911 • 2,555
Yorklyn, DE 19736 • 600
Yorkshire, NY 14173 • 1,340
Yorktown, IN 47396 • 4,106
Yorktown, NY 10598 • 5,270
Yorktown, TX 78164 • 2,207
Yorktown, VA 23690-93 • 270
Yorktown Heights, NY 10598 • 7,690
Yorktown Manor, RI 02852 • 2,520
Yorkville, IL 60560 • 3,925
Yorkville, NY 13495 • 2,972
Yorkville, OH 43971 • 1,246
Yosemite National Park, CA 95389 • 1,073
Young □, TX • 18,126
Youngstown, NY 14174 • 2,075
Youngstown, OH 44501-15 • 95,732
Youngsville, PA 16371 • 1,775
Youngtown, AZ 85363 • 2,542
Youngwood, PA 15697 • 3,372
Ypsilanti, MI 48197-98 • 24,846
Yreka, CA 96097 • 6,948
Yuba □, CA • 58,228
Yuba City, CA 95991-92 • 27,437
Yucaipa, CA 92399 • 20,000
Yucca Valley, CA 92284-86 • 13,701
Yukon, OK 73099 • 20,935
Yulee, FL 32097 • 6,915
Yuma, AZ 85364-69 • 54,923
Yuma, CO 80759 • 2,719
Yuma □, AZ • 106,895
Yuma □, CO • 8,954

Z

Zachary, LA 70791 • 9,036
Zanesville, OH 43701-02 • 26,778
Zapata, TX 78076 • 7,119
Zapata □, TX • 9,279
Zavala □, TX • 12,162
Zebulon, GA 30295 • 1,035
Zebulon, NC 27597 • 3,173
Zeeland, MI 49464 • 5,417
Zeigler, IL 62999 • 1,746
Zelienople, PA 16063 • 4,158
Zenith, WA 98188 • 1,100
Zephyr Cove, NV 89448 • 1,700
Zephyrhills, FL 33539-44 • 8,220
Ziebach □, SD • 2,220
Zillah, WA 98953 • 1,911
Zilwaukee, MI 48604 • 1,850
Zimmerman, MN 55398 • 1,350
Zion, IL 60099 • 19,775
Zionsville, IN 46077 • 5,281
Zolfo Springs, FL 33890 • 1,219
Zumbrota, MN 55992 • 2,312
Zuni (Zuni Pueblo), NM 87327 • 5,857
Zwolle, LA 71486 • 1,779